T0203092

Lecture Notes in Computer Science 14103

Founding Editors

Gerhard Goos
Juris Hartmanis

Editorial Board Members

Elisa Bertino, *Purdue University, West Lafayette, IN, USA*
Wen Gao, *Peking University, Beijing, China*
Bernhard Steffen ⓘ, *TU Dortmund University, Dortmund, Germany*
Moti Yung ⓘ, *Columbia University, New York, NY, USA*

The series Lecture Notes in Computer Science (LNCS), including its subseries Lecture Notes in Artificial Intelligence (LNAI) and Lecture Notes in Bioinformatics (LNBI), has established itself as a medium for the publication of new developments in computer science and information technology research, teaching, and education.

LNCS enjoys close cooperation with the computer science R & D community, the series counts many renowned academics among its volume editors and paper authors, and collaborates with prestigious societies. Its mission is to serve this international community by providing an invaluable service, mainly focused on the publication of conference and workshop proceedings and postproceedings. LNCS commenced publication in 1973.

Chao Li · Zhenhua Li · Li Shen · Fan Wu ·
Xiaoli Gong

Editors

Advanced Parallel Processing Technologies

15th International Symposium, APPT 2023
Nanchang, China, August 4–6, 2023
Proceedings

Springer

Editors
Chao Li 🆔
Shanghai Jiao Tong University
Shanghai, China

Zhenhua Li 🆔
Tsinghua University
Beijing, China

Li Shen
National University of Defense Technology
Changsha, China

Fan Wu 🆔
Shanghai Jiao Tong University
Shanghai, China

Xiaoli Gong 🆔
Nankai University
Tianjin, China

ISSN 0302-9743　　　　　　ISSN 1611-3349 (electronic)
Lecture Notes in Computer Science
ISBN 978-981-99-7871-7　　　ISBN 978-981-99-7872-4 (eBook)
https://doi.org/10.1007/978-981-99-7872-4

© The Editor(s) (if applicable) and The Author(s), under exclusive license
to Springer Nature Singapore Pte Ltd. 2024

This work is subject to copyright. All rights are reserved by the Publisher, whether the whole or part of the material is concerned, specifically the rights of translation, reprinting, reuse of illustrations, recitation, broadcasting, reproduction on microfilms or in any other physical way, and transmission or information storage and retrieval, electronic adaptation, computer software, or by similar or dissimilar methodology now known or hereafter developed.
The use of general descriptive names, registered names, trademarks, service marks, etc. in this publication does not imply, even in the absence of a specific statement, that such names are exempt from the relevant protective laws and regulations and therefore free for general use.
The publisher, the authors, and the editors are safe to assume that the advice and information in this book are believed to be true and accurate at the date of publication. Neither the publisher nor the authors or the editors give a warranty, expressed or implied, with respect to the material contained herein or for any errors or omissions that may have been made. The publisher remains neutral with regard to jurisdictional claims in published maps and institutional affiliations.

This Springer imprint is published by the registered company Springer Nature Singapore Pte Ltd.
The registered company address is: 152 Beach Road, #21-01/04 Gateway East, Singapore 189721, Singapore

Paper in this product is recyclable.

Preface

Welcome to the 15th International Symposium on Advanced Parallel Processing Technology (APPT)! It is our great pleasure to serve as the Program Co-Chairs of this prestigious event. This year, APPT is an in-person event co-located with CCFSys 2023, the flagship computer system conference organized by China Computer Federation (CCF). The theme of CCFSys 2023 is "Computer Systems in the Era of Artificial Intelligence: From Research to Industrialization." Computer systems, rooted in fundamental hardware and core software, serve as the foundation for the information industry and digital economy. In recent years, the significant improvement in hardware computing power and the expansion of system scale have formed various new computing systems, nurturing next-generation artificial intelligence technologies such as ChatGPT. With a focus on cutting-edge technology, APPT 2023 aims to explore the development trends in technology and emphasizes the integration of intelligence and computer systems through collaboration between academia, industry, and research.

The conference attracted researchers engaged in parallel computing, distributed computing, and emerging computing techniques to submit their work. The papers cover a wide range of topics, including architecture, systems, data management, algorithms, and programming. We received 49 paper registrations in total. Each submission was reviewed by three program committee (PC) members on average. There was also an online discussion stage to guarantee that consensus was reached for each submission. Finally, the program committee decided to accept 24 submissions. Authors of all the accepted papers were asked to submit a revised version based on the review comments.

We sincerely thank all the authors who submitted their papers, whether they were accepted or not. Your contributions played a crucial role in the success of this conference. We would like to express our special thanks to all the reviewers who took the time out of their busy schedules to review the papers and provide valuable feedback and suggestions. Their expertise and hard work have made significant contributions to ensuring a high-quality conference program and maintaining a high academic standard. We would also like to thank the General Co-Chairs (Chenggang Wu and Prof. Xiaofei Liao), the Organization Co-Chairs (Tao Li, and Prof. Baoliu Ye), the Local Co-Chairs (Zichen Xu, and Nan Jiang), and the Publication Chair (Xiaoli Gong). Lastly, we would like to thank all the individuals involved in this conference, including the organizing committee members, program committee members, conference secretaries, and volunteers. Our thanks also go to Springer for its assistance in putting the proceedings together. Without your hard work and support, this conference would not have been possible.

August 2023

Chao Li
Zhenhua Li
Li Shen
Fan Wu

Organization

General Chairs

Chenggang Wu — Institute of Computing Technology, Chinese Academy of Science, China

Xiaofei Liao — Huazhong University of Science and Technology, China

Program Committee Chairs

Chao Li — Shanghai Jiao Tong University, China

Zhenhua Li — Tsinghua University, China

Li Shen — National University of Defense Technology, China

Fan Wu — Shanghai Jiao Tong University, China

Steering Committee

Weimin Zheng — Tsinghua University, China

Songlin Zhuang — University of Shanghai for Science and Technology, China

Zuoning Chen — Jiangnan Institute of Computing Technology, China

Guoliang Chen — University of Science and Technology of China, China

Jiangxing Wu — National Digital Switching System Engineering Technology Research Center, China

Jifeng He — Tongji University, China

Yaoxue Zhang — Tsinghua University, China

Mengfei Ynag — Xidian University, China

Min Gu — University of Shanghai for Science and Technology, China

Huaimin Wang — National University of Defense Technology, China

Ninghui Sun — Institute of Computing Technology, Chinese Academy of Science, China

Depei Qian	Beijing University of Aeronautics and Astronautics, China
Hai Jin	Huazhong University of Science and Technology, China
Chenggang Wu	Institute of Computing Technology, Chinese Academy of Science, China
Xiaofei Liao	Huazhong University of Science and Technology, China

Program Committee

Helei Cui	Northwestern Polytechnical University, China
Laizhong Cui	Shenzhen University, China
Haipeng Dai	Nanjing University, China
Dezun Dong	National University of Defense Technology, China
Fang Dong	Southeast University, China
Juan Fang	Beijing University of Technology, China
Xiaoli Gong	Nankai University, China
Yu Gu	Northeastern University, China
Rong Gu	Nanjing University, China
Guangjie Han	Hohai University, China
Bingsheng He	National University of Singapore, Singapore
Yuan He	Tsinghua University, China
Shibo He	Zhejiang University, China
Xiaofeng Hou	Shanghai Jiao Tong University, China
Yang Hu	Tsinghua University, China
Qianyi Huang	Sun Yat-sen University, China
Xu Huanle	University of Macau, China
Lei Jiao	University of Oregon, USA
Meng Jin	Shanghai Jiao Tong University, China
Yibo Jin	Huawei Technologies Co. Ltd., China
Chao Li	Shanghai Jiao Tong University, China
Peng Li	University of Aizu, Japan
Wei Li	University of Sydney, Australia
Zhenhua Li	Tsinghua University, China
Cheng Li	University of Science and Technology of China, China
Xin Li	Nanjing University of Aeronautics and Astronautics, China
Shigang Li	Beijing University of Posts and Telecommunications, China

Yusen Li	Nankai University, China
Fuliang Li	Northeastern University, China
Zhen Ling	Southeast University, China
Sicong Liu	Nothwestern Polytechnical University, China
Jia Liu	Nanjing University, China
Kai Liu	Chongqing University, China
Li Lu	Zhejiang University, China
Yingwei Luo	Peking University, China
Yongqiang Lyu	Tsinghua University, China
Xiaohui Peng	Institute of Computing Technology, Chinese Academy of Sciences, China
Zhuzhong Qian	Nanjing University, China
Jianbin Qin	Shenzhen University, China
Li Shen	National University of Defense Technology, China
Zhaoyan Shen	Shandong University, China
Meng Shen	Beijing Institute of Technology, China
Xiaohua Tian	Shanghai Jiao Tong University, China
Yongxin Tong	Beihang University, China
Lei Wang	National University of Defense Technology, China
Zeke Wang	Zhejiang University, China
Ying Wang	Key Laboratory of Computer System and Architecture Institute of Computing Technology, Chinese Academy of Sciences, China
Lei Wang	Dalian University of Technology, China
Xiaofei Wang	Tianjin University, China
Jizeng Wei	Tianjin University, China
Weiwei Wu	City University of Hong Kong, China
Fan Wu	Shanghai Jiao Tong University, China
Yuan Wu	University of Macau, China
Wei Xi	Xi'an Jiaotong University, China
Jiang Xiao	Huazhong University of Science and Technology, China
Zichen Xu	Nanchang University, China
Mengwei Xu	Beijing University of Posts and Telecommunications, China
Liu Yan	Hunan University, China
Hailong Yang	Beihang University, China
Deze Zeng	China University of Geosciences, China
Yu Zhang	Huazhong University of Science and Technology, China

Yiming Zhang	National University of Defense Technology, China
Hao Zhang	Chinese University of Hong Kong, China
Zhiwei Zhang	Beijing Institute of Technology, China
Shenglin Zhang	Nankai University, China
Yanfeng Zhang	Northeastern University, China
Sheng Zhang	State Key Laboratory for Novel Software Technology, Nanjing University, China
Yi Zhao	Tsinghua University, China
Dong Zhao	Beijing University of Posts and Telecommunications, China
Laiping Zhao	Tianjin University, China
Zhenzhe Zheng	Shanghai Jiao Tong University, China
Zhi Zhou	Sun Yat-sen University, China
Ruiting Zhou	Southeast University, China

Contents

High Performance Computing
and Parallelized Computing

Enhancing Multi-physics Coupling on ARM Many-Core Cluster

Wencheng Shi, Nan Hu, Jiangsu Du, Dan Huang$^{(\boxtimes)}$, and Yutong Lu

Sun Yat-sen University, Guangzhou, China
{shiwch,hunan5}@mail2.sysu.edu.cn,
{dujiangsu,huangd79,luyutong}@mail.sysu.edu.cn

Abstract. In scientific and engineering computing, there are a large number of complex physical simulations involving multiple physical fields. This complex physical simulation in which multiple physical fields superimpose and interact with each other is aiming at solving the multiphysics coupling problem. A typical approach to solving a complex physics problem is decoupling it into multiple separate physical models. These models are solved independently and coupled by explicitly exchanging data with each other. A key to the method is the design of the multiphysics coupler, that transmits data between two physical models with high fidelity and high efficiency. However, current multiphysics data transmission algorithms have scalability and performance bottlenecks caused by communication and computation overhead. In this paper, we take full advantage of modern multi-core hardware to improve the performance of multiphysics data transfer algorithms. At the same time, the scalability of the coupler is improved by optimizing the communication algorithm, search algorithm, and KD-Tree reusing strategies. Experimental results on the ARM multi-core platform show that our improved multiphysics coupling methods achieve more than $10\times$ acceleration compared with the original program. The scalability of the our method has also been greatly improved.

Keywords: MultiPhysics · Parallel Computing · Data Transfer

1 Introduction

The constantly increasing computing power makes it possible for scientists to tackle previously unsolvable complex problems, with multiphysics coupling problems being a prime example. These multiphysics coupling problems link multiple disciplines and involve collaborators with specific knowledge [17]. According to the degree of coupling between physical models, multiphysics coupling problems can be divided into three types: fully coupled, tightly coupled, and loosely coupled. The fully coupled algorithm completes the solution in one solver to achieve implicit coupling. For tightly coupled and loosely coupled algorithms [19], each physics model has an independent solver, and data is explicitly transferred

© The Author(s), under exclusive license to Springer Nature Singapore Pte Ltd. 2024
C. Li et al. (Eds.): APPT 2023, LNCS 14103, pp. 3–18, 2024.
https://doi.org/10.1007/978-981-99-7872-4_1

between multiple physics models to complete the coupling. The optimization of this data transfer process is the focus of our follow-up research.

Traditionally, multiphysics coupling simulations were achieved by linking individual simulation tools built by researchers, which is time-consuming, error-prone, and problematic for taking advantage of modern parallel computing [17]. In order to provide a more flexible development environment, researchers developed multiphysics coupling frameworks such as MOOSE [9]. We focus on the efficiency of data transfer (aka. couplers) between multiphysics in these frameworks. For easy understanding, we simplify the coulper to a data transfer from the source physics grid to the target physics grid. Specifically, it computes the value of each target grid point based on the values of the source grid points and elements.

We evaluated the performance bottlenecks of the data transfer algorithm on the MOOSE framework. MOOSE implements multiphysics coupling simulation through multiapp module and transfer module [3]. The multiapp module is designed for multiple physical model simulations and the transfer module is designed for data transfer between them. MOOSE provides transfer based on interpolation, finite element shape evaluation, projection, and other data analysis methods. Our experimental results show that two transfers in MOOSE have obvious performance and scalability bottlenecks. The shape transfer sends the target grid point to process in which the source grid range contains it, and then queries which element contains the target grid point, finally uses the element shape function to evaluate the value of it. The interpolation transfer uses KD-Tree to find the K nearest neighbors around the target grid point and then calculates the value of the target grid point by interpolation.

As shown in Fig. 1, the shape evaluation transfer has lower performance on computing tasks, mainly due to the degradation problem of search trees. The shape evaluation transfer searches the tree to find a specific mesh element. However, if the target element does not exist in the search tree, the search tree will degenerate into a linear search to query again. This will eventually lead to an exponential increase in search time, occupying over 99% runtime of the transfer. Besides, after reducing the calculation task time, the procedure that determines which process the target grid point should be sent to, also reduces the scalability of the program. The interpolation transfer has very limited scalability. This is caused by communication overhead for gathering data to build kd-tree, kd-tree building overhead and kd-tree searching overhead. Motivated by the problems in the above preliminary experiments, we propose a set of optimization strategies aimed at the performance and scalability bottlenecks of different data transmission algorithms to enhance the multiphysics coupling simulation.

For the data transmission method based on **shape evaluation**:

1) We propose a new pruning strategy to improve the pruning efficiency of search tree recursive search. In addition, threads are used to accelerate searching and calculation tasks. We achieved more than 3× acceleration benefit with 4 threads.

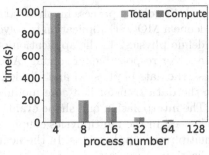

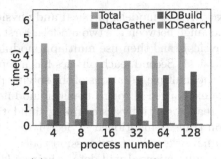

(a) Shape evaluation transfer test   (b) Interpolation transfer test

Fig. 1. Performance and scalability testing of the two types transfer

2) For the procedure of determining which process the target grid point should be sent to, we propose a pre-judge method to reduce the number of loops, and propose pre-store method to improve traversal efficiency. We successfully improve the program scalability by accelerating this procedure.

For the data transmission method based on **interpolation**:

1) We design a mixed parallel method which creates and handles the thread in the MPI process to accelerate the calculation task. And we successfully achieved more than $3.2\times$ acceleration benefit with 4 threads.
2) We propose a new communication strategy based on MPI shared memory which will significantly improve the efficiency of process communication within the same MPI node. The ever-increasing communication overhead of the original MOOSE program was significantly reduced.
3) We design the KD-Tree reusing strategy to eliminate the huge overhead of repeatedly building KD-Tree. In the end, this overhead was reduced to one percent of the original, which improved the scalability of the program.

In the Sect. 2 of the follow-up paper, we will introduce the situation about MOOSE and the wide application of the shape evaluation coupler and interpolation coupler. In the Sect. 3, we propose optimization strategies for the performance bottlenecks. In Sect. 4, we conduct a performance comparison between the original program and the optimized program. In Sect. 5, we summarize our work and propose future optimization ideas.

2   Related Work

2.1   MOOSE

The Multiphysics Object Oriented Simulation Environment (MOOSE [9]) is an open-sourced, finite-element, multiphysics framework. The process of using MOOSE for multiphysics simulation is shown in the Fig. 2. Suppose we now have two physical models, physics1 and physics2, and the solving process involves data exchange between the two models. First, we define a MOOSE application to solve physics1, and then use multiapp module to define physics2 in the application of physics1. Second, each physics has a separate solver responsible for solving. And in the multiple iterations of the solving process, the data of physics1 and physics2 are exchanged through transfer module. So the data transfer is a core module to realize multiphysics coupling simulation. The interpolation and shape evaluation transfer mentioned in Sect. 1 were widely used in the multiphysics coupling frameworks, data transmission tools, and multiphysics applications. In the next two subsections, I will detail their wide application.

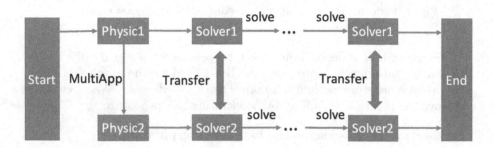

Fig. 2. Process for multiphysics coupling simulation with MOOSE

2.2   Shape Evaluation Transfer

The Warthog team [4] proposed a data transmission tool Warthog, which coupled the neutronics code and the fuel performance code. And the data transmission between the above three applications is completed by using the transfer of shape evaluation. Scrimieri et al. [18] performed a physics simulation during the fabrication of an aerospace engine blade assembly using the data transfer based on the finite element shape function. The transfer is responsible for the data transmission between two non-matched meshes from the heat treatment process to the macro machining process. Nieminen [15] realize the two-way fluid-structure interaction simulation. The pressure of the flow field and the displacement data of the solid structure field are transferred to each other through the finite element shape function simulation. Leitão et al. [8] constructed a chemo-thermal model based on the chemical affinity concept to analyze the temperature distribution of concrete arch dams during the construction phase. The data transmission among multiple physical field grids in this model is mainly realized by finite element shape function simulation. Afazov et al. [1] developed a finite element data transfer tool FEDES based on elemental shape functions. And the authors use FEDES to implement data transfer between different meshes in a typical manufacturing chain simulation (casting, forging, heat treatment).

2.3   Interpolation Transfer

Miao et al. [14] used MOOSE to conduct a multiphysics simulation of molten metal fuel microreactor. The heat conduction module used the power distribution of reactor physics application as a heat source to calculate the temperature distribution inside the fuel and then transmitted it back to reactor physics application through the interpolation type transfer. Park et al. [16] assembled the reactor physics field, the thermal fluid field and the MOOSE thermal conduction module into a high-fidelity temperature distribution for lead-cooled fast reactor (LFR) design. The interpolation transfer was responsible for transferring the solid temperature from the reactor module to the temperature transfer module. Mei et al. [11] used loose coupling method to couple the thermochemical flow field and thermal temperature mechanical field. The data exchange of non-matching grids used the interpolation method based on KD-Tree. Khamayseht et al. [5] used the KD-Tree and mean method to map the orographic field data (discrete altitude data) to a distinct mesh to drive an r-adaptive mesh motion algorithm. And in the follow-up study [6], the method was applied to the coupled data transmission between the earth terrain science and the climate simulation model. The MBCoupler, a solution transfer tool based on MOAB [21], provided a data transfer based on KD-Tree and interpolation method. In these projects [10,12,13], the interpolation in MBCoupler was used to complete data transfer of neutronics and thermal hydraulics coupling problems.

As can be seen from the above, the two types of transfer are widely used in multiphysics coupling simulations, so they can be regarded as two general grid data transfer algorithms. Our optimizations for the two types of transfer can be applied to other multiphysics coupling frameworks, data transmission tools, and multiphysics applications.

3   Methodology

In Sect. 1, we conduct preliminary performance analysis on two types of transfer and propose a set of optimization strategies. We will introduce the specific details of our optimization strategies in this section. Firstly, we introduce the specific operation of the shape evaluation and interpolation transfer.

The shape evaluation transfer mainly consists of three steps.

1. **Build Boundary**: Each process calculates the boundary of the local source grid, and then uses MPI's collective communication to collect the source grid boundaries of all processes.
2. **Build Outgoing**: For each target grid point, it will be sent to the process which boundary contains it.
3. **Compute**: Each process builds a search tree using local source grid elements. For each target grid point sent by other process, use the search tree to find the element that contains it. And then the value of the target grid point is calculated by using the element shape function.

The interpolation transfer mainly consists of three steps.

1. **Data allgather**: Each process collects the source grid points of all processes and the values at these points.
2. **KD-Tree Build**: All the processes use the entire source grid points from the step 1 to build a local KD-Tree.
3. **KD-Tree Search**: For a target grid point. First, use the KD-Tree to search for the K nearest neighbors of target grid point. The value of the target grid point is calculated based on the interpolation method by using the values of the K nearest neighbor points.

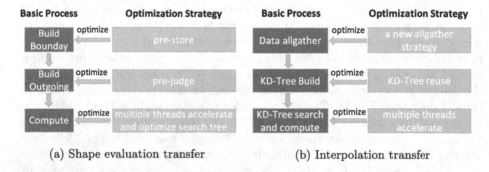

(a) Shape evaluation transfer   (b) Interpolation transfer

Fig. 3. The process and optimization of two types of transfer

The processes of the two types of transfer are shown in Fig. 3, and we propose corresponding optimization strategies for each step. For shape evaluation transfer, we propose double boundary method to optimize the efficiency of search tree, the multi-thread method to accelerate recursive search tasks of the search tree, the pre-store method to speed up the building boundary processes, and the pre-judge method to accelerate building outgoing processes. For interpolation transfer, we propose a new allgather algorithm based on MPI shared memory to reduce communication overhead, the KD-Tree reusing strategy to reduce KD-Tree building overhead, the multi-thread method to accelerate KD-Tree search calculation tasks. We discuss the details in the next two subsections.

3.1   Shape Evaluation Transfer

Build Boundary and Build Outgoing Optimization. MOOSE covers all source grid points with a rectangle or cuboid, called the boundary. The construction method of the boundary is to traverse all the local source grid points, and then count the points in the lower left corner and upper right corner to form a rectangle or cuboid. MOOSE uses a custom data structure to store grid points, and designs an iterator for it. When the iterator needs to traverse all the local grid points, it will first traverse all the grid points, and then perform a predicate to determine whether it is a local point. This calculation process involves all the grid points, and obviously does not change as the number of processes increases, the time for building boundary will gradually remain unchanged. To solve this problem, we propose a pre-store method which allocate another memory space dedicated to store the local grid points, so that there is no need to access complex iterators. The advantage of the iterator is that it has high versatility and can easily access active points or local points, but for local grid points which are commonly used, it can be stored in advance for quick access.

As for "Build Outgoing", the original MOOSE program goes through a double loop, the first layer of loops is the local target grid points, and the second layer of loops is all the MPI processes. As the number of processes increases, the number of the first layer will be halved, but at the same time the number of the second layer will be doubled. Therefore, the overall number of loops does not change which will affect the overall performance of the program. We propose a pre-judge strategy to reduce the number of loops in the second layer. Only when there is an intersection between the boundary of local target grid and the boundary of source grid, the target grid point may be sent to the process of the source grid. In this case, there is no need to traverse all MPI processes in the second layer of loops, thereby reducing program running time and increasing scalability.

Search Tree Optimization. The shape evaluation transfer uses all source grid elements to build a search tree. The search tree consists of many nodes, each node contains a boundary variable and the node can only store elements that intersect with its boundary. When the number of elements in a node reaches the storage capacity, the parent node boundary will be split into K small boundaries. Then the parent node uses the child boundaries to create K child nodes, and inserts its elements into these child nodes. In Fig. 4a is a schematic diagram of the search tree. Each rectangular area in the figure is the boundary of a node. Initially, the complete grid boundary is divided into four smaller boundaries, forming four child nodes. As elements are continuously inserted, the boundaries in the lower left and upper right corners are further divided, and finally the small boundary in the lower left corner is divided again.

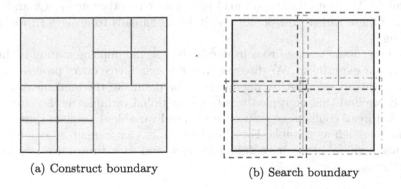

(a) Construct boundary   (b) Search boundary

Fig. 4. The process of building search tree

When a grid point recursively searches for the element which contains it in the search tree, we select the next child node according to the node's boundary. However, we found a problem during our experiments. If the element containing the grid point cannot be found, this search operation will become highly time-consuming. This is because, in such cases, transfer will search the unsearched nodes of the entire search tree, resulting in an exponential increase of search time. The problem commonly arises in unstructured grids due to their irregular shape. Although the boundary of a grid area is a rectangle or a cube during segmentation, the irregular shape of grid causes more empty areas within the boundary. Points located in these empty areas are impossible to find the corresponding element when searching.

We design a double boundary method to solve this problem. The double boundary method adds a new boundary variable called the search boundary, while the original node's boundary is called the construct boundary. When we add an element to a node, judge whether the element can be inserted into the current node according to the construct boundary. And if it can be inserted, take the union of the element's boundary and the construct boundary to update the search boundary. During the search, if a grid point is outside the search boundary, we can conclude that it cannot be contained within the current node, and hence avoid traversing all tree nodes. The dotted line part of Fig. 4b is the search boundary. For clarity, only the search boundaries of the largest four nodes are displayed.

Multi-thread Optimization. For each target grid point sent by other processes, we need to find which element it belongs to and then calculate its value. This is an extremely time-consuming task, especially when dealing with a large number of target grid points. In order to improve program performance and make good use of computing resources, we utilize threads within each process to accelerate the computing task.

At the beginning, our idea is that each thread is responsible for receiving and calculating all the target grid points sent by one process. However, we find the number of grid points sent by each process varied greatly, resulting in an unbalanced load among threads. So our group modify the calculation tasks of each thread. We collect all target grid points sent by other processes, and then distribute these target grid points evenly to all threads to achieve thread load balancing.

The other issue we need to consider in the specific implementation is thread safety. In our experiment, We discover that the search tree query process cannot guarantee thread safety. After digging into the details of the implementation of MOOSE, we find that multiple threads access global variables at the same time will cause thread conflicts, so we use thread local variables to replace these global variables as much as possible. For global variables that cannot be removed, we try to use a global array or container instead, and each thread accesses one of the locations.

3.2 Interpolation Transfer

Allgather Optimization. MOOSE uses the allgather function in MPI3 to collect the points and values of the source grid. However, as the number of processes increases, the time of the allgather algorithm also increases. To solve this problem, we propose a new communication strategy based on MPI shared memory and allgather algorithm, which can significantly reduce communication overhead. The algorithm pseudocode can be seen in Algorithm 1.

Algorithm 1. AllGather

1: **procedure** ALLGATERDATA($Data$)
      //build local node communication subset
2:     $MPI\_Split(MPI\_COMM\_WORLD, \cdots, \&localnode\_comm)$;
      //allocate the shared memory
3:     $allnodedatasize = Data.size() * sizeof(Data)$;
4:     $MPI\_Win\_allocate\_shared(allnodedatasize, ...,$
                    $localnode\_comm, \&allnodedata)$;
      //build allgather communication subset
5:     $MPI\_Split(MPI\_COMM\_WORLD, \cdots, \&allgather\_comm)$;
      //allgather operation
6:     $MPI\_Allgatherv(localnodedata, \cdots ,$
                    $\&allnodedata[offset], \cdots, allgather\_comm)$;
7: **end procedure**

Firstly, we divide the processes belonging to the same MPI node into one communication domain called *localnode_comm*. And then we use the *localnode_comm* to allocate a piece of MPI shared memory on each MPI node. Secondly, we divide the i-th process of each MPI node into one communication domain called *allgather_comm*. Thirdly, the allgather result of the i-th *allgather_comm* will be put into the i-th block of the shared memory applied in the first step. Through the above three steps, we can complete the collection of all source grid points.

The details of the strategy are illustrated in Fig. 5, which shows an example with 4 MPI nodes and 16 processes. First of all, we need to emphasize that each MPI node has applied for a shared memory space. In our strategy, allgather operation is performed by processes belonging to different MPI nodes. In Fig. 5, Process 0, Process 1, Process 2, and Process 3 belong to different MPI nodes. These four processes perform an allgather operation and store the result in block 0 of their respective MPI node's shared memory. Process 4 to Process 7 perform an allgather operation, and store the results in the block 1 of the shared memory. Process 8 to Process 11 perform an allgather operation, and store the result in the third block of the shared memory. Process 12 to Process 15 execute an allgather operation, and store the result in the fourth block of the shared memory. In this way, the data from 16 processes is collected in the shared memory of each MPI node, effectively completing the allgather operation of 16 processes. And these four allgather operations can be executed in parallel.

The allgather operation of MOOSE involves P processes, where P is the total number of processes. But our new allgather strategy only involves M processes each time, where M is the number of MPI nodes. Since M is generally much smaller than P and its change range is also smaller or even unchanged, so our program experiences a significant improvement in communication overhead.

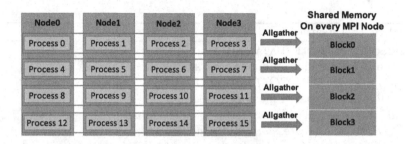

Fig. 5. The optimized allgather strategy

KD-Tree Reusing Strategy. In the interpolation Transfer, the KD-Tree is rebuilt for each time step iteration, which is a highly time-consuming operation. Furthermore, building KD-Tree requires using the source grid points of all processes. When the number of source grid points is fixed, the time to build KD-Tree will remain constant as the number of processes increases. This will significantly impact the performance of parallel programs.

If the overall source grid remains unchanged, KD-Tree can be reused theoretically, but the value on each source grid point will change as the solver runs. We separate the source grid points and the values at each source grid point. When running transfer for the first time, we collect the source grid points and the values on these source grid points into two arrays respectively. The size of the source grid points array and the values array are equal. And the same position of the two arrays saves the source grid point and the value on this source grid point respectively. Then we use the source grid points to build the KD-Tree. When running transfer for the second time, we only collect the values on the source grid points and maintain the same data order as the first running. This allows the points in the KD-Tree to map to the updated values. By reusing the KD-Tree built in the first iteration, the fixed time of building KD-Tree can be saved in subsequent iterations, which significantly improves the scalability of the program.

Multi-thread Optimization. For all local target grid points, we need to search the KD-Tree and perform interpolation calculations. When the number of target grid points is too large, this calculation tasks will be highly time-consuming. In order to make better use of the multi-core architecture of modern computers, we use the nesting threads inside the MPI process to accelerate the calculation tasks. Specifically, we divide the local target grid points evenly into N parts and allocate them to N threads. However, There are two problems to be solved in modifying transfer to a hybrid parallel mode.

Firstly, the KD-Tree in MOOSE is implemented based on the nanoflann [2]. The search operation of nanoflann is thread-safe, but the interpolation calculation does not guarantee thread safety. The reason is the same as in the Sect. 3.1, due to the conflict of multiple threads accessing the same global variable. The solution is similar, so I won't repeat it here. Secondly, the value of a grid point is stored by the *petsc_vector* type variable, and each grid point corresponds to a value of *petsc_vector*. MOOSE modifies each value of *petsc_vector* through a locked way to ensure thread safety. This causes multiple threads to modify *petsc_vector* serially, which has a great impact on the performance of the entire program. We solve this problem by separating the process of modifying *petsc_vector* from the loop used for KD-Tree search calculation. After the necessary information is preserved inside the loop, the *petsc_vector* is modified outside the loop by the master thread.

4 Experiment

In this section, we configure the ARM cluster to conduct a performance comparison between the original MOOSE program and the optimized program from 4 processes to 128 processes. The specific experimental setting is to open the same number of processes on each machine and open 4 threads for each process.

Table 1. The experiment grid used by transfer

Transfer Type	Grid Type	Source Grid		Target Grid	
		Points	Elements	Points	Elements
Shape evaluation	2D structured Grid	5166529	5161984	6723649	6718464
	2D unstructured Grid	2616406	5199980	3670976	6702656
	3D structured Grid	2146689	2097152	3581577	3511808
	3D unstructured Grid	807676	2029328	1292984	3650689
Interpolation	2D structured Grid	4218916	4214809	5290000	5285401
	2D unstructured Grid	4216741	7445645	5287359	9458288
	3D structured Grid	5268024	5177717	6331625	6229504
	3D unstructured Grid	5168848	3465936	6266532	4279147

4.1   Experiment Environment

Hardware: we have a Huawei ARM cluster with four nodes. Each ARM machine contains 128 CPU cores, divided into 4 NUMA nodes on average, and the CPU architecture is aarch64. **Software**: the operating system is Linux version 4.14.0-115.el7a.0.1.aarch64, GCC-8.5.0, MPI-3.2.1. The program we used is the basic example of performing a transient diffusion simulation in MOOSE. We tested the performance of the optimized transfer on structured and unstructured grids to ensure that our optimization works on multiple types of grids. The unstructured grid is generated by CUBIT [20]. The structured grid is generated using the LibMesh [7]. The detailed grid parameters are provided in Table 1.

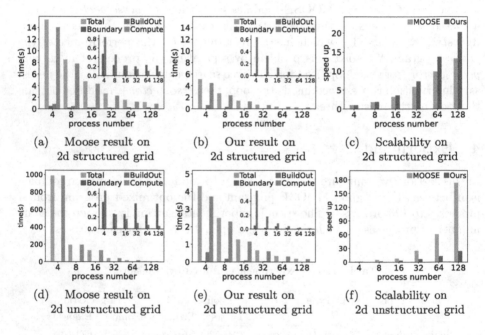

Fig. 6. Data transfer results on shape evaluation

4.2   Shape Evaluation Transfer Result

The experimental results show that there is a significant variance in the performance of shape evaluation transfer between structured and unstructured grids. Because the results on 2D structured grid and 3D structured grid are similar, and the results on 2D unstructured grid and 3D unstructured grid are similar. For the convenience of observation, we only present the results of 2D structured grid and 2D unstructured grid. We analyze it respectively.

Structured Grid Result. In Fig. 6, the three figures in the first row are the results of structured grid. The Fig. 6a shows the running time of each stage of the MOOSE original transfer, the Fig. 6b shows the running time of each stage of the optimized transfer, and the Fig. 6c shows the comparison of scalability. We first conduct performance analysis of the structured grid with Fig. 6a and Fig. 6b.

1) From the perspective of building boundary time, the building boundary time of original MOOSE program hardly change, but the optimized program can decrease the time as the number of processes increases.
2) From the perspective of building outgoing time, when the number of processes increases to a certain number, the building outgoing time of the original MOOSE program tends to be flat. However, after pre-judge optimization, the optimized program has a good halving trend.
3) From the perspective of multi-thread computing time, compared with the original MOOSE program, the optimized program achieves more than 3.0× speedup. The thread utilization reaches more than 75%.

Finally, from the overall performance analysis, compared with the original MOOSE program, the optimized program achieves a 3× speedup with 4 processes and a 4.6× speedup with 128 processes. As for the scalability, it can be found that the optimized program has a better scalability in Fig. 6c. The original MOOSE program with 128 processes has only achieved 13× speedup compared to the original MOOSE program with 4 processes. However, the optimized program achieves 20× speedup.

Unstructured Grid Result. For unstructured grids, we see the second row of the Fig. 6. In Fig. 6d, it can be seen that the MOOSE program is very time-consuming, and each iteration takes nearly 1000 s. The reason is caused by a large number of grid points not found in the search tree mentioned in the Sect. 3.1. After we use double boundary method to optimize the search tree, the program performance is greatly improved. As shown in Fig. 6d and Fig. 6e, compared with the original MOOSE program, the optimized program achieves a nearly 230× speedup with 4 processes and a nearly 32× speedup with 128 processes.

In terms of scalability, the original MOOSE program has an "exceptional" speedup in Fig. 6f. From 4 processes to 128 processes, MOOSE yields a 172× speedup. The main reason for this is that as the number of processes increases, the boundary of each process will gradually become smaller, resulting in less occurrence of not found in search tree. But this does not mean how good the performance of the original MOOSE program is, on the contrary, it is caused by poor performance. As can be seen from the Fig. 6f, we have successfully eliminated this anomaly. The optimized program with 128 processes achieves a 24× speedup compared to the optimized program with 4 processes.

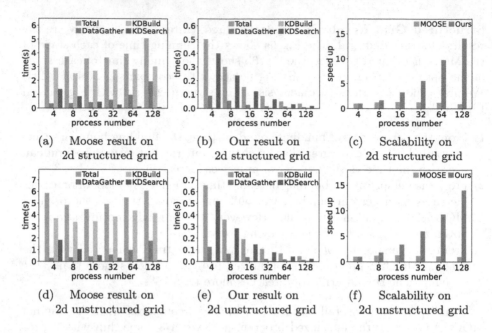

Fig. 7. Data transfer results on interpolation

4.3 Interpolation Transfer Result

Because the results on the four grids have little difference, we only display the results of 2D structured grid and 2D unstructured grid. We first conduct performance analysis, compare and analyze the detailed running time of each stage of MOOSE and our optimized program. The Fig. 7a and Fig. 7b show the detailed running time of each stage of MOOSE and our program on 2D structured grid. The Fig. 7d and Fig. 7e are the results on 2D unstructured grid.

1) From the perspective of communication time, the time of allgather algorithm in MOOSE has a tendency of doubling as the number of processes increases. In contrast, our optimized communication algorithm shows a decreasing trend. Up to 128 processes, compared with the original communication time, we achieve more than 100× speedup.
2) From the perspective of KD-Tree building time, as the process increases, the KD-Tree building time of the original MOOSE program remains unchanged. However, our optimized program completely eliminates the impact of this fixed time through the KD-Tree reusing strategy. And as the number of iterations increases, the speed-up effect will be more obvious. Because after optimization we only need to build KD-Tree once in the first iteration.
3) From the perspective of KD-Tree search calculation time. With the same number of processes, the optimized program achieves more than 3.4 speedup compared to the original MOOSE. The thread utilization rate has generally reached above 85%.

Finally, make a summary through the overall optimization benefits. Compared with the original MOOSE program, our optimized program achieves an 8× speedup when 4 processes are used, and then achieves a nearly 100× speedup when 128 processes are used.

We have also achieved a good optimization result on scalability. As shown in the Fig. 7c and Fig. 7f, It can be seen that the original program of MOOSE has poor scalability, and the speedup has almost no change. But for the optimized program, when using 128 processes, the optimized program achieved a nearly 15× speedup compared to the optimized program with only 4 processes. This is a significant improvement compared to the scalability of original MOOSE program.

5 Conclusion

In this paper, we propose two optimization schemes for commonly used multi-physics coupling data transmission methods based on the MOOSE framework. We conducted a performance test on the ARM platform cluster, and experimental results show that our optimization scheme has a certain improvement in performance and parallel scalability. However, there is still room for optimization in the part of adaptive grid optimization. The follow-up research mainly focuses on how to optimize the two commonly used data transmission algorithms in the case of grid adaptation.

Acknowledgement. This work was supported by the Key-Area Research and Development Program of Guangdong Province 2021B0101190003, the Major Program of Guangdong Basic and Applied Research: 2019B030302002, National Natural Science Foundation of China (NSFC): 62272499 and Guangdong Province Special Support Program for Cultivating High-Level Talents: 2021TQ06X160.

References

1. Afazov, S.M., Becker, A.A., Hyde, T.: Development of a finite element data exchange system for chain simulation of manufacturing processes. Adv. Eng. Softw. **47**(1), 104–113 (2012)
2. Blanco, J., Rai, P.: Nanoflann: a C++ header-only fork of FLANN, a library for nearest neighbor (NN) with KD. Trees (2014)
3. Gaston, D.R., et al.: Physics-based multiscale coupling for full core nuclear reactor simulation. Ann. Nucl. Energy **84**, 45–54 (2015)
4. Hart, S.W., Rearden, B.T.: Warthog: coupling status update. Technical report, Technical Report ONRL/LTR-2017/325, Oak Ridge National Laboratory (2017)
5. Khamayseh, A., Hansen, G.: Use of the spatial KD-tree in computational physics applications. Commun. Comput. Phys. **2**(3), 545–576 (2007)
6. Khamayseh, A., Kuprat, A.: Deterministic point inclusion methods for computational applications with complex geometry. Comput. Sci. Discov. **1**(1), 015004 (2008)

7. Kirk, B.S., Peterson, J.W., Stogner, R.H., Carey, G.F.: libMesh: a c++ library for parallel adaptive mesh refinement/coarsening simulations. Eng. Comput. **22**, 237–254 (2006)
8. Leitão, N.S., Castilho, E., Farinha, M.L.B.: Towards a better understanding of concrete arch dam behavior during the first filling of the reservoir. CivilEng **4**(1), 151–173 (2023)
9. Lindsay, A.D., et al.: 2.0-MOOSE: enabling massively parallel multiphysics simulation. SoftwareX **20**, 101202 (2022)
10. Mahadevan, V.S., et al.: High-resolution coupled physics solvers for analysing fine-scale nuclear reactor design problems. Philos. Trans. Royal Soc. A Math. Phys. Eng. Sci. **372**(2021), 20130381 (2014)
11. Mei, Z., Shi, C., Fan, X., Wang, X.: Coupled simulation for reentry ablative behavior of hypersonic vehicles. In: IOP Conference Series: Materials Science and Engineering, vol. 892, p. 012028. IOP Publishing (2020)
12. Merzari, E., et al.: Full core multi-physics simulation with offline core deformation. ANL/NE **15**, 42 (2015)
13. Merzari, E., et al.: Multi-physics demonstration problem with the sharp reactor simulation toolkit. Technical report, Argonne National Lab. (ANL), Argonne, IL (United States) (2015)
14. Miao, Y., Mo, K., Fei, T., Cao, Y.: Multiphysics simulations of self-regulating performance of an optimized molten metal fuel microreactor design. Nucl. Eng. Des. **406**, 112244 (2023)
15. Nieminen, V.: Fluid-structure interaction simulation utilising MpCCI (2015)
16. Park, H., Yu, Y., Shemon, E., Novak, A.: Progress on demonstration of a moose-based coupled capability for hot channel factors in fast reactors. Technical report, Argonne National Lab. (ANL), Argonne, IL (United States) (2022)
17. Permann, C.J., et al.: MOOSE: enabling massively parallel multiphysics simulation. SoftwareX **11**, 100430 (2020)
18. Scrimieri, D., Afazov, S.M., Becker, A.A., Ratchev, S.M.: Fast mapping of finite element field variables between meshes with different densities and element types. Adv. Eng. Softw. **67**, 90–98 (2014)
19. Slaughter, A.E., Permann, C.J., Kong, F.: NEAMS-IPL MOOSE framework activities. Technical report, Idaho National Lab. (INL), Idaho Falls, ID (United States) (2016)
20. Stimpson, C., et al.: CUBIT v. 16. x. Technical report, Sandia National Lab. (SNL-NM), Albuquerque, NM (United States) (2022)
21. Tautges, T.J., Ernst, C., Stimpson, C., Meyers, R.J., Merkley, K.: MOAB: a mesh-oriented database. Technical report, Sandia National Laboratories (SNL), Albuquerque, NM, and Livermore, CA (2004)

Polaris: Enhancing CXL-based Memory Expanders with Memory-side Prefetching

Zhe Zhou[1,2], Shuotao Xu[4], Yiqi Chen[1], Tao Zhang[4], Ran Shu[4], Lei Qu[4], Peng Cheng[4], Yongqiang Xiong[4], and Guangyu Sun[1,2,3(✉)]

[1] School of Integrated Circuits, Beijing, China
{pkuzhou,cyq1009,gsun}@pku.edu.cn
[2] School of Computer Science, Beijing, China
[3] Beijing Advanced Innovation Center for Integrated Circuits, Beijing, China
[4] Microsoft Research Asia, Beijing, China
{shuotaoxu,zhangt,ran.shu,lei.qu,pengc,yongqiang.xiong}@microsoft.com

Abstract. The use of CXL-based memory expanders introduces increased latency compared to local memory due to control and transmission overheads. This latency difference negatively impacts tasks that are sensitive to latency. While cache prefetching has traditionally been used to mitigate memory latency, addressing this performance gap requires improved CPU prefetch coverage. However, tuning a CPU prefetcher for CXL memory necessitates costly CPU modifications and can result in cache pollution and wasted memory bandwidth. To address these challenges, we propose a solution called POLARIS, a novel CXL memory expander that integrates a hardware prefetcher in the CXL memory controller chip. POLARIS analyzes incoming memory requests and prefetches cachelines to a dedicated SRAM buffer without requiring modifications to CPUs or software. In cases where prefetch hits occur, POLARIS establishes a "shortcut" for rapid memory access, significantly reducing the performance gap between CXL and local DDR memory. Furthermore, if small CPU changes are allowed, such as extending Intel's DDIO, POLARIS can further minimize CXL memory access overheads by actively pushing high-confidence prefetches to the CPU's last-level cache (LLC). Extensive experiments demonstrate that, in conjunction with various CPU-side prefetchers, POLARIS enables up to 85% of common workloads (on average, 43%) to effectively tolerate CXL memory's longer latency.

Keywords: CXL · Cache Prefetching · Near-memory processing

1 Introduction

Recently, Compute Express Link (CXL) interconnected memory expanders (CXL memory) have been proposed as a new expansion approach to scale up a single server's memory capacity and bandwidth [19,23,42]. Unlike previous methods such as memory expansion through PCIe [29] or RDMA over

© The Author(s), under exclusive license to Springer Nature Singapore Pte Ltd. 2024
C. Li et al. (Eds.): APPT 2023, LNCS 14103, pp. 19–39, 2024.
https://doi.org/10.1007/978-981-99-7872-4_2

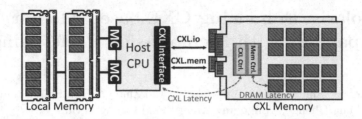

Fig. 1. A server system with both local DDR memory and CXL memory.

Table 1. Feature comparison across different memory types

Type	Interconnect	Latency	Bandwidth	Access Semantic
Local Memory	DDR Channel	80-140 ns	38.4 GB/s$^{\#}$	Load/Store
Memory Blade	PCIe	450 ns [29]	64 GB/s*	DMA
RDMA [20]	Infiniband	>1 μs	6 GB/s	DMA
CXL Memory	**CXL Channel**	**170–250 ns** [30]	**64 GB/s**	**Load/Store**

$^{\#}$DDR5-4800, single channel. *Scaled to DDR5 & PCIe 5.0 x16.

InfiniBand/Ethernet networks [3–5,18,20,37,40,45] , CXL memory is byte-addressable via normal CPU load/store instructions and exposes a coherent, unified memory space with the local memory. Because a host accesses CXL memory directly without invoking page faults or DMA operations, CXL memory achieves much lower latency than the RDMA and Memory Blade [29] counterparts. This sheds new light on memory expansion in data centers.

However, due to non-negligible control and transmission overheads of the CXL interconnect (the *CXL Latency* in Fig. 1), CXL memory still has ∼2× access latency than local memory accesses, as shown in Table 1. Consequently, many latency-sensitive workloads even suffer up to 50% slowdown on CXL memory [28]. Considering that the CPU accesses CXL memory through normal `load/store` interfaces at a cacheline granularity, one strawman solution to mitigate such a performance gap is to adopt cache prefetching. Theoretically, if most of cache misses are covered by prefetching, average access latency to both local and CXL memory is reduced substantially, and so is the performance gap. However, our profiling reveals that even the state-of-the-art CPU prefetchers cannot provide sufficiently high prefetch coverage to achieve this goal for CXL memories. For a certain CPU prefetcher to hide CXL memory latency, it often requires expanding its prefetch coverage via more aggressive prefetching, and is usually at the cost of lower prefetch accuracy [9]. More aggressive CPU-side prefetching often results in extraneous DRAM accesses that lead to *cache pollution* and *bandwidth waste* issues. This paradox between prefetch coverage and accuracy makes it challenging to improve CPU prefetchers' performance further for CXL memories. Moreover, incorporating a more accurate prefetcher for CXL memory incurs *costly modifications to CPUs* and may *demand much more core-side resources*. All these limitations indicate that one shall

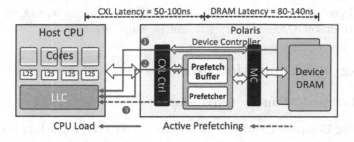

Fig. 2. Illustration of POLARIS. Path ❶: CPU loads from device DRAMs. Path ❷: CPU loads from the prefetch buffer. Path ❸: The memory-side prefetcher directly pushes data to CPU's LLC via DDIO.

go beyond CPU side and seek new prefetch opportunities on the CXL side to hide long memory access latency.

In this paper, we propose POLARIS, a novel CXL memory expander that reduces the CXL memory latency by *prefetching on the memory side*. The overall architecture of POLARIS is illustrated in Fig. 2. A standard CXL memory expander only has Path ❶, where CPU accesses would suffer from CXL latency and DRAM latency. POLARIS creates fast paths for CPU accesses (Paths ❷ and ❸) by adding prefetch functionality to CXL memory. POLARIS incorporates a hardware prefetcher in its controller chip, which predicts CPU cacheline accesses and prefetches them to a dedicated SRAM buffer (Prefetch Buffer) for quick future accesses. In events of prefetch hits, POLARIS redirects CPU requests to a *shortcut* (Path ❷) to substantially reduce the access latency.

The base design of POLARIS (Path ❷) already brings several advantages: (1) Hardware modifications are restricted to memory expanders, which facilitates a drop-in compatible solution to existing data-center servers. (2) With a dedicated prefetch buffer, POLARIS can unlock more prefetch coverage than CPU prefetchers by aggressive prefetching without polluting the CPU cache. (3) POLARIS can harvest the higher device-side DRAM bandwidth than CPU-side for prefetching. (4) Memory-side prefetchers in standalone off-chip silicons have more budget for sophisticated prefetchers than CPU-side prefetchers to yield higher prefetch accuracy. In particular, POLARIS ensembles multiple prefetchers and proposes a score-based selector to choose the best-performing prefetcher dynamically. Besides POLARIS-Base, we further present POLARIS-Active to make the most of memory-side prefetching capability. It actively pushes prefetched cachelines to CPU's LLC to reduce prefetch hit latency (Path ❸) further. We propose that POLARIS-Active only requires minimal modifications to the existing direct-cache-access interfaces like Intel's DDIO (Data-Direct-IO) [24]. Extensive experiments on 33 representative workloads demonstrate that together with different CPU prefetchers, POLARIS helps up to 85% of workloads, 43% on average, effectively tolerate[1] CXL memory's longer latency (Sect. 4).

2 Background and Motivation

2.1 CXL-Based Memory Expansion

The emerging Compute Express Link protocol (CXL) [17] is the first open industry standard to support cache-coherent interconnect between the host CPU and various accelerators or memory devices. It is composed of three sub-protocols: CXL.io creates high-speed I/O channels called *FlexBus* based on the PCIe-5.0 physical layer. It provides a basic, non-coherent load/store interface for general I/O devices. CXL.cache further adds cache coherence abilities to *FlexBus*, which works on MESI coherence protocol and enables the CXL devices to cache the host memory. The third one, CXL.mem, allows the host to have coherent, byte-addressable access to the device-attached memory.

The CXL-based memory expanders (*CXL memory*) are built upon CXL.io and CXL.mem. As shown in Fig. 1, in a system that equips CXL memory, the local and CXL memory have a unified physical memory space. LLC (Last-Level-Cache) misses to CXL memory addresses are translated into CXL requests and sent via CXL channels. At the CXL memory side, these requests will first be decoded by a CXL controller and then fed into the memory controller to access device DRAMs. Responses carrying missed cachelines are sent back to the CPU without invoking page faults or DMAs. Recently, Samsung [42] and SK Hynix [23] have launched commodity CXL memory expanders. They can extend the single server memory capacity to several TBs and provide hundreds of GB/s of extra memory bandwidth. Gouk et al. also implemented an FPGA prototype [19] to demonstrate CXL memory's unmatched advantages over RDMA-based solutions.

2.2 The Long Latency Issue of CXL Memory

As compared in Table 1, though CXL memory has much lower latency than the RDMA/PCIe-based counterparts, it is still slower than local DDR memory. According to Fig. 1, we can formulate the CXL memory latency as follows:

$$t\_CXL\_Mem = t\_CXL + t\_Device\_DRAM \tag{1}$$

In the formula, t_CXL is the latency caused by the CXL stack (including the CXL packets processing, data transmission, etc.). t_Device_DRAM denotes the latency of device-side DRAMs. Although CXL-enabled CPU [33] and memory expanders [23,42] have not been commercially available till now, it has been confirmed that t_CXL_Mem is close to the latency of one-hop NUMA access

---

[1] We say the CXL latency is "effectively tolerated" if the performance gap between CXL and local memory is within 5%.

(i.e., CPU-0 accessing CPU-1's main memory in a dual-socket system) [28,30]. Therefore, *t_CXL is estimated to be 50–100ns*. [30].

To tackle CXL memory's long latency issue, some recent works focus on system-level optimizations [28,30,38]. Their main idea is to keep "hot" data in local memory while placing "cold" data in the CXL memory. Such a data mapping/migration can happen in VM instance [28] or memory page [30,38] granularity. However, these methods require complex modifications to OS kernels [30] or applications [38]. What's worse, the coarse-grained swapping methods will incur read/write amplification problems [15] and cannot fully leverage the byte-addressable and fine-grained-access advantages of CXL memory. In brief, *there still lacks an efficient approach to reduce the CXL memory access latency directly.*

2.3 Cache Prefetching to the Rescue?

As mentioned before, a key advantage of CXL memory is the compatibility with normal CPU load/store interfaces, which transfer data in a cacheline granularity. Therefore, it is natural to wonder whether cache prefetching, a primary method to tolerate data access latency in conventional memory systems, can also help offset the side effects of CXL memory.

According to previous profiling [28], commercial CPU with hardware prefetchers enabled fails to tolerate the CXL latency on many tasks effectively. Given that commercial CPUs tend to equip simple and conservative hardware prefetchers [44], we also turn our eyes to some complex yet powerful prefetchers. For instance, the recently-proposed Pythia [10] prefetcher adopts Reinforcement-Learning to obtain the best prefetch policy from multiple program features and system-level feedback information. It claims to achieve the highest *coverage* and *accuracy* among CPU prefetchers. Without loss of generality, we inspect Pythia's performance under CXL memory scenarios and mainly answer two questions:

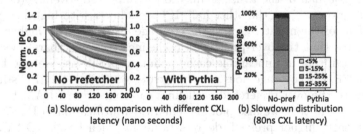

Fig. 3. Pythia's Performance on the CXL Memory.

(1) Can Powerful CPU Prefetchers Help? To answer this question, we evaluate Pythia on various SPEC2006 and SPEC2017 tasks. The simulation configurations are detailed in Sect. 4.1. As shown in Fig. 3-(a), we set *t_CXL*

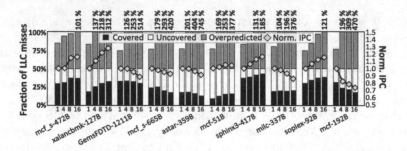

Fig. 4. Pythia's Performance with Different Prefetch Degrees.

from $0ns$ to $200ns$ and evaluate the caused slowdown. Compared to the no-prefetcher baseline, Pythia achieves more gentle slowdown curves, indicating that it can, to some extent, help tolerate the CXL latency. We also plot the slowdown distribution in Fig. 3-(b). Under a typical 80ns of CXL latency, 6% of tasks have >35% slowdown without a prefetcher, and 42% get a 25% to 35% slowdown. The fraction of unaffected tasks (slowdown <5%) is merely 12%. With Pythia, the slowdown caused by CXL latency is obviously mitigated. The fraction of unaffected tasks increases to 47% (+35%), and no task has a higher than 35% slowdown. However, 53% of cases are still heavily affected even with Pythia: 31% of tasks get a 5%–15% slowdown, and still, 22% of tasks bear a 15%–35% slowdown. *Even powerful cache prefetchers like Pythia still leave a huge room for improvement in tolerating CXL latency.*

(2) The Impact of Prefetch Aggressiveness? In general, we can increase the aggressiveness of prefetchers (i.e., the prefetch degree) for potentially higher prefetch coverage. Therefore, we set Pythia's prefetch degree from 1 to 16 and evaluate the IPC performance, coverage, and over-prediction (i.e., the fraction of useless prefetches). As Fig. 4 shows, increasing the aggressiveness boosts the performance on half of the tasks, thanks to the improved coverage (denoted by black bars). However, on the other half, IPC gets lower with higher aggressiveness. On four of the negative cases, the coverage decreases with higher degrees. This indicates that the over-prefetched cachelines (the grey bars) evict useful cachelines, resulting in unbearable cache pollution problems. We also find that for `milc-337B`, the coverage does not change obviously, but the IPC still drops. This is due to the over-prefetched cachelines causing severe DRAM bandwidth waste. To confirm this, we also plot the bandwidth utilization in Fig. 5. For the `milc-337B` task, higher prefetch degrees result in much heavier DRAM bandwidth utilization, reflected by the increased fraction of black bars in the figure.

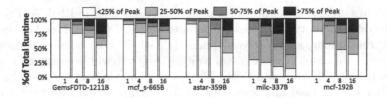

Fig. 5. Bandwidth Utilization with Different Prefetch Degrees.

Conclusions: According to these analyses we demonstrate that the prefetch coverage is the main affecting factor. Even the state-of-the-art CPU cache prefetcher, Pythia, can only help 35% of tasks tolerate the CXL latency. For the remaining tasks, it is difficult to improve the prefetch coverage further due to severe **cache pollution** and **bandwidth waste** issues. Note that these are general problems faced by CPU prefetchers since Pythia already has the (almost) highest prefetch accuracy [9,10]. Moreover, although one may want to propose better CPU prefetchers tuned for CXL memory, putting them into the host CPU will incur considerable **CPU modification overheads.** In a word, it is less feasible to effectively mitigate the performance gap between CXL and local DDR memory purely relying on CPU-side prefetchers.

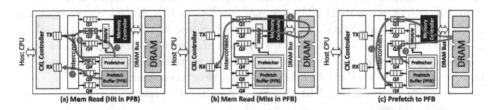

Fig. 6. Architecture and Data Path Overview of POLARIS-Base.

3   Polaris

In this section, we propose to tackle the challenges mentioned above via **memory-side prefetching**. We introduce our designed **prefetchable** CXL memory architectures, including POLARIS-Base and POLARIS-Active.

3.1   Polaris-Base Architecture

We first introduce the base design of POLARIS. Figure 6 illustrates the architecture and data paths of POLARIS-Base. Compared to standard CXL memory, we add a *Prefetcher* and a *Prefetch Buffer* (PFB) in the device-side controller chip. The prefetcher feeds into memory read requests decoded by the CXL controller, performs data prefetching, and stores prefetched cachelines in PFB. As Fig. 6-(a) shows, decoded memory addresses are fed into both $Q2$ (normal read queue) and $Q4$ (PFB read queue) simultaneously, namely Path ❶. If a cacheline address hits in PFB while the same request is still waiting in $Q2$, it will be removed from $Q2$ (Path ❷) to save DRAM bandwidth. The hit cacheline is read out from PFB via $Q5$ (PFB return queue) and sent back to the CXL controller for packetization (Path ❸). If a request hits in PFB but its fork request has already been issued to the memory controller (no longer in $Q2$), the CXL controller will receive the same cacheline twice, one from PFB and the other from DRAM. It directly drops the latter one. Such a parallel-querying design removes PFB from the critical path of DRAM accesses.

If the CPU read request misses in PFB, device memory returns the missed cachelines as usual. Such a PFB-miss case is illustrated by data path ❹ in Fig. 6-(b): the memory access requests are served by the memory controller, and the read data is fed back to the CXL controller via $Q1$ (DRAM return queue). Here we omit operation ❶ in this sub-figure for clarity. Received read requests are analyzed by the memory-side prefetcher. As illustrated in Fig. 6-(c), the prefetcher fetches the read addresses deposited in $Q4$, analyzes them, and issues prefetch requests to the memory controller. As path ❺ denotes, the cacheline addresses to prefetch (the prefetcher should guarantee the addresses are valid) are put into $Q3$ (prefetch queue). An arbiter schedules the requests from $Q2$ and $Q3$ to guarantee that normal memory read has a higher priority. The prefetched data will be stored in PFB via the PFB-fill queue, $Q6$ (data path ❻). Note that these queues are logically separated to explain ideas better. Some of them can be merged in physical implementation. CPU writes are not illustrated in the figure. The only thing to notice is that upon receiving a memory-write request, POLARIS updates the cacheline in both PFB (if hits) and DRAM to keep consistent.

We claim that such a POLARIS-Base architecture leveraging memory-side prefetching brings four main advantages:

(1) Non-intrusive Modifications: POLARIS-Base restricts all modifications to the CXL memory expander and avoids costly substrate systems (e.g., the host CPU, CXL interface, OS kernels [30], system software [28], memory allocation libraries [38], etc.) modifications.

(2) Avoid CPU Cache Pollution: POLARIS-Base prefetches data to the dedicated PFB buffer to create a ***Shortcut*** for future CPU accesses. It avoids polluting the host CPU cache even when an aggressive prefetcher is equipped.

(3) Harvest Device-side Memory Bandwidth: As Fig. 1 shows, the CXL memory bandwidth exposed to the hosts is jointly determined by the CXL channel bandwidth and the device-side memory bandwidth. Specifically, a standard PCIe 5.0 x16 channel provides, at most, 64 GB/s [46] of unidirectional bandwidth. However, a typical two-channel DDR5-4800 memory can provide up to 76.8 GB/s peak bandwidth, already 20% higher than the x16 channel. POLARIS can harvest such over-provisioned DRAM bandwidth to facilitate memory-side prefetching.

(4) Support Complex Prefetchers: Unlike CPU prefetchers, memory-side prefetchers in standalone chips have more area/power budgets to adopt complicated prefetching mechanisms, e.g., ensembling hybrid prefetchers to improve the prefetch accuracy. We detail this idea in the following subsection.

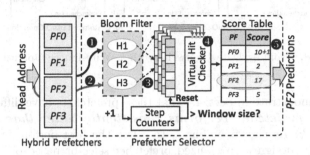

Fig. 7. Ensembled Memory-Side Prefetchers with Score-based Selector.

3.2 Ensembled Memory-Side Prefetchers

POLARIS's main goal is to redirect as many memory requests as possible to the fast path (namely, improve the coverage of memory-side prefetchers) so as to reduce the average latency. However, improving the coverage of memory-side prefetchers is not an easy job. Unlike some CPU-side prefetchers, memory-side prefetchers cannot see some useful core-side information such as PC (Program Counter) [7,11,12] and branch instruction [10], etc.. Moreover, after being filtered by CPU's cache hierarchy, the memory-access patterns exposed to CXL memory become highly irregular and are harder to predict. Fortunately, POLARIS equipping standalone controller chip has more resource budget for complex prefetchers. Therefore, we propose *ensemble hybrid prefetchers in* POLARIS *and use a score-based selector to choose the best-performing prefetcher dynamically.* Compared to individual prefetchers, our method shows much better coverage and accuracy. Here we introduce four existing prefetchers purely adopting physical addresses as inputs that can be ensembled in POLARIS:

BOP: Offset prefetching prefetches X+D where X is a line of requested address and D is the prefetch offset. Best-Offset prefetcher (BOP) [31] adopts a simple learning mechanism to help select the best offsets.

Domino is a temporal prefetcher [6] that records the correlations of memory accesses and prefetches correlated addresses on a trigger event (i.e., one or two cache misses).

SPP compresses the history of memory accesses to create a page signature [25]. It then correlates the signature with future likely delta patterns to make the prediction.

VLDP [41] also relies on recorded memory access history to predict future memory requests. It makes predictions based on multiple previous deltas (i.e.,the difference between two successive miss addresses in a physical page).

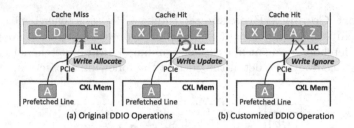

Fig. 8. Avoiding Data Overwrite with a Write-Ignore Operation.

We will demonstrate in Sect. 4.5 that these prefetchers have different advantages, and *no prefetcher performs consistently better than the others on every task*. As shown in Fig. 7, to select the best-performing prefetcher dynamically, we design a specialized prefetcher selector based on the *Virtual Prefetching* mechanism [31,36]. To be specific, When receiving a memory read address, all the prefetchers (four prefetchers, *PF0* to *PF3*) generate the prefetch candidates according to their diverse prefetching mechanisms. However, these candidates *will not actually trigger a prefetching*. Instead, they are sent to a *Bloom filter* [13] (operation ❶). Bloom filter is a low overhead probabilistic data structure used to examine whether an element is *not* a member of a set. The hash functions of the Bloom filter map each prefetcher's predictions to multiple entries of the corresponding *Bit vector* (operation ❸). These target entries are then set to 1. The CPU read address is mapped to certain entries of all the bit vectors to check whether this address could have been prefetched (operation ❷). For example, if all the three mapped entries in bit vector 0 have been set to 1, we assume prefetcher-0 (PF0) has prefetched the address before (*Virtual Hit*). Otherwise, if any entry's value is still zero, it means PF0 has not prefetched the address. This job is done by a virtual hit checker (❹). There is also a *Score Table* recording the gained score of each prefetcher (❺). A virtual hit increments the prefetcher's score by one each time. We always adopt the prefetcher with the highest score (e.g., *PF2* in the figure) to output the actual prefetching addresses.

The bit vectors should be reset at the beginning of each *Step Window*: We use a per-predictor *Step Counter* to record the number of predictions fed into the bloom filter. The counter is reset to zero once reaching a predefined *Window Size*) and then a new window begins. The implications are that inserting predictions (we call each bloom filter insertion a *Step*) will gradually saturate the filter. To maintain accuracy, we have to reset the bit vectors periodically. Also, we right-shit all the scores if a score reaches the maximum number. All the components work in a pipelined manner to achieve high throughput.

3.3   Polaris-Active Architecture

POLARIS-Base effectively mitigates the performance gap to local memory if the PFB-hit ratio is high enough. However, we still wonder whether we can *make the most of* POLARIS*'s memory-side prefetching ability to boost the system performance further.* Therefore, we also propose a POLARIS-Active architecture. It is featured by an *Active Prefetching* mechanism, which pushes prefetched cachelines to CPU's LLC to hide the CXL memory access latency entirely. To this end, we should answer two critical questions:

How to Push Cachelines to LLC? The mechanisms of pushing data from PCIe (CXL) devices to the CPU cache are usually referred to as Direct-Cache-Access (DCA) techniques [22,26,27,43]. For instance, Intel's DDIO (Data-Direct I/O) [24] enables a PCIe-connected device to push data into CPU's LLC cache directly. It is important to note that DDIO uses *Write-Allocate* and **Write-Update** policies. When a DDIO-write hits, it views the device's data as the newest and will overwrite the LLC's data (see Fig. 8-(a)). However, in our scenarios, the data in CXL memory can be older than CPU's, if CPU's dirty cachelines have not been written back. *Directly using DDIO for active prefetching will cause severe data coherence issues.*

We argue that we can add a **Write-Ignore** operation to the standard DDIO protocol to solve this problem. As shown in Fig. 8-(b), if the direct-cache access request is issued by the CXL memory and the prefetched cacheline hits in CPU's LLC, the CPU just ignores the request. To support Write-Ignore, the CPU only needs to modify its DDIO control logic slightly and add a flag bit in the DDIO packets to distinguish active prefetching from normal DDIO requests.

What to Push to LLC? Considering that active prefetching consumes both the LLC's DDIO ways and the CXL channel bandwidth, it is costly to push all the prefetched data to LLC. To make better use of active prefetching, *we only push the data with high confidence to CPU's LLC.* Specifically, we reuse the scores (see Fig. 7) to estimate a prefetch accuracy (Acc):

$$Acc = \frac{Score - Score_{i-1}}{Steps\ in\ the\ i_{th}\ Window} \tag{2}$$

In this formula, $Score$ denotes the running score of the best prefetcher and $Score_{i-1}$ is the old score value in the previous *Step Window*. Similar to the ensembled prefetching mechanism in Sect. 3.2, we measure the accuracy in each step window to guarantee timeliness. The prefetching accuracy is estimated by calculating the fraction of virtual prefetch hit in the current step window. When $Acc > T$, where T is a predefined threshold, we assume the prefetcher has good enough accuracy and push the cachelines to LLC via DDIO, otherwise we still store them in PFB. In practice, we can set threshold T as a power-of-two decimal like $T = 2^{-t}$. Then the controller only needs to calculate $\triangle Score = Score - Score_{i-1}$ and compare it with a $T' = \#Steps >> t$ in each step. In this way, the multi-cycle division operation is avoided. Note that the Acc calculation skips the first few steps (128 by default) in each window to guarantee stability. We also set an *Active Degree* parameter to limit the maximum number of cachelines that can be pushed to LLC in each prediction.

4   Evaluation

4.1   Methodology

Table 2. Default System Parameters

Core	4 GHz, 4-wide OoO, 256-entry ROB, 72/56-entry LQ/SQ
Branch Pred.	Perceptron-based, 20-cycle misprediction penalty
L1/L2 Caches	Private, 32KB/256KB, 64B line, 8 way, LRU, 16/32 MSHRs, 4 cycle/14-cycle round-trip latency
LLC	2MB/core, 64B line, 16 way, SHiP replacement, 64 MSHRs per bank, 20-cycle latency
PFB	4MB, 16 way, LRU, 20-cycle latency
CXL memory	**CXL Channel:** PCIe 5.0 x16, $t\_CXL = 80ns$ (round-trip) **DRAM:** DDR5-4800, 1 Channel, tRP, tRCD, tCAS = 16ns
CPU Prefetcher	Streamer, BOP, Pythia. Degree = 4
CXL Prefetcher	BOP, Domino, SPP, VLDP (Ensembled). Degree = 10

We compare POLARIS-equipped systems against several baselines using the cycle-accurate ChampSim simulator [16]. More specifically, we adopt a modified version [2] as the code base. We customize the simulator to simulate the behavior of CXL channels and enable arbitrary CXL latency injection. We also implement the prefetch buffer (PFB) and memory-side prefetcher in the simulator.

Table 2 lists the host CPU, CXL channel, and memory configurations. We simulate a 4 GHz CPU with 1,4,8 core. Each core has a 32KB L1 cache, 256KB L2 cache, and 2 MB shared LLC. The default PFB size is 4 MB and has a 20-cycle latency. For the CXL memory, we assume the expander is based on the PCIe-5.0 x16 physical channel and has 80 ns of CXL latency. The device DRAM is a single-channel DDR5-4800 memory by default. We set $t\_CXL = 0$ and disable the PFB when simulating a local memory. The host CPU can equip one of the three CPU-side prefetchers and adopt four prefetchers to compose the ensembled memory-side prefetcher.

CPU Prefetchers: We assume the host CPU equips one of the following prefetchers: The Streamer prefetcher used by commercial CPUs [44], the Best-Offset Prefetcher (BOP) used in open-sourced RSIC-V CPU [35], and the state-of-the-art Pythia [10] prefetcher adopting reinforcement-learning techniques. The Streamer, BOP, and Pythia prefetchers are trained on L1-cache misses and fill prefetched lines into L2 and LLC. For the single-core system, the default CPU prefetching degree is set to four to achieve high coverage.

Memory-Side Prefetchers: POLARIS ensembles four hardware prefetchers introduced in Sect. 3.2, which only rely on physical addresses for prediction: BOP [31], Domino [6], SPP [25] and VLDP [41]. For the score-based prefetcher selector, we set a 512B binary vector (used by the bloom filter) per prefetcher. The window size is set to 4096, and the active prefetching threshold T is empirically set to 2^{-5}. The *Active Degree* is set to 4 by default. The detailed configurations of these hardware prefetchers are summarized in Table 3.

Table 3. Benchmarking Prefetchers

Prefetchers	Configuration	Overhead
Streamer [44]	64 trackers	0.5KB
BOP [31]	256 entry RR, MR=100, MaxScore=31, BadScore=1	1.3KB
SPP [25]	256-entry ST, 2K-entry PT, 1024-entry PF, 8-entry GHR	6.2KB
Domino [6]	128B LogMiss, 2KB Prefetch Buffer, 256B PointBuf, 64B FetchBuf.	2.4KB
Pythia [10]	2 Features, 2 Vaults, 3 Plances, 16 Actions	25.5KB

4.2 Workloads

We adopt 91 instruction traces collected from 33 workloads of SPEC2006 [21], SPEC2017 [14], PARSEC-2.1 [1] and GAPBS [8] benchmarks for evaluation. They are summarized in Table 4. These traces, except for GAPBS, are obtained from Pythia's repo [2]. We record GAPBAS traces manually using Champsim's tracer with a [-u 20] running arguments. For GAPBS, we use 150M instructions for warmup and 50M for evaluation. The other traces use 100M instructions for warmup and 100M for evaluation. All traces have higher than 3 MPKI running on a no-prefetcher system.

Table 4. Workloads for evaluation

Benchmark	#Workloads	#Traces	Example Workloads
SPEC2006	13	38	gcc,mcf,lbm,libquantum,
SPEC2017	10	35	gcc,mcf,pop2,fotonik3d,
PARSEC	4	12	canneal,facesim,fluidanimate,
GAPBS	6	6	bfs,pagerank,spmv,bc

4.3   Performance Metric

We first define a **Slowdown** function as the performance metric to compare among different system configurations:

$$Slowdown(\Omega, \Pi) = \frac{IPC(\Omega, \Pi)_{CXL} - IPC(\Omega)_{Local}}{IPC(\Omega)_{Local}} \tag{3}$$

In this formula, Ω and Π represent the adopted CPU-side and memory-side prefetching mechanisms, respectively. Specifically, $\Omega \in \{None, Streamer, BOP, Pythia\}$ and $\Pi \in \{Polaris - Base, Polaris - Active\}$. Our primary goal is to make the system's IPC on CXL memory, namely $IPC(\Omega, \Pi)_{CXL}$, close to or higher than the baseline system's, which adopts the same CPU-side prefetcher but using local DDR memory, namely $IPC(\Omega)_{Local}$. Ideally, the slowdown should be close to or even higher than zero to indicate that the performance gap between CXL and local memory is effectively mitigated.

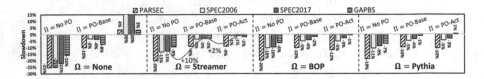

Fig. 9. Slowdown Mitigation with POLARIS

4.4   Performance Overview

Performance with Single Task: We first evaluate POLARIS's performance on the single-core system, which runs a single task each time. We compare the average slowdown under various (Ω, Π) configurations in Fig. 9. In the figure, No PO denotes the baseline system with no memory-side prefetchers, PO-Base and PO-Act are short for POLARIS-Base and POLARIS-Active architectures. We can observe that with POLARIS, the average slowdown on all four benchmarks is substantially mitigated. Without memory-side prefetching (Π =NO PO), the system bears –6% (Ω = BOP, GAPBS) to –25% (Ω=None, PARSEC and SPEC2006) average slowdown. With POLARIS-Base, the average slowdown is only –1% to –10%. POLARIS-Active mitigates the slowdown further on many cases. For instance, as annotated by the red line, with Ω = Streamer, POLARIS-Base has already reduced the slowdown on SPEC2017 (the dark bars) by 10%. POLARIS-Active reduces the value by 2% further. Surprisingly, POLARIS-Active even achieves higher IPC than the local-memory system without CPU-side prefetchers (Ω =None). This is because POLARIS-Active can directly push cachelines to CPU's LLC, compensating for the absence of a CPU-side prefetcher. In rare cases, POLARIS-Active performs slightly worse than POLARIS-Base (Ω = BOP, PARSEC). This may be because some useful cachelines are evicted by prefetched ones, even with the DDIO capacity constraints. Fortunately, the negative case still outperforms the NO PO baseline by eight points.

Figure 10 also presents the breakdown of the slowdown on all traces. POLARIS-Base and POLARIS-Active can increase the percentage of unaffected tasks (slowdown <5%) by 26% (Pythia) to 85% (No Pref.), 43% on average. They can also substantially mitigate the ratio of heavily-affected tasks denoted by the dark bars. For example, POLARIS-Act saves 43 out of 44 tasks from suffering >25% slowdown in the No Pref. ($\Omega = $ None) system. The ratio ranges from 70% to 98% with different CPU prefetchers.

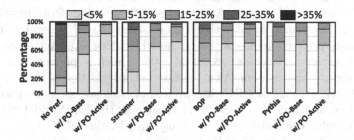

Fig. 10. Breakdown of Slowdown on All Tasks.

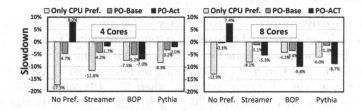

Fig. 11. Performance with Multi-Tasks.

Performance with Multi-tasks: We then evaluate POLARIS's performance on multi-core systems, with each core running a different task. We increase the number of cores to 4 and 8 and set two DRAM channels to match the bandwidth requirements. For an N-core system, we randomly select N traces from the 91 traces to build a mixed trace. We prepare eight mixed traces for each configuration and calculate the geomean IPC of all the cores as the multi-core IPC. The CPU prefetch degrees are reduced from four to two in the multi-core systems. As shown in Fig. 11, in the four-core system, POLARIS-Base mitigates a 2.3% to 12.6% slowdown when cooperating with different CPU-side prefetchers.

POLARIS-Active gets a higher IPC than the local-memory baseline by +8.0%. With Streamer or Pythia as the CPU prefetcher, POLARIS-Active pushes the

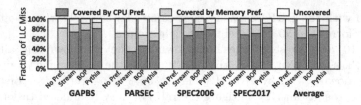

Fig. 12. Coverage Improvement with POLARIS-Base.

slowdown to a much lower value than POLARIS-Base, merely -1.7% and -2.0%, respectively. However, POLARIS-Active is less effective than POLARIS-Base on a BOP-equipped system. We infer that this is because BOP generates too many miss-predicted prefetch requests, based on which POLARIS-Active can hardly ensure high active-prefetching accuracy, either. Such a phenomenon is more severe in the eight-core system. As we can see in the right figure, POLARIS-Active works perfectly without a CPU-side prefetcher, but works more poorly than POLARIS-Base and even hurts the performance in the BOP and Pythia-based systems. We infer that with more working threads, the DDIO ways and CXL bandwidth are stressed greatly. More conservative active prefetching parameters (i.e., higher threshold T and lower *Active Degree*, etc.) may be beneficial. We leave the study of the optimal parameters setting to our future work.

4.5   Performance Analysis

Coverage Improvement: To better interpret POLARIS's effectiveness, we profile the prefetch coverage in the baseline systems equipping POLARIS-Base. As shown in Fig. 12, we break down total LLC misses into three parts: 1) Covered by CPU prefetcher. 2) Covered by POLARIS's prefetcher and 3) Uncovered LLC misses. Firstly, we can easily observe that, when $\Omega = \{\texttt{Streamer},\texttt{BOP},\texttt{Pythia}\}$ the CPU-side prefetchers can cover 35% to 80% LLC misses. Based on CPU prefetchers, POLARIS can further reduce 34% to 66% of uncovered LLC misses, 54% on average. We also find that, when the host CPU does not equip a prefetcher, about 70% to 85% of LLC misses are hit in the PFB.

Score-Based Ensembled Prefetchers: We compare the score-based ensembled prefetcher (see Sect. 3.2) with every individual prefetcher. We adopt the representative SPEC traces used in Fig. 4 for demonstration. As shown in Fig. 13, no individual prefetcher performs consistently better than the others among all tasks (Red circles annotate the best-performing tasks of each prefetcher). We also find that the proposed ensembled prefetcher (the black bars) can achieve near-optimal speedup on almost all tasks.

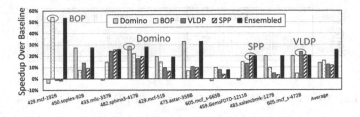

Fig. 13. Benefits of the Ensembled Memory-side Prefetcher.

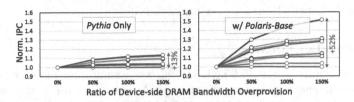

Fig. 14. Speedup Comparison with Different Over-provision Ratio η.

4.6 Sensitivity Analysis

DRAM Bandwidth Over-provision: As claimed before, an advantage of POLARIS is the ability to harvest the higher device-side DRAM bandwidth for prefetching. We use the over-provision ratio $\eta = \frac{DRAM\_Bandwidth}{CXL\_Bandwidth} - 1$ to measure how much device-side DRAM bandwidth is over-provisioned. Without loss of generality, we compare the performance of a Pythia + POLARIS-Base and a Pythia-only system under different η values. Following Pythia's practice [10], we constrain the single-core system's CXL bandwidth to 8 GB/s and set the default DRAM IO speed to 1000MTPS ($\eta = 1$) to emulate the bandwidth budget in multi-core systems. We test on PARSEC tasks since they have the worst performance among all four benchmarks. As compared in Fig. 14, for the baseline system without POLARIS, over-providing 150% device-side DRAM bandwidth only brings 13% IPC improvement. With POLARIS, the system's performance improves by up to 52% with higher device-side DRAM bandwidth. This indicates that POLARIS effectively leverages the over-provided DRAM bandwidth to facilitate memory-side prefetching.

PFB Size: We set different PFB sizes ranging from 512KB to 8 MB and use the SPEC traces for a quick exploration on the POLARIS-Base system. The results are shown in Fig. 15. It is interesting to find that an accurate CPU-side prefetcher, namely Pythia is more sensitive to the PFB size. An 8MB PFB brings about a 14% performance improvement over the 512KB PFB. While for Ω =None or Streamer, the IPC increases slowly. We infer that this is because POLARIS does not distinguish between demand cache misses and CPU prefetch misses. If the CPU prefetcher's predictions are accurate, POLARIS's prefetcher is more likely to generate useful prefetch-on-prefetch requests, which demand a larger PFB to

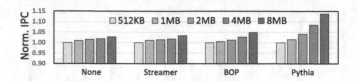

Fig. 15. Polaris-Base's Performance with Different PFB Sizes.

store. Otherwise, Polaris may generate too many inaccurate prefetches, which does not easily benefit from a larger prefetch buffer.

4.7   Overhead of Polaris

Similar to previous works [6,25,31,36,39], we assume the main overhead of Polaris's prefetcher comes from the storage. As listed in Table 3, the ensembled prefetchers consume roughly 35.9KB of SRAM. Taking into consideration the bit vectors and score tables, etc., we assume a 40KB budget. We estimate the power and area using Synopsys Design Compiler 2016 with FreePDK 45 nm library [34]. The registers have $2.82\,mm^2$ total cell areas and consume about 240.8 mW of power. We also estimate the overhead of the 4MB PFB via CACTI [32] under the 40 nm technology. The 16-way PFB consumes $24.28\,mm^2$ of area and 1.53 W of peak power. Putting them together, Polaris roughly requires $27.1\,mm^2$ more area and a 1.77 W additional power budget.

5   Conclusion

This paper presents Polaris, a novel CXL memory featured by memory-side prefetching. It enhances the system's prefetching capability while avoiding CPU cache pollution and mitigating bandwidth waste. Polaris's base design does not incur substrate-system modifications to be drop-in compatible with data center servers. If one permits small CPU changes, Polaris can actively push prefetched cachelines to CPU's LLC to boost performance further. Polaris is the first attempt to bring some conventional CPU-side tasks, like cache prefetching, to the CXL-device side for more opportunities.

Acknowledgment. This work is supported by Key-Area Research and Development Program of Guangdong Province (2021B0101310002), NSFC (61832020, 62032001, 92064006) and 111 Project (B18001).

References

1. Parsec 2.1, 2022.9. https://parsec.cs.princeton.edu/
2. Pythia's github repo, 2022.9. https://github.com/CMU-SAFARI/Pythia
3. Aguilera, M.K., et al.: Remote regions: a simple abstraction for remote memory. In: 2018 USENIX Annual Technical Conference (USENIX ATC 18), pp. 775–787 (2018)

4. Al Maruf, H., Chowdhury, M.: Effectively prefetching remote memory with leap. In: 2020 USENIX Annual Technical Conference (USENIX ATC 20), pp. 843–857 (2020)
5. Amaro, E., et al.: Can far memory improve job throughput? In: Proceedings of the Fifteenth European Conference on Computer Systems, pp. 1–16 (2020)
6. Bakhshalipour, M., Lotfi-Kamran, P., Sarbazi-Azad, H.: Domino temporal data prefetcher. In: 2018 IEEE International Symposium on High Performance Computer Architecture (HPCA), pp. 131–142. IEEE (2018)
7. Bakhshalipour, M., Shakerinava, M., Lotfi-Kamran, P., Sarbazi-Azad, H.: Bingo spatial data prefetcher. In: 2019 IEEE International Symposium on High Performance Computer Architecture (HPCA), pp. 399–411. IEEE (2019)
8. Beamer, S., Asanović, K., Patterson, D.: The gap benchmark suite, arXiv preprint arXiv:1508.03619 (2015)
9. Bera, R., et al.: Hermes: accelerating long-latency load requests via perceptron-based off-chip load prediction. In: 55th IEEE/ACM International Symposium on Microarchitecture, MICRO 2022, Chicago, IL, USA, 1–5 October 2022. IEEE, 2022, pp. 1–18 (2022). https://doi.org/10.1109/MICRO56248.2022.00015
10. Bera, R., Kanellopoulos, K., Nori, A., Shahroodi, T., Subramoney, S., Mutlu, O.: Pythia: a customizable hardware prefetching framework using online reinforcement learning. In: MICRO-54: 54th Annual IEEE/ACM International Symposium on Microarchitecture, 2021, pp. 1121–1137 (2021)
11. Bera, R., Nori, A.V., Mutlu, O., Subramoney, S.: Dspatch: dual spatial pattern prefetcher. In: Proceedings of the 52nd Annual IEEE/ACM International Symposium on Microarchitecture, 2019, pp. 531–544 (2019)
12. Bhatia, E., Chacon, G., Pugsley, S., Teran, E., Gratz, P.V., Jiménez, D.A.: Perceptron-based prefetch filtering. In: 2019 ACM/IEEE 46th Annual International Symposium on Computer Architecture (ISCA), pp. 1–13. IEEE (2019)
13. Bloom, B.H.: Space/time trade-offs in hash coding with allowable errors. Commun. ACM **13**(7), 422–426 (1970). https://doi.org/10.1145/362686.362692
14. Bucek, J., Lange, K.-D., Kistowski, J.V.: SPEC CPU2017: next-generation compute benchmark. In: Companion of the 2018 ACM/SPEC International Conference on Performance Engineering, pp. 41–42 (2018)
15. Calciu, I., et al.: Rethinking software runtimes for disaggregated memory. In: Proceedings of the 26th ACM International Conference on Architectural Support for Programming Languages and Operating Systems, pp. 79–92 (2021)
16. ChampSim, Champsim simulator, 2022.9. https://github.com/ChampSim/ChampSim
17. C. foundation, Cxl 3.0 specification, 2022.9. https://www.computeexpresslink.org/download-the-specification
18. Gao, Y., et al.: When cloud storage meets {$RDMA$}. In: 18th USENIX Symposium on Networked Systems Design and Implementation (NSDI 21), pp. 519–533 (2021)
19. Gouk, D., Lee, S., Kwon, M., Jung, M.: Direct access,{$High - Performance$} memory disaggregation with {$DirectCXL$}. In: 2022 USENIX Annual Technical Conference (USENIX ATC 22), pp. 287–294 (2022)
20. Gu, J., Lee, Y., Zhang, Y., Chowdhury, M., Shin, K.G.: Efficient memory disaggregation with infiniswap. In: 14th USENIX Symposium on Networked Systems Design and Implementation (NSDI 17), pp. 649–667 (2017)
21. Henning, J.L.: SPEC CPU2006 benchmark descriptions. ACM SIGARCH Comput. Archit. News **34**(4), 1–17 (2006)

22. Huggahalli, R., Iyer, R., Tetrick, S.: Direct cache access for high bandwidth network i/o. In: 32nd International Symposium on Computer Architecture (ISCA'05), pp. 50–59. IEEE (2005)

23. Hynix, S.: Sk hynix cxl memory expander, 2022.9. https://news.skhynix.com/sk-hynix-develops-ddr5-dram-cxltm-memory-to-expand-the-cxl-memory-ecosystem/

24. Intel, Intel data-direct io, 2022.9. https://www.intel.cn/content/www/cn/zh/io/data-direct-i-o-technology.html

25. Kim, J., Pugsley, S.H., Gratz, P.V., Reddy, A.N., Wilkerson, C., Chishti, Z.: Path confidence based lookahead prefetching. In: 2016 49th Annual IEEE/ACM International Symposium on Microarchitecture (MICRO), pp. 1–12. IEEE (2016)

26. Kumar, A., Huggahalli, R., Makineni, S.: Characterization of direct cache access on multi-core systems and 10gbe. In: 2009 IEEE 15th International Symposium on High Performance Computer Architecture, pp. 341–352. IEEE (2009)

27. León, E.A., Ferreira, K.B., Maccabe, A.B.: Reducing the impact of the memorywall for I/O using cache injection. In: 2007 15th Annual IEEE Symposium on High-Performance Interconnects (HOTI), pp. 143–150. IEEE (2007)

28. Li, H., et al.: First-generation memory disaggregation for cloud platforms, arXiv preprint arXiv:2203.00241 (2022)

29. Lim, K., Chang, J., Mudge, T., Ranganathan, P., Reinhardt, S.K., Wenisch, T.F.: Disaggregated memory for expansion and sharing in blade servers. ACM SIGARCH Comput. Archit. News 37(3), 267–278 (2009)

30. Maruf, H.A., et al.: TPP: transparent page placement for cxl-enabled tiered memory, arXiv preprint arXiv:2206.02878 (2022)

31. Michaud, P.: Best-offset hardware prefetching. In: 2016 IEEE International Symposium on High Performance Computer Architecture (HPCA), pp. 469–480 (2016)

32. Muralimanohar, N., Balasubramonian, R., Jouppi, N.P.: Cacti 6.0: a tool to model large caches. HP Lab. 27, 28 (2009)

33. Nassif, N., et al.: Sapphire rapids: the next-generation intel Xeon scalable processor. In: 2022 IEEE International Solid-State Circuits Conference (ISSCC), vol. 65, pp. 44–46. IEEE (2022)

34. NCSU, Freepdk45. https://www.eda.ncsu.edu/wiki/FreePDK45:Contents

35. OpenXiangShan, Xiangshan riscv cpu, 2022.9. https://github.com/OpenXiangShan/XiangShan

36. Pugsley, S.H., et al.: Sandbox prefetching: safe run-time evaluation of aggressive prefetchers. In: IEEE 20th International Symposium on High Performance Computer Architecture (HPCA), pp. 626–637. IEEE (2014)

37. Ruan, Z., Schwarzkopf, M., Aguilera, M.K., Belay, A.: $\{AIFM\}$:$\{High -$ $Performance\}$,$\{Application - Integrated\}$ far memory. In: 14th USENIX Symposium on Operating Systems Design and Implementation (OSDI 20), pp. 315–332 (2020)

38. Samsung, Smdk, 2022.9. https://github.com/OpenMPDK/SMDK.git

39. Shakerinava, M., Bakhshalipour, M., Lotfi-Kamran, P., Sarbazi-Azad, H.: Multi-lookahead offset prefetching. The Third Data Prefetching Championship (2019)

40. Shan, Y., Huang, Y., Chen, Y., Zhang, Y.: $\{LegoOS\}$: a disseminated, distributed $\{OS\}$ for hardware resource disaggregation. In: 13th USENIX Symposium on Operating Systems Design and Implementation (OSDI 18), pp. 69–87 (2018)

41. Shevgoor, M., Koladiya, S., Balasubramonian, R., Wilkerson, C., Pugsley, S.H., Chishti, Z.: Efficiently prefetching complex address patterns. In: 2015 48th Annual IEEE/ACM International Symposium on Microarchitecture (MICRO), pp. 41–152. IEEE (2015)

42. Sumsung, Expanding the limits of memory bandwidth and density: Samsung's cxl dram memory expander, 2022.9. https://semiconductor.samsung.com/newsroom/tech-blog/expanding-the-limits-of-memory-bandwidth-and-density-samsungs-cxl-dram-memory-expander/

43. Tang, D., Bao, Y., Hu, W., Chen, M.: DMA cache: using on-chip storage to architecturally separate I/O data from CPU data for improving I/O performance. In: HPCA-16: The Sixteenth International Symposium on High-Performance Computer Architecture, pp. 1–12. IEEE (2010)

44. Viswanathan, V.: Disclosure of H/W prefetcher control on some intel processors. Intel SW Developer Zone (2014)

45. Wang, C., et al.: Semeru: a {$Memory-Disaggregated$} managed runtime. In: 14th USENIX Symposium on Operating Systems Design and Implementation (OSDI 20), pp. 261–280 (2020)

46. Wiki, Pcie 5.0, 2022.9. https://en.wikipedia.org/wiki/PCI_Express

ExtendLife: Weights Mapping Framework to Improve RRAM Lifetime for Accelerating CNN

Fan Yang[1], Yusen Li[1(✉)], Zeyuan Niu[2], Gang Wang[1], and Xiaoguang Liu[1]

[1] College of Computer Science, Nankai University, Tianjin, China
{yangf,liyusen,wgzwp,liuxg}@nbjl.nankai.edu.cn
[2] College of Information Engineering, Southeast University, Nanjing, China

Abstract. Process-in-memory (PIM) engines based on Resistive random-access memory (RRAM) are used to accelerate the convolutional neural network (CNN). RRAM performs computation by mapping weights on its crossbars and applying a high voltage to get results. The computing process degrades RRAM from the fresh status where RRAM can support high data precision to the aged status where RRAM only can support low precision, potentially leading to a significant CNN training accuracy degradation. Fortunately, many previous studies show that the impact of loss caused by the RRAM precision limitation across various weights is different for CNN training accuracy, which motivates us to consider mapping different weights on RRAM with different statuses to keep high CNN training accuracy and extending the high CNN training accuracy iterations of PIM engines based on RRAM, which is regarded as the lifetime of the RRAM on CNN training. In this paper, we propose a method to evaluate the performance of the weights mapping on extending the lifetime of the RRAM and present a weights mapping framework specifically designed for the hybrid of aged and fresh RRAM to extend the lifetime of the RRAM engines on CNN training. Experimental results demonstrate that our weights mapping framework brings up to 6.3× on average lifetime enhancement compared to the random weights mapping.

Keywords: RRAM · CNN · Weights Mapping · Process-In-Memory

1 Introduction

Convolutional neural networks have gained remarkable performances in various fields such as facial recognition [1], image classification [2], and pattern recognition [3]. CNN can usually be deployed on different devices to support the corresponding service. Since the low power consumption of RRAM and its ability to calculate matrix multiplication quickly, PIM engines based on RRAM are often used to deploy CNN [4]. Compared with the traditional von-Neumann architectures, e.g., CPUs and GPUs, PIM engines based on RRAM can efficiently perform amounts of vector-matrix multiplications by using RRAM crossbars

© The Author(s), under exclusive license to Springer Nature Singapore Pte Ltd. 2024
C. Li et al. (Eds.): APPT 2023, LNCS 14103, pp. 40–53, 2024.
https://doi.org/10.1007/978-981-99-7872-4_3

as shown in Fig. 1 to implement these computations, where the matrix data G is mapped onto RRAM and the voltage vector V representing input vector is applied to the crossbar, and then each column of RRAM generates current indicating results according to Kirchoff's Law.

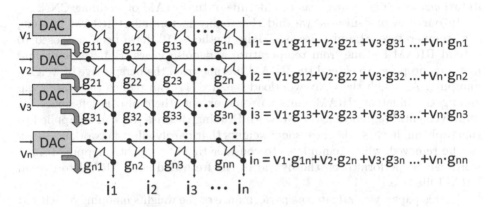

Fig. 1. The RRAM crossbar computation progress

Fig. 1 illustrates how to perform the vector-matrix multiplication on the RRAM crossbar. As Fig. 1 shows, g_{11} means the RRAM unit in the first row and the first column of the RRAM crossbar, and the g_{11} value presents the conductance of the RRAM unit, which can be programmed according to the data on the specific location of the matrix so that all the matrix data can be mapped onto the RRAM crossbar. After mapping matrix data on the RRAM crossbar, we need to apply the input vector to the RRAM crossbar to finish the vector-matrix multiplication. On the RRAM crossbar, the input vector is programmed to the voltage vector $V = [v_1, v_2, v_3, ..., v_n]$, where v_1 is applied to the first row in the crossbar.

According to Kirchoff's Law, the output current value of each column on the RRAM crossbar equals the dot product result of the input voltage vector V and the vector consisting of the RRAM units conductance in the corresponding column. For example, the first column current is $i_1 = v_1 \cdot g_{11} + v_2 \cdot g_{21} + v_3 \cdot g_{31} + ... + v_n \cdot g_{n1}$. With the crossbar computing process above, the RRAM crossbar can be used to efficiently perform vector-matrix multiplications within a few cycles, which is crucial for accelerating CNN. And the crossbar architecture has been widely integrated into different accelerators such as ISAAC [5], Prime [6], and Timely [7].

To train CNN on the RRAM crossbar, a common method is online tuning, which means the conductance of the RRAM units is firstly programmed according to the initialized weights and then tuned in further iterations. During online tuning, RRAM is reprogrammed by applying the high voltage many times, which causes subtle changes in RRAM units, resulting in a decrease in the data precision that RRAM supports, which is called aging. RRAM units that are never used are in the fresh status, where they can support the highest data precision, and ones that have been programmed many times are in the aged status, where they cannot support high data precision. If the precision of the mapped data exceeds what the RRAM units support, this may result in the data loss of the mapped data, that ultimately influences the high CNN training accuracy iterations, which is regarded as the lifetime of the RRAM on training CNN.

In our previous surveys, we find that many factors affect RRAM lifetime, e.g., temperature [8] and noise [9]. Many methods [10] have been proposed to extend RRAM lifetime from temperature and noise views. But we don't find methods proposed to extend the RRAM lifetime from the perspective of weights mapping. Although the CNN workload balance [11] can reduce the status gap among the different RRAM units to some extent, there also is left space for improvement. We find that the Network Pruning theories [12] can be applied to this problem, in these theories, some weights that hardly affect network accuracy can be removed, which reminds us to consider that the weights mapping framework can be performed on the hybrid of the fresh and aged RRAM to extend RRAM lifetime.

In this paper, we evaluate the performance of the weights mapping on RRAM lifetime based on Taylor expansion. According to our analysis, we propose the weights mapping framework to improve RRAM lifetime in the hybrid environment of aged and fresh RRAM. Our contributions are:

- We propose an evaluating method based on Taylor expansion to compare two opposite weights mappings performance.
- According to our evaluating method, we propose the weights mapping framework consisting of two methods: 1. Weights mapping based on the layer position in CNN, 2. Weights mapping based on the characteristic of the groups which split weights in the same kernel.
- We do experiments about three VGG-like networks as shown in Table 1 (NN5, NN7, NN9) on two datasets (MNIST, Fashion). Compared with the random weights mapping, our weights mapping framework can improve the RRAM lifetime by 6.3× on average.

2 Background and Motivation

In this section, we will review the CNN training on RRAM crossbars, RRAM aging, and other related backgrounds.

2.1 CNN Training on RRAM

The convolution operator is the most common operator in CNN, which extracts information from the input data by applying the convolution kernel. Figure 3 depicts the kernel weights W mapping on RRAM, where the convolution kernel, with 3 channels, convolutes on the input data X. The weights W within each channel are converted into a one-dimensional vector, which is mapped on a

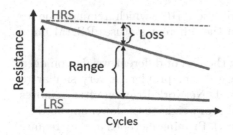

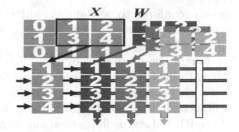

Fig. 2. The aging progress of RRAM

Fig. 3. Mapping the convolution kernel weights on RRAM

column of the crossbar, and then, as Fig. 1 shown, the input data is also converted to a one-dimensional voltage vector and this voltage vector is applied to the crossbar to generate the results.

After W is mapped on the RRAM crossbar, the output of the network is compared with the expected output in the training data, and the difference between them is defined as the $Cost$, which is used as the feedback to the neural network to adjust the weights. $\mathcal{LR}$ denotes the learning rate. According to $Cost$, the backpropagation is then applied to update the weights as below equation in CNN to reduce the $Cost$ for higher training accuracy.

$$W = W - \mathcal{LR} \cdot \frac{\partial Cost}{\partial W} \qquad (1)$$

2.2 RRAM Aging

Both Mapping weights on RRAM and adjusting the weights need applying the high voltage to RRAM, inducing tiny changes within the RRAM cells [13]. Regrettably, these tiny changes are irreparable, leading to RRAM aging and a permanent decrease in its supporting precision. The phenomenon of RRAM aging is depicted in Fig. 2, where HRS and LRS denote the upper and lower resistance of the RRAM. The interval between HRS and LRS denotes the range that RRAM uses to support data precision. The latest single RRAM cell can store 3 bits and the byte is usually represented by a fixed number RRAM units [14]. As the times of RRAM applied to high voltage increases, tiny changes accumulate in the RRAM cells, and finally, the accumulated changes decrease the precision that RRAM supports.

2.3 Weights Distribution and Network Pruning

To avoid gradient disappearance and gradient explosion, many initialization methods such as Kaiming initialization have been integrated into PyTorch [15]. These initialization methods normalize the distribution of weights across each layer of CNN, and prior research has demonstrated that the trained weights mostly conform to a Gaussian-alike distribution [16], which reminds me to explore the influence of weights mapped on the different statuses RRAM units on CNN training.

Furthermore, we need to determine how the loss of different weights on aged RRAM affects network training. In this regard, our problem is very similar to Network Pruning, but with two differences: 1. Network Pruning often removes useless weights, while RRAM reduces the value of weight to the lower one because of the RRAM status limitation, and 2. Network Pruning methods usually require complete network training and repeat fine-tuning, and these methods need much computation and may further age RRAM. Additionally, as RRAM computes based on the crossbars, many Network Pruning methods like unstructured pruning are also difficult to adapt to RRAM.

In the following sections, we discuss the evaluating methods of the two opposite weights mapping methods and propose the weights mapping framework suitable for RRAM crossbars and our framework achieves better performance compared to the random weights mapping baseline.

3   Evaluate Weights Mapping

To map different weights to RRAM with different statuses in a reasonable way, we want to know how to evaluate the weights mapping to some extent in advance. Consider a set of training examples $\mathcal{D} = \{\mathcal{X} = \{x_0, x_1, \ldots, x_n\}, \mathcal{Y} = \{y_0, y_1, \ldots, y_n\}\}$, where x_i, y_i respectively represent an input and a target output. The weights $\mathcal{W} = \{w_0, w_1, \ldots, w_n\}$ are optimized to minimize the cost value $Cost(\mathcal{D}, \mathcal{W})$.

We find the weights update magnitude from backpropagation usually drops out of the range that aged RRAM supports. Because the update of the weights in the layer follows $\frac{\partial Cost}{\partial w^l} = \delta^l \cdot \sigma\left(z^{l-1}\right)$, where $\sigma\left(z^{l-1}\right)$ is the previous layer output and δ^l means the derivative of $Cost$ to z^l. To avoid gradient disappearance and gradient explosion, each layer output needs to be normalized, causing the absolute value of $\sigma\left(z^{l-1}\right)$ and δ^l is less than 1.0. So the update magnitude on weights following Eq. 1 is less than $\mathcal{LR}$. $\mathcal{LR}$ is usually related to iteration speed and overfitting, to take a good compromise, it's common to pick 0.0001 as $\mathcal{LR}$. This means the update magnitude on weights is usually less than 0.0001. The aged RRAM can not support such high precision, so the weights in CNN training on the aged RRAM are not precisely updated, and eventually, the effects of backpropagation will be useless on the aged RRAM.

In this situation, we evaluate the weights mapping on the training network based on Taylor expansion. As $|\Delta Cost| = |\mathcal{C}(\mathcal{D}, \mathcal{W}') - \mathcal{C}(\mathcal{D}, \mathcal{W})|$ shows, where $\mathcal{W}$ means the original weights and $\mathcal{W}'$ is the weights mapped on the RRAM with different statuses, $|\Delta Cost|$ means the difference caused by weights change because of the RRAM statuses limitation.

For notational convenience, we temporarily consider the weights mapped on the aged RRAM as $\alpha \mathcal{W}$, where α is an aged factor ranging from 0.0 to 1.0. The larger α indicates the weights mapped on the fresher RRAM. Then, the $|\Delta Cost|$ is can be expressed as $|\Delta Cost| = |\mathcal{C}(\mathcal{D}, W) - \mathcal{C}(\mathcal{D}, \alpha W)|$.

To approximate $|\Delta Cost|$, we use the first-degree Taylor polynomial. For a function $f(x)$, the Taylor expansion at point $x = a$ is $f(x) = \sum_{p=0}^{P} \frac{f^{(p)}(a)}{p!}(x - a)^p + R_p(x)$, where $f^{(p)}(a)$ is the p-th derivative of f evaluated at point a, and $R_p(x)$ is the p-th order remainder. Approximating $\mathcal{C}(\mathcal{D}, \alpha W)$ with a first-order Taylor polynomial near αW, we have: $\mathcal{C}(\mathcal{D}, \alpha W) = \mathcal{C}(\mathcal{D}, W) - \frac{\partial \mathcal{C}}{\partial W}(W - \alpha W) + R_1(W = \alpha W)$. The remainder $R_1(W = \alpha W)$ can be neglected largely because of the significant calculation required, but also in part because the widely-used ReLU activation function encourages a smaller second order term [17], so we substitute the above equations, we have: $|\Delta Cost| = |\mathcal{C}(\mathcal{D}, W) - \mathcal{C}(\mathcal{D}, \alpha W)| = |\frac{\partial \mathcal{C}}{\partial W}(W - \alpha W)| = |(1 - \alpha)\frac{\partial \mathcal{C}}{\partial W}W|$. $\frac{\partial \mathcal{C}}{\partial W}$ usually needs enormous amounts of computation, many studies [18] choose to neglect its effect temporarily. Intuitively, $|\Delta Cost|$ is much related to $(1 - \alpha)$ and W. It shows that the RRAM aged factor and the weights themselves can affect $|\Delta Cost|$. Based on that, we can infer that we should avoid mapping the weights with the high value on the aged RRAM.

For this, we conduct experiments to compare the opposite weights mapping methods in advance, which are illustrated in detail in the next section. We assume that we map weights on the RRAM which has half aged units and half fresh units. In Fig. 4, we accumulate the loss between the original value and the value mapped on the different statuses RRAM units to get information loss, and *back-front* means that we map the weights of the front/back half of the network on the aged RRAM and map the left half weights on the fresh RRAM. We can observe that the *back* has less information loss than *front* in NN5, NN7 and more information loss in NN9, these networks structure will be illustrated in Table 1. According to the information loss, we can predict the *back* performs better compared with *front* in NN5, NN7, and has worse performance than *front* in NN9.

We also compare the information loss between *over* and *below* weights mapping, which groups the weights within the same kernel and maps the groups on the different statuses RRAM according to the absolute sum of the groups. Based on Fig. 4, we find that *below* has less information loss than *over* and we predict *below* has better performance than *over*. The final experiments results show that our evaluation between the opposite weights mapping methods is effective.

4   Weights Mapping Framework

According to the comparison of information loss in the above section, we propose two weights mapping methods. The first is to map all the weights of different convolutional kernels to the RRAM with different statuses based on the layer position of weights in the network. The second is to group the weights of each convolution kernel for RRAM crossbar computation and map them based on the values of the grouped weights.

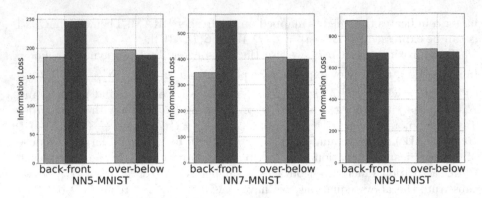

Fig. 4. Compare information loss of different weights mappings. The bar means the information loss of weights mapping.

4.1   Dataflow

As shown in Fig. 5, there are three RRAM crossbars with varying degrees of aged, labeled as Fresh, Old and Older, with Fresh exhibiting the minimum degree of aged, followed by Old, and Older. In training CNN, the weights in the convolution kernels need to be mapped on the RRAM crossbar. There are two simple mapping directions in Fig. 5: Dataflow1 maps the Conv1 weights on the Fresh crossbar, the Conv2 weights on the Old crossbar, and the Conv3 weights on the Older crossbar, while Dataflow2 sets the Conv1 weights to the Older crossbar, the Conv2 weights to the Old crossbar, and the Conv3 weights to the Fresh crossbar, with the input data streams going through Conv1 followed by Conv2 and Conv3.

In the real case, our usual choice is Dataflow2. The weights in the back half of the network are mapped on the aged RRAM and the front half weights are mapped on the fresh RRAM, this weights mapping, called *back*, results in less information loss compared with the opposite weights mapping in some networks as shown in Fig. 4.

4.2   Grouping and Mapping Groups

In the above section, we observe that the approach of mapping weights to RRAM with different statuses based on the layer position may become ineffective as CNN becomes deep as shown in Fig. 4. This challenge leads us to explore a weights mapping approach that applies to all deep CNN for RRAM crossbars.

As illustrated in Fig. 6, we extract the kernel weights in the stripe-wise direction and map them to the column in the RRAM crossbar. Similarly, we extract input data in the same direction to apply it on the crossbar. Each crossbar generates a part of this layer output, and all the results from the crossbars must be summed on the position of the next layer. As shown in Fig. 6, $K \times K$ crossbars are required for computation, and $K \times K$ outputs must be aggregated to derive the output at the intended position of the next layer.

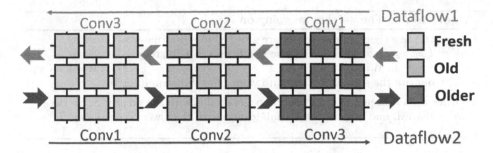

Fig. 5. Two dataflows: Dataflow1 maps the front half of weights in the network on the aged RRAM, and Dataflow2 maps the back half of weights in the network on the aged RRAM.

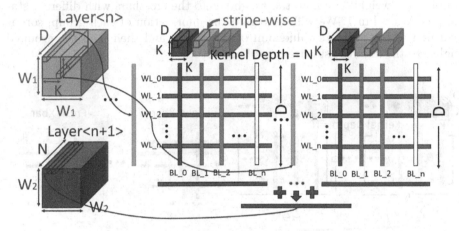

Fig. 6. We group weights in the stripe-wise direction and the input data that is extracted in the stripe-wise direction is applied to the crossbar.

Compared to the traditional weights mapping shown in Fig. 3, the grouping in the stripe-wise direction brings significant advantages. Since the traditional mapping method converts the weights of each channel into a one-dimensional vector and maps it to the column of the RRAM crossbar, and this method requires a large RRAM crossbar with the size of $N \times (K \times K \times D)$. Our mapping as Fig. 6 shows groups the weights in the stripe-wise direction and maps the groups to many little size RRAM crossbars with different statuses, and avoid using the one whole large size RRAM crossbar consisting of different statuses RRAM units.

Algorithm 1: The weights mapping on crossbars

---

1 **Input:** The weights in one kernel are grouped in the stripe-wise direction
  $W = \{w_1, w_2, ..., w_n\}$, w_i means the weights set in i-th group.

2 **for** *each w_i in W* **do**   // Traverse all w_i

3 ⌊ Compute the sum of the absolute value of w_i $S_i = sum(\|w_i\|)$

4 Order S_i in descending order and map the groups with the greater S_i on the
  fresh RRAM, and map the other half groups with the lower S_i on the aged
  RRAM.

From Fig. 4, we know that the weights information loss caused by RRAM with different statuses has different impacts on CNN. As shown in Fig. 7, after grouping the weights, we map the weights onto the crossbars with different statuses as Algorithm 1. We will aggregate the information of each group, sort it according to the absolute value sum of the group, and then map the grouped weights to the different statuses crossbars.

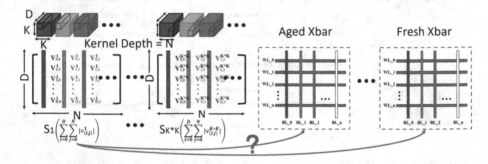

Fig. 7. After we group the weights, we map the groups on the crossbars with different statuses as Algorithm 1 describes.

5   Experiments

To evaluate the performance of our weights mapping approaches, we test three different neural networks, NN5, NN7, and NN9, on two datasets, MNIST and Fashion [19]. We use three VGG-like networks shown in Table 1, where NN5 has 5 convolution layers, NN7 has 7 convolution layers, and NN9 has 9 convolution layers to explore the effect of different weights mapping on networks with different depths. Because the simulation continuously changes the weights according to the RRAM units' statuses, the simulation will cost much time even though we test small datasets such as MNIST and Fashion at first. MNIST and Fashion both contain 60,000 images, and the images are divided into 10 classes. We conduct simulation experiments in the hybrid environment of aged and fresh RRAM, where the number of fresh RRAM units is the same as the aged RRAM ones. All network implementations and the weights mapping framework are implemented using Numpy [20]. The experiments are tested on an Intel Xeon Silver 4114 CPU @ 2.20GHz.

Table 1. CNN Configuration

CNN Configuration		
NN5	NN7	NN9
5 conv layers	7 conv layers	9 conv layers
input (28×28 image)		
conv3-16	conv3-16	conv3-16
maxpool		
conv3-16	conv3-16	conv3-16
maxpool		
conv3-16	conv3-16	conv3-16
conv3-32	conv3-32	conv3-32
conv3-64	conv3-32	conv3-32
	conv3-64	conv3-32
	conv3-64	conv3-64
		conv3-64
		conv3-64
FC-128		
FC-10		
soft-max		

Table 2 shows the performance of different weights mapping methods on different datasets and networks, where the data represents the RRAM lifetime improvement compared to the random weights mapping, which maps the weights on the same RRAM randomly. The lifetime is the iteration when the CNN training batch accuracy drops down the borderline, which usually is defined as 80% of the original final accuracy from the test data [21], and we use the same rule. The crosses in the next figures mark the lifetime of the RRAM. The *front-half* means we map the weights of the front half of CNN on the aged RRAM and map the other weights on the fresh RRAM, and the *back-half* is opposite to the *front-half*. It can be seen that the *front-half* weights mapping is inferior to the random weights mapping in all networks, and does not exhibit significant changes on the networks of different depths.

Unlike the *front-half*, the *back-half* maps the weights of the back half of the CNN to the aged RRAM, and maps the front half to the fresh RRAM. Table 2 shows that the back-half significantly extends 4.9× lifetime in NN7. Although the performance of the back-half on NN5 is not outstanding, Fig. 8 shows that *back-half* still extends the lifetime around 0.6 accuracy in NN5. Comparing Fig. 9 and Fig. 10, we can see that the lifetime improvement of the *back-half* becomes less significant with the depth of CNN increasing, indicating that the simple front or back half weights mapping on RRAM may become ineffective in the deep CNN.

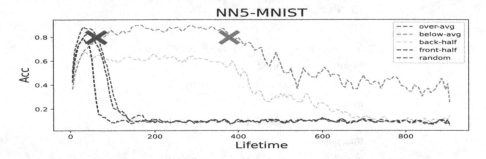

Fig. 8. NN5-MNIST lifetime improvement

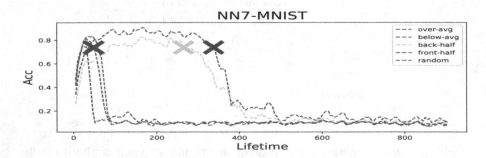

Fig. 9. NN7-MNIST lifetime improvement

Interestingly, we find the results from Table 2 are different from Fig. 4 in NN7 and NN9. But if we lower the borderline determining the lifetime, we can easily find that in NN5 and NN7, *back-half* has better performance, and in NN9 it has almost worse performance than *front-half* from Fig. 8, Fig. 9 and Fig. 10 which corresponds to the Fig. 4.

For solving the issue of possible inefficiency of *back-half* in deep CNN, we also propose a mapping method that groups the weights and maps them to the crossbars with different aged statuses. The main criterion for this mapping is the absolute sum of grouped weights as Algorithm 1 describes. The *over-avg* means that we map the half groups that have the greater absolute sum on the aged RRAM, and map the other half groups on the fresh RRAM. As shown in

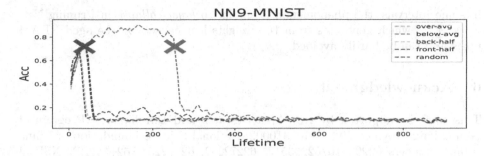

Fig. 10. NN9-MNIST lifetime improvement

Table 2, the *over-avg* shows a similar speedup to the random weights mapping among all the networks.

The *below-avg* is opposite to the *over-avg*, *below-avg* maps the half groups with less absolute value sum to the aged crossbar and maps the other half groups on the fresh crossbar. As shown in Table 2, the *below-avg* demonstrates a significant and stable lifetime improvement across all networks. This highlights the meaningfulness of weights grouping in the convolution kernel, which not only allows a more flexible and friendly mapping for the RRAM crossbars but also significantly enhances lifetime.

Table 2. Weights mapping lifetime improvment

NN	Dataset	back-half	front-half	over-avg	below-avg
NN5	MNIST	0.8×	0.8×	1.3×	7.1×
	Fashion	1.1×	0.7×	0.7×	5.5×
NN7	MNIST	4.8×	0.5×	0.9×	5.6×
	Fashion	5.0×	0.7×	1.0×	7.2×
NN9	MNIST	0.8×	0.6×	0.9×	5.7×
	Fashion	1.0×	0.7×	1.3×	7.2×

Although Fig. 4 shows the loss of the four weights mapping, the *back/front-half* loss is difficult to be compared with the *below/over-avg* one. Because the loss between *back-half* and *front-half* is primarily caused by the weights distribution difference in the different layers. But the loss between *below-half* and *over-half* generates from the same kernel, its difference is dramatically smaller than the loss between *back-half* and *front-half*. Even though the information loss cannot be compared with the weights mapping *back/front-half* based on the dataflow and the one *below/over-avg* within the kernel directly, it can be used to compare the weights mappings based on the same way such as *back-half* and *front-half* or *below-half* and *over-half*. In the above figures, the accuracy drops very fast in some intervals, the phenomenon is similar to *layer-collapse* in Pruning Networks [22], which generates from the weights loss caused by the aged RRAM units and can be hardly avoided.

6 Acknowledgment

This work is supported by Key-Area Research and Development Program of Guangdong Province 2021B0101310002; National Science Foundation of China (grant numbers 62293510/62293513, 62272252, 62272253, 62141412), NSF of Tianjin 21JCYBJC00070; Fundamental Research Funds for the Central Universities.

7 Conclusions

In this paper, we analyze the impact of aged RRAM on training CNN and proposed a method to evaluate the performance of weights mapping on the hybrid of aged and fresh RRAM through Taylor expansion in advance. Based on this method, we propose a weights mapping framework specifically designed for the hybrid of aged and fresh RRAM to extend RRAM engines lifetime consisting of two weights mapping methods. The *back-half* maps the weights of the back half of the network to aged RRAM, and the *below-avg* groups the weights and maps the groups with smaller absolute value sum to aged RRAM. Experimental results show that both *back-half* and *below-avg* can improve the lifetime of RRAM accelerators. However, in experiments, *back-half* varies in lifetime improvement in CNN with different depths, while *below-avg* can stably improve the RRAM lifetime in all CNN. Compared with random weights mapping baseline, *below-avg* can improve the RRAM lifetime by 6.3× on average.

References

1. Cokun, M., et al.: Face recognition based on convolutional neural network. In: International Conference on Modern Electrical and Energy Systems (2017)
2. Li, Q., et al.: Medical image classification with convolutional neural network. In: 13th International Conference on Control Automation Robotics & Vision (2014)
3. Chen, L., et al.: Beyond human recognition: a CNN-based framework for handwritten character recognition. In: 3rd IAPR Asian Conference on Pattern Recognition (2015)
4. Tang, T., et al.: Binary convolutional neural network on RRAM. In: 22nd Asia and South Pacific Design Automation Conference (2017)
5. Shafiee, A., et al.: ISAAC: a convolutional neural network accelerator with in-situ analog arithmetic in crossbars. In: ACM SIGARCH Computer Architecture News, vol. 44, no. 3, pp. 14–26 (2016)
6. Chi, P., et al.: Prime: a novel processing-in-memory architecture for neural network computation in reram-based main memory. In: ACM SIGARCH Computer Architecture News, vol. 44, no. 3, pp. 27–39 (2016)

7. Li, W., et al.: Timely: pushing data movements and interfaces in pim accelerators towards local and in time domain. In: ACM/IEEE 47th Annual International Symposium on Computer Architecture (2020)
8. Chen, P.Y., et al.: WRAP: weight RemApping and processing in RRAM-based neural network accelerators considering thermal effect. In: Design, Automation & Test in Europe Conference & Exhibition (2022)
9. Zhang, G.L., et al.: Reliable and robust RRAM-based neuromorphic computing. In Proceedings of the 2020 on Great Lakes Symposium on VLSI (2020)
10. Zhang, S., et al.: Lifetime enhancement for rram-based computing-in-memory engine considering aging and thermal effects. In: 2nd IEEE International Conference on Artificial Intelligence Circuits and Systems (2020)
11. Zhu, Z., et al.: Mixed size crossbar based RRAM CNN accelerator with overlapped mapping method. In: International Conference on Computer-Aided Design (2018)
12. Liang, T., et al.: Pruning and quantization for deep neural network acceleration: a survey. Neurocomputing **461**, 370–403 (2021)
13. Chen, B., et al.: Physical mechanisms of endurance degradation in TMO-RRAM. In: International Electron Devices (2011)
14. Le, B.Q., et al.: Resistive RAM with multiple bits per cell: array-level demonstration of 3 bits per cell. IEEE Trans. Electron Dev. **66**(1), 641–646 (2018)
15. Yong, H., Huang, J., Hua, X., Zhang, L.: Gradient centralization: a new optimization technique for deep neural networks. In: Vedaldi, A., Bischof, H., Brox, T., Frahm, J.-M. (eds.) ECCV 2020. LNCS, vol. 12346, pp. 635–652. Springer, Cham (2020). https://doi.org/10.1007/978-3-030-58452-8_37
16. Huang, Z., Shao, W., Wang, X., Lin, L., Luo, P.: Rethinking the pruning criteria for convolutional neural network. Adv. Neural Inf. Process. Syst. **34**, 16305–16318 (2021)
17. Molchanov, P., et al.: Pruning convolutional neural networks for resource efficient inference. In: International Conference on Learning Representations (2017)
18. LeCun, Y., Denker, J., Solla, S.: Optimal brain damage. In: Conference on Neural Information Processing Systems (1989)
19. Xiao, H., Rasul, K., Vollgraf, R.: Fashion-mnist: a novel image dataset for benchmarking machine learning algorithms. arXiv Machine Learning (2017)
20. Walt, S., Colbert, S.C., Varoquaux, G.: The NumPy array: a structure for efficient numerical computation. Comput. Sci. Eng. **13**(2), 22–30 (2011)
21. Zhang, S., et al.: Lifetime enhancement for rram-based computing-in-memory engine considering aging and thermal effects. In: IEEE International Conference on Artificial Intelligence Circuits and Systems (2020)
22. Tanaka, H., et al.: Pruning neural networks without any data by iteratively conserving synaptic flow. Adv. Neural Inf. Process. Syst. **33**, 6377–6389 (2020)

The Optimization of IVSHMEM Based on Jailhouse

Jiaming Zhang, Fengyun Li, Liu Yang, Yucong Chen, Hubin Yang, Qingguo Zhou, Yan Li$^{(\boxtimes)}$, and Rui Zhou$^{(\boxtimes)}$

School of Information Science and Engineering, Lanzhou University, Lanzhou, Gansu, China
{jmzhang2020,220220941880,220220942471,chenyc18, yanghb2019,zhouqg,ynali,zr}@lzu.edu.cn

Abstract. The hypervisor, with its resource isolation, security guarantees, and ability to meet high real-time requirements, offers significant advantages in real-time scenarios. Furthermore, its communication capabilities play a crucial role in enabling collaborative computation tasks across different virtual machines. The Jailhouse hypervisor, known for its real-time capabilities and secure embedded platform, demonstrates outstanding performance in real-time scenarios. However, the inter-virtual machine (inter-VM) communication protocol based on Jailhouse is not yet mature, necessitating optimization to enhance its suitability for real-time communication scenarios. Firstly, the existing communication mechanism underwent reconstruction, involving the disabling of the one-shot interrupt mode and expanding the shared memory area. Secondly, an experimental platform was established on the Raspberry Pi-4B, configuring the real-time system and adopting the io_uring methods. Finally, experimental evaluations were conducted to assess the differences in communication delay, throughput, and data transmission delay before and after the communication protocol reconstruction. Additionally, the mitigating effect of the new communication mechanism on VMexit behavior was also evaluated. The experimental results demonstrate that the enhanced communication mechanism significantly reduces both the system call overhead and the number of VMexit compared to the native communication protocol (Inter-VM Shared Memory, IVSHMEM). Moreover, the throughput exhibits a notable improvement of approximately 200 MB/s.

Keywords: Virtualization · Jailhouse · IVSHMEM · communication mechanism · RTOS

1 Introduction

Amidst the escalating software complexity and the prevailing shift towards heterogeneous computing platforms, consolidating multiple functionalities within

---

J. Zhang and F. Li—These authors contributed equally to this work.

© The Author(s), under exclusive license to Springer Nature Singapore Pte Ltd. 2024
C. Li et al. (Eds.): APPT 2023, LNCS 14103, pp. 54–75, 2024.
https://doi.org/10.1007/978-981-99-7872-4_4

a single hardware platform is considered an optimal approach to tackle issues related to space, weight, power consumption, and economic considerations [1]. One effective strategy for resource consolidation is the utilization of virtualization technology. By employing a hypervisor, it becomes possible to operate multiple cells with different operating systems on a single platform, thereby enhancing the integration capabilities of the hardware platform. Consequently, the concept of distributed systems becomes highly significant, as it allows for the deployment and execution of applications across multiple physical or virtual machines, further enhancing system flexibility and efficiency. This combination of virtualization and distributed processing has stimulated the development of Mixed Critical Systems (MCS), where tasks with varying levels of criticality are executed by corresponding operating systems [22]. Virtualization technology plays a central role in resource partitioning and task execution within MCS.

Solutions for implementing mixed critical systems within a single system can be classified into two categories [3]: dual-kernel solutions and resource partitioning solutions [30]. The former category comprises RTLinux, RTAI, and Xenomai, while the latter includes Bao [15], ACRN [12], and Jailhouse [2]. This article specifically focuses on the resource partitioning solution-Jailhouse.

Jailhouse [18,23,24] represents a typical static partitioning hypervisor that emphasizes static resource allocation. Its compact codebase stems from its lack of a scheduler or virtualization services. This characteristic not only facilitates the certification of security features but also contributes to the vibrant development of the Jailhouse community [7]. When constructing MCS, Jailhouse exhibits two primary advantages [13,21]. Firstly, in comparison to virtualization managers such as KVM and Xen, which are more tailored to server environments, Jailhouse better fulfills the real-time requirements of embedded platforms. Secondly, Jailhouse conforms to the demands of safety-critical design due to its small footprint, aligning well with certification requirements. In contrast, other hypervisors similar to Jailhouse, such as SafeG [20] and Quest-V [27,28], have limited application scenarios or lower adaptability in practical usage.

Inter-VM communication functionality serves as a crucial component of hypervisors. To optimize Inter-Process Communication (IPC) efficiency, shared memory technology has been explored [5,6], aiming to reduce data replication and transmission overhead. While Jailhouse provides a socket interface based on the TCP/IP protocol [17] for inter-VM communication, which establishes communication channels between multiple physical machines, its suitability for latency-sensitive tasks is restricted due to protocol stack requirements, frequent data copying, and multiple context switches [12]. Jailhouse offers the IVSHMEM (Inter-VM Shared Memory) protocol at the lower level, which enables efficient data communication with minimal overhead and is particularly well-suited for local environment implementation. However, the absence of an extensive user-level API and concerns about the maturity of the shared memory protocol impose limitations on IVSHMEM, preventing it from becoming the prevailing inter-VM communication method in Jailhouse.

Based on this premise, the primary focus of this research is to enhance the inter-VM shared memory protocol, IVSHMEM, in Jailhouse, specifically for real-time communication scenarios. The objective is to facilitate communication between two virtual machines, meeting the demands of predictability and high throughput required by real-time systems, while abstaining from the utilization of virtual networks for data exchange. The main contributions of this article are as follows:

1. Investigating the inter-cell[1] communication protocol based on shared memory in Jailhouse, with a particular emphasis on the performance overhead and optimization directions for real-time communication.
2. Reshaping the current communication mechanism by optimizing the communication process, expanding the shared memory region, addressing issues related to excessive VMexit behavior and small shared memory, and designing memory barriers and synchronization mechanisms to ensure synchronized data access.
3. Establishing a Linux and RTOS experimental environment based on Jailhouse on the Raspberry Pi 4B platform, configuring real-time systems, and exploring the use of the asynchronous I/O mechanism, io_uring, to enhance I/O performance.
4. Conducting experimental evaluations to assess the changes in communication latency, throughput, and data transfer latency before and after the reconstruction. The aim is to validate the applicability, feasibility, and advantages of the new communication mechanism in real-time communication scenarios between two cells.

2 Related Works

Communication plays a crucial role in building MCS. Data exchange is required between Host-Guest and Guest-Guest through communication. However, communication between Guest-Guest cells may incur higher costs compared to Guest-Host communication. Hence, optimizing communication mechanisms is essential to ensure the efficiency and reliability of MCS. The design and optimization of inter-cell communication mechanism is a key research area in Jailhouse. This section explores the communication process between cells, provides an overview of the IVSHMEM communication protocol and the background of the io_uring technology, and reviews the relevant research progress.

2.1 IVSHMEM Communication Protocol

Figure 1 provides an example using a Linux cell to illustrate the communication flow between the root cell (cell 0) and the Linux cell (cell 1). Inter-cell communication is facilitated through the utilization of shared memory. During this

---

[1] It is worth noting that in Jailhouse, a virtual machine is commonly referred to as a "cell". Therefore, the terms "inter-VM" and "inter-cell" are equivalent in meaning.

process, the application program in the root cell copies user space data from the kernel space and writes it into the shared memory using a PCI device. The Linux cell, on the other hand, reads the data from the shared memory and transfers it through various layers until it reaches the application program within the Linux cell. To facilitate these operations, the IVSHMEM PCI device is managed by the UIO (Userspace I/O) device driver. Through the override of the mmap system call, the driver enables efficient read and write access to diverse memory regions within the device and the shared memory.

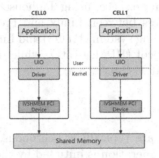

Fig. 1. Inter-cell communication process

The IVSHMEM communication protocol, based on Jailhouse, establishes specifications for inter-cell communication, enabling seamless communication between cells through shared memory and interrupt signaling mechanisms. The IVSHMEM PCI device acts as an interface between the host's shared memory interface (POSIX) and the applications running within the cells. It utilizes Linux event file descriptors to facilitate the transmission of interrupt signals between virtual machines [14]. The functionality and configuration of the IVSHMEM PCI device are primarily determined by three components: the device configuration register set, the device register region, and the shared memory region. The configuration section, visible to the operating system, contains relevant information such as the vendor ID and device ID, which enables the operating system to load the appropriate driver.

The latest version of the IVSHMEM protocol, version 2.0, provides a range of functionalities and features [8]. These functionalities encompass support for up to 65536 interconnected communication nodes, multiple types of shared memory regions, interrupt-based signaling for node communication, support for different shared memory protocols, and memory mapping implementation for the device register region. Initially completed in Jailhouse version 0.9 in 2018, the protocol has undergone improvements in the latest version of Jailhouse (0.12, released in 2020), which address specific communication protocol issues and add support for the Raspberry Pi-4B platform [9].

In 2017, Masaki Miyagawa et al. conducted a comparative study and testing of the IVSHMEM shared memory protocol and the traditional TCP/IP communication protocol. The study focused on different stages of the Jailhouse boot

process and performed in-depth analysis of the memory regions in the cell configuration files, using QEMU (v2.8.1) and Jailhouse (v0.6) on an industrial platform
[16]. In 2019, the official Jailhouse community announced the release of IVSH-
MEM 2.0 version [11]. Ramos et al. investigated the process of inter-partition
communication using the IVSHMEM protocol on the BananaPi-M1 platform
managed by Jailhouse. The study specifically focused on the transmission of messages between two partitions [17]. In another study, Schade et al. developed an
intelligent industrial controller for a computer numerical control (CNC) machine
on the same BananaPi-M1 platform. The controller implemented tool overload
detection and predictive maintenance, using Jailhouse to coordinate concurrent
execution and resource access between Linux and FreeRTOS. Communication
between the real-time operating system (RTOS) and Linux was achieved through
the simplified RPMsg protocol (RPMsg-Lite), while data exchange and transmission utilized the IVSHMEM interface.

2.2   IO_uring

Traditional I/O operations are typically synchronous, also known as blocking
I/O. In this approach, each operation is initiated by the application, which then
pauses and waits for the operation to complete. Read/write functions are used
to perform read and write operations on the underlying files. However, compared
to asynchronous I/O, blocking I/O's performance is limited by the file type and
device capabilities, resulting in potential program blocking. Clearly, blocking I/O
is inadequate for meeting the demands of high real-time scenarios. Asynchronous
I/O allows the application to execute other tasks during the waiting period, significantly reducing the frequency and overhead of system calls and improving
efficiency. As shown in Fig. 2, Linux I/O operations involve data reading and
writing, and a typical I/O operation goes through two stages: data preparation and data copying. After a user-level process initiates an asynchronous I/O
request, it promptly receives status information returned by the kernel. The process can continue its execution rather than being in a blocked state. The kernel
awaits data completion, performs data copying to the user's memory, and eventually sends a signal to the user process, notifying it that the I/O operation has
been completed.

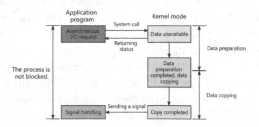

Fig. 2. Asynchronous I/O operation flow

Io_uring is an asynchronous I/O implementation provided by the Linux kernel starting from version 5.1. Its main feature is the ability to reduce the overhead of system calls and alleviate the cost of data copying. The reason for considering the integration of io_uring technology into Jailhouse primarily lies in its capability to achieve zero-copy transfers by constructing a shared ring buffer between the kernel and user space. This eliminates the need for data copying involved in traditional data transfers between the kernel and user space. Although the overhead of a single system call is minimal, frequent system calls can become a performance bottleneck in high-performance applications. Optimizing I/O performance is an important direction for improving real-time systems and contributes to enhancing system predictability [29].

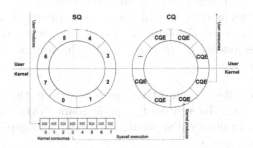

Fig. 3. io_uring Framework

In Fig. 3, io_uring establishes a shared memory region between the user and the kernel using mmap. It constructs two lockless ring queues, namely the submission queue (SQ) and the completion queue (CQ), based on memory barriers. The SQ queue is used for the user program to submit I/O tasks to the kernel, and the completed tasks are placed in the CQ queue, from which the user program retrieves the results. During the submission of tasks and the return of task results, the user program and the kernel share the data in the ring queues. I/O requests and completion events no longer need to be passed through system calls, completely avoiding the overhead of copy_to_user/copy_from_user operations.

In Linux, when using synchronous or asynchronous programming interfaces, each I/O request typically requires at least one system call. However, in io_uring, multiple requests can be submitted at once, with each Submission Queue Entry (SQE) describing an I/O operation. This is achieved through a single system call, further reducing the overhead of system calls. Additionally, the polling mode of io_uring further reduces system calls and interrupt notifications.

Related studies have explored the implementation of asynchronous I/O using the ivshmem shared memory protocol with io_uring, as demonstrated by Reichenbach et al. [19].

3   Design and Implementation

According to the actual application case (ivshmem demo) source code of IVSH-MEM officially provided by Jailhouse, it is analyzed that the communication process of IVSHMEM has the following drawbacks and performance overhead.

1. Low-frequency interrupt signal sending: The use of the alarm command limits the sending of interrupt signals to once per second, resulting in a low frequency.
2. Frequent VMexit: The communication protocol requires writing to the interrupt enable register and device status register in the device register area through VMexit. This behavior occurs frequently during interrupt handling and status updates, leading to performance overhead.
3. Waste of shared memory space: In the current practical application of the communication protocol, the same data is written separately to the rw and out regions corresponding to the current cell. This approach results in wasted shared memory space.

These factors can affect the real-time communication, throughput, and overall system performance. To address the performance overhead of the current IVSHMEM protocol in practical applications, this paper proposes optimizations in the following four aspects.

3.1   Reconstruction and Mapping of IVSHMEM Shared Memory Regions

The current IVSHMEM protocol divides the shared memory region into three regions with different read and write permissions (a Read-Only State Table region used to define and describe the status and attributes of cells, a Read/Write Region used for data sharing and a In Region used to read data from other cells). When communicating between two or three cells, a significant amount of unused memory space is present. Therefore, in this paper, we have reconstructed the shared memory region of the IVSHMEM device by modifying the Jailhouse and Linux device driver code. The original 36 KB Read-Write Region has been modified to 64 KB, providing two new designs for shared memory types to support structured data and maximize the utilization of the shared memory region, thus improving communication efficiency. Additionally, the practice of identifying the current cell's status by writing to the device status register has been eliminated. This approach consumed a significant portion of memory space while offering minimal status information.

The two shared memory structures are shown in Fig. 4. Shared Memory Type I divides the shared memory into 16 fixed-length frames, with each frame being 4KB. It supports concurrent usage of shared memory by multiple processes, where different frames are used by different applications to avoid data synchronization overhead. Shared Memory Type II treats the 64KB shared memory region as a unified whole and dynamically allocates memory using the malloc tool. Based on the Sender ID and Receiver ID in the protocol header, this type of memory primarily serves the data communication between two cells' processes. The Semaphore field indicates data availability, and the Semaphore and other shared memory region data are promptly updated using device memory barrier primitives. The communication protocol fields also encompass current data frame length, total number of data frames, current frame number, and data pointer, among others. For the two shared memory types, mapping is performed separately. The mapping process uses a character pointer array to index different types of shared memory regions to their respective memory locations. By designing the two shared memory types, structured data can be used in shared memory, supporting concurrent access by multiple processes, meeting dynamic shared memory requirements, and expanding the shared memory region of the IVSHMEM PCI device.

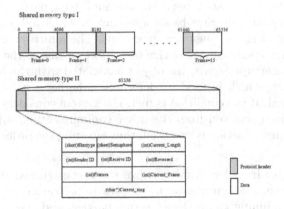

Fig. 4. Two types of shared memory

In the user-space program, the prot field in the mmap system call is modified to set the read-write attributes of the memory mapping region. Moreover, modifications are necessary in the cell configuration file, Jailhouse code, device driver code, and user-space code. Subsequently, the kernel needs to be recompiled and installed, and Jailhouse must be enabled.

3.2   Device Memory Barriers and Synchronization Mechanisms

Mechanism Design. Considering the selected platform architecture, the design also takes into account the memory barrier and synchronization mechanisms when operating on device memory regions. A memory barrier for device memory is a method of controlling the order of execution of CPU or other device instructions, aimed at maintaining data consistency in multi-threaded or multi-process environments. Synchronization mechanisms, such as mutex locks and semaphores, are common programming techniques used to regulate the access order of shared resources among multiple processes or threads to prevent data race conditions. Proper application of device memory barriers and synchronization mechanisms can ensure timely synchronization of device memory regions between two cells, improving operational stability, efficiency, and preventing data conflicts.

In the ARMv8 architecture, the device memory barrier mechanism adjusts the order of memory operations by differentiating between instruction and data caches and employing three different memory barrier instructions: instruction synchronization barrier (ISB), data memory barrier (DMB), and data synchronization barrier (DSB). By setting the cache attribute of the shared memory region to MAP_CACHED and using memory barrier primitives, the timeliness of the data is ensured.

Although memory barriers ensure consistency in CPU memory access order, prevent data races and out-of-order execution, the order of shared memory operations also needs to be consistent between communicating parties. To achieve the desired consistency, an interrupt-based approach is employed, effectively guaranteeing the order of shared memory operations. The interrupt-based approach listens for interrupt events on the device file object to ensure the order of operations. Once an interrupt occurs, the object associated with the interrupt event saves a semaphore, which is used to determine whether a specific I/O event behavior is satisfied. If the condition is met, the system considers that an interrupt signal has been received from the other communicating object, and then the interrupt handler function is executed, thus ensuring the order of operations.

Modules Design. In order to fully utilize the reconstructed shared memory regions, we propose a design approach for data initialization and the send/receive modules, combining knowledge of kernel barriers and synchronization. We have redesigned the data preparation and communication processes, dividing them into the communication initialization module and the data communication module. The former is responsible for two types of memory mapping and io_uring initialization, while the latter handles the initialization, sending, and receiving of data for the two types of shared memory.

Taking shared memory type II as an example (as shown in Fig. 5), the communication initialization module is divided into two parts: mapping and reconstructing the shared memory, and io_uring initialization. The specific steps are as follows:

1. Map the discrete IVSHMEM PCI device's shared memory to virtual memory and consolidate it into a unified block divided into 16 data frames of 4 KB each.
2. After memory mapping, format the communication protocol data structure in the memory header. For shared memory type I, the header of each data frame needs to be individually initialized.
3. Utilize io_uring as a replacement for the read operation to perform I/O operations for reading data from external storage devices. The read data is seg-

mented according to the frame length and the data pointers are filled into the corresponding fields of the shared memory protocol area.

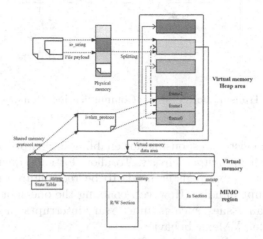

Fig. 5. Initialization Module (Communication Memory Type II)

After initialization, data frames are sent in parallel for shared memory types I and II, with type I sending frames concurrently and type II sending frames sequentially. Memory barriers and semaphores are used to ensure data consistency and synchronization. This process represents the data sending process for both shared memory types, and the data receiving process is the reverse of the data sending process. Taking shared memory type II as an example (Fig. 6), after initialization, each frame is sequentially sent. The first data frame is written into the shared memory data area, then an interrupt vector value is written to the doorbell register in the register area to send an interrupt signal to the communication object. Finally, the critical section is entered, where memory barriers ensure data consistency. Within the critical section, the process waits for the semaphore indicating that the data has been read and receives the interrupt signal sent by the communication object before exiting the critical section. Once the current frame data is sent, the next frame data sending process begins.

3.3 Disabling the One-Shot Interrupt Mode

Disabling the one-shot interrupt mode can improve system predictability and reliability, as well as enhance system performance in real-time communication scenarios. Instead of using periodic alarm-based interrupts, direct manipulation of the mmio region's registers is employed to increase the frequency of interrupt signal transmission.

Enabling the one-shot interrupt mode involves setting the Privilege Control Register in the device's feature extension register group to 1. In this mode, the

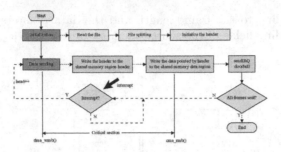

Fig. 6. Data Transmission Module (Communication Memory Type II)

Interrupt Control Register, responsible for enabling interrupts, is automatically reset to 0 after each interrupt delivery. To allow for subsequent interrupts to occur, the interrupt enable register needs to be reconfigured to 1 within the application's interrupt handler. However, enabling the one-shot interrupt mode may introduce certain issues, such as unnecessary interrupts and additional processing overhead (i.e., VMexit behavior).

To tackle this issue, the approach of disabling the one-shot interrupt mode is adopted. Within the IVSHMEM device driver, the pertinent statements responsible for writing to the device's memory are commented out, thereby maintaining the interrupt enable register at 1 and preventing unnecessary operational overhead. By deactivating the one-shot interrupt mode, there is no longer a requirement to perform the re-enable interrupt operation in the interrupt handler, which is commonly used to ensure proper reception of the subsequent interrupt.

3.4   Applications of IO_uring

To further enhance performance, the traditional read method is replaced with the asynchronous I/O approach of io_uring, resulting in lower system call overhead and improved latency benefits.

The liburing tool is utilized to implement asynchronous I/O operations. Liburing is an open-source library designed to simplify and manage the io_uring interface, allowing developers to more conveniently implement asynchronous I/O operations. It provides a higher-level interface that eliminates the need to directly interact with the native io_uring interface, thereby streamlining the process. Consequently, the invocation interface of the liburing tool differs from the native io_uring interface, as shown in Fig. 7.

The specific workflow for using io_uring is as follows:

1. Initialize the circular buffer by calling the io_uring_queue_init() function. This function accepts two parameters: the Queue Depth (QD) and a ring object (struct io_uring). The QD value is shared between the Submission Queue Entries (SQEs) and Completion Queue Entries (CQEs), with the number of CQEs being twice the number of SQEs.

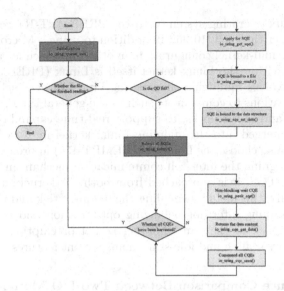

Fig. 7. io_uring data reading process

2. Perform the necessary preparations before submitting the requests, ensuring that all QDs are utilized. This involves allocating SQEs, associating them with file objects and readv operations, reading data, and binding the data with the SQEs. Each read operation reads BS bytes (approximately the size of the shared memory region) and is repeated QD times.
3. Submit the I/O requests. Once all the QDs are fully utilized, the requests are collectively submitted using the io_uring_submit(ring) system call. The io_uring method significantly reduces the number of system calls. In traditional approaches, each request requires at least one system call. However, with io_uring, multiple requests (each represented by a distinct SQE, corresponding to an I/O operation) can be added at once, and the submission is completed with a single system call, io_uring_submit(). Moreover, by employing polling, the kernel can process the SQEs without relying on io_uring_submit(), thereby reducing system performance overhead.
4. The kernel processes the submitted requests and appends the completion events (CQEs) to the end of the completion buffer. Each SQE corresponds to a CQE and contains the status of the respective request.

4   Evaluation and Analysis

The experimental platform used in this study is Raspberry Pi-4B, with a Linux and RTOS system built on Jailhouse. The Linux kernel version used is 5.4.16, and during the kernel compilation process, the kernel configuration file needs to be selected. The Jailhouse version used in this setup is 0.12.

Based on the specific requirements of the Raspberry Pi-4B platform and considering the prototype validation process of Jailhouse, Ralf Ramsauer et al. chose to run a slim Linux operating system with the PREEMPT-RT real-time extension in the secure critical cell [10,26]. In addition to using a Micro-Kernel as the RTOS kernel in a dual-kernel configuration, another approach for achieving real-time capabilities within the Linux kernel itself is Linux (PREEMPT-RT) [25]. This approach involves modifying the existing Linux kernel, including but not limited to modifications to components such as the general timer, interrupt handling structures, and mutex locks, to support real-time capabilities. This work was successfully merged into the mainline Linux kernel in 2004 [4]. Therefore, in this study, we also choose the Linux (PREEMPT-RT) approach as the target RTOS cell for designing the inter-cell communication mechanism.Regarding the configuration of RTOS, it is approached from both the kernel and cell configurations. Specifically, this includes enabling the dynamic tick and tickless options in the kernel, disabling interrupt balancing optimization and the RCU (read-copy-update) callback mechanism, enabling kernel preemption, and disabling processor frequency scaling and idle-state management features.

4.1   Performance Comparison Between Two I/O Methods

To compare the system call counts and latency differences between the two I/O methods of read and io_uring when reading data from a file, this article utilizes a system call count testing script and a latency testing script for the purpose of conducting the tests.

Listing 1.1. System Call Count Evaluation Script

```
sudo strace -o strace.log -c tools/ivshmem-demo ${DATA_file} ${QD}
cat strace.log | grep "total" | awk {print $3}
```

Listing 1.2. Latency Testing Script

```
static unsigned long emul_division(u64 val, u64 div)
{
    unsigned long cnt = 0;
    while (val > div) {
        val -= div;
        cnt++;
    }
    return cnt;
}

u64 timer_ticks_to_ns(u64 ticks)
{
    return emul_division(ticks * 1000, timer_get_frequency() / 1000 / 1000);
}
```

Comparison of System Call Counts Between Read and io_uring. By using the testing script (Listing 1.1), the data file was consecutively read 10 times, and the results are shown in Fig. 8. The QD value represents the maximum number of concurrent tasks that an application can handle. The appropriate selection of the QD value depends on the system hardware performance and the requirements of the application. To fully utilize system resources, enhance system throughput, and improve performance, it is essential to determine the suitable QD value for the current target platform through experimentation. To optimize system call overhead on the experimental platform used in this paper, we recommend selecting a QD value higher than 64, such as 128.

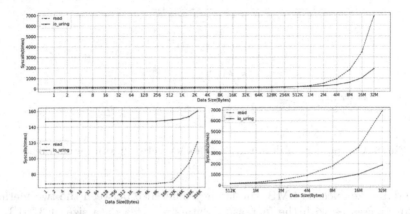

Fig. 8. Comparison of system call frequencies between io_uring and read

The results demonstrate that the read method incurs lower system call overhead when the data size is below the 1 MB threshold. However, as the data size exceeds 1 MB, the system call count of the read method gradually increases, highlighting the disparity between the read method and the io_uring method. At a data size of 32 KB, the system call count of the read method sharply rises. Starting from a data size of 512 KB, the difference in system call counts between the two methods becomes less significant, but the read method experiences a much higher increment compared to the io_uring method. When the data size reaches 32 MB, the read method falls behind the io_uring method by approximately 5000 system call counts. This difference may be attributed to the cache sizes of the experimental platform (L1-Dcache: 32 KB, L2-cache: 1 MB). In contrast to the rapid increase in system call counts of the read method, the io_uring method exhibits a slower increase, making it more suitable for scenarios with larger data sizes.

Comparison of Latency in Data Retrieval Between Read and io_uring.
With the help of the latency testing script (Listing 1.2), the latency differences between the two methods were tested when reading text content of different data sizes. A suitable QD value was selected as the latency result for the io_uring method, and the experiments indicate that a QD value of 8 has a positive impact on improving data read latency.

As shown in Fig. 9, considering the latency differences between the two methods across all data sizes, the io_uring method consistently exhibits better latency performance than the read method. Below the threshold of 1 MB data size, the read method demonstrates more noticeable latency jitter compared to io_uring.

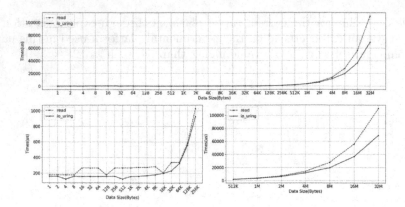

Fig. 9. Comparison of data retrieval latency between io_uring and read

As the data size exceeds 1 MB, the latency difference between the two methods gradually increases with the increasing data size. At a data size of 32 MB, the maximum difference is observed, with the io_uring method showing a latency advantage of approximately 40 ms over the read method. This difference may be attributed to the cache size of the experimental platform. When the cache is filled with data, cache flushing operations occur, resulting in a significant increase in latency.

4.2 Comparison Between Two Types of Shared Memory

In this article, we have constructed two distinct types of shared memory, as depicted in Fig. 4. We designate the first type as new-IVSHMEM (I) and the second type as new-IVSHMEM (II). The former supports parallel transmission and has 16 segments, with each segment capable of accommodating 4 KB of data. The latter supports sending a larger amount of data (64 KB) in one go. The data submission methods for new-IVSHMEM(I) and new-IVSHMEM(II) differ: new-IVSHMEM(I) submits the data once after filling all 16 segments, while new-IVSHMEM(II) submits the data after filling each segment, requiring 16 consecutive submissions.

Comparison of Transmission Latency. As shown in Fig. 10, as the data size increases, both new-IVSHMEM(I) and new-IVSHMEM(II) experience an increase in transmission latency. However, the segmented design of type I, which allows for parallel transmission of 16 frames of data, results in better latency performance compared to the non-segmented design of type II. The experimental results demonstrate a latency difference of at least 15 ms between the two types.

Comparison of VMexit. The number of VMexit is an important metric for evaluating a hypervisor. The design goal of Jailhouse is to minimize interference

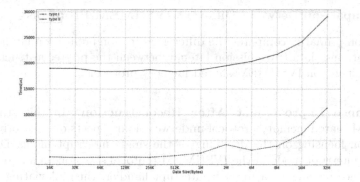

Fig. 10. Transmission latency

with the transactions running inside a cell. The VMexit count indirectly reflects the level of involvement of Jailhouse in the transactions running within the cell.

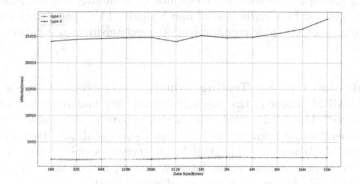

Fig. 11. VMexit counts

As shown in Fig. 11, the evaluation results of the VMexit count during data transmission for new-IVSHMEM(I) and new-IVSHMEM(II) align with the latency results, with type I outperforming type II. Higher latency is typically accompanied by a higher number of VMexit, showing a positive correlation between the two. The experiments indicate a minimum difference of 20,000 VMexit per transmission. The designed communication mechanism aims to mitigate VMexit behavior, aligning with Jailhouse's design philosophy of providing partitioning functionality without excessive interference in the internal transactions of the cell. Additionally, this approach contributes to system stability and enhances reliability in real-time communication scenarios.

4.3   Comparison Between Different IVSHMEM Protocols

This section primarily compares the differences in communication latency, data throughput, and data transmission latency between the pre-reconstruction and post-reconstruction IVSHMEM shared memory protocols.

Performance Improvement After Reconstruction. In this study, the IVSHMEM shared memory protocol underwent four aspects of refactoring, with this section focusing on the disabling of the single interrupt mode. Disabling the single interrupt mode in the IVSHMEM protocol saves one mmio operation on the device register area in each interrupt handler, thus alleviating VMexit behavior.

To evaluate the benefits in terms of VMexit and time brought by disabling the single interrupt mode, we conducted evaluations in the root cell using a Linux-based cell. Through simulation and statistical measurement of actual time costs using the latency testing script (Listing 1.2), we measured the time cost for each operation (a total of 100,000 times) and calculated the mean, resulting in a time cost saving of 1.076497 microseconds by disabling the single interrupt mode, accompanied by a reduction of one VMexit. This observation highlights the effectiveness of the new communication mechanism in mitigating VMexit behavior.

Communication Latency Testing. Through reconstructing specific aspects of the IVSHMEM protocol, the processes of sending and receiving interrupts were optimized. The sender transmits a single byte of data and receives an acknowledgment signal from the receiver upon successful data reception. Both new-IVSHMEM (I) and new-IVSHMEM (II) types exhibit consistent performance in terms of communication latency. Taking new-IVSHMEM (I) as an example, Fig. 12 illustrates a comparison of communication latency between the original IVSHMEM protocol (IVSHMEM-demo) and the communication mechanism proposed in this study (new-IVSHMEM (I)).

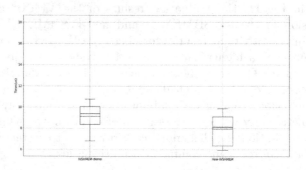

Fig. 12. Comparison of Communication Latency

By comparing the average and median values, it is observed that the new-IVSHMEM method exhibits a difference of approximately 1–2 ms in communication latency compared to the IVSHMEM-demo method. The latter outperforms the former in terms of latency performance, thanks to the disabling of the single interrupt mode, which reduces the VMexit overhead during each communication.

Throughput Testing. To compare the latency and estimate the difference in throughput between IVSHMEM-demo based on the IVSHMEM protocol and new-IVSHMEM based on the communication mechanism proposed in this paper when transmitting 100MB data, the test was conducted 10 times. The specific test results are shown in Table 1, and the differences between the two are illustrated in Fig. 13.

Table 1. Latency Data (Throughput Test)

IVSHMEM-demo/us	new-IVSHMEM/us
84804	74006
83960	70346
84197	71931
87615	71551
86727	75218
88841	70918
82429	70657
83287	71340
84919	71313
87905	74218

Through the comparison, it was found that the throughput of IVSHMEM-demo based on the IVSHMEM protocol is 1170.02 MB/s, while the throughput of new-IVSHMEM designed in this study reaches 1386.01 MB/s, achieving an approximately 200 MB/s throughput improvement. This difference is mainly attributed to the redesigned shared memory region. As new-IVSHMEM can utilize a larger shared memory region, its data throughput is superior to that of IVSHMEM-demo.

Data Transmission Latency Testing. The difference in data transmission latency (median) between new-IVSHMEM and IVSHMEM-demo methods is compared in Fig. 14. For different data sizes, new-IVSHMEM outperforms IVSHMEM-demo, and the latency gap gradually increases with the increase in data volume. When the data size is 32 MB, new-IVSHMEM brings a latency benefit of approximately 5–6 ms. This is attributed to the reconstructed shared memory region and optimization of the native communication protocol described in

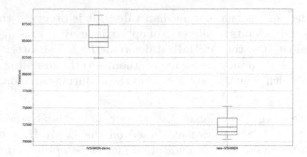

Fig. 13. Data transmission latency difference (Throughput Test)

this paper. When the data volume exceeds 32 KB, the latency difference between the two becomes more significant, which may be related to the cache size of the experimental platform. Additionally, the new communication mechanism has a larger shared memory region, reducing the number of data submissions and lowering latency. This advantage is particularly prominent when handling large volumes of data.

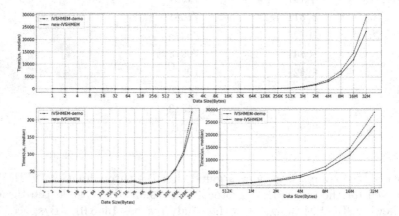

Fig. 14. Comparison of data transmission latency between new-IVSHMEM and IVSHMEM-demo

Based on the comprehensive analysis of the experimental data, the results demonstrate that the communication mechanism designed in this study exhibits lower system call overhead and reduced VMexit compared to the native communication protocol (IVSHMEM). These findings highlight the advantages of the proposed mechanism in enhancing system predictability in real-time communication scenarios.

5 Conclusion

Given the increasing complexity of software, the increasing demand for deploying different systems on the same platform has contributed to the development of mixed critical systems. In this context, the hypervisor assumes a pivotal role in resource partitioning and task execution. Jailhouse, as a lightweight and safety critical design hypervisor, has broad practical application prospects in fields that require real-time virtualization such as intelligent driving and industrial automation. This article aims to provide practical support and solutions for communication issues in future vehicle systems and automation systems by optimizing the Jailhouse IVSHMEM communication protocol.

This study centers on the IVSHMEM communication protocol in Jailhouse and presents a redesign of the shared memory region, proposing two novel design schemes that optimize the communication process and reduce redundant performance overhead. By introducing io_uring to replace traditional read methods, the efficiency of I/O reading is improved. Comparative experiments conducted on both a Linux and RTOS experimental platform based on Jailhouse illustrate that the newly devised mechanism offers advantages in terms of throughput and communication latency.

The IVSHMEM communication protocol remains an ongoing area of development. While the enhanced communication protocol presented in this paper outperforms the performance of the official native communication protocol, it is essential to acknowledge that there are lingering unresolved issues, including:

1. System predictability offers potential for improvement.Currently, the memory-mapped portion of device registers lacks caching, while the shared memory region uses caching, which could impact the system's predictability owing to cache behavior.
2. To facilitate inter-cell communication in Jailhouse, it is conceivable to provide better encapsulation of the current communication protocol's behavior or apply mature alternative communication protocols to Jailhouse. Particularly in scenarios involving communication among multiple cells, a new mechanism may be required to achieve synchronization of operations, further enhancing the work presented in this paper.
3. To minimize Jailhouse's interference in inter-cell communication activities, exploration can be done on how to further avoid VMexit behavior, thereby improving communication performance and aligning with Jailhouse's design philosophy.

Acknowledgements. This work was partially supported by Gansu Province Key Research and Development Plan - Industrial Project under Grant No. 22YF7GA004, Gansu Province Science and Technology Major Project - Industrial Project under Grant No. 22ZD6GA048, the Fundamental Research Funds for the Central Universities under Grant No. lzujbky-2022-kb12, lzujbky-2021-sp43, lzujbky-2020-sp02, lzujbky-2019-kb51 and lzujbky-2018-k12, National Natural Science Foundation of China under Grant Nos. U22A20261 and 61402210. Science and Technology Plan of Qinghai

Province under Grant No.2020-GX-164, and Supercomputing Center of Lanzhou University. We appreciate co-author Mr. Jiaming Zhang's hard work during his postgraduate for the contribution of this paper is inspired by his master thesis [30].

References

1. Biondi, A., Marinoni, M., Buttazzo, G., Scordino, C., Gai, P.: Challenges in virtualizing safety-critical cyber-physical systems. In: Proceedings of Embedded World Conference 2018, pp. 1–5 (2018)
2. Cao, H.: Research on Communication Between Virtual Machines Based on Soft-RoCE in Jailhouse. Master's thesis, Lanzhou University (2022)
3. Corbet, J.: Linux in mixed-criticality systems. https://lwn.net/Articles/774217/. Accessed 7 June 2023
4. Corbet, J.: Safety-critical realtime with linux. https://lwn.net/Articles/734694/. Accessed 7 June 2023
5. Druschel, P.: A high-bandwidth cross-domain transfer facility. In: Proceedings of the 14th ACM Symposium on Operating Systems Principles 1993 (1993)
6. Gamsa, B., Krieger, O., Stumm, M.: Optimizing IPC performance for shared-memory multiprocessors. In: 1994 International Conference on Parallel Processing, vol. 1, pp. 208–211. IEEE (1994)
7. Hernandez, C., et al.: Selene: self-monitored dependable platform for high-performance safety-critical systems. In: 2020 23rd Euromicro Conference on Digital System Design (DSD), pp. 370–377. IEEE (2020)
8. Kiszka, J.: ivshmem-v2-specification. https://github.com/siemens/jailhouse/blob/master/Documentation/ivshmem-v2-specification.md. Accessed 3 June 2023
9. Kiszka, J.: Jailhouse 0.12 released. https://lwn.net/Articles/811509/. Accessed 3 June 2023
10. Kiszka, J.: Jailhouse: a linux-based partitioning hypervisor. https://lwn.net/Articles/574273/. Accessed 7 June 2023
11. Kiszka, J.: Reworking the inter-vm-shared-memory devices. https://static.sched.com/hosted_files/kvmforum2019/4b/KVM-Forum19_ivshmem2.pdf. Accessed 7 June 2023
12. Li, H., Xu, X., Ren, J., Dong, Y.: ACRN: a big little hypervisor for IoT development. In: Proceedings of the 15th ACM SIGPLAN/SIGOPS International Conference on Virtual Execution Environments, pp. 31–44 (2019)
13. Lu, D.: Research on the Impact of Jailhouse on Dynamic Execution Paths in Linux. Master's thesis, Lanzhou University (2021)
14. Macdonell, A.C.: Shared-memory optimizations for virtual machines. Ph.D. thesis, University of Alberta (2011)
15. Martins, J., Tavares, A., Solieri, M., Bertogna, M., Pinto, S.: Bao: a lightweight static partitioning hypervisor for modern multi-core embedded systems. In: Workshop on Next Generation Real-Time Embedded Systems (NG-RES 2020). Schloss Dagstuhl-Leibniz-Zentrum für Informatik (2020)
16. Miyagawa, M.: Applying jailhouse to the civil infrastructure system. https://elinux.org/images/f/ff/JapanTechnicalJamboree61_JailhouseR1_eng.pdf. Accessed 7 June 2023
17. Ramos, D.: Exploring IVSHMEM in the Jailhouse Hypervisor. Ph.D. thesis, Instituto Superior de Engenharia do Porto (2019)

18. Ramsauer, R., Kiszka, J., Mauerer, W.: Building mixed criticality linux systems with the jailhouse hypervisor. In: Embedded Lunux Conference + OpenIoT-Summit, Portland, OR, 21–23 February 2017 (2017). https://www.youtube.com/watch?v=pvs0fv-gnvw
19. Reichenbach, K.A.: System-call offloading via linux' io_uring on the jailhouse partitioning hypervisor (2021). https://osg.tuhh.de/Theses/2021/2021_ba_kelvin_reichenbach.pdf
20. Sangorrin, D., Honda, S., Takada, H.: Integrated scheduling in a real-time embedded hypervisor. IPSJ SIG Technical Reports 2010–18(2) (2010)
21. Shen, Y., Wang, L., Liang, Y., Li, S., Jiang, B.: Shyper: an embedded hypervisor applying hierarchical resource isolation strategies for mixed-criticality systems. In: 2022 Design, Automation & Test in Europe Conference & Exhibition (DATE), pp. 1287–1292. IEEE (2022)
22. Sinha, S.: Scheduling policies and system software architectures for mixed-criticality computing. Department of Computer Science, Boston University, Technical report (2018)
23. Sinitsyn, V.: Understanding the jailhouse hypervisor, part 1. https://lwn.net/Articles/578295/. Accessed 5 June 2023
24. Sinitsyn, V.: Understanding the jailhouse hypervisor, part 2. https://lwn.net/Articles/578852/. Accessed 5 June 2023
25. torvalds: linux-jailhouse-enabling. https://github.com/siemens/linux/. Accessed 7 June 2023
26. Wang, C., Yang, F., Wang, H., Guo, P., Hou, J.: Improving real time performance of linux system using rt-linux. In: Journal of Physics: Conference Series, vol. 1237, p. 052017. IOP Publishing (2019)
27. West, R., Li, Y., Missimer, E.: Quest-v: a virtualized multikernel for safety-critical real-time systems. arXiv preprint arXiv:1310.6349 (2013)
28. West, R., Li, Y., Missimer, E.: Quest-v: a virtualized multikernel for safety-critical real-time systems. arXiv e-prints arXiv:1310.6349 (2013)
29. Yugang, M., Shiyou, J.: Research on predictability of distributed real-time systems. Comput. Res. Dev. **37**(6), 661–667 (2000)
30. Zhang, J.: Optimal Design of Communication Mechanism between Linux and RTOS based on Jailhouse. Master's thesis, Lanzhou University (2023)

Multi-agent Cooperative Computing Resource Scheduling Algorithm for Periodic Task Scenarios

Zheng Chen[1] , Ruijin Wang[1(✉)], Zhiyang Zhang[1], Ting Chen[1(✉)], Xikai Pei[1,2], and Zhenya Wu[2]

[1] School of Information and Software Engineering, University of Electronic Science and Technology of China, Chengdu 611731, Sichuan, China
{ruijinwang,brokendragon}@uestc.edu.cn, peixikai@cdatc.com
[2] The Second Research Institute of Civil Aviation Administration of China, Chengdu 610041, Sichuan, China
wuzhenya@cdatc.com

Abstract. The scheduling of large-scale service requests and jobs usually requires the service cluster to fully use node computing resources. However, due to the increasing number of server devices, the dependence between resource allocation and request, and the periodic external request received, the scheduling process of edge-oriented service requests is a complicated scientific problem. Existing studies do not take into account the periodic characteristics of service requests in different periods, leading to inaccurate scheduling decisions on external requests. This paper proposes a coordinated Multi-Agent recurrent Actor-Critic, based on a recursive network. CMARAC is used to solve the problem of computing resource allocation for periodic requests in edge computing scenarios. According to different resource information in the server cluster and the status of the task queue, the system state information and historical information are captured and maintained by integrating LSTM, and then the most appropriate service resources are selected by processing them in the Actor-Critic network. Tracking experiments using actual request data show that CMARAC can successfully learn the periodic state between external requests in the face of large-scale service requests. Compared with the baseline, the average throughput rate of the system implemented by CMARAC is improved by 2.1%, and the algorithm convergence rate is improved by 0.69 times. Finally, we optimized the parameters through experiments and determined the best parameter configuration of CMARAC.

Keywords: Service request · Multi-agent cooperative scheduling algorithm · Edge computing · Task scheduling

1 Introduction

The popularity of Chat GPT shows that AI is moving towards "big models, big data", and often has limited hardware resources to support the training of large

© The Author(s), under exclusive license to Springer Nature Singapore Pte Ltd. 2024
C. Li et al. (Eds.): APPT 2023, LNCS 14103, pp. 76–97, 2024.
https://doi.org/10.1007/978-981-99-7872-4_5

models. In the traditional cloud computing mode, there is a large delay in data transmission [1], so to realize the training and application of large-scale models, edge computing technology has become a field of concern. Edge computing is increasingly popular in the existing academic and industrial computing frameworks [2,3], and users are more inclined to share large hardware platforms [4,5], so the dynamic allocation and balance of limited hardware resources is the main problem facing edge computing.

The dynamic workload of the edge cluster environment brings a high challenge to the service request of the front-end application. When the request arrives, how to optimize the allocation of computing resources between the edge node and the cloud is a complex scientific problem [6].

In the existing work, there are a variety of solutions for task unloading and resource optimal allocation, such as meta-heuristic algorithms [7], dynamic programming [8,9], reinforcement learning [6,10], which can solve the problem of resource allocation to a certain extent. However, it is difficult to capture the periodicity of the task when completing the periodic task scheduling in the above scheme, so the optimal scheduling effect cannot be achieved. Using historical data to predict the future often means potential advantages [11]. Therefore, in marginal scenarios, how considering the periodic relationship of service requests in time and adjusting the plan of resource allocation is a key issue in resource allocation and request scheduling.

Aiming at the above problems, a method of coordinated Multi-Agent recurrent Actor-Critic (CMARAC) based on the recursive network is proposed in this paper. First, the reward function and network updating scheme of reinforcement learning are defined. Secondly, the history and reality of the server cluster are combined into a matrix with temporal characteristics and input into the network model to obtain the node selection probability vector. Finally, the node most suitable for the current request is selected according to the probability vector, and the state changes of the system after selecting this node are calculated and applied to the network input in the next period.

The specific scheme of this paper is as follows: (i) The introduction of a time series network in reinforcement learning can learn long-term strategy information and improve the performance of agents. (ii) The parameters and network structure of the temporal network are designed, and the reward function of reinforcement learning is defined to ensure the convergence of the network. (iii) Apply the proposed model to the experimental process of specific data sets to prove the effectiveness and superiority of the model. Therefore, the major challenges facing this scheme are arranging the time scale of the recursive network, how to design the reward function that can make the network converge, and finally proving the validity of the model.

In response to the above challenges, this paper adopts the method of dual time scale for resource scheduling and recursive network input design and sets the product of throughput rate and normalized negative exponential function of resource consumption variance within a period as the reward function. Finally, the validity of the model is proved by mathematical proof and experimental proof.

Based on the above work, the main contributions are as follows.

1. A multi-agent reinforcement learning method based on the recursive network is proposed. According to the distribution of requests in time and the deployment of servers in edge scenarios, a multi-agent reinforcement learning method based on the recursive network is designed. Based on the recursive network method, the input design under double time scales is adopted. The model can grasp the distribution characteristics of requests in time and output a more appropriate resource scheduling scheme. Multi-agent reinforcement learning can handle dynamic request information and cope with distributed time-varying resource systems.

2. A reward function is designed to consider both the system throughput rate and load balance within a period. Different from calculating the reward function once in each resource allocation process, this paper takes the negative exponential function value of the system throughput rate in multiple time units as a partial reward. At the same time, the normalized result of the variance of resource utilization ratio of different nodes is used as the index of cluster load balancing, and the negative exponential function value is also used as another part of the reward, and the product of the two parts is the complete reward function.

3. The experiment of the Alibaba cluster tracking data set is completed, which has obvious advantages compared with other scheduling algorithms. The parameters of the neural network structure are optimized and the optimal parameters are found through experiments. Compared with the algorithm without recursive network, the experiment shows that the convergence speed of CMARAC is faster. Finally, the feasibility of the algorithm in the real scheduling scenario is tested.

2   Related Research

Recent studies on similar resource scheduling problems have focused on reinforcement learning algorithms. In 2020, Chen et al. studied the joint power control of MECs in the Industrial Internet of Things and the dynamic resource management of computing resource allocation. To minimize the long-term average delay of the task, the original problem is transformed into a Markov decision process (MDP). A dynamic resource management (DDRM) algorithm based on deep reinforcement learning is proposed to solve the MDP problem.

In summary, the existing solution uses a single strategy for the scheduling process. It can not adapt to the complex and changing workshop production scene, with long order completion times, large system computational complexity, and poor stability of the scheduling effect achieved for different orders. This paper proposes an innovative RGA algorithm based on learning and meta-inspiration, which can adapt to the intelligent scheduling in the FJSP scenario and is closer to the real workshop production environment [12]. Cui et al. describe the long-term resource allocation problem as a stochastic game that maximizes expected

returns, in which each drone becomes a learning agent and each resource allocation scheme corresponds to an action taken by the drone. Then, a multi-agent
reinforcement learning (MARL) framework is developed, where each agent finds
its optimal strategy based on its local observations of use learning [13]. In 2021,
Farhadi et al. proposed a two-time-scale framework that combines optimization
of service (data and code) placement and request scheduling within the storage,
communication, computing, and budget constraints. By analyzing the difficulty
of various situations to fully describe the complexity of the problem, a polynomial time algorithm is developed to achieve a constant factor approximation
under certain conditions [8]. In the same year, Han et al. used the CMMAC
algorithm to share a centralized state value function with multiple agents, and
each actor only observed the local state [14]. However, the above paper does not
consider the dynamic and time periodicity of the task queue in the server in the
distributed scenario, so the timing relationship between inputs is not considered
in the mentioned scheme.

To sum up, the existing computing resource allocation and scheduling scheme
only analyzes the existing system status upon the arrival of each task and selects
the node server to process the task through model judgment, without considering
the time sequence relationship in the updating process of the task queue of the
node server. The CMARAC algorithm proposed in this paper adopts the method
of combining the recursive network and strategy to schedule each task and makes
full use of the timing relationship of the task queue of the edge server node in
each task scheduling process. Compared with the traditional scheme network,
the convergence speed is faster and fewer data is required in the training process.

3   Scheduling Problem

3.1   Problem Definition

We consider the task scheduling process in the edge cluster environment and use
the system throughput rate of the task scheduling process as one of the indicators
to measure the algorithm effect, that is, the proportion of tasks completed on
schedule in the total of all tasks during the long-term operation of the system.
Given edge cluster $\mathcal{M} = \{1, 2, \ldots, M\}$, the index is m. To better complete
the task scheduling process, each cluster is assigned a master responsible for
managing cluster tasks. The nodes of each cluster are $\mathcal{N}_m = \{1, 2, \ldots, N_m\}$
is managed by master m. In each edge cluster, all nodes are represented as
$\mathcal{N} = \{1, 2, \ldots, N\}$. All the masters are responsible for distributing the tasks
allowed to be processed to the managed edge nodes or cloud. All nodes of an edge
cluster communicate through the local area network. The edge cluster master
m arranges a queue to record the ID of the task, $\mathcal{Q}_m$, which represents all the
tasks to be completed and the order of task scheduling. A queue of tasks to be
processed q_σ is arranged on all servers for which tasks can be assigned. σ is less
than or equal to the total number of servers in a cluster or edge cluster. Tasks
in the queue are prioritized according to time requirements.

To illustrate the number of tasks that each node can handle, this paper records a matrix $\mathcal{D} = \{d_1, d_2, \ldots, d_T\}$, including d_T record a server, can handle task types of one-hot vector, which $T = M + \sum_{i=1}^{m} N_i$, said the total number of all except the cloud cluster server. Compared with edge servers and edge nodes, the cloud has sufficient computing resources and task processing capacity and can complete all kinds of task processing by default. Therefore, matrix $\mathcal{D}$ does not contain information about the cluster.

The task scheduling time in this paper is strictly constrained. To correspond to the time unit t required by task scheduling in the data set, the resource scheduling system adjusts the time needed for a scheduling task $\tau = \alpha t (\alpha \in (0, 1))$. In each τ, the master m of each edge cluster will distribute a task to the edge node $\mathcal{N}_m$ with sufficient computing resources, or to the cluster processing, and each task will consume the computing resources and network bandwidth of the edge or cloud. However, because the edge master is typically close to the end device but not the cloud, sending a task to the cloud may result in additional communication overhead. Therefore, This paper's algorithm will lower the priority of the cloud processing task. When the system schedules tasks based on time, if any task is not processed in time, the system will check and discard it at each τ.

In this paper, the optimization of the target for throughput, in the process of system scheduling system to complete tasks $\Omega = \sum_{s}^{\infty} \sum_{\sigma}^{T+1} \omega_s(q_\sigma)$, $\omega_s(q_\sigma)$ indicates the number of tasks completed by the server σ in time s, and $T+1$ indicates the number of all servers in the system. However, with the increase of time, Ω will continue to increase, which is not conducive to the subsequent calculation and optimization of the model. Throughput $\Phi \in [0, 1]$, the said system within the required time to complete the ratio of the total number of jobs and tasks, the total number of tasks $\Omega' = \sum_{s}^{\infty} \sum_{m}^{M} \omega'_s(\mathcal{Q}_m)$. Where $\omega'_s(\mathcal{Q}_m)$ represents the number of tasks received by edge cluster master m in time s. Therefore, the system throughput rate can be expressed as:

$$\Phi = \frac{\Omega}{\Omega'} = \frac{\sum_{s}^{\infty} \sum_{\sigma}^{T+1} \omega_s(q_\sigma)}{\sum_{s}^{\infty} \sum_{m}^{M} \omega'_s(\mathcal{Q}_m)} \tag{1}$$

4 Algorithm Design

4.1 CMARAC Algorithm Framework

The main body of the CMARAC algorithm contains two time scales, namely, the time scale of resource allocation and the time scale of recursive network input. The algorithm hierarchy diagram is as follows:

CMARAC algorithm is applied to hundreds of distributed edge clusters. Traditional learning algorithms, such as DQN [15] and DDPG [16], usually use a centralized learning agent, but it is difficult to realize for edge clusters, because distributed master will lead to the explosion of scheduling action space [17]. In order to ensure the real-time scheduling, CMARAC adopts a decentralized way to schedule requests at the place where the requests arrive.

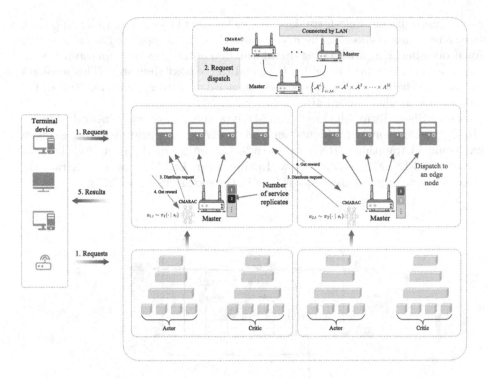

Fig. 1. Distributed request scheduling process based on CMARAC

We consider a typical distributed edge cluster scenario for request distribution. The complete request scheduling process is shown in Fig. 1. (i) the terminal device sends a request to the nearest edge cluster $\mathcal{M}$, and master m of the edge cluster receives the request and adds it to the request queue $\mathcal{Q}_m$. (ii) After completing the previous request scheduling process in queue $\mathcal{Q}_m$, the task is taken out of the queue. In addition, an agent of CMARAC deployed in the master is used to complete the scheduling process of the request, and finally the task is assigned to the appropriate node server for processing.

4.2 Identification of Temporal Characteristics of the Request

In a cluster environment, the arrival process of external requests usually follows a periodic rule. When Alibaba tracked the process of processing requests in their server cluster in 2020, it found the following rule: In a day, the situation of the server submitting tasks presents a periodic change with the change of time. Capturing such a change of task submission plays an important role in the scheduling process of external requests. The system can make preparations for task scheduling by predicting the arrival of peak request in advance.

Recurrent Neural networks (RNN) are neural networks with recurrent feedback connections that can be used to process data with sequential structure. The internal self-feedback of neurons gives them an inherent "depth" structure, which can obtain sufficient long-term dependence by using historical data [18,19]. Each time a new data is entered, the RNN passes the current input to the hidden layer for processing along with the state information of the previous time step, resulting in a new state output, which is passed to the next time step. This feedback connection enables RNNS to process sequence data with memory and the ability to consider previous information.

Long Short-Term Memory (LSTM) is a special recursive neural network (RNN), which solves problems such as gradient disappearance and gradient explosion in traditional RNN by introducing gating mechanism [20]. The cell structure of LSTM is shown below. In this paper, LSTM is used to extract the time characteristics of the request flow in the server cluster (Fig. 2).

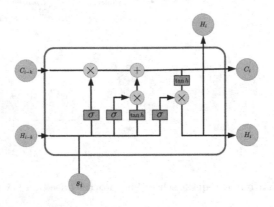

Fig. 2. Input cell diagram of system scheduling state

In this article, we overlay multiple LSTM layers onto the model to capture the time feature of higher level request flows. LSTM layer1 edge processing services in the cluster operation sequence $\mathbf{s} = [s_i, s_{i+k}, s_{i+2k}, ..., s_{i+ck}]$. Where s_i represents the system state at time i, k represents the time step, c represents the number of cells, and the system hidden state sequence $\mathbf{H} = [H_i, H_{i+k}, H_{i+2k}, ..., H_{i+ck}]$ at each time point is calculated. The hidden layer state sequence is then input to LSTM layer 2 to calculate the hidden layer state sequence $\mathbf{H}'$. Finally, the system state $\mathbf{H}_{i+ck}$ containing the past to present time characteristics is output.

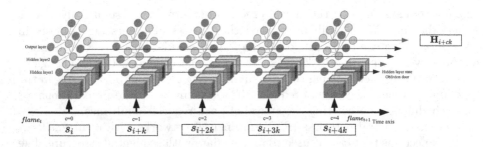

Fig. 3. Request timing feature recognition based on LSTM

Figure 3 shows the identification process of request features. The time axis of request arrival contains a time series of five time points, corresponding to $c = 0, 1, 2, 3, 4$, respectively. This time series corresponds to the system state characteristics corresponding to the first five time points including the current time. The final output $\mathbf{H}_{i+ck}$ is a combination of the system state characteristics of the whole period of time series, can effectively capture the timing characteristics of the system at five time points of the request, so as to make a better task scheduling scheme. Specific parameters are calculated as follows:

$$f_i = \sigma \left(W_{gf} s_i + b_{jf} + W_{hf} H_{(i-k)} + b_{hf} \right) \tag{2}$$

The calculation mode of f_i in Formula (2) represents the forgetting gate, W_{gf} and W_{hf} correspond to the weight parameters of the state input and hidden state input respectively, b_{jf} and b_{hf} represent the offset after the state input and hidden input respectively, s_i is the system state under the condition that the time corresponds to i. $H_{(i-k)}$ is the hidden state input, and σ is the sigma activation function.

$$I_i = \sigma \left(W_{gj} s_i + b_{jj} + W_{hj} H_{(i-k)} + b_{hj} \right) \tag{3}$$

$$g_i = \tanh \left(W_{jg} s_i + b_{jg} + W_{hg} H_{(i-k)} + b_{hg} \right) \tag{4}$$

$$C_i = f_i C_{(i-k)} + I_i g_i \tag{5}$$

The formulas for I_i, g_i, and C_i represent the update gate, W_{gj} and W_{hj} correspond to the weights of state inputs and hidden state inputs, b_{jj} and b_{hj} represent their respective offsets, and tanh represents the tangent function. Finally, the sequential state of the cell will be determined jointly by the calculated output of the forgetting gate and the output of the updaters in Formula (2), and the previous state $C_{(i-k)}$ will be transformed into the current state C_i.

$$o_i = \sigma \left(W_{go} s_i + b_{jo} + W_{ho} H_{(i-k)} + b_{ho} \right) \tag{6}$$

$$H_i = o_i \tanh \left(C_i \right) \tag{7}$$

Formula (6) represents the output gate, where W_{go} and W_{ho} are the weight parameters corresponding to the input state and hidden state of the system respectively, b_{jo} and b_{ho} are the offset respectively, and o_i is the calculation result of the output gate. The final output H_i from LSTM is determined by both the output gate and the cell update state C_i, as described in Formula (7). Finally, we will get the system state at the time step $i + ck$ and input it into the actor network and critic network.

Figure 4 shows the composition of CMARAC algorithm. On the whole, CMARAC algorithm is composed of two parts. The first part is responsible for collecting the request state information of the system in a period of time series and the time sequence relationship between the states, and finally obtaining the system state $\mathbf{H}_i$ containing the time sequence features. $\mathbf{H}_i$ is input into the Actor and Critic network, the state value is calculated, and the appropriate node in the edge cluster is selected to process the next task in the request queue $\mathcal{Q}_m$.

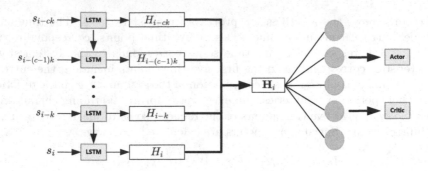

Fig. 4. CMARAC model structure diagram

4.3   Task Scheduling Procedure

In recent years, a revolutionary breakthrough has been made in the field of multi-agent deep reinforcement learning, which has been successfully applied to a variety of complex scenarios, proving that pure cooperative tasks can be represented by monotone hybrid networks, and agents based on neural networks can learn their actions in multi-agent environments through interaction [21].

In contrast to the general RL training process, DQN relies on a small batch of random sampling to experience the transition in the replay buffer, rather than just selecting a single transition. In addition, the target network with the same network structure as $Q(s_t, a_t)$ is used to reduce the correlation. And the target network is only updated at certain intervals.

DQN cannot be directly applied to solve continuous value control problems, so we adopt the most popular actor-critic method to deal with the computing resource scheduling problem in the edge cluster scenario. Specifically, actor-critic consists of a DNN acting as an actor network and a DQN called critic network [22]. The Actor represents our mapping function $\pi(s_t \mid \theta^\pi)$, and the critic performs the function $Q(s_t, a_t \mid \theta^Q)$. Actor can generate the optimal action a_t based on state s_t.

This chapter will introduce the multi-agent reinforcement learning method based on recursive network. Deploy critic network in the cloud, and deploy an actor network in each master at the edge. Usually, an agent does not fully understand all the knowledge of the environment state $\mathcal{S}$, so we express the process of each master to schedule the tasks in the queue as a Markov game Γ for cloud edge cluster, $\Gamma = \left(\mathcal{M}, \mathcal{S}, \{\mathcal{A}^i\}_{i\in\mathcal{M}}, \mathcal{P}, \{R^i\}_{i\in\mathcal{M}}, \gamma\right)$. Where $\mathcal{M} = \{1, 2, \ldots, M\}$ represents the agent of M edge clusters, $\mathcal{S}$ represents the state space, $\mathcal{A}^i$ represents the action taken by the ith master in the edge cluster, that is, the first task in the queue is selected and dispatched to a node, $\mathcal{P}$ represents the selection probability of each action, R^i represents the reward obtained after the ith master takes the action. We adopt the mechanism that all agents share the same reward function to deal with the computational resource scheduling problem proposed in this paper. $\gamma \in (0, 1)$ is a discount factor that can be used to control the influence of an agent on other agents. When the agent considers future rewards, it can take into account the actions and strategies that other agents may take.

In this case, the discount factor can be used to measure the agent's impact on future rewards, and thus influence its behavior and strategy.

S represents the state space, where in each time unit t, a state value $s_{t,m}$ is constructed for node σ in each edge cluster m. The composition of the state value is shown in the following table:

Table 1. Environment status

State	Description
$q_{\sigma,t}$	The queue of tasks to be processed in Node σ
$\mathcal{Q}_{m,t}$	The queue of tasks to be completed in Master m
L	Transmission delay between the cloud and the edge cluster master
Re	Remaining CPU and storage space resources of each cluster node N_m
St	N_m service type deployed on each cluster node
N	Number of nodes N_m in an edge cluster m

Table 1 shows the status information of time unit t. $q_{\sigma,t}$ represents the task queue that has not been processed since time t in node σ; $\mathcal{Q}_{m,t}$ represents the task queue information that has not been dispatched since time t in master m; L represents the transmission delay between the cloud and the edge cluster master. Re represents the remaining CPU and storage space resources of each cluster node N_m at time t, St represents the service type deployed by each cluster node N_m, and N represents the number of node N_m in an edge cluster m. The above parameters are combined into $s_{t,m}$. In order to concentrate the status information and facilitate the update of critic network, We maintain a global state $s_t \in S$, which not only contains the state information of all cluster nodes N_m, but also includes the task queue information $\mathcal{Q}_{C,t}$ in the cloud.

The action space of Markov game $\left\{\mathcal{A}^i\right\}_{i \in \mathcal{M}}$ is expressed as $\{\mathcal{A}^1, \mathcal{A}^2, \ldots, \mathcal{A}^M\}$, represents the action space of the state space of the agent deployed in each edge cluster m. For edge cluster, we regard all available edge nodes as a resource pool, that is, the mutual cooperation among the masters in the enabled state. All $\mathcal{A}^i$ contains the number of all available edge nodes and the cloud $\{1, 2, 3, \ldots, N_1 + N_2 + \cdots + N_m + M\}$, and the sum of all edge nodes, masters, and the cloud is the size of the action space $\mathcal{A}^i$. In particular, when $\mathcal{A}^i = 0$, the cloud handles the current request. We only allow each master agent to schedule one request within time unit t.

Generally speaking, the master of an edge server cluster needs to balance the system throughput rate and resource scheduling costs when allocating resources to server nodes. Therefore, a reward function is needed to teach the agent to learn the potential resource allocation plan. The return function derived from ensuring the throughput rate of the system and realizing the load balancing of the cluster can be obtained:

$$r_1 = e^\mu, \mu \in [0, 1] \tag{8}$$

$$r_2 = e^{-\beta}, \beta \in [\frac{1}{2}, 1] \tag{9}$$

$$R = r_1 r_2 \tag{10}$$

Reward function contains two parts, the first part of the throughput rate of the system, as shown in Formula (8). The value range of r_1 is $[e^{-1}, 1]$, μ represents the system throughput rate at time $[\lambda t, \lambda(t+1)]$, $\lambda = 1, 2, \ldots, n$, λ represents the time step, that is, the system throughput rate within a period of time is calculated after a period of time unit t. The second part considers cluster load balancing, as shown in Formula (9), $\beta = 1/(1 + e^{-\xi})$ is the variance of normalized node resource consumption ξ. Finally, the total reward R is the product of r_1 and r_2.

In an edge cluster environment, the state transition probability of multi-agent reinforcement learning is the joint state transition probability of all agents, which is expressed as follows:

$$P\left(s_{t+1} \mid s_t, s_{t-1}, \cdots, s_1, s_0\right) = P\left(s_{t+1} \mid s_t\right) = p\left(s_{t+1} \mid s_t, a_{1,t}, a_{2,t}, \ldots, a_{n,t}\right) \tag{11}$$

Formula (11) shows that the state s_t conforms to the Markov property, that is, the state of the next time node only depends on the current state and an action made in the current state, and the state is the environment that the system can achieve through some way [23]. In multi-agent reinforcement learning, we construct an observable Markov model [24]. The status s_{t+1} of the next point in time is only related to the status s_t of the current point in time and the action $\{a_{1,t}, a_{2,t}, \ldots, a_{n,t}\}$ taken by all agents.

The state value function of agent in edge cluster master is the function of joint strategy $\pi : \mathcal{S} \to \Delta(\mathcal{A})$, which can be defined as:

$$\pi(a_t | s_t) = \prod_{i \in \mathcal{M}} \pi_i\left(a_{i,t} | s_{i,t}\right) \tag{12}$$

Therefore, for every joint strategy π and state $s_t \in \mathcal{S}_t$, the common state value function $V_{m,\pi}$ of agents can be derived by minimizing Bellman equation:

$$V_{m,\pi}(s_t) = \mathbb{E}\left[\sum_{t \geq 0} \gamma R\left(s_t, a_{m,t}, s_{t+1}\right) \mid a_{m,t} \sim \pi_m\left(\cdot \mid s_t\right), s_0 = s\right] \tag{13}$$

The multi-agent collaborative resource scheduling algorithm proposed by us is designed based on the actor-critic algorithm framework, including the actor network deployed in different edge clusters and the critic network deployed in the cloud. The coordinated learning method of centralized critic and distributed actor is adopted. When training critic network, all actors share a centralized state value function, while in the training and reasoning process of distributed actor network, each actor only observes the local state.

The Critic network is divided into target value network θ' and value network θ. We used the target value network θ' to calculate TD (Temporal Difference) errors, and kept updating them in the training process, but at a slow speed.

Generally, parameters of Critic network θ will not be copied to target value network θ' until a certain time interval is required, so the objective function V of target network can be expressed as Formula (14):

$$V(s_{t+1}; \theta', \pi) = \sum_{m \in \mathcal{M}, t \geq 0} \pi(a_{m,t} \mid s_{m,t})(R + \gamma V'(s_{m,t+1})) \tag{14}$$

$$\mathcal{L}(\theta') = (R + \gamma V'(s_{m,t}; \theta') - V(s_{m,t}; \theta'))^2 \tag{15}$$

The objective function in Formula (14) is the weighted sum of agent action value and reward function under different strategies. The weight is the probability of edge cluster m taking relative action $a_{m,t}$ against state $s_{m,t}$ at time point t. For all edge clusters $\mathcal{M}$ in edge server cluster m, each time t has a unique state value $\{V(s_{m,t}), m \in \mathcal{M}\}$. Formula (15) represents the loss function of the target network, $V(s_{m,t}; \theta')$ represents the value estimate of the target value network for the current state, $V'(s_{m,t}; \theta')$ represents the value estimate of the target value network for the next state.

We define an advantage function $A(s_{t,m}, a_{m,t})$ and calculate gradient ∇_a to update actor networks, where the advantage function $A(s_{t,m}, a_{m,t})$ is shown in Formula (16):

$$A(s_{t,m}, a_{m,t}) = R + \gamma V'(s_{m,t}; \theta') - V(s_{m,t}; \theta') \tag{16}$$

γ is the discount factor, $V(s_{m,t}; \theta')$ represents the value estimate of the target value network for the current state, $V'(s_{m,t}; \theta')$ represents the value estimate of the target value network for the next state, R represents the reward after taking action $a_{m,t}$ in the current state, and then calculate the gradient used to update the actor network, as shown in Formula (17):

$$\nabla_a = \nabla \log \pi(a_{m,t} \mid s_{t,m}) A(s_{t,m}, a_{m,t}) \tag{17}$$

where $\pi(a_{m,t} \mid s_{t,m})$ is the strategy of corresponding state $s_{t,m}$ in edge cluster m which takes related action $a_{m,t}$, after calculating the gradient of actor network, the network can be updated. The overall algorithm flow is as follows:

The above algorithm flow is the whole process of training and scheduling of CMARAC. In each system scheduling time unit, each edge cluster master will realize the scheduling of the first task in queue $\mathcal{Q}_m$, and eject it from the queue and distribute it to a node in the cluster for processing according to the action $a_{m,t}$ output by the actor network. Each time to complete the scheduling process of a specific time, according to the recorded status, action and training parameters, calculate the loss function value $\mathcal{L}(\theta')$ and gradient ∇_a to update the actor network and critic network.

5   Experiment and Analysis

In this paper, the optimization of the target for the throughput, in the process of system scheduling system to complete tasks $\Omega = \sum_s^\infty \sum_\sigma^{T+1} w_s(q_\sigma)$, including $w_s(q_\sigma)$ said the server σ number of tasks in a timely manner.

Algorithm 1. CMARAC training and scheduling process

1: Initialize the system environment and neural network structure
2: **for** τ in 1, 2, 3, ... **do**
3:     **for** each m in $\mathcal{M}$ **do**
4:         Update task queue $\mathcal{Q}_m$ in edge cluster m
5:         Update CPU and storage resource Re of each node in cluster m
6:         Remove a task from the task queue $\mathcal{Q}_m$
7:         Action $a_{m,t}$ is taken to assign tasks by formula 12
8:         **if** $\tau \% reward\ cycle$ **then**
9:             Formulas (8), (9), and (10) were used to calculate the current cluster
        return R_m
10:             Formula (8): $r_1 = e^{\mu}, \mu \in [0, 1]$
11:             Formula (9): $r_2 = e^{-\beta}, \beta \in [\frac{1}{2}, 1]$
12:             Formula (10): $R = r_1 r_2$
13:             Calculate the dominant functions $A(s_{t,m}, a_{m,t})$ and gradient ∇_a using
        formulas (16) and (17)
14:             Formula (16): $A(s_{t,m}, a_{m,t}) = R + \gamma V'(s_{m,t}; \theta') - V(s_{m,t}; \theta')$
15:             Formula (17): $\nabla_a = \nabla \log \pi(a_{m,t} \mid s_{t,m}) A(s_{t,m}, a_{m,t})$
16:             Record the critic network training parameters $[s_t, V(s_{t+1}; \theta', \pi)]$
17:             Record the actor network training parameters
        $[s_{t,m}, a_{m,t}, A(s_{t,m}, a_{m,t}), R_m]$
18:         **end if**
19:     **end for**
20:     The loss function $\mathcal{L}(\theta')$ and gradient ∇_a are calculated using formulas (14) and
    (15)
21:     Update actor and critic network parameters
22:     Formula (14): $V(s_{t+1}; \theta', \pi) = \sum_{m \in \mathcal{M}, t \geq 0} \pi(a_{m,t} \mid s_{m,t})(R + \gamma V'(s_{m,t+1}))$
23:     Formula (15): $\mathcal{L}(\theta') = (R + \gamma V'(s_{m,t}; \theta') - V(s_{m,t}; \theta'))^2$
24: **end for**

5.1   Experimental Setup and Data Set

The data set of this experiment is Alibaba cluster tracking data set [25], which makes detailed statistics on the workload tracking data collected in the production MLaaS cluster of more than 6000 GPUs for two months. Alibaba Cluster Trace data set comes from Alibaba Cluster Trace Program, which makes a comprehensive analysis of Alibaba's large-scale workload tracking and reveals the benefits of GPU sharing in the production of GPU data centers [26]. It is widely used in academia and industry. We modified these server trace data sets to external request data sets, and the data structure of this data set and its examples are shown in Table 2:

We used task_type, start_time, end_time, plan_cpu and plan_mem in the data set as experimental data. Other data were not used in this experiment. This is because this experiment deals with the scheduling of different types of external requests, one for each service, and the service deployment status of the server is reflected in deploy_state.

Table 2. Data items and examples in the data set

Columns	Example Entry
task_name	task_ODk2MzU0ODg1MTY5MTExNTUwMg==
inst_id	9
job_name	j_18443
task_type	3
status	Terminated
start_time	86442
end_time	86446
plan_cpu	300
plan_mem	0.39

5.2 Experimental Results and Analysis

In order to evaluate the effectiveness of CMARAC algorithm and the advantages compared with other algorithms, this paper obtained some high quality performance of CMARAC algorithm from different dimensions through 5 comparison experiments with other algorithms, and carried out optimization experiments on the parameters of CMARAC algorithm.

5.2.1 Overall Performance

Table 3. Scheduling effect comparison between CMARAC and random scheduling, greedy policy and cMMAC

Contrast round	Random scheduling	Greedy strategy	cMMAC	CMARAC
1	0.277	0.679	0.808	0.819
2	0.316	0.674	0.81	0.842
3	0.317	0.673	0.823	0.85
4	0.33	0.734	0.824	0.849
5	0.337	0.688	0.83	0.85
6	0.336	0.694	0.832	0.854
7	0.314	0.651	0.835	0.854
8	0.347	0.695	0.833	0.853
9	0.434	0.661	0.839	0.854
10	0.315	0.666	0.84	0.852
11	0.304	0.662	0.84	0.851
12	0.348	0.698	0.842	0.854
13	0.342	0.653	0.843	0.856
14	0.36	0.7	0.842	0.854
15	0.331	0.712	0.844	0.855

This experiment adopted cluster-trace-Gpu-V2020, the Alibaba cluster tracking data set published by Alibaba Group. We compared the scheduling effects of random scheduling, greedy strategy, cMMAC [12] and CMARAC algorithm. There were 15 rounds of experiments. The experimental data used in each round contains all the requests in the 50,000 time units, which are different for different rounds. The same cloud edge system adopts different scheduling algorithms respectively, and the throughput rate after each algorithm is compared. The comparison effect is shown in Table 3. The best result of each instance is shown in boldface.

It can be seen from the above comparison that the scheduling effect of the proposed CMARAC is generally better than that of random scheduling, greedy strategy and cMMAC. Taking the throughput rate of all requests in the same time period with a range of 50,000 time units as the index, the CMARAC algorithm improves 1.545 times compared with random scheduling, 24.5% compared with greedy policy scheduling, and 2.1% compared with baseline cMMAC algorithm scheduling. This indicates that CMARAC has a higher scheduling effect than other algorithms when facing a large number of request data with timing characteristics.

Request timing feature identification is a key step in CMARAC scheduling process, which determines whether the system can learn the timing feature in the process of request arrival, and thus determines the scheduling performance of CMARAC. The following experiments show that the convergence rate of CMARAC algorithm is faster than that of baseline cMMAC algorithm.

Figure 5 shows the training process of CMARAC algorithm and cMMAC algorithm. The training data adopts all requests within 50000 time units in cluster-trace-gpu-v2020 data set, and a total of 50 rounds of training are conducted. Each round of training includes 50 calculations of loss value and network updates. The label data in the figure is the median of loss value in each round

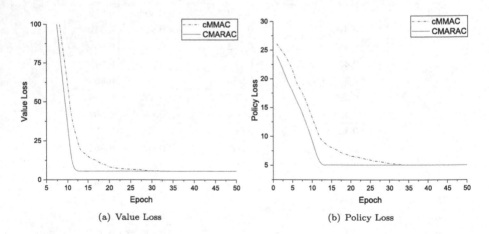

(a) Value Loss   (b) Policy Loss

Fig. 5. Comparison of network convergence effect of CMMARAC and cMMAC algorithm, (a) represents the convergence of loss value of actor network, and (b) represents the convergence of loss value of critic network. In the figure, the algorithm achieves convergence of loss value with as few training cycles as possible, which indicates that the algorithm has better performance.

of data. The hidden layer nodes of both algorithm cMMAC and CMARAC network are [128, 32], and the number of cells participating in the comparison of CMARAC algorithm is 4.

In the CMARAC algorithm, the request feature recognition network proposed by us adopts the LSTM recursive network, which can capture the time sequence dependence in the input sequence, remember the past information, and apply it to the current context. By iterating through multiple time steps, LSTM can gradually build an abstract representation of the sequence data, capturing key patterns and features in the input. In cloud edge systems with significant periodic request arrival processes, using LSTM to extract temporal features from requests can help understand and model the temporal patterns and behaviors of requests. By utilizing LSTM's sequential modeling capabilities, we can better understand and process timing data related to computing resource scheduling.

Figure 5 respectively shows the change of loss value of CMARAC and cMMAC with the training rounds. For the calculation process of the loss value of actor network, the loss value of CMARAC is always lower than that of cMMAC. When the training cycle is 1, the loss value of CMARAC is 304 and the loss value of cMMAC is 302. When the training cycle is 13, CMARAC reaches the state of convergence. cMMAC converges, and the final loss converges to about 5.53. For critic network, the initial loss value of CMARAC was 23.97, and reached convergence in the 13th round of training; the initial loss value of cMMAC was 26.08, and reached convergence in the 34th round, with the final loss converging to about 5.07.

Compared with cMMAC algorithm, the convergence speed of CMARAC is 1.69 times faster. This is because LSTM can capture the timing characteristics in a large number of requests, so as to achieve the best scheduling effect in fewer training rounds. Moreover, the calculation method of our return function considers the scheduling failure rate and load balancing rate in a period of time. The network has a better scheduling effect. Compare the throughput of CMARAC and cMMAC in the training process, as shown in Fig. 6.

It can be seen that CMARAC showed a high system throughput rate of 0.852 in the fourth round, and reached a convergence state of 0.855 in the eighth round. The system throughput rate based on cMMAC algorithm converges to 0.854 in the 13th round. Taking the system throughput rate as the indicator, the convergence rate of CMARAC is 62.5% faster than that of cMMAC, and the system throughput rate of Cmarac is 0.1% higher than that of cMMAC when it reaches the convergence state.

5.2.2   Load Balancing Effect

In edge clusters, task load balancing is an important aspect of computing resource allocation [27]. Load balancing distributes tasks and traffic evenly to edge nodes to ensure load balance among each node and avoid overloads on individual nodes, thus improving overall performance and scalability.

As scheduling tasks and recorded the resource usage of each edge node. In the experiment, it is assumed that each task occupies corresponding resources

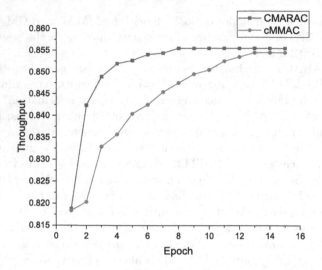

Fig. 6. Comparison of throughput between CMARAC and cMMAC algorithms in the training process

after being distributed to a node, and the load rate of the node will keep a rising trend. The number of nodes of the network hidden layer of cMMAC is [128, 32], the number of nodes of the network hidden layer of CMARAC is [64, 16], and the number of cells is 7. The operating environment is two edge clusters. Each edge cluster contains three edge nodes, and the service deployment of each node is fixed. The changes of resource load rates of six edge nodes were recorded in the test, as shown in Fig. 7:

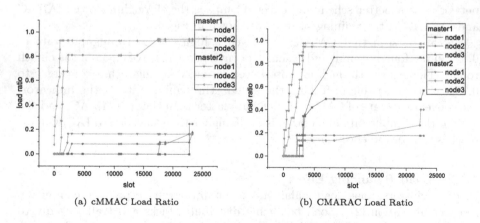

(a) cMMAC Load Ratio   (b) CMARAC Load Ratio

Fig. 7. Changes in the algorithm load rate of each node in the edge cluster. (a) represents the change of node load rate based on cMMAC algorithm, and (b) represents the change of node load rate based on CMARAC algorithm.

There are two reasons for the load difference between nodes. (1) Different nodes deploy different kinds of services. Since a service can only be used to process one kind of request, the quantity difference of different kinds of request data will cause the node load difference. (2) When a service is deployed on different nodes at the same time, the algorithm considers the resource usage of the node, the ability of the node to process the request, the communication cost between the node and the master and other factors, and then selects one of the nodes to process the current request and allocate resources, which will also cause the difference in node load. In Fig. 7(a), the load rate of the three nodes of the cluster where master1 resides and node1 of the cluster where master2 resides are all at a low level, while the overall load rate of node2 and node3 of the cluster where master2 resides is high, and the load rate reaches 0.8 or above in a short time. In Fig. 7(b), node3 of the cluster where master1 resides and node1 and node3 of the cluster where master2 resides have high load rates, while the load rates of other nodes are low.

By calculating the load balancing index of the system using different algorithms for resource scheduling, namely the standard deviation of node resource consumption, we can compare the load balancing effect of different algorithms. The comparison effect is shown in Fig. 8:

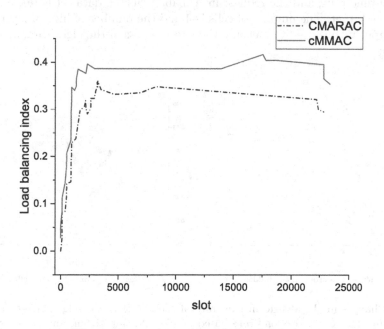

Fig. 8. Comparison of load balancing index

It can be seen that the standard deviation of the system resource consumption using CMARAC algorithm is smaller than that using cMMAC algorithm in most of the scheduling time, with the maximum standard deviation being 0.360 and

0.417. In the computing resource scheduling scenario of distributed edge clusters, the load status may dynamically change with the increase or decrease of external request traffic. LSTM can adjust the model adaptively according to the real-time observed load information. By learning the timing pattern of the load, the LSTM network can adjust the decision-making strategy in time to adapt to the requirements of different load states. Therefore, compared with cMMAC without LSTM network model, CMARAC achieves better cluster load balancing effect.

5.2.3   Parameter Optimization Experiment

Parameter optimization is a very important problem in CMARAC, because it determines the performance and training efficiency of the algorithm. Optimizing parameters can make the model better adapt to the specific environment and improve its generalization ability for various scenarios. For example, the number of hidden layers in the recursive network, the number of neurons in each hidden layer, the network structure of actor-critic network, payback function and so on. Based on the throughput rate of task scheduling process, this paper conducts relevant experiments on the influence of the number of neurons in the hidden layer of recursive network on scheduling effect in the process of time sequence feature recognition. 25000 time units are taken as the interval, 1 frame is defined as 25000 time unit, and the request in Alibaba tracking data set is taken as the scheduling target. The number of cells is 4 and the number of hidden layers is 2. Throughput rate is used to measure the effectiveness of the algorithm, as shown in Fig. 9:

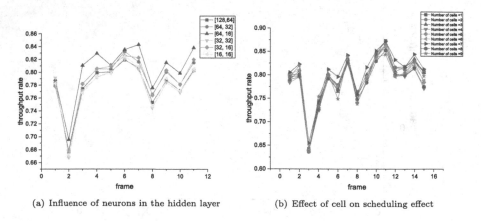

(a) Influence of neurons in the hidden layer   (b) Effect of cell on scheduling effect

Fig. 9. Changes in the algorithm load rate of each node in the edge cluster. (a) represents the change of node load rate based on cMMAC algorithm, and (b) represents the change of node load rate based on CMARAC algorithm.

According to Fig. 9, when other parameters of the recursive network and the number of hidden layers remain unchanged, the number of neurons in different networks corresponds to different throughput rates. On the whole, when the neuronal structure is [64,16], the system throughput rate is the highest in different time periods. In the whole experiment, the average system throughput rate is 0.80. When the neuronal structure is [32, 32], the average system throughput is the lowest 0.77, while when the neuronal structure is other structures in the figure, the average system throughput is concentrated around 0.78. It can be clearly seen from the figure that when the hidden layer is [64, 16], the line graph is at the top and the system throughput is the highest. Therefore, the optimal neuron structure of the hidden layer is [64, 16].

We continue to optimize the structure of the LSTM part of the neural network, and explore the influence of the number of cells on the system request throughput rate when 1 frame is 25000 scheduling time unit and the number of neurons in the hidden layer is [128, 32].

We can see that when the number of cells is 7, the best effect is achieved in the test area. After taking Alibaba tracking requests of different time periods and inputting them into the system, the average system throughput rate can be obtained at 0.80. When the number of cells is other numbers, the average system throughput rate is between [0.78, 0.79]. Therefore, the experiment proves that the task scheduling effect of the system is the best when the number of cells is 7. When the number of cells is too small, the network cannot capture the time sequence feature in the process of request arrival; when the number of cells is too large, the network appears the phenomenon of overfitting, which leads to the degradation of the scheduling performance of the model.

6   Summary

In order to solve the problem of periodic computing resource scheduling for external requests, this paper proposes the CMARAC algorithm. Its main idea is to take the system state including multiple time nodes in the present and the past and the request information in the current server cluster as the input, and use LSTM to extract the time characteristics of the request flow in the server cluster. Finally, it is output to the actor-critic network, and the most suitable edge node is selected for processing, so as to achieve the function of resource scheduling for external requests. Experiments show that the proposed multi-agent cooperative computing resource scheduling algorithm (CMARAC) for periodic task scenarios has better scheduling effect than random scheduling algorithm, greedy strategy and cMMAC. In addition, compared with the baseline, the request timing feature recognition function proposed in this paper can capture the change of task submission, and the convergence speed is faster. Compared with the actor-critic algorithm alone, the system computation cost is less, and the scheduling scheme produced by greedy strategy judgment is better. CMARAC can schedule computing resources when multiple edge clusters are combined, improving the processing efficiency of external requests. Subsequently, we plan to further improve this algorithm and perfect the time step between the input time series of the algorithm.

References

1. Wang, R., Lai, J., Zhang, Z., Li, X., Vijayakumar, P., Karuppiah, M.: Privacy-preserving federated learning for internet of medical things under edge computing. IEEE J. Biomed. Health Inform. **27**, 854–865 (2022)
2. Deng, S., Zhao, H., Fang, W., Yin, J., Dustdar, S., Zomaya, A.Y.: Edge intelligence: the confluence of edge computing and artificial intelligence. IEEE Internet Things J. **7**(8), 7457–7469 (2020)
3. Khan, W.Z., Ahmed, E., Hakak, S., Yaqoob, I., Ahmed, A.: Edge computing: a survey. Futur. Gener. Comput. Syst. **97**, 219–235 (2019)
4. Zhang, J., Chen, B., Zhao, Y., Cheng, X., Hu, F.: Data security and privacy-preserving in edge computing paradigm: survey and open issues. IEEE Access **6**, 18209–18237 (2018)
5. Lu, C., Ye, K., Xu, G., Xu, C.Z., Bai, T.: Imbalance in the cloud: an analysis on alibaba cluster trace. In: 2017 IEEE International Conference on Big Data (Big Data), pp. 2884–2892. IEEE (2017)
6. Tianqing, Z., Zhou, W., Ye, D., Cheng, Z., Li, J.: Resource allocation in IoT edge computing via concurrent federated reinforcement learning. IEEE Internet Things J. **9**(2), 1414–1426 (2021)
7. Houssein, E.H., Gad, A.G., Wazery, Y.M., Suganthan, P.N.: Task scheduling in cloud computing based on meta-heuristics: review, taxonomy, open challenges, and future trends. Swarm Evol. Comput. **62**, 100841 (2021)
8. Farhadi, V., et al.: Service placement and request scheduling for data-intensive applications in edge clouds. IEEE/ACM Trans. Netw. **29**(2), 779–792 (2021)
9. Liu, B., Liu, C., Peng, M.: Resource allocation for energy-efficient MEC in NOMA-enabled massive IoT networks. IEEE J. Sel. Areas Commun. **39**(4), 1015–1027 (2020)
10. Chen, X., Zhu, F., Chen, Z., Min, G., Zheng, X., Rong, C.: Resource allocation for cloud-based software services using prediction-enabled feedback control with reinforcement learning. IEEE Trans. Cloud Comput. **10**(2), 1117–1129 (2020)
11. Wang, R., et al.: Multivariable time series forecasting using model fusion. Inf. Sci. **585**, 262–274 (2022)
12. Chen, Y., Liu, Z., Zhang, Y., Wu, Y., Chen, X., Zhao, L.: Deep reinforcement learning-based dynamic resource management for mobile edge computing in industrial internet of things. IEEE Trans. Industr. Inf. **17**(7), 4925–4934 (2020)
13. Cui, J., Liu, Y., Nallanathan, A.: Multi-agent reinforcement learning-based resource allocation for UAV networks. IEEE Trans. Wirel. Commun. **19**(2), 729–743 (2019)
14. Han, Y., Shen, S., Wang, X., Wang, S., Leung, V.C.: Tailored learning-based scheduling for Kubernetes-oriented edge-cloud system. In: IEEE INFOCOM 2021-IEEE Conference on Computer Communications, pp. 1–10. IEEE (2021)
15. Mnih, V., et al.: Human-level control through deep reinforcement learning. Nature **518**(7540), 529–533 (2015)
16. Lillicrap, T.P., et al.: Continuous control with deep reinforcement learning. arXiv preprint arXiv:1509.02971 (2015)
17. Wang, F., Wang, F., Liu, J., Shea, R., Sun, L.: Intelligent video caching at network edge: A multi-agent deep reinforcement learning approach. In: IEEE INFOCOM 2020-IEEE Conference on Computer Communications, pp. 2499–2508. IEEE (2020)
18. Fei, J., Liu, L.: Real-time nonlinear model predictive control of active power filter using self-feedback recurrent fuzzy neural network estimator. IEEE Trans. Ind. Electron. **69**(8), 8366–8376 (2021)

19. Funahashi, K., Nakamura, Y.: Approximation of dynamical systems by continuous time recurrent neural networks. Neural Netw. **6**(6), 801–806 (1993)
20. Zheng, H., Lin, F., Feng, X., Chen, Y.: A hybrid deep learning model with attention-based conv-LSTM networks for short-term traffic flow prediction. IEEE Trans. Intell. Transp. Syst. **22**(11), 6910–6920 (2020)
21. Hu, J., Jiang, S., Harding, S.A., Wu, H., Liao, S.W.: Rethinking the implementation tricks and monotonicity constraint in cooperative multi-agent reinforcement learning. arXiv preprint arXiv:2102.03479 (2021)
22. Wang, L., Wang, K., Pan, C., Xu, W., Aslam, N., Hanzo, L.: Multi-agent deep reinforcement learning-based trajectory planning for multi-UAV assisted mobile edge computing. IEEE Trans. Cogn. Commun. Netw. **7**(1), 73–84 (2020)
23. Dorronsoro, B., Bouvry, P.: Improving classical and decentralized differential evolution with new mutation operator and population topologies. IEEE Trans. Evol. Comput. **15**(1), 67–98 (2011)
24. Littman, M.L: Markov games as a framework for multi-agent reinforcement learning. In: Machine Learning Proceedings 1994, pp. 157–163. Elsevier (1994)
25. Weng, Q., et al.: MLaaS in the wild: workload analysis and scheduling in large-scale heterogeneous GPU clusters. In: 19th USENIX Symposium on Networked Systems Design and Implementation (NSDI 22), pp. 945–960. USENIX Association (2022)
26. Gao, W., et al.: Deep learning workload scheduling in GPU datacenters: taxonomy, challenges and vision. arXiv preprint arXiv:2205.11913 (2022)
27. Jena, U., Das, P., Kabat, M.: Hybridization of meta-heuristic algorithm for load balancing in cloud computing environment. J. King Saud Univ.-Comput. Inf. Sci. **34**(6), 2332–2342 (2022)

Storage Systems and File Management

CLMS: Configurable and Lightweight Metadata Service for Parallel File Systems on NVMe SSDs

Qiong Li[1,2], Shuaizhe Lv[1], Xuchao Xie[1(✉)], and Zhenlong Song[1]

[1] College of Computer, National University of Defense Technology, Changsha, China
xiexuchao@nudt.edu.cn
[2] Defense Innovation Institute, Academy of Military Sciences, Beijing, China

Abstract. With the tendency of running large-scale data-intensive applications on High-Performance Computing (HPC) systems, the I/O workloads of HPC storage systems are becoming more complex, such as the increasing metadata-intensive I/O operations in Exascale computing and High-Performance Data Analytics (HPDA). To meet the increasing performance requirements of the metadata service in HPC parallel file systems, this paper proposes a Configurable and Lightweight Metadata Service (CLMS) design for the parallel file systems on NVMe SSDs. CLMS introduces a configurable metadata distribution policy that simultaneously enables the directory-based and hash-based metadata distribution strategies and can be activated according to the application I/O access pattern, thus improving the processing efficiency of metadata accesses from different kinds of data-intensive applications. CLMS further reduces the memory copy and serialization processing overhead in the I/O path through the full-user metadata service design. We implemented the CLMS prototype and evaluated it under the MDTest benchmarks. Our experimental results demonstrate that CLMS can significantly improve the performance of metadata services. Besides, CMLS achieves a linear growth trend as the number of metadata servers increases for the unique-directory file distribution pattern.

Keywords: High-Performance Computing · Parallel File System · CLMS · Metadata Service · Storage System

1 Introduction

Integrating the new emerging NVMe SSDs and Non-Volatile Memory (NVM) into the storage hierarchy of High-Performance Computing (HPC) systems is attractive, especially as the growing tendency of running large-scale data-intensive applications on HPC systems [2]. Nowadays, almost all the top supercomputers in the world employ a large number of NVMe SSDs to build Burst Buffer which provides applications with a high-performance I/O acceleration layer [8,20]. Typically, compared with the HDD-based parallel file system (PFS),

© The Author(s), under exclusive license to Springer Nature Singapore Pte Ltd. 2024
C. Li et al. (Eds.): APPT 2023, LNCS 14103, pp. 101–112, 2024.
https://doi.org/10.1007/978-981-99-7872-4_6

the NVMe SSD-based BB can improve HPC I/O performance by one to two orders of magnitude. In terms of Burst Buffer implementations, NVMe SSDs can be placed on a dedicated I/O Node (ION) between compute nodes and PFS as shared Burst Buffer, or simply placed on compute node as node-local Burst Buffer [17,19].

With the price of NVMe SSDs continuously decreasing, HPC systems are trying to construct PFS using only NVMe SSDs to achieve high I/O performance with a fixed Total Cost of Ownership (TCO) for storage systems. The legacy PFS implementations for HPC storage systems are specially designed to provide high bandwidth for parallel file accesses [4,14,15]. For metadata-intensive workloads with a large number of data synchronization, non-continuous random access, and small I/O requests, PFS potentially incurs high I/O latency and low throughput for its inefficiency of metadata performance [5,9,11,18]. Thus, how to design the specific PFS for NVMe SSDs and break through the metadata performance bottleneck of existing PFS is critical for HPC storage systems.

Data-intensive applications will inevitably generate hot data directories, therefore a large number of file and sub-directory create, delete, modify, and find operations will be frequently triggered in the hot directories. Once the metadata of the hot data is located in a single or small number of metadata servers (MDS), the load unbalance issue of MDS will result in poor metadata scalability, and the overall PFS performance is severely limited [10]. For example, BeeGFS adopts a static directory partition method for load balancing, metadata accesses to a large directory will be redirected to a single MDS. BeeGFS cannot efficiently handle the metadata operations to hot directories. GekkoFS can appropriately solve such hot directory problems through a hash-based metadata distribution strategy. However, the hash-based metadata distribution will lead to a poor locality of metadata accesses, which generates a large number of inter-server I/O communication overhead in PFS.

Existing PFS is usually constructed in a superimposed style that metadata and data in PFS are stored on the local filesystem of MDS and OSS, such as EXT4, XFS, etc. However, due to the small size of PFS metadata, storing each PFS metadata as a single file in the local filesystem is inefficient [3,6,12]. This is because the getattr, setattr, and other system calls in the I/O path will incur significant user and kernel mode switching overhead. In addition, the inode and directory blocks of the local filesystem are not optimized for parallel I/O [7,16]. Each block can only be accessed by one process at a time, and it will bring a large number of serial processing operations when there are multiple processes to access a single PFS directory, resulting in serious locking competitive overhead.

In this paper, we propose CLMS, a configurable and lightweight metadata service for the parallel file systems on NVMe SSDs. CLMS introduces a configurable metadata distribution policy that simultaneously enables the directory-based and hash-based metadata distribution strategies and can be activated according to the application I/O access pattern, thus improving the processing efficiency of metadata accesses from different kinds of data-intensive applications. CLMS further reduces the memory copy and serialization processing overhead in the I/O path through the userspace metadata service design. We implemented the CLMS prototype and evaluated it under the MDTest benchmarks. Our experimental results demonstrate that CLMS can significantly improve the performance of metadata services. Besides, CMLS achieves a linear growth trend as the number of metadata servers increases for the unique-directory file distribution pattern.

The rest of this paper is organized as follows. Section 2 summarizes the related work. Section 3 provides an overview of CLMS architecture. Section 4 and Sect. 5 describe the detailed configurable metadata distribution and lightweight metadata service designs of CLMS. We evaluate CLMS in Sect. 6 and conclude the paper in Sect. 7.

2 Related Work

HPC storage systems usually equip a limited number of metadata servers for PFS. As the th increasing metadata-intensive I/O operations in Exascale computing and High-Performance Data Analytics (HPDA), the metadata performance has been one of the PFS performance bottleneck. Chen et al. [3] proposed to redirect the metadata operations to high-performance NVMe SSDs, thereby achieving higher metadata performance. Wang et al. [19] build a distributed key-value store based on the local burst buffer for metadata to alleviate the performance bottleneck of the key-value store under burst and concurrent I/O workloads. Ren et al. [13] propose IndexFS that each server is responsible for managing part of the PFS metadata. IndexFS dynamically divides the metadata according to the directory set and package file metadata and small files into SSTable based on the LSM Tree, thus the random metadata can be written in sequential and the performance of metadata can be significantly improved.

However, managing metadata in IndexFS needs to deploy a dedicated metadata management server and may cause resource waste for a large number of MDS. Zheng et al. [21] propose DeltaFS to provide a private local metadata server for each application process, and use the data path of the underlying PFS to realize the metadata management. The application obtains the metadata snapshot required through a public registration service before runtime. All metadata operations are completed on local private servers, thereby avoiding unnecessary metadata synchronization overhead. Once the application finishes its execution, DeltaFS will push the output result as a new snapshot to the global registration service. However, DeltaFS is not suitable for applications that need frequent inter-process interaction during the running process.

3 System Overview

In the scenario of data-intensive computing, PFS has to handle a large number of metadata-intensive I/O workloads. Metadata is usually divided into dentry and inode. Specifically, dentry of a file or directory is used to record the file and sub-directory ID, stat data, parent directory ID, strip distribution information, etc. inode of a directory is used to record the directory ID, the number of file and sub-directory of this directory, stat data, parent directory ID, strip distribution information, etc. The efficiency of metadata service depends mainly on two factors. One is whether the metadata distribution has good locality and parallelism, the other is the access efficiency of a single metadata service. When providing parallel file system services with different I/O workloads, PFS is difficult to satisfy all application I/O modes through a single metadata distribution strategy. To effectively improve the PFS metadata performance under different types of data-intensive applications, and fully utilize the performance advantage of NVMe SSDs, this paper proposes CLMS that enables a configurable metadata distribution method for PFS and matches metadata distribution strategies according to the application I/O characteristics. CLMS also designs metadata services based on NVMe SSD features and the key-value store to achieve high-performance metadata handling in MDS.

There are two kinds of hot data in PFS, i.e., the hot directory where most data operations are concentrated in a single directory, and the hot files that are intensively accessed but distributed in multiple directories. Once the metadata of the hot directory or files are distributed in a small amount of MDS, the overall PFS performance will be limited by the metadata handling efficiency of each MDS. As a result, PFS cannot provide desired high-performance and scalable parallel file access services for large-scale HPC systems. Different from existing PFS, CLMS enables both directory-based and hash-based metadata distribution to simultaneously provide access locality and parallelism for the metadata of hot data.

Traditional PFS directly stores its metadata and data on the local file system on MDS and OSS, which potentially brings serious performance problems to PFS. This is because these file systems strictly follow the POSIX semantics and frequently perform system calls such as file open, close, etc., which will cause frequent user and kernel mode switching and eventually lead to low local file system performance. Besides, the legacy I/O software stack introduces significant performance overhead in PFS as each PFS metadata and data go through local file systems, I/O scheduling layers, general block layers, and block device drivers in MDS and OSS, resulting in additional system management overhead and performance reduction. CLMS designs and implements a high-performance local storage engine for metadata services based on NVMe SSD features and Key-Value store, and relaxes POSIX semantics to achieve fast persistent storage of directory and file metadata, thus reducing the software performance overhead introduced by the local file system.

4   Configurable Metadata Distribution

4.1   Directory-Based Distribution

In the directory-based metadata distribution strategy, each directory in PFS will be attached to a metadata service that processes its metadata operations, as shown in Fig. 1, the metadata of directory A is processed by MDS0, then the metadata of all files in directory A will be stored on MDS0. When creating a

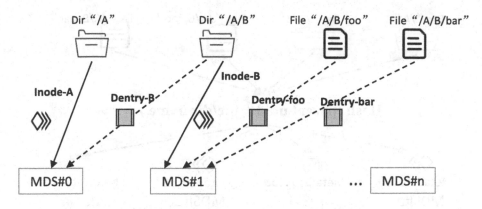

Fig. 1. Directory-based Metadata Distribution

subdirectory B in directory A, CLMS needs to randomly pick a new MDS node from the available metadata service nodes to store the inode of directory B, but the dentry information of directory B is still stored on MDS0. It should be noted that in the directory-based metadata distribution strategy, the metadata operations of the root directory are always handled by MDS0, which contains the information of all subdirectories under the root directory, including the link to the MDS where the subdirectory is located, so that there is a defined fixed entry point in the CLMS directory tree, and PFS clients can find the metadata service node responsible for a specific directory by traversing the directory tree. In the directory-based metadata distribution strategy, all files in a single directory are distributed in the same MDS node, and when the application intensively processes a large number of files in a single directory, PFS performance will be limited by the efficiency of the metadata service of a single MDS node.

4.2   Hash-Based Distribution

For applications where hot data is centralized in a few directories, CLMS provides a metadata distribution strategy based on the hash of the file path. In this hash-based metadata distribution design, the metadata of directories and files is hashed under the VFS schema and distributed to multiple MDS nodes, and the files are no longer distributed on the same MDS nodes following the parent directory. Ash shown in Fig. 2, CLMS executes the hash function on ¡parent_directory_uuid, file_name¿ combination, selects the MDS node responsible for processing file metadata requests, and forwards the subsequent operations of the file to the daemon process of the MDS node for execution, to achieve the uniform distribution of file metadata among all MDS nodes. In this way, the metadata of files and directories is distributed pseudo-randomly among MDS nodes. In the hash-based distribution policy, the number of MDTs can be configured for directory hash distribution. CLMS will select the MDT that meets the satisfaction according to this information, the MDT with the lowest utilization will be selected by default and prioritized in the MDT list. Once the

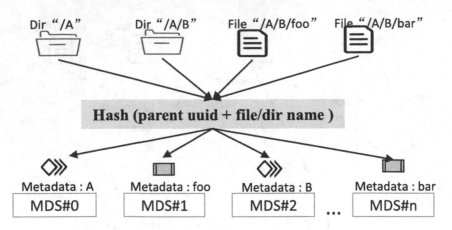

Fig. 2. Hash-based Metadata Distribution

selection is completed, the directory metadata will record the user-configured MDT list, and the subdirectory and file metadata will be distributed according to the MDT list.

5   Lightweight Metadata Service

5.1   Efficient Key-Value Store

CLMS designs and implements a high-performance metadata storage engine based on NVMe SSD features and user-mode key-value store for metadata services. This MDS-specific storage engine can achieve fast storage performance for metadata and reduce the software performance overhead introduced by traditional local file systems. CLMS implements user-mode key-value store instead of the local file system as a metadata storage engine, as shown in Fig. 3, the metadata storage engine divides the NVMe SSD address space into fixed-size slots, each slot is used to store directory or file-related metadata, and all slots are organized by a simple and efficient hash table data structure, where key is the ID of the directory or file, and value is the address pointer of the metadata. To accelerate the insertion, deletion, and search of metadata in the hash table, CLMS further introduces region locks and locates the region locks to be used according to the Key. This region lock design is used to improve the parallel processing capabilities of the metadata storage engine and abandon the inefficient mutex lock to further reduce the lock overhead in the metadata storage path.

CLMS assigns a UUID (Universally Unique Identifier) to each directory or file and uses the UUID as part of the directory and file metadata index. To save memory, only the key fields of inodeID, parentID, name, and entryType of file and directory metadata are stored and organized in memory, and the remaining fields are stored in NVMe SSDs and read when needed. There are three types of hash tables, one is the UID Hash Table (UHT) with the object

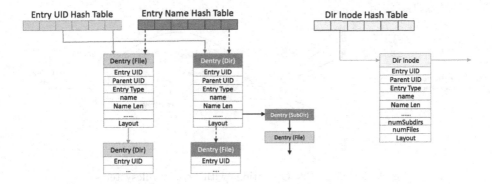

Fig. 3. MDS-Specific Key-Value Store in CLMS

entry UID as the key, which is used to quickly find the metadata of the object according to the entry UID. The second is the Name Hash Table (NHT) with the object entry name as the key, which is used to quickly find the metadata of the object according to the entry name. The third is the Inode Hash Table (IHT) built specifically for directory inodes, which is used to retrieve directory inode information. For the same catalog item, join UHT with object UID as key and NHT with object name as the key. Based on this design, CLMS metadata service provides two types of API interfaces, one is to find the corresponding directory or file metadata according to the parent directory UUID (parent_uuid) and name. The second is to directly manipulate the corresponding metadata according to the UUID of the directory or file. Therefore, whether it is based on directory-based distribution metadata or hash-based distribution metadata, the local KV storage engine can effectively support it.

5.2   POSIX Semantic Relaxation

The inode and directory blocks of traditional file systems are not designed for parallel access, as only one block can be accessed by one process at a time. When a large number of files are created from multiple processes in a single directory, this introduces significant serial processing and performance penalty. As shown in Fig. 4, the same is true in distributed file systems, for example, for file and directory creation and deletion operations, the parent directory must be locked first, and the parent directory is updated after the file and directory operation is completed. To relax POSIX semantics in CLMS, instead of using directory blocks that are difficult to use in a distributed environment, each directory entry is stored in the KV store of the daemon process, and the current state of the directory is not guaranteed to be returned in these indirect file system operations when the directory contents are requested. For example, the readdir() operation follows the eventual consistency model, that is, operations such as creating and deleting files in the same directory are no longer processed serially with parent directory updates, and the serial lock of the parent directory is removed. When

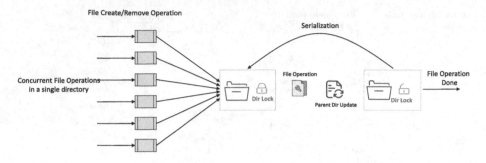

Fig. 4. Serialized File Operations with Legacy Filesystems

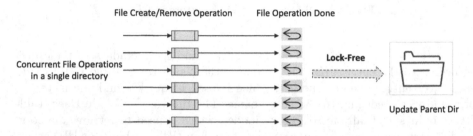

Fig. 5. Parallel File Operations with POSIX Semantic Relaxation

deleting a file, the data corresponding to the file also needs to be deleted, which requires communication with the data storage server and is a time-consuming process. In CLMS, we can also configure this strategy, implement asynchronous processing, and delete file data in the background.

As shown in Fig. 5, CLMS relaxes POSIX directory semantics. The creation of directories is similar to files, and directories are configured with hash-based distribution, and the contents of directories can only be collected from distributed inode entries, that is, the contents of directories must be traversed through the hash distribution nodes associated with the directory. Although there are multiple node communications, the problem can be mitigated by reading as many directory entries as possible into the buffer at once. In the rename operation, metadata may need to be re-migrated to the new MDS based on hash values due to the directory or file name changes, but due to the unchanged UUID of the directory or file and the path traversal lookup mechanism, unlike GekkoFS and LocoFS that use the path of a file system object as an index within a flat namespace, when a directory is moved to a different file system path, the path of all its contents must also be modified recursively.

6   Performance Evaluation

6.1   Experimental Setup

We built a 10-node HPC system to evaluate the performance of CLMS, each compute node is equipped with 2 Intel Xeon Gold 6134 CPUs, 512 GB of node memory, 2 NVMe SSDs to build RAID for storing metadata, and 8 NVMe SSDs for object storage. In the experiment, the cluster interconnects all compute nodes using a 100 Gbps RDMA network. We evaluate CLMS performance using the MDTest [1] benchmarks in both Unique Dir and Single Dir modes, where Unique Dir means that the files and file operations of each process are in separate directories, and Single Dir means that the files and file operations of all processes are in the same directory. MDTest simulates common metadata-intensive HPC workloads to evaluate the metadata performance of CLMS and BeeGFS.

To comprehensively evaluate the behavior of CLMS, we introduce BeeGFS, CLMS-Dir, and CLMS-Hash as comparison candidates. Both CLMS-Dir and CLMS-Hash implementations follow the basic principles of CLMS designs but with different metadata distribution schemes, i.e., CLMS-Dir uses directory-based distribution and CLMS-Hash uses hash-based distribution. In HPC systems, the concurrent metadata operations in a single directory are an important workload in many applications, we tested the performance of file Create, Stat, and Remove operations using 100,000 zero-byte files per process and 16 processes per node. The x-axis of the evaluation results shown in Sect. 6.2 represents the number of nodes, up to 10 nodes, and the y-axis represents OPS for each kind of I/O workload.

6.2   Evaluation Results

In the first set of tests, we use Single Dir workload, i.e., all processes of MDTest run in a single directory, to evaluate the performance of the metadata distribution strategy and the dedicated storage engine design in CLMS. Figure 6 shows the OPS of file Create, Stat, and Remove operations. CLMS-Dir uses the same directory-based metadata distribution strategy as BeeGFS, and CLMS-Dir introduces the local metadata storage engine with full userspace key-value store rather than the legacy EXT4 filesystem configured with BeeGFS, thus the performance of metadata service for Create, Stat, and Remove are improved by 14.86×, 3.61×, and 7.49× on average. However, because all metadata operations target a single metadata server under Single Dir workload, the metadata performance of the file system is limited by the performance of a single MDS and does not improve as the system scales. In contrast, CLMS-Hash can distribute metadata operations to all MDSs in the file system through hash functions, so parallel metadata services can be implemented and metadata performance can be greatly improved. Specifically, CLMS-Hash can further improve the OPS of file Create, Stat, and Remove operations by 1.6× when the number of MDS increases from 1 to 2, and by 10.48 when the number of MDS increases from 1 to 10. The metadata service scalability of CLMS-Hash outperforms BeeGFS and CLMS-Dir under the Single Dir workloads.

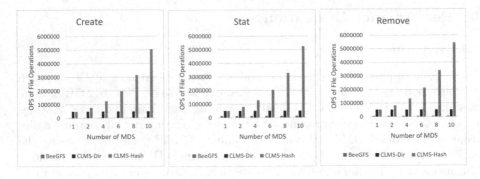

Fig. 6. OPS of File Operations under Single Dir Workloads

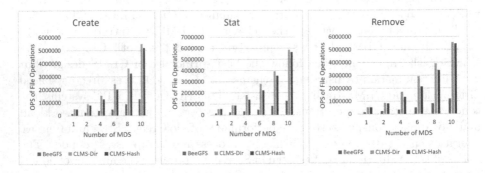

Fig. 7. OPS of File Operations under Unique Dir Workloads

We further compare BeeGFS, CLMS-Dir, and CLMS-Hash under the Unique Dir workloads that each process only accesses its directory. As shown in Fig. 7, different from the Single Dir workload, BeeGFS shows obvious metadata scalability as the number of MDS increases. Specifically, as the number of MDS increases from 1 to 10, the OPS of file Create, Stat, and Remove operations in BeeGFS get 8.82× improvements on average. This is mainly because the inherited directory-based metadata distribution strategy in BeeGFS achieves good metadata scalability. Compared with BeeGFS, CLMS-Dir achieves 4.21×, 4.75×, and 4.69× for Create, Stat, and Remove while CLMS-Hash achieves 3.72×, 4.22×, and 4.09× for Create, Stat, and Remove respectively. The metadata performance improvements are mainly from the efficient key-value store and POSIX semantic relaxation implementations in CLMS. Furthermore, as CLMS-Hash always distributes file and directory metadata across all the MDS, it inevitably incurs more inter-server networking communication overhead on the metadata access path. As a result, the metadata performance of CLMS-Hash is lower than that of CLMS-Dir under the Unique Dir workload. For file Create, Stat, and Remove operations, the OPS of CLMS-Dir is 11.59%, 9.94%, and 11.41% higher than that of CLMS-Hash.

7 Conclusion

This paper proposes CLMS, a configurable and lightweight metadata service for the parallel file systems on NVMe SSDs to meet the increasing performance requirements of the PFS metadata service. CLMS introduces a configurable metadata distribution policy that simultaneously enables the directory-based and hash-based metadata distribution strategies and can be activated according to the application I/O access pattern, thus improving the processing efficiency of metadata accesses from different kinds of data-intensive applications. CLMS further reduces the memory copy and serialization processing overhead in the I/O path through the full-user metadata service design. CLMS is comprehensively evaluated under the MDTest benchmarks. The experimental results demonstrate that CLMS can significantly improve the performance of metadata services and achieve a linear growth trend as the number of metadata servers increases.

Acknowledgements. This work was partially supported by the Foundation of National Key Research and Development Program of China under Grant 2021YFB 0300101, the Foundation of State Key Lab of High-Performance Computing under Grant 202101-09, and the Natural Science Foundation of NUDT under Grant ZK21-03.

References

1. IOR/mdtest (2020). https://github.com/hpc/ior
2. Amvrosiadis, G., Park, J.W., Ganger, G.R., Gibson, G.A., Baseman, E., DeBardeleben, N.: On the diversity of cluster workloads and its impact on research results. In: 2018 USENIX Annual Technical Conference (USENIX ATC 2018), pp. 533–546 (2018)
3. Chen, Y., Shu, J., Ou, J., Lu, Y.: HiNFS: a persistent memory file system with both buffering and direct-access. ACM Trans. Storage (ToS) **14**(1), 1–30 (2018)
4. Devarakonda, M.V., Mohindra, A., Simoneaux, J., Tetzlaff, W.H.: Evaluation of design alternatives for a cluster file system. In: USENIX, pp. 35–46 (1995)
5. Dorier, M., Antoniu, G., Ross, R., Kimpe, D., Ibrahim, S.: CALCioM: mitigating I/O interference in HPC systems through cross-application coordination. In: 2014 IEEE 28th International Parallel and Distributed Processing Symposium, pp. 155–164. IEEE (2014)
6. Dulloor, S.R., et al.: System software for persistent memory. In: Proceedings of the Ninth European Conference on Computer Systems, pp. 1–15 (2014)
7. Hua, Y., Jiang, H., Zhu, Y., Feng, D., Tian, L.: SmartStore: a new metadata organization paradigm with semantic-awareness for next-generation file systems. In: Proceedings of the Conference on High Performance Computing Networking, Storage and Analysis, pp. 1–12 (2009)
8. Kougkas, A., Devarajan, H., Sun, X.H.: Hermes: a heterogeneous-aware multi-tiered distributed I/O buffering system. In: Proceedings of the 27th International Symposium on High-Performance Parallel and Distributed Computing, pp. 219–230 (2018)
9. Lensing, P.H., Cortes, T., Hughes, J., Brinkmann, A.: File system scalability with highly decentralized metadata on independent storage devices. In: 2016 16th IEEE/ACM International Symposium on Cluster, Cloud and Grid Computing (CCGrid), pp. 366–375. IEEE (2016)

10. Leung, A.W., Shao, M., Bisson, T., Pasupathy, S., Miller, E.L.: Spyglass: fast, scalable metadata search for large-scale storage systems. In: FAST, vol. 9, pp. 153–166 (2009)
11. Li, S., Lu, Y., Shu, J., Hu, Y., Li, T.: LocoFS: a loosely-coupled metadata service for distributed file systems. In: Proceedings of the International Conference for High Performance Computing, Networking, Storage and Analysis, pp. 1–12 (2017)
12. Patil, S., Gibson, G.A.: Scale and concurrency of giga+: file system directories with millions of files. In: FAST, vol. 11, p. 13 (2011)
13. Ren, K., Zheng, Q., Patil, S., Gibson, G.: IndexFS: scaling file system metadata performance with stateless caching and bulk insertion. In: SC 20: Proceedings of the International Conference for High Performance Computing, Networking, Storage and Analysis, pp. 237–248. IEEE (2014)
14. Ross, R.B., Thakur, R., et al.: PVFS: a parallel file system for Linux clusters. In: Proceedings of the 4th Annual Linux Showcase and Conference, pp. 391–430 (2000)
15. Schmuck, F.B., Haskin, R.L.: GPFS: a shared-disk file system for large computing clusters. In: FAST, vol. 2 (2002)
16. Sim, H., Kim, Y., Vazhkudai, S.S., Vallée, G.R., Lim, S.H., Butt, A.R.: TagIt: an integrated indexing and search service for file systems. In: Proceedings of the International Conference for High Performance Computing, Networking, Storage and Analysis, pp. 1–12 (2017)
17. Thapaliya, S., Bangalore, P., Lofstead, J., Mohror, K., Moody, A.: Managing I/O interference in a shared burst buffer system. In: 2016 45th International Conference on Parallel Processing (ICPP), pp. 416–425. IEEE (2016)
18. Vef, M.A., et al.: GekkoFS-a temporary distributed file system for HPC applications. In: 2018 IEEE International Conference on Cluster Computing (CLUSTER), pp. 319–324. IEEE (2018)
19. Wang, T., Mohror, K., Moody, A., Sato, K., Yu, W.: An ephemeral burst-buffer file system for scientific applications. In: SC 2016: Proceedings of the International Conference for High Performance Computing, Networking, Storage and Analysis, pp. 807–818. IEEE (2016)
20. Wang, T., Yu, W., Sato, K., Moody, A., Mohror, K.: BurstFS: a distributed burst buffer file system for scientific applications. Technical report, Lawrence Livermore National Lab. (LLNL), Livermore, CA (United States) (2016)
21. Zheng, Q., et al.: DeltaFS: a scalable no-ground-truth filesystem for massively-parallel computing. In: Proceedings of the International Conference for High Performance Computing, Networking, Storage and Analysis, pp. 1–15 (2021)

Combining Cache and Refresh to Optimize SSD Read Performance Scheme

Jinli Chen[1,2,3,4], Peixuan Li[1,2,3,4], and Ping Xie[1,2,3,4](✉)

[1] College of Computer of Qinghai Normal University, Xining 810016,
People's Republic of China
xieping@qhnu.edu.cn
[2] The State Key Laboratory of Tibetan Intelligent Information Processing and Application,
Xining 810016, People's Republic of China
[3] The Key Laboratory of Internet of Things of Qinghai Province, Xining 810016,
People's Republic of China
[4] Academy of Plateau Science and Sustainability, Xining 810016, People's Republic of China

Abstract. In the era of continuous advances in flash technology, the storage density of NAND flash memory is increasing, but the availability of data is declining. In order to improve data availability, low-density parity check codes (LDPC), which have been highly corrected in recent years, are used in flash memory. However, although LDPC can solve the problem of low data availability, it also brings the problem of long decoding time. Moreover, the LDPC decoding delay time is related to its decoding level, and the higher the LDPC decoding level, the longer the delay time. Long decoding delays can have an impact on the read performance of the flash. Therefore, in order to improve the speed of reading data in flash memory, this paper proposes a scheme combining cache and flushing, the main idea of which is to use the cache to reduce LDPC decoding time, and at the same time refresh the pages with high latency replaced by the cache, so that the pages with high latency can be restored to the state of low latency pages Experimental results show that this scheme can significantly reduce LDPC decoding delay and improve data availability with less overhead, and optimize the read performance of flash memory. The experimental results show that compared with the original strategy, the average response time is reduced by 24%, and the average IOPS value is increased by 32%.

Keywords: Cache · Refresh · LDPC · Flash memory

1 Introduction

Solid-state drives (SSDs) based on NAND flash memory are non-volatile and have slowly developed into dominant secondary storage due to their small size, high performance, and low energy consumption [1, 2]. In order to increase the storage capacity of SSD, the memory cell density of flash memory has slowly increased from single-level cell flash memory (SLC) to multi-level cell (MLC) or three-level cell (TLC). As the memory density of flash memory increases, the gap between flash memory cells becomes smaller and smaller [3, 4], and the voltage of the memory cell is more likely to shift. As a result, the endurance of flash memory will be reduced, and the bit error rate will increase.

© The Author(s), under exclusive license to Springer Nature Singapore Pte Ltd. 2024
C. Li et al. (Eds.): APPT 2023, LNCS 14103, pp. 113–129, 2024.
https://doi.org/10.1007/978-981-99-7872-4_7

With the increasing density of flash memory cells leading to the continuous increase of bit error rate, users have higher and higher requirements for erasure coding in flash memory, and BCH erasure coding (Bose, Ray Choudhury, and Huo Quinheng) can no longer meet people's requirements for flash memory reliability [5]. In recent years, LDPC (Low-Density Parity-Check Codes), as a high-cost, error-correcting ECC, has become the default ECC scheme for the most advanced flash-based storage devices [6]. However, although the error correction ability of LDPC coding is strong, it also has disadvantages. LDPC code is highly complex to compile and requires up to 7 read retries to take full advantage of its error correction capabilities. Larger read-retry operations contain more fine-grained read voltages. In order to successfully decode, this data may waste more time to decode, and the long decoding delay reduces the read performance of the flash memory. Therefore, in order to improve the read performance of flash memory, this paper starts from reducing the number of read retries in the LDPC decoding process of the LDPC decoding process, and proposes a scheme to apply cache and flushing to the LDPC decoding process of flash memory, and experiments show that this scheme improves the read performance and prolongs the life of flash memory to a certain extent.

2   Research Background and Motivation

2.1   Introduction to the Basics of Flash Memory

Flash memory is a non-volatile memory device, also known as solid-state memory [7], which is widely used in various devices. Flash memory consists of many memory cells, each of which can store one or more bits. A storage unit is usually composed of a transistor and a capacitor, and the transistor is used to control the charging and discharging of the capacitor to realize data storage. Flash memory can be divided into various types according to the structure and working principle of the storage unit. NAND flash memory is the most common type of flash memory, and it is usually used in large-capacity storage media, such as solid-state drives (SSD). NAND flash memory connects multiple storage units into a block, multiple blocks form a plane, multiple planes form a core, and multiple cores form a chip. Read and write operations for NAND flash are performed on a page-by-page basis, while erase operations are performed on a per-block basis [8]. Therefore, when a storage unit needs to be updated or deleted, the block where the storage unit is located needs to be erased, and the data in other data pages is copied to the new block. Compared to traditional hard drives, flash memory offers faster read and write speeds, lower power consumption, smaller size, and higher reliability.

2.2   LDPC in Flash Memory

In order to solve the reliability problem of flash memory, BCH code with high performance and error correction capability is applied to flash memory [9]. However, as the reliability of flash memory decreases, the error correction capability of BCH can no longer meet the reliability requirements. To meet the reliability requirements of state-of-the-art flash systems, LDPC codes are recommended [10]. LDPC codes, also known as low-density parity codes, were proposed in the 1960s and have been widely used in storage in recent years [11]. LDPC code has high error correction ability, can achieve high error correction performance, and high coding efficiency, so it is used in flash memory devices. In the following, we will discuss the decoding process of LDPC.

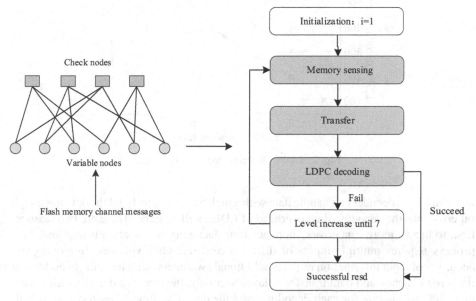

Fig. 1. Tanner diagram of LDPC

LDPC codes generally use an iterative belief propagation decoding algorithm to complete the input of decoding information. The basic idea is to XOR the received code word and code book to obtain the constraints involved in each check node, and then the algorithm converts these constraints into a Tanner graph, where nodes represent the variable nodes and check nodes of the code word, and edges represent the relationships between them, as shown in Fig. 1. When decoding fails, multiple read retries are required, as shown in Fig. 1. Although increasing the number of read retries can increase the probability of successful decoding. However, the decoding delay also increases significantly.

2.3 Research Motivation

LDPC code is an error-correcting code that has been commonly used in storage systems in recent years to correct data errors. The decoding level of LDPC code refers to the trade-off between error correction performance and computational complexity in the process of LDPC code decoding, and the decoding level is mainly adjusted to achieve the optimal balance between decoding performance and computational complexity. The decoding level of LDPC code can be divided into seven levels, among these seven levels, the higher the decoding level, the higher the success rate, but the longer the data decoding delay time, as shown in Fig. 2.

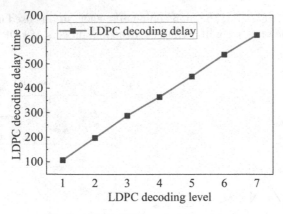

Fig. 2. LDPC different decoding delays.

The LDPC decoder can handle data with a high bit error rate, but if the data has a high bit error rate, the decoding time overhead of LDPC will be large. There are two reasons, first, to handle more data errors, more accurate data entry information is required. This process requires multiple inputs of different read reference voltages. Improving the accuracy of input information requires additional awareness, which results in additional flash read latency and data transfer delays. Secondly, the iterative decoding algorithm of LDPC will iterate for each decoding, and the decoding time of each decoding will iteratively accumulate until all errors are corrected. When the bit error rate of data is high, the time overhead of decoding will be very large. For these two reasons, this paper proposes a new method combining caching and refreshing. The main idea is to utilize caching to reduce LDPC decoding time for pages with high latency, thereby reducing the performance overhead of LDPC.

3   Related Work

In recent years, as the storage density of flash memory cells increases, the size of storage devices and the gap between flash memory cells gradually decrease [3, 4], and the possibility of data errors gradually increases. The disadvantages of LDPC codes in flash memory are more prominent. To this end, in order to reduce the decoding time of LDPC, many optimization methods have been proposed. There are many of these methods, which are briefly introduced below.

The first approach is to improve the reliability of flash memory by using refresh [12–14]. For the first method, most of them suggest to refresh data by in-place charging [5] or non-in-place updating [12, 15]. In the literature [12], a lightweight data refreshing method is utilized, which primarily relies on soft sensing to reduce read latency. By leveraging the characteristics of read-hot data, only a small portion of the data is refreshed, requiring only a few PE cycles. Furthermore, the refresh granularity of this solution is performed at the page level. By only moving one or a few hot pages during each refresh operation, it can reduce the cost of heavy block migration in the current refresh method.

This literature borrows the idea of refreshing to reset the long LDPC read latency and soft sensing back to the cheapest latency and hard sensing, in order to reduce RBER (Raw Bit Error Rate) and improve flash memory read performance.

The second method is to use caching [16] to reduce the process of LDPC read retries, thereby improving the read performance of flash memory. The main idea of this scheme is to correct most of the errors that occur in the requested Flash page before the LDPC decoding process begins, by caching the detected errors. This method improves the read performance of flash memory by speeding up the decoding process of LDPC.

Both solutions reduce LDPC decoding time, but they have their own respective drawbacks. Although refresh operation can reduce the decoding latency of LDPC, it also incurs additional migration costs, especially in the case of frequent refreshes. Using caching can indeed reduce the decoding time of LDPC. However, in the early stages of flash memory, the bit error rate is low, and using LDPC hard decision decoding can recover most of the data. Therefore, in the early stages of flash memory, using a larger cache would result in wasted space. Therefore, this article proposes an optimized LDPC read-retry scheme that combines refresh and caching. In this proposed scheme, refresh operations are employed in the early stages of flash memory to transform high-latency pages into low-latency states. Due to the low bit error rate in the early stages of flash memory, there are not many pages with high latency. As a result, the number of refresh operations required is minimal, significantly reducing the cost associated with refreshing. In the later stages of flash memory, cache techniques can be employed to store pages with high latency in a cache. When the same read request occurs again, the data can be directly retrieved from the cache, reducing LDPC decoding time and improving space utilization.

4 Design of the Scheme

Due to the increase in flash memory density, the reliability of flash memory data has decreased. To enhance data reliability, LDPC (Low-Density Parity-Check) codes are applied in flash memory. But using LDPC decoding directly can introduce significant latency. The increased decoding latency is primarily caused by the multiple read retry steps in LDPC decoding. To address this issue, this paper proposes a hybrid approach combining caching and refreshing to reduce LDPC read retries. By leveraging high-latency caching pages, LDPC decoding process can be reduced, thereby improving data reading performance and reliability.

This chapter focuses on the combination of caching and flushing to optimize the performance of flash reads, the CR solution. First, the first step is to distinguish between hot and cold reading data, and apply different recovery methods to the data according to the hot and cold nature of the data. This paper distinguishes hot read data and cold read data according to the number of data reads. When the number of data reads exceeds 1, it is hot read data, otherwise it is cold read data. The second step is to migrate high-latency pages with LDPC decoding level greater than or equal to 3 to the cache for hot-read data. The third step is to refresh the replaced high-latency pages. Due to the limited size of the cache, high-latency data cannot be stored infinitely. Therefore, when the cache space is exhausted, pages in the cache that have not been accessed for a long time are replaced according to the cache replacement algorithm, and then these pages are refreshed. This scheme reduces the LDPC decoding time of high-latency data and improves the speed of reading data from flash memory to a certain extent. The implementation of this scheme includes three parts: the determination of high-latency pages, the selection of cache size, and the selection of cache replacement algorithm. Below, I will briefly explain the choice of these three parts.

4.1   Determining the Latency Threshold T

The choice of the T threshold is critical for performance improvement. First of all, if T is set too small, a large amount of data will be put into the cache, due to the limited cache space, a large amount of data into the limited cache will cause high-latency pages to be frequently replaced, which will cause frequent refresh operations. Frequent refreshing not only brings additional read and write operations to the device, but also introduces wear and tear, which will further reduce reliability. If T is set too large, data with long access latency will significantly affect performance, especially for frequently accessed data. As stated in the review, the T-threshold should not be set too large or too small. In order to select the appropriate T, we performed experiments and analyzed the normalized delay time comparison of each load at different LDPC levels. From Fig. 3, it can be seen that the latency cost of each load is higher after LDPC decoding level 3, so setting the threshold for high latency to 3 is reasonable.

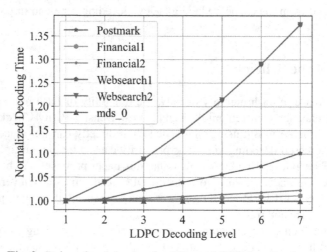

Fig. 3. Delay of each load under different LDPC decoding levels

4.2   Choice of Cache Size M

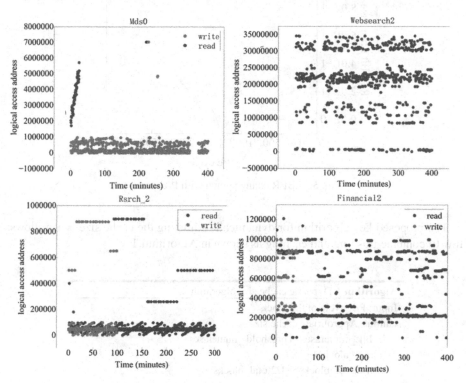

Fig. 4. Data access under different Workload

Another threshold cache size M setting of the scheme is also very important, M is not the bigger the better [17]. In this article, the size of M affects the number of refreshes, so it must be set within a reasonable range. Figure 4 intercepts access to a part of the payload Mds0, Rsrch_2, Financial2 and Websearch2. From the Fig. 4, we can see that the user's access to the data is local to the group, and through the analysis and calculation of the relevant load, it is found that only about 8% of the data is hot read data, and most of the remaining data is cold data. We set the cache size based on this.

The bit error rate of flash memory increases with the number of P/E times. As shown in Fig. 5, in the early stage of flash memory, due to the small number of P/E times of blocks, there are fewer pages with high latency. Therefore, if a fixed cache size is used all the time, it will cause a large waste of space in the early stage of the flash memory. In order to improve space utilization, a dynamic cache size adjustment scheme is proposed. The main idea is to set a P/E threshold C, if the P/E period of the block exceeds the set threshold, the block will be recorded as a late block, and count the number of blocks that exceed the P/E period threshold, when the late block is greater than or equal to half of the total number of blocks T, the size of the cache will be increased, otherwise the size of the cache will not change.

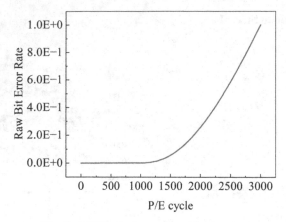

Fig. 5. RBER change graph with P/E cycle

The proposed key algorithm for dynamically adjusting the cache size is as follows: How to combine flushing and caching as shown in Algorithm 1.

Algorithm 1 Dynamic cache size algorithm

Input: P/E cycle of the block
Output: Appropriate cache size
   if blk_numerases>Threshold _numerases
   target_blocks++
     if target_blocks>=1/2total_blocks
        cache size changed from 4MB to 8MB
  else
    end if
  end if

4.3   Choice of Cache Replacement Algorithm

The function of the cache replacement algorithm is how to better manage the cache, whether it is caching in Memory or caching in SSD controllers, its main purpose is to make the cache play the maximum role as much as possible, so as to better improve the performance of the storage system. Different application scenarios and data access patterns may require different cache replacement strategies [18], and appropriate replacement strategies can be selected according to different application scenarios and requirements to achieve the best performance and efficiency [19]. Currently common cache replacement algorithms include least recently used (SLRU) algorithm, least frequently used (LFU) algorithm [20], random replacement (RR) algorithm, first-in-first-out (FIFO) algorithm, etc., each algorithm has its own advantages. Disadvantages and applicable scenarios, as shown in Table 1. In this experimental environment, due to the large read ratio of the load used, the data read access frequency is high, and the LFU algorithm mainly selects the cache replacement according to the access frequency of the data, in order to reduce unnecessary space overhead, the LFU cache replacement algorithm is selected.

Table 1. Comparison of different cache replacement algorithms

	LFU	LRU	FIFO	Random
Main basis	access frequency	time	time	random
advantage	effective identify of hot data	high space utilization	easy to implement	easy to implement
disadvantage	low space utilization	not flexible	unable to identify hot data	low hit rate
applicable Scenario	high read frequency, low write frequency	read and write frequency is high	stable access frequency	irregular access time

4.4 CR Program

In the traditional LDPC usage process in flash memory, the user sends a write request to the SSD controller. The ECC (Error Correction Code) module in the controller temporarily stores the write request data in an I/O buffer and then encodes it using LDPC before sending it to the flash memory cells. When there is a read request from the user, the data is retrieved from the flash memory cells. The LDPC decoder is then used to recover the correct data, which is then transferred to the I/O buffer. Finally, the data is returned to the user. In the traditional approach, reading data requires LDPC decoding, and when the read data has a high error rate, the LDPC decoding time will also be longer. To reduce read latency, this solution stores high-latency pages in the cache. When the data being read is hit in the cache, it is directly accessed from the cache without going through LDPC decoding. This reduces the decoding latency of LDPC and improves the read performance of flash memory. If there is a cache miss, the data will be read from the flash memory chip unit. After that, it will go through LDPC code decoding, and once successfully decoded, the data will be returned to the user. Figure 6 illustrates the comparison of data retrieval before and after optimization.

In this scheme, the first step is to differentiate between hot and cold read data, and adopt different recovery methods for each. For hot read data, the first step is to check if there is enough space in the cache. If there is sufficient space, the hot read data is placed into the cache. If there is not enough space, the Least Frequently Used (LFU) replacement algorithm is used. The page with the least number of accesses is evicted from the cache and refreshed. Then, the newly identified hot read data is placed into the cache. When a new read request comes in, the first step is to check if the data is present in the cache. If it is a cache hit, the data is directly read and returned to the user after the read operation is completed. In this process, LDPC code decoding is not required, reducing the decoding latency of LDPC code. If there is a cache miss, the data is read from the flash memory chip unit. After that, it goes through LDPC code decoding. Upon successful decoding, the data is returned to the user. The structure of this scheme is illustrated in Fig. 7.

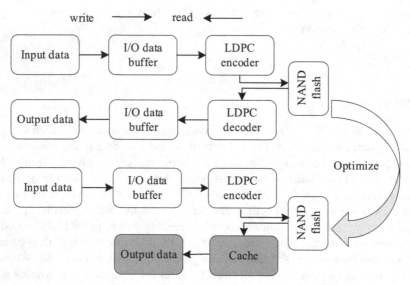

Fig. 6. Flash memory read and write process before and after optimization

The key algorithm of the caching and refreshing combined optimization scheme proposed in this paper is as follows: how to combine flushing and caching as shown in Algorithm 2.

Algorithm 2 Combination of cache and refresh

Input: Quantization level for LDPC soft decoding

Output: suitable decoding method

if data is hot data and high latency data

  if data_size<cache_size

    cache_add(new_blkno,new_data)

else

  cache_replace_lfu(int blkno,void* data)

  cache_add(new_blkno,new_data)

  cache_refresh(blkno,data

    end if

else

direct use of LDPC decoding

end if

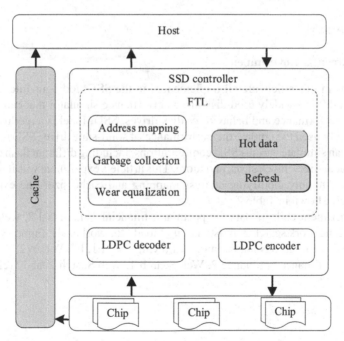

Fig. 7. Flash memory read and write process before and after optimization

The detailed reading process of the scheme is as follows:

1) Distinguish hot and cold data, and classify the hot and cold data according to the number of data reads. If the number of reads exceeds 1, it is hot read data, otherwise it is cold data. For hot-read data, determine the LDPC decoding method when the second read is successful, direct decoding if it is LDPC hard decoding, and record it if it is LDPC soft judgment decoding.
2) For hot-read data, determine the LDPC decoding method when the second read is successful, direct decoding if it is LDPC hard decoding, and record it if it is LDPC soft judgment decoding.
3) Determine whether the LDPC level of the hot read data is greater than or equal to 3. If it is greater than or equal to 3, check whether the cache space is sufficient. If it is sufficient, put it into the cache. If it is insufficient, use the LFU replacement algorithm to access it in the cache The page with the least number of times is replaced to make room for newly identified hot read data.
4) Refresh the replaced page
5) When there is a new read request, it is first looked up in the cache, if found in the cache, it is read directly, and vice versa, the data is read from the flash memory chip cell.
6) Detects whether the data has completed error correction, and if it is complete, returns the data to the user, and vice versa.

5 Experiment

5.1 Experimental Environment

The solutions in this article are all implemented in the SSDModel module in disksim-4.0. Disksim-4.0 is a widely used disk drive performance simulator that can be used to evaluate the performance and behavior of disk drives. SSDModel is a module added to disksim, mainly used to simulate the performance of solid-state drive (SSD) simulators. SSDModel can simulate various SSD configurations, including different flash chip types, read/write cache sizes, block sizes, and more. This article's experiment was implemented in SSDModel, mainly modifying address mapping and cache size. The experimental parameters are shown in Table 2.

This experiment collects data for postmark, financial 1, financial 2, web search 1, web search 2, network search 3, mds0, rsrch_2 loads for workloads. Figure 8 shows the read/write ratios for various loads. In the following text, F1, F2, W1, W2, W3 are used to represent the Finance 1, Finance 2, Web Search 1, Web Search 2, and Web Search 3 workloads.

Table 2. Flash memory parameter configuration

parameter configuration	value
Planes per pack	8
Block per planes	2048
Page per block	64
Page size	16
Page read transfer time	0.0002384
Page write transfer time	0.0002384
chip transmission delay	0.000025
page read delay	0.025
page write latency	0.200
block erase delay	1.5

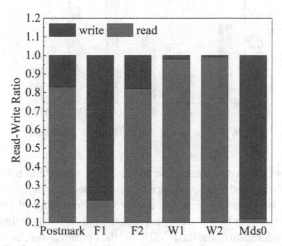

Fig. 8. Reading and Writing Ratios for Different Workload

5.2 Experimental Analysis

In our experiments, we evaluated three strategies.

1) Original strategy(NS): In the original strategy, only the garbage collection module, ECC module, and wear leveling module inherent in flash memory could be relied on to ensure data reliability.

2) Traditional refresh strategy(TRS): In the traditional refresh strategy, only when the quantization level of LDPC reaches 7 will the refresh condition be triggered and the data will be refreshed.

3) Strategy combining cache and refresh(CR): In this scheme, mainly for hot read data, when the read request arrives, first check whether the data exists in the cache, if it

exists, read directly, if it does not exist, check whether the cache has free space, if there is, put the hot read data into the cache, if not, use the LRU algorithm to put the recently infrequently accessed data into the cache, and refresh the replaced page.

Figure 9 shows the cache hit ratio under different loads. It can be seen from the Fig. 9 that the load with a higher read ratio has a higher hit rate, but not all loads are higher read ratio, and the higher the hit rate. For example, the read ratio of load Financial2 is 82%, and the hit rate is indeed 0.25. This is because although the read ratio of Financial2 is high, it can be seen from Fig. 4 that the access logical address of Financial2 is relatively scattered, and there are not many data that belong to hot reading, so the hit rate of Financial2 is low.

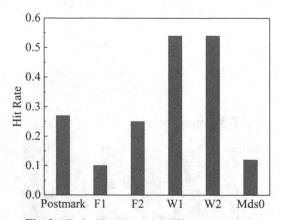

Fig. 9. Cache hit ratio under different Workload

Figure 10 shows the average response time of the caching and refresh combination scheme with the normalized average response time of the original and traditional refresh strategies. As can be seen in Fig a, the average response time of the CR scheme is reduced under all loads, but by different proportions. This is because this solution mainly optimizes the read operation of the flash SSD, and the optimization effect is more obvious for the load with more read operations. Such as Websearch1, Websearch2, Postmark, Financial2 These loads have a large read ratio, and their fluctuations are larger than the original scheme. However, the change of Financial1 is relatively stable, which is because the load of Financial1 has more write requests. As you can see from Fig b, the total average response time of Websearch1 and Financial2 has been reduced by 28% and 29%, respectively, compared to the traditional refresh strategy, and by 26% and 2%, respectively, compared to the traditional refresh strategy. It can be seen from this that the solution combining caching and refreshing has a better optimization effect under read-intensive loads.

Figure 11 shows the comparison of the normalized IOPS of the combined cache and refresh scheme with the original strategy and the traditional refresh strategy, and the comparison with the growth rate of the original strategy and the traditional refresh scheme. IOPS refers to the number of input/output operations that can be performed per second and is one of the important indicators to measure the performance of storage

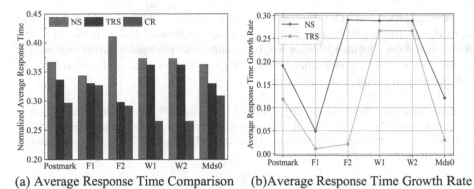

(a) Average Response Time Comparison   (b)Average Response Time Growth Rate

Fig. 10. Average Response Time and Reduction Rate under Different Workloads

devices. The higher the IOPS, the stronger the read and write capability of the storage device and the faster the data transmission speed. From Figure a, we can see that the IOPS of the CR solution performs higher than the IOPS of the other two solutions in these workloads.And the load with a small read ratio of the load changes more smoothly in IOPS, and the load with a larger read ratio has a greater increase in IOPS, such as Websearch1 and Financial2 for loads with a large read ratio. It can be seen from Figure B that compared with the original strategy, the I/O performance of Websearch1 and Financial2 has been improved by 43% and 46%.

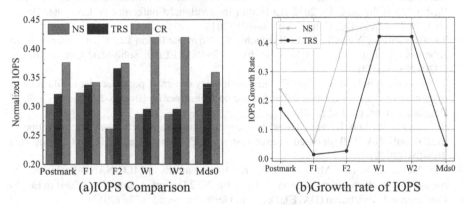

(a)IOPS Comparison   (b)Growth rate of IOPS

Fig. 11. IOPS vs. growth rate under different workloads

6   Conclusion

LDPC, as a powerful error correction ECC, is the default use of erasure coding by state-of-the-art flash memory. However, the large time overhead caused by LDPC decoding delay cannot be ignored. In order to solve this problem, this paper proposes a scheme combining cache and flushing, which aims to use cache and refresh technology to reduce the decoding process of LDPC, further reduce the decoding delay of LDPC, and improve the read performance of flash memory. Combined load-based testing proves that this scheme is feasible, but using flushes will bring additional read and write operations, and we will continue to consider whether other ways to improve the read performance of flash memory in future further research.

Acknowledgments. This work is supported by The National Natural Science Foundation of China under Grant No. 61762075. It is also supported in part by the Provincial Natural Science Foundation Team Project of Qinghai under Grant 2020-ZJ-903. Ping Xie is the corresponding author of this paper.

References

1. Bjrling, M., Gonzalez, J., Bonnet, P.: LightNVM: the Linux open-channel SSD subsystem. In: 15th USENIX Conference on File and Storage Technologies, FAST 2017, USA 27 February–2 March 2017, Santa Clara, CA, pp. 359–374 (2017)
2. Zuolo, L., Zambelli, C., Micheloni, R., et al.: Solid-state drives: memory driven design methodologies for optimal performance. Proc. IEEE **105**(9), 1589–1608 (2017)
3. Lee, S., et al.: A 128 Gb 2b/cell NAND flash memory in 14 nm technology with tprog = 640 μs and 800 MB/s I/O Rate. In: 2016 IEEE International Solid-State Circuits Conference (ISSCC), Digest of Technical Papers, San Francisco, USA, pp. 138–139 (2016)
4. Jeong, W., et al.: A 128 Gb 3b/cell V-NAND flash memory with 1 Gb/s I/O rate. IEEE J. Solid-State Circuits **51**(1), 204–212 (2016)
5. Cai, Y., et al.: Flash correct-and-refresh: Retention-aware error management for increased flash memory lifetime. In: 2012 IEEE 30th International Conference on Computer Design (ICCD), Montreal, QC, Canada, pp. 94–101 (2012)
6. Tanakamaru, S., Yanagihara, Y., Takeuchi, K.: Error-prediction LDPC and error-recovery schemes for highly reliable solid-state drives (SSDs). IEEE J. Solid-State Circuits **48**(11), 2920–2933 (2013)
7. Tseng, Y.-F., Shieh, M.-D., Kuo, C.-H.: Low latency design of polar decoder for flash memory. In: 2021 IEEE International Conference on Consumer Electronics-Taiwan (ICCE-TW), Penghu, Taiwan, pp. 1–2 (2021)
8. Shi, L., Lv, Y., Luo, L., et al.: Read latency variation aware performance optimization on high-density NAND flash based storage systems. CCF Trans. High Perform. Comput. **4**(3), 265–280 (2022)
9. Cai, Y., Haratsch, E.F., Mutlu, O., Mai, K.: Error patterns in MLC NAND flash memory: measurement, characterization, and analysis. In: 2012 Design, Automation & Test in Europe Conference & Exhibition (DATE), Dresden, Germany, pp. 521–526 (2012)
10. Yu, C., Haratsch, E.F., Mutlu, O., et al.: Threshold voltage distribution in MLC NAND flash memory: characterization, analysis, and modelling. In: Design, Automation & Test in Europe Conference & Exhibition, pp.1285–1290. IEEE (2013)
11. Kou, Y., Lin, S., Fossorier, M.P.C.: Low-density parity-check codes based on finite geometries: a rediscovery and new results. IEEE Trans. Inf. Theory **47**(7), 2711–2736 (2001)
12. Du, Y., Li, Q., Shi, L., Zou, D., Jin, H., Xue, C.J.: Reducing LDPC soft sensing latency by lightweight data refresh for flash read performance improvement. In: 2017 54th ACM/EDAC/IEEE Design Automation Conference (DAC), Austin, TX, USA, pp. 1–6 (2017)
13. Li, Q., Shi, L., Xue, C.J., et al.: Access characteristic guided read and write cost regulation for performance improvement on flash memory. In: 14th FAST 2016, Santa Clara, CA, USA, pp.125–132 (2016)

14. Du, Y., Zou, D., Qiao, L., et al.: LaLDPC: latency-aware LDPC for read performance improvement of solid state drives. In: 33rd International Conference on Massive Storage Systems and Technology (MSST 2017) (2017)
15. Shi, L., Wu, K., Zhao, M., et al.: Retention trimming for lifetime improvement of flash memory storage systems. IEEE Trans. Comput. Aided Des. Integr. Circuits Syst. **35**(1), 58–71 (2015)
16. Liu, R.-S., Chuang, M.-Y., Yang, C.-L., Li, C.-H., Ho, K.-C., Li, H.-P.: EC-Cache: exploiting error locality to optimize LDPC in NAND flash-based SSDs. In: 2014 51st ACM/EDAC/IEEE Design Automation Conference (DAC), San Francisco, CA, USA, pp. 1–6 (2014)
17. Gu, B., Luo, L., Lv, Y., et al.: Dynamic file cache optimization for hybrid SSDs with high-density and low-cost flash memory. In: 2021 IEEE 39th International Conference on Computer Design (ICCD), pp. 170–173 (2021)
18. Yoon, J., Ro, W.W.: Access characteristic-based cache replacement policy in an SSD. In: ICCV Workshops, pp. 1–4 (2019)
19. Tripathy, S., Satpathy, M.: SSD internal cache management policies: a survey. J. Syst. Archit. (122), 122 (2022)
20. International Conference on Networking, Architecture and Storage (NAS), pp. 1–10. EnShi, China (2019)

CCS: A Motif-Based Storage Format for Micro-execution Dependence Graph

Yawen Zheng[1,2,3]([✉]), Chenji Han[1,2,3], Tingting Zhang[2,4], Chao Yang[5], and Jian Wang[1,2,3]

[1] State Key Lab of Processors, ICT, CAS, Beijing, China
zhengyawen@ict.ac.cn
[2] Institute of Computing Technology, CAS, Beijing, China
[3] University of Chinese Academy of Sciences, Beijing, China
[4] Loongson Technology Corporation Limited, Beijing, China
[5] Electric Power Research Institute of State Grid Liaoning Electric Power Co., Ltd., Shenyang, China

Abstract. Micro-execution dependence graphs model the program execution on a microprocessor as relationships of micro-execution events intra- and inter-instructions for performance analysis. Each instruction constitutes a motif whose structure is defined by the dependence graph model. With the size of the application increasing dramatically, storing a large-scale dependence graph with billions of instructions becomes difficult. However, popular graph storage formats, such as CSR and CSC, are inefficient for motifs. And the current motif-based compression methods involve the time-consuming process of subgraph isomorphism checking, which is NP-hard. To reduce redundancy, we propose a novel motif-based lossless storage format called *compressed common subgraph* (CCS) for micro-execution dependence graphs. The key idea is to divide the graph into the intra- and inter-motif parts and compress the common subgraph structures in the intra-motif part by storing the same structures only once. Our method avoids subgraph isomorphism checking because the motifs (instructions) are regularly arranged. Furthermore, the CCS format has two variant implementations, *compressed common single subgraph* (CCSS) and *compressed common multiple subgraphs* (CCMS) to adapt to various dependence graph models. Experimental results show that our CCSS and CCMS formats use 16.66% and 8.67% less memory size than the CSC graph format, respectively.

Keywords: Graph compression method · Graph storage format · Micro-execution dependence graph · Network motifs

1 Introduction

Critical path analysis plays an important role in bottleneck analysis of microarchitecture design, and the key technology is based on a micro-execution dependence graph [7–12, 18, 24, 25, 27, 28]. By modeling the execution of a program as a

© The Author(s), under exclusive license to Springer Nature Singapore Pte Ltd. 2024
C. Li et al. (Eds.): APPT 2023, LNCS 14103, pp. 130–146, 2024.
https://doi.org/10.1007/978-981-99-7872-4_8

micro-execution dependence graph, hardware designers can easily calculate the critical path and identify the key performance bottlenecks on the microarchitectural level.

Unfortunately, a micro-execution dependence graph can be very large and it keeps growing in recent years. A micro-execution dependence graph is a directed acyclic graph, whose nodes represent specific micro events in the CPU pipeline to process an instruction and edges denote the dependency between those events. The size of the micro-execution dependence graph is determined by the number of dynamic instructions of the running program and the model complexity. For example, when applying a 5-node and 12-edge model to a program with 10 million instructions, the average number of nodes and edges of the dependence graph can reach 50 million and 95.13 million, respectively. What's worse, the average number of instructions in the SPEC CPU benchmark suite increased from 1.96 trillion in 2006 to 22.19 trillion in 2017 [23].

An efficient memory storage method is crucial for effectively managing the escalating size of micro-execution dependence graphs. In offline critical path analysis, dynamic tracing tools like the gem5 simulator [15] generate micro-execution dependence graphs which are subsequently stored for further analysis including event relationships and locations. The compression of dependence graphs can reduce memory/disk usage and copying time for faster performance analysis.

To reduce memory usage of general graph storage, previous works fall into two main categories: designing specific graph storage formats and optimizing graph compression methods.

For graph storage formats, there are two approaches: (1) removing the no-meaning zeros in *adjacent matrix* (AM) format, such as *adjacency list* (AL) and *coordinate list* (COO); (2) compressing the common information by splitting matrix into certain discrete units and storing them in a specific order, such as *compressed sparse row/column* (CSR/CSC), *diagonal* (DIA), and *block compressed sparse row* (BCSR) formats. However, these formats are not suitable for micro-execution dependence graphs for two reasons: (1) The basic compression units cannot match the size of the subgraphs in the dependence graph appropriately. (2) It is unnecessary to store all basic units because the isomorphic subgraphs are frequently repeated.

As for graph compression methods, motif-based graph compression methods collapse a given part of a graph (e.g., a clique or a subgraph) into a smaller entity (e.g., a vertex) to save storage space [2]. Motifs are defined as frequent isomorphic subgraphs occurring in networks [1]. However, motif-based graph compression needs to check the isomorphism between the subgraph and motif [22,26], which is NP-hard [31]. This time-consuming task can be avoided in the dependence graph, in which the network motifs are defined as the recurring subgraphs to represent the execution process of each instruction and are arranged in order of the instruction stream.

To solve the problems mentioned above, we designed a lossless *compressed common subgraph* (CCS) format to match the features of the dependence graph and reduce the redundancy inside the storage of motifs. The main contributions of this work are:

- We propose a *compressed common subgraph* (CCS) format, which divides the graph into intra- and inter-motif parts according to the dependence graph feature and thus compresses the common subgraphs by storing the same structures of intra-motif parts only once.
- We design the CCS as two variants, *compressed common single subgraph* (CCSS) and *compressed common multiple subgraphs* (CCMS), to meet the different demands of various dependence graph models consisting of single or multiple kinds of motifs.
- Our method avoids the time-consuming process of subgraph isomorphism checking, which is NP-hard because the motifs (instructions) defined in the dependence graph model are regularly arranged.
- Experimental results show that the CCSS and CCMS formats save 16.66% and 8.67% memory space respectively compared with the CSC graph format, and the total time for compression and decompression is less.

This paper is organized as follows. Section 2 introduces the background and motivation. Section 3 describes the CCS format. Section 4 evaluates our work. Section 5 summarizes related work and Sect. 6 concludes.

2   Background and Motivation

2.1   Micro-execution Dependence Graph

Critical Path Analysis Method. Assuming that the working process of a system can be described by a directed acyclic graph, it may exist the longest path that determines the total time spent. The longest path, called the critical path, is the most time-consuming execution sequence in the system dealing with that workload. Optimizing the design to shorten the critical path can improve the overall performance of the system because the critical path is the performance bottleneck [20, 21, 29].

Dependence Graph Model. The dependence graph model [10, 24] depicts how instructions make their way through various pipeline stages and the relationship between instructions. According to the dependence graph model, nodes in the micro-execution dependence graph represent pipeline stages, edges represent dependency caused by bandwidth limitations, data dependencies, resource conflicts, and control dependencies, and the weights labeled on edges represent the delays to resolve the dependence. For example, as shown in Fig. 1(a), *Fetch*, *Execute* and *Commit* are nodes, edge $E \rightarrow C$ indicates that the operation completes execution and commits, and the number on the arrow is the latency.

Micro-execution Dependence Graph. Micro-execution dependence graph is dynamic directed acyclic graph generated according to the dependence graph model when the processor executes instructions. It reflects the relationship of micro-events inside and between instructions during dynamic execution. Figure 1 shows two micro-execution dependence graphs respectively for single and multiple motif types, each consisting of 4 instructions (motifs). As for single motif type shown in Fig. 1(a), each motif has the same structure. The multiple motif types in Fig. 1(b) represent instructions with multiple structures.

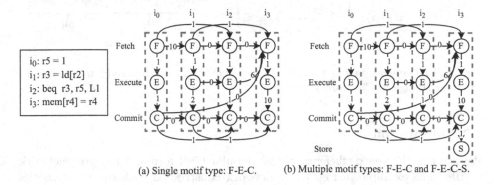

i_0: r5 = 1
i_1: r3 = ld[r2]
i_2: beq r3, r5, L1
i_3: mem[r4] = r4

(a) Single motif type: F-E-C.   (b) Multiple motif types: F-E-C and F-E-C-S.

Fig. 1. Micro-execution dependence graphs with four motifs in red rectangles. (Color figure online)

The Role of Graph Compression and Decompression. The micro-execution dependence graphs are generated dynamically by processor simulators. Critical path analysis typically acquires a complete dependence graph for subsequent offline analysis. Therefore, the dependence graph is saved during generation and analysis. Unfortunately, the size of the dependence graph is large, depending on the graph model and the number of dynamic instructions. In order to minimize storage requirements, the graph is stored in a compressed format and then decompressed before further analysis, as shown in Fig. 2. Both compression and decompression must be lossless to ensure the integrity of the graph used for analysis.

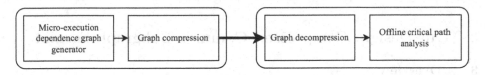

Fig. 2. The role of graph compression and decompression in a critical path analysis framework based on micro-execution dependence graph.

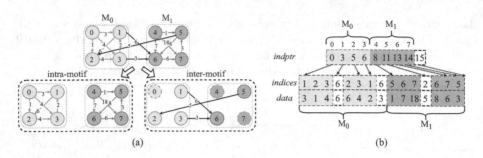

Fig. 3. Two network motifs M_0 and M_1: (a) Their divided intra- and inter parts, and (b) their storage in CSR format.

2.2 Motivation

We studied the space efficiency of the popular CSR format for storing network motifs. The example in Fig. 3 is a network constructed with two same motifs M_0 and M_1. As shown in Fig. 3(a), The edges can be divided into two parts for intra- and inter-links of motifs. Figure 3(b) shows its storage in CSR format. CSR format uses three arrays to store the nonzero elements in a sparse matrix: row pointer (*indptr*), column index (*indices*), and value (*data*) array. The *indices* array contains the column indices of the nonzero elements. The *indptr* array stores the start locations of each row in the *indices*, and its last element is the length of the *indices*.

As shown in Fig. 3(b), the edges distinguished as the blue and green items are respectively the intra-motif parts from M_0 and M_1. We find that in *indices* array, each element in the intra-motif part of M_1, i.e. {5,6,7,6,7,5}, can be obtained by adding 4 to the elements in M_0 {1,2,3,2,3,1}, and 4 is the number of vertices in a motif. This means the network has repetitive intra-motifs connections. We can deduce that for micro-execution dependence graphs with a high fraction of repetitive intra-motifs, the storage redundancy space for the intra-part of *indices* array can be high. The repeated storage of the same motif structures is unnecessary but occupies a considerable part of space usage in the CSR format.

3   Our Design: Compressed Common Subgraph Format

3.1 Overview

Compared with the CSR format, the CCS format can eliminate the repeated storage of isomorphic motifs in *indices* array. It splits the original CSR format into two separate parts, intra- and inter-motif. As for intra-motif parts, the CCS format stores the repeated motif structures in *indices* array only once.

As Fig. 4 shown, CCS format has two implement variants for different constructions of network motifs. One variant is *compressed common single subgraph* (CCSS), which is for the network constructed with a single kind of motif

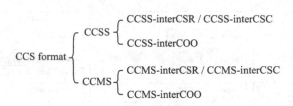

Fig. 4. CCS format and its implement variants.

structure. The other variant is *compressed common multiple subgraphs* (CCMS), which is designed for network with multiple motif structures.

For each CCSS and CCMS, we design two additional sub-variants to store the inter-motif part in CSR/CSC or COO format. Because for a matrix with few nonzero elements, the COO format can save more space than CSR/CSC that unnecessarily stores all the row/column items in *indptr* array even only a few nodes have connections. We use the suffix *interCSR/CSC* and *interCOO* to distinguish these two variants.

3.2   CCSS Format

The CCSS format is suitable for network motifs constructed with a single kind of subgraph. It consists of two parts for intra- and inter-motif connections, as shown in Fig. 5(a), the upper is the intra-motif and the lower is the inter-motif.

Similar to the CSR format, the intra-motif part also consists of three arrays, *intra-indptr*, *intra-indices*, and *intra-data*. The difference from the original CSR format is that the *intra-indptr* and *intra-indices* arrays only store the first one of repeated motifs as the common subgraph. The content of *indices* array for all intra-motifs in the original CSR format is regularly repeated with an interval of the motif node number. Therefore, in the CCSS format, only the first intra-motif is saved in the *indices* array and the corresponding *indptr* array. The *intra-data* array stores values of each intra-motif successively in motif order.

The inter-motif part of the CCSS format stores the remaining inter-motif links in the CSR or COO format. Figure 5(b) and (c) show the example in Fig. 3 stored in CCSS-interCSR and CCSS-interCOO formats, respectively.

The space usage of CCSS format can be calculated by network parameters. Assuming the network has m motifs, all the motifs are in the same structure. The motif structure is a subgraph with k nodes and l edges. The mixing parameter of the network is μ, which is the fraction of the inter-edges to total edge [30, 32]. Then we can get the space usage as following (1) and (2).

$$CCSS\text{-}interCSR : k + 2 + l + lm + km + 2\frac{\mu lm}{1 - \mu} \tag{1}$$

$$CCSS\text{-}interCOO : k + 1 + l + lm + 3\frac{\mu lm}{1 - \mu} \tag{2}$$

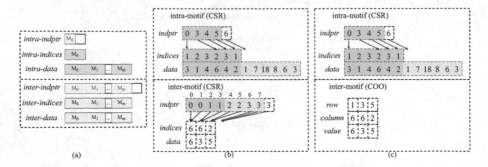

Fig. 5. CCSS format and its sub-variants. (a) CCSS format. (b) CCSS-interCSR: applying CSR format for both intra- and inter-motif parts. (c) CCSS-interCOO: applying CSR format for intra-motif and COO format for inter-motif part.

The only difference between CCSS-interCSR and CCSS-interCOO is the first array in the inter-motif part. We define the recommended coefficient $R_{interCSR} \in \{0, 1\}$ to represent whether to choose the CCSS-interCSR format. We use intra-degree d_{intra} to represent the ratio of the intra-edge number l to the node number k of a motif, as in Formula (3):

$$d_{intra} = \frac{l}{k}.\tag{3}$$

And we use c_{intra} to interpret the concentration of motif, which is defined as the ratio of the intra-motif links to the inter-motif links, as in Formula (4):

$$c_{intra} = \frac{1 - \mu}{\mu}.\tag{4}$$

Assuming the network is a large-scale network that m is large enough to ignore the influence of $\frac{1}{m}$. Then we can deduce the recommended coefficient $R_{interCSR}$ as following Formula (5):

$$R_{interCSR} = \begin{cases} 1 & (d_{intra} \geq c_{intra}) \\ 0 & (d_{intra} < c_{intra}) \end{cases}.\tag{5}$$

3.3   CCMS Format

The CCMS format is proposed for network motifs constructed with multiple subgraph structures. It consists of three parts: intra-motif structure, intra-motif data, and inter-motif.

The intra-motif structure is a list of all types of motif structures. Each list item points to a subgraph structure consisting of *intra-indptr* and *intra-indices* arrays like CSR format. Each intra-motif structure will be stored only once and

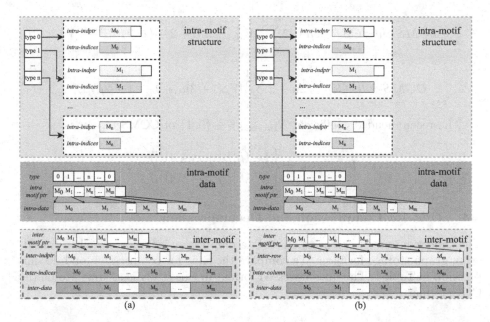

Fig. 6. CCMS format: (a) CCMS-interCSR format. (b) CCMS-interCOO format. The parts in red dash circles are the difference of two variants. (Color figure online)

allocated a type id as its position in the list. The length of the list is the number of total motif structure types.

The intra-motif data consists of three arrays: *type*, *intra motif ptr*, and *intra-data*. To map each type to the particular motif, the *type* array stores each motif type id assigned in the intra-motif structure. The *intra motif ptr* array is designed to access a certain motif more conveniently. The *intra motif ptr* array stores the start positions of each motif in the *intra-data* array and the length of the *intra-data* array. The *intra-data* array stores the data of each intra-motif in order.

The inter-motif part stores the inter-motif edges. As shown in Fig. 6, we have variants of the inter-motif part as stored in CSR or COO format. Similar to the CCSS format, the CCMS-interCSR stores all the row indices and the CCMS-interCOO only stores the row indices of inter-motif edges. The *inter motif ptr* array stores the start positions of each motif and the length of the *inter-indptr* array in CCMS-interCSR; and stores the start positions of the *inter-row* array in CCMS-interCOO.

The space usage of the CCMS format and its variants can be calculated. Giving a network with m motifs (i.e., M_0, M_1, ..., M_{m-1}), and the total motif types is n, we use the set $V_m = \{|V_{M_0}|, |V_{M_1}|, ..., |V_{M_{n-1}}|\}$ and $E_m = \{|E_{M_0}|, |E_{M_1}|, ..., |E_{M_{n-1}}|\}$ to represent the node size and edge size of each motif structure type, respectively. The ith element of these two sets is associated with the ith type of motif structures. Then the space usage is represented as following (6) and (7).

$$CCMS\text{-}interCSR : 2n + 2\sum_{i=0}^{n-1}|V_{M_i}| + 2m + 2 + (1+\mu)|E| + |V| \qquad (6)$$

$$CCMS\text{-}interCOO : 2n + 2\sum_{i=0}^{n-1}|V_{M_i}| + 3m + 2 + (1+2\mu)|E| \qquad (7)$$

The recommended coefficient $R_{interCSR} \in \{0,1\}$ of CCMS format is:

$$R_{interCSR} = \begin{cases} 1 & (\mu|E| + m \geq |V|) \\ 0 & (\mu|E| + m < |V|) \end{cases}. \qquad (8)$$

3.4   Time for Compression and Decompression

The time required for compression and decompression is important when considering graph storage formats. We compare the time for compression and decompression in Table 1. The uncompressed format in this study is assumed to be the COO format.

Table 1. Compression and decompression time of CSR and CCS format.

Format	Compression time	Decompression time
CSR	$T_{intra} + T_{inter} + T_{data}$	$|V| \times D$
CCSS-interCSR	$Const_{intra} + T_{inter} + T_{data}$	$|V| \times (D_{intra} + D_{inter})$
CCSS-interCOO	$Const_{intra} + T_{data}$	$|V| \times D_{intra}$
CCMS-interCSR	$2T_m + Const_{intra} + T_{inter} + T_{data}$	$2T_m + |V| \times (D_{intra} + D_{inter})$
CCMS-interCOO	$2T_m + Const_{intra} + T_{data}$	$2T_m + |V| \times D_{intra}$

The compression process of CSR involves traversing all edges to generate the *indptr* and *indices* arrays $(T_{intra} + T_{inter})$, as well as copying data to the *data* array (T_{data}). The times T_{intra} and T_{inter} refer to the time associated with the size of intra- and inter-connections. CCSS stores the structure of the intra-motif part only once, resulting in the generation of the *indptr* and *indices* arrays in the intra-motif part once, which consumes a constant time $Const_{intra}$. Typically, $Const_{intra}$ is considerably smaller than T_{intra}, where the latter increases with the size of intra-links. Specifically, interCOO variant requires less compression time than interCSR because the inter-motif part in interCOO is directly obtained from the COO format. In the case of CCMS, additional time $2T_m$ is required to generate two pointer arrays that store the corresponding type of each motif in the intra-motif data and inter-motif part, respectively.

During the decompression process, each vertex is accessed and its outgoing edges in CSR format (or incoming edges in CSC format) are recovered. The symbol D represents the average number of outgoing (or incoming) edges per vertex, while D_{intra} and D_{inter} represent the number of intra-edges and inter-edges, respectively. CCSS requires more decompression time than CSR as both the intra- and inter-motif parts need to be decompressed. The interCOO variant requires less decompression time since only the intra-part needs to be decompressed. CCMS requires an additional decompression time of $2T_m$ to access the motif type pointer array in both the intra-motif data and inter-motif part.

4   Evaluation

4.1   Experimental Setup

Table 2. Parameters of dependence graphs of SPEC CPU 2006.

Graph model	Parameters									
Fields's	$|V|$	$|E|$	m	k	l	μ	d_{intra}	c_{intra}	$R_{interCSR}$	
	5.00E+07	9.51E+07	1.00E+07	5	4	0.579	0.8	0.727	1	
Tanimoto's	$|V|$	$|E|$	m	n	$|V_{M_0}|$	$|V_{M_1}|$			$R_{interCSR}$	
	5.21E+07	1.01E+08	1.00E+07	2	5	6			1	

We modified gem5 [15] to generate micro-execution dependence graphs and ran 10M instructions per SPEC CPU 2006 test with reference input sets to evaluate the memory usage of our CCS format in 4.2. Fields's model [10] and Tanimoto's model [24] are used to evaluate the CCS variants, respectively for CCSS and CCMS formats. The parameters for the dependence graphs of these two models are shown in Table 2. $|V|$ and $|E|$ are the average number of nodes and edges, m is the number of motifs (instructions) of the graphs. For Fields's model with a single type of motif, each instruction is represented as a 5-node and 4-edge motif ($D \rightarrow R \rightarrow E \rightarrow P \rightarrow C$). Parameters k, l, and μ are described in 3.2 and parameters d_{intra}, c_{intra}, and $R_{interCSR}$ can be calculated by Formula (3)~(5). Tanimoto's model has two types of motifs: the same motif as Fields's model for non-store instructions, and a 6-node and 5-edge motif ($D \rightarrow R \rightarrow E \rightarrow P \rightarrow C \rightarrow S$) for store instructions. Parameters n and $|V_{M_n}|$ are described in 3.3 and parameter $R_{interCSR}$ can be calculated by Formula (8).

Synthetic network motifs with diverse parameters and similar structures to micro-execution dependence graphs are generated by C++ to evaluate the time consumption (4.3) and analyze parameter sensitivity (4.4) of CCS format.

4.2   Memory Consumption

Figure 7 shows the memory usage of the CCS format variants and other formats for storing the dependence graphs of SPEC CPU 2006. For Fields's model, Fig. 7(a) shows that CCSS-interCSC saves the most space while COO consumes

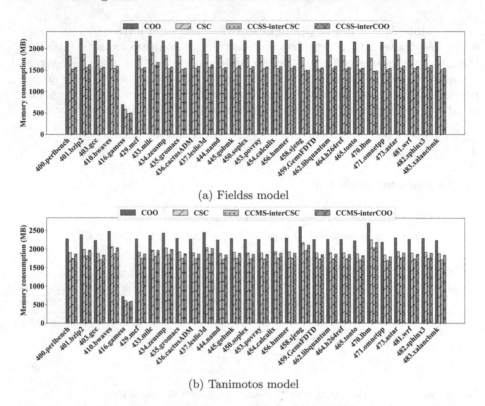

(a) Fieldss model

(b) Tanimotos model

Fig. 7. Memory consumption of micro-execution dependence graphs for 10M dynamic instructions per SPEC CPU 2006 test.

the most space for all benchmark tests. The average memory usage of CCSS-interCSC format is 1490.48 MB, which is respectively 29.83%, 16.66%, and 2.47% less than COO (2124.03 MB), CSC (1788.30 MB), and CCSS-interCOO (1528.39 MB). Figure 7(b) shows the same result trend for Tanimoto's model that the average memory usage of CCMS-interCSC is 1733.42 MB, which is respectively 23.46%, 8.67%, and 6.87% less than COO (2265.09 MB), CSC (1898.01 MB), and CCMS-interCOO (1861.46 MB). These results indicate that interCSC uses less memory space than the other CCS variant. The experimental results match with the calculated recommended coefficient $R_{interCSR} = 1$ in Table 2, i.e., the graphs are more space efficiency stored in interCSR (or interCSC) than interCOO.

4.3 Compression and Decompression Time

We generated graphs in respective CSR and CCS formats to compare the compression time and decompressed the respective CSR and CCS data into COO format to evaluate the decompression time.

Figure 8 depicts the time usage of our CCS variants and CSR formats. It can be seen that, for either single (Fig. 8(a)) or multiple (Fig. 8(b)) motif types,

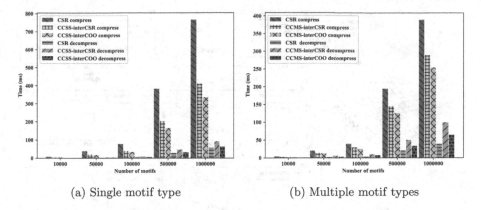

(a) Single motif type   (b) Multiple motif types

Fig. 8. Compression and decompression time of CSR and CCS (CCSS or CCMS) formats. Total number of motifs varies from 1000 to 1000000. (a) Single motif type with motif node number $k = 5$. (b) Ten motif types with motif node number $k = 5$.

CCS variants use significantly less compression time than CSR format for various motif number setups, with only slightly more but absolutely low decompression time. As shown in Fig. 8(a), when the number of motifs is 1M, the compression times are respectively 766 ms for the CSR format and 411 ms for the CCSS-interCSR format, indicating CCSS-interCSR can save 46.34% (i.e. 355 ms) spent time compared with the CSR format. While the decompression time is 92 ms for the CCSS-interCSR format, which is only absolutely 34 ms more than that of the CSR format (58 ms). The reduction in compression time is because CCS avoids compression of the internal structure of motifs, while the increase in decompression time is due to the more complex storage format. The total time of the CCS format is less than CSR by 36.04% because compression takes more time than decompression. We also find that the interCSR uses more time than the interCOO variant because CSR is more complex than COO.

4.4 Parameter Sensitivity

Memory Efficiency of CCSS Format with Variable Motif Structure and Mixing Parameter. We constructed random networks that have single motif type: the motif size k is 100, motif number m is 1 M, d_{intra} differs from 0.1 to 2, and μ from 0.1 to 1. Figure 9 shows that the CCSS format always uses less memory than the CSR format at any d_{intra} and μ. However, whether interCSR or interCOO uses less memory is influenced by the variable parameters d_{intra} and μ that depend on $R_{interCSR}$. As Fig. 9(b) shows, the points below the curve are the situations of d_{intra} and μ values when CCSS-interCOO is recommended, and the upper are situations when CCSS-interCSR is better. For example, ($\mu = 0.5$, $d_{intra} = 1$) is a point on $R_{interCSR} = 1$ curve, then CCSS-interCOO is better when $d_{intra} = 1$ and $\mu < 0.5$ (Fig. 9(d)), or $d_{intra} < 1$ and $\mu = 0.5$ (Fig. 9(g)).

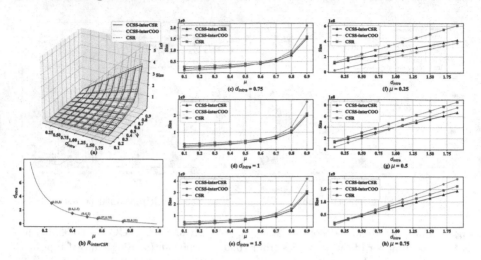

Fig. 9. Memory usage of CCSS and other formats with variable parameters. (a) $d_{intra} = 0.1 \sim 2$, $\mu = 0.1 \sim 1$. (b) (d_{intra}, μ) values when $R_{interCSR} = 1$. (c)(d)(e) $\mu = 0.1 \sim 1$ and $d_{intra} = 0.75, 1, 1.5$, respectively. (f)(g)(h) $d_{intra} = 0.1 \sim 2$ and $\mu = 0.25, 0.5, 0.75$, respectively.

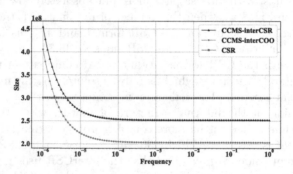

Fig. 10. Memory usage of CCMS with variable motif frequency.

Memory Efficiency of CCMS Format with Variable Motif Frequency.

We constructed multiple network motifs with the following network parameters: the motif size k is 100, the total motif number m is 1M, d_{intra} is 0.5, and μ is 0.5. To be simple, we assumed that different motif structures are in different topologies but have the same number of nodes and edges. Each type of motif has a equal proportion in the network, and the proportion value is the average frequency of the motif. Figure 10 shows the memory usage of CCMS format and CSR format with variable motif frequency from 10^{-6} to 1. We find that as for the network with multiple motifs, the efficiency of the CCMS format has a positive association with motif frequency. For those networks with extremely low motif frequency ($< 10^{-5}$), it is better to use the CSR format.

5   Related Work

There are lots of studies on graph compression [2]. We focus our overview on those related works that exploit structural characteristics of common subgraphs to compress large-scale graphs such as web graphs and biology networks.

WebGraph [3] compresses the web graphs by exploiting their features such as locality, similarity, and consecutiveness to obtain a high compression ratio. S-Node [19] collapses subgraphs into supervertices. Virtual node compression [6,13] generates virtual nodes from frequent itemsets in vertex adjacency lists. Khalili et al. [14] group similar vertices together and collapse edges between groups into single superedges. Boldi et al. [4] leverage the encoding methods to use fewer bytes to represent the adjacency list. SCMD [26] compresses symmetric subgraphs in biological networks for storage reduction. SEG [22] groups the motifs (such as cliques) into single vertices to compress the network traffic graphs. Maneth and Peternek [16,17] propose a scheme that recursively detects repeating substructures and uses grammar rules to represent them. Bouritsas et al. [5] propose the Partition and Code (PnC) framework to compress graphs losslessly by partitioning them into subgraphs, learning a dictionary and a probability distribution over it, and encoding the subgraphs with an entropy encoder.

These motif-based graph compression methods employ different techniques to identify, represent, and compress motifs, catering to specific compression goals and application requirements. This paper eliminates the time-consuming process of motif identification, which is known to be NP-hard, due to the regular arrangement of motifs (instructions) in the dependence graph model.

6   Conclusion

This paper presents a novel CCS format to meet the storage demands of micro-execution dependency graphs. The CCS format stores the same structures in the intra-motif only once to avoid repeated storage of the common motif structures. We propose two variants, CCSS and CCMS, for single and multiple kinds of motifs, respectively. Our experiment results show that the CCS format can save more memory space and use less compression time than the most popular CSR format. CCS format can effectively reduce the overhead of storing and copying to save disk space and transfer time for further analyzing dependence graphs. It can also be applied to the storage of networks with similar subgraph structures.

Acknowledgements. This work is supported by the National Key Research and Development Program of China (under Grant 2022YFB3105103).

References

1. Alon, U.: Network motifs: theory and experimental approaches. Nat. Rev. Genet. **8**(6), 450–461 (2007). https://doi.org/10.1038/nrg2102
2. Besta, M., Hoefler, T.: Survey and taxonomy of lossless graph compression and space-efficient graph representations. CoRR abs/1806.01799 (2018). http://arxiv.org/abs/1806.01799
3. Boldi, P., Vigna, S.: The webgraph framework I: compression techniques. In: Proceedings of the 13th International Conference on World Wide Web, WWW 2004, pp. 595–602. Association for Computing Machinery, New York, NY, USA (2004). https://doi.org/10.1145/988672.988752
4. Boldi, P., Santini, M., Vigna, S.: Permuting web and social graphs. Internet Math. **6**(3), 257–283 (2009). https://doi.org/10.1080/15427951.2009.10390641
5. Bouritsas, G., Loukas, A., Karalias, N., Bronstein, M.M.: Partition and code: learning how to compress graphs. CoRR abs/2107.01952 (2021). https://arxiv.org/abs/2107.01952
6. Buehrer, G., Chellapilla, K.: A scalable pattern mining approach to web graph compression with communities. In: Najork, M., Broder, A.Z., Chakrabarti, S. (eds.) Proceedings of the International Conference on Web Search and Web Data Mining, WSDM 2008, Palo Alto, California, USA, 11–12 February 2008, pp. 95–106. ACM (2008). https://doi.org/10.1145/1341531.1341547
7. Fields, B., Bodik, R., Hill, M.: Slack: maximizing performance under technological constraints. In: Proceedings 29th Annual International Symposium on Computer Architecture, pp. 47–58 (2002). https://doi.org/10.1109/ISCA.2002.1003561
8. Fields, B., Rubin, S., Bodik, R.: Focusing processor policies via critical-path prediction. In: Proceedings 28th Annual International Symposium on Computer Architecture, pp. 74–85 (2001). https://doi.org/10.1109/ISCA.2001.937434
9. Fields, B., Bodik, R., Hill, M., Newburn, C.: Using interaction costs for microarchitectural bottleneck analysis. In: Proceedings. 36th Annual IEEE/ACM International Symposium on Microarchitecture, MICRO-36, pp. 228–239 (2003). https://doi.org/10.1109/MICRO.2003.1253198
10. Fields, B.A., Bodik, R., Hill, M.D., Newburn, C.J.: Interaction cost and shotgun profiling. ACM Trans. Archit. Code Optim. **1**(3), 272–304 (2004). https://doi.org/10.1145/1022969.1022971
11. Fields, B.A.: Using Criticality to Attack Performance Bottlenecks. Ph.D. thesis, EECS Department, University of California, Berkeley (2006). http://www2.eecs.berkeley.edu/Pubs/TechRpts/2006/EECS-2006-176.html
12. Golestani, H., Sen, R., Young, V., Gupta, G.: Calipers: a criticality-aware framework for modeling processor performance. In: Proceedings of the 36th ACM International Conference on Supercomputing, ICS 2022. Association for Computing Machinery, New York (2022). https://doi.org/10.1145/3524059.3532390
13. Karande, C., Chellapilla, K., Andersen, R.: Speeding up algorithms on compressed web graphs. In: Proceedings of the Second ACM International Conference on Web Search and Data Mining, WSDM 2009, pp. 272–281. Association for Computing Machinery, New York (2009). https://doi.org/10.1145/1498759.1498836
14. Khalili, H., Yahyavi, A., Oroumchian, F.: Web-graph pre-compression for similarity based algorithms. In: Proceedings of the Third International Conference on Modeling, Simulation and Applied Optimization, pp. 20–22 (2009). https://ro.uow.edu.au/dubaipapers/55/

15. Lowe-Power, J., Ahmad, A.M., Akram, A., Alian, M., Amslinger, R., Andreozzi, M., et al.: The gem5 simulator: version 20.0+. CoRR abs/2007.03152 (2020). https://arxiv.org/abs/2007.03152

16. Maneth, S., Peternek, F.: Compressing graphs by grammars. In: 2016 IEEE 32nd International Conference on Data Engineering (ICDE), pp. 109–120 (2016). https://doi.org/10.1109/ICDE.2016.7498233

17. Maneth, S., Peternek, F.: Grammar-based graph compression. Inf. Syst. **76**, 19–45 (2018). https://doi.org/10.1016/j.is.2018.03.002

18. Qin, F., Wang, L., Deng, Y., Wang, Y., Zhao, T.: HMCPA: heuristic method utilizing critical path analysis for design space exploration of superscalar microprocessors. In: Xu, W., Xiao, L., Li, J., Zhang, C., Zhu, Z. (eds.) NCCET 2014. Communications in Computer and Information Science, vol. 491, pp. 20–35. Springer, Berlin (2015). https://doi.org/10.1007/978-3-662-45815-0_3

19. Raghavan, S., Garcia-Molina, H.: Representing web graphs. In: Proceedings 19th International Conference on Data Engineering (Cat. No.03CH37405), pp. 405–416 (2003). https://doi.org/10.1109/ICDE.2003.1260809

20. Saidi, A.G., Binkert, N.L., Reinhardt, S.K., Mudge, T.: Full-system critical path analysis. In: ISPASS 2008 - IEEE International Symposium on Performance Analysis of Systems and software, pp. 63–74 (2008). https://doi.org/10.1109/ISPASS.2008.4510739

21. Saidi, A.G.: Full-system critical-path analysis and performance prediction. Ph.D. thesis, Department of Computer Science and Engineering, University of Michigan (2009). https://hdl.handle.net/2027.42/62309

22. Shi, L., Liac, Q., Sun, X., Chen, Y., Lin, C.: Scalable network traffic visualization using compressed graphs. In: 2013 IEEE International Conference on Big Data, pp. 606–612 (2013). https://doi.org/10.1109/BigData.2013.6691629

23. Singh, S., Awasthi, M.: Memory centric characterization and analysis of spec cpu2017 suite. In: Proceedings of the 2019 ACM/SPEC International Conference on Performance Engineering, ICPE 2019, pp. 285–292. Association for Computing Machinery, New York (2019). https://doi.org/10.1145/3297663.3310311

24. Tanimoto, T., Ono, T., Inoue, K.: Dependence graph model for accurate critical path analysis on out-of-order processors. J. Inf. Process. **25**, 983–992 (2017). https://doi.org/10.2197/ipsjjip.25.983

25. Tanimoto, T., Ono, T., Inoue, K., Sasaki, H.: Enhanced dependence graph model for critical path analysis on modern out-of-order processors. IEEE Comput. Archit. Lett. **16**(2), 111–114 (2017). https://doi.org/10.1109/LCA.2017.2684813

26. Wang, J., Huang, Y., Wu, F.X., Pan, Y.: Symmetry compression method for discovering network motifs. IEEE/ACM Trans. Comput. Biol. Bioinf. **9**(6), 1776–1789 (2012). https://doi.org/10.1109/TCBB.2012.119

27. Wang, L., Deng, Y., Gong, R., Shi, W., Luo, L., Wang, Y.: CSMO-DSE: fast and precise application-driven DSE guided by criticality and sensitivity analysis. J. Emerg. Technol. Comput. Syst. **16**(2) (2020). https://doi.org/10.1145/3371406

28. Wang, L., et al.: A scalable and fast microprocessor design space exploration methodology. In: 2015 IEEE 9th International Symposium on Embedded Multicore/Many-core Systems-on-Chip, pp. 33–40 (2015). https://doi.org/10.1109/MCSoC.2015.30

29. Yang, C.Q., Miller, B.: Critical path analysis for the execution of parallel and distributed programs. In: [1988] Proceedings of the 8th International Conference on Distributed, pp. 366–373 (1988). https://doi.org/10.1109/DCS.1988.12538

30. Yin, H., Benson, A.R., Leskovec, J., Gleich, D.F.: Local higher-order graph clustering. In: Proceedings of the 23rd ACM SIGKDD International Conference on Knowledge Discovery and Data Mining, KDD 2017, pp. 555–564. Association for Computing Machinery, New York (2017). https://doi.org/10.1145/3097983.3098069
31. Yu, S., Feng, Y., Zhang, D., Bedru, H.D., Xu, B., Xia, F.: Motif discovery in networks: a survey. Comput. Sci. Rev. **37**, 100267 (2020). https://doi.org/10.1016/j.cosrev.2020.100267
32. Zhang, Y., Wu, B., Liu, Y., L., J.: Local community detection based on network motifs. Tsinghua Sci. Technol. **24**(6), 716–727 (2019). https://doi.org/10.26599/TST.2018.9010106

Hydis: A Hybrid Consistent KVS with Effective Sync Among Replicas

Junsheng Lou and Zichen Xu[✉]

School of Mathematics and Computer Sciences, Nanchang University,
Nanchang, China
xuz@ncu.edu.cn

Abstract. Distributed storage systems distribute user loads across regions. User requests from different geographical locations are directed to the nearest data center, benefiting reduced service latency and improved service quality. However, the consistency among regions holds against availability and richness of the underlying data services. To address these constraints, our study proposes Hydis, a hybrid consistency distributed key-value storage system based on optimized replica synchronization. Hydis guarantees high availability and scalability for geographically distributed systems and uses Conflict-free Replicated Data Types to construct HybridLattice that supports various consistency models. A novel Writeless-Consistency strategy is proposed to improve the synchronization efficiency between replicas, and a dynamic synchronization optimization based on this strategy is implemented for consistency algorithm to effectively reduce the synchronization overhead of distributed storage systems. A performance evaluation of the Hydis cluster deployed on Alibaba Cloud showed that the strong consistency algorithm in Hydis outperformed the Raft algorithm by 1.8X. Additionally, the causal consistency algorithm in Hydis outperformed the traditional Vector Clock algorithm by 2.5X.

Keywords: Replica Synchronization · Data Consistency · Distributed System

1 Introduction

Distributed databases improve storage efficiency and availability by storing data in geographically distributed nodes, and serve as the backbone for supporting large-scale applications today, including social networking, online shopping, and large-scale machine learning frameworks. Distributed databases, particularly distributed key-value databases [26], cannot be ignored in these applications. As a non-relational NoSQL database, distributed key-value databases store data in key-value pairs and are not limited by the relational model, making it easier to achieve horizontal scaling for high availability.

A single level of consistency cannot meet the diverse requirements of higher-level applications for consistency level [7,8]. Multi-level consistency allows users

© The Author(s), under exclusive license to Springer Nature Singapore Pte Ltd. 2024
C. Li et al. (Eds.): APPT 2023, LNCS 14103, pp. 147–161, 2024.
https://doi.org/10.1007/978-981-99-7872-4_9

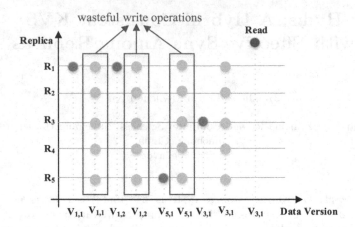

Fig. 1. $V_{i,j}$ means the version j of the data written by replica R_i. Blue represents write operations, and yellow represents synchronization operations between replicas. (Color figure online)

to choose the level that is most suitable for their needs and to better match their application scenarios. For example, Cassandra [14] implements Tunable Consistency based on the number of read and write requests, while Azure Cosmos DB [24] implements Strong Consistency, Bounded Staleness, and other consistency levels in the system, supporting users to switch between them through API calls. The implementations [25] of these multi-level consistency algorithms only provide users with a consistency switching interface, without considering dynamically matching the user's workload. Therefore, when there is a fluctuation in the workload, there may be a sudden drop in performance.

We research the cost of replica synchronization strategy from the perspective of dynamically matching the user's workload. In distributed key-value databases, regardless of using strong or weak consistency, the system's workload is mainly generated by write operations because write operations trigger replica synchronization strategies, resulting in overhead, while read operations do not cause data replication between nodes. Although replica synchronization strategies provide guarantees for data consistency, they also bring some seemingly unnecessary overhead, as shown in the Fig. 1. In some business scenarios with frequent write operations, there may be a large number of **"wasteful write operations"**. We constructed a business scenario about periodically broadcasted the minimum transaction price based on a real-world electronic currency transaction dataset [1]. The database logs showed that for the same key-value pair data, there were 5-10 write operations between most consecutive read operations. These write operations would be immediately overwritten by the next write operation, resulting in a lot of invalid coordination overhead, and only the result of the last write operation could be used.

In this paper, we propose Hydis, a hybrid consistency distributed key-value storage system based on dynamically optimizing replica synchronization strategies. Hydis builds a hybrid consistency data structure that supports multiple consistency levels, enabling lightweight construction of different consistency levels and reducing the amount of coordination operations required for strong consistency. We address the issue of wasted replica synchronization overhead in write operations between replicas by using machine learning algorithms to predict the next read operation, effectively reducing the synchronization overhead of invalid write operations between replicas.

Our contributions are as follows:

- We identify the performance problem of replica synchronization strategy, the core of consistency algorithm, and evaluated the problem based on a real business dataset.
- We propose the Writeless replica synchronization strategy, which dynamically optimizes consistency algorithms based on the historical characteristics of workloads, and explores how to achieve efficient synchronization between replicas while ensuring consistency.
- We built a prototype system Hydis that employs the Writeless strategy and deployed it on public clouds. We evaluated the performance using workloads based on a real dataset. The results show that the throughput of the strong consistency algorithm in Hydis is 1.8X that of Raft, the throughput of the causal consistency algorithm is 2.5X that of Vector Clock algorithm.

2 Background

In this section, we will provide an overview of the hybrid consistency and replica synchronization strategies to briefly illustrate the problem targeted in this work.

2.1 Hybrid Consistency

The basic requirement for the design of modern distributed database systems is to support multiple levels of consistency, rather than being limited to a single consistency level. This is particularly important in distributed database systems that aim to provide integrated storage services, ranging from user-level data storage to system-level metadata storage. For example, developers of social media applications often want their users to quickly see changes in social content, and consistency of data may not be their primary concern. However, they still want strong consistency for certain infrequently updated system-level metadata. Hybrid consistency is what they need. Developers can use the same distributed storage system throughout the development process and configure the appropriate consistency level in different deployment environments.

Hybrid Consistency is not a recognized vocabulary and may also be referred to as "Tunable Consistency" in other works [14,25]. Cassandra has realized different consistency levels based on different read-write strategies: ONE, QUORUM, ALL, etc. MongoDB also uses a similar scheme to implement multiple coexisting consistency levels. As shown in the Fig. 2, distributed database systems with hybrid consistency features are mostly divided into two consistency routing schemes: one is a static consistency routing scheme [14,25,31], in which

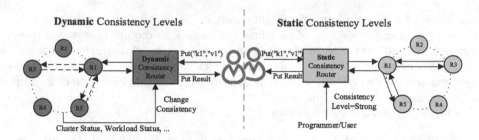

Fig. 2. Showing two hybrid consistency strategies: blue represents Dynamic Consistency Levels that can be dynamically adjusted based on other parameters such as cluster node status, workload status or characteristics, or write operations with different consistency requirements; red represents Static Consistency Levels that are set by programmers or users, and read-write requests are executed according to the corresponding consistency algorithm, without the ability to dynamically adjust the consistency level or perform dynamic optimization of the consistency algorithm. (Color figure online)

developers set the consistency level for the application scenario and the system executes the consistency algorithm according to the set level; the other is a dynamic consistency routing scheme [6,17], which often assumes that developers or users do not know which consistency level is most suitable for them, so the system will switch the consistency level or perform dynamic optimization based on some conditions. This work is based on CRDTs [16,27] to implement a hybrid consistency model, providing a static consistency level switching interface, while also supporting dynamic optimization of consistency algorithms to adapt to the unique workload of the application.

2.2   Replica Synchronization Strategy

The synchronization operation between replicas ensures data consistency, the synchronization strategy is also the core of the consistency algorithm. According to the synchronization timing, replica synchronization strategies can be divided into two types: synchronous replication strategy and asynchronous replication strategy. The synchronous replication strategy requires replica nodes to synchronize data updates immediately, and only returns processing results to the client after receiving a message of successful synchronization from over half of the nodes (in more strict consistency scenarios, all replicas may be required to synchronize successfully). Strong consistency algorithms like Paxos [15] and Raft [23] adopt synchronous replication strategies, which ensure strong consistency, but also impose a significant time cost on the users. The asynchronous replication strategy allows replica nodes to return processing results to the client immediately after processing write operations locally. Eventual consistency algorithms like Gossip [11] adopt asynchronous replication strategies, greatly reducing the operation latency for clients, but also increase risk of data inconsistency.

Some works have recognized the overhead caused by replica synchronization. PANDO [32] introduced erasure coding into the two-phase commit plan to reduce

Table 1. Common notations

Symbol	Meaning
r_i	the i-th replica
f_i^k	the k-th operation on replica r_i
s_i^k	the state of replica r_i after the f_i^k has been executed
S	the set of statuses of all replica nodes
F	the set of f
F_i'	the subset of F that includes f^i

$$f(t_{n-1}) = t_n$$

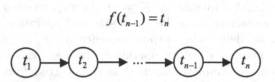

Fig. 3. Prediction model for the number of write operations between read operations

data synchronization overhead and reduce communication latency between nodes with delegation mechanism. Similarly, CRaft [35] introduced erasure coding into the Raft algorithm to reduce network overhead. DYNAMIC Consistency [29] takes a different approach and estimates the currency of replica data from client read operations to reduce other unnecessary read operations. This work targets the "wasteful write operations" problem between replicas, combining machine learning methods with replica synchronization strategies to reduce ineffective synchronization between replicas and greatly reduce latency.

3 Design

In this section, we will present the design of the hybrid consistency model and Writeless replica synchronization strategy in this work, and explain how the strategy reduces the number of invalid synchronizations between replicas (Table 1).

3.1 Writeless Replica Sync Strategy

In KVS that employs overwrite updates as the primary write mode, the performance under the heavy-write workload may be very poor. The main reason for this is not only the cost of the write update, but also the existence of a large number of invalid write updates. To demonstrate this, we built a read-write frequency dataset based on the Btcusd dataset [1], which reports on the lowest price of bitcoin-dollar trading. Between two read operations, there is about a 75% chance that the number of write operations is between 5 and 10 times. Considering that if weak consistency is required, not every write request needs to be immediately synchronized. As shown in the Fig. 1, if only the last update is read, then the synchronization of previous write operations is invalid.

To reduce the number of invalid synchronization operations, we have designed and implemented a replica synchronization strategy called **Writeless**. This strategy can predict the timing of the next read operation based on the historical characteristics of the read-write workload, and synchronize the latest version of the data before the read operation occurs, thus minimizing the number of invalid synchronization operations. Furthermore, it is possible to **dynamically optimize** the replica synchronization strategy based on changes in the read-write load. As shown in the Fig. 3, Writeless uses an LSTM [6] model as f for prediction, where t_n represents the number of write operations experienced between the $n - 1_{th}$ and n_{th} read operations.

We define the input sequence as: $X = (x_1, ..., x_n)$, where x_i represents the number of write operations from the $(i - 1)$-th read operation to the i-th read operation. Then, we define the output sequence as: $Y = (y_1, ..., y_n)$, where y_i represents the number of write operations between the i-th and $(i + 1)$-th read operations. A sample dataset D is constructed from the input and output sequences, where each sample consists of an input sequence composed of historical time steps and the output sequence for the next occurrence, i.e., $D = \{(x_1, ..., x_t), (y_t) \mid t = T, ..., n\}$. During training, the LSTM model predicts the number of write operations y_{t+1} experienced in the next read operation based on the input sequence X of historical time steps.

The main reason for using the LSTM model is that it predicts time series data more accurately, and it is small enough to be used as the basis for distributed training models, which is convenient for propagation between different nodes.

Replicated State Machine Model with Writeless. Consider a distributed system consisting of k replicas, denoted as $r_0, ..., r_{k-1}$. The state that is potentially present at all replica nodes in the system can be summarized as S, where $s_i \in S$ denotes the state of r_i. For simplicity, we assume that the system is fully connected. Every synchronization operation of a replica will eventually propagate to all replicas, and each synchronization operation is based on a state merging rather than an operation merging strategy.

The k-th operation on replica r_i is denoted as f_i^k, and the initial state of replica r_i is s_i^0, such that the state change that is synchronized from the kth operation received from other replicas to replica r_i can be represented as:

$$s_i^0 \cup f_i^k = s_i^k \tag{1}$$

We can verify the feasibility of the Writeless strategy. The partial order relationship $\prec$ exists between operations. For a set of partially ordered operations $F = \{f^1, f^2, ..., f^k\}$, where $f^1 \prec f^2 \prec ... \prec f^k$, no matter how many times replica r_i executes the operations in the set and in what order, as long as the last operation f^k has been executed, it will reach the state s_i^k:

$$s_i^0 \cup F_k = s_i^0 \cup F_k' = s_i^0 \cup f^k = s_i^k \tag{2}$$

where F_k' is any subset of F that includes f^k. All replicas can reach a converged state, that is, a state where data consistency is achieved.

Algorithm 1. WritelessCausal

Require:
    vcLocal, vcGlobal, vcClient
1: **function** PUT_WLCAUSAL(*key,value, node*)
2:    *node.persister* ← < *key, value* >
3:    **for** *server* **in** *vcClient*
4:       **if** *vcClient*[*server*] > *vcLocal*[*server*]
5:          *vcLocal*[*server*] ← *vc*[*server*]
6:       **break**
7:    *vcLocal*[*self*] + +
8:    **var** *hlSync* ← GENERATE_HL(*key,value*)
9:    *putCountsInProxy*[*key*]++
10:   *putCountsByNodes*[*key*] ← *node.addr*
11:   **if** *putCountsInProxy*[*key*] ≥ *predictPutCounts*[*key*]
12:      *syncBuffer*[*node*] ← *hlSync*
13:     **wait receive** SYNC_ACK(*key, hl*) **from others**
14:   **return** *vcLocal, STATUS*

1: **function** GET_WLCAUSAL(*key, node*)
2:    **if** *putCountsInProxy*[*key*] == 0
3:      **var** *resHL* ← GENERATE_HL(*key, value*)
4:      **return** *resHL*
5:    *nodeCountsHash* ← *putCountsByNodes*
6:    **if** *len*(*nodeCountsHash*) > 1
7:      **send** SYNC(*key*)
8:      **wait receive** SYNC_ACK(*key, hl*) **from others**
9:    **var** *resHL* ← GENERATE_HL(*key, value*)
10:   **return** *resHL*

3.2 Hybrid Consistency with Writeless

Considering the data format of KVS and the Hybrid consistency model, we use the lattice structure [9] with ACI properties to construct a Hybrid consistency data structure, HybridLattice. In Hydis, strong consistency, causal consistency, and bounded staleness consistency have been implemented.

We optimize the consistency algorithm based on the Writeless replica synchronization strategy, as shown in the Algorithm 1. WritlessCausal is a causal consistency algorithm that combines the Writeless strategy and implements GET and PUT interfaces for client calls. *putCountsInProxy* counts the write operations for each key and sets a threshold to trigger the Writeless strategy. When the number of write operations for a certain key exceeds this threshold, the Writeless model will be used to predict its future read and write operations. *predictPutCounts* is the prediction result of the Writeless model based on a single key-value, and *predictPutCounts*[*k*] represents the number of write operations for the key-value pair where the key is "k". When a client calls the PUT operation, *putCountsInProxy* will be updated and compared with *predictPutCounts*. If *putCountsInProxy*[*k*] ≥ *predictPutCounts*[*k*], a synchronization operation

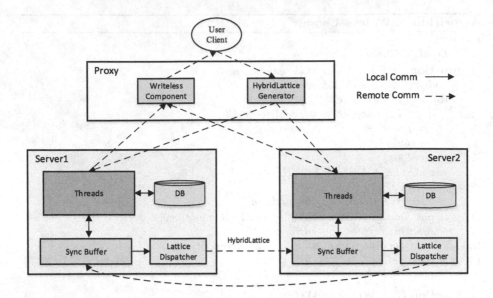

Fig. 4. System architecture of Hydis

will be triggered; otherwise, the operation will be executed locally and the result will be immediately returned.

If clients call the GET operation, in order to avoid data inconsistency between replicas, we will synchronize the replica node that has performed the last write operation. The GET operation will be executed and return the corresponding data only after all replica nodes confirm their completion of synchronization.

4   Implementation

The Hydis system is implemented based on the Go language. We use gRPC [4] and Google Protocol Buffers [3] for distributed communication, with a total of about 3000 lines of Go code, including the implementation of Hybrid Consistency, the Writeless replica synchronization strategy, and the Hydis components.

The architecture of the Hydis system is shown in the Fig. 4, and the cluster consists of two parts: Proxy and Server. Next, we will explain the system architecture based on the previously mentioned hybrid consistency scheme constructed using HybridLattice and Writeless replica synchronization strategy.

4.1   Proxy

Clients calls various consistency read-write APIs provided by Hydis and sends requests to the Proxy. The Proxy controls the global variables in hybrid consistency, and also acts as a load balancer, directing user requests to the appropriate Server based on its workload and latency.

HybridLattice Generator. HybridLattice Generator in the Proxy is an important component for implementing hybrid consistency in Hydis. It generates HybridLattice data based on the Timestamp and Vector Clock of client requests and sends the data to the corresponding Server according to the consistency level corresponding to the clients' API call.

Writeless Component. After the server processes the request, the result is returned to the Writeless Component in the Proxy. Writeless Component implements the Writeless strategy and predicts the read-write frequency for each key-value unit, while setting some variables to track the read-write frequency of the keys. If the number of write operations for a key reaches the predicted value, then the write operation will be synchronized. Otherwise, a message indicating a successful write operation is returned to the client. When a client sends a read request, the Writeless Component checks the number of pending write operations for the key $t[key]$. If $t[key] > 0$, the Server that performed the last write operation will send a synchronization operation to other nodes. After the write operation is synchronized, the read operation can be performed.

4.2 Server

Proxy redirects requests from clients to Server. Hydis Server uses LevelDB [5] as the storage engine to achieve distributed key-value storage databases. To meet the requirements of distributed high concurrency scenarios, we utilize Goroutines to implement multithreaded processing of high-load request workloads. Each request's processing or synchronization operation is determined to be synchronized or asynchronously processed by the Goroutines based on the consistency level.

Sync Buffer. Hydis uses a buffer channel to implement data buffer for replica synchronization. The Goroutines write HybridLattice data to the Sync Buffer through intercom communication. The Sync Buffer continuously sends the data in the channel to the Lattice Dispatcher, which then determines the target replica node. The existence of the Sync Buffer means that non-strong consistency operations do not need to wait for execution, which is wait-free. At the same time, because the workload of a single thread is reduced, it avoids performance degradation caused by multi-thread contention.

Lattice Dispatcher. Lattice Dispatcher is responsible for getting the update data to be synchronized from the Sync Buffer and sending it to other replica nodes. The data transmitted between nodes are all Hybrid Lattice structures. The Lattice Dispatcher internally tracks the communication latency between this node and other nodes and updates it regularly. Therefore, it can send update operations to nodes with lower latency waiting, reducing the time delay caused by consistency coordination as much as possible.

5   Evaluation

Hydis aims to implement a hybrid consistency model for multiple workload loads and dynamically optimize consistency algorithms using the Writeless replica synchronization strategy. In this section, we evaluate the performance of Hydis prototype system by implementing and deploying it on Alibaba Cloud platform.

5.1   Evaluation Setup

System Setup. We deployed Hydis to instances on Alibaba Cloud (ecs.c5. xlarge), with two regions, Beijing (North China) and Shanghai (East China), each with a varying number of instances depending on the experimental environment. Each instance is equipped with a 8-core 2.5 GHz CPU (Intel(R) Xeon(R) Platinum 8163), 8 GiB of running memory, 40 GiB SSD, and a 100 Mb/s Ethernet card. We built and expanded the same workload as YCSB based on real-world read-write data sets and evaluated the performance of Hydis using this workload.

Software Setup. The instance operating system uses Ubuntu 20.04 LTS. Our experiment is based on a client-server model, as shown in the Fig. 4. The client sends batched workload with different read-write ratios. In this paper, we mainly evaluated the performance of Hydis from the following two consistency levels:

- *Strong Consistency*: A strong consistency algorithm based on Raft implementation. Raft is a widely used strong consistency algorithm in the industry. We implement a state-of-the-art Raft design from Ongaro et al. [23];
- *Causal Consistency*: Causal consistency is widely used in scenarios where consistency requirements, such as social applications, are not very strong. We referred to related work and implemented a causal consistency algorithm based on Vector Clock.

Workloads. We build a dataset on reading and writing frequency of trade price data based on the trading data of "Bitcoin vs. US$" (public price) from the Bitfinex exchange [1], and extensively expanded it to construct a workload similar to YCSB. Workloads are random reads/writes, controlled ratio R/W batches, and read/write-only workloads.

- **Read** is a workload for read-only queries.
- **Write** is a workload with all writes.
- α-**Static** is an α controlled workload, where α is the read-write ratio.

5.2   Evaluation Results

In this section, we compare the two consistency algorithms optimized in Hydis using the Writeless strategy, **WritelessStrong** (strong consistency) and **WritelessCausal** (causal consistency), with the traditional strong consistency algorithm Raft and the causal consistency algorithm based on Vector Clock(referred to as Causal). We conduct detailed comparisons in various experimental environments and provide explanations.

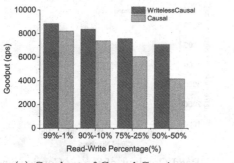 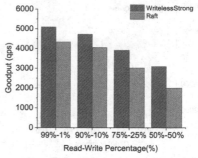

(a) Goodput of Causal Consistency   (b) Goodput of Strong Consistency

Fig. 5. Goodput under different read/write ratio workloads.

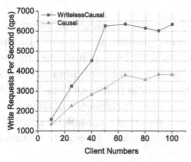 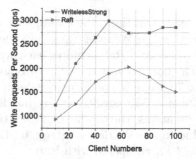

(a) Write Goodput of Causal Consistency (b) Write Goodput of Strong Consistency

Fig. 6. Write goodput comparison with different numbers of client.

Goodput Under Different R/W Ratio Workload. In the Fig. 5, we evaluated the performance of Hydis using the same workload as YCSB. We evaluated the Goodput(correct execution of application-level queries) of WritelessStrong and WritelessCausal based on workloads with different read/write ratios.

In the Fig. 5(a), the tests with different read/write ratios show that the average throughput of WritelessCausal is 1.2X–2.5X that of the conventional Causal consistency algorithm based on vector clocks.When the proportion of write operations is high, the optimization effect is significant. In the Fig. 5(b), WritelessStrong greatly enhances performance in high-write scenarios compared to Raft due to its ability to minimize coordination overhead in strong consistency settings by reducing data synchronization operations.

Performance Under Different Levels of Concurrency. In the case of write-only workload shown in the Fig. 6(a), WritelessCausal's throughput is 1.98X higher than that of Causal, thanks to the Writeless strategy, which reduces most of the ineffective write synchronization. We updated each key-value pair data more than ten times on average in this workload, but because we did not

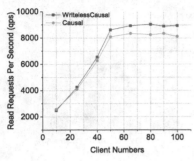
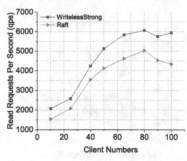

(a) Read Goodput of Causal Consistency (b) Read Goodput of Strong Consistency

Fig. 7. Read goodput comparison with different numbers of client.

invoke read operations, there were a lot of ineffective synchronization operations in Causal, while WritelessCausal avoided the above problems very well. In the Fig. 6(b), because Raft requires each write operation to be synchronized in the form of a quorum every time, the throughput is lower, when the number of clients is above 70, there is a performance decline due to its single point bottleneck problem. Because WritelessStrong continually triggers the Writeless Component for write operations, the overhead of updating related metadata cannot be ignored. Still, due to the Writless strategy, it still achieved a performance improvement of up to 1.8X compared with Raft.

In the case of read-only workload, as shown in the Fig. 7(a), WritelessCausal has no significant throughput advantage over Causal. The main reason is that the read operation is not the core optimization point of Writeless write optimization strategy. In the Fig. 7(b), Raft's leader bears most of the work (i.e., log replication, membership maintenance), leading to performance degradation under high concurrency workloads. WritelessStrong reduces the responsibility of Proxy in the cluster, and since this is a read-only load, the problem of single point bottleneck is greatly improved compared to Raft.

6   Related Work

Consistency Algorithm and Related System. Distributed databases have always been a focus of research in the field of data services, among which consistency algorithms are the core. Some of them focus on providing causal consistency and its variants, allowing users to obtain locally better consistency experience at low cost [20–22]. In some businesses, such as bank transfer business, strong consistency is a basic requirement, so some work optimizes traditional strong consistency algorithms such as [15,23,30,33]. ChainPaxos [13] combines the pipeline communication mode similar to the ChainReplication algorithm [33] with the Paxos algorithm, minimizing the propagation of messages among nodes and reducing additional communication costs. BW-Raft [12] introduces low-cost Secretary and Observer roles to divert the workload of a single Leader, effectively reducing deployment costs and improving performance. This survey [34] provides a comprehensive introduction to related consistency semantics, from eventual consistency to strong consistency.

Hybrid Consistency. In order to make effective trade-offs between low latency and stronger consistency, many works [2,10,28,36] have begun to focus on providing multiple consistency levels. Gemini [17] distinguishes the consistency levels based on the user's operations, minimizing the coordination overhead of blue operations. Olisipo [18] proposed the PoR consistency, minimizing consistency coordination overhead at a granular level. Pileus [31] provides multiple consistency levels around SLA to provide the best static consistency level for the best user experience. Stabilizer [19] supports domain-specific languages for consistency levels to define multiple granular consistency levels accurately.

7   Conclusion

In distributed systems, the performance of consistency algorithms is essential for large-scale intensive data services. In this paper, we propose Hydis, a distributed key-value database that supports hybrid consistency and dynamically optimizes consistency algorithms based on workload. Hydis builds the underlying data transmission structure HybridLattice based on CRDTs and implements the Writeless replica synchronization strategy based on LSTM model training using historical workload data. In practice, we implement two dynamically optimized consistency algorithms, WritelessCausal and WritelessStrong, and establish a prototype key-value storage service.

Experimental results show that compared with Raft, Hydis can improve throughput up to 1.8X while ensuring strong consistency. In the comparison under causal consistency, the throughput of the WritelessCausal implemented in Hydis can be improved up to 2.5X that of traditional causal consistency algorithms. At the same time, there are still some unfinished work in Hydis, such as reducing the training cost of the Writeless strategy model or introducing some non-prior methods for write frequency prediction. We look forward to optimizing and implementing them in future work.

Acknowledgments. This work was supported by the National Key R&D Program of China, No. 2022YFB4501703, the National Natural Science Foundation of China (KY0402022036), and the Provincial Key Research and Development Program of Jiangxi (012031379055).

References

1. 400+ crypto currency pairs at 1-minute resolution. https://www.kaggle.com/datasets/tencars/392-crypto-currency-pairs-at-minute-resolution. Accessed 15 May 2023

2. Azure DocumentDB. https://azure.microsoft.com/en-us/products/. Accessed 6 June 2023
3. Google Protocol Buffers. https://github.com/protocolbuffers/protobuf. Accessed 10 June 2023
4. gRPC. https://grpc.io/. Accessed 10 June 2023
5. LevelDB. https://github.com/google/leveldb. Accessed 10 June 2023
6. Bravo, M., Gotsman, A., de Régil, B., Wei, H.: Unistore: a fault-tolerant marriage of causal and strong consistency. In: USENIX Annual Technical Conference, pp. 923–937 (2021)
7. Brewer, E.: A certain freedom: thoughts on the cap theorem. In: Proceedings of the 29th ACM SIGACT-SIGOPS Symposium on Principles of Distributed Computing, pp. 335–335 (2010)
8. Brewer, E.: Cap twelve years later: how the "rules" have changed. Computer **45**(2), 23–29 (2012)
9. Conway, N., Marczak, W.R., Alvaro, P., Hellerstein, J.M., Maier, D.: Logic and lattices for distributed programming. In: Proceedings of the Third ACM Symposium on Cloud Computing, pp. 1–14 (2012)
10. DeCandia, G., et al.: Dynamo: Amazon's highly available key-value store. ACM SIGOPS Oper. Syst. Rev. **41**(6), 205–220 (2007)
11. Demers, A., et al.: Epidemic algorithms for replicated database maintenance. In: Proceedings of the Sixth Annual ACM Symposium on Principles of Distributed Computing, pp. 1–12 (1987)
12. Du, Y., Xu, Z., Zhang, K., Liu, J., Huang, J., Stewart, C.: Cost-effective strong consistency on scalable geo-diverse data replicas. IEEE Trans. Cloud Comput. (2022)
13. Fouto, P., Preguiça, N., Leitão, J.: High throughput replication with integrated membership management. In: 2022 USENIX Annual Technical Conference (USENIX ATC 22), pp. 575–592 (2022)
14. Lakshman, A., Malik, P.: Cassandra: a decentralized structured storage system. ACM SIGOPS Oper. Syst. Rev. **44**(2), 35–40 (2010)
15. Lamport, L.: Paxos made simple. ACM SIGACT News (Distributed Computing Column) **32**, 4 (Whole Number 121, December 2001) 51–58 (2001)
16. Letia, M., Preguiça, N., Shapiro, M.: CRDTs: consistency without concurrency control. arXiv preprint arXiv:0907.0929 (2009)
17. Li, C., Porto, D., Clement, A., Gehrke, J., Preguiça, N., Rodrigues, R.: Making geo-replicated systems fast as possible, consistent when necessary. In: Presented as part of the 10th {$USENIX$} Symposium on Operating Systems Design and Implementation ({$OSDI$} 12), pp. 265–278 (2012)
18. Li, C., Preguiça, N., Rodrigues, R.: Fine-grained consistency for geo-replicated systems. In: 2018 {$USENIX$} Annual Technical Conference ({$USENIX$}{ATC} 18), pp. 359–372 (2018)
19. Li, P., Pan, L., Yang, X., Song, W., Xiao, Z., Birman, K.: Stabilizer: geo-replication with user-defined consistency. In: 2022 IEEE 42nd International Conference on Distributed Computing Systems (ICDCS), pp. 359–369. IEEE (2022)
20. Lloyd, W., Freedman, M.J., Kaminsky, M., Andersen, D.G.: Don't settle for eventual: scalable causal consistency for wide-area storage with cops. In: Proceedings of the Twenty-Third ACM Symposium on Operating Systems Principles, pp. 401–416 (2011)
21. Lykhenko, T., Soares, R., Rodrigues, L.: FaaSTCC: efficient transactional causal consistency for serverless computing. In: Proceedings of the 22nd International Middleware Conference, pp. 159–171 (2021)

22. Mehdi, S.A., Littley, C., Crooks, N., Alvisi, L., Bronson, N., Lloyd, W.: I can't believe it's not causal! scalable causal consistency with no slowdown cascades. In: NSDI, vol. 17, pp. 453–468 (2017)
23. Ongaro, D., Ousterhout, J.: In search of an understandable consensus algorithm. In: 2014 {USENIX} Annual Technical Conference ({USENIX}{ATC} 14), pp. 305–319 (2014)
24. Reagan, R., Reagan, R.: Cosmos db. Web Applications on Azure: Developing for Global Scale, pp. 187–255 (2018)
25. Schultz, W., Avitabile, T., Cabral, A.: Tunable consistency in MongoDB. Proc. VLDB Endowment **12**(12), 2071–2081 (2019)
26. Seeger, M., Ultra-Large-Sites, S.: Key-value stores: a practical overview. Comput. Sci. Med. Stutt. (2009)
27. Shapiro, M., Preguiça, N., Baquero, C., Zawirski, M.: A comprehensive study of convergent and commutative replicated data types. Ph.D. thesis, Inria-Centre Paris-Rocquencourt; INRIA (2011)
28. Sreekanti, V., et al.: Cloudburst: stateful functions-as-a-service. arXiv preprint arXiv:2001.04592 (2020)
29. Sun, Y., Zheng, Z., Song, S., Chiang, F.: Confidence bounded replica currency estimation. In: Proceedings of the 2022 International Conference on Management of Data, pp. 730–743 (2022)
30. Terrace, J., Freedman, M.J.: Object storage on CRAQ: high-throughput chain replication for read-mostly workloads. In: USENIX Annual Technical Conference (2009)
31. Terry, D.B., Prabhakaran, V., Kotla, R., Balakrishnan, M., Aguilera, M.K., Abu-Libdeh, H.: Consistency-based service level agreements for cloud storage. In: Proceedings of the Twenty-Fourth ACM Symposium on Operating Systems Principles, pp. 309–324 (2013)
32. Uluyol, M., Huang, A., Goel, A., Chowdhury, M., Madhyastha, H.V.: Near-optimal latency versus cost tradeoffs in geo-distributed storage. In: NSDI, vol. 20, pp. 157–180 (2020)
33. Van Renesse, R., Schneider, F.B.: Chain replication for supporting high throughput and availability. In: OSDI, vol. 4 (2004)
34. Viotti, P., Vukolić, M.: Consistency in non-transactional distributed storage systems. ACM Comput. Surv. (CSUR) **49**(1), 1–34 (2016)
35. Wang, Z., et al.: Craft: an erasure-coding-supported version of raft for reducing storage cost and network cost. In: FAST, pp. 297–308 (2020)
36. Wu, C., Faleiro, J.M., Lin, Y., Hellerstein, J.M.: Anna: a kvs for any scale. IEEE Trans. Knowl. Data Eng. **33**(2), 344–358 (2019)

Networking and Cloud Computing

An Automatic Deployment Method for Hybrid Cloud Simulation Platform

Xilai Yao[1]([✉]), Yizhuo Wang[1], Weixing Ji[1], and Qiurui Chen[2]

[1] Beijing Institute of Technology, Beijing, China
{3120211069,frankwyz,jwx}@bit.edu.cn
[2] Beijing Simulation Center, Beijing, China
qiuruich@126.com

Abstract. The simulation resources are now virtualized and deployed on cloud platform. It can provide on-demand simulation tests, improving the efficiency of simulation systems. Simulation resources are packaged into virtual machines or containers. Complex software are packaged into virtual machines, and simple simulation services are packaged into containers. However, how to deploy simulation systems under resource constraints is a problem worth studying. This paper studies a virtual machine and container based hybrid cloud simulation platform. An automatic deployment method is proposed to reduce labor costs and errors of manual deployment. A simulation case is applied to verify the usefulness and efficiency of our approach.

Keywords: System simulation · Cloud computing · Virtual machine · Container · Automated deployment

1 Introduction

With the rapid development of cloud computing, PaaS hosts a number of development tools and provides a framework for various applications. Simulation system represented by test beds involve various simulation resources such as physical models, simulation engines, and shared services. These simulation resources are virtualized and deployed on cloud platforms, which can save costs, provide on-demand simulation testing, and improve the efficiency of simulation systems.

Given that, researchers proposed a cloud simulation framework [10]. By comprehensively utilizing distributed simulation, computer network, and resource virtualization, cloud computing provides external services such as infrastructure, support platforms, and software applications, achieving full sharing and reuse of software and hardware resources, such as computing, storage and network, supporting distributed modeling and simulation for multiple users.

© The Author(s), under exclusive license to Springer Nature Singapore Pte Ltd. 2024
C. Li et al. (Eds.): APPT 2023, LNCS 14103, pp. 165–179, 2024.
https://doi.org/10.1007/978-981-99-7872-4_10

However, existing cloud simulation adopt traditional virtualization technology, encapsulating various simulation resources into virtual machines and deploying them on cloud platforms for users to use on demand. The deployment requires a significant amount of human involvement. Encapsulating lightweight simulation resources into virtual machines can lead to low utilization of hardware resources and operational efficiency.

In response to the above issues, this paper investigates a simulation cloud platform that combines virtual machines and containers, encapsulating various simulation resources into virtual machines or containers based on their own features, and deploying them cooperatively on the cloud. Virtual machines and containers that connected in a sub-network work together to complete simulation system experiments, avoiding resource waste caused by deploying small modules in virtual machines. In addition, most existing cloud platforms separate virtualization machines from containers, and requires manually deployment for cooperated simulation. This work investigates a hybrid and automatic deployment system for virtual machines and containers, providing a unified interface for applications and achieving unified management of virtual machine networks and container networks.

2   Architecture of Hybrid Cloud Simulation Platform

The architecture of the hybrid simulation cloud platform investigated in this work is shown in Fig. 1, which is mainly composed of application layer, service layer, resource layer, and simulation security management system.

The resource layer virtualizes and en-services the hardware resources and simulation resources used in simulation experiments, which can further dynamically invoke and allocate these resources with respect to users' demands. Among them, the hardware resources for simulation mainly include computing resources, network resources, and storage resources. Virtual simulation resources include both virtual machines and containers, which are stored in an image repository.

The service layer provides functions such as resource allocation, network construction, service scheduling, access control, and version control. These functions are specifically implemented by the virtual machine management system and container management system, and the unified management module is responsible for coordinating the virtual machine management system and container management system.

The application layer mainly includes the platform frontend and platform management console, which enable users to use and configure the required simulation services in the browser or console, and conduct simulation experiment scenario design, experiment process monitoring, data analysis, etc.

The simulation security management system mainly ensures the information security of the network, storage, data, models, and various applications during the operation of the cloud simulation. It also provides backup and disaster recovery, ensuring the data security of the entire cloud simulation.

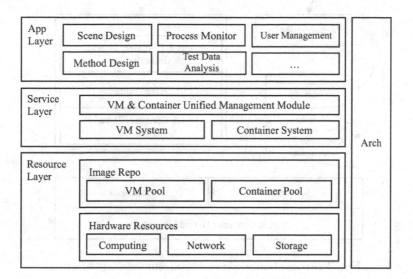

Fig. 1. Architecture of Hybrid VM and container simulation platform

The application of the hybrid cloud simulation platform is shown in Fig. 2. Firstly, various simulation resources are virtualized and described. Then, based on the configuration file, packaged virtual machine and container are pushed into the image repository. Afterwards, based on the user's simulation requirements, automated deployment of virtual machines and containers on the simulation cloud platform is carried out.

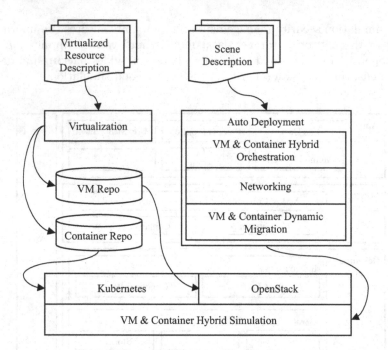

Fig. 2. Application mode of hybrid simulation platform

This work implements a virtual machine and container hybrid cloud simulation platform based on OpenStack [2] and Kubernetes [14]. Kubernetes is used as the management and deployment platform for container virtualization, and OpenStack is used as the management and deployment platform for virtual machine simulation resources. The deployment plan generated by the automated deployment system is executed by OpenStack and Kubernetes.

The design and implementation of a hybrid cloud simulation platform involves the following key points:

1. Combination and orchestration of virtual machines and containers. Establish an automated deployment system and optimize resource scheduling algorithms during the deployment to meet the needs of hybrid cloud platforms.
2. Hybrid networking of virtual machines and containers. It is necessary to meet the connectivity requirements between various simulation testing modules, while also achieving isolation between subnets.
3. Dynamic virtual machine and container migration. Consider issues such as load balancing on cloud simulation platforms, and achieve dynamic deployment optimization through the migration of virtual machines and containers.

3   Automated Deployment of Cloud Simulation Applications

3.1   Overall Workflow

The automatic deployment system needs to address the following issues [8,17]:

1. How users can submit task to the simulation cloud platform.
2. How the system converts user requirements into information required for automatic deployment such as resource requirements.
3. How does the system deploy the required virtualization simulation resources for users.

After the user submit a task, the system instantiates the user requirement into an XML file, which is the user requirement file. Then the system obtains actual resource information such as computing, storage, and networking from the OpenStack and Kubernetes platforms. Based on the actual total amount of resources, check the resources required by users to determine whether the current total amount of resources can meet the demand.

Converting user requirements into resource requirements information for OpenStack and Kubernetes to complete the automated deployment work, it is necessary to implement an automatic platform recognizable deployment plan generation subsystem. A deployment plan is a plan file that can ultimately execute deployment services for users. The purpose of the generation subsystem is to convert requirement information into an automated deployment plan that can be practically carried out according to the current resource amount. In order to complete automatic deployment, it is necessary to convert the deployment plan into a script language that can be recognized by the cloud simulation platform, and then complete the deployment task.

We first create XML configuration files and YAML configuration files for the virtual machine and container, respectively, to define their resource requirements and network communication requirements, as well as achieving network communication between virtual machines and containers. The hybrid and automatic deployment model is shown in Fig. 3.

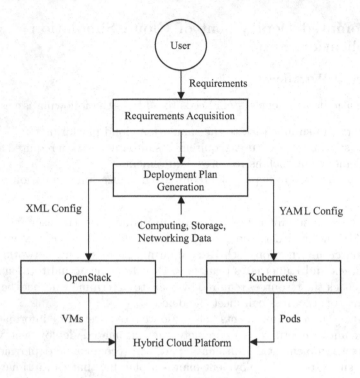

Fig. 3. Automatic deployment of a hybrid simulation system.

Both OpenStack and Kubernetes have their own Python API interfaces, which can be invoked by scripts, thus achieving unified deployment and management of VMs and containers. In OpenStack and Kubernetes, in addition to command-line interfaces and RESTful APIs, native Python API interfaces are also provided for administrators and users to use. We use the Python API to deploy VMs and containers.

The creation of virtual machines is shown in Figure ??. Firstly, authentication is required to obtain access permissions to OpenStack. On successful authentication, it is necessary to obtain information such as image, flavor, network, etc. which are required for instance creation. As a result, we first upload the image through the Glance service, create a network through the Neutron service [13], and then create a Flavor for use when creating an instance ahead of time. Flavor, also known as virtual machine hardware template, defines information such as the number of CPUs, memory size, and hard disk size required to create an instance.

In Kubernetes, Pod is the smallest unit that can be created and deployed. So we need to deploy containers by creating Pods. Before we creating a Pod, it is necessary to write a YAML configuration file for the Pod. A full YAML file for the Pod description consists of over seventy key-value pairs, but in normal use, it is not necessary to use all of them. After writing the YAML file, we can import the *yaml* module into the Python. We can call *yaml.safe_load()* to obtain the configuration information in the YAML file, and then call the K8s API to create a Pod [15].

After deploying virtual machines and containers on OpenStack and Kubernetes, it is necessary to configure a network to achieve mutual inter-communication between virtual machines and containers. OpenStack's network services are provided by the Neutron component. When deploying Neutron services, we chose the *Selfservice* mode to better achieve network environment isolation between virtual machines. Kubernetes' network services are provided by Calico plugins to enable communication between containers in different hosts.

In order to achieve communication between virtual machines and containers, we need to connect the Neutron service with the containers' network. Regarding the integration of these two, the Kuryr project is adopted [1]. The emergence of Kuryr is to integrate Docker and Neutron, using Neutron to provide network services for Docker. With the development of container technologies, two branches of container networks have emerged. One is Docker's native container network model CNM, and the other is the container network interface CNI. In order to meet the corresponding requirements, Kuryr also has two branches, *Kuryr-libnetwork* and *Kuryr-kubernetes*. Due to the Calico plugin used by Kubernetes in this article, the container only relies on three-layer routing. Therefore, we use *Kuryr-kubernetes* to integrate OpenStack and Kubernetes' networks. *Kuryr-kubernetes* mainly consists of two components, *Kuryr Controller* and *Kuryr CNI*. *Kuryr Controller* is mainly responsible for calling Neutron services and providing actual network functions for Kubernetes, while *Kuryr CNI* is responsible for binding Neutron ports for newly created Pods.

3.2 Rule-Based Resource Allocation

The key issue in the automated deployment process mentioned above is how to generate deployment plans for virtual machines and containers for a certain simulation system experiment, which is the resource allocation problem of the cloud simulation platform. We propose a rule-based resource allocation algorithm to address this issue.

We have set up a number of constraint rules and target rules for the hybrid cloud simulation. Constraint rules include instance constraints on the number of CPUs, memory capacity, disk capacity, network bandwidth, communication topology, etc. Target rules include the most balanced resource usage, optimal resource utilization rate, and minimum communication overhead. Administrators can also add and modify rule libraries to achieve more comprehensive scheduling strategies.

Using built-in rules as an example, we build a constraint rule library and a target rule library. First, we define the description identifier of the rule, as shown in Table 1, Table 2, and Table 3.

Next, we show how to define constraint rules. Assuming we have m instances to be scheduled and n nodes available for scheduling. The following constraint rules can be defined.

Table 1. Symbols for Instances (VMs and containers)

Number	Name	Description	Symbol
1	Encapsulation Type	VM = 0, Container = 1	SIM_Type
2	Simulation Component Name	String	SIM_Name
3	CPU Core	CPU Cores needed	SIM_CPU
4	Min Memory	Minimum memory	SIM_MemMin
5	Max Memory	Maximun memory	SIM_MemMax
6	Port	Network ports used	SIM_NetPort
7	Architecture	X86 = 0, ARM = 1	SIM_ARCH
8	OS	Windows = 0, Linux = 1	SIM_OS
9	GPU	Enabled = 1, Disabled = 0	SIM_GPU
10	Subnet ID	Which subnet it belongs to	SIM_SubNet

Table 2. Symbols for Nodes

Number	Name	Description	Symbol
1	Architecture	X86 = 0, ARM = 1, etc	PLT_ARCH
2	OS	Windows = 0, Linux=1, etc	PLT_OS
3	CPU Core	CPU Cores in a node	PLT_CPU
4	GPU	Enabled = 1, Disabled = 0	PLT_GPU
5	Memory	Memory of a node (MB)	PLT_Mem
6	Port	Available ports	PLT_NetPort

The basic constraint rule is that each instance i can and can only be scheduled to one node j, and its formal rule expression is

$$\sum_{j=1}^{n} p_{ij} = 1, i = 1, ..., m \qquad (1)$$

To define memory constraint rule, assuming a total of m simulation components, the per-task memory on each node j must meet the minimum requirement

$$\sum_{i=1}^{m} p_{ij} \cdot SIM\_MemMin_i \leq PLT\_Mem_j, j = 1, ..., n \qquad (2)$$

Table 3. Other symbols for resource allocation

Number	Description	Type	Symbol
1	Represents whether a simulation component i is to run on platform j, with values of 1 or 0	Var	p_{ij}
2	Maximum simulation components number difference allowed to run on two different platforms	Const	C_i
3	Represents the optimal CPU and memory utilization rate empirically	Const	$ubest_j$

The CPU usage on each node j must not exceed the total amount of CPU that the node can provide

$$\sum_{i=1}^{m} p_{ij} \cdot SIM\_CPU_i \leq PLT\_CPU_j, j = 1, ..., n \qquad (3)$$

To define operating system constraint rule, that for the i-th simulation component, if the operating system needs to match (Docker container needs to be deployed on the matching OS), the following constraint rule can be constructed

$$SIM\_Type_i \cdot \sum_{j=1}^{n} p_{ij} \cdot (SIM\_OS_i == PLT\_OS_j) = 1, i = 1, ..., m \qquad (4)$$

GPU requirements are similar to OS, that each instance i that requires GPU must be able to match to a node j that equipments with GPU.

$$\sum_{j=1}^{n} p_{ij} \cdot (SIM\_GPU_i == PLT\_GPU_j) = 1, i = 1, ..., m \qquad (5)$$

For each instance i, it has to match the architecture of some node j.

$$\sum_{j=1}^{n} p_{ij} \cdot (SIM\_ARCH_i == PLT\_ARCH_j) = 1, i = 1, ...m \qquad (6)$$

The most common targets of resource dispatches include load balancing and minimum communication overhead. To define the load balancing target rule, the distribution of the simulation components must meet the following constraint.

$$\sum_{i=1}^{m} p_{ij} \leq m/n + C_j, j = 1, ..., n \qquad (7)$$

The number of simulation components distributed on each node should be similar, fluctuating around the average plus C_j.

To ensure that components of the same subnet run on the same platform as much as possible, the following rules are constructed.

$$\begin{cases} Sum_j = \sum_{i=1}^{m} p_{ij} \cdot SIM\_SubNet_i \\ Cnt_j = \sum_{i=1}^{m} p_{ij} \\ Avg_j = Sum_j/Cnt_j \end{cases} \qquad (8)$$

where Sum_j is the sum of subnet numbers of all simulation components on platform j, Cnt_j is the number of simulation components, and Avg_j is the average of subnet numbers. We can now set the optimization target as the minimum standard deviation of each subnet numbers.

$$min \sum_{i=1}^{m} \delta_i \tag{9}$$

where δ_i represents the standard deviation of subnet numbers on platform i.

We use the Z3 solver to solve the above constraint problem. Z3 is an open-source constraint solver produced by Microsoft, which can solve the problem of seeking a set of solutions that meet the given constrains. Z3 can check if a logical expression is satisfiable, and get a model which satisfy all the constrains. Through Z3, we can get a model of p_{ij}, which is a mapping from simulation component to platform.

4 Simulation Validation

4.1 Experimental Setup

To verify the approach presented in this work, we setup a cluster of three physical machines with a single master node and two slave nodes. The machine configurations are shown in Table 4. OpenStack Train and Kubernetes 1.21 are installed on each node.

Table 4. Experiment Machine Configurations

Name	OS	CPU	Mem	IP
Master	CentOS 7.9.2009	8	16 GB	192.168.3.65
Node1	CentOS 7.9.2009	4	8 GB	192.168.3.82
Node2	CentOS 7.9.2009	4	8 GB	192.168.3.83

4.2 Simulation Scenario

To verify the automated deployment of simulation system on hybrid cloud platforms, we designed a simulation scenario. There are two types of equipment involved. Both types of equipment are simulated by multiple software and have different requirements for computing and network resources. The specific requirements are shown in Table 5.

Software 1 to *Software 4* are used for the simulation of *Equipment 1*, and the others are used for *Equipment 2*. From the table above, we can see the specific resource requirements of each simulation software. We package *Software 1* as well as the *Software 2* which occupies a lot of system resources as virtual machines, while others are packaged in containers. The requirements and parameters for these software in the simulation scenario are described in an XML file.

Table 5. Simulation software resource requirements

Software	Mem	GPU	Network
Software 1	2 GB	✓	192.168.X.Y
Software 2	2 GB	✓	192.168.X.Y
Software 3 & 4	1 GB		192.168.X.Y
Software 5	1 GB		192.168.X.Y
Software 6	1 GB		Independent Subnet
Software 7 & 8	2 GB		Independent Subnet

4.3   Automated Deployment of Instances

The automated deployment creates the required virtual machines and containers by parsing the extended simulation scenario description file. As shown in Table 6 and Table 7, the virtual machine section displays the ID, name, state, subnet used, and IP address of the created instance, while the container section displays information such as Pod's IP address, name, state, owning node, and namespace.

Table 6. VM information

Name	IP
vm_6	10.224.48.102
vm_5	10.224.2.102
vm_4	10.224.2.101
vm_3	10.224.48.101
vm_2	10.224.1.102
vm_1	10.224.1.101

Table 7. Container information

Node	Name	IP
192.168.3.82	qwe-6769c78b8f-cls58	10.224.1.105
192.168.3.82	qwe-6769c78b8f-cls58	10.224.1.104
192.168.3.82	qwe-6769c78b8f-cls58	10.224.1.103
192.168.3.83	qwe-6769c78b8f-cls58	10.224.1.105
192.168.3.83	qwe-6769c78b8f-cls58	10.224.1.104
192.168.3.83	qwe-6769c78b8f-cls58	10.224.1.103
192.168.3.83	qwe-6769c78b8f-cls58	10.224.1.101

According to the requirements, the network masks composed of various parts of the software need to be assigned in the form of 10.244.X.Y, where X is the equipment identifier, and Y changes according to different software. The network segments of each part of the simulation software need to be allocated in the form of independent subnets. Here, 10.244.16.0/28 subnet is selected to be assigned to the simulation software 6, and 10.244.48.0/28 subnet is selected to be assigned to the simulation software 7 and 8. The configuration results are shown in Fig. 4.

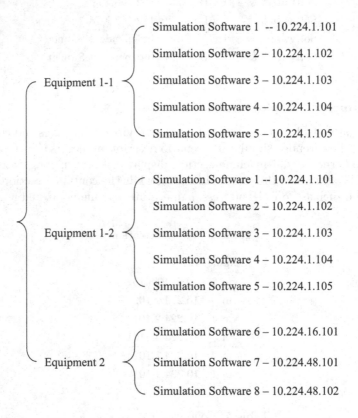

Fig. 4. IP Addresses of the Simulation Modules

The experimental result shows that the simulation instance can be deployed and run correctly on the hybrid cloud platform we have built. The automated deployment process takes about 50 s from receiving the extended simulation scenario description file to completing the deployment, greatly reducing the deployment time compared to manual deployment.

4.4   Optimization Results

We use Z3 [12] to solve the constraint optimization problem. It's guaranteed to get the optimal solution of the target function, or can't get a solution at all. For small problem size, it's almost guaranteed to achieve the optimal solution. For the simulation configurations described in Sect. 4.2, the optimization results are shown in Table 8. We can see from the results, that the high resource demanding software are deployed on Master node, which is more performant. The other software are deployed on Node 1 and Node 2. The subnet target is also fitted. We also tested the optimization time, which varies between 2 min to 10 min. Since the optimize result can be reused every deployment, as long as the configuration is not changed, we consider the optimization time acceptable.

Table 8. Optimization Result

	Master	Node1	Node2
Software 1	✓		
Software 2	✓		
Software 3	✓		
Software 4	✓		
Software 5		✓	
Software 6		✓	
Software 7			✓
Software 8			✓

5 Related Work

Accompanying with the growing complexity of software systems, it's not always possible to perform a full test in real machines. Some tests might be too complicated to be performed in a single instance. With the development of cloud technology, cloud based simulation is an intuitive way to perform software simulation. Cloud based systems tend to provide virtualization technologies to improve hardware utilization. Several methods are proposed to simulate based on cloud platforms. CloudSim [5] is a well-known and open-source simulation system, but it doesn't provide optimization for individual simulation software. DartCSim [11] is based on CloudSim, which enhanced CloudSim by providing a user interface, and the abilities to select nodes and topology manually. OptorSim [3] and Green-Cloud [9] are similar to CloudSim, which are dedicated to cloud infrastructure simulation. The authors of [4] proposed an algorithm to orchestrate virtualized resources on different physical nodes, in order to benefit hardware utilization and energy consumption. This method is also employed by CloudSim. However, this method didn't take the difference of individual container or VM into account. Several works [6] are dedicated to large scale simulation, where simulation resources can be geographically parted. Some works [7,16] are dedicated to the security problem in cloud.

6   Conclusion

This work investigates a hybrid cloud simulation platform and presents an optimization algorithm for virtual machines and containers, which is implemented based on OpenStack and Kubernetes. In response to the issues of low efficiency and error prone manual deployment of complex simulation system, an automated deployment method on the hybrid cloud is studied, and automated deployment is verified use examples.

References

1. Kuryr official documentation (2021). https://github.com/openstack/kuryr
2. Openstack official documentation (2021). https://docs.openstack.org/train/index.html
3. Bell, W.H., Cameron, D.G., Millar, A.P., Capozza, L., Stockinger, K., Zini, F.: Optorsim: a grid simulator for studying dynamic data replication strategies optorsim: a grid simulator for studying dynamic data replication strategies. https://api.semanticscholar.org/CorpusID:52874296
4. Beloglazov, A., Buyya, R.: Optimal online deterministic algorithms and adaptive heuristics for energy and performance efficient dynamic consolidation of virtual machines in cloud data centers. Concurrency Comput. Pract. Experience **24**, 1397–1420 (2012). https://api.semanticscholar.org/CorpusID:10061036
5. Calheiros, R.N., Ranjan, R., Beloglazov, A., Rose, C.A.F.D., Buyya, R.: Cloudsim: a toolkit for modeling and simulation of cloud computing environments and evaluation of resource provisioning algorithms. Softw. Pract. Experience **41** (2011). https://api.semanticscholar.org/CorpusID:14970692
6. Chen, D., Theodoropoulos, G.K., Turner, S.J., Cai, W., Minson, R., Zhang, Y.: Large scale agent-based simulation on the grid. Future Gener. Comput. Syst. **24**, 658–671 (2008). https://api.semanticscholar.org/CorpusID:2324254
7. He, H., Chen, L., Yuan, P., Xu, X., Wang, X.: A security architecture for grid-based distributed simulation platform. In: 2008 IEEE Pacific-Asia Workshop on Computational Intelligence and Industrial Application, vol. 1, pp. 207–212 (2008). https://api.semanticscholar.org/CorpusID:15314143
8. Hu, C.: Research and implementation of automated deployment system based on docker (2017)
9. Kliazovich, D., Bouvry, P., Khan, S.U.: Greencloud: a packet-level simulator of energy-aware cloud computing data centers. J. Supercomput. **62**, 1263–1283 (2010). https://api.semanticscholar.org/CorpusID:9615195
10. Li, B., et al.: Networked modeling simulation platform based on concept of cloud computing-cloud simulation platform. J. Syst. Simul. **21**, 5292–5299 (2009)
11. Li, X., Jiang, X., Huang, P., Ye, K.: DartCSim: an enhanced user-friendly cloud simulation system based on Cloudsim with better performance. In: 2012 IEEE 2nd International Conference on Cloud Computing and Intelligence Systems, vol. 01, pp. 392–396 (2012). https://api.semanticscholar.org/CorpusID:13224042
12. de Moura, Leonardo, Bjørner, Nikolaj: Z3: an efficient SMT solver. In: Ramakrishnan, C.. R.., Rehof, Jakob (eds.) TACAS 2008. LNCS, vol. 4963, pp. 337–340. Springer, Heidelberg (2008). https://doi.org/10.1007/978-3-540-78800-3_24. https://api.semanticscholar.org/CorpusID:15912959

13. Santos, J.L., Kimmerlin, M.: Massive-scale deployments in cloud: the case of open-stack networking. In: 2018 IEEE International Conference on Cloud Engineering (IC2E), pp. 225–232 (2018)
14. Sindhu, G., Mtech, N.P., PavithraD., R.: Deploying a kubernetes cluster with kubernetes-operation (kops) on AWS cloud: Experiments and lessons learned. Int. J. Eng. Adv. Technol. (2020)
15. Wu, Z.: Design and implementation of cloud management platform based on open-stack (2019)
16. Yan, L., Rong, C., Zhao, G.: Strengthen cloud computing security with federal identity management using hierarchical identity-based cryptography. In: International Conference on Cloud Computing (2009), https://api.semanticscholar.org/CorpusID:12098812. https://api.semanticscholar.org/CorpusID:12098812
17. Zhang, R.: An automatic deployment mechanism based on cloud computing platform (2015)

Reliability Optimization Scheduling and Energy Balancing for Real-Time Application in Fog Computing Environment

Ruihua Liu[1], Huijuan Huang[2], Yulei He[2], Xiaochuan Guo[2], Can Yan[2], Junhao Dai[2], and Wufei Wu[2(✉)]

[1] School of Mathematics and Computer Science, Nanchang University, Nanchang, Jiangxi, China
`4161002100116@email.ncu.edu.cn`
[2] School of Information Engineering, Nanchang University, Nanchang, Jiangxi, China
`{41610021065,heyulei,416100220228,6105121102,daijunhao}@email.ncu.edu.cn,`
`wuwufei@ncu.edu.cn`

Abstract. Fog computing has the characteristics of stronger localized computing power and less data transmission load, thus better meeting the high energy efficiency, reliability, and real-time response requirements required by intelligent connected vehicle technology applications. Currently, research on fog computing task scheduling has become a hot topic, with existing research mainly focusing on low energy consumption or high real-time parallel task scheduling, which cannot meet the high reliability requirements in intelligent connected vehicle scenarios. Therefore, this paper establishes a fog computing task model based on Directed acyclic graph (DAG) to achieve accurate definition of energy, time and reliability. To achieve quantitative optimization of time and reliability indicators under energy constraints, a fog computing task scheduling algorithm was proposed and compared with existing scheduling algorithms. Then, the proposed algorithm is used to solve the DAG task list optimization problem based on fast Fourier transform (FFT) and Gaussian elimination (GE) structure. The experimental results show that compared with the existing ECLL method, ECLLRS has a more significant effect in satisfying the real-time and reliability of the system under the premise of limited energy budget.

Keywords: fog computing · energy constraint · reliability · task scheduling

1 Introduction

1.1 Background

With the development of information and communication technology (ICT), fog computing architecture provides high-performance computing resources for

ⓒ The Author(s), under exclusive license to Springer Nature Singapore Pte Ltd. 2024
C. Li et al. (Eds.): APPT 2023, LNCS 14103, pp. 180–200, 2024.
https://doi.org/10.1007/978-981-99-7872-4_11

applications such as intelligent networked vehicles. Task scheduling in fog computing environment has become a research hotspot in recent years [1]. Fog computing is an extended concept of cloud computing that focuses on managing data from sensors and edge devices, centralizing data, processing, and applications in network edge devices rather than storing it all in cloud data centers [2]. The main idea of fog computing is to add another layer of fog between the terminal device and the cloud data center (the network edge layer). This layer of fog directly processes and stores some data that does not need to be placed in the cloud. The existence of fog can greatly reduce the pressure of cloud computing and storage, improve efficiency and transmission rate, and reduce latency [3]. The fog calculation concept diagram is shown in Fig. 1.

Intelligent made cars (Intelligent Connected Vehicle, ICV) refers to the organic joint car networking and intelligent car, eventually alternative to operation of a new generation of cars. Intelligent connected vehicles are equipped with advanced on-board sensors, controllers, actuators and other devices, integrating modern communication and network technology to achieve intelligent information exchange and sharing between vehicles and people, roads, backstage and other intelligent information, focusing more on solving the core problems of safety, energy saving, environmental protection and other constraints on industrial development, and its own independent environmental perception ability [4]. The development focus is to improve vehicle safety, and in the information exchange and sharing link, the computer determines the processing order and the final execution position of the task is an important link to improve the high response and reliability of the networked vehicle [5].

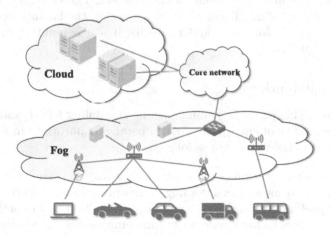

Fig. 1. Concept diagram of fog calculation.

Typically, a mobile application generated on the user equipment (UE) can be broken down into a number of tasks with priority constraints that can be arbitrarily complex [6]. Some typical models describe parallel applications with prioritized tasks, such as directed acyclic graphs (DAGs), hybrid DAGs (HDAGs), and task interaction graphs (TiGs), etc. [7–9]. Meanwhile, the tasks may have very different computing and communication requirements, and the existing research results of heterogeneous distributed systems can not directly adapt to the fog computing environment, which makes the problem more difficult to solve [10–12].

1.2   Motivation

With the increasing popularity of intelligent mobile user devices, people expect more and more devices to be able to undertake the operation of mobile applications with intensive farming and reading [13]. These applications typically consume a lot of energy, require a lot of computing power, and have strict latency constraints. However, terminals are usually resource-constrained, with limited computing power and batteries, making it impractical to run complex applications on them [14]. In fog computing, computing unloading can effectively improve the computing power and battery life of mobile devices. By offloading computous-intensive tasks to the mobile edge cloud (MEC) server, UE can perform more tasks in the same amount of time, thus demonstrating greater computing power [15]. In addition, by moving power-hungry tasks to MEC servers, the UE uses less energy to process the same set of tasks, resulting in longer battery life.

Most of the existing researches focus on real-time performance and low energy consumption optimization of the system [16], but lack of attention to the reliability of the system. Similarly, the results of existing fog computing task scheduling strategies are not as mature as those of common heterogeneous distributed systems, and there is still a lot of room for development. Therefore, considering the importance of safety of intelligent networked vehicles, the balance between task scheduling energy consumption and reliability in fog computing environment remains to be studied.

1.3   Our Contributions

The objective of this paper is to minimize the scheduling length and maximize application reliability of energy-constrained parallel applications in fog environment. Its main contributions are as follows:

- We propose a task allocation strategy under equal energy allocation scheme (LRSEC), allocating servers according to the optimal execution results of each node, and preliminarily realizes the accurate definition and quantification of reliability indexes in fog environment, and emphasizes the feasibility of this scheme.
- We propose an energy-constrained task scheduling algorithm with priority constraints to further improve the performance of task scheduling (ECLLRS), which attempts to quantify and optimize the time and reliability indexes under energy constraints.

- Experiments are conducted based on fast Fourier transform (FFT) and Gaussian elimination (GE) structure structural model, and the results verify that the algorithm has different degrees of optimization under different indexes under the constraint of energy consumption compared with the existing methods.

The rest of this paper is organized as follow. Section 3 introduces the four models of the system, Sect. 4 introduces the problems to be solved, Sect. 5 proposes the LRSEC algorithm, and on the basis of this proposed ECLLRS algorithm. Section 6 verifies the ECLLRS and LRSEC algorithms and Sect. 7 concludes this study.

2 Related Works

Reliability is defined as the probability that the execution is successful, and the commonly used reliability model was presented in [17]. Liu et al. [18,19] focused on minimizing cost through efficient task allocation on heterogeneous embedded systems, while meeting the response time target of end-to-end distributed function. From the perspective of application function security, minimizing resource cost under reliability objective is a hot topic in recent years.

In [20], Xie et al. proposed the MRCRG method, which assumed that each unassigned follow-up task assigned the maximum reliability value to the processor to minimize the cost of resource consumption. However, the proposed algorithm was not mature enough in the partition stage of reliability index. On this basis, Yuan et al. [21] proposed an algorithm RGAGM to define two kinds of geometric mean values of tasks and functions respectively, and preassign reliability values based on geometric mean values to unassigned tasks, so as to effectively ensure reliability objectives and reduce resource consumption costs.

Because of the difference between clouds and fog, there are more possibilities and diversity for task unloading between clouds and fog. Minh et al. [4] proposed a new context-aware service decentralization mechanism to conduct analytical experiments and comprehensive evaluations of real Intelligent Transportation system (ITS) services in a fog environment, providing delay-sensitive services while optimizing virtualized resources. Khan et al. [22] proposed the MSCA algorithm to solve the task unloading problem in 5G IoHT cloud computing environment with the aid of fog. However, when fog cannot complete task calculation independently, heavy computation will be transferred from fog to cloud, and when to transfer task from fog to cloud is a big decision. In [2], MTFCT algorithm proposed by Jindal et al. solves this problem, but it is only theoretically proposed algorithm.

Li [16] strictly defined two problems of optimal computational unloading under energy constraints and optimal computational unloading under time constraints. Further work is done to study the computational unloading under the background of traditional task scheduling [23]. At the same time, considering the new characteristics and unique features of fog computing, the author divides the application program based on DAG into levels, and scheduled tasks step by step to eliminate the priority constraints carried by application. In the intra-level scheduling method, greedy algorithm is adopted to ensure that the response time of all MEC servers in the same level, which realizes the optimization of response time index. Although the minimum total response time of the application is guaranteed, the quantification and optimization of the reliability value of the application cannot be guaranteed.

The limitation of these most advanced algorithms [16,23] is that they only support DVFS and local energy-saving scheduling algorithms to optimize real-time performance, but cannot ensure that the reliability of applications is also relatively optimized, thus limiting the overall effect. In this study, we aim to achieve joint optimization of real-time performance and reliability under energy constraints through priority constrained scheduling algorithm.

3   Establishment of Model

3.1   Application Model

Suppose a terminal has a mobile application $Q=(L,\prec)$ as follows: There is a task list $L=(t_1,t_2,...,t_m)$, where each task t_i is specified as $t_i=(r_i,d_i)$, where r_i is the computational requirement of t_i (that is, the computational amount, measured by the number of billion processor cycles or billion instructions to execute (BI)), d_i is the communication requirement of t_i (that is, the amount of data communicated between the terminal UE and the server MEC, Measured in millions of bits (MB). There are also precedence constraints between tasks, which are specified in partial order.

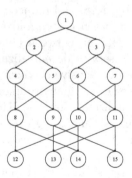

Fig. 2. FFT example at level 5.

If $t_1 \prec t_2$, then t_1 is the predecessor of t_2, and t_2 can only start executing after t_1 has finished executing. A mobile application with priority constrained tasks can be described by a Directed Acyclic Graph (DAG), Fig. 2 and Fig. 3 show the classical DAG based on FFT and GE structures respectively. The

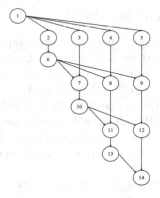

Fig. 3. GE example at level 8.

vertices in G are m tasks in L. The arc in G is defined as follows: there is an arc from t_1 to t_2 if and only if $t_1 \prec t_2$.

In order to verify the validity of our algorithm, we used a model of FFT and GE structure in this study.An obvious feature of the task structure in the FFT structure model is that the number of nodes in each layer decreases as it gets closer to the upper layer.In the GE architecture model, the number of nodes in each layer increases as you get closer to the upper layer, and at the same time each layer has a single task as a layer.

3.2   The Computation and Communication Models

For the list L of tasks to be executed, each task can be executed on the terminal or MEC. Suppose there is a server queue n composed of N heterogeneous servers MEC, that is, N = $(MEC_1, MEC_2,..., MEC_n)$. Each MEC_j has a computational speed s_j processor execution speed, measured in GHz or billion instructions per second ($1 \leq j \leq n$), which cannot be changed by a terminal UE. The execution time of task t_i includes computation time and communication time.

If t_i is directly executed locally on the terminal without being sent out, the calculation speed $s_{0,i}$ is determined by the terminal. Since the local execution does not generate communication time, the time (in seconds) calculated on the terminal is:

$$ct_i = r_i/s_{0,i}(1 \leq i \leq m). \tag{1}$$

If t_i is sent to a MEC_j and executed remotely on MEC_j, then the computation time of t_i on MEC_j is r_i/s_j. For t_i, the communication speed between UE and MEC_j is $c_{i,j}$(that is, the data transmission rate, measured in millions of bits per second that can be transmitted), which can be determined by UE. For t_i, the communication time (in seconds) between UE and MEC_j is $d_i/c_{i,j}$. The execution time of t_i on MEC_j is:

$$ct_i = r_i/s_j + d_i/c_{i,j}(1 \leq i \leq m, 1 \leq j \leq n). \tag{2}$$

3.3   The Power Consumption Models

Consider the terminal side first, there are two components in the UE's power consumption P in watts used for calculation, namely the dynamic power consumption and the static power consumption. The dynamic component P_d is usually expressed as $P_d = \xi s_0{}^\alpha$, where ξ and α are constants determined by the technique. The static component P_s is usually a constant. We obtain $P = Pd + Ps = \xi s_0{}^\alpha + Ps$. For all cases $1 \le i \le m$, when t_i is not unloaded and is directly executed on UE at the computation speed of $s_{0,i}$, its power consumption is $P_0 = \xi s_{0,i}{}^\alpha + P_s$, and the energy consumption of t_i calculated on UE (in joules) is:

$$E_i = P(r_i/s_{0,i}) = ((\xi s_{0,i}{}^\alpha + Ps)/s_{0,i})r_i. \tag{3}$$

At the same time, it should be noted that in addition to computing energy consumption, there will also be communication energy consumption. Let be the transmission power (in watts) of the transmission task t_i from UE to MEC_j ($1 \le j \le n$). Communication speed (e.g. data transfer rate, 1 s in the number of millions of bits that can travel) from problem to MEC_j:

$$c_j = w_j \log_2(1 + P_{t,j} g_j/(I_j + \sigma_j{}^2)) \tag{4}$$

where w_j represents the channel band width, g_j is the channel gain between UE and MEC_j, is the interference to the communication channel caused by other devices transmitting data to the same MEC, and is the background noise power. To make a summary of it, the following formula can be obtained:

$$c_j = w_j \log_2(1 + P_{t,j}\beta_j). \tag{5}$$

So the energy consumption for communication (measured by Joules) of t_i from the UE to $MEC_j i$ is

$$E_i = P_{t,j}(d_i/c_{i,j}) = (2^{c_{i,j}/\omega_j} - 1)/(\beta_j c_{i,j})d_i. \tag{6}$$

3.4   The Reliability Models

The ISO26262 standard states that the probability of random hardware failure (that is, instantaneous failure) follows a certain distribution. In general, the occurrence of transient faults of tasks based on DAG function follows the Poisson distribution.

Set λ_j to represent the constant failure rate per time unit of the processor MEC_j, then the reliability $RE_{i,j}$ of t_i executed on MEC_j in its execution time can be expressed as:

$$RE_{i,j} = e^{-\lambda_j T_{i,j}}. \tag{7}$$

Therefore, the minimum and maximum reliability values of each task can be obtained from the following formula:

$$RE_{\max}(ti) = \max_{MEC_j \in N} RE_{i,j}, \tag{8}$$

$$RE_{\min}(ti) = \min_{MEC_j \in N} RE_{i,j}. \tag{9}$$

The reliability value of function G is the product of the reliability values of all tasks, namely:

$$RE(G) = \prod_{t_i \in L} (RE(t_i, MEC_{proc}(t_i))). \tag{10}$$

Specifies the server MEC to which task t_i is assigned to execute. Meanwhile, the minimum and maximum reliability values of function G can be obtained as follows:

$$RE_{\max}(G) = \prod_{t_i \in L} RE_{\max}(ti), \tag{11}$$

$$RE_{\min}(G) = \prod_{t_i \in L} RE_{\min}(ti). \tag{12}$$

Assuming that the reliability goal of the application is $RE_{goal}(G)$, then $RE_{goal}(G)$ must fall within the scope of $RE_{\min}(G)$ and $RE_{\max}(G)$:

$$RE_{\min}(G) \leq RE_{goal}(G) \leq RE_{\max}(G). \tag{13}$$

In terms of task transfer, network reliability is an appropriate performance indicator, defined as the probability of the amount of data that can be successfully transferred through the terminal. If $task_i$ is determined to be unloaded to MEC_j during scheduling, the network reliability of transmission $task_i$ is affected by the transmission time of data transmission quantity (d_i) in $task_i$, and its influence function is linearly correlated with the transmission time.

4   Problem Definitions

In this section, we formally define the optimization problems that this article addresses.

$L = (t_1, t_2, ..., t_m)$ is the independent task list of DAG-based application $G = (L, \prec)$ generated on terminal UE $= (s_0, \xi, P_s)$, where $t_i = (r_r, d_i)$ $(1 \leq i \leq m)$. Suppose there are n edge servers in a fog environment MEC: MEC_1, MEC_2, ..., MEC_n, $MEC_j = (s_j, c_j, W_j)$ for all $j \in [1, n]$. The task scheduling policy S of mobile application G is to determine when (the starting time of execution) and where (the location of execution : UE or MEC) each task t_i executes the task $(1 \leq i \leq m)$.

R_j is defined as the total execution requirement (r_i sum) of all tasks t_i transmitted to MEC_j $(0 \leq j \leq n)$ (UE is defined as MEC_0 for easy reading and understanding), and D_j is the total data (d_i sum) of tasks transmitted to MEC_j $(1 \leq j \leq n)$. In terms of time, the execution time of L_0 is $T_0 = R_0/s_0$ (local execution does not consider the transmission time), the execution time of L_j is $T_j = R_j/s_j + D_j/r_j$, and the total time of L is T:

$$T = \frac{R_0}{s_0} + \sum_{j=1}^{n} \left(\frac{R_j}{s_j} + \frac{D_j}{c_j}\right). \tag{14}$$

In terms of energy consumption, since local execution does not consider transmission energy consumption, the energy consumed by executing L_0 is

$$E_0 = T_0 * P_0 = (R_0/s_0) * P_0 = ((\xi s_0^\alpha + P_s)/s_0) * R_0, \qquad (15)$$

and since MEC execution does not consider execution energy consumption. Therefore, the energy consumed by executing L_j is

$$E_j = (D_j/c_j) * P_{i,j} = (P_{i,j}/c_j) * D_j, \qquad (16)$$

then the total energy consumption of L, E is the sum of the energy consumption of UE and all MEC_s, as shown below:

$$E = (\frac{\xi s_0^\alpha + P_s}{s_0})R_0 + \sum_{j=1}^{n}(\frac{2^{c_j/w_j} - 1}{\beta_j c_j})D_j. \qquad (17)$$

In terms of task reliability, the reliability required to perform L_j is $RE_j = e^{-\lambda(R_j/s_j)}$, then the total reliability of L is the product of task reliability (execution reliability multiplied by communication reliability) on all MEC_s (UE set MEC_0), i.e.

$$RE = \prod_{j=0}^{n} e^{-\lambda(R_j/s_j)} = e^{-\lambda(\sum_{j=0}^{n} R_j/s_j)}. \qquad (18)$$

Now we are ready to define a combinatorial optimization problem for task scheduling optimization in fog computing.

Problem:(Scheduling optimization of task execution time and reliability with energy constraints). Given a DAG-based task list L = $(t_1, t_2, ..., t_m)$, where $t_i = (r_i, d_i)$ $(1 \leq i \leq m)$, a UE = (ξ, α, P_s), n MEC: MEC_1, MEC_2, ..., MEC_n, $MEC_j = (s_j, c_j, W_j)$ $(1 \leq j \leq n)$, and energy constraints $\tilde{E}$. To explore a task scheduling strategy S = $(L_0, L_1, ..., L_n)$, and determine the computation speed s_0 and communication speed c_j $(1 \leq j \leq n)$, so that RE is maximized and E does not exceed $\tilde{E}$.

5   Algorithm

5.1   Task Scheduling Without Priority Constraints

At present, many methods have been proposed in the research of prepower allocation. In constant velocity method, all the tasks with the same calculating speed, but the idea is not feasible in the fog to calculate, because UE can't change the calculation speed of MEC, this leads to a UE can't control terminal MEC task execution time, made all the tasks in the time methods, such as have the same execution time this goal cannot be reached. Therefore, in this paper, we adopt the equal energy method that all tasks consume the same energy, namely : E/m.

Algorithm 1. List reliability optimization schedule under the energy constraint(LRSEC)

Input: $L=(t_1,t_2,...,t_m)$,where $t_i=(r_i,d_i)$,for all $1{\leq}i{\leq}m$, $UE=(\xi,\alpha,P_s)$,MEC_j = (s_j,c_j,W_j),for all $1{\leq}j{\leq}$n,and $\widetilde{E}$.

Output: A computation offloading strategy and a power allocation strategy such that E does not exceed $\widetilde{E}$ and RE is maximized.

1: Initialize data of servers and tasks;
2: **for** $(j = 0; j \leq n; j + +)$ **do**
3:    $RE_j \leftarrow 1$;
4: **end for**
5: **for** $(i = 1; i \leq m; i + +)$ **do**
6:    **for** (each MEC_j) **do**
7:       Schedule t_i on MEC_j at time T_j;
8:       $REsum_j \leftarrow$ the overall reliability of t_i;
9:    **end for**
10:    $REcompare \leftarrow RE_j * REsum_0$;
11:    $j' \leftarrow 0$;
12:    **for** $(j = 1; j < n; j + +)$ **do**
13:       **if** $RE_j * REsum_j < REcompare$ **then**
14:          $j' \leftarrow$ subscript of the current RE_j;
15:       **end if**
16:    **end for**
17:    $RE_j' \leftarrow RE_j' + REsum_j'$;
18: **end for**
19: $RE = RE_1 * RE_2 * RE_3 * RE_4 * ... * RE_n$;
20: **return** S, s_0, c_j for all j $\in [1, n]$,and RE;

In Algorithm 1, the energy constrained scheduling algorithm of equal-energy method without priority constraints is presented, namely, the energy constrained List reliability Optimization scheduling (LRSEC).

The key idea of **Algorithm 1** is to assign tasks to UE or other MECs with the same energy allocation so that the total reliability RE decreases at the slowest rate (its initial value is 1). Line (1) first initializes and enters server and task data. The reinitialization variable RE_j represents the total reliability of the tasks performed by each mec (lines (2)–(4)). The For loop in lines (7)–(10) transfers the first task to all MECs at time 0 (line (8)) and records the calculated reliability as RE_j (line (9)), where RE_j contains the calculated reliability and communication reliability of the task (for all $0 \leq j \leq$ n, We set UE $= MEC_0$ for easy computation).

In line (11), we first set the product value of RE_0 and $REsum_0$ owned by UE as $REcompare$ as the standard quantity to judge the degree of optimization. The for loop in lines (13) through (17) traverses all MECs except UE, doing the following in each loop:

1) Determine whether the product of RE_j and $REsum_j$ of the current MEC is less than $REcompare$(Line (14)).

2) If so, assign the subscript j of the current MEC_j to line (15) of j' (j' is initially set to 0, which is UE's subscript).

When the loop is complete, you get the maximum value of $MEC_{j'}$ for the total reliability of the current task. Then loop through the other tasks (lines (5)–(19)) to get the total reliability of the task list and calculate the unload strategy corresponding to the reliability.

LRSEC algorithm's time complexity is $O(|M| \times |N|)$, within the time $O(|M|)$ all tasks scheduling, in $O(|N|)$ time calculating minimum time consumption value of each task.

5.2   Analysis

In this section, the lower limit of calculation speed s0, lower limit of energy consumption E_0, and upper limit of calculation time T_0 on UE can be obtained through calculation in advance [16].

Theorem 1. *For UE, the following conditions must exist:* $s_0 \geq s_0^*$ *and* $s_0^* = (P_s/\xi(\alpha-1))^{1/\alpha}$, *therefore,* $E_0 \geq E_0^* = R_0 P_s^{1-1/\alpha} \xi^{1/\alpha} \alpha/(\alpha-1)^{1-1/\alpha}$, *and* $T_0 \leq T_0^* = R_0(\xi(\alpha-1)/P_s)^{1/\alpha}$.

Theorem 2. E_j *is an increasing function of* c_j, *and when* c_j *approaches 0,* E_j *approaches* $E_j^* = ln2/(w_j\beta_j) D_j$. *Hence, the following conditions must exist:* $E_j > E_j^* = (ln2/w_j\beta_j) D_j$, *and* $T_j > T_j^* = R_j/s_j$, *for all* $1 \leq j \leq n$.

5.3   Task Scheduling with Priority Constraints

We divide the directed acyclic graph into v levels, $L = (L_1, L_2, ..., L_v)$, so that all tasks in L_1 are initial tasks (that is, no successor tasks). If the number of nodes on the longest path from an initial task to task ti is l, then level l contains task t_i ($1 \leq l \leq v$). Let L_1 denote the set of tasks in level l, then for all $1 \leq l \leq v$, we have $L = L_1 \cup L_2 \cup ... \cup L_v$. Step by step scheduling method is adopted, that is, tasks in L are scheduled step by step. This means that tasks in L_2 can only start executing when all tasks in L_1 have been completed. Each phase of the schedule is carried out separately, independently and separately.

At the same time, in order to make the data integration traversal and the result intuitive, the task set in L_x is classified ($x \in [1,v]$) in the case of stepwise scheduling, and divided into n+1 sublists $L_x = (Lx_0, Lx_1, Lx_2, ..., Lx_n)$, so that all tasks in Lx_0 are directly executed on UE, and all tasks in Lx_j are transferred and executed on MEC_j ($j \in [1,n]$). The summary of policy rules is defined as $S = (L_0, L_1, ..., L_n)$, where L_j refers to the set of tasks ($i \in [1,n]$) performed by MEC_j in all levels.

Since all tasks at the same level are independent of each other, we can use the proposed algorithm 1 to schedule independent tasks. Meanwhile, the initial energy constraintE_x of a single level is determined as follows: let $R_x = \sum_{t_i \in L_x} ri$

and $D_x = \sum_{t_i \in L_x} d_i$, for all $1 \le l \le v$. Then, the following formula can be obtained through [16] :

$$E_x = R_x P_s^{1-1/\alpha} \xi^{1/\alpha} \frac{\alpha}{(\alpha-1)^{1-1/\alpha}} + (\frac{\ln 2}{\min_{1 \le j \le n}(\omega_j \beta_j)}) D_x. \tag{19}$$

Algorithm 2 . Energy-Constrained Level-by-Level reliability optimization Scheduling(ECLLRS)

Input: $G = (L, \prec)$ with $L = (t_1, t_2, ..., t_m)$, where $t_i = (r_i, d_i)$, for all $1 \le i \le m$, $UE = (\xi, \alpha, P_s)$, $MEC_j = (s_j, c_j, W_j)$, for all $1 \le j \le n$, and $\widetilde{E}$.

Output: A computation offloading strategy and a power allocation strategy such that E does not exceed $\widetilde{E}$, T is relative minimized and RE is maximized.

1: **for** (x = 1;x $\le$ v;x++) **do**
2:    $RE_x \leftarrow LRSEC(H_x, E_x)$;
3: **end for**
4: $remainingE \leftarrow \widetilde{E} - (E_1 + E_2 + ... + E_v)$;
5: $E' \leftarrow (\widetilde{E} - (E_1 + E_2 + ... + E_v))/K$;
6: **while** ($remainingE > 0$) **do**
7:    **if** ($remainingE \le E'$) **then**
8:       $\Delta E \leftarrow remainingE$;
9:    **else**
10:       $\Delta E \leftarrow \gamma E'$,where $\gamma \in [0.5, 1.0]$;
11:    **end if**
12:    $x' \leftarrow$ indexmax $_{1 \le x \le v}(LRSEC(H_x, E_x + \Delta E) - RE_x)$;
13:    $E_x' \leftarrow E_x' + \Delta E$;
14:    $R_x' \leftarrow LTSEC(H_x', E_x')$;
15:    $remainingE \leftarrow remainingE - \Delta E$;
16: **end while**
17: $T \leftarrow T_1 + T_2 + ... + T_v$;
18: $RE \leftarrow RE_1 * RE_2 * ... * RE_v$;
19: **return** S, s_0, c_j for all j $\in [1, n]$, T and RE;

In Algorithm 2, an energy constrained scheduling algorithm with priority constraints is proposed, namely, hierarchical reliability optimal scheduling under the energy constraints (ECLLRS).

The key problem in step energy constrained scheduling is to determine how to reasonably allocate a given energy threshold to v levels. Let $H(L_1, E_1)$ be the total reliability value when algorithm 1 is applied to the first layer task L_1 under energy limit E_1.

At the beginning of the algorithm operation, each level of L_1 uses the H algorithm with initial energy (the calculation of initial energy is referred to equation (19)), which allocates E_1 (lines (1)–(3)) for scheduling calculation. Then, the remaining energy is obtained from the energy threshold E' minus the sum of the energy consumption of each layer $(E_1 + E_2 + ... + E_v)$ to get (line (4)), and the obtained value is divided by K to get E'(line (5)), which is the upper limit of the energy value of a single distribution. The while loop in lines 6–16 has to be repeated slightly more than K times. In each repetition, the following operation is performed:

1) Determine ΔE, which is a random number γ times E', where γ is evenly distributed at $[0.5, 1.0]$ (line (10)).
2) In lines (11)–(12), the variation amplitude of level reliability when different levels receive additional energy (ΔE) is $H(L_1, E_1) - H(L_1, E_1 + \Delta E)$, and the level with the largest optimization is determined .
3) In lines (13)–(18), the extra energy ΔE is allocated according to the result obtained in the previous step. The above while loop ends after all remaining energy is allocated (line (6)). The overall reliability of the mobile application is $H(L_1, E_1) * H(L_2, E_2) * ... * H(L_v, E_v)$, and the overall time of the application under the current reliability condition can also be obtained .

The time complexity of ECLLRS is $O(K \times |M| \times |N|)$, where scheduling all tasks can be done in $O(|M| \times |N|)$ time, the distribution of the remaining energy costs $O(K \times |M| \times |N|)$ Time.

6   Experiment

6.1   Parameter Setting

A fog computing environment with one UE and n $= 7$ MEC_s is considered. The UE is configured with the following parameters: $\xi = 0.1$, $\alpha = 2.0$, $P_s = 0.05$ W. The MEC_j is configured with the following parameters: $s_j = 3.1 - 0.1j$ BI/second, $w_j = 2.9 + 0.1j$ MB/second, $\beta_j = 2.1 - 0.1j$ Watts^{-1}, for all $1 \leq j \leq n$.

Task calculation and communication requirements are randomly generated. The r_i is independent and uniformly distributed over the range $[1.5, 5.0]$. Correspondingly, d_i is also independent and equally evenly distributed in the range $[1.0, 3.0]$.

6.2   Comparative Experiments Under Different Transmission Error Rates

The purpose of this experiment is to observe the overall reliability and real-time optimization effect of FFT and GE based applications under the same number of tasks and different transmission error rate intervals. The experimental parameters in this section use the parameters in Subsect. 6.1.

The directed acyclic graph based on FFT structure and GE structure application program is generated by using the parameters mentioned in the previous section, and several comparative experiments are carried out under the premise of the same number of servers and the same number of tasks. The communication error rate is set according to the linear relationship between task communication reliability and transmission time class, set three intervals as representative

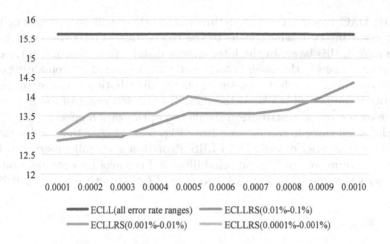

Fig. 4. Execution time comparison of FFT structures (all error rate ranges).

0.01%–0.1%, 0.001%-0.01% and 0.0001%-0.001%, and the results are shown in
Fig. 4, 5, 6 and 7.

It can be seen from both Fig. 4 and Fig. 6 that the computational response
time of ECLLRS algorithm under FFT and GE structure models is better than
that of ECLL algorithm, which is consistent with the overall expectation of the
experiment. The optimization effect of the algorithm in FFT structure model
ranges from 8.01% to 17.06%, and in GE structure model from 11.36% to 24.45%,
and the response time increases gradually with the increase of task transmission
error rate. However, there is some reverse trend in the error rate range of 0.001%-
0.01% in GE structure, which is speculated to be caused by the particularity of
GE structure.

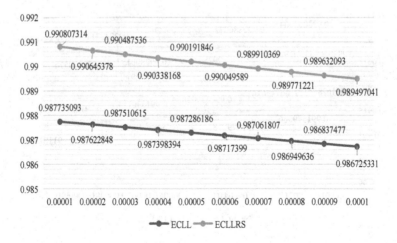

Fig. 5. Reliability comparison of FFT structures (0.001%-0.01% error rate).

In the DAG based on GE structure model, there will be a single task as a layer at every interval, which leads to the calculation of only the lower limit of a single task in this layer. In the later energy distribution environment, because the number of tasks in this layer is too small and the size of the remaining energy slice, the optimization effect of a single energy distribution is not stronger than that of other multi-task levels, so the final distribution result of the floor will be the same as the initial distribution result (no optimization effect).

At the same time, it can be seen from Fig. 5 and Fig. 7 that under the condition of fixed number of tasks, ECLLRS algorithm is overall superior to ECLL algorithm in terms of application reliability, and the average optimization effect of FFT structure model is 0.1455% and that of GE structure model is 0.2932%.

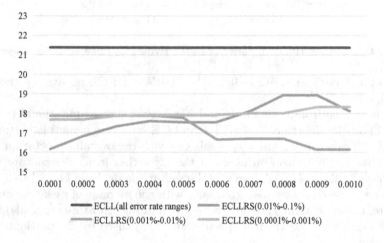

Fig. 6. Excution time comparison of GE structures (all error rate ranges).

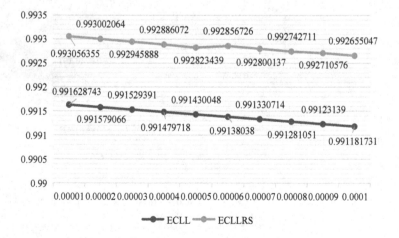

Fig. 7. Reliability comparison of GE structures (0.001%–0.01% error rate).

6.3 Comparative Experiment Under Different Number of Tasks

The purpose of this experiment is to observe the overall reliability and real-time optimization effect of FFT and GE based applications under the same transmission error rate interval and different number of tasks. The experimental parameters in this section use the parameters in Subsect. 6.1.

Under the same number of servers and different number of tasks, we conducted several experiments on the directed acyclic graph of FFT structure and GE structure generated in the previous section (the number of experimental tasks of FFT structure is 15, 39, 95,223,511, and the number of experimental tasks of GE structure is 14, 27, 35, 54,154). In the experiment, the transmission error rate is set to range from 0.01% to 0.1%. The simulation results of FFT structure application program are shown in Table 1, 2 and 3, and the simulation results of GE structure application program are shown in Table 4, 5 and 6.

Table 1. Experimental Data for Energy-Constrained Level-by-Level Scheduling (Total application time - FFT).

error rate	15	39	95	223	511
0.001%	6.729440309	9.905387101	10.85058808	15.48664380	18.86995269
0.002%	6.729440309	9.96462299	10.85058808	15.48664380	18.86995269
0.003%	6.729440309	9.96462299	10.85058808	15.48664380	18.86995269
0.004%	6.729440309	9.96462299	10.85058808	15.48664380	18.86995269
0.005%	6.729440309	9.96462299	10.85058808	15.48664380	18.86995269
0.006%	6.729440309	10.48419344	11.12426817	15.67704809	19.28312955
0.007%	6.729440309	10.48419344	11.12426817	15.67704809	19.28312955
0.008%	6.729440309	10.48419344	11.12426817	15.67704809	19.28312955
0.009%	6.729440309	10.48419344	11.12426817	15.67704809	19.28312955
0.010%	6.729440309	10.48419344	11.12426817	15.60439699	19.28312955
Control group	9.409484288	12.09314996	15.25300687	36.97735914	85.92192500

As can be seen from Table 1, when the number of tasks and parameters are the same, ECLLRS algorithm has a significant improvement in the total response time of the application compared with ECLL algorithm. The overall optimization effect is between 13.304%-78.0383%, and the greater the number of tasks, the more significant the optimization effect.

As can be seen from Table 2 and 3, in the FFT structural model, ECLLRS algorithm also has an intuitive improvement in the overall reliability compared with ECLL algorithm. The smaller the transmission error rate is, the more significant the optimization effect is, and the overall optimization effect ranges from 0.072% to 0.698%. At the same time, the optimization effect decreases with the increase of the number of computing tasks.

Table 2. Experimental Data for Energy-Constrained Level-by-Level Scheduling (Experimental group application reliability - FFT).

error rate	15	39	95	223	511
0.001%	0.996942188	0.995098896	0.988763852	0.960826021	0.904455326
0.002%	0.996920158	0.994857076	0.988673977	0.960503486	0.903680112
0.003%	0.996898128	0.994615312	0.988584111	0.960181058	0.902914099
0.004%	0.996876099	0.994373604	0.988494252	0.959858737	0.902165473
0.005%	0.99685407	0.994131953	0.988404402	0.959536524	0.901425918
0.006%	0.996832042	0.993890359	0.988314559	0.959214418	0.900696642
0.007%	0.996810014	0.993648821	0.988224724	0.958892419	0.899979695
0.008%	0.996787986	0.993407339	0.988134898	0.958570528	0.899275433
0.009%	0.996765959	0.993165914	0.988045079	0.958248744	0.89858664
0.010%	0.996743932	0.992924545	0.987955268	0.957927066	0.89790415

Table 3. Experimental Data for Energy-Constrained Level-by-Level Scheduling (Compare group application reliability - FFT).

error rate	15	39	95	223	511
0.001%	0.996217945	0.993291117	0.982148492	0.956149236	0.9033258
0.002%	0.996196831	0.993234229	0.982026384	0.955792438	0.902525395
0.003%	0.996175717	0.99317888	0.981907137	0.955443913	0.901725698
0.004%	0.996154603	0.993127083	0.981788988	0.955106421	0.900926707
0.005%	0.99613349	0.993077974	0.981670979	0.954772348	0.900128421
0.006%	0.996112377	0.993030681	0.98155501	0.954443438	0.899330841
0.007%	0.996091265	0.992983707	0.981439882	0.954122772	0.898533964
0.008%	0.996070153	0.992936736	0.981327159	0.953808804	0.897737792
0.009%	0.996049042	0.992889767	0.981215586	0.95349843	0.896942322
0.010%	0.99602793	0.9928428	0.981104534	0.953195335	0.896147555

As can be seen from Table 4, when the number of tasks and other parameters are the same, the optimization effect of ECLLRS algorithm in GE model is not as significant as that of FFT model compared with ECLL algorithm, and the number of tasks to be executed will only show better scheduling effect when the number of tasks to be executed is in a specific interval (the sub-interval determined by multiple experiments is [27,54]). The scheduling optimization effect basically fluctuates in the range of 5%-12%, which is caused by the special structure of GE model (subsection B).

Table 4. Experimental Data for Energy-Constrained Level-by-Level Scheduling (Total application time - GE).

error rate	14	27	35	54	135
0.001%	12.01486565	16.08391497	19.41808497	21.21150432	35.30960003
0.002%	12.01486565	16.04563502	18.00561638	21.21150432	35.31312679
0.003%	12.01486565	16.04957164	17.90797669	21.20875001	35.21045173
0.004%	12.01486565	14.7232746	17.87559062	21.90324894	35.12290436
0.005%	12.01486565	14.72496127	17.86227043	21.44372675	35.06617427
0.006%	12.01486565	14.72891988	17.85645764	21.30104841	35.04328888
0.007%	12.01486565	14.73424505	17.8545009	21.01072187	35.03393247
0.008%	12.01486565	14.73995102	17.81106102	20.9627853	35.03180945
0.009%	12.01486565	14.74613978	17.5380364	21.66762031	35.0333124
0.010%	12.01486565	14.75103909	17.40914545	22.16118764	34.83113352
Control group	11.19551055	16.08905857	17.97676662	23.96358911	34.06946943

Table 5. Experimental Data for Energy-Constrained Level-by-Level Scheduling (Experimental group application reliability - GE).

error rate	14	27	35	54	135
0.001%	0.996967606	0.99463972	0.993013444	0.988902978	0.973602714
0.002%	0.996943299	0.994704703	0.993095273	0.988844635	0.973370064
0.003%	0.996918993	0.994685008	0.993059125	0.988786294	0.973222091
0.004%	0.996894688	0.994671725	0.993010666	0.988727957	0.973227879
0.005%	0.996870383	0.994644231	0.992958612	0.988669624	0.97307319
0.006%	0.996846078	0.994609747	0.992905144	0.988611294	0.972887108
0.007%	0.996821774	0.994574651	0.992850952	0.988552967	0.972688298
0.008%	0.99679747	0.994538776	0.992818797	0.988494643	0.972484449
0.009%	0.996773167	0.994501488	0.992806829	0.988436323	0.972276417
0.010%	0.996748865	0.994465111	0.992788496	0.988378005	0.972072007

As can be seen from Table 5 and 6, ECLLRS algorithm has better optimization effect than ECLL algorithm in a specific interval, and the scheduling optimization effect fluctuates between 0.025%–0.1%, and the optimization effect becomes more obvious with the increase of the number of tasks. However, once the task order is too large, the calculation result becomes worse.

Table 6. Experimental Data for Energy-Constrained Level-by-Level Scheduling (Compare group application reliability - GE).

error rate	14	27	35	54	135
0.001%	0.996616697	0.994189678	0.992623048	0.988056576	0.983630332
0.002%	0.996603619	0.994149333	0.992573647	0.987956023	0.983515232
0.003%	0.996590541	0.99410899	0.992524249	0.987870504	0.983400145
0.004%	0.996577464	0.994068648	0.992474852	0.98781349	0.983285071
0.005%	0.996564386	0.994028307	0.992425458	0.987761875	0.98317001
0.006%	0.996551309	0.993987968	0.992376067	0.987702651	0.983054962
0.007%	0.996538232	0.993947631	0.992326677	0.987631292	0.982939928
0.008%	0.996525155	0.993907295	0.99227729	0.987553276	0.982824907
0.009%	0.996512078	0.99386696	0.992227906	0.987473089	0.982709898
0.010%	0.996499001	0.993826627	0.992178523	0.987392513	0.982594903

7   Conclusion

This study aims to maximize the overall reliability of the application in fog computing environment, while meeting the real-time requirements of the system under energy constraints. Therefore, a reliability optimization scheme without priority constraints under energy constraints is proposed. In addition, through experiments, we find that considering the relationship between response time and reliability can greatly improve scheduling performance when designing scheduling algorithms for systems with priority constraint structure, which is not taken into account by existing algorithms. Therefore, this paper proposes a step - by - step reliability optimization scheduling algorithm under energy constraint.

This scheduling was an early static deployment design where the execution plan was known before the task was executed to meet specific requirements, such as task-structured application processors. Considering the real-time performance and reliability of the application is very effective for improving the performance of the algorithm.

The experimental results show that compared with the existing ECLL method, ECLLRS has a more significant effect in satisfying the real-time and reliability of the system under the premise of limited energy budget. At the same time, this paper only considers the application simulation of FFT and GE structure models, and the application model experiments of different structures and parameters need to be carried out in the future.

Therefore, in future work, we will explore methods to generalize task structure in various abstract models, and try to find scheduling algorithms suitable for different task structures, while realizing real-time and reliable multi-objective optimization on this basis. In addition, further research on energy allocation in scheduling algorithm is another research direction in the future.

Acknowledgment. This work was supported in part by the National Natural Science Foundation of China under Grant No. 62002147, and the China Postdoctoral Science Foundation under Grant No. 2020TQ0134. The authors would like to express their gratitude to the anonymous reviewers for their constructive comments, which have helped to improve the quality of the paper.

References

1. Hong, H.-J.: From cloud computing to fog computing: unleash the power of edge and end devices. In: 2017 IEEE International Conference on Cloud Computing Technology and Science (CloudCom), pp. 331–334. Hong Kong, China (2017). https://doi.org/10.1109/CloudCom.2017.53
2. Jindal, R., Kumar, N., Nirwan, H.: MTFCT: a task offloading approach for fog computing and cloud computing. In: 2020 10th International Conference on Cloud Computing, Data Science & Engineering (Confluence), Noida, India, pp. 145–149 (2020). https://doi.org/10.1109/Confluence47617.2020.9058209
3. Garcia, J., Simó, E., Masip-Bruin, X., Marín-Tordera, E., Sánchez-López, S.: Do we really need cloud? estimating the fog computing capacities in the city of Barcelona. In: 2018 IEEE/ACM International Conference on Utility and Cloud Computing Companion (UCC Companion), Zurich, Switzerland, pp. 290–295 (2018). https://doi.org/10.1109/UCC-Companion.2018.00070
4. Minh, Q.T., Kamioka, E., Yamada, S.: CFC-ITS: context-aware fog computing for intelligent transportation systems. IT Prof. **20**(6), 35–45 (2018). https://doi.org/10.1109/MITP.2018.2876978
5. Xue, D.: Task offload optimization management of networked vehicles in edge computing environment. In: 2nd International Signal Processing, Communications and Engineering Management Conference (ISPCEM). Montreal, ON, Canada, vol. 2022, pp. 38–42 (2022). https://doi.org/10.1109/ISPCEM57418.2022.00014
6. Ra, M.-R., Sheth, A., Mummert, L., Pillai, P., Wetherall, D., Govindan, R.: Odessa: enabling interactive perception applications on mobile devices. In: Proceedings of the 9th International Conference on Mobile Systems, Applications, and Services, pp. 43–56, Bethesda, Maryland (2011)
7. Xiao, X., Xie, G., Li, R., Li, K.: Minimizing schedule length ofenergy consumption constrained parallel applications on heterogeneous distributed systems. In: Trustcom/BigDataSE/ISPA, 2016 IEEE, pp. 1471–1476. IEEE (2016)
8. Niu, J., Liu, C., Gao, Y., Qiu, M.: Energy efficient task assignment with guaranteed probability satisfying timing constraints for embedded systems. IEEE Trans. Parallel Distrib. Syst. **25**(8), 2043–2052 (2014)
9. Naghibzadeh, M.: Modeling and scheduling hybrid workflows of tasks and task interaction graphs on the cloud. Future Generation Comput. Syst. **65**, 33–45 (2016)
10. Tang, Z., Qi, L., Cheng, Z., Li, K., Khan, S.U., Li, K.: An energy-efficient task scheduling algorithm in DVFS-enabled cloud environment. J. Grid Comput. **14**(1), 55–74 (2016)
11. Xie, G., Jiang, J., Liu, Y., Li, R., Li, K.: Minimizing energy consumption of real-time parallel applications using downward and upward approaches on heterogeneous systems. IEEE Trans. Ind. Inform. **13**, 108–1078 (2017)
12. Xie, G., Zeng, G., Li, R., Li, K.: Energy-aware processor merging algorithms for deadline constrained parallel applications in heterogeneous cloud computing. IEEE Trans. Sustain. Comput. **2**(2), 62–75 (2017)

13. Kwak, J., Kim, Y., Lee, J., Chong, S.: DREAM: dynamic resource and task allocation for energy minimization in mobile cloud systems. IEEE J. Sel. Areas Commun. **33**(12), 2510–2523 (2015)
14. Cuervo, E., et al.: Maui: making smartphones last longer with code offload. In: Proceedings of the 8th International Conference on Mobile Systems, Applications, and Services, San Francisco, CA, USA, pp. 49-62 (2010)
15. Contini, D., De Castro, L.F.S., Madeira, E., Rigo, S., Bittencourt, L.F.: Simulating smart campus applications in edge and fog computing. In: 2020 IEEE International Conference on Smart Computing (SMARTCOMP), Bologna, Italy, pp. 326–331 (2020). https://doi.org/10.1109/SMARTCOMP50058.2020.00072
16. Li, K.: Heuristic computation offloading algorithms for mobile users in fog computing. ACM Trans. Embed. Comput. Syst. (TECS) **20**(2), 1–28, 11 (2021). Article no. 11
17. Shatz, S.M., Wang, J.P.: Models and algorithms for reliability-oriented task-allocation in redundant distributed-computer systems. IEEE Trans. Reliab. **38**(1), 16–27 (1989)
18. Liu, J., Li, K., Zhu, D., Han, J., Li, K.: Minimizing cost of scheduling tasks on heterogeneous multicore embedded systems. ACM Trans. Embed. Comput. Syst. (TECS) **16**(2), 36 (2016)
19. Liu, J., Zhuge, Q., Gu, S., Hu, J., Zhu, G., Sha, E.H.M.: Minimizing system cost with efficient task assignment on heterogeneous multicore processors considering time constraint. IEEE Trans. Parallel Distrib. Syst. **25**(8), 2101–2113 (2014)
20. Xie, G., Chen, Y., Liu, Y., Wei, Y., Li, R., Li, K.: Resource consumption cost minimization of reliable parallel applications on heterogeneous embedded systems. IEEE Trans. Ind. Inform. **13**(4), 1629–1640 (2016)
21. Yuan, N., Xie, G., Li, R., Chen, X.: An effective reliability goal assurance method using geometric mean for distributed automotive functions on heterogeneous architectures. In: 2017 IEEE International Symposium on Parallel and Distributed Processing with Applications and 2017 IEEE International Conference on Ubiquitous Computing and Communications (ISPA/IUCC), pp. 667–674 (2017). https://doi.org/10.1109/ISPA/IUCC.2017.00105
22. Khan, S.M.T., Barik, L., Adholiya, A., Patra, S.S., Brahma, A.N., Barik, R.K.: Task offloading scheme for latency sensitive tasks In: 5G IOHT on Fog Assisted Cloud Computing Environment, 3rd International Conference for Emerging Technology (INCET). Belgaum, India, vol. 2022, pp. 1–5 (2022). https://doi.org/10.1109/INCET54531.2022.9824699
23. Li, K.: Scheduling precedence constrained tasks for mobile applications in fog computing. IEEE Trans. Serv. Comput. **16**, 2153–2164 (2022)

Federated Classification for Multiple Blockchain Systems

Zhanyi Yuan[1], Fuhui Sun[2(✉)], Yurong Cheng[1], and Xiaoyan Wang[2]

[1] School of Computer Science and Technology, Beijing Institute of Technology, Beijing, China
yrcheng@bit.edu.cn
[2] Information Technology Service Center of People's Court, Chennai, Tamil Nadu, India
sunfh6732@163.com

Abstract. As blockchain technology continues to advance, it has become increasingly utilized as a fundamental infrastructure in various industries, such as business, justice, and finance. The widespread adoption of blockchain technology has created a pressing need for effective information exchange among different institutional units within blockchain networks. Fortunately, cross-chain technology has emerged as a promising solution for enhancing information interaction among diverse blockchain units. In this study, we examined several variables and employed multiple methodologies to validate our proposed hypothesis. Using cross-chain technology, we introduce a blockchain cross-chain federated learning framework (BCFL) that facilitates the interaction and mutual verification of data and parameters across different blockchains. This approach enables federated learning without the need to collect or coordinate model weights on a central server, while also enhancing the security of the federated learning process through the consensus algorithm mechanism of blockchains. Finally, we conduct a comparative analysis of the effectiveness of BCFL compared to traditional machine learning and centralized federated learning.

Keywords: Blockchain Cross-Chain · Federated Learning · Machine-learning · Blockchain

1 Introduction

In recent years, cross-chain blockchain technology [4] has emerged as a significant research topic. With the maturation and advancement of contemporary big data technology and related applications, the practical effectiveness of blockchain technology in diverse industries has been demonstrated, leading to its increasing utilization as a fundamental infrastructure by numerous industries and government units. As a result, the importance of blockchain infrastructure has become increasingly prominent, and the exchange of data and information between blockchain networks has emerged as a key challenge to be addressed.

© The Author(s), under exclusive license to Springer Nature Singapore Pte Ltd. 2024
C. Li et al. (Eds.): APPT 2023, LNCS 14103, pp. 201–209, 2024.
https://doi.org/10.1007/978-981-99-7872-4_12

In contemporary business scenarios, distinct companies or organizations in various industries often establish their own dedicated blockchain systems to store their business data. At times, these disparate organizations engage in collaborative business ventures, sharing each other's data to jointly train a collaborative model for mutual benefit.

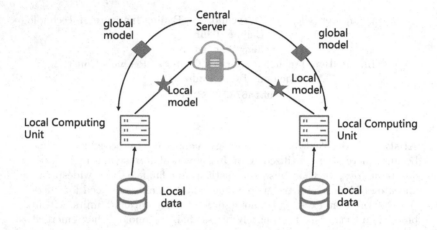

Fig. 1. Centralized federated learning's architecture

In order to tackle the challenge of collaborative training, Google has proposed a federated learning framework referred to as centralized FL [6,9]. In this framework, each computing unit generates locally trained gradients and weights, which are then submitted to a central server for computation, thereby avoiding the possibility of leaking the original data. As illustrated in Fig. 1, the centralized FL's exchange is facilitated through the intermediary of a central server, which aggregates all of the local model updates and takes an ensemble average to produce a global model update. Subsequently, each computing unit downloads the global model update and computes its next local update until the global model training is completed.

The advent of cross-chain blockchain technology [8,10] represents a novel approach to addressing the challenge of data and information transfer between distinct blockchain networks. Cross-chain technology has its roots in the earliest atomic transfers (atomic transfers) [1,3] concept, which represents the most fundamental technical solution for atomic digital assets. As cross-chain technology has continued to mature, various cutting-edge cross-chain methodologies have emerged, including notary schemes [12], relay-chains [2], and sidechain [11], which represent the current mainstream cross-chain technologies.

Notably, some organizations with data sensitivity concerns, such as banks and courts, store their data on their individual blockchains to ensure data traceability and security. Consequently, the use of the centralized FL framework for federated learning is rendered impractical, as it involves the transfer of data to computational units for training, thereby increasing the risk of data tampering. Furthermore, the central server of the centralized FL framework is also susceptible to attacks, which may permit attackers to reverse-engineer certain data information by exploiting the trained gradients or weights.

This paper proposes a blockchain cross-chain federated learning framework to tackle this issue. This framework involves two or more distinct institutions, and multiple computing units from each institution jointly maintain the corresponding institution's blockchain, with these units also owning the associated data. During the blockchain cross-chain federated learning, these computing units upload the weights and gradients generated during training to their own institution's blockchain, and concurrently invoke the cross-chain smart contract to retrieve weights and gradients from the collaborating institution's blockchain. These retrieved weights and gradients are then merged and updated to the blockchain of the current institution. Subsequently, the computing units obtain the updated weights, and repeat these steps until the local model training is completed. In summary, the contributions of this paper are as follows:

1. Proposing a federated learning framework between blockchains.
2. Utilizing cross-chain technology to share model weights and ensuring data security and traceability.

2   Related Work

Previous research has extensively studied the combination of blockchain and federated learning. In [5], the authors propose a blockchain-based approach to federated learning, called BlockFL, which utilizes a blockchain network as a substitute for the central server to upload trained weights onto a central blockchain while providing verification and incentives. In addition, the authors analyze the delay caused by the blockchain network in BlockFL. They consider adjusting the block generation rate, namely the POW difficulty, to minimize the delay and increase the system's practicality. In [14], the authors further improved the federated learning system using blockchain by proposing the DeepChain model, in which each participant individually encrypts their trained model gradient before uploading it. Before uploading the encrypted gradient, participants are required to provide proof of correctness to ensure the accuracy of gradient collection and parameter updates. This approach enhances the security and privacy of the federated learning process in blockchain applications. In [7], the author constructed data models and shared them through federated learning instead of sharing raw data, thus transforming the data sharing problem into a machine learning problem. This approach ensured that data owners could exercise further control over access to data sharing while integrating differential privacy into federated learning to further protect data privacy.

However, the above works all use a single blockchain to replace a central server, which is limiting in certain specific scenarios. Some institutions store their data on their own blockchain to ensure data security and traceability. Our proposed BCFL framework is designed to address this situation where data participating in federated learning is stored on a blockchain.

3   Architecture and Operation

In this section, we elaborate in detail on the architecture(as shown in Fig. 2) and operation flow of the BCFL framework, which involves two operations: federated learning and cross-chain operation.

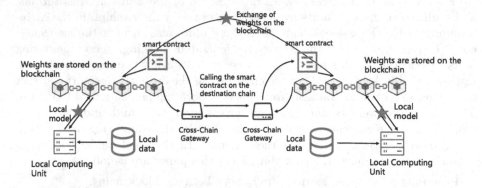

Fig. 2. Cross-Chain Federated Learning's architecture

FL Operation in BCFL: The federated learning process comprises a series of institutions, each equipped with its own blockchain $B = \{1, 2, \cdots, N_B\}$ and data samples to train local models, N_B represents the total number of institutions participating in BCFL. The computational units of each institution located beneath the chain calculate and upload the model weights to the respective blockchain. The i-th institution with a blockchain B_i owns a set of data samples D_i with $|D_i| = N_i$, D_i is the dataset owned by each blockchain institution and $|D_i| = N_i$ is the total amount of data held by this institution.

In this study, federated learning is employed to tackle the task of binary classification between blockchains of different institutions, considering a set of the entire blockchains' data samples $\mathcal{D} = \cup_{i=1}^{N_B} D_i$ with $|\mathcal{D}| = N_D$, $\mathcal{D}$ is the dataset of all institutions participating in the federated learning, and N_D is the total amount of data from all institutions participating in the federated learning. The k-th data sample $d_k \in \mathcal{D}$ is given as $d_k = \{x_k, y_k\}$ for a n-dimensional column vector $x_k \in \mathbb{R}^d$ and a scalar value $y_k \in \{0, 1\}$. Its objective is to minimize the loss function of the global weight vector $w \in \mathbb{R}^d$. The loss function $f(w)$ is chosen as the Binary Cross Entropy (BCEloss): $f(w) = \frac{1}{N_D} \sum_{i=1}^{N_B} \sum_{d_k \in D_i} f_k(w)$, where $f_k(w) = y_k \cdot \log x_k + (1 - y_k) \cdot \log(1 - x_k)$. Each blockchain B_i institution trains their model by stochastic gradient descent, and the local weights for all blockchains are aggregated using distributed approximate Newton methods. For each epoch, each institution that owns the blockchain B_i iterates the model for N_i times. At the t-th local iteration of the ℓ-th epoch, the local weight $w_i^{(t,\ell)} \in \mathbb{R}^d$ is calculated from the following equation:

$$w_i^{(t,\ell)} = w_i^{(t-1,\ell)} - \frac{\beta}{N_i} \left([\nabla f_k(w_i^{(t-1,\ell)}) - \nabla f_k(w^{(\ell)})] + \nabla f(w^{(\ell)}) \right)$$

where β is the learning rate, $w^{(\ell)}$ represents the global weight at the ℓ-th epoch, and $\nabla f(w^{(\ell)}) = \frac{1}{N_D} \sum_{i=1}^{N_B} \sum_{d_k \in \mathcal{D}_i} \nabla f_k(w^{(\ell)})$. So the global weight at the ℓ-th epoch is:

$$w^{(\ell)} = w^{(\ell-1)} + \sum_{i=1}^{N_B} \frac{N_i}{N_D} \left(w_i^{(\ell)} - w^{(\ell-1)} \right) \qquad (1)$$

In the vanilla federated learning framework, each computational unit uploads weights and gradients to the central server. However, in our proposed BCFL framework, the parameters and gradients are first stored on the institution's own blockchain, and then each institution calls each other to obtain updated data of the model. In the following sections, we will provide a detailed explanation of these steps.

Cross-Chain operation in BCFL: In our proposed BCFL framework, the parameters and gradients generated by each computational unit's local training in each epoch will first be stored on the institution's own blockchain after being verified by the consensus algorithm. In the distributed ledger, each block can be divided into two parts: the header and body parts. The body part is used to store the locally trained weights and gradients denote as $\left(w_i^{(\ell)}, \{\nabla f_k (w^{(\ell)})\}_{d_k \in \mathcal{D}_i} \right)$, i.e., the updated of the blockchain B_i at ℓ-th epoch, as well as the number of epochs ℓ and the time $T_{local,i}^{(\ell)}$ of local training of the blockchain institution. The header section primarily stores information related to the previous block and the output of the consensus algorithm.

To facilitate the transfer of model updates between blockchains with different structures (e.g., Ether and Hyperledger Fabric), we have standardized the data format for cross-chain transactions. Figure 3 shows the unified data format that we have designed (Table 1).

Table 1. Cross-chain transaction data format

Parameter	Description
From	The launch chain's id
To	The destination chain's id
Index	Cross-chain transaction number
Content	Including cross-chain model updates

We begin by assigning numbers to the blockchains participating in BCFL. "From" denotes the blockchain ID that needs to send model updates to other blockchains in this epoch, "To" denotes the blockchain ID that needs to receive model updates in this epoch. "Index" is the serial number of each cross-chain transaction, used to ensure the transaction's orderly transmission and verify if it has been lost. "Content" contains the model updates generated by each blockchain in this epoch, and it is used to provide data for the subsequent cross-chain update of the model. After packaging the cross-chain parameters or weight data into a standardized format, as shown in Fig. 2, the cross-chain gateway routes the cross-chain transaction to the corresponding destination blockchain.

Then, the blockchain throws a cross-chain transaction that invokes the smart contract on the target blockchain, which is used to push model updates to the blockchain that initiated the transaction. At the same time, the cross-chain gateway listens and captures the cross-chain transactions thrown by the blockchains it is responsible for. Upon arrival of the cross-chain transaction at the cross-chain gateway, the transaction's orderliness is validated by the gateway based on its "Index". Once verified by the gateway, the transaction is routed to the appropriate blockchain via the distributed hash table maintained by the gateway, which tracks the interconnections between blockchains. After the cross-chain transaction arrives at the target blockchain, the smart contract on the blockchain is called. This smart contract first obtains the data containing the model updates in the blockchain and transforms it into a unified data format, and then sends it to the blockchain that initiated the transaction. Once the initiating blockchain receives the model updates sent by other blockchains, it stores them on its own blockchain and sends them to its corresponding computing unit for aggregation.

One-epoch BCFL operation: As shown in Fig. 2, the BCFL operation of blockchain B_i in ℓ-th epochs is described as the following steps:

1. Compute local model updates: The blockchain's Calculation units B_i calculate the model update in ℓ-th epoch according to equation (1) in T_{local}^{ℓ}.
2. Model updates uploaded to the blockchain: After verification by the consensus algorithm of the local blockchain, the model updates $\left(w_i^{(\ell)}, \{\nabla f_k\left(w^{(\ell)}\right)\}_{d_k \in \mathcal{D}_i}\right)$ of ℓ-th epoch are stored in the blockchain with a waiting time of T_{upload}^{ℓ}.
3. Calling the smart contract on the destination blockchain: The blockchain throws a cross-chain transaction to invoke the smart contract on the target blockchain through the cross-chain gateway, and the time consumed during this process is denoted as T_{call}^{ℓ}.
4. Get model updates on the target blockchain: The target blockchain pushes updates of the model stored on its own chain to the blockchain that initiated the call. The time required is T_{push}^{ℓ}.
5. Update local models: After receiving the model updates from the target blockchain, the blockchain stores and sends them to the corresponding computing unit. The local computing unit aggregates the received model updates with Eq. (1) for the next epoch training, which takes T_{agg}^{ℓ} time.

This process continues until the local model converges, i.e., $|w^{\ell} - w^{\ell-1}| \le \varepsilon$. The communication time required for each epoch is $T_{total}^{\ell} = T_{local}^{\ell} + T_{upload}^{\ell} + T_{call}^{\ell} + T_{push}^{\ell} + T_{agg}^{\ell}$.

In our proposed BCFL framework, model updates are exchanged through cross-chain technology, while model aggregation and training are performed locally, and verified on the blockchain. This not only ensures the security of model parameters but also makes the data traceable, which satisfies specific business scenarios.

4   Experimental Results and Analysis

4.1   Datasets and Setup

In order to validate the feasibility of our proposed approach, we conducted experiments on a real dataset, which is the Breast Cancer dataset from UCL. This database contains microscopic biopsy images of benign and malignant breast tumors, with a total of 569 samples, 30 input variables, and 2 classifications.

Regarding the blockchain aspect, we chose to use BCOS and Hyperledger Fabric for cross-chain operations, and the WeCross [13] cross-chain gateway was utilized.

4.2   Analysis of Results

The receiver operating characteristic (ROC) curve is commonly used to illustrate the classification performance of a model. In this study, we evaluated the accuracy of the model using the area under the ROC curve (AUC) and presented the AUC of the models obtained through federated learning under different modes, as well as the time required for model training to be completed.

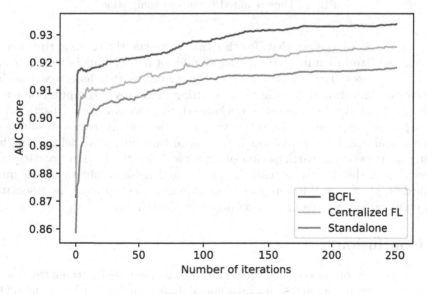

Fig. 3. Test AUC

Figure 4 illustrates the AUC scores of models trained under different modes at various iteration numbers. It can be observed from the figure that the AUC scores of BCFL and centralized federated learning are comparable, both converging around 0.92. In contrast, the AUC performance of single machine learning is relatively lower than the above two approaches due to the lack of additional data for learning.

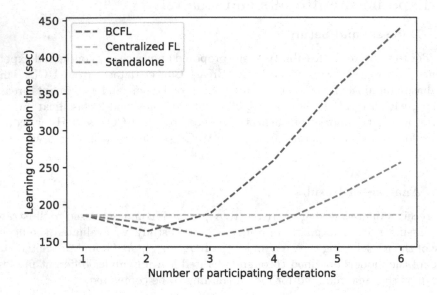

Fig. 4. Time required for model completion

From Fig. 5, we can see that, for the same datasets, the running time generally decreases and then increases as the number of participants in the federated learning increases. The reason for this phenomenon is that federated learning performs computation simultaneously, resulting in improved computation speed while the total data set remains unchanged. As the number of participants increases, the communication cost between parties also increases, resulting in longer model training time.Although the completion time of model training has slightly increased, the participation of multiple federated learning participants has expanded the data scale, enabling each participant to obtain higher quality models. Moreover, this approach also addresses security concerns associated with cooperative training of data on multiple blockchains.

5   Conclusion

In this paper, we proposed a blockchain cross-chain federated learning framework to address some application scenarios where data is stored on the blockchain. Our approach improves model quality while ensuring data security and traceability. The numerical results demonstrate that our proposed approach slightly sacrifices time efficiency but still yields high-quality models. These results indicate the effectiveness of our proposed framework.

In future work, we will consider more factors to speed up the model training time of BCFL, such as optimizing our proposed framework by taking into account transaction scheduling on the blockchain, fast processing of cross-chain transactions, and other related factors.

References

1. Borkowski, M., McDonald, D., Ritzer, C., Schulte, S.: Towards atomic cross-chain token transfers: State of the art and open questions within tast. Distributed Systems Group TU Wien (Technische Universit at Wien), Report 8 (2018)
2. Cao, L., Song, B.: Blockchain cross-chain protocol and platform research and development. In: 2021 International Conference on Electronics, Circuits and Information Engineering (ECIE), pp. 264–269. IEEE (2021)
3. Deshpande, A., Herlihy, M.: Privacy-preserving cross-chain atomic swaps. In: Bernhard, M., et al. (eds.) FC 2020. LNCS, vol. 12063, pp. 540–549. Springer, Cham (2020). https://doi.org/10.1007/978-3-030-54455-3_38
4. Hameed, K., Barika, M., Garg, S., Amin, M.B., Kang, B.: A taxonomy study on securing blockchain-based industrial applications: an overview, application perspectives, requirements, attacks, countermeasures, and open issues. J. Ind. Inf. Integr. **26**, 100312 (2022)
5. Kim, H., Park, J., Bennis, M., Kim, S.L.: On-device federated learning via blockchain and its latency analysis. arXiv preprint arXiv:1808.03949 (2018)
6. Konečný, J., McMahan, H.B., Ramage, D., Richtárik, P.: Federated optimization: distributed machine learning for on-device intelligence. arXiv preprint arXiv:1610.02527 (2016)
7. Lu, Y., Huang, X., Dai, Y., Maharjan, S., Zhang, Y.: Blockchain and federated learning for privacy-preserved data sharing in industrial IoT. IEEE Trans. Industr. Inf. **16**(6), 4177–4186 (2019)
8. Lys, L.: Security and reliability of cross-chain exchanges. (Sécurité et fiabilité des échanges inter-blockchain). Ph.D. thesis, Sorbonne University, Paris, France (2022). https://tel.archives-ouvertes.fr/tel 03847642
9. McMahan, B., Moore, E., Ramage, D., Hampson, S., y Arcas, B.A.: Communication-efficient learning of deep networks from decentralized data. In: Artificial intelligence and statistics, pp. 1273–1282. PMLR (2017)
10. Ou, W., Huang, S., Zheng, J., Zhang, Q., Zeng, G., Han, W.: An overview on cross-chain: mechanism, platforms, challenges and advances. Comput. Networks **218**, 109378 (2022)
11. Singh, A., Click, K., Parizi, R.M., Zhang, Q., Dehghantanha, A., Choo, K.K.R.: Sidechain technologies in blockchain networks: an examination and state-of-the-art review. J. Netw. Comput. Appl. **149**, 102471 (2020)
12. Sun, Y., Yi, L., Duan, L., Wang, W.: A decentralized cross-chain service protocol based on notary schemes and hash-locking. In: 2022 IEEE International Conference on Services Computing (SCC), pp. 152–157. IEEE (2022)
13. WeBankFinTech: Wecross: Open source cross-blockchain protocol (2019). https://doi.org/github.com/WeBankFinTech/WeCross
14. Weng, J., Weng, J., Zhang, J., Li, M., Zhang, Y., Luo, W.: Deepchain: auditable and privacy-preserving deep learning with blockchain-based incentive. IEEE Trans. Dependable Secure Comput. **18**(5), 2438–2455 (2019)

Towards Privacy-Preserving Decentralized Reputation Management for Vehicular Crowdsensing

Zhongkai Lu, Lingling Wang[✉], Ke Geng, Jingjing Wang, and Lijun Sun

School of Information and Science Technology, Qingdao University of Science and Technology, No. 99 Songling Road, Qingdao 266061, Shandong, China
{luzhongkai,gengke}@mails.qust.edu.cn,
{wanglingling,wangjingjing,lijunsun}@qust.edu.cn

Abstract. The reputation of a vehicle is a critical role in most vehicular crowdsensing applications, which incentivizes vehicles to perform crowdsensing tasks by submitting high-quality data and getting remunerated accordingly. Unfortunately, existing centralized reputation systems are vulnerable to collusion attacks, and decentralized approaches are susceptible to Sybil attacks. What's worse, both of them have privacy leakage and fairness problems. To address these issues, we take advantage of various cryptographic primitives and the blockchain technology to present a privacy-preserving decentralized reputation management system. Specifically, a compact traceable ring signature is proposed to provide identity privacy protection and resist Sybil attacks. To ensure fairness, the quantification of data quality is fulfilled by combining the rating feedback mechanism with comprehensive updating factors. Additionally, our system allows the reputation update automatically through smart contracts deployed on the consortium blockchain. The authenticity of the reputation can be verified by a zero-knowledge proof when a vehicle shows its reputation. Finally, a proof-of-concept prototype system by Parity Ethereum is presented. Extensive security analysis and implementations demonstrate the feasibility and efficiency of the proposed system.

Keywords: Vehicular crowdsensing · Reputation management · Privacy-preservation · Fairness

1 Introduction

Vehicular crowdsensing (VCS) [1] is an emerging paradigm where vehicles use onboard sensors to collect and share real time traffic information [2] without establishing extra dedicated infrastructure, which can help drivers to improve users' driving experiences and offer other services on roads. Due to these benefits, some practical VCS applications have emerged [3]. In a VCS application,

Z. Lu, K. Geng, J. Wang and L. Sun—Contributed equally.

© The Author(s), under exclusive license to Springer Nature Singapore Pte Ltd. 2024
C. Li et al. (Eds.): APPT 2023, LNCS 14103, pp. 210–240, 2024.
https://doi.org/10.1007/978-981-99-7872-4_13

reputation systems are used to maintain and update the reputation value, which is usually the benchmark for reliable worker selection, rewards calculation [4], and user-level classification, etc. Therefore, a well-designed reputation system is essential for VCS applications.

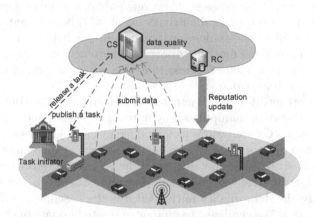

Fig. 1. A centralized reputation system in vehicular crowdsensing

Existing reputation systems in VCS are mainly divided into two types: centralized and decentralized systems. As shown in Fig. 1, in a centralized system, vehicles are assigned with the reputation according to their past behaviours in the former crowdsensing tasks. A central server CS is in charge of sensing tasks distribution and data collection. A reputation center RC is responsible for storing and updating the reputation. Although centralized reputation systems provide some benefits and conveniences, they simultaneously suffer from a single point of failure and collusion attacks. Specifically, RC is the Achilles's heel of the reputation systems. Dishonest vehicles may collude with compromised RC to increase their reputations illegally, or take advantage of system's vulnerabilities to keep large reputations even when they provide poor-quality data [5], thereby incurring fairness problem and revenue losses to VCS applications.

Blockchain, as the most popular distributed technology, has enabled a decentralized reputation system. Although blockchain originally acts as a fundamental technology in Bitcoin, it has been recently adopted in many domains, such as Artificial Intelligence [6], Internet of Things [7], etc. We could achieve a public and tamper-resistant record of the reputation as well as the open access to the reputation by using blockchain. However, existing blockchain-based reputation systems [8–11], do not apply well to the VCS scenario. Specifically, most existing systems are put forward under E-commerce environment, in which the reputation is evaluated in different ways. Besides, in the existing works, almost all reputation opinions and interaction histories are stored on the blockchain, and most interactions of the system are performed via the consensus protocol, where consensus efficiency is a problem that affects communication efficiency. In a VCS scenario, it is inefficient and impractical for vehicles to frequently access the blockchain. So, it is highly desirable to develop a decentralized reputation system that minimizes the frequency of access to the blockchain. Due to the "open" nature, another problem the decentralized system faces is the Sybil attacks [12]. To avoid Sybil attacks, identity authentication is essential to perform each time when a vehicle submits a message. However, public key authentication might lead to privacy disclosure (e.g., the drivers' identity, driving speed, and driving path), which may affect the vehicle's willingness to participate in a task.

As a consequence, these motivate our research problem to be *"how to evaluate and update the reputation with fairness in a VCS scenario without revealing any privacy of participating vehicles?"*

Though important, it is still a non-trivial task to solve the above challenges in a decentralized system manipulated by untrusted vehicles and attakers. First, authentication in a VCS scenario is usually done by edge nodes, such as roadside units (RSUs), which are usually curious about the privacy of vehicles. Moreover, the reputation is attached to the identity of the vehicle, so recording all reputations on the ledger directly will also result in privacy disclosure. Second, it is not easy to quantify the data quality fairly, which is the baseline of evaluating the reputation. Third, it is a challenge to guarantee trusted update of the reputation while reducing interactions with the blockchain.

To address the privacy issue, anonymous mechanisms, i.e. vehicles generate multiple pseudonyms or anonymous credentials, can protect the vehicles' privacy. However, simply leveraging pseudonyms for vehicle's anonymity cannot resolve this issue, which is vulnerable to de-anonymization attacks [13]. Moreover, anonymous credentials are often issued by a trusted party, and may incur a lot of additional computation and storage overhead [14], which are not suitable to our system. Hence, we present a privacy-preserving mechanism to protect vehicles' privacy while resisting sybil attacks. Moreover, we accomplish a trustworthy anonymous record on the blockchain and apply a zero-knowledge proof to bind the reputation to a specific vehicle.

To address the fairness issue, it is necessary to update the reputation according to the data quality impartially, which requires that the system knows whether the data provided by a vehicle is authentic or not and to what extent is it accurate. Rating feedback mechanisms [15] is a straightforward solution to quantify data quality, which allow other users in the proximity to provide a feedback rating (viz., positive, negative, or neutral) for a submitted data. However, existing works [16,17] either utilize the proportion of only positive feedback to measure data quality, or lack comprehensive consideration about the data structure, leading to unsatisfactory quantitative results and unfairness. So, we present a new reputation evaluating method by modifying existing rating feedback mechanisms. To address the trusted reputation update, we propose a solution for vehicles to update their reputation trustworthily by generating corresponding proofs. Our solution needs not frequent accesses to the blockchain.

To summarize, the main contributions of this paper are as threefolds.

- We propose a privacy-preserving decentralized reputation management system for VCS (PPDR-VCS). Specifically, as for the privacy-preserving mechanism, we construct a traceable ring signature by leveraging non-interactive zero-knowledge proof [18] and the Schnorr signature scheme [19] to fulfill anonymous authentication in a VCS scenario. The proposed system guarantees the vehicles' privacy and also resists Sybil attacks existing in decentralized systems.
- We propose two updating factors to evaluate the reputation impartially. Thereinto, the truthfulness-based factor is quantified by leveraging the rating feedback mechanism where both the total number and ratio of feedback is taken into account for the fairness. The time-based factor ensures the validity of the data to meet the time-sensitive VCS scenario. Moreover, we design smart contracts to automatically update the reputation value once a task finishes, and generate zero-knowledge proofs to confirm the trusted reputation update.
- We make theoretical security and privacy analysis of the proposed system and verify the feasibility of the proof-of-concept prototype by implementing it on Parity Ethereum, and provide a comprehensive evaluation of the performance.

The remainder of this paper is organized as follows. In Sect. 2, we present the system model, threat model, and design goals. Some preliminaries are in Sect. 3. In Sect. 4, we propose PPDR-VCS. Subsequently, privacy and security analysis and performance evaluation are presented in Sect. 5 and 6. Then, we review some related works in Sect. 7. Finally, Sect. 8 draws the conclusion.

2 Problem Statement

In this section, we formalize the system model of PPDR-VCS, threat model and the underlying assumptions, and also identify our design goals.

2.1 System Model

Our PPDR-VCS system is a reputation management system auxiliary to the VCS. The system model mainly consists of four entities: Blockchain network, fog servers, vehicles and certificate authority as shown in Fig. 2.

Blockchain network refers to the consortium blockchain of fog servers in different traffic areas. It has a permissioned ledger, which is shared with the legitimate fog servers, and serves for the reputation management system. The reputation update is executed in a verifiable manner according to smart contracts without a central third party.

Fog servers act as consensus nodes (i.e. validators) in the consortium blockchain. Fog servers can be RSUs, base stations, or any other edge devices equipped with powerful computation and storage capabilities, and they verify and seal new blocks for maintaining the blockchain network. Moreover, fog servers are also in charge of identity and message authentication, data quality calculation and sensory data aggregation. The local fog server maintains a

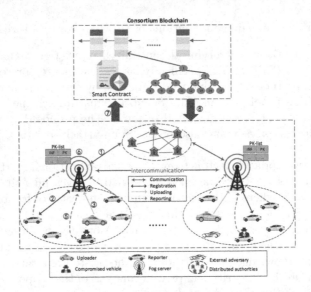

Fig. 2. System model

public key list (called PK-list), including public keys of the registered vehicles in the vicinity of it at a certain time. We assume that fog servers can only be accessed by vehicles from nearby location (e.g., by means of radio networks). Besides, transaction fees and mining rewards involved in the blockchain network are provided as the incentives for supporting fog servers.

Vehicles are divided into two categories: *Uploader* and *Reporter*. An *Uploader* always generates a data report with regard to some traffic information in a VCS task. Meanwhile, *Reporters* will give their feedback on this report to the fog server. In our system, we assume that there are plenty of *Reporters* submitting feedback on a data report. Once a data report is received by the fog server, it will reject another data report with the same traffic information. In this paper, we focus on the privacy protection and reputation update of the *Uploader* not the *Reporters*. Before diving into the details of our system, we firstly give a formal definition of the reputation of vehicles.

Definition 1 (Reputation of Vehicles): The reputation of a vehicle V_i, denoted as R_i, is the synthesized evaluation of the quality of vehicles to complete crowdsensing tasks. The reputation value ranges from 0 to 1. The bigger the reputation value, the better the past behavior of the vehicle, and the more likely it is able to complete the crowdsensing task with high quality. A vehicle can obtain an initial reputation R_i^0 before its first VCS task, and it can apply for the initial reputation only once. Without loss of generality, R_i^0 is set as 0.3 in our system.

Certificate Authority (*CA*) is responsible for generating system parameters and cryptographic keys for vehicles and fog servers. The *CA* receives registration requests from vehicles and fog servers. It also assists the initial reputation distribution and the anonymity revoke of misbehaved vehicles. The *CA* maintains a list called IR-list, which records the public keys of vehicles who have applied for the initial reputation before. This is to prevent malicious vehicles from applying for initial reputation multiple times when their reputation is lower than the initial value. It does not conflict with the decentralized feature of our system because it stays offline when vehicles are performing crowdsensing tasks and the reputation are updated.

In our model, we assume task initiators, who are interested in some traffic information, have released crowdsensing tasks via the fog servers or the blockchain network. Winning vehicles are selected to upload the data report by some worker selection algorithms in VCS, and they will get rewards that are subject to their reputation values after the task. The details of the above procedure are not our concern. In this paper, we only focus on the decentralized reputation management system with privacy preservation. The workflow is as follows: ① Vehicles and fog servers register with the CA. They get their public keys, and legitimate vehicles get their initial reputation. ② Selected vehicles ($Uploaders$) submit encrypted sensory data along with a ring signature. ③ Local fog server decrypts and verifies the data, and then broadcasts the traffic message to nearby vehicles. ④ $Reporters$ in the proximity submit their feedback reports about this message. ⑤ Local fog server calculates the updating factors. ⑥ Local fog server runs the deployed smart contracts to update the reputation of the vehicle. Consortium fog servers verify all transactions about the reputation updating and build a new block periodically. ⑦ Vehicles update their reputation by accessing the blockchain.

2.2 Threat Model and Assumptions

We assume that the CA is fully trusted, and no adversary can breach it. Fog servers are honest-but-curious, i.e. they follow the protocol, but are also curious about others' privacy by launching passive attacks. Dishonest vehicles may be selfish or malicious, who may forge their reputation values and try to get private information of other vehicles. A dishonest $Uploader$ is a legitimate vehicle that is selected to submit data reports, and a dishonest $Reporter$ is also a legitimate vehicle that generates correct feedback reports intermittently, with the purpose of maximizing their reputation value via some illegal ways.

Malicious attackers are either compromised vehicles or external adversaries that may eavesdrop to violate vehicles' privacy or intentionally act to cripple the reputation system. A compromised $Reporter$ may destroy the system by submitting incorrect feedback of a submitted data generated by an honest $Uploader$, or in collusion with a compromised $Uploader$. In our system, we assume that the number of honest $Reporters$ is always higher than the number of compromised $Reporters$, which is also in accord with reality. As for the external adversary, it may forge the legitimate vehicles to perform VCS tasks and identify a vehicle's track from a set of submitted data by observing over time.

2.3   Design Goals

We summarize the design goals of PPDR-VCS under the threat model and assumptions.

- Privacy. ① Data privacy. A submitted data containing in-time traffic information should be hidden from other vehicles, and only revealed to the local fog server, who can verify the data, broadcast the traffic information and wait for the feedback from the *Reporters* in the vicinity. ② Identity privacy. The *Uploader*'s identity can be protected, i.e. when an *Uploader* performs a VCS task, anyone including the fog server cannot identify its real identity. Furthermore, attackers cannot trace the *Uploader*'s driving trajectory via different reports. However, the anonymity of the *Uploader* can be revoked in case of any misbehavior.
- Security. The reputation system must resist two attacks, i.e., Sybil attacks and collusion attacks. No one can impersonate a legitimate vehicle to submit a data report even when some attackers want to generate a large number of fake vehicles to manipulate the reputation system. Any vehicle can not collude with a fog server to boost its reputation, which can pass the verification of the proof.
- Fairness. The reputation is updated depending on the data quality. The reputation value of *Uploaders* who submit high-quality data increases, and vice versa. Dishonest vehicles can not boost their reputation illegally. Moreover, anyone can not successfully re-upload a sensory data collected by other *Uploader*. Reputation update should be transparent and publicly verifiable to legitimate members of the consortium blockchain.
- Decentralization. Any central point of failure and any single point of control should be avoided. Therefore, the PPDR-VCS can still work well even if some fog server is compromised.

3   Preliminaries

3.1   zk-SNARK

The zero-knowledge succinct non-interactive arguments of knowledge (*zk-SNARK*) [20] is a novel form of zero-knowledge proof. It allows a prover convince a verifier that he knows some secret information without leaking any useful knowledge and the proof can be verified in a few milliseconds. A *zk-SNARK* algorithm $ZS = (Setup, Prove, Verify, Sim)$ is composed by the following probabilistic polynomial time (PPT) algorithms:

- $Setup(R_{el})$: input the constraint relations R_{el}, output the common reference string crs and the trapdoor τ. R_{el} is the non-interactive linear proof output constructed by the quadratic arithmetic program generated by the constraint condition.
- $Prove(crs, x, \omega)$: input a common reference string crs, a statement x and an evidence ω, return an argument π.

- $Verify(crs, x, \pi)$: input a common reference string crs, a statement x and an argument π, return a bit b.
- $Sim(R_{el}, \tau, x)$: input the constraint relations R_{el}, a simulation trapdoor τ and statement x, return an argument π.

3.2 Schnorr Signature Scheme with Re-randomizable Keys

Signatures with re-randomizable keys is a digital signature scheme [19], where the public and private keys can be re-randomized separately. It requires that the distribution of the re-randomized keys is the same as the original keys. So, the signer can sign a message m with a brand new key and prove the relationship between the original key pair (pk, sk) and the new key pair (pk', sk') in zero-knowledge, which guarantees the unlinkability of the signature. In this paper, we use the Schnorr signature scheme with re-randomizable keys $SSS = (KGen, Sig, Ver, RandSK, RandVK)$ to design our traceable ring signature. It mainly consists of the following algorithms:

- $KGen(1^\lambda)$: given the security parameter λ, select a private key $sk \leftarrow Z_q$, compute a public key $pk = g^{sk}$ and output the key pair (pk, sk).
- $Sig(sk, m)$: given the private key sk and the message to be signed m, select $\alpha \leftarrow Z_q$ randomly, calculate $R = g^\alpha$, $c = H(m||R)$, $y = \alpha + sk \cdot c(mod\ q)$, and output the signature $\sigma = (c, y)$.
- $Ver(pk, m, \sigma)$: given the public key pk, message m and the signature σ, parse σ as (c, y), and check whether the equation $c = H(pk^{-c}, g^y, m)$ holds and output a bit b.
- $RandSK(sk, \rho)$: given the private key sk and the re-randomizable number ρ which is chosen by signer randomly, calculate the re-randomizable private key $sk' = sk + \rho(mod\ q)$ and output sk'.
- $RandVK(pk, \rho)$: given the public key pk and the re-randomizable number ρ, calculate the re-randomizable public key $pk' = pk \cdot g^\rho(mod\ q)$ and output pk'.

3.3 Ring Signature

Ring signatures enable a signer to include his/herself in an ad-hoc group (called a ring) and sign a message as a user in the ring without disclosing which one of them is the signer [21]. Ring signatures are often used to implement anonymous authentication, especially suitable for the ad-hoc network, such as Internet of vehicles [14]. In this paper, we construct a traceable ring signature $ZKTRS = (RSetup, RKGen, RSig, RVerify)$ shown in Fig. 3 for the sake of identity privacy protection of vehicles. The proposed ring signature consists of the output of SSS and a zero-knowledge arguement [18] of the randomization factor of the new public key with respect to original public key in a ring. Furthermore, the traceable ring signature includes an extra tracing algorithm.

$RSetup(1^\lambda, R_{el})$	$RSig(r_i, M, S, \Phi)$	$RVerify(S, \Sigma_i, M)$
$(G, q, g, h) \leftarrow \mathcal{G}(1^\lambda)$ $H : \{0,1\}^* \rightarrow Z_q^*$ $(crs, \tau) \leftarrow Setup(R_{el})$ Return $((G, q, g, h),$ $H, crs, \tau)$	Parse $S = (P_1, ..., P_n)$ if $\nexists i : S_{[i]} = P_i$ return $\perp$ $\rho \leftarrow \{0,1\}^\lambda$ $P_i' \leftarrow RandVK(P_i, \rho), r_i' \leftarrow RandSK(r_i, \rho)$ $r_{tag} \leftarrow Z_q, l = H(S \| M \| r_{tag})$ $\Delta \leftarrow (ct_1 = h^l, ct_2 = P_i \cdot \Phi^l)$	Parse $S = (P_1, ..., P_n)$ Parse $\Sigma_i = (\pi, P_i', \sigma_i, \Delta)$ $b_1 \leftarrow Verify(crs, x, \pi)$ $b_2 \leftarrow Ver(P_i', M \| S \| \Delta, \sigma_i)$ Return (b_1, b_2)
$RKGen(1^\lambda)$	$x = (S, P_i', \Phi, ct_2), \omega = ((\rho, i), r_i, l)$ $\pi \leftarrow Prove(crs, x, \omega)$	
$\phi \leftarrow Z_q, \Phi \leftarrow h^\phi$ $(P_i, r_i) \leftarrow KGen(1^\lambda)$ Return $((\phi, \Phi), (P_i, r_i))$	$\sigma_i \leftarrow Sig(r', M \| S \| \Delta)$ $\Sigma_i = (\pi, P_i', \sigma_i, \Delta)$ Return Σ_i	

Fig. 3. The proposed traceable ring signature scheme $ZKTRS$

3.4   Rating Feedback Mechanism

The rating feedback mechanism [15] is a trust model which can represent the
degree of the trust on the received data. This trust model was originally designed
to solve the trust problem of certificates between users. Recently, the rating feedback mechanism is used in many real crowdsensing applications such as Waze,
eBay, etc., to provide a rating by feedback (positive, negative and uncertainty)
which are received from the consumers of these services. The benefits of using a
feedback rating paradigm in VCS are that it is fast, less expensive, and exudes
the essence of a vehicular crowdsensing paradigm. In our system, due to the lack
of knowledge of an event, we can not assert the uploaded data is true or false.
Thus, the rating feedback mechanism is used for measuring the truthfulness of
uploaded data. Unlike some existing rating feedback mechanisms, we comprehensively consider both the amount of feedback and the proportion of positive
and uncertainty feedback.

4   The Proposed System PPDR-VCS

In this section, we firstly present the privacy-preserving mechanism of PPDR-
VCS, and then describe the detailed PPDR-VCS.

4.1   The Privacy-Preserving Mechanism of PPDR-VCS

When a vehicle performs a crowdsensing task, the identity privacy and data
privacy are protected in our system. We propose $ZKTRS = (RSetup, RKGen,$
$RSig, RVerify)$ shown in Fig. 3 to protect the identity privacy. We will detail
four algorithms of $ZKTRS$ in the VCS scenario. The data privacy is accomplished by encryption algorithms, such as ElGamal.

System Setup *RSetup*

The CA sets the security parameter λ and generates the public parameters of the system. Let G be a group of a prime order $q > 2^\lambda$, g and h are two generators of group G. $H : \{0,1\}^* \rightarrow Z_q^*$ is a collision-resistant hash function. The CA also runs the $Setup(R_{el})$ in zk-$SNARK$ algorithm to generate the common reference string and the trapdoor (crs, τ). Finally, the system public parameters are $para = \{G, q, g, h, H, crs\}$.

Key Generation *RKGen*

The CA publishes the public key $\Phi = h^\phi$, where $\phi \in Z_q$ is its private key. The fog server F selects $sk_f \leftarrow Z_q$ as its private key, and computes the public key $pk_f = g^{sk_f}$. Vehicles generate their public-private key pair $(pk_i = g^{sk_i}, sk_i)$, where $sk_i \in Z_q$. All legitimate entities can get their public key certificates.

Signature Generation *RSig*

Assume a vehicle V_i enters the vicinity of a fog server F, it broadcasts the public key pk_i and the corresponding certificate. The fog server will add the legitimate public key into the PK-list. When the V_i performs a crowdsensing task and uploads a sensory data M, it first selects a ring set, i.e. n ring members, from the PK-list published by the local fog server.

Assume the V_i gets a ring set $S = \{pk_1, pk_2, ..., pk_n\}$ according to the (n, k)-privacy ring selection algorithm [22]. Then, it encrypts the data M as $Enc_{pk_f}(M)$, generates a traceable ring signature $\Sigma_i = (\pi, pk_i', \sigma_i, \Delta)$ on M and sends $(Enc_{pk_f}(M), \Sigma_i)$ to the F as following.

Firstly, the V_i selects a random number $\rho \leftarrow \{0,1\}^\lambda$, runs the re-randomizable algorithms $RandVK(pk_i, \rho)$ and $RandSK(sk_i, \rho)$ to generate the new key pair (pk_i', sk_i') where

$$pk_i' = pk_i \cdot g^\rho$$
$$sk_i' = sk_i + \rho$$

Secondly, the V_i selects a random number $r_{tag} \in Z_q$, calculates $l = H(S||M||r_{tag})$, generates the tracing tag $\Delta = (ct_1, ct_2)$ where $ct_1 = h^l$ and $ct_2 = pk_i \Phi^l$ and sets the statement $x = (S, pk_i', \Phi, ct_2)$, and the witness $\omega = ((\rho, i), sk_i, l)$. Then the V_i constructs a non-interactive zero-knowledge proof by leveraging the zk-$SNARK$ algorithm:

$$\pi \leftarrow Prove\left(\left(\begin{matrix} pk_i g^\rho = pk_i' \\ ct_2 = pk_i \Phi^l \end{matrix}\right) : crs, x, \omega\right)$$

Thirdly, the V_i generates a signature via $Sig(sk_i', M||S||\Delta)$ in SSS, i.e. $\sigma_i \leftarrow (c, y)$, where $c = H(M||S||g^\alpha||\Delta)$, $y = \alpha + sk_i' \cdot c(mod q)$, and $\alpha \in Z_q$.

Finally, the V_i generates a ring signature $\Sigma_i = (\pi, pk_i', \sigma_i, \Delta)$.

Signature Verification *RVerify*

Upon receiving $(Enc_{pk_f}(M), \Sigma_i)$, the F firstly decrypts $Enc_{pk_f}(M)$ to get the data M, and then parses S as $\{pk_1, pk_2, ..., pk_n\}$ and Σ_i as the tuple $(\pi, pk_i', \sigma_i, \Delta)$. Then the *Verify* algorithm in *zk-SNARK* algorithm takes as input the tuple (crs, x, π) and checks whether the proof π holds. The notation b_1 is defined as a result of the above procedure which can be described as:

$$b_1 \leftarrow Verify(crs, x, \pi)$$

Later, the equation $H(M||S||g^y pk_i'^{-c}||\Delta) \stackrel{?}{=} c$ is calculated to verify the validity of the signature. It outputs $b_2 = 1$ when the equation holds, otherwise output $b_2 = 0$.

If all the above verifications are valid, i.e. $b_1 = b_2 = 1$, the M is accepted by the F, who will then broadcast the M to the nearby vehicles. Otherwise, the M will be rejected.

4.2　The Detailed PPDR-VCS

Our proposed PPDR-VCS consists of four phases: system initialization, entities registration, initial reputation distribution, and reputation update.

Algorithm 1. PPDR-VCS

Input: Security parameter
Output: System parameters, public key list, reputation transaction, new block, new reputation and the proof.

　　/* **System initialization** */
1: The CA generates the system parameters;
　　/* **Entities registration** */
2: Vehicles and fog servers register with the CA and get their certificated public-private key pairs;
　　/***Initial reputation distribution** */
3: A vehicle authenticates itself to the local fog server F;
4: The F generates a reputation transaction;
5: The vehicle accesses an initial reputation from the blockchain, and generates a proof on the reputation.
　　/***Reputation update** */
6: An *Uploader* submits a sensory data M to the F which verifies and broadcasts the M, and receives feedback about the M from the *Reporters* in the vicinity of the F.
7: The reputation of the *Uploader* is re-calculated according to the data quality, which is quantified by two factors: the truthfulness of the data and the response time.
8: The F generates a reputation updating transaction;
9: A new block is created;
10: The *Uploader*'s reputation is updated and the *Uploader* generates the proof of its current reputation.

System Initialization

The CA initializes the whole reputation system via the algorithm $RSetup$. After that, the system parameters $para$ are public to all entities. The CA also initializes an empty set using bloomfilter $\Omega = \{\varnothing\}$ to maintain the IR-list for the query efficiency.

Entities Registration

All vehicles firstly provide the unique identification (e.g. vehicle identification number (VIN) and driver's ID number) to the CA for the registration. The CA will verify the correctness of the identification and check whether the vehicle has registered before. Each vehicle is only allowed to be registered once. Fog servers also need to register with the CA. All entities get their public-private key pair (pk, sk) via the algorithm $RKGen$.

Initial Reputation Distribution

A registered vehicle can get an initial reputation anonymously on its first task within an area of a fog server F. As shown in Fig. 4, the F will send an identifier query to the CA for the initial reputation identifiers in advance. The CA generates an identifier N_i by encrypting a random number a_i and signing it: $N_i \leftarrow Sig_\phi(Enc_\Phi(a_i))$. Here, we can take $ECDSA$ as the signature algorithm $Sig(.)$, and ElGamal encryption scheme as the algorithm $Enc(.)$.

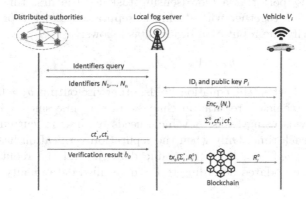

Fig. 4. The distribution of the initial reputation

The F randomly selects and encrypts an identifier N_i by using the V_i's public key pk_i, and sends $Enc_{pk_i}(N_i)$ to the V_i. The V_i decrypts it and gets N_i. Then, the V_i generates a one-time public and private key pair (pk_i'', sk_i''), encrypts N_i and sk_i'' by using pk_i'' and Φ, respectively.

$$\eta_1 \leftarrow Enc_{pk_i''}(N_i), \eta_2 \leftarrow Enc_\Phi(sk_i'').$$

The V_i also generates a ring signature Σ_i^0 on η_1 and η_2 via the algorithm $RSig$ and sends it to the F along with η_1 and η_2. The F parses and verifies Σ_i^0, and sends $\eta_1, \eta_2, \Delta = (ct_1, ct_2)$ to the CA, who will firstly check whether the vehicle applies for the initinal reputation before by computing $pk_i = \frac{ct_2}{ct_1^\phi}$, and searching for the public key pk_i in the IR-List. If pk_i is in the Ω, the CA will inform the F to reject the initial reputation request from the vehicle. Otherwise, the CA gets the one-time private key sk_i'' by decrypting η_2, and then it will get N_i by decrypting η_1 via sk_i''. After that, the CA verifies the signature and decrypts N_i to obtain a_i. If the verification succeeds and a_i is correct, the CA will send a bit $b_0 = 1$ to the F to inform that this vehicle is legitimate and applys for the initial reputation for the first time. Otherwise, $b_0 = 0$ will be sent.

If the F receives $b_0 = 1$, it will generate a reputation transaction tx_0 about (Σ_i^*, R_i^0), where $\Sigma_i^* = H(\Sigma_i^0)$. The tx_0 is then verified, sealed in a block, and appended to the consortium blockchain. Otherwise, the V_i is rejected. Finally, the V_i generates a proof π_0 on (Σ_i^*, R_i^0) by leveraging the $zk\text{-}SNARK$ algorithm:

$$\pi_0 \leftarrow Prove\left(\begin{pmatrix} \alpha + sk_i' \cdot c(modq) = y \\ \Sigma_i^* = H(\Sigma_i^0) \end{pmatrix} : crs, x_0, \omega_0 \right) \tag{1}$$

where $x_0 = (S, (c, y), \Sigma_i^0, \Sigma_i^*)$ is the statement, and $\omega_0 = (sk_i', \alpha)$ is the witness. π_0 indicates that R_i^0 is indeed the reputation of a legitimate vehicle of which the ring sinature is Σ_i^0, and π_0 also confirms the relationship between R_i^0 and pk_i anonymously.

When the V_i performs a crowdsensing task for the first time, it submits a sensary data M together with its initial reputation and the proof (R_i^0, π_0). Anyone can verify the reputation proof π_0 as follows:

$$b_3 \leftarrow Verify(crs, x_0, \pi_0)$$

It outputs $b_3 = 1$ when the equation holds, otherwise output $b_3 = 0$.

Note that a vehicle's reputation changes all the time since it is constantly engaged in crowdsensing tasks. A vehicle needs to show its current reputation and the proof each time. Only when the reputation verification has passed, the fog server will then broadcast the traffic data M and the reputation of the $Uploader$ will be updated according to the quantified data quality.

Reputation Update

Assume the F broadcasts the M submitted by an authenticated $Uploader$, and $Reporters$ in the vicinity of the F can provide positive, negative or neutral ratings on the M, which is quantified by the truthfulness-based factor Q_r and the time-based factor Q_t (The details of Q_r and Q_t are shown in the next section). Smart contracts are created and deployed on the ledger. Once the updating factors have been calculated, it triggers the $Reputation\ update\ algorithm$ to execute automatically. In Algorithm 2, the parameter γ controls the degree of importance of Q_r and Q_t. The value of γ is specified according to the requirements of the task initiator. When Q_d is positive, the data has a tendency to be true and uploaded within survival time, the vehicle's reputation will increase. Otherwise, if Q_d is negative which means $0 < (1 + Q_d) < 1$, the vehicle's reputation will be decreased. And then, the V_i's updated reputation is calculated based on Q_d and its current reputation R_i. Since the range of R_i^* is [0,1], we use the arctan function $atan$ for the normalization as $R_i^* = 2atan(R_i^{*'})/\pi$. Besides, if a normalized reputation of some vehicle is less than a threshold (we take 0.05 as an example), which means the vehicle frequently submit low-quality data or engage in improper behavior, the vehicle should be not allowed to participate in the task or be punished.

Algorithm 2. Reputation Update Algorithm

Input: The V_i's ring signature Σ_i, current reputation R_i, the reputation updating factors Q_r and Q_t

Output: The updated reputation R_i^*

1: **if** $Q_r > 0$ **then**
2:     $Q_d = \gamma Q_r + (1 - \gamma)Q_t$;
3: **else**
4:     $Q_d = Q_r$;
5: **end if**
6: $R_i^{*'} = (1 + Q_d)R_i$;
7: $R_i^* = 2atan(R_i^{*'})/\pi$;
8: **if** $R_i^* \geq 0.05$ **then**
9:     $\Sigma_i^* = H(\Sigma_i)$
10:     **return** (Σ_i^*, R_i^*);
11: **else**
12:     **return** (Σ_i, R_i^*);
13: **end if**

After executing the reputation update algorithm, the F generates a reputation updating transaction Tx, which includes the transaction number, the V_i's ring signature and the corresponding reputation value (Σ_i^*, R_i^*) or (Σ_i, R_i^*), and the F's public key and signature, as shown in Fig. 5. The transaction Tx is then verified and sealed in a block by the fog validator. Assuming a block has the capacity of v transactions, the fog validator with the highest priority generates a new block, which consists of a blockheader, the validator's updated reputation (vital assets to be authorized as validator), v transactions and a signature from the validator. And the blockheader includes a block number, a hash of previous blockheader, a hash root of Merkle tree constructed from v transactions and a timestamp, etc. Then the validator appends this block to the consortium blockchain and informs the network.

Case I: the V_i accesses the blockchain and gets (Σ_i^*, R_i^*). The V_i computes $H(\Sigma_i)$ and gets his new reputation R_i^* by comparing with Σ_i^*. Then, the V_i updates his reputation by himself and generates a proof by leveraging the zk-SNARK algorithm:

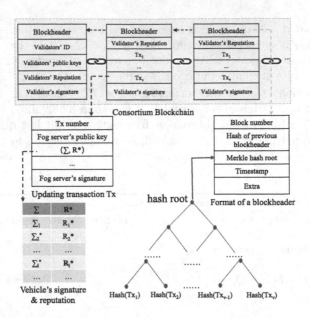

Fig. 5. Construction of the consortium blockchain

$$\pi_1 \leftarrow Prove\left(\left(\begin{array}{c}\alpha + sk'_i \cdot c(mod q) = y \\ \Sigma_i^* = H(\Sigma_i)\end{array}\right) : crs, x_1, \omega_1\right) \tag{2}$$

where $x_1 = (S, (c, y), \Sigma_i, \Sigma_i^*)$ and $\omega_1 = (sk'_i, \alpha)$. This proof confirms the relationship between R_i^* and pk_i anonymously.

Case II: If a vehicle's R_i^* is lower than the threshold on the blockchain, the CA can unite the fog server F to revoke the anonymity of the V_i by calculating $pk_i = \frac{ct_2}{ct_1^\phi}$, and mapping the public key pk_i to the V_i. The vehicle will be punished, and the CA will send pk_i to the F, who can remove pk_i from the PK-list. That means the vehicle is not allowed to perform the crowdsensing task for a time.

4.3 Updating Factors Calculation

The truthfulness of the data is calculated based on the feedback from *Reporters* in the proximity. To ensure fairness, the truthfulness-based factor Q_r is calculated by the total number of the feedback, the belief and uncertainty masses. Meanwhile, each task has a lifetime and the submitted data beyond its lifetime will be discarded. So the time-based factor Q_t is modeled as an exponential decay function. The V_i's reputation updating factors are computed as shown in Algorithm 3.

Algorithm 3. Updating Factors Calculation

Input: Sensory data M from the *Uploader* V_i, the V_i's current reputation R_i, the number of three kinds of feedback from repoters N_b, N_f and N_u

Output: V_i's reputation updating factors Q_r and Q_t

1: Calculate posterior probability (b, f, u) and the weights of belief and uncertainty ω_b, ω_u;

2: $\tau_r = \omega_b \cdot b + \omega_u \cdot u$;

3: **if** $\tau_r \geq 0.5$ **then**

4:     $Q_r = (\tau_r)^\theta$;

5:     **if** $t - t_0 < T$ **then**

6:         $Q_t = \frac{1}{e^{\rho(t-t_0)}}$;

7:     **else**

8:         drop;

9:     **end if**

10: **else**

11:     $Q_r = -(0.5 - \tau_r)^\mu$;

12: **end if**

---

① Calculation of Q_r: Let $N = N_b + N_f + N_u$ represents the total number of the feedback. According to the Bayesian theorem based on the feedback, the posterior probabilities of belief, disbelief and uncertainty are given as: $b = \frac{N_b+1}{N+3}$, $f = \frac{N_f+1}{N+3}$, $u = \frac{N_u+1}{N+3}$. We consider that the expected truthfulness of a submitted data depends on the belief and uncertainty masses which is modeled as nonlinear weighted regression model. Then the expected truthfulness can be represented as:

$$\tau_r = \omega_b \cdot b + \omega_u \cdot u \tag{3}$$

where $0 < \omega_b < 1$ is the weight of belief feedback and $0 < \omega_u < 1$ is the weight of uncertainty feedback.

We apply Richard's generalized curve [23] to model ω_b while considering the total number of the feedback. The proportion of belief feedback is also taken into consideration. Less N should have lower ω_b, in other words, ω_b should gradually increase with N, represented as follows:

$$\omega_b = \frac{1}{(1 + \delta e^{-v_b N})^{\frac{1}{\delta}}} \cdot \frac{N_b}{N} \tag{4}$$

where $\delta(\delta > 0$ and $\delta \neq \infty)$ controls the initial value of the weight and the point that ω_b turns to exponential growth. If the F receives a mass of feedback, the value of δ should be set higher, or vice-versa. v_b, the rate of growth, controls the speed of ω_b to reach the maximum value.

Intuitively, most of the *Reporters* are unaware of the event when it just happens. Thus ω_u will increase when the number of feedback is small. However, it will decrease as more feedback is received. Hence, we set N_{thres} denotes the threshold value of the feedback and $\omega_u^{max} = 0.5$ as the maximum value of the weight which means that the belief feedback would make more contributions to the expected truthfulness of the report. After that, ω_u is modeled as a piecewise function that has a growthing part and a decaying part. The growth part is similar to ω_b while the decayed part is modeled by the Kohlrausch relaxation function [24]. The equation of ω_u is represented as:

$$\omega_u = \begin{cases} \dfrac{1}{2(1+\delta e^{-v_u N})^{\frac{1}{\delta}}} \cdot \dfrac{N_u}{N} & N < N_{thres} \\ e^{-(N-N_{thres})^\epsilon} & N \geq N_{thres} \end{cases} \tag{5}$$

where ϵ is the Kohlrausch factor, controls the decreasing speed of ω_u after N reaches N_{thres}. A higher value of ϵ can eliminate the effect of uncertainty immediately. The threshold value N_{thres} controls the attenuation point of ω_u where the effect of uncertainty feedback starts to reduce. The concept of other parameters are similar to ω_b.

After achieving the expected truthfulness τ_r, a link function which is treated as the truthfulness-based updating factor Q_r based on Cumulative Prospect theory [25], is described as follows:

$$Q_r = \begin{cases} (\tau_r)^\theta & \tau_r \geq 0.5 \\ -(0.5 - \tau_r)^\mu & \tau_r < 0.5 \end{cases} \tag{6}$$

where Q_r has the value in the interval $[-1, 1]$. θ and μ control the rate of the change of upper and lower parts of Q_r, respectively. $\tau_r = 0.5$ is a reference point. $\tau_r > 0.5$ means that the data tends to be true and the vehicle's reputation should be improved, or vice versa.

② Calculation of Q_t: Another factor that influences the Uploader's reputation is the task response time. When a task is completed within task survival time T (i.e. $t - t_0 < T$), the F will accept the data report and calculate the time-based updating factor Q_t. The contribution of the data M decreases with the increases of the response time, and the time-based updating factor Q_t should be quantified according to the contribution. Therefore Q_t is modeled as an exponential decay function:

$$Q_t = \frac{1}{e^{\rho(t-t_0)}} \quad t - t_0 < T \tag{7}$$

where t is the data uploading time, t_0 is the task release time and ρ is the time factor which controls the decay rate of Q_t. A higher ρ can be chosen if the task is an emergency or time-sensitive. The shorter the response time, the bigger the time-based factor, because a "fresh" report can make more contributions.

5   Privacy and Security Analysis

5.1   Privacy

Data privacy is protected by the encryption algorithm. In our PPDR-VCS, vehicles encrypt their submitted data via ElGamal encryption algorithm. Only the fog server can decrypt the data before being broadcast. That is, an adversary can get the data submitted by other uploaders only if he can solve the discrete logarithm problem on G. So, the data privacy is preserved in our system.

When a vehicle uploads a message, it will be authenticated by our proposed $ZKTRS$ which has properties of the unforgeability, anonymity and traceability.

Theorem 1. Let $zk\text{-}SNARK$ be a computationally sound argument of knowledge, SSS be a signature scheme with re-randomizable keys which is unforgeable in the random oracle model. Our $ZKTRS$ is an unforgeable traceable ring signature scheme in the random oracle model.

Proof. Let H be a random oracle hash function. Assume that there exists a PPT adversary $\mathcal{A}$ who can forge a valid traceable ring signature successfully with the probability of $\epsilon(\lambda)$ that is non-negligible. Then the following reduction $\mathcal{R}$ can be constructed to break the unforgeability of the signature scheme with re-randomizable keys. If $\mathcal{A}$ can forge a valid signature successfully, then there exists a forgery in the SSS.

First, the unforgeability of the tracing tag $\Delta = (ct_1, ct_2)$ is guaranteed by the ElGamal [26] of which DDH assumption is hard. The sound of $zk\text{-}SNARK$ ensures the ciphertext ct_2 as the form $ct_2 = g^{sk_i}\Phi^l$. Next, we construct the reduction $\mathcal{R}$ which breaks the unforgeability of the SSS and $Adv_{vk}(\mathcal{R}^{\mathcal{A}}) \leq \frac{\epsilon(\lambda)}{q}$. The reduction $\mathcal{R}^{\mathcal{A}}(pk)$ is given as follows.

- Choose an index $i \leftarrow \{1, ..., q\}$ uniformly at random, and set $pk_i = P$.
- For all indices $k \neq i$, $\mathcal{R}$ sets $(pk_k, sk_k) \leftarrow KGen(1^\lambda)$, The adversary $\mathcal{A}$ is provided with the public keys $\mathbf{P} = (pk_1, ..., pk_q)$.
- For all indices $k \neq i$, $\mathcal{A}$ is allowed to make the corrupt query and sign query.
  - Corrupt query(k): A corrupt query is in the form of $k \in \{1, ..., q\}$. The challenger sends sk_k to $\mathcal{A}$ and appends pk_k to the corrupted user list $\mathcal{C}$.
  - Sign query (k, S, m): A sign query is in the form of (k, S, m), where m is the uploaded message, S is a set of public keys and k is an index such that $pk_k \in S$, The challenger responds with $RSig(sk_k, m, S, \Phi)$.
- $\mathcal{A}$ makes the form (i, S, m) of the sign query, and $\mathcal{R}$ responds as follows.
  - Select a random ρ.
  - Compute the re-randomized public key $pk'_i \leftarrow RandVK(S_i, \rho)$, where S_i is the i-th member of the S, the tracing tag $\Delta = (ct_1, ct_2)$, and the $zk\text{-}SNARK$ proof:

$$\pi \leftarrow Prove\left(\left(\begin{matrix} pk_i g^\rho = pk'_i \\ ct_2 = pk_i \Phi^l \end{matrix}\right) : crs, x, \omega\right)$$

  - On input of $(m||S||\Delta, \rho)$, and query the signing oracle. Assume the challenger responses with σ.
  - Return $(\pi, pk'_i, \sigma, \Delta)$.
- $\mathcal{A}$ outputs a forged signature (S^*, Σ^*, m^*).
- $\mathcal{R}$ parses the signature as $\Sigma^* = (\pi^*, pk^*, \sigma^*, \Delta^*)$ and gets $(S^*||pk^*||\Delta^*, \omega^*, \pi^*)$, where ω^* is the form of (ρ^*, i^*, sk^*, l^*) and $i^* = i$, $\mathcal{R}$ aborts if $i^* \neq i$.

- $\mathcal{R}$ returns the tuple of a signature $(m^*||S^*||\Delta^*, \sigma^*, \rho^*)$ and finishes the simulation.

Assume $\mathcal{A}$ successfully forges a valid signature $\Sigma^* = (\pi^*, pk^*, \sigma^*, \Delta^*)$ which satisfies the following conditions: $\mathcal{A}$ doesn't make any corrupt oracle on i, where $pk_i \in S^*$ and $S^* \subseteq \mathbf{P} \setminus \mathcal{C}$; $\mathcal{A}$ doesn't make any signing oracle in the form of $(., S^*, m^*)$; and the equation $RVerify(S^*, \Sigma^*, m^*) = 1$ holds. When $\mathcal{A}$ queries the signing oracle in the form of (i, S, m), the challenger responds $\sigma \leftarrow Sig(RandSK(sk_i, \rho), m||S||\Delta)$ to $\mathcal{R}$. Therefore, we know that $\mathcal{R}$ perfectly simulates the inputs of $\mathcal{A}$. From the above, in the case $i^* = i$, we have the re-randomizable key

$$pk^* = RandVK(pk_{i^*}, \rho^*) = RandVK(pk_i, \rho^*)$$

such that $RVerify(S^*, \Sigma^*, m^*) = 1$, which implies that

$$Verify(crs, (S^*, pk^*, \Phi, ct_2), \pi^*) = 1;$$
$$Ver(pk^*, m^*||S^*||\Delta^*, \sigma^*) = 1.$$

It shows that $(m^*||S^*||\Delta^*, \sigma^*, \rho^*, \Delta^*)$ is the tuple of a valid signature. In other words, if $\mathcal{A}$ successfully forges a valid signature, $\mathcal{R}$ can forge a valid signature with the same probability. That is

$$Adv_{vk}(\mathcal{R}^{\mathcal{A}}) = \sum_{j=1}^{p} Pr[i^* = j] \cdot Pr[\mathcal{R}^{\mathcal{A}}|i^* = j]$$
$$+ Pr[\overline{i^* = j}] \cdot Pr[\mathcal{R}^{\mathcal{A}}|\overline{i^* = j}]$$
$$\geq \sum_{j=1}^{p} Pr[i^* = j] \cdot Pr[\mathcal{R}^{\mathcal{A}}|i^* = j]$$
$$\geq \frac{1}{q} \cdot Pr[\mathcal{R}^{\mathcal{A}}|i^* = j] \geq \frac{\epsilon(\lambda)}{q}$$

which is non-negligible. This contradicts to the unforgeability of SSS.

Theorem 2. Let $zk\text{-}SNARK$ be perfect zero-knowledge, SSS be a signature scheme with re-randomizable keys in the random oracle model, then $ZKTRS$ is anonymous in the random oracle model.

Proof. Consider the following games:

- $Game_0$: For all indices $i \in \{1, ..., q\}$, the reduction sets $(pk_i, sk_i) \leftarrow KGen(1^\lambda)$. The public keys $\mathbf{P} = (pk_1, ..., pk_q)$ are provided to the adversary $\mathcal{A}$. $\mathcal{A}$ can make queries in the form of (k, S, m), where m is the uploaded message, S is a set of public keys and k is an index such that $pk_k \in S$. The challenger responds with $RSig(sk_k, m, S, \Phi)$. $\mathcal{A}$ sends the tuple (i_0, i_1, S, m)

to request a challenge, where i_0, i_1 are indices such that $pk_{i_0}, pk_{i_1} \in S$. The challenger chooses a bit $b \leftarrow \{0, 1\}$ randomly and sents $RSig(sk_{i_b}, m, S, \Phi)$ to $\mathcal{A}$. Also, random numbers $(\omega_1, ..., \omega_q)$ are given to $\mathcal{A}$. $\mathcal{A}$ outputs b' and makes a success if $b' = b$.

- $Game_1$: The proof π in the challenge step is computed as

$$\pi \leftarrow Sim(\tau, x)$$

where $x = (S^*, pk'_{i_b}, \Phi, ct_2)$. The other part of $Game_1$ is similar to $Game_0$.
- $Game_2$: Is similar to $Game_1$ except that the challenge signature is $(\pi, pk', Sig(sk', m^*||S^*||\Delta), \Delta)$, where $(pk', sk') \leftarrow KGen(1^\lambda)$.
- $Game_3$: Is defined as $Game_2$ except that the tracing tag Δ' is computed by r'_{tag} which is freshly chosen randomly.

We can find that adjacent games are indistinguishable.

$Game_0 \approx Game_1$: In these two games, all the parameters are generated honestly except the proof π. Because of the zero-knowledge property of $zk\text{-}SNARK$, the proof generated by $Sim(\tau, x)$ and the proof generated by $(x, (\rho, i))$ are statistically close.

$Game_1 \approx Game_2$: The two games are different only in the sampling step of the key pair (pk', sk') which are used to compute the challenging signature. In $Game_1$, the signature computed by (pk', sk'), while in $Game_2$ the pair is freshly sampled. Since the keys of signature scheme are perfectly re-randomizable, the two games are identical.

$Game_2 \approx Game_3$: The two games differ only in the choosing procedure of random numbers used to compute the tracing tag. In $Game_2$ the signature computed by r'_{tag}, while in $Game_3$ the random number is freshly sampled. Since the pseudo-random property of the tracing tag is derived from pseudo-random numbers, the tracing tags are computationally indistinguishable. Therefore the games are identical.

From the above, the challenge signature computed in $Game_3$ is irrelevant to b which means that $\mathcal{A}$ wins the $Game_3$ with the probability $\frac{1}{2}$. Besides, we have $Game_1 \approx Game_2$ and $Game_0 \approx Game_1$. Thus, we can conclude that any $\mathcal{A}$ cannot win the game with negligible probability greater than guessing.

To sum up, anonymity means the vehicle's identity is hidden in the ring. Anyone including the fog server cannot distinguish which secret key has been used to generate the ring signature. Furthermore, the ring selection algorithm in our system can achieve (n, k)-privacy, thus any attackers cannot trace a vehicle's identity by observing different ring signatures of the same vehicle. Then the identity anonymity and driving trajectory of the vehicles are protected.

Theorem 3. The proposed $ZKTRS$ achieves traceability if $zk\text{-}SNARK$ is perfectly correct and zero-knowledge, as well as the variant ElGamal encryption is sound.

Proof. The correctness and soundness of *zk-SNARK* guarantee that the tracing tag is generated by the signer. We set (Φ, ct_2) as the statement and (sk_i, l) as the witness. The signer can calculate the proof using its private key. In other words, the proof of *zk-SNARK* guarantees that ct_2 is generated as the form $ct_2 = g^{sk_i}\Phi^l$. If we take the hash function H as a random oracle, we can prove that it is computationally infeasible to find another $l' = H(S'||m'||r'_{tag})$ as a collision, given the output l. Based on the correctness of variant ElGamal, we can ensure that the decryption is correct which means the signer's identity can be revoked. Only the CA can decrypt the ciphertext using the private key ϕ and find out the identity of the poorly behaved signer, whose reputation is lower than the threshold value. The privacy of good behaved vehicles, whose reputation is bigger than the threshold value, is protected unconditionally. Nobody even the CA can revoke the anonymity of them, because (Σ_i^*, R_i^*) are recorded on the blockchain rather than (Σ_i, R_i^*) and ct_2 can not be obtained via Σ_i^*.

In conclusion, the traceable ring signature can be generated by the *Uploader* in a ring S, no one can forge others' signature. Moreover, the CA can revoke the anonymity of a poorly behaved vehicle. Hence, conditional anonymity is preserved in our PPDR-VCS.

5.2 Security

In our PPDR-VCS, all vehicles need to register with the CA firstly. When a vehicle is performing a VCS task in a coverage area of a fog server, the public key of the registered vehicle will be maintained in the PK-list by the local fog server. The public key is certificated by the CA, which prevents an illegal vehicle from generating multiple public keys and launching Sybil attacks. When vehicles perform crowdsensing tasks, all transmitting messages are required to be authenticated to the fog server. Sybil devices cannot damage our reputation system through misbehaviors without successful registration and authentication.

An external adversary can launch Sybil attacks in the following two ways: The first one is to generate a large number of Sybil vehicles [12] to manipulate the reputation system. Since the fake vehicle has no legal filing information with DMV, it can not register with the CA successfully. Second, it tries to compromise a legitimate vehicle and forge a signature of its submitted message. Since the unforgeability of the signature is guaranteed by the proposed $ZKTRS$, the adversary can not forge a valid signature which can pass the verification process. In case an attacker creates a ring signature by using his secret key, generated by running $KGen(1^\lambda)$ algorithm, along with a ring set. Since its public key is not in the PK-list, the signature cannot pass the verification $RVerify$. So the proposed system can resist Sybil attacks.

In our system, there is no such reputation center, which is responsible for evaluating and updating the reputation. Although the fog server is responsible for the calculation of updating factors, it follows the protocol and computes Q_r and Q_t honestly based on the feedback responded by *Reporters*. The reputation is updated by the smart contracts on the blockchain, which is tamper-resistant. So, there is no opportunity for collusion between the vehicle and the fog server.

5.3   Fairness

Firstly, the crowdsensing data is encrypted by the *Uploader*, which will prevent some lazy *Uploader* from re-uploading the data report to earn profit. Secondly, fairness is guaranteed by the reputation update algorithm, which is influenced by the data quality quantification. Since we quantify the data quality by using the truthfulness-based and time-based updating factors detailed as Q_r and Q_t in Algorithm 3. So our analysis will focus on how the calculation of Q_r and Q_t can ensure the fairness.

Q_r is calculated based on τ_r (i.e. $\tau_r = \omega_b \cdot b + \omega_u \cdot u$), where the weight of belief feedback ω_b and the weight of uncertainty feedback ω_u are modeled as Richard's generalized curve and kohlrausch relaxation function, respectively. Since the Richard's generalized curve can control the initial lower asymptote, inflection point, and the rate of change, so fog servers can set appropriate parameters to control ω_b for different tasks. This makes the calculation of τ_r objective and authentic. Besides, the proportion of the belief feedback is taken into consideration. It is obviously that the data supported by more feedback is more reliable. What's more, the amount of all received feedback is also added into our expression (Eq. 2) in order to compute ω_b fairly. Consider the following situation, there is an *Uploader* uploading a wrong data and manipulating several *Reporters* to give wrong feedback. If we leave out the amount of feedback, the proportion will be high when the amount of the received feedback is small. Then ω_b is calculated to be a bigger value than its normal one. And this malicious *Uploader*'s reputation will be increased illegally. Similarly, the growth part of ω_u is also modeled as Richard's generalized curve. Hence, the truthfulness-based updating factor Q_r can be calculated via ω_b and ω_u fairly.

As for Q_t, it is modeled as an exponential decay function on account of the contribution of the data. This is fair because the data which is uploaded earlier has better accuracy and does more contributions to the task initiator. Moreover, the updating procedure is accomplished by the smart contract so that no one can change it, and the reputation can be checked by all authority nodes.

5.4   Decentralization

In this work, when a vehicle firstly registers with the CA, the initial reputation is distributed via the CA and the local fog server instead of a reputation center. The reputation update is realized by smart contracts automatically, and there is no central reputation center, which might be compromised allowing illegal reputation updating or even impairing the reputation system. The local fog server only assists in distributing the initial reputation and calculating the updating factors. Vehicles access the blockchain to update their reputation and generate the corresponding proof via *zk-SNARK* algorithm after a task. Any central party is not needed to maintain the updated reputation of vehicles.

In addition, the local fog server also acts as a validator candidate in the PoA consensus mechanism. These validators are responsible for verifying and signing the blockchain and one of them will package all transactions into the block. If a fog server is compromised, other validators will vote out the malicious fog server and another fog server in this area will be selected to take its place. Thus the compromised fog server can not damage the system which means that the PPDR-VCS can still work well even there exist some malicious nodes.

6   Performance Evaluation

6.1   Implementation Overview

We present a proof-of-concept implementation of our system based on Parity Ethereum, and accomplish extensive experiments to evaluate the performance of PPDR-VCS.

We implement our PPDR-VCS on a notebook with AMD Core R7-5800H CPU@3.20 GHz and 16.00 GB memory. The operating system is Ubuntu 20.04.3 LTS AMD64. We use libsnark to implement the *zk-SNARK* [18]. The hash function is SHA-256. The security-parameter of the Schnorr&ECDSA signature scheme and the ElGamal encryption scheme are 256 bits. We construct a blockchain testing network based on Proof of Authority (PoA) [27], which consists of Authority nodes and User nodes. In particular, fog servers play the role of Authority nodes in Parity PoA network, and they can be selected as validators to verify the transactions and issue blocks. While local fog servers can also perform the function of the User nodes that send reputation update transactions to the blockchain.

We deployed a few fog nodes in our experiments. Eclipse as the JAVA client communicates with the Parity blockchain via web3j to fulfill the interaction with smart contracts. We specify the validator list as configurations in the blockchain file, and we also encode the public parameters of the system in Java clients. The off-chain and on-chain performance are tested to reveal the system efficiency.

6.2   Off-Chain Performance

We evaluate the off-chain performance of the initial reputation distribution, the anonymous authentication based on ring signatures and updating factors calculation.

In the initial reputation distribution, the main computational costs come from the identifiers generation and verification as well as the ring signature. As shown in Fig. 6, we set the number of identifiers as $\{10, 30, 50, 70, 100\}$. The computation cost of identifier generation and verification is linearly increasing with the number of identifiers. From Fig. 6, it costs less than 1400ms to generate 100 identifiers. As for the verification process, the cost of verifying 100 identifiers at the same time is less than 2500ms. The procedure of ring signatures is similar to the message authentication in the Reputation update phase, we will discuss below.

We set a PK-list of the local fog server containing 1000 vehicles. The ring selection algorithm chooses n vehicles to generate a traceable ring signature of η_1

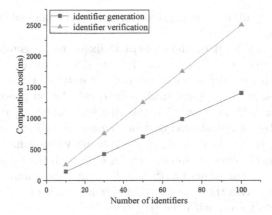

Fig. 6. Computation costs of identifier generation and verification

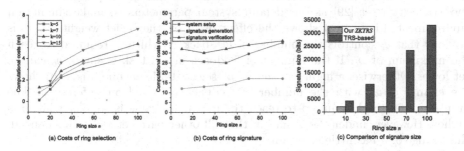

(a) Costs of ring selection   (b) Costs of ring signature   (c) Comparison of signature size

Fig. 7. Performance of the proposed *ZKTRS*

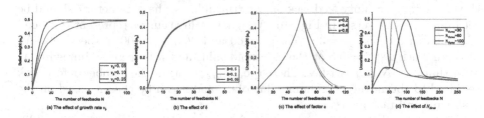

(a) The effect of growth rate v_b (b) The effect of δ (c) The effect of factor ε (d) The effect of N_{thre}

Fig. 8. The effects of parameter choices on ω_b and ω_u

and η_2 or the sensory data M. The computational cost varies with the ring size n. In each set of experiments with different n, which is set as $\{10, 20, 30, 50, 100\}$, we adopted an average result of 100-times round.

As shown in Fig. 7(a), we can see that the time cost for ring selection is increasing as the privacy level k increases. Because keeping k ring members of S_1 takes more time than randomly selecting k members from the PK-list. Given a fixed privacy level k, the computational cost of ring selection algorithm also increases as the ring size n grows. Because it also takes some time to randomly select n-k new ring members from the PK-list. Nevertheless, the ring selection algorithm takes very little or negligible time, which is efficient while improving privacy protection.

When the privacy level of the system is fixed, the execution time of the ring signature is shown in Fig. 7(b). As the ring size increases, the time cost on the ring generation and verification are both maintains a fixed value because the compact ring signature algorithm has fixed calculation procedure. The cost of setup algorithm will increase with the ring size, however, it is still tens of milliseconds. So the computational cost of ring signature is acceptable.

Moreover, our traceable ring signature scheme yields small signature size. The Fig. 7(c) shows the comparison of our $ZKTRS$ with the baseline TRS-based scheme [28]. The signature size of TRS-based scheme [28] is multiple times larger than ours and grows with the ring size. The signature size of the $ZKTRS$ is only 2040 bits and doesn't grow with the ring size.

We test the performance of updating factors calculation by considering the truthfulness-based factor and time-based factor. We obtain the parameters from the Waze data set [29] as our default system parameters to make simulation environment. Figure 8(a) shows the effect of v_b on the belief weight ω_b. It is obvious that v_b controls the number of feedback N which is required to reach the maximum of ω_b. If the number of feedback in the task is small, v_b can be set lower. Otherwise, a higher v_b should be selected. Meanwhile, Fig. 8(b) shows the change of ω_b with the number of feedback N based on different δ. The number of feedback required to reach the maximum value is smaller while δ is higher. However, under the situation that all other parameters are unchanged, the change of δ has little effect on ω_b.

Figure 8(c) shows how ϵ affects the uncertainty weight ω_u. We can see that the higher the ϵ, the faster the decrease of ω_u. If the task initiator wants to decrease the effect of uncertainty feedback on the truthfulness, the parameter ϵ should be set higher, or vice versa. In Fig. 8(d), we can see three curves represent the trend of ω_u based on $N_{thres} = 30$, $N_{thres} = 60$ and $N_{thres} = 100$, respectively. All of them reach $\omega_u^{max} = 0.5$ at the threshold value and will decrease immediately after that $N = N_{thres}$ satisfies. Therefore, N_{thres} controls the number of feedback required to obtain the maximum value of ω_u and it can be chosen based on the task time and task area.

Figure 9(a) shows the trend of truthfulness-based factor Q_r is based on different θ and μ which controls the growth rate above and below zero, respectively. When $\tau_r > 0.5$, Q_r is positive and that the one based on a higher θ grows faster than the one based on a lower θ. On the contrary, when $\tau_r < 0.5$, Q_r is negative. As τ_r gradually decreases from 0.5, Q_r will decreases faster if it has a lower μ. The growth curve of time-based factor Q_t is described in Fig. 9(b) which shows that Q_t with a higher ρ decreases faster. When the task is time-sensitive or the task initiator needs data urgently, a higher value can be given to the parameter ρ, otherwise a lower value is a good choice.

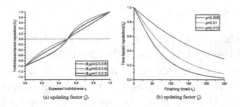

Fig. 9. The effects of different factors on Q_r and Q_t

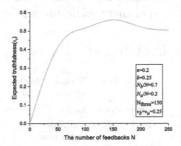

Fig. 10. The truthfulness variation with the number of feedback

Figure 10 describes the trend of τ_r with the number of feedback N where we assume that the ratio of belief feedback, the ratio of uncertainty feedback, v_b, v_u, δ, ϵ and N_{thres} are fixed. When $N < N_{thres}$, τ_r is increasing with the growth of N and obtains the maximum value at $N = N_{thres}$. On the contrary, τ_r is decreasing with N after the point $N = N_{thres}$. It is reasonable that the data which has more belief feedback has a higher truthfulness and it will decrease if more uncertainty feedback are received. We also evaluate the data quality Q_d based on Q_r and Q_t as shown in Fig. 11. Apparently, Q_d will increase with Q_r and Q_t. However, the weight of two parameters is controlled by γ. If a task acquires more truthful data, the γ can be set higher(> 0.5), and if a task is time-sensitive, γ can be set lower.

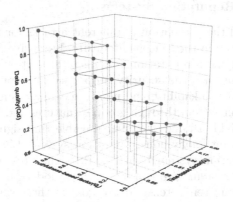

Fig. 11. The variation of Q_d based on Q_r and Q_t

6.3   On-Chain Performance

We evaluate the on-chain performance of smart reputation update through the confirmation time of the update transaction and the gas costs of deploying the contract and executing its functions on Parity Ethereum. Local fog server sends an updating transaction Tx by calling the reputation update algorithm in the update contract. Then, the fog validator verifies the correctness of the transaction. We conduct 20 sets of experiments to evaluate the on-chain performance, the average transaction confirmation time of the updating transaction Tx is 129 ms, which is efficient in the experiment environment.

Table 1. The comparison of PPDR-VCS with existing reputation systems

Proposal	Scenarios	Architecture	Technologies for identity privacy	Transparency	Fairness
Blomer [30]	Not given	Centralized	Group signatures	No	Yes
Zhai [31]	Online services	Decentralized	Linkable ring signatures	No	Yes
Soska [8]	E-commerce	Blockchain	Ring signatures	Yes	No
ARS-PS [9]	Retail marketing	Blockchain	Anonymous credentials	Yes	No
RepChain [11]	E-commerce	Blockchain	Blind signatures	Yes	Yes
BC-DRS [10]	E-commerce	Blockchain	None	Yes	Yes
PPDR-VCS	Vehicular crowdsensing	Decentralized	Traceable ring signatures	Yes	Yes

7   Related Work

In this section, we compare the existing works with our system from five aspects in Table 1.

7.1   Anonymous Reputation Systems

Privacy concerns and the prevention of different attacks for reputation systems are frequently discussed in the rencent literature. Extensive research have made efforts to design anonymous reputation systems to protect users' privacy. Blomer et al. [30] pointed out that the security properties for reputation systems are anonymity, traceability, linkability, and non-frameability, and they proposed an anonymous reputation system through group signatures and Σ-protocol. Zhai et al. [31] utilized verifiable shuffles [32] and linkable ring signatures [33] to propose a tracking-resistant anonymous reputation system. Liu et al. [9] proposed an anonymous reputation system based on PS signatures in retail marketing. Almost all proposed systems are combined with modern e-commerce services, such as eBay, Amazon, Yelp, etc., and the goal of these systems is to protect raters' privacy.

There exist a few works addressing the issues on privacy-preserving reputation system in mobile crowdsensing applications. Wang et al. [34] proposed an anonymous reputation management scheme. In their scheme, honest participants are vulnerable to tracking attacks, while malicious participants can keep large reputation values for some time even when they provide false data. To conquer the drawbacks of the work [34], Ma et al. [35] presented a privacy-preserving reputation management scheme for edge computing enhanced mobile crowdsensing. The scheme in [35] updates the reputation values based on the deviations of the sensing data to the final aggregating result. However, the scheme is based on centralized model, which can not meet our decentralized requirement. Different from the existing works, we focus on the privacy presevation of the *Uploader* and provide a scheme which can combine with a specific VCS application.

7.2 Reputation Calculation Model

Jøsang [15] and Yu et al. [36] proposed trust models to calculate reputation scores based on rating feedback, which leverage the ratio of positive feedback to the all. However, there exist threats such as ballot and obfuscation stuffing in Jøsang's belief models [15], and Dempster-Shafer model [36] does not consider the degree of participation and data quality when computing the reputation score. To address these issues, Bhattacharjee et al. [16] proposed a quality and quantity-unified QoI metric for published information in a mobile crowdsensing system. In order to model the expected truthfulness of the published information, they use generalized Richard's curve and Kohlsrausch relaxation function to calculate the weights to belief and uncertainty masses, respectively. They pointed out that their approach outperforms Jøsang's belief and Dempster-Shafer based reputation models in some aspects of classification, incentivization, and scalability.

We presented our data quality quantification for vehicular crowdsensing scenario. Different from QnQ [16], we modify the design of the belief and uncertainty coefficient to satisfy our scenario. Furthermore, QnQ only considers the truthfulness of an event to calculate the aggregate reputation score. In our system, another time-based factor, which affects the reputation value in time-sensitive crowdsensing tasks, is also taken into account.

7.3 Blockchain-Enabled Reputation Systems

To build a decentralized system, the blockchain has been taken into consideration to construct reputation systems [8–11] in E-commerce environment. Soska et al. [8] proposed an anonymous reputation system based on ring signature and the robust transaction chain property. Different from our system, the ring signature in [8] is used to protect the identity privacy of the customer, but the size of the ring signature is not constant. Liu et al. [9] proposed an anonymous reputation system based on the PoS Blockchain architecture [37]. And they focus on the efficiency and scalability issues of a blockchain-based architecture. Zhou et al. [10] gave a blockchain-based decentralized reputation system in the E-commerce environment. They did not consider the privacy pretection of users, whose reputation scores are stored on the blockchain and can be accessed by others. Li et al. [11] presented RepChain, a privacy preserving reputation system for E-commerce platforms based on the blockchain. Different from the existing work, our system is proposed under the VCS scenario. And we aim to accomplish privacy-preserving trusted reputation update on the premise of minimizing the number of times accessing the blockchain.

8   Conclusion

In this paper, we have investigated the security and privacy issues of reputation systems in VCS scenarios. We propose a privacy-preserving decentralized reputation system by utilizing zk-$SNARK$, traceable ring signature and the blockchain technology. The privacy of vehicles is protected unconditionally for their good behaviors. Any dishonest vehicle cannot boost their reputation arbitrarily. Sybil attacks and collusion attacks are resisted in our system. The reputation of vehicles is updated trustworthily depending on the quantified data quality. We have also implemented a prototype system based on Ethereum to verify its performance and feasibility. For future work, we will study how to enrich our current design and improve the decentralized feature [38] of our system. Besides, multiple updating factors should also be taken into account to meet the demands of different tasks since there are different factors that affect the performance.

Acknowledgments. This work was supported by National Natural Science Foundation of China under Grant 61802217, in part by the Natural Science Foundation of Shandong Province under Grant ZR2023MF082, in part by Qingdao Science and Technology Plan Key Research and Development Project under Grant 22-3-4-xxgg-10-gx, and in part by Original Exploration Project of Qingdao Natural Science Foundation under Grant 23-2-1-164-zyyd-jch.

References

1. Ni, J., Zhang, A., Lin, X., Shen, X.: Security, privacy, and fairness in fog-based vehicular crowdsensing. IEEE Commun. Mag. **55**(6), 146–152 (2017)
2. Li, M., Chen, Y., Zheng, S., Hu, D., Lal, C., Conti, M.: Privacy-preserving navigation supporting similar queries in vehicular networks. IEEE Trans. Dependable Secure Comput. **19**(2), 1133–1148 (2020)
3. Work-Brows by the Type of Client. https://www.pentagram.com/work/waze
4. Wang, L., Cao, Z., Zhou, P., Zhao, X.: Towards a smart privacy-preserving incentive mechanism for vehicular crowd sensing. Secur. Commun. Netw. **2021**, 1–16 (2021)
5. Wang, X., Cheng, W., Mohapatra, P., Abdelzaher, T.F.: Enabling reputation and trust in privacy-preserving mobile sensing. IEEE Trans. Mob. Comput. **13**(12), 2777–2790 (2013)
6. Singh, S.K., Rathore, S., Park, J.H.: BlockIoTIntelligence: a blockchain-enabled intelligent IoT architecture with artificial intelligence. Futur. Gener. Comput. Syst. **110**, 721–743 (2020)

7. Xu, Y., Ren, J., Wang, G., Zhang, C., Yang, J., Zhang, Y.: A blockchain-based nonrepudiation network computing service scheme for industrial IoT. IEEE Trans. Industr. Inf. **15**(6), 3632–3641 (2019)
8. Soska, K., Kwon, A., Christin, N., Devadas, S.: Beaver: a decentralized anonymous marketplace with secure reputation. Cryptology ePrint Archive (2016)
9. Liu, D., Alahmadi, A., Ni, J., Lin, X., Shen, X.: Anonymous reputation system for IIoT-enabled retail marketing atop POS blockchain. IEEE Trans. Industr. Inf. **15**(6), 3527–3537 (2019)
10. Zhou, Z., Wang, M., Yang, C.N., Fu, Z., Sun, X., Wu, Q.J.: Blockchain-based decentralized reputation system in e-commerce environment. Futur. Gener. Comput. Syst. **124**, 155–167 (2021)
11. Li, M., Zhu, L., Zhang, Z., Lal, C., Conti, M., Alazab, M.: Anonymous and verifiable reputation system for e-commerce platforms based on blockchain. IEEE Trans. Netw. Serv. Manage. **18**(4), 4434–4449 (2021)
12. Wang, G., Wang, B., Wang, T., Nika, A., Zheng, H., Zhao, B.: Defending against sybil devices in crowdsourced mapping services. In: Proceedings of the 14th Annual International Conference on Mobile Systems, Applications, and Services, pp. 179–191 (2016)
13. Li, H., Chen, Q., Zhu, H., Ma, D., Wen, H., Shen, X.: Privacy leakage via deanonymization and aggregation in heterogeneous social networks. IEEE Trans. Dependable Secure Comput. **17**(2), 350–362 (2017)
14. Wang, L., Lin, X., Zima, E., Ma, C.: Towards airbnb-like privacy-enhanced private parking spot sharing based on blockchain. IEEE Trans. Veh. Technol. **69**(3), 2411–2423 (2020)
15. Jsang, A.: An algebra for assessing trust in certification chains (1999)
16. Bhattacharjee, S., Ghosh, N., Shah, V., Das, S.: Q n Q: quality and quantity based unified approach for secure and trustworthy mobile rowdsensing. IEEE Trans. Mob. Comput. **19**(1), 200–216 (2018)
17. Xu, Z., Yang, W., Xiong, Z., Wang, J., Liu, G.: TPSense: a framework for event-reports trustworthiness evaluation in privacy-preserving vehicular crowdsensing systems. J. Signal Process. Syst. **93**(2–3), 209–219 (2021)
18. Groth, J.: On the size of pairing-based non-interactive arguments. In: Fischlin, M., Coron, J.-S. (eds.) EUROCRYPT 2016, Part II. LNCS, vol. 9666, pp. 305–326. Springer, Heidelberg (2016). https://doi.org/10.1007/978-3-662-49896-5_11
19. Fleischhacker, N., Krupp, J., Malavolta, G., Schneider, J., Schröder, D., Simkin, M.: Efficient unlinkable sanitizable signatures from signatures with re-randomizable keys. In: Cheng, C.-M., Chung, K.-M., Persiano, G., Yang, B.-Y. (eds.) PKC 2016, Part I. LNCS, vol. 9614, pp. 301–330. Springer, Heidelberg (2016). https://doi.org/10.1007/978-3-662-49384-7_12
20. Gennaro, R., Gentry, C., Parno, B., Raykova, M.: Quadratic span programs and succinct NIZKs without PCPs. In: Johansson, T., Nguyen, P.Q. (eds.) EUROCRYPT 2013. LNCS, vol. 7881, pp. 626–645. Springer, Heidelberg (2013). https://doi.org/10.1007/978-3-642-38348-9_37
21. Wang, L., Zhang, G., Ma, C.: A survey of ring signature. Front. Electr. Electron. Eng. China **3**, 10–19 (2008)
22. Wang, L., Lin, X., Qu, L., Ma, C.: Ring selection for ring signature-based privacy protection in VANETs. In: ICC 2020–2020 IEEE International Conference on Communications (ICC), pp. 1–6 (2020)
23. Ram, N., Grimm, K.: Growth curve modeling and longitudinal factor analysis (2015)

24. Anderssen, R., Husain, S., Loy, R.: The Kohlrausch function: properties and applications. Anziam J. **45**, 800–816 (2003)
25. Kahneman, D., Tversky, A.: Prospect theory: an analysis of decision under risk. In: Handbook of the Fundamentals of Financial Decision Making: Part I, pp. 99–127 (2013)
26. Fujisaki, E., Okamoto, T.: Secure integration of asymmetric and symmetric encryption schemes. In: Wiener, M. (ed.) CRYPTO 1999. LNCS, vol. 1666, pp. 537–554. Springer, Heidelberg (1999). https://doi.org/10.1007/3-540-48405-1_34
27. Alofs, M.: Blockchain: proof of authority (2018)
28. Fujisaki, E., Suzuki, K.: Traceable ring signature. In: Okamoto, T., Wang, X. (eds.) PKC 2007. LNCS, vol. 4450, pp. 181–200. Springer, Heidelberg (2007). https://doi.org/10.1007/978-3-540-71677-8_13
29. Barnwal, R., Ghosh, N., Ghosh, S., Das, S.: Enhancing reliability of vehicular participatory sensing network: a Bayesian approach. In: 2016 IEEE International Conference on Smart Computing (SMARTCOMP), pp. 1–8 (2016)
30. Blömer, J., Eidens, F., Juhnke, J.: Practical, anonymous, and publicly linkable universally-composable reputation systems. In: Smart, N.P. (ed.) CT-RSA 2018. LNCS, vol. 10808, pp. 470–490. Springer, Cham (2018). https://doi.org/10.1007/978-3-319-76953-0_25
31. Zhai, E., Wolinsky, D.I., Chen, R., Syta, E., Teng, C., Ford, B.: AnonRep: towards tracking-resistant anonymous reputation. In: 13th $\{USENIX\}$ Symposium on Networked Systems Design and Implementation ($\{NSDI\}$ 2016), pp. 583–596 (2016)
32. Neff, C.A.: A verifiable secret shuffle and its application to e-voting. In: Proceedings of the 8th ACM Conference on Computer and Communications Security, pp. 116–125 (2001)
33. Liu, J.K., Wong, D.S.: Linkable ring signatures: security models and new schemes. In: Gervasi, O., Gavrilova, M.L., Kumar, V., Laganà, A., Lee, H.P., Mun, Y., Taniar, D., Tan, C.J.K. (eds.) ICCSA 2005. LNCS, vol. 3481, pp. 614–623. Springer, Heidelberg (2005). https://doi.org/10.1007/11424826_65
34. Wang, X., Cheng, W., Mohapatra, P., Abdelzaher, T.: Enabling reputation and trust in privacy-preserving mobile sensing. IEEE Trans. Mob. Comput. **13**(12), 2777–2790 (2013)
35. Ma, L., Liu, X., Pei, Q., Xiang, Y.: Privacy-preserving reputation management for edge computing enhanced mobile crowdsensing. IEEE Trans. Serv. Comput. **12**(5), 786–799 (2018)
36. Yu, B., Singh, M.: An evidential model of distributed reputation management. In: Proceedings of the First International Joint Conference on Autonomous Agents and Multiagent Systems: Part 1, pp. 294–301 (2002)
37. Kiayias, A., Russell, A., David, B., Oliynykov, R.: Ouroboros: a provably secure proof-of-stake blockchain protocol. In: Katz, J., Shacham, H. (eds.) CRYPTO 2017. LNCS, vol. 10401, pp. 357–388. Springer, Cham (2017). https://doi.org/10.1007/978-3-319-63688-7_12
38. Wang, L., Zhao, X., Lu, Z., Wang, L., Zhang, S.: Enhancing privacy preservation and trustworthiness for decentralized federated learning. Inf. Sci. **628**, 449–468 (2023)

Delay Optimization for Consensus Communication in Blockchain-Based End-Edge-Cloud Network

Shengcheng Ma[1]($\boxtimes$) (iD), Shuai Wang[1] (iD), Wei-Tek Tsai[1,2], and Yaowei Zhang[3]

[1] School of Computer Science and Engineering, Beihang University, No. 37 Xueyuan Road, Beijing, China
mashengcheng@163.com
[2] Digital Society and Blockchain Laboratory, Beihang University, No. 37 Xueyuan Road, Beijing 100191, China
[3] China Mobile Information Security Management and Operation Center, Beijing, China

Abstract. With the rapid development of smart IoT technology, various innovative mobile applications improve many aspects of our daily life. End-edge-cloud collaboration provides data transmission in connecting heterogeneous IoT devices and machines with improvements in high quality of service and capacity. However, the end-edge cloud architecture still remains some challenges including the risks of data privacy and tolerance transmission delay. Blockchain is a promising solution to enable data processing in a secure and efficient way. In this paper, blockchain is considered as an infrastructure of the end-edge-cloud network and the time cost of the PBFT consensus is analyzed from the perspective of the leader's position. Considering the concurrent processing of tasks in cellular networks, multi-intelligent deep reinforcement learning is used to train the assignment strategy of the edge server. The numerical results show that the proposed method can achieve better performance improvement in terms of the time consumption of data processing.

Keywords: End-Edge-Cloud · Blockchain · Delay Optimization · Multi-Agent Deep Reinforcement Learning

1 Introduction

The development of mobile communication technologies fully supports emerging wireless applications. In particular, 5G/6G has facilitated the widespread use of the Internet of Things (IoT). Various applications are based on IoT technologies that provide users with friendly services, such as the Internet of Vehicles (IoV) [1], electronic payments, smart homes, virtual and augmented reality(VR/AR) [2], and unmanned aerial vehicles(UAV) [3]. Massive data will be generated by endpoint devices, processed and stored as valuable information. End-edge-cloud collaboration, integrated with smart IoT devices, edge computing, and the cloud,

© The Author(s), under exclusive license to Springer Nature Singapore Pte Ltd. 2024
C. Li et al. (Eds.): APPT 2023, LNCS 14103, pp. 241–262, 2024.
https://doi.org/10.1007/978-981-99-7872-4_14

is considered a promising architecture to cope with a large amount of data [4]. To enhance data security and availability during data communication, blockchain is integrated with end-edge-cloud network. Blockchain is a tamper-proofed and traceable distributed ledger that can prevent the data from tampering or contamination by attackers [6]. The consensus algorithm guarantees reliable data consistency across all nodes of the blockchain [7]. Therefore, blockchain is widely considered a promising technology that integrated in mobile communication [8].

Though great benefits can be gained through the application of cloud-edge-end collaboration, there are still some problems. The tasks can be offloaded to edge servers, while the edge server is not enough to take all the tasks. Sending all data to cloud may cause long propaganda latency, and the latency will degrade system performance [5]. Moreover, blockchain protects data from tampering, but the consensus mechanism leads to more communication and increased data processing delays.

To improve the performance of the end-edge-cloud network, many studies attempt to coordinate tasks at different layers. Article [9,10] exploit the game-theoretical method to design an incentive mechanism to promote the system performance. Resource allocation is an ordinary research orientation to boost system efficiency [11,12]. Yang et al. [13] schedule the computing and network resources effectively and build an intelligence measurement model for healthcare systems. Reinforcement learning, as an optimization method, is often used to solve resource allocation problems. Liao [14] proposes a multi-timescale resource allocation model based on reinforcement learning. The model can optimize physical-layer task offloading in a large timescale. Delay is an important performance indicator. Richard Yu's team [15,16] employs reinforcement learning to solve a resource allocation model for reducing delay in Blockchain-based IoT networks. However, they do not take into account the case of parallel processing of tasks when calculating the processing delay.

The work of [17] builds an edge computing environment among IoT devices with blockchain technologies to support the embedding of security-focused offloading algorithms. Zhang et al. [18] propose a blockchain empowered federated learning framework in digital twin empowered 6G networks. This framework improves the reliability and security of the system and enhances data privacy. Due to the public blockchain having the disadvantages of low transaction throughput, many researchers prefer using permissioned-blockchain in mobile networks. PBFT [19] is a classic consensus algorithm widely used in the permissioned-blockchain. These studies [20,21] attempt to optimize the PBFT consensus algorithm to improve the performance of the blockchain network. Owing to the different volume of resources at each level in the end-edge-cloud network and the algorithmic rules of PBFT, the position of the leader node is also an important factor in the performance of the blockchain networks. Yet, the impact of the position of the leader in the blockchain has not been well investigated in these studies.

The main contributions of our paper can be summarized as follows:

- First, we establish a blockchain-based end-edge-cloud task assignment model based on reinforcement learning. In considering task processing times, we take into account the situation where tasks are processed in parallel on multiple edge servers. The model aims to reduce task processing latency by assigning tasks to appropriate positions for execution.

- Second, according to the computing, communication, and storage capabilities of layers in the end-edge-cloud architecture, we analyze the time consumption of the PBFT consensus algorithm where the leader deployed on edge and cloud, respectively. The edge server is near the task side but has a small computational power, whereas the cloud has high computational power but the transmission delay is large. Since the leader node broadcasts more communication than the replica node, there is a difference in the total time consumption of the consensus algorithm when the leader is deployed in different locations.
- Third, we implement an optimization method to solve the task assignment problem using the MADDPG algorithm. Our approach uses multi-agent to manage the task assignment for multiple edge servers, and the experimental results demonstrate the superiority of our proposed method.

The rest of this paper is organized as follows: In Sect. 2, we introduce the system model of the blockchain-enabled end-edge-cloud network and analyze the time cost for the PBFT consensus algorithm. Next, we present a reinforcement learning optimization framework to select the appropriate equipment for task processing in Sect. 3. We design a reward function to fit the scenario and implement the framework using the MADDPG method in this section. Then, we provide the experimental and analyze the result to illustrate the improvement of performance. Finally, we conclude this paper in Sect. 5.

2   System Model

To illustrate our system, we first describe the architecture of blockchain-based end-edge-cloud collaboration. Then we build a model to represent the system operation mechanism. Finally, we use the MADDPG deep reinforcement learning method to optimize the policy for blockchain.

2.1   The Architecture of the Blockchain-Enabled End-Edge-Cloud Collaboration

For a typical end-edge-cloud collaboration architecture, there are three layers that constitute the network. As the name is called, those are the device layer, the mobile edge computing layer, and the cloud layer.

For the device layer, it is the endpoint of the architecture and it usually represents the IoT network. In the edge layer, the edge computing servers are usually deployed near the base station. Blockchain service is also supported in the edge layer. The edge computing servers act as the consensus nodes in the blockchain network. The offloading data can be recorded in a block and saved in the blockchain after consensus operation. The cloud layer is deemed as the data

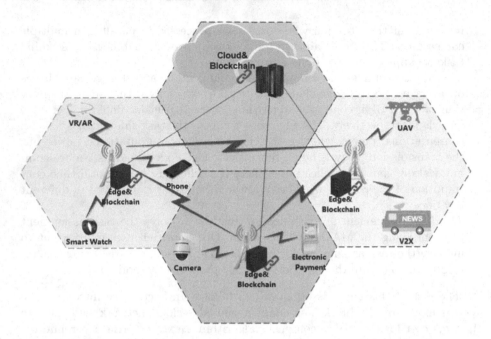

Fig. 1. The Architecture of Blockchain-enabled End-Edge-Cloud Collaboration

center which has sufficient computation, storage, and bandwidth resources. The cloud layer also provides the blockchain service. The cloud server can participate in the consensus communication with the edge servers.

The device layer, the edge layer, and the cloud collaborate with each other and integrate together to consist of a blockchain-based cloud-edge-end architecture. The proposed architecture is shown in Fig. 1.

2.2 Network Model

In the device layer, we assume that a base station covers a cellular network. In each cellular network, there are N active IoT devices connected to the base station. The set of all active IoT devices can be denoted as $\mathcal{D} = \{d_1, d_2, ..., d_N\}$ The ith $(i = 1, 2, ...N)$ active IoT device d_i means that it has a job need to be processed at the time slot t.

In the edge layer, we consider that there are M edge servers represented by the set $\mathcal{E} = \{e_1, e_2, ..., e_M\}$ in the network. Each edge server, like the jth $(j = 1, 2, ..., M)$ edge server, is deployed at the base station and provides a blockchain service. The edge server is responsible to provide service for IoT devices in the cellular network which is covered by the base station. Therefore, we combine the concept of the edge server with the base station, and the jth cellular network also means the network serviced by the edge server e_j. The amount of IoT devices in the whole network is $N \times M$.

We assume that a cloud server C with sufficient resources in the cloud layer, and it is connected to the edge servers by a wired link. All the edge servers and the cloud server constitute a blockchain platform.

The IoT device has lightweight storage and computing capacity, and it only can execute the low load task. A job from the IoT device d_i connected with edge server e_j denotes as $J_{i,j} <s_{i,j}, f_{i,j}>$, and it requires two kinds of resource, $s_{i,j}$ is the data size and $f_{i,j}$ is the required CPU cycles of the job. If the ith IoT device has enough resources to process the job $J_{i,j}$ in time, the job will be handled on the local device. Otherwise, the job will be offloaded to the edge server.

2.3   Wireless Communication

When the IoT device's own resources are insufficient to complete task processing, it will offload the job to the edge server through wireless communication. For wireless communication, the data transmission power on the ith IoT device is represented as P_{I_i,E_j}, and the channel gain from the jth edge server to the ith IoT device is g_{I_i,E_j}. The actual effective transmission data rate is defined as Eq. 1.

$$B_{I_i,E_j} = W \log_2(1 + \frac{P_{I_i,E_j} g_{I_i,E_j}}{N_0 W}) \tag{1}$$

where W is the bandwidth of the channel, and N_0 is the noise power. Consequently, the speed of task offloading between the ith IoT device to the jth edge server is B_{I_i,E_j}.

2.4   Offloading and Computation

The determinant of where a task will be executed is based on the processing time. Our goal is to minimize the processing time. For the different positions of the job executing, the processing time will be discussed as followed:

Computing on Local Device. For the local computation, the job will be executed immediately without data transferring. The time cost is only generated by the CPU computing, so the time to execute a job on a local device $T_{Local,i}$ can be expressed as

$$T_{Local,i} = \frac{f_{i,j}}{F_i^I}. \tag{2}$$

where F_i^I the CPU cycles per second of the ith IoT device. In addition, we assume that the data size of the job $s_{i,j}$ should be less than the storage capacity of the IoT device S_i^I.

Computing on Edge Server. When a job is too complex, it will be time-consuming to execute on the local device and impact on quality of service (QoS). Therefore, the job will be offloaded to the edge computing server to reduce the processing time. When the job is processed on the edge server, the time cost includes transmission time and computation time.

The transmission time from the ith IoT device to the jth edge server $T_{Edge_j,i}^{trans}$ is represented as

$$T_{Edge_j,i}^{trans} = \frac{s_{i,j}}{B_{I_i,E_j}}. \tag{3}$$

The computation time for job $J_{i,j}$ on the jth edge server $T_{Edge_j,i}^{comp}$ is denoted as

$$T_{Edge_j,i}^{comp} = \frac{f_{i,j}}{F_j^E} \tag{4}$$

where F_j^E is the CPU cycle of the jth edge server. The processing time of $J_{i,j}$ on the jth edge server $T_{Edge_j,i}$ is defined as Eq. (5).

$$T_{Edge_j,i} = T_{Edge_j,i}^{trans} + T_{Edge_j,i}^{comp} = \frac{s_{i,j}}{B_{I_i,E_j}} + \frac{f_{i,j}}{F_j^E} \tag{5}$$

Computing on Cloud Server. If the resource of the edge server is also not enough to process the job, edge server will transfer the job to the cloud server. The processing time of the job in the cloud server consists of three parts. The transmission time from the IoT device to the edge server $T_{Edge_j,i}^{trans}$, the transmission time from the edge server to the cloud server $T_{Cloud,j}^{trans}$, and the computation time on the cloud server $T_{Cloud,i}^{comp}$. The transmission time $T_{Edge_j,i}^{trans}$ is shown as Eq. (3). The transmission time $T_{Cloud,i}^{trans}$ can be represent as:

$$T_{Cloud,i}^{trans} = \frac{s_{i,j}}{B_{Eth}} + T_{route}, \tag{6}$$

where B_{Eth} is the bandwidth of the wire link between the edge server and the cloud server, and T_{route} is the delay generated by routers from the edge server to the cloud server.

The computation time $T_{Cloud,i}^{comp}$ is denoted as:

$$T_{Cloud,i}^{comp} = \frac{f_{i,j}}{F^C}, \tag{7}$$

where F^C is the CPU cycle frequency allocated by the cloud server.

The processing time of job $J_{i,j}$ on the cloud server $T_{Cloud,i}$ is presented as Eq. (8).

$$T_{Cloud,i} = T_{Edge_j,i}^{trans} + T_{Cloud,i}^{trans} + T_{Cloud,i}^{comp} = \frac{s_{i,j}}{B_{I_i,E_j}} + \frac{s_{i,j}}{B_{Eth}} + T_{route} + \frac{f_{i,j}}{F^C} \tag{8}$$

Processing Time of Tasks in Entire Network. For jobs in a cellular network, we assume that a, b, and c are the number of jobs executed on the local device, the edge server, and the cloud server. The range of values of these variables should satisfy $0 \leq a, b, c \leq N$, and $a + b + c = N$. The whole processing time in the mth cellular network can be represented as:

$$T_{cell_j} = \max\{\max_{i \in a}\{T_{Local,i}\}, \sum_{i \in b} T_{Edge_j,i}, \sum_{i \in c} T_{Cloud,i}\}. \tag{9}$$

We calculate the max value of these three parts to support concurrent execution. It means that three layers of servers can process tasks concurrently, which can greatly improve the efficiency of the system. Every IoT device can execute the job respectively, so we use the max function to calculate the processing time of the device layer. In addition, the total amount of data size for jobs offloaded to the edge server should be less than the storage capacity of the edge server. That is $\sum_{i \in b} s_{i,j} \leq S_j^E$. The cloud server is considered to have enough storage capacity to accommodate all offloading jobs, and computing supports parallel processing of offloading jobs from multiple cellular networks.

For all tasks in the network, the total task processing time at the current moment T_{total_t} can be expressed as:

$$T_{total\_t} = \max_{j \in M}\{T_{cell_j}\} \tag{10}$$

2.5   Time Consumption of Blockchain Consensus

After processing, the job should be stored securely. To ensure the traceability and non-tampering of data, this storage process is done by the blockchain system. In this paper, we investigate the PBFT algorithm as the typical blockchain consensus method. In the cloud-edge-end architecture, the blockchain network contains two situations on the basis of the position of the leader node. One is the leader node voted in an edge server, the other one is the leader node in the cloud server. Next, we discuss the time cost in two situations respectively.

Leader Node on the Edge Server. For the case of the leader node on the edge server, we analyzed the time consumption of the different algorithm phases.

In the request phase, a client as the sponsor sends the request of consensus for the $J <i, j>$ to the leader node. The client is an edge server that has completed job J. The transmission from the client to the leader node can be denoted as:

$$T_{req,j}^{trans} = \frac{R + s_{i,j}}{B_{j^c,j^l}} \tag{11}$$

where B_{j^c,j^l} is the bandwidth between the client and the leader node, and R is the REQUEST message except $s_{i,j}$. The REQUEST message includes operation which is the information requiring consensus $s_{i,j}$, timestamp, and client ID. In addition, the client calculates the digest of the request message and signs it. Then, it appends the signature to the plaintext of the REQUEST messages and sends them to the leader node. In the pre-prepare phase, the leader node receives the REQUEST message and validates the signature of the client. Then, the leader composes a PRE-PREPARE message. The PRE-PREPARE message contains the view number, sequence number, and digest of the REQUEST message. The leader node signs the digest of the PRE-PREPARE message and combines the signature with the plaintext and the REQUEST message. Next, the leader multicasts the combination of the PRE-PREPARE message to all the replica nodes. The time cost for multicast can be denoted as:

$$T_{pre-pre,j}^{trans} = \frac{(PP + R + s_{i,j}) \cdot (M-1)}{B_{j^l,j^r}} + \frac{PP + R + s_{i,j}}{B_{Eth}} + T_{route} \qquad (12)$$

where PP is the PRE-PREPARE message and the signature, B_{j^l,j^r} is the bandwidth between the leader node and the replica node. There are $M-1$ nodes deployed on the edge servers and one node deployed on the cloud server. The replica nodes receive the message from the leader node and check its correctness. It contains the signature of the leader's PRE-PREPARE message, the signature of the client's REQUEST message, and the digest of the REQUEST message. If this information is right, the replica node accepts the message and turns into the prepare phase.

In the prepare phase, the replica node multicasts the PREPARE message to other nodes. Similar to the PRE-PREPARE message, the PREPARE message also contains the view number, sequence number, and digest. Besides, it adds its node identification to the message. The time cost for transmission can be denoted as:

$$T_{pre,j}^{trans} = \frac{P \cdot (M-1)}{B_{j',j}} + \frac{P}{B_{Eth}} + T_{route} \qquad (13)$$

where P is the PREPARE message and the signature, $B_{j',j}$ is the bandwidth between replica nodes. For the special case, a replica node is deployed on the cloud server. The time cost of the transmission for this node can be represented as:

$$T_{pre,c}^{trans} = \left(\frac{P}{B_{Eth}} + T_{route}\right) \cdot M \qquad (14)$$

Considering the concurrent communications, the total time cost of this phase can be expressed as:

$$T_{pre}^{trans} = \max_{j \in M}(T_{pre,j}^{trans}, T_{pre,c}^{trans}) \qquad (15)$$

If each node (including leader and replica) in the blockchain receives at least $2f$ valid PREPARE messages, it will enter the commit phase.

In the commit phase, each node sends the COMMIT message to other nodes. The contents of the COMMIT message are the same as the PREPARE message, so the time cost of the node on the edge server can be denoted as:

$$T_{com,j}^{trans} = \frac{C \cdot (M-1)}{B_{j',j}} + \frac{C}{B_{Eth}} + T_{route} \qquad (16)$$

where C is the COMMIT message and the signature, $B_{j',j}$ is the bandwidth between different edge servers. For the node deployed on the cloud server, the time cost can be represented as:

$$T_{com,c}^{trans} = (\frac{C}{B_{Eth}} + T_{route}) \cdot M \tag{17}$$

The total time cost of the commit phase can be expressed as:

$$T_{com}^{trans} = \max_{j \in M}(T_{com,j}^{trans}, T_{com,c}^{trans}). \tag{18}$$

If the number of the COMMIT messages accepted by the consensus node is equal to or greater than $2f+1$, including its own message, the node will send a REPLY message to the client.

In the reply phase, the majority of nodes in the blockchain attain the consensus for a normal situation. Each node will save $s_{i,j}$ on the blockchain and send the REPLY message to the client. The REPLY message contains the view number, timestamp, client ID, node ID, and the result. The time cost of transmission for node deployed on the edge server can be expressed as:

$$T_{rep,j}^{trans} = \frac{RP}{B_{j^r,j^c}} \tag{19}$$

For the node deployed on the cloud server, the time cost can be denoted as:

$$T_{rep,c}^{trans} = \frac{RP}{B_{Eth}} + T_{route} \tag{20}$$

The total time cost of the reply phase can be expressed as:

$$T_{rep}^{trans} = \max_{j \in M}(T_{rep,j}^{trans}, T_{rep,c}^{trans}). \tag{21}$$

The total time cost of the consensus for the leader deployed on the edge server is:

$$\begin{aligned}
T_{total\_c} &= T_{req,j}^{trans} + T_{pre-pre,j}^{trans} + T_{pre}^{trans} + T_{com}^{trans} + T_{rep}^{trans} \\
&= \frac{R + s_{i,j}}{B_{j^c,j^l}} + \frac{(PP + R + s_{i,j})(M-1)}{B_{j^l,j^r}} \\
&\quad + \frac{PP + R + s_{i,j}}{B_{Eth}} + T_{route} + \max_{j \in M}(T_{pre,j}^{trans}, T_{pre,c}^{trans}) \\
&\quad + \max_{j \in M}(T_{com,j}^{trans}, T_{com,c}^{trans}) + \max_{j \in M}(T_{rep,j}^{trans}, T_{rep,c}^{trans}).
\end{aligned} \tag{22}$$

Leader Node on the Cloud Server. In the case of a leader deployed on a cloud server, its consensus communication is different from a leader on an edge server. The difference is mainly concentrated in the transmission path, so the time cost changes accordingly.

In the request phase, the client sends the REQUEST message to the leader on the cloud server. The time cost of the transmission is:

$$T_{req,c}^{trans} = \frac{R + s_{i,j}}{B_{Eth}} + T_{route} \tag{23}$$

In the pre-prepare phase, the leader node sends the PRE-PREPARE message to all replicas on the edge servers. The time cost in this phase can be expressed as:

$$T_{pre-pre,c}^{trans} = (\frac{PP + R + s_{i,j}}{B_{Eth}} + T_{route}) \cdot M \tag{24}$$

In the prepare phase, the replica sends the PREPARE message to other nodes in the blockchain network. The leader node does not participate in message transmission. Therefore, the time cost in this phase can be represented as:

$$T_{pre}^{trans} = \frac{P}{B_{j',j}} \cdot (M - 1) + \frac{P}{B_{Eth}} + T_{route} \tag{25}$$

In the commit phase, each node sends the COMMIT message to others. Whatever the leader node is deployed on which position, the communications are identical. Hence, the time cost in this phase is the same as Eq. 18.

In the reply phase, all nodes reply to the client, so the transmission time is the same as Eq. 21.

The total time consumption of consensus for the leader deployed on the cloud server can be denoted as:

$$\begin{aligned} T_{total\_c} &= T_{req,c}^{trans} + T_{pre-pre,c}^{trans} + T_{pre}^{trans} + T_{com}^{trans} + T_{rep}^{trans} \\ &= \frac{R + P + M \cdot PP + (M + 1) \cdot s_{i,j}}{B_{Eth}} \\ &\quad + (M + 2) \cdot T_{route} + \frac{P}{B_{j',j}} \cdot (M - 1) \\ &\quad + \max_{j \in M}(T_{com,j}^{trans}, T_{com,c}^{trans}) + \max_{j \in M}(T_{rep,j}^{trans}, T_{rep,c}^{trans}) \end{aligned} \tag{26}$$

2.6 Optimization Model of Minimizing Time for Task Processing and Consensus

In the proposed cloud-edge-end network, we assume that each IoT device has a job to process at a time period. In a time period, all jobs in the network should be completed. Then, the model enters the next stage and devices generate new tasks. Though we suppose the cloud server has adequate resources, the task offloading should satisfy the resource limitation of the edge server. In order to minimize the processing time, the selection of the job processing position needs to be optimized. Combining the above factors, we define the task offloading model as follows:

$$\begin{aligned} \mathbf{P1} : &\min \ T_{total\_t} + T_{total\_c} \\ s.t. \ &C1 : \ 0 \leqslant a, b, c \leqslant N \\ &C2 : \ a + b + c = N \\ &C3 : \ s_{i,j} \leqslant s_i^I, \forall i \in \{1, .., N\} \\ &C4 : \ \sum_{i \in b} s_{i,j} \leqslant s_j^E, \forall j \in \{1, .., M\} \\ &C5 : \ \sum_{i \in b} B_{I_i, E_j} \leqslant B_{E_j}, \forall i \in \{1, .., M\} \end{aligned} \tag{27}$$

Constraint $C1$ represents that the number of jobs assigned in the end, edge, and cloud should be valid values. Constraint $C2$ represents that all the jobs should be appointed in a position and processed. Constraint $C3$ indicates that the size of the job should be less than the storage capacity of the IoT device that generates the job. Constraint $C4$ indicates that the total data volume of tasks offloaded to the edge server should be less than the storage capacity of the edge server. For IoT devices that offload tasks, constraint $C5$ shows that the total bandwidth allocated to these devices should be less than the total bandwidth of the edge servers.

3   Reinforcement Learning Optimization Framework

The goal of the model is to minimize the task processing time, so we need to assign the tasks to the appropriate servers for processing. Because of Eq. (27) is an NP-hard problem, we cannot obtain a solution using traditional methods within a certain period of time. In addition, each cellular network in the model need an agent, we use Multi-Agent Deep Deterministic Policy Gradient (MAD-DPG) [22] algorithms to support the parallel processing and solve this problem. For task assignment, we can consider the current network model as the state in RL, and we deem the assignment of tasks as the action. We also need to define a reasonable incentive function as the reward. With the help of the algorithm, the agent completes the position selections for tasks and achieves the goal of minimizing the task processing time.

3.1   State Space

In our model, the cloud-edge-end architecture is constructed by M cellular networks. For a cellular network, we define the environment as the system state $o_j = \{J_j, F_j^I, B_j, S^E, F^E, S^C, F^C\}, j \in [1, M]$. Where $J_j = \{J_{1,j}, J_{2,j}, ..., J_{N,j}\}$ is the set of tasks generated at time slot t in the jth cellular network. For a task $J_{i,j}$, it can be denote as $J_{i,j} = <s_{i,j}, f_{i,j}>, i \in [1, N]$. The element $s_{i,j}, i \in [1, N], j \in (1, M)$ is the data size of task from device d_i in the jth cellular network. Similarly, the element $f_{i,j}, i \in (1, N), j \in (1, M)$ is the required CPU cycles of the task. $F_j^I = \{F_{1,j}^I, F_{2,j}^I, ..., F_{N,j}^I\}$ is the set of computation capacity of the IoT devices. For B_j, it can be written as $B_j = \{B_{I_1,E_j}, B_{I_2,E_j}, ..., B_{I_N,E_j}\}$, and it represents the set of the required bandwidth of tasks which need to be allocated by edge server. S^E, F^E are the storage capacity and CPU frequency of the edge server respectively. S^C, F^C are the resources of the cloud server including storage and calculation. In each time slot, the parameters of tasks generated by the device layer will be stochastic values. For the whole network, we should combine all the cellular networks, so the state space of the environment can be written as S which is $S = \{o_1, o_2, ..., o_M\}$.

3.2   Action Space

The action space is defined as the processing position selection for tasks. The processing position includes local which is IoT device, edge server, and cloud server. In the time slot t, the action $a_j(t), j \in [1, M]$ denotes the selection in the jth cellular network. It can be expressed as $a_j(t) = \{a_{1,j}(t), a_{2,j}(t), ..., a_{N,j}(t)\}$. For $a_{i,j}(t)$, its value represents the selection of processing locations for task $J_{i,j}$. It can be written as $a_{i,j}(t) = 0, 1, 2$, where $a_{i,j}(t) = 0$ means the decision of task processing position is in the local device, while $a_{i,j}(t) = 1$ means the task will be offloaded to the edge server e_j, and the task will be processed by cloud server when $a_{i,j}(t) = 2$. For the entire model, the action space can be represented as $A = \{a_1(t), a_2(t), ..., a_M(t)\}$.

3.3   Reward Function

An efficient incentive function is a key factor for the RL algorithm. When the agent chooses the right action, the reward function should give positive incentives, otherwise the reward function will punish the agent to avoid making wrong decisions. After the action executing in each time slot, the reward function will return a value. The accumulated value is related to the achievement of the optimization objective in the model. Our goal of the proposed architecture network is to minimize the task processing time, so we consider the time cost as criterion in the reward function. Moreover, the action for the processing position selection should be valid. This implies that the resources consumed by the selection must be within the capacity of the servers. Consequently, the reward function for a cellular network can be defined as:

$$
\begin{aligned}
r_j(t) = &\; \alpha(T + T_{local_t} - 2T_{total_t}) \\
&+ \beta(s_j^E - \sum_{i \in (b \cup c)} s_{i,j}) \\
&+ \gamma(B_{E_j} - \sum_{i \in (b \cup c)} B_{I_i, E_j}), j \in [1, M]
\end{aligned} \tag{28}
$$

where T is the time span of the slot t, T_{local_t} is the time cost of processing all tasks on local devices, which means that there is no offloading. T_{total_t} is the time cost after the task assignment of action $a_j(t)$ executing, α, β, and γ are the weight for turning the reward value.

Normally, all the tasks should be completed in the time slot, so $T - T_{total_t}$ will be a positive number. Otherwise, the value of $T - T_{total_t}$ is negative, which is a punishment. Similarly, utilizing edge or cloud computing should enhance the processing efficiency of the task, or else such operations are futile. Therefore, a larger positive difference of $T_{local_t} - T_{total_t}$ indicates more efficient processing and better incentives. This is a good decision. $s_j^E - \sum_{i \in (b \cup c)} s_{i,j}$ denotes that the agent will be punished if the obtained storage space caused by the action is beyond the capacity of the edge server. $(B_{E_j} - \sum_{i \in (b \cup c)} B_{I_i, E_j})$ means that the savings in bandwidth resources will also be rewarded. For the two cases above, $i \in (b \cup c)$ is the same as $a_{i,j}(t) = 1$ or $a_{i,j}(t) = 2$, and they both confine the case in which the task is offloaded to the edge or the cloud server to perform. For the whole system, the reward function should be $R(t) = \{r_1(t), r_2(t), ..., r_M(t)\}$.

3.4   Optimization Solution by MADDPG Algorithm

We apply the MADDPG algorithm to solve the task processing location selection problem. Since our model represents a multiple cellular network scenario, the multi-agent mode of the MADDPG can be effectively compatible with this situation. In addition, the cellular networks share one cloud computing center, so we expect that cellular networks can cooperate rather than compete. The algorithm can well support this situation. By setting the number and policy of adversaries, the cooperative relationship between agents can be realized. To be suitable for multi-agent environments, the basic idea of the MADDPG algorithm is centralized training and decentralized execution, which is the fusion and extension of Deep Deterministic Policy Gradient(DDPG) [23] and Actor-Critic [24] methods. Therefore, we adopt MADDPG to optimize the task assignments in multiple cellular networks. To achieve the goal of minimizing task execution time, we transform the problem into the assignment of tasks in different service locations. We input the state information of the environment into the agents of the RL model. The state information includes the requirements of tasks in multiple cellular networks and the computing resources of each service node in the end-edge-cloud system. In the proposed model, each agent is responsible for task allocation in a cellular network, and multiple agents work together on the selection of task processing locations for the entire network.

In the agent, a DDPG algorithm is constructed with four neural networks: the Actor network, Critic network, Actor Target network, and Critic Target network. The four networks have the same structure, each with three fully connected layers and 64 nodes per layer. The policy in the agent can be defined as μ with parameter θ.

For the Actor network, it generates an action based on the inputting state information of the environment. It can be expressed as $a - \mu_\theta(o|\theta)$. To increase the exploration of the environment, noise is added to the output of the Actor network to form the final Action. The training goal of the Actor network is to maximize the Q value of the accumulated rewards, and the gradient of the expected reward for a cellular network can be denoted as below:

$$\nabla J(\theta) = E[\nabla_\theta \mu_\theta(a|o) \nabla_a Q^\mu(o,a)|_{a=\mu_\theta(o)}]. \tag{29}$$

After the interaction between the action and environment, the agent receives a reward, and the environment transforms into a new state. The quadruple (o, a, r, o') will be stored in the memory buffer. The agent samples a mini-batch of quadruples from the memory buffer, and utilizes experience replay to update parameters of the Critic Target network and Actor Target network. When updating the target networks, a soft update is used in order to avoid too fast parameter changes. The parameters of the Actor Target network and Critic Target network are updated by:

$$\theta^{\mu'} = \tau\theta^\mu + (1-\tau)\theta^{\mu'}$$
$$\theta^{Q'} = \tau\theta^Q + (1-\tau)\theta^{Q'} \tag{30}$$

where $\tau \in (0,1)$ is the learning rate. The Actor Target network computes the new action $a' = \mu'(o'|\theta^{\mu'})$ and sends the result to the Critic Target network. This action does not require the addition of noise. The Critic Target network adopts the result from the Actor Target network to calculate the target value as below:

$$y = re + \gamma Q'(o', \mu'(o'|\theta^{\mu'})|\theta^{Q'})$$ (31)

For the Critic network, the output is the estimated Q value of the current state and the corresponding action. The training updates θ^Q by minimizing the difference between the action-value function Q^μ and the target value y. The loss function of the Critic network is calculated by:

$$L(\theta^Q) = E[(Q^\mu(o,a|\theta^Q) - y)^2]$$ (32)

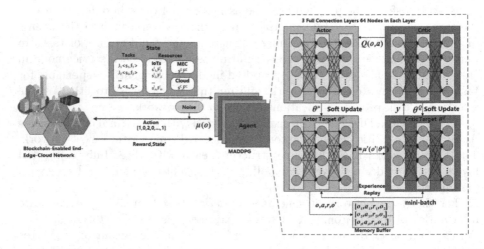

Fig. 2. The MADDPG Model of Task Assignment for Blockchain-enabled End-Edge-Cloud Network

The detail of the task assignment optimization by MADDPG is shown in Fig. 2.

4   Experimental Environment and Results

In this section, we will first introduce our simulation setting. Then, we discuss the performance of our proposed method.

4.1   Simulation Setting

In this simulation, TensorFlow 2.8.0 with Python 3.9 is employed to build the experiment environment, and the OS is Windows 11. We consider an end-edge-cloud network that includes a cloud server and some cellular networks. The number of edge servers can be set as {3, 9, 15}. We set the number of edge servers according to the principle that the number of edge and cloud servers meets the $3f + 1$ relationship required for Byzantine fault tolerance. In each cellular network, the number of IoTs can be set as {10,20,30,40,50}. Each IoT generates a task in slot time. The size of the task is from 0.5 MB to 10 MB, and the required CPU cycles of the task are from 3.5G to 4.5G. The CPU cycle frequency of the IoT device, edge server, and cloud server are 0.5GHz, 2.4GHz, and 20GHz, respectively. Some wireless resource parameters refer to the article [11]. To analyze the consumption of consensus, we assume that both edge servers and cloud servers are blockchain nodes that are involved in consensus communication. For the PBFT algorithm, the message size of R, PP, P, C, and RP is set to 1 KB, and the timeout for consensus was set to ≤ 1 min. In addition, other parameters in the simulation environment are shown in the Table 1.

Table 1. Simulation Parameters

Parameters	Value
Path loss between the IoT and the edge server l_{I_i, E_j}	$140.7+36.7 log_{10}(d)$dB
Radio power of the IoT P_i	10 mW
Noise power N_0	-174 dBm
Storage capacity of the edge server S_j^E	100 MB
Total bandwidth of the edge server B_{E_j}	30 MHz
Data rate of wire link from edge to cloud server B_{Eth}	1 GB/s
Delay between the edge and cloud server T_{router}	0.5 s
Slot time T	5 s
Reward value weight α, β, γ	0.5,0.25,0.25

4.2   Result and Discussion

Figure 3 shows the comparison of system reward in our proposed task assignment method with different learning rates. The value of the reward is the average of 1000 training episodes. For learning rates 0.1 and 0.01, the system cannot reach better rewards when it converges. When the learning rate is 0.001, the system can obtain a high reward value and converge quickly. The reward has a negative value because our incentive function has a penalty mechanism, and when tasks are not allocated properly, the reward will have a negative value. Continuing to reduce the learning rate to 0.0001 does not give better results, so we set the learning rate to 0.001 for the following test.

Figure 4 shows the variation of reward with different numbers of edge servers. We selected 3, 9, and 15 as the number of edge servers. These three numbers were chosen because the total number of edge servers plus cloud servers meets the Byzantine requirement of $3f + 1$ for fault tolerance. Each edge server is

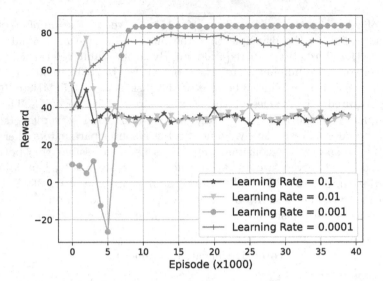

Fig. 3. Reward with Different Learning Rate.

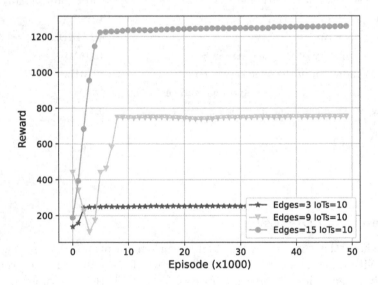

Fig. 4. Reward with Different Numbers of Edge Servers.

responsible for the processing tasks of 10 IoT devices. As the number of edge server grows, our proposed model is still able to consistently guarantee a high reward value. When the number of edge servers is 15, the system's reward figure exceeds 1200. This is because the increase in edge nodes means that more IoT devices are covered and more tasks are handled, so the system gain increases. Each agent can output better decision results for the task, and the model can converge steadily at a high reward value. This validates the stability of the model's decision making capability.

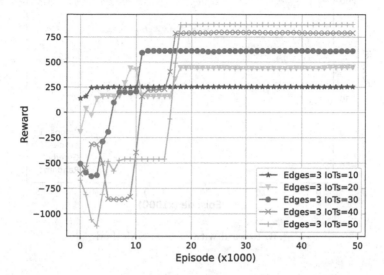

Fig. 5. Reward with Different Numbers of IoT devices.

Figure 5 shows the change in system reward when increasing the number of IoT devices served by the edge server. The number of edge servers is set as 3, and the number of IoT tasks served by each edge node has been increased from 10 to 50. When the number of tasks increases to 50, there are many negative rewards at the beginning of training. This is because our model has a penalty mechanism. Failure to complete all tasks within the current time slot will result in a negative value, and decisions that exceed the capacity of the edge server will also result in a negative reward. As the number of tasks increases, it becomes more difficult for the system to make decisions with constant resources. However, after continuous training of the system, it can eventually converge to a relatively optimal reward value. This illustrates the good adaptability of our method.

Figure 6 shows a comparison of the reward values obtained by the different methods for the case of three edge servers, each handling the task of 10 IoT devices. We compare with some existing schemes, such as the greedy strategy, the random strategy, and similar to the method proposed in the article [15]. As shown in the figure, the rewards of random method do not converge well to higher values and the values fluctuate continuously. For the greedy algorithms, although the reward value has been increasing, the value may be limited to the local optimum without achieving higher gains. Article [15] presents an improved dueling DQN method that is able to converge to a better value, but its convergence speed is slower compared to our proposed method and the convergence value is lower than the value obtained by our method. This demonstrates the advantages of our approach and also illustrates that the adoption of our proposed approach

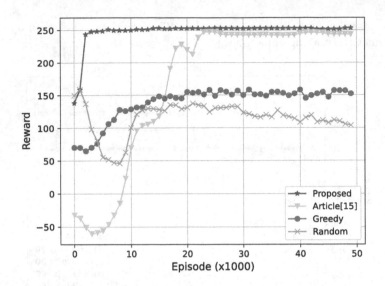

Fig. 6. Reward with Different Method.

allows blockchain networks with end-to-end cloud architecture to process tasks faster and with less transaction latency.

Figure 7 shows the task processing time of different methods under different IoT task. The number of edge servers is set as 3, and the number of IoT tasks for each edge server increased from 10 to 50. We can see that the results of the random method are still inferior to the other three methods. The greedy algorithm has significant time fluctuations due to converging to local optimal values during execution. The method in article [15] is superior to the first two methods, but slightly worse than our proposed method. This demonstrates the advantages of the proposed method.

We also simulated the time consumption of PBFT consensus communication. We conduct comparative experiments on the main factors affecting consensus time, including the number of consensus nodes and the transmission delay of the communication line between edge servers and the cloud server. Figure 8 shows the comparison of time consumption under different consensus node numbers. In this figure, we set the block size to 1MB and the latency between the edge server and cloud server is 0.5 s. In this setting, the consensus time for deploying leader on edge nodes and cloud server is similar and does not differ much. The time consumption of consensus increases with the number of consensus nodes whether the leader node is deployed on the edge server or on the cloud server. When the number of consensus nodes is small, the time consumption of the leader on the edge server is greater than on the cloud server, but as the number of nodes increases, the time consumption is less when the leader is deployed on the edge server than on the cloud server. When the delay is 0.5 s and the number of nodes participating in consensus is 22, the time consumption of consensus exceeds 20 s,

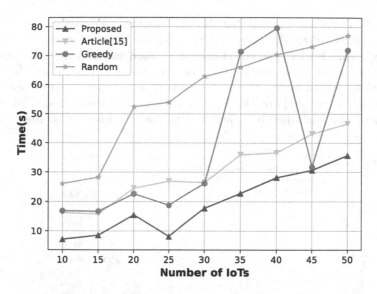

Fig. 7. Task Processing Time with Different Method.

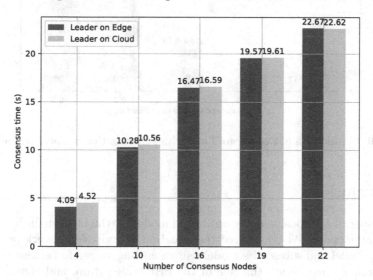

Fig. 8. Comparison of Consensus Time with Different Number of Nodes.

which is hardly acceptable in practical applications. This also indicates that it is inefficient for a large number of nodes to perform consensus in a network with large latency. Figure 9 shows the consensus time of the PBFT algorithm as it varies with the link delay. There are four nodes involved in consensus communication. The delay here mainly refers to the communication delay between the edge server and the cloud server, which is the meaning represented by T_{route}.

From the figure, it can be seen that the consensus time increases with the delay. When the delay is low, the consensus time for the entire blockchain network is smaller when the leader is on the cloud server. As delay increases, the consensus time for the blockchain network is smaller when the leader is on the edge server. Compared to replica nodes, the leader node takes on more communications in the pre-prepare and prepare phases of consensus. The leader node suffers from the delay on the link when it is deployed on the cloud server, so the consensus time increases.

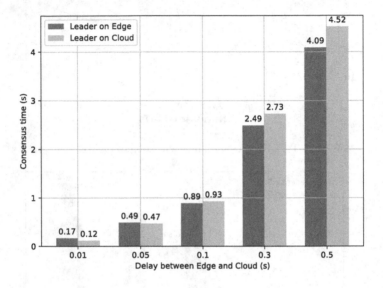

Fig. 9. Comparison of Consensus Time with Different Communication Delay.

5   Conclusions

In this paper, we propose a delay optimized model for the blockchain-based end-edge-cloud network. We considered the situation of multiple network processing tasks in parallel and solved the model using multi-agent reinforcement learning. In addition, we investigate the rule of the PBFT algorithm, and compared the consensus time when leader node is on edge servers and cloud servers. In the experiment, our proposed method can obtain better performance, adaptability, and convergence speed. For the analysis of consensus time, the number of consensus nodes and the delay between the edge and cloud are the main factors. When the delay is large, the leader on the edge is more appropriate. When the number of consensus nodes is large, the leader on the cloud makes the consensus time shorter. With the further development of the research, we will implement a leader generation algorithm that takes into account the resource of the nodes. The algorithm attempts to elect leaders on resource-rich nodes to improve consensus efficiency while ensuring consistency.

Acknowledgements. This work was supported by the National Key R&D Program of China under Grant 2018YFB1402700, and in part by the National Natural Science Foundation of China under Grant 61690202.

References

1. Lu, Y., Huang, X., Zhang, K., Maharjan, S., Zhang, Y.: Blockchain empowered asynchronous federated learning for secure data sharing in internet of vehicles. IEEE Trans. Veh. Technol. **69**(4), 4298–4311 (2020)
2. Maksymyuk, T., et al.: Blockchain-empowered framework for decentralized network management in 6G. IEEE Commun. Mag. **58**(9), 86–92 (2021)
3. Shubhani, A., Neeraj, K., Sudeep, T.: Blockchain-envisioned UAV communication using 6G networks: open issues, use cases, and future directions. IEEE Internet Things J. **8**(7) (2021)
4. Jiang, M., Wu, T., Wang, Z., Gong, Y., Zhang, L., Liu, R.P.: A multi-intersection vehicular cooperative control based on end-edge-cloud computing. IEEE Trans. Veh. Technol. **71**(3), 2459–2471 (2022)
5. Duan, S., et al.: Distributed artificial intelligence empowered by end-edge-cloud computing: a survey. IEEE Commun. Surv. Tutor. **25**(1), 591–624 (2023)
6. Zhang, S., Wang, Z., Zhou, Z., Wang, Y., Zhang, H., et al.: Blockchain and federated deep reinforcement learning based secure cloud-edge-end collaboration in power IoT. IEEE Wirel. Commun. **29**(2), 84–91 (2022)
7. Mafakheri, B., Heider-Aviet, A., Riggio, R., Goratti, L.: Smart contracts in the 5G roaming architecture: the fusion of blockchain with 5G networks. IEEE Commun. Mag. **59**(3), 77–83 (2021)
8. Li, W., Su, Z., Li, R., Zhang, K., Wang, Y.: Blockchain-based data security for artificial intelligence applications in 6G networks. IEEE Netw. **34**(6), 31–37 (2020)
9. Wang, X., Zhao, Y., Qiu, C., Liu, Z., Nie, J., Leung, V.C.M.: InFEDge: a blockchain-based incentive mechanism in hierarchical federated learning for end edge-cloud communications. IEEE J. Sel. Areas Commun. **40**(12), 3325–3342 (2022)
10. Ding, Y., Li, K., Liu, C., Li, K.: InFEDGe: a blockchain-based incentive mechanism in hierarchical federated learning for end-edge-cloud communications. IEEE Trans. Parallel Distrib. Syst. **33**(6), 1503–1519 (2022)
11. Feng, J., Yu, F.R., Pei, Q., Du, J., Zhu, L.: Joint optimization of radio and computational resources allocation in blockchain-enabled mobile edge computing systems. IEEE Trans. Wirel. Commun. **19**(6), 4321–4334 (2020)
12. Zhang, X., Peng, M., Yan, S., Sun, Y.: Joint communication and computation resource allocation in fog-based vehicular networks. IEEE Internet Things J. **9**(15), 13195–13208 (2022)
13. Yang, Z., Liang, B., Ji, W.: An intelligent end-edge-cloud architecture for visual IoT-assisted healthcare systems. IEEE Internet Things J. **8**(23), 16779–16786 (2021)
14. Liao, H., Jia, Z., Zhou, Z., Wang, Y., Zhang, H., et al.: Cloud-edge-end collaboration in air-ground integrated power IoT: a semi-distributed learning approach. IEEE Trans. Ind. Inform. **18**(11), 8047–8057 (2022)
15. Li, M., Yu, F.R., Si, P., Wu, W., Zhang, Y.: Resource optimization for delay-tolerant data in blockchain-enabled IoT with edge computing: a deep reinforcement learning approach. IEEE Internet Things J. **7**(10), 9399–9412 (2020)

16. Liu, M., Yu, F.R., Teng, Y., Leung, V.C.M., Song, M.: Performance optimization for blockchain-enabled industrial internet of things (IIoT) systems: a deep reinforcement learning approach. IEEE Trans. Ind. Inform. **15**(6), 3559–3570 (2019)

17. Qu, G., Cui, N., Wu, H., Li, R., Ding, Y.: ChainFL: a simulation platform for joint federated learning and blockchain in edge/cloud computing environments. IEEE Trans. Ind. Inform. **18**(5), 3572–3581 (2022)

18. Lu, Y., Huang, X., Zhang, K., Maharjan, S., Zhang, Y.: Low-latency federated learning and blockchain for edge association in digital twin empowered 6G networks. IEEE Trans. Ind. Inform. **17**(7), 5098–5107 (2021)

19. Castro, M., Liskov, B.: Practical Byzantine fault tolerance. In: Proceedings of the Third Symposium on Operating Systems Design and Implementation, vol. 17, no. 7, pp. 173–186 (1999)

20. Cao, B., Wang, X., Zhang, W., Song, H., Lv, Z.: A many-objective optimization model of industrial internet of things based on private blockchain. IEEE Netw. **34**(5), 78–83 (2020)

21. Chunlin, L., Jing, Z., Xianmin, Y., Luo, Y.: Lightweight blockchain consensus mechanism and storage optimization for resource constrained IoT devices. Inf. Process. Manag. **58**(4), 102602 (2021)

22. Ryan, L., Yi, W., Aviv, T., Jean, H., Pieter, A., Igor, M.: Multi-agent actor-critic for mixed cooperative-competitive environments. In: 31st International Conference on Neural Information Processing Systems (NIPS 2017). Curran Associates Inc., Red Hook (2017)

23. Lillicrap, T.P., et al.: Continuous control with deep reinforcement learning. In: 4th International Conference on Learning Representations, ICLR 2016 (2016)

24. Barto, A.G., Sutton, R.S., Anderson, C.W.: Neuronlike adaptive elements that can solve difficult learning control problems. IEEE Trans. Syst. Man Cybern. **13**(5), 834–846 (1983)

Computer Architecture and Hardware Acceleration

A Low-Latency Hardware Accelerator
for YOLO Object Detection Algorithms

Aibin Wang[1,2], Youshi Ye[2], Yu Peng[2], Dezheng Zhang[1], Zhihong Yan[1],
and Dong Wang[1(✉)]

[1] Institute of Information Science, Beijing Jiaotong University, Beijing 100044, China
wangdong@bjtu.edu.cn
[2] Beijing Institute of Control Engineering, Beijing 100190, China

Abstract. Object detection is an important computer vision task with
a wide range of applications, including autonomous driving, smart security, and other domains. However, the high computational requirements
poses challenges on deploying object detection on resource-limited edge
devices. Thus dedicated hardware accelerators are desired to delever
improved performances on detection speed and latency. Post-processing
is a key step in object detection. It involves intensive computation on the
CPU or GPU. The non-maximum suppression (NMS) algorithm is the
core of post-processing, which can eliminate redundant boxes belonging
to the same object. However, NMS becomes a bottleneck for hardware
acceleration due to its characteristics of multiple iterations and waiting
for all predicted boxes to be generated.

In this paper, we propose a novel hardware-friendly NMS algorithm
for FPGA accelerator design. Our proposed algorithm alleviates the performance bottleneck of NMS by implementing the iterative algorithm
into an efficient pipelined hardware circuit. We validate our algorithm on
the VOC2007 dataset and show that it only brings 0.27% difference compared to the baseline NMS. Additional, the exponential function and sigmoid function are also extremely hardware-costly. To address this issue,
we propose an approximate exponential function circuit to calculate the
two functions with minimum logic cost and zero DSP cost.

We deploy our post-processing accelerator on Xilinx's Alveo U50
FPGA board. The final design achieves a end-to-end detection latency
of 283us for YOLOv2 model, According to the user guide provided by
Xilinx and Intel, we converted the logic resources of different implementations on the FPGA into LUT resources. After that, we compared the
resource utilization of acceleration module in the current state-of-the-
art object detection system deployed on Intel with ours. Compared with
it, we consumed 13.5× lower LUT resources and used much fewer DSP
resources.

Keywords: Object detection · Neural network accelerator ·
Hardware-friendly NMS algorithm

This work was partially supported by Open Fund (NO. OBCandETL-2022-06) of Space
Advanced Computing and Electronic Information Laboratory of BICE.

© The Author(s), under exclusive license to Springer Nature Singapore Pte Ltd. 2024
C. Li et al. (Eds.): APPT 2023, LNCS 14103, pp. 265–278, 2024.
https://doi.org/10.1007/978-981-99-7872-4_15

1   Introduction

In the field of computer vision, object detection algorithms based on deep learning have received wide attention and are widely applied [16]. According to the different detection methods, object detection algorithms can be divided into single-stage and two-stage detection algorithms. Generally, single-stage object detection algorithms have faster detection speed than two-stage algorithms, but there is a slight loss in accuracy. Single-stage object detection algorithms are often more preferred for embedded devices such as autonomous driving applications, as they simplify the object detection process and are more suitable for mobile embedded devices. Traditional single-stage object detection network frameworks include SSD [8] and YOLO series [11–13]. The YOLO network unified the feature extraction, object classification, and object bounding box regression into a complete convolutional neural network, simplifying the object detection process and making it more suitable for mobile devices.

However, due to the high computational complexity and excessive parameter count, deployment of convolutional neural networks (CNNs) on embedded devices still faces challenges. Recently, various hardware accelerators have been proposed, such as UNPU [5], Eyeriss [3], and TPU [4], which are designed for general neural network operations (i.e., convolutions). Some other researchers make efforts to the deployment of neural networks on FPGAs with low-bitwidth or sparse representations to reduce the excessive parameter count [10, 14]. However, the post-processing stage of object detection algorithms, which involves removing redundant boxes and generating bounding boxes, has not been previously designed with hardware acceleration in mind.

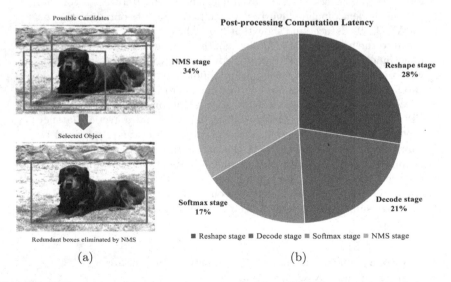

Fig. 1. (a) The process of non maximum suppression; (b) The computation latency of NMS in the post-processing stage

Most CNN hardware accelerators implement the post-processing stage on the CPU, where processing speed is slow, making it a bottleneck in achieving fast object detection. Non-maximum suppression (NMS) is a common algorithm for the post-processing stage of object detection, aimed at removing redundant boxes belonging to the same object, as shown in Fig. 1(a). The standard NMS algorithm is a greedy algorithm that requires all bounding boxes to be sorted. This property creates a strict sequential dependency between the prediction head and NMS algorithm, which is not friendly to hardware acceleration. NMS must wait for all bounding boxes to be generated before processing them, resulting in significant delay overhead throughout the entire system. The computation latency of NMS in the post-processing stage is shown in Fig. 1(b).

To address the aforementioned challenges in achieving high-speed object detection on edge devices, we propose a novel NMS algorithm to eliminate the strict sequential dependency between the NMS algorithm and the prediction head, while achieving minimal functionality degradation. Additionally, We exploit the property that the output of the convolution layer of a neural network is a fixed-point number with a fixed range after quantization. This allows us to simplify the computational complexity of complex functions in the post-processing process. We propose a configurable post-processing hardware acceleration structure that can be deployed on datasets with varying numbers of classes in a pipelined manner. In summary, our contributions are as follows:

- We proposed a novel NMS algorithm that is suitable for hardware pipeline implementation eliminating the strict sequence dependency. The hardware-friendly NMS algorithm exhibited a negligible performance decrease of 0.27% on the VOC2007 dataset and 0.03% on SAR ship images. This suggests that the algorithm is well-suited for hardware acceleration, while maintaining high accuracy.
- Accordingly, we developed a low-latency hardware accelerator design to implement the improved NMS algorithm on FPGA device with the flexible capability of multi-class and single-class object detection.
- Finally, we use a fixed-point implementation of the sigmoid function to simplify the computational complexity in the post-processing process. This is a more accurate approximation of the sigmoid function than the Taylor series expansion implementation, and it can be implemented efficiently in hardware.

2 Background and Related Work

2.1 The Network Architecture of Yolov2

Object detectors mainly include one-stage and two-stage detectors. One-stage detectors directly perform regression and classification on the input image, outputting the position, size, and category of the target. In contrast, two-stage detectors first generate candidate boxes and then perform regression and classification on each candidate box, outputting the final target. Common one-stage object detectors include SSD [8] and YOLOv2 [12]. In this work, we prefer one-stage object detectors, especially YOLOv2, because of its better real-time performance. The overall architecture of YOLOv2 is shown in Fig. 2.

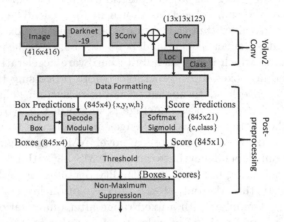

Fig. 2. YOLOv2 Structure Overview

As shown in Fig. 2, after the input image has been extracted features by Darknet-19, the prediction head outputs bounding box location information relative to anchor boxes. Anchor boxes are idealized boundaries that are predefined in different sizes and aspect ratios during model training for bounding objects in the image. The purpose of using anchor boxes is to improve the efficiency and accuracy of object detection. When the input image resolution is 416 × 416, after 32-times downsampling, YOLOv2 will divides the input image into 13 × 13 grids, and each grid has 5 anchor boxes. Therefore, a total of 845 candidate box information is generated.

The output feature map (13 × 13 × 125) generated after passing through darknet-19 for feature extraction undergoes data formatting operations (e.g. reshapes, divisions, convert fixpoint to float) to produce a list of 845 boxes (each described by $\{x, y, w, h\}$) and score information (each described by $\{c, cls\}$) for downstream processing. These generated box information are then passed through a decode module and matched with predefined anchor boxes to produce a series of predicted boxes, as shown in Eq. 1. Moreover, sigmoid and softmax functions are applied to the score list to generate prediction scores for 20 classes, as shown in Eq. 2. The resulting lists (containing boxes and scores) are passed through a threshold function, such that only boxes with scores higher than a predefined threshold are processed by NMS.

$$
\begin{aligned}
b_x &= \delta(t_x) + c_x \\
b_y &= \delta(t_y) + c_y \\
b_w &= P_w e^{t_w} \\
b_h &= P_h e^{t_h}
\end{aligned}
\tag{1}
$$

where b_x, b_y, b_w, b_h are the center and width and height of the predicted bounding box. c_x, c_y are the distances from the top left corner of the current grid to the top left corner of the image. P_w, P_h are the width and height of the anchor. δ is the sigmoid function. tx, ty, tw, th are the parameters to be learned, which are used to predict the center and width and height of the bounding box respectively. Here they refer to the outputs of the convolutional layer.

$$Sigmoid = \frac{1}{1 + e^{-x}}, \quad Softmax = \frac{exp(S_i)}{\sum_{i=1}^{N} exp(S_i)} \tag{2}$$

2.2   Non-maximum Suppression

The baseline NMS algorithm implemented in the object detection system based on YOLOv2 is shown in Algorithm 1. The NMS algorithm is used to filter out redundant and overlapping boxes and select the ones with the highest confidence scores. The algorithm takes as input a list of boxes and scores and outputs a list of final detections. The algorithm works as follows: (1) For each of the 21 classes, sorting the boxes by their scores of this class in descending order by using the argSort function. (2) Initialize an empty list for selected boxes. (3) For each class, while the list of candidate boxes is not empty, pop the box with the highest score from the candidate list and append it to the selected boxes. For each remaining box in the candidate boxes, calculate the intersection over union (IoU) between the popped box and the current box. If IoU is greater than a predefined threshold, remove the current box from the list. (4) Repeat step 3 until there are no more boxes left.

Algorithm 1. Baseline NMS algorithm

1: **procedure** NON-MAXIMUM SUPPRESSION
2:      $D \leftarrow$ sorted list of bounding boxes and their scores
3:      $S \leftarrow$ empty set of selected bounding boxes
4:      **while** $D \neq \varnothing$ **do**
5:          $B \leftarrow$ bounding box with highest score in D
6:          add B to S
7:          **for** $B' \in D$ **do**
8:              **if** $IoU(B, B') > threshold$ **then**
9:                  remove B' from D
10:             **end if**
11:         **end for**
12:     **end while**
13:     **return** S
14: **end procedure**

2.3 Bottleneck Analysis

Implement of Complex Function. Complex functions such as exponential functions consume a large amount of DSP resources when implemented on hardware circuits [6]. If deployed on edge embedded devices, a more resource-optimized deployment method needs to be considered. In the post-processing stage of calculating coordinates and scores, there will be a large number of calculations involving complex functions composed of exponential functions (such as softmax function, sigmoid function). We use the characteristics of quantized networks to design simplified calculation methods for corresponding functions according to their mapping relationships.

Limitations of NMS Implement. Firstly, the sorting operation at the beginning of the baseline NMS algorithm poses a challenge for hardware deployment. The sorting operation brings extra time and space overhead to the hardware. The sorting operation requires waiting for all the boxes to be generated, which causes a considerable time delay. Moreover, the process of removing redundant boxes by NMS has a strict sequential dependency, and the hardware cannot execute it in a pipelined manner, which reduces the throughput of the entire processing process. In addition, waiting for all the boxes to be generated requires more intermediate storage space.

2.4 FPGA-Based Object Detection System.

Although most previous works have deployed object detection systems on FPGA, most of them did not implement the post-processing stage on FPGA, but rather executed them on CPU [2,9]. A few works proposed hardware acceleration for various modules in the post-processing stage (including the NMS module), but these works did not have corresponding quantization schemes for the post-processing stage after low-bit quantization. Most convolutional outputs had to be dequantized and calculated in floating-point format in function [1,7,15].

The authors of [13] built an FPGA-based object detection system on YOLO. They deployed an NMS module with bubble sorting on the FPGA, which leveraged the parallelization and reuse of IOU computation units to enhance the computational efficiency of the NMS algorithm. The final latency of the two modules working together on the Xilinx Viertex-7 FPGA was 680us. The authors of [15] implemented an end-to-end object detection system on the FPGA (including the post-processing stage) with extremely low latency and high throughput. The NMS module only introduced a negligible delay (only 0.13us) on the Xlinx Stratix 10 GX2800 FPGA. Compared to previous work, they were the first eliminated the sorting constraint in the NMS stage, and validated their approach on the COCO dataset with a mean average precision (mAP) of 22.5%. However, their NMS module consumed a large amount of resources (the post-processing module consumed 695 DSP resources), which posed a great challenge for deployment on resource-constrained embedded edge devices.

3   Proposed Design

3.1   Hardware-Friendly NMS Algorithm

The flow of the proposed hardware-friendly NMS algorithm is depicted in Algorithm 2.

Sorting are often essential in the Baseline NMS algorithm, but due to their high iteration and the limit of waiting for all candidate boxes to be generated, deploying them on hardware can cause significant delays. Unlike Baseline NMS,

---

Algorithm 2. Novel hardware-friendly NMS algorithm

Input: $scores, boxes, IOU_{thr}$
Output: $detected\_objects$
1: **Instantiate** $selected\_boxes$
2: **for** each box in $boxes$ **do**
3:     $box\_inserted = Ture$;
4:     $box\_deleted = False$;
5:     $box\_replaced = False$;
6:     $box\_suppressed = False$;
7:     **for** each box in $sboxes$ **do**
8:         $IOU =$ **Calculate_IOU**$(box, sbox)$
9:         **if** $same\_class(box, sbox)$ & $IOU > IOU_{thr}$ **then**
10:             $box\_inserted = False$;
11:             **if** $box.score > sbox.score$ **then**
12:                 $box\_replaced = Ture$;
13:                 Remember the sbox index
14:             **if** $!box\_replaced$ **then**
15:                 $box\_deleted = Ture$;
16:                 Remember the sbox index
17:             **end if**
18:             **else**
19:                 $box\_suppressed = Ture$;
20:             **end if**
21:         **end if**
22:     **end for**
23:     replaceIf$(box\_suppressed, box\_replaced, boxes, sbox)$;
24:     deleteIf$(box\_suppressed, box\_deleted, boxes, sbox)$;
25: **end for**
26: $detected\_objects = selected\_boxes$;

27: **replaceIf(**$flag, boxes, sbox$**)is**
28: **if** $!box\_suppressed$ & $box\_replaced$ **then**
29:     $sbox[r\_index]$.replaceWith(box)
30: **end if**

31: **deleteIf(**$flag, boxes, sbox$**)is**
32: **if** $!box\_suppressed$ & $box\_deleted$ **then**
33:     **delete** $sbox[d\_index]$
34: **end if**

---

which sorts all candidate boxes at the beginning and requires boxes to be input in descending order of score, our algorithm does not require candidate boxes to be sorted by score. Our algorithm initializes a selected box list as empty at the beginning. For each input candidate box, it is first declared as the candidate object to be inserted (line 3), and then the IOU calculation operation and score comparison are performed between the input candidate box and all elements in the selected box list one by one.

The goal of NMS is to search for local maximum values and suppress non-maximum values. However, algorithms with sequential structures are not easy to search for local maximum values. The same data input in different orders may result in different outcomes. To solve this problem and make the results of Novel NMS more accurate, we have imposed some constraints on the insertion and replacement of new candidate boxes. When the result of IOU calculation between candidate box and select box is greater than the threshold, we compare their scores (line 7–11). If the candidate box is better, we mark it (it may replace the selected box later, line 12). We still need to compare the candidate boxes with the remaining part of the selected box list to remove the boxes that were previously selected from the same category with lower prediction scores and IOUs higher than the threshold. We mark it when the predicted score of the input candidate box is lower than that of the selected box and IOU is higher than the threshold (not allowing it to replace any candidate box, line 19). We perform replacement and deletion operations only after comparing all elements in the selected box list (line 23–24, 27–34).

Although our algorithm does not involve sorting scores, it achieves consistent functionality with baseline algorithms and ensures consistent results even under conditions of different order inputs. Sorting is implicitly performed because we replace, delete, insert and suppress selected boxes based on their scores and calculated IOUs.

3.2   Post-processing Implementation Overview

The proposed architecture of the Post-Processing Accelerator is presented in Fig. 3. The convolution layers of Yolov2 predicts 845 box coordinates as described in Sect. 2, each with score predictions for the 20 classes and 1 Confidence. These outputs are processed in dataflow by the Decode module and Softmax module to consolidate the boxes for the final detection.

3.3   Post-processing Implementation Details

In order to effectively complete NMS calculations, we have proposed some circuit improvements in the following sections.

Approximated Method of Exponential Arithmetic. Exponential and sigmoid functions are very challenging for hardware implementation, but they are essential for Softmax computation. Since our quantization algorithm can quantize the post-processing input to -128 to 127, we can design an approximate

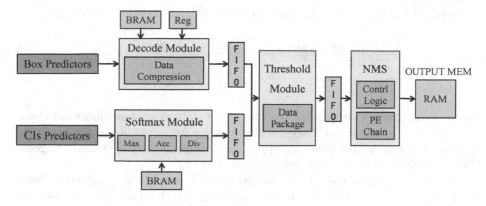

Fig. 3. Architecture of Post-Processing Accelerator

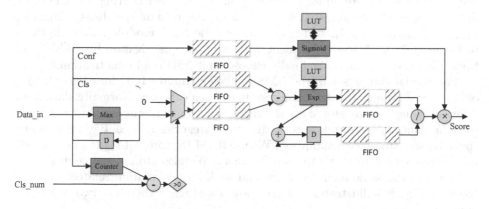

Fig. 4. The Process of Softmax Module

exponential function circuit easily. As shown in Fig. 4, we use a lookup table to store the dequantized function values in Block RAM (BRAM). In the post-processing stage, we need to compute exponential and sigmoid functions for Score calculation. The dequantized values of these functions are stored in different BRAMs for parallel access.

Moreover, we exploit the property of Softmax computation to compress some of the dequantized outputs. Because Softmax involves normalization, the normalized output ranges from negative infinity to zero, and the corresponding exponential output ranges from zero to one. This can be easily quantized with 8-bit fixed-point numbers. By doing so, we further reduce the storage space consumption.

Overall, we only need 3 M32K BRAMs to store all the dequantized results. This method introduces very small errors compared with function approximation methods such as Taylor series expansion, and most importantly, it does not consume any DSP resources. As shown in Table 1, we compare the resource utilization with different method of sigmoid function implement.

Table 1. Comparation of implementations of sigmoid function approximations

	Logic	Register	Memory	DSP	M32K BRAMs
[15]	67	134	2304	2	–
Ours	38	23	–	0	1.5

Data and Space Compression. The object detection algorithm produces a large number of candidate boxes, which poses a great challenge for hardware storage. To address this issue, we apply data compression and spatial compression techniques to reduce the storage space demand.

For data compression, the convolution layer outputs are converted back to floating-point numbers after dequantization in the Decode and Softmax modules. Floating-point numbers offer higher accuracy for computation, but they also require more storage space. A single-precision floating-point number needs 4 bytes of storage space. To quantize the output coordinate data(i.e., $\{x_{min}, y_{min}, x_{max}, y_{max}\}$, which are fed into the NMS module), we scale them to between 0 and 1. We experiment with different quantization bit-widths and their effects on accuracy. We finally choose 8-bit fractional quantization.

For spatial compression, the NMS module computes IOU for each category of boxes and obtains the detection results for each category. Normally, data from different categories are stored separately, which avoids interference but also leads to redundancy. We store data from different categories in a contiguous memory space to save storage consumption. We use RAM to store data contiguously and use category tags to mark them in memory. We also store some control logic for NMS in the same memory space and pack all information related to a box together. Figure 7 illustrates how data are stored when there are two categories (Fig. 5).

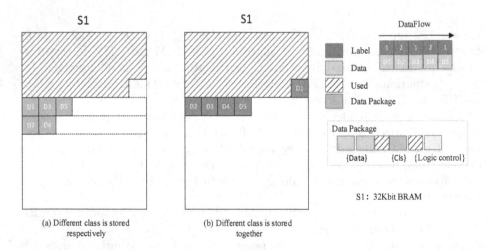

(a) Different class is stored respectively

(b) Different class is stored together

Fig. 5. The Process of Data Package

NMS Hardware Implementation. As shown in Fig. 6, the post-processing module is composed of a processing element (PE) and a control logic block. The PE contains a buffer that stores a packed data of a single bounding box (including coordinates, score, class and control logic) and an IOU computation unit. The PE traverses the select boxes in the buffer and performs a series of comparisons and IOU calculations with the new input box. The control logic block determines whether to replace, ignore or delete the local or incoming bounding box based on the results. Each bounding box in the PE has a suppression flag to prevent erroneous deletion in the sequential structure, which is explained in detail previously. The NMS module does not wait for all bounding boxes to be generated by the convolutional layer and Decode/Softmax module of Yolov2. Instead, it uses a first-in first-out (FIFO) queue to buffer the input.

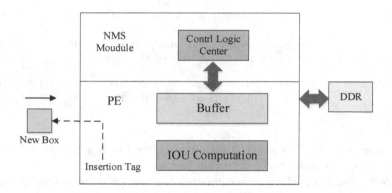

Fig. 6. NMS Hardware Implementation.

4 Experiment Result

We implemented and deployed neural network accelerators and post-processing accelerators on Xilinx Alveo U50 FPGA attached as a PCIe accelerator card to an AMD RyZenq 5950X server with 16 dual-threaded cores, a working frequency of 3.4 GHz and 64 GB RAM. In this setup, the host CPU sends input images to the FPGA accelerator card and receives the returned output prediction via the PCIe link. Similarly, the post-processing acceleration module is part of the entire system and outputs the corresponding results to the host CPU via the PCIe link after processing the convolution layer output results. The actual execution time of the post-processing module is measured using Xilinx Runtime Library (XRT) analysis API. The resource consumption of the post-processing module on the entire development board was also calculated using Vivado2022 tools.

We tested our post-processing accelerator on multi-class datasets and single-class datasets separately. We validated the system's functionality on 4952 validation images from VOC2007 dataset and 232 validation images from remote

Table 2. Comparison with general-purpose hardware

	Frequency (MHz)	Accuracy	Latency (us)	Dataset
AMD Ryzenq 5950X	3400	75.09%	555	VOC
		90.41%	141	SAR
Our Work	300	74.82%	**283**	VOC
		90.38%	**78**	SAR

Table 3. Comparison of our work to prior FPGA-based postprocessing accelerator

	LUTRAM	DSPs	BRAMs	FF	Latency	FPGA Device	Frequency (Mhz)	Boxes number	Best boxes	Multi Class
F. Liang et al. [7]	2890	36	203	11842	680 us	Viertex-7 485T	100	1960	3	No
H. Zhang et al. [15]	714	22	32	11139	32 us	Zynq-7 VC 706	100	3000	5	No
A. Anupreetham et al. [1]	–	695	425	86,704	0.13 us	Stratix 10 GX2800	350	1917	–	Yes
This work	1364	77	24.5	13929	283 us	Alveo U50	300	845	128	Yes
	1181	77	11	16071	78 us	Alveo U50	300	845	5	No

sensing ship dataset. This proves that our architecture is versatile and suitable for not only single-class object detection tasks.

Table 2 present a performance comparison of our post-processing accelerator with general hardware on the VOC2007 dataset and SAR image ship dataset. The post-processing accelerator uses a hardware-friendly NMS algorithm to significantly reduce latency while only incurring an acceptable loss of accuracy. Specifically, the mAP decreases by 0.17% on the VOC2007 dataset and only 0.03% on the SAR image ship dataset. Our results demonstrate that the post-processing accelerator is a promising approach for FPGA neural network acceleration. The accelerator achieves significant latency reductions while maintaining high accuracy, making it a valuable tool for real-time applications.

Table 3 compares our work with other object detectors that deploy post-processing on FPGAs. Some of the works in the Table 3 are implemented on different feature extraction networks and object detectors, but this does not affect the comparison and evaluation of their post-processing modules. The most relevant comparison is against the work of [1], which is implemented on the same generation of Intel FPGA and is the only object detection accelerator that verifies processing acceleration modules on multi-class datasets. Compared with its high throughput and low latency implementation, our accelerator has lower resource utilization. According to the user guide provided by Xilinx and Intel, we converted the logic resources of different implementations on the FPGA into LUT resources. The work of [1] used 86704 Adaptive Logic Module (ALM) resources in the post-processing module, each containing 2 LUT resources and 1 register resource. We converted this and compared it to the 13929 register

Fig. 7. The detection examples of Yolov2

resources and 12837 LUT resources we used in our work, we consumed 13.5×
lower LUT resources and 6× lower register resources.

We also deployed a single-class object detection task on FPGA based on
the post-processing architecture proposed in this paper using the VITIS HLS
toolchain. In order to ensure its versatility, we still retain the calculation process
that can be omitted, because this will affect its normal operation under multi-
class object detection tasks. The post-processing accelerator implemented by [15]
has lower resource utilization on DSP and LUTRAM. Nevertheless, our solution
ensures that the post-processing accelerator architecture we proposed is feasible
for different object detection tasks, and our solution still achieves lower resource
utilization and delay at higher detection accuracy.

5   Conclusion

In this paper, we propose a post-processing accelerator for FPGA-based
YOLOv2 object detection. We propose a novel hardware-friendly NMS algorithm for FPGA accelerator design, which alleviates the performance bottleneck
of NMS and deploys the corresponding hardware architecture. We validate our
algorithm on the VOC2007 dataset. In addition, we propose an approximate
exponential function circuit to simplify the computational complexity in the
post-processing stage. Our work achieves considerable detection accuracy while
using much fewer resources. This makes it possible to deploy object detection
on edge devices with more limited resources.

References

1. Anupreetham, A., et al.: End-to-end FPGA-based object detection using pipelined
   CNN and non-maximum suppression. In: 2021 31st International Conference on
   Field-Programmable Logic and Applications (FPL), pp. 76–82 (2021). https://doi.
   org/10.1109/FPL53798.2021.00021

2. Cai, L., Dong, F., Chen, K., Yu, K., Qu, W., Jiang, J.: An FPGA based heterogeneous accelerator for single shot multibox detector (SSD). In: 2020 IEEE 15th International Conference on Solid-State & Integrated Circuit Technology (ICSICT), pp. 1–3. IEEE (2020)

3. Chen, Y.H., Krishna, T., Emer, J.S., Sze, V.: Eyeriss: an energy-efficient reconfigurable accelerator for deep convolutional neural networks. IEEE J. Solid-State Circuits **52**(1), 127–138 (2016)

4. Jouppi, N.P., et al.: In-datacenter performance analysis of a tensor processing unit. In: Proceedings of the 44th Annual International Symposium on Computer Architecture, pp. 1–12 (2017)

5. Lee, J., Kim, C., Kang, S., Shin, D., Kim, S., Yoo, H.J.: UNPU: a 50.6 TOPS/W unified deep neural network accelerator with 1b-to-16b fully-variable weight bit-precision. In: 2018 IEEE International Solid-State Circuits Conference-(ISSCC), pp. 218–220. IEEE (2018)

6. Li, Z., Zhang, Y., Sui, B., Xing, Z., Wang, Q.: FPGA implementation for the sigmoid with piecewise linear fitting method based on curvature analysis. Electronics **11**(9), 1365 (2022)

7. Liang, F., Yang, S., Mai, T., Yang, Y.: The design of objects bounding boxes non-maximum suppression and visualization module based on FPGA. In: 2018 IEEE 23rd International Conference on Digital Signal Processing (DSP), pp. 1–5 (2018). https://doi.org/10.1109/ICDSP.2018.8631668

8. Liu, W., et al.: SSD: single shot multibox detector. In: Leibe, B., Matas, J., Sebe, N., Welling, M. (eds.) ECCV 2016. LNCS, vol. 9905, pp. 21–37. Springer, Cham (2016). https://doi.org/10.1007/978-3-319-46448-0_2

9. Ma, Y., Zheng, T., Cao, Y., Vrudhula, S., Seo, J.: Algorithm-hardware co-design of single shot detector for fast object detection on FPGAs. In: 2018 IEEE/ACM International Conference on Computer-Aided Design (ICCAD), pp. 1–8. IEEE (2018)

10. Mo, R., Xu, K., Liu, L., Liu, L., Wang, D.: Adaptive linear unit for accurate binary neural networks. In: 2022 16th IEEE International Conference on Signal Processing (ICSP), vol. 1, pp. 223–228 (2022). https://doi.org/10.1109/ICSP56322.2022.9965306

11. Redmon, J., Divvala, S., Girshick, R., Farhadi, A.: You only look once: unified, real-time object detection. In: Proceedings of the IEEE Conference on Computer Vision and Pattern Recognition, pp. 779–788 (2016)

12. Redmon, J., Farhadi, A.: YOLO9000: better, faster, stronger. In: Proceedings of the IEEE Conference on Computer Vision and Pattern Recognition, pp. 7263–7271 (2017)

13. Redmon, J., Farhadi, A.: YOLOv3: an incremental improvement. arXiv preprint arXiv:1804.02767 (2018)

14. Wang, Z., Xu, K., Wu, S., Liu, L., Liu, L., Wang, D.: Sparse-YOLO: hardware/software co-design of an FPGA accelerator for YOLOv2. IEEE Access **8**, 116569–116585 (2020). https://doi.org/10.1109/ACCESS.2020.3004198

15. Zhang, H., Wu, W., Ma, Y., Wang, Z.: Efficient hardware post processing of anchor-based object detection on FPGA. In: 2020 IEEE Computer Society Annual Symposium on VLSI (ISVLSI), pp. 580–585 (2020). https://doi.org/10.1109/ISVLSI49217.2020.00089

16. Zou, Z., Chen, K., Shi, Z., Guo, Y., Ye, J.: Object detection in 20 years: a survey. Proc. IEEE **111**(3), 257–276 (2023). https://doi.org/10.1109/JPROC.2023.3238524

SCFM: A Statistical Coarse-to-Fine Method to Select Cross-Microarchitecture Reliable Simulation Points

Chenji Han[1,2,3]($\boxtimes$), Hongze Tan[1,2,3], Tingting Zhang[2,4], Xinyu Li[1,2,3], Ruiyang Wu[4], and Fuxin Zhang[1,2]

[1] State Key Lab of Processors, ICT, CAS, Beijing 100190, China
[2] Institute of Computing Technology, CAS, Beijing 100190, China
[3] University of Chinese Academy of Sciences, Beijing 100049, China
hanchenji16@mails.ucas.ac.cn
[4] Loongson Technology Co., Ltd., Beijing 100190, China

Abstract. With computer microarchitectures advancing and benchmark sizes expanding, the need for agile pre-silicon performance estimation becomes increasingly crucial. SimPoint is a widely used sampling method to solve this problem, making it a promising research area. However, previous studies mainly focus on how to enhance the estimation accuracy, speedup, and usability of SimPoint, while ignoring the critical problem of cross-microarchitecture estimation reliability. We have observed that although SimPoint can provide an accurate performance estimation, it could fail in yielding reliable estimations across different microarchitectures due to the difficulties in **(a)** rapidly evaluating the cross-microarchitecture reliability of SimPoint and **(b)** effectively selecting reliable simulation points.

To address this problem, we propose SCFM, a statistical coarse-to-fine method to select cross-microarchitecture reliable simulation points. The SCFM introduces two key metrics: the micro-independent metric E_{repre} and micro-dependent metric $Loss$, to rapidly evaluate the simulation points. Our method could efficiently scan a large SimPoint parameter space by rapidly evaluating their program characteristic representation abilities and precisely assessing their cross-microarchitecture estimation capabilities. To verify the effectiveness of SCFM, we conducted thorough evaluations, configuring thirty distinct machine models to select reliable simulation points and preparing three test models to implement the verification. Experimental results demonstrate that the final-selected reliable simulation points could yield statistically accurate estimations for SPEC CPU 2006 on the test models, giving average errors of less than 1%.

Keywords: SimPoint · Performance Analysis · Statistical Analysis · Coarse-to-Fine Method · Emulation Accelerators

© The Author(s), under exclusive license to Springer Nature Singapore Pte Ltd. 2024
C. Li et al. (Eds.): APPT 2023, LNCS 14103, pp. 279–296, 2024.
https://doi.org/10.1007/978-981-99-7872-4_16

1   Introduction

Nowadays, fast and agile computer microarchitecture designs depend heavily on accurate and efficient simulation. With the rapid growth of the microarchitecture complexity and the benchmark size, the simulation time gradually becomes unacceptable. It usually takes several months to simulate the SPEC CPU 2006 with the reference input on cycle-accurate simulators [17]. To address this problem, several solutions have been proposed from aspects of the input set reduction [11], systematic sampling [29], representative sampling [24], and others. Among these methods, SimPoint [6,20,24] is a fast and accurate simulation tool and has drawn considerable attention from researchers and engineers.

However, existing studies mainly focus on how to enhance the estimation accuracy [7,10,14,16,20,23,28], speedup [3,22,26], and usability [12,15,18,31] of SimPoint, while ignoring the critical problem of cross-microarchitecture estimation reliability. Although SimPoint is able to give an accurate estimation [4,17,27,30], we observed that it could fail in yielding reliable estimations across various microarchitectures with inappropriate simulation points selected. This phenomenon suggests the existence of inherent errors in SimPoint, arising from issues like the imperfect representation ability of the basic block vector [14], suboptimal clustering [7], and insufficient warm-up [1]. Compared with giving accurate estimation on a single microarchitecture, accurately estimating performance across various microarchitectures is more significant for SimPoint. The large variances in estimation accuracy across different microarchitectures would significantly mislead the pre-silicon performance analysis, leading to incorrect design decisions.

The challenges of selecting cross-microarchitecture reliable simulation points mainly stem from **(a)** how to rapidly evaluate the cross-microarchitecture reliability of SimPoint and **(b)** how to effectively guide the selection of reliable simulation points, as explained below.

Firstly, to precisely assess the estimation accuracy of the SimPoint, it necessitates the information of both the complete run time and the extrapolated run time given by SimPoint of the same program on the same microarchitecture. To further evaluate the cross-microarchitecture reliability, the simulation points are required to be evaluated on distinct microarchitectures. However, existing works [4,15,31] primarily utilize the simulators as the evaluation platforms to assess the estimation accuracy of simulation points, which are quite time-consuming, especially when the number of microarchitecture configurations is large. Therefore, it requires a platform to rapidly and precisely evaluate the estimation accuracy of SimPoint.

Secondly, there are several significant parameters in the SimPoint [8], and each SimPoint parameter configuration corresponds to a set of simulation points. Because of the obscure and uncertain relationship between the SimPoint parameters and the cross-microarchitecture reliability, the traversal of parameter configurations are necessary to experimentally measure (rather than theoretically calculate) their cross-microarchitecture reliability and pick the optimal simulation points. However, the excessively large parameter space makes this process

impractical due to the limited time budgets. Therefore, it requires an agile approach to effectively assess the simulation points and rapidly select the desired
reliable simulation points.

In this work, responding to these challenges, we propose SCFM, a Statistical
Coarse-to-Fine Method to Select Cross-Microarchitecture Reliable Simulation
Points. The SCFM introduces two key metrics: the micro-independent[1] metric
E_{repre} and micro-dependent metric $Loss$, to rapidly evaluate the program characteristic representation abilities and precisely assess the cross-microarchitecture
estimation capabilities, respectively. Therefore, the SCFM could effectively scan
a large SimPoint parameter space and select the desired cross-microarchitecture
reliable simulation points. The main contributions of this paper include:

1. We designed a platform to rapidly and precisely evaluate the estimation accuracy of SimPoint based on real machines and their calibrated RTL-model
   emulation accelerators.
2. We proposed SCFM, a statistical coarse-to-fine method. SCFM leverages two
   key metrics E_{repre} and $Loss$ to rapidly assess the simulation points and efficiently select the reliable simulation points.
3. We configured thirty distinct machine models to select reliable simulation
   points and prepared three test models to implement the verification. Experimental results demonstrate that the final-selected reliable simulation points
   could yield statistically accurate estimations for SPEC CPU 2006 on the test
   models, giving average errors of less than 1%

The rest of this paper is organized as follows: Sect. 2 introduces the SimPoint
methodology in detail; Sect. 3 presents the statistical coarse-to-fine method to
select the reliable simulation points; Sect. 4 introduces our experiment platform;
Sect. 5 reports and discusses the experimental results; Sect. 6 talks about the
related work; and Sect. 7 concludes the paper.

2   Background

SimPoint is a representative sampling method that utilizes Basic Block Vector
(BBV) as the code signature to profile and extracts the simulation points of
the program's dynamic execution. The basic block is a sequential code block
with a single entrance and exit, and BBV is the vector of the total number
of instructions executed by each basic block. SimPoint works on the premise
that intervals with similar BBV would exhibit similar performance behaviors
[13]. The process of the SimPoint method are depicted in Fig. 1. ① Initially,
SimPoint profiles the benchmark to collect the BBV. ② The random linear
projection is conducted to reduce the dimensions of BBV. ③ SimPoint then
uses the K-Means algorithm to cluster different phases of BBV and picks the

---

[1] We will use micro-independent and microarchitecture-independent interchangeably
   in this paper. Similar to micro-dependent and microarchitecture-dependent, simulation points and SimPoints.

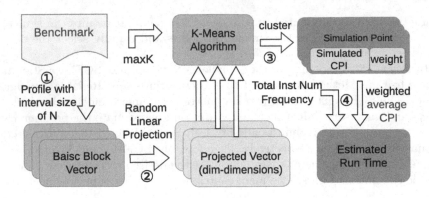

Fig. 1. The Procedures of SimPoint Methodology.

points that are closest to the centroids of each phase as the simulation points. Besides, each simulation point is assigned a weight according to the percentage of instructions in the cluster where it belongs. ④ Finally, after simulating these points, the run time can be extrapolated according to the weighted average CPI, frequency, and the number of dynamic instructions.

The selection of simulation points is determined by multiple nontrivial parameters [8], as illustrated in Fig. 1. Firstly, SimPoint divides the program stream into non-overlapping intervals of a fixed length N. Determining the appropriate value of N can be quite challenging due to the varying granularity of the repetitive phases in the benchmark, which may not always align with the interval of fixed length [12]. Secondly, in order to prevent dimension explosion, SimPoint utilizes random linear projection to convert the BBVs into vectors of dim dimensions. A higher value of dim indicates that more information is retained following projection, but may result in a heavier burden on clustering. Thirdly, the K-Means algorithm requires specification of the maximum number of clusters, $maxK$. If the value is too small, the representative clusters may not be fully extracted. However, if the value is too large, redundant simulation points would be selected and result in an excessively large simulation budgets. Different benchmarks or binaries under various compilation options prefer distinct configurations of SimPoint parameters [6]. Therefore, a delicate tuning process is necessary to obtain high accuracy [19,25]. For instance, Nair et al. [17] and Ganesan et al. [4] employ the parameters of $N = 100$ million, $dim = 15$, and $maxK = 30$ for the SPEC CPU 2006 benchmark, which gives an accurate estimation of the average CPI error below 3%. What's more, Grayson et al. [5] also mention the usage of SimPoint with $N = 100$ million.

Previous studies have pointed out that SimPoint is not immune to inherent errors. Firstly, the BBV provides an imperfect representation of program behaviors as it only captures the execution frequency of basic blocks while disregarding their execution order [14]. Besides, intervals that execute the same instructions may exhibit different performance behaviors in the phase transitions due to the influence of the different descendants [21,29]. Secondly, the intervals of fixed length may fail to track the program's inherent phases of varying length [12]. Thirdly, in programs characterized by intricate behaviors, the BBVs may be dispersed in the hyperspace in a random manner, rendering them unsuitable for clustering due to the absence of discernible patterns. What's more, the insufficient warm-up would introduce error [1,2] which may behave differently on various microarchitectures. The above-mentioned errors could vary across different microarchitectures and are directly influenced by the SimPoint parameter configurations. As a consequence, by selecting the appropriate simulation points, it is possible to minimize these inherent errors, thereby demonstrating a reliable estimation ability across different microarchitectures.

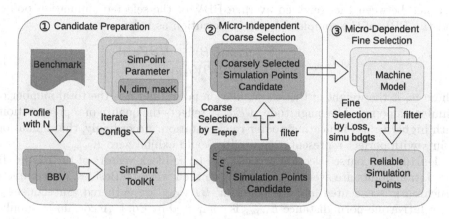

Fig. 2. Overview of the Procedures of SCFM.

3   Our Methodology

3.1   Overview of the SCFM

The selection of reliable simulation points using the novel coarse-to-fine method involves three stages: candidate preparation, coarse selection, and fine selection, as illustrated in Fig. 2. ① Initially, a range of possible values is assigned to the parameters N, $maxK$, and dim respectively, which are then combined to generate a list of candidate SimPoint parameter configurations. The SimPoint toolkit is then employed to iterate through these configurations to generate the corresponding simulation points using the Basic Block Vector (BBV) profiled from the benchmark. ② Next, the coarse selection process utilizes a micro-independent metric to quantify each candidate's ability to represent the code-level characteristics of the entire program, which serves as the foundation for SimPoint. Only the simulation points with good representation ability could pass through the coarse selection. ③ Finally, the fine selection process evaluates the simulation points on multiple machine models to statistically assess their estimation ability. Among the candidates that satisfy the desired requirement of cross-microarchitecture estimation accuracy, which is quantified by a micro-dependent metric, the simulation points with the least simulation budgets are finally selected.

3.2   Coarse Selection: Based on Micro-independent E_{repre}

SimPoint works on the basis that the simulation points are representative of the programmatic characteristics of the complete program dynamic stream. Therefore, we could quantify such representation ability and utilize it as a metric to guide the coarse selection of simulation points. Specifically, the micro-independent metric E_{repre} is proposed, which calculates the relative one-norm distance between the weighted average BBV of the selected simulation points and the BBV of the complete dynamic execution as follows:

$$E_{repre} = \frac{|\sum_i^n w_i \times BBV_i - BBV_{full}|}{|BBV_{full}|} \tag{1}$$

where w_i is the weight of the ith simulation point, and n is the total number of simulation points. The magnitude of E_{repre} reflects the quality of representation, with higher values indicating poorer representation. Accordingly, the simulation points with perfect representation ability would exhibit zero E_{repre}.

During the coarse selection process, the basic block vectors of the candidate simulation points are averaged according to their weights. Besides, the complete benchmark is executed and the resulting BBV_{full} are gathered. Subsequently, the relative one-norm distance E_{repre} is computed by Eq. 1. Accordingly, simulation points that exhibit large values of E_{repre} are considered unreliable and thus excluded from the next fine selection stage. By adopting the coarse selection, the unnecessary candidates of the fine selection could be largely eliminated and the whole iterative process would be expedited significantly.

3.3   Fine Selection: Based on Micro-dependent $Loss$

The selection of reliable simulation points should rely on the understanding of the inherent errors of SimPoint. With these errors, the selection process should be treated carefully because the simulation points may be over-tuned to exhibit high estimation accuracy on a certain machine model while losing general cross-microarchitecture accuracy. To quantify the estimation ability of SimPoint, we propose the correction factor, which is defined as follows:

$$Correction\ Factor(i) = \frac{T_{machine}(i)}{T_{simpoint}(i)} \tag{2}$$

where $T_{machine}(i)$ is the full run time on machine model i, and $T_{simpoint}(i)$ is the estimation given by SimPoint. Besides, equipped with multiple machine models, the statistical error of the correction factor could be calculated as follows:

$$e_{cf} = z_{\frac{1}{2}\alpha, N-1} \times \frac{\sigma_{cf}}{\mu_{cf}} \tag{3}$$

where σ_{cf}, μ_{cf} is the standard deviation and mean value of the correction factor respectively, and $z_{\frac{1}{2}\alpha, N-1}$ is the significance multiplier, that is determined by the confidence interval α and the number of machine models N.

For reliable simulation points that are able to yield accurate estimations across distinct microarchitectures, the mean value μ_{cf} of the correction factor should be close to **one**, which indicates the average accuracy. On the other hand, the error σ_{cf} of the correction factor should be near to **zero**, which suggests the cross-microarchitecture reliability. By taking both issues into consideration, a micro-dependent metric $Loss$ is proposed as follows:

$$Loss = 0.5 \times e_{cf} + 0.5 \times |\mu_{cf} - 1| \qquad (4)$$

where the cross-microarchitecture average estimation accuracy μ_{cf} and statistical estimation error e_{cf} have the same coefficient, indicating equal importance in the selection process. Besides, to guide the fine selection, the maximum allowed value of $Loss$ needs to be assigned as $Loss_{max}$.

Specifically, in the fine selection process, the statistical evaluations are implemented based on both the real machines with different microarchitectures and their corresponding RTL-model emulation accelerators, which are commercial devices utilized to expedite the behavior simulation. Firstly, the benchmark is executed on real machines to collect the full run time, while the candidate simulation points are simulated on the emulation accelerators to extrapolate the estimated run time by the SimPoint method. With the confidence interval α assigned, the micro-dependent metric $Loss$ can be calculated to guide the fine selection. Among the candidates satisfying the $Loss_{max}$, simulation points with the smallest simulation budgets are finally selected. If none of the candidate simulation points selected after the coarse selection meet the required $Loss_{max}$, there are two options available: increase the number of candidates in the fine selection process or choose the simulation points with the smallest $Loss$. In the latter case, it is acknowledged that the required $Loss_{max}$ may not be attainable due to the limitations inherent in the SimPoint methodology.

3.4 Further Correction

After the coarse-to-fine selection process, the distribution of the correction factor across different microarchitectures is collected at the same time, which describes the inherent errors of the selected simulation points. We could apply it to reform the raw SimPoint estimation and give the estimation error as follows:

$$Mean(\frac{T_{machine}}{T_{simpoint}}) = \mu_{cf} \rightarrow Corrected\ Estimation = Raw \times \mu_{cf} \qquad (5)$$

$$Error(\frac{T_{machine}}{T_{simpoint}}) = e_{cf} \rightarrow Estimation\ Error = Raw \times e_{cf} \qquad (6)$$

where Raw represents the raw SimPoint estimation, μ_{cf} and e_{cf} denote the mean value and error of the correction factor respectively. The motivation is that μ_{cf} indicates the average systematic deviation of the real run time over the estimated run time given by SimPoint, and the discrepancy between *Raw* and the theoretical run time could be statistically eliminated by such multiplication. Similarly, e_{cf} represents the statistical error of the correction factor and can be used to assign estimation error by Eq. 6.

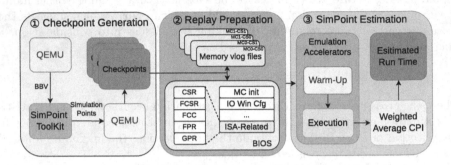

Fig. 3. Experiment Procedures of the SimPoint Implementation.

4   Our Platform Design

4.1   SimPoint Setup

The implementation of SimPoint on our platform involves the following procedures: checkpoint generation, replay preparation, and SimPoint estimation, as illustrated in Fig. 3.

Firstly, in the process of checkpoint generation, the benchmark is executed on the modified systematic-mode QEMU to collect the full-system BBVs. The benchmark that we use here is the SPEC CPU 2006, which provides a reliable and consistent way to assess the performance across different microarchitecture configurations [9]. The SimPoint toolkit is then utilized to generate the simulation points according to the BBVs. Accordingly, the benchmark is executed on QEMU for the second time to dump the checkpoints, which include the memory image and the ISA-related registers.

Secondly, the checkpoints go through the replay preparation, which involves two tasks: memory reorganizing and ISA-related register recovery. Memory reloading requires converting the memory images dumped from QEMU into a specific format for each Memory Controller(MC) and Chip Select(CS) of DDR. To facilitate the recovery of ISA-related registers, such as General Purpose Register(GPR), Floating Point Register(FPR), Control and Status Register(CSR), Flag Condition Code(FCC), and Float Control and Status Register(FCSR), the BIOS is modified to insert instructions that recover the aforementioned content and jump to the first instruction of the simulation point to initiate the warm-up.

Thirdly, the checkpoints are executed on the emulation accelerators to generate the weighted average CPI. As a result, the estimated run time could be extrapolated according to the SimPoint method as described in Sect. 2.

4.2   Machine Models

The real machines used in SCFM is the Loongson 3A5000 and 2K2000 chips, whose configurations are listed in Table 1. Besides, to statistically assess the simulation points on different microarchitectures, we configure up to 30 machine models based on the 3A5000 and 2K2000 by modifying the firmware, as listed in Table 2. These machine models are distinct in many aspects, including the pipeline width, the size of OoO windows, issue width, the number of arithmetic units, branch predictors, and the memory subsystem. Equipped with these diverse models and their RTL emulation accelerators, we are able to measure the inherent errors of the SimPoint methodology from a statistical perspective.

Table 1. Description of Loongson 3A5000 and 2K2000 CPU.

	3A5000	2K2000		3A5000	2K2000
Fetch Width	8	4	FP Arith Units	2	2
Rename Width	4	3	L1 Cache Capacity	64 KB	64 KB
OoO Windows	128	128	L2 Cache Capacity	256 KB	2 MB
MEM Units	2	2	L3 Cache Capacity	16 MB	N/A
INT Arith Units	4	3	DDR Channel(s)	2	1

Table 2. List of Our Machine Models.

Model	Description	Model	Description
M01	original 3A5000 configuration	M16	M08, but with 4MB LLC
M02	M01, but w.o inst prefetcher	M17	original 2K2000 configuration
M03	M01, but w.o data prefetcher	M18	M17, but w.o data prefetcher
M04	M01, but w.o prefetcher	M19	M17, but w.o inst prefetcher
M05	M01, but w.o L2 Cache	M20	M17, but w.o prefetcher
M06	M01, but w.o ld-st anti-violation	M21	M17, but w.o BTB
M07	M01, but with only one mem unit	M22	M17, but with only one mem unit
M08	M01, but w.o RAS & BTB	M23	M17, but with only one float unit
M09	M01, but with 4MB LLC	M24	M17, but with 1MB LLC
M10	M02, but with 4MB LLC	M25	M18, but with 1MB LLC
M11	M03, but with 4MB LLC	M26	M19, but with 1MB LLC
M12	M04, but with 4MB LLC	M27	M20, but with 1MB LLC
M13	M05, but with 4MB LLC	M28	M21, but with 1MB LLC
M14	M06, but with 4MB LLC	M29	M22, but with 1MB LLC
M15	M07, but with 4MB LLC	M30	M23, but with 1MB LLC

What's more, to scrutinize the cross-microarchitecture accuracy of the selected reliable simulation points, three test models are prepared as follows:

1. **Test Model I** is founded on the 3A5000, but with only one mem unit, 4MB LLC, and without prefetcher, ld-st anti-violation, BTB, RAS, and L2 Cache.
2. **Test Model II** is founded on the 2K2000, but with only one mem unit, only one FPU, only 1MB LLC, and without prefetcher, BTB, and RAS
3. **Test Model III** is the next generation of the 3A5000, with wider issue width, smarter prefetcher, and better branch predictors.

5   Evaluation

5.1   Validation of Our Platform

To guarantee the full run time on real machines and the estimated run time on emulation accelerators are comparable, a calibration process is conducted. Because the CPU cores of the real machines and their RTL-model emulation accelerators are identical, we only need to calibrate their DDR system by configuring the same parameters of the memory controller to guarantee they have similar memory latency and bandwidth. Specifically, the programs *Stream Copy* and *lat-mem-rd* are utilized to measure the bandwidth and latency of the memory system respectively. The benchmarks *Coremark* and *Dhrystone* are fully executed on both the real machines and the emulation accelerators to compare and quantify their difference. The test results for these benchmarks are listed in Table 3, where good consistency is observed between the real machines and the emulation accelerators. As a result, our platform is validated to reliably assess the estimation accuracy of the simulation points.

Table 3. Test Results of real machines and their Emulation Accelerators.

test	3A5000			2K2000		
	Machine	Emu	Error	Machine	Emu	Error
Stream Copy(MB/sec)	15398.7	15497.9	0.64%	10440.5	10463.0	0.22%
DDR Latency(ns)	99.944	99.672	−0.27%	123.221	123.589	0.29%
Coremark(10^3 iters/sec)	12.121	12.102	−0.16%	8.223	8.217	−0.07%
DhryStone(10^6 iters/sec)	17.362	17.380	0.10%	13.120	13.124	0.03%

5.2   Examination of the Base Simulation Points

Similar to previous studies [4,5,17], the parameters of $N = 100$ million, $dim = 15$, and $maxK = 30$ are utilized as the base configuration to assess the SimPoint methodology and to conduct the statistical correction factor analysis on the prepared 30 machine models. Initially, 30 machine models are utilized to statistically evaluate the base simulation points and collect the distributions of the correction factors. Specifically, the distributions of correction factor are displayed for six representative tests are shown in Fig. 4. These distributions show large variances in the accuracy of the base simulation point estimations, suggesting the inherent errors in SimPoint. The remaining tests exhibit similar large variances in the distributions of correction factor. Besides, the mean value and error of the correction factor for all the tests in the SPEC CPU 2006 on the 30 machine models are displayed in Fig. 5, where the large error is observed for many tests, which indicates the base simulation points are lack of cross-microarchitecture accuracy.

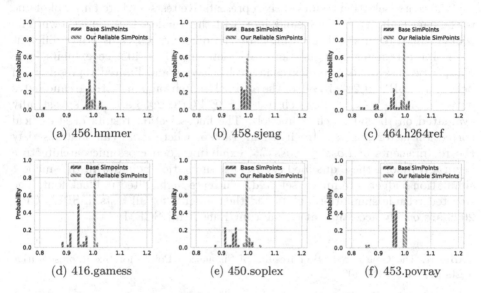

Fig. 4. The Distributions of the Correction Factor for Six Representative Tests in SPEC CPU 2006. The Remaining Tests Exhibit Similar Tendencies.

Moreover, the base simulation points are evaluated on the three test models. The estimation errors of the base simulation points for SPEC CPU 2006 are listed in Table 6, where the errors vary largely on different test models, ranging from 1.82% to 6.24% for CINT and from −0.59% to 1.88% for CFP. Such large variance in the estimation accuracy can be highly misleading for architects, as the error variance may exceed the actual performance improvement arising from the introduction of new microarchitecture designs. Specifically, the correction factor for each test in SPEC CPU 2006 on test model I is shown in Fig. 6, where the base simulation points are capable to give a good estimation with the average run time error of 1.82% for CINT and −0.59% for CFP. However, we also observe that for tests like 401.bzip2, 464.h264ref, 416.gamess, and 459.GemsFDTD, the base simulation points exhibit relatively large estimation errors.

5.3   Selection of the Reliable Simulation Points

To select the reliable simulation points, the novel coarse-to-fine selection procedures are implemented, where we set $Loss_{max} = 0.05$, and the confidence interval $\alpha = 0.95$. Besides, we scan the parameters of interval size N from 40 million to 320 million with the step of 20 million(total 15 candidates), dim from 15 to 30 with the step of 5(total 4 candidates), and $maxK$ from 15 to 60 with the step of 15(total 4 candidates). To sum up, the total number of candidate SimPoint parameter configurations is 240 for each test in SPEC CPU 2006.

The coarse selection results of six representative tests are listed in Table 4 due to the page limit, where three candidates with the smallest E_{repre} are shown. The coarse-tuning results in Table 4 indicate that different programs prefer different SimPoint parameter configurations. We note that test 403.gcc exhibits large E_{repre}, because of its complex code-level behavior and limited representation behavior of BBV [9, 20]. To select the optimal simulation points, three candidates with the smallest E_{repre} for each test in SPEC CPU 2006 are then statistically evaluated on the 30 machine models. The fine selection results of statistical correction factor analysis are listed in Table 5, where most candidates satisfy the requirements of $Loss \leq Loss_{max}$, exhibiting good cross-microarchitecture accuracy. Among these qualified candidates, simulation points with the smallest simulation budgets are finally selected, which are highlighted in black font. The selected reliable simulation points and their weights for all tests in SPEC CPU 2006 are openly accessible at github.com/HanChenji/SCFM.

Table 4. The Coarse Selection Results of Simulation Points for Six Representative Tests in SPEC CPU 2006.

test	Candidate 1				Candidate 2				Candidate 3			
	N (10^6)	max K	dim	E_{repre} (%)	N (10^6)	max K	dim	E_{repre} (%)	N (10^6)	max K	dim	E_{repre} (%)
401.1	300	45	25	0.77	320	45	15	0.82	200	60	30	0.96
403.1	100	60	30	8.78	120	45	15	8.88	160	60	15	9.45
462	140	60	20	0.19	100	60	20	0.20	140	60	30	0.25
410	40	60	25	0.15	200	60	30	0.16	120	60	25	0.17
416.1	320	60	30	1.04	300	60	20	1.10	260	60	15	1.15
482	200	60	20	0.13	260	60	15	0.15	300	30	20	0.15

Besides, Fig. 4 depicts the change of the distributions of the correction factor before and after the SimPoint parameter tuning, where we observe that compared with the base simulation points, the selected reliable simulation points by our approach own more compact distributions, exhibiting more accurate average estimation and smaller error. What's more, the mean value and the error of the correction factor of our selected reliable simulation points are plotted in Fig. 5, where we observe that after the coarse-to-fine selection, the correction factor of most tests locate close to one and own short error bar. We note

Table 5. The Fine Selection Results of Simulation Points for Six Representative Tests. The Final-Selected Results are Highlighted in Bold.

test	Candidate 1				Candidate 2				Candidate 3			
	μ_{cf}	e_{cf} (10^{-2})	Loss (10^{-2})	bgt. (10^{9})	μ_{cf}	e_{cf} (10^{-2})	Loss (10^{-2})	bgt. (10^{9})	μ_{cf}	e_{cf} (10^{-2})	Loss (10^{-2})	bgt. (10^{9})
401.1	1.01	1.1	1.2	7.8	1.00	1.8	1.1	8.0	**0.98**	**1.0**	**1.5**	**6.0**
403.1	**1.03**	**3.1**	**3.1**	**2.7**	1.04	5.3	4.5	3.5	1.11	2.5	6.7	2.6
462	1.01	7.0	3.7	4.9	**1.00**	**3.6**	**3.1**	**3.9**	1.06	4.6	5.4	5.3
410	**1.02**	**3.7**	**2.8**	**1.6**	1.02	4.2	2.8	8.6	1.02	1.7	2.0	4.9
416.1	1.00	0.4	0.3	11.5	**1.01**	**0.4**	**0.8**	**11.1**	1.00	2.1	1.0	11.7
482	1.01	4.2	2.8	5.6	1.02	4.4	3.0	9.4	**1.03**	**5.1**	**3.9**	**5.1**

that for tests like 400.perlbench, 401.bzip2, 410.bwaves, and 482.sphinx3, their cross-microarchitecture accuracy is greatly improved compared with the base simulation points. However, we also observe that the mean value of the correction factor for tests like 403.gcc exhibits a large deviation from one, which is consistent with their poor representation ability as can be seen in Table 4.

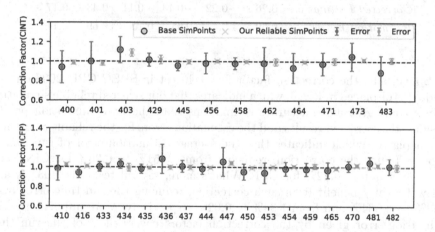

Fig. 5. The Mean Value and Error of Correction Factor for All Tests in SPEC CPU 2006. The Error is Calculated According to Eq. 3.

5.4   Verification of the Reliable Simulation Points

To scrutinize the ability of the selected reliable simulation points in generating accurate estimations across different microarchitectures, evaluations on the three test models are implemented. These test models, especially test model III, which is the next generation of 3A5000 CPU, have distinct microarchitecture configurations with the 30 machine models used to implement the coarse-to-fine selection.

The estimation errors on the test models are listed in Table 6, where our reliable simulation points exhibit small errors, only from -0.32% to 0.64% for CINT and from 0.09% to -0.89% for CFP, giving accurate cross-microarchitecture estimations. What's more, according to Eq. 5 and Eq. 6, the raw estimations given by our selected simulation points are corrected by the mean value of correction factor μ_{cf}, and the estimation errors are assigned according to the error of correction factor e_{cf}, as listed in Table 6. The experimental results suggest that the estimation accuracy on these test models is improved and the assigned estimation errors could cover the difference between real run time and estimated run time in most cases, exhibiting more statistically valid estimations.

Table 6. Estimation Errors for SPEC CPU 2006 on the Test Models.

	Test Model I Error(%)		Test Model II Error(%)		Test Model III Error(%)	
SPEC CPU 2006	CINT	CFP	CINT	CFP	CINT	CFP
Base SimPoints	1.82	−0.59	−5.08	−1.73	6.24	1.88
Our Reliable SimPoints	−0.51	−0.89	−0.32	−0.16	0.64	0.09
Corrected Estimation	0.26	−0.22	−0.43	−0.11	0.43	0.17
Estimation Error	0.69	1.03	0.65	0.10	0.69	0.11

Specifically, the correction factor for each test in SPEC CPU 2006 on test model I is displaced in Fig. 6, which indicates that our selected reliable simulation points could give more accurate estimations than the base simulation points. Besides, the corrected results and the estimation errors for the reliable SimPoints are displayed, which indicates that the average estimation error of run time is improved after the correction, reducing from -0.51% to 0.26% for CINT and from -0.89% to -0.22% for CFP. What's more, several tests like 403.gcc and 481.wrf greatly benefit from such correction, reducing the run time error from 6.68% to -1.64% and from 1.94% to 0.02% respectively. More importantly, the estimation error given by the correction factors covers most of the run time discrepancy, indicating the statistical reliability of the selected simulation points.

6   Related Work

Being an effective and rapid simulation approach, SimPoint has drawn considerable attention from both researchers and engineers as a promising research area. Many works have been proposed to improve SimPoint from aspects of accuracy, speed-up, and usability.

There have been several attempts to substitute BBV and K-Means with alternatives to further improve the accuracy of SimPoint. Studies conducted by Lau et al. [14], Luo et al. [16], and Vengalam et al. [28] have explored the effectiveness of various code-related signatures in extracting phases from program streams.

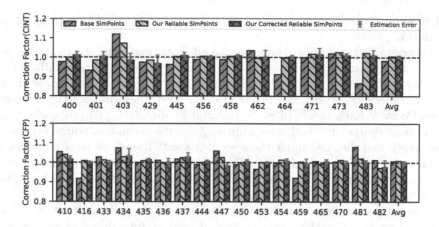

Fig. 6. The Correction Factor for All Tests in SPEC CPU 2006 on the Test Model I. The Estimation Error is Assigned According to Eq. 6.

However, none of the tested signatures have demonstrated clear advantages over BBV. Harmerly et al. [7] and Sanghai et al. [23] examine the efficacy of the multinomial algorithm and conclude that a combination of K-means and multinomial could reduce the number of simulation points needed without compromising the accuracy. What's more, Johnston et al. [10] propose a novel EDCM model, which could outperform the K-Means algorithm when the simulation budgets are limited. To yield the statistically valid performance estimation, Perlman et al. [20] utilize the bootstrap method to evaluate the error of the K-means clustering and then use it to guide the selection of SimPoint parameter $maxK$. However, the obtained statistical error only applies to the machine model where the bootstrap methodology is implemented and the cross-microarchitecture estimation accuracy is not guaranteed.

Some works try to further reduce the simulation budgets. Eeckhout et al. [3] put forth a technique that evaluates program similarity and extracts fewer simulation points by considering the benchmark suite in its entirety, rather than focusing solely on individual programs. Soares et al. [26] propose a method to analyze the phase similarities among multiple inputs of the benchmark and thus extract the simulation points from these grouped executions to reduce the simulation budgets. What's more, to avoid checkpointing or functional fast-forwarding, Ringenberg et al. [22] present a novel method to analyze and modify the binaries of benchmarks and insert intrinsic checkpoints, which exhibits promising speed-up.

To enhance the usability of SimPoint, many works have been proposed. Patil et al. [18] set up a novel tool-chain to convert the checkpoints into executable files based on the PinPlay platform. Perelman et al. [20] propose the idea of early simulation points that are more likely to locate in the early stage of program execution. The early simulation points could increase the usability and reduce the simulation budgets in cases where checkpoint restoring is not allowed and functional fast-forwarding is required before the detailed simulation of the simulation points.

There are also attempts to enhance the SimPoint methodology itself. Because of the varying granularity of the repetitive phases in program streams which may not always align with the interval of fixed length, Lau et al. [12] suggest incorporating intervals of varying lengths in order to further enhance the accuracy of SimPoint. What's more, Li et al. [15] and Zhang et al. [31] propose a novel multi-phase analysis method, which initially obtains simulation points with large interval size and then re-sample these segments with a small value of interval size N. This multi-phase method can maximize the benefits of different granularity of interval size and is more likely to generate the early simulation points, achieving higher speed-up and accuracy. However, these studies didn't statistically measure the estimation errors of SimPoint and ignored the critical question of how to give accurate estimations across different microarchitecture configurations.

7   Conclusion

Previous SimPoint studies mainly focus on how to give an accurate estimation on a specific microarchitecture, while ignoring the critical problem of how to guarantee the general cross-microarchitecture estimation accuracy, which is more significant in the early-stage design space exploration.

This work presents a novel statistical coarse-to-fine method, SCFM, to accurately estimate performance across various microarchitectures. SCFM implements both the micro-independent metric E_{repre} and micro-dependent metric $Loss$ to select reliable simulation points. By applying various real machine models and their corresponding RTL-model emulation accelerators as the platform to conduct the statistical coarse-to-fine method, the reliable simulation points are selected and evaluated on three test models with distinct microarchitecture configurations. The evaluation results show that such selected reliable simulation points could give accurate estimations on various machine models, giving average errors of less than 1%.

Acknowledgment. We would like to thank all the anonymous reviewers for their helpful comments and suggestions. This work is partially supported by the National Key Research and Development Program of China (under Grant 2022YFB3105104).

References

1. Biesbrouck, M.V., Calder, B., Eeckhout, L.: Efficient sampling startup for SimPoint. IEEE Micro **26**, 32–42 (2006)
2. Van Biesbrouck, M., Eeckhout, L., Calder, B.: Efficient sampling startup for sampled processor simulation. In: Conte, T., Navarro, N., Hwu, W.W., Valero, M., Ungerer, T. (eds.) HiPEAC 2005. LNCS, vol. 3793, pp. 47–67. Springer, Heidelberg (2005). https://doi.org/10.1007/11587514_5

3. Eeckhout, L., Sampson, J., Calder, B.: Exploiting program microarchitecture independent characteristics and phase behavior for reduced benchmark suite simulation. In: IEEE International. 2005 Proceedings of the IEEE Workload Characterization Symposium, pp. 2–12 (2005)

4. Ganesan, K., Panwar, D., John, L.K.: Generation, validation and analysis of SPEC CPU2006 simulation points based on branch, memory and TLB characteristics. In: Kaeli, D., Sachs, K. (eds.) SBW 2009. LNCS, vol. 5419, pp. 121–137. Springer, Heidelberg (2009). https://doi.org/10.1007/978-3-540-93799-9_8

5. Grayson, B., et al.: Evolution of the Samsung Exynos CPU microarchitecture. In: 2020 ACM/IEEE 47th Annual International Symposium on Computer Architecture (ISCA), pp. 40–51 (2020)

6. Hamerly, G., Perelman, E., Calder, B.: How to use SimPoint to pick simulation points. SIGMETRICS Perform. Eval. Rev. **31**, 25–30 (2004)

7. Hamerly, G., Perelman, E., Calder, B.: Comparing multinomial and k-means clustering for SimPoint. In: 2006 IEEE International Symposium on Performance Analysis of Systems and Software, pp. 131–142 (2006)

8. Hamerly, G., Perelman, E., Lau, J., Calder, B.: SimPoint 3.0: faster and more flexible program analysis (2005)

9. Henning, J.L.: SPEC CPU2006 benchmark descriptions. SIGARCH Comput. Archit. News **34**, 1–17 (2006)

10. Johnston, J., Hamerly, G.: Improving SimPoint accuracy for small simulation budgets with EDCM clustering (2008)

11. KleinOsowski, A.J., Lilja, D.J.: MinneSPEC: a new spec benchmark workload for simulation-based computer architecture research. IEEE Comput. Archit. Lett. **1**, 7 (2002)

12. Lau, J., Perelman, E., Hamerly, G., Sherwood, T., Calder, B.: Motivation for variable length intervals and hierarchical phase behavior. In: IEEE International Symposium on Performance Analysis of Systems and Software, ISPASS 2005, pp. 135–146 (2005)

13. Lau, J., Sampson, J., Perelman, E., Hamerly, G., Calder, B.: The strong correlation between code signatures and performance. In: IEEE International Symposium on Performance Analysis of Systems and Software, ISPASS 2005, pp. 236–247 (2005)

14. Lau, J., Schoenmackers, S., Calder, B.: Structures for phase classification. In: IEEE International Symposium on - ISPASS Performance Analysis of Systems and Software, pp. 57–67 (2004)

15. Li, J., Zhang, W., Chen, H., Zang, B.: Multi-level phase analysis for sampling simulation. In: 2013 Design, Automation & Test in Europe Conference & Exhibition (DATE), pp. 649–654 (2013)

16. Luo, Y., Joshi, A.M., Phansalkar, A., John, L.K., Ghosh, J.: Analyzing and improving clustering based sampling for microprocessor simulation. In: 17th International Symposium on Computer Architecture and High Performance Computing (SBAC-PAD 2005), pp. 193–200 (2005)

17. Nair, A.A., John, L.K.: Simulation points for SPEC CPU 2006. In: 2008 IEEE International Conference on Computer Design, pp. 397–403 (2008)

18. Patil, H., Isaev, A., Heirman, W., Sabu, A., Hajiabadi, A., Carlson, T.E.: ELFies: executable region checkpoints for performance analysis and simulation. In: 2021 IEEE/ACM International Symposium on Code Generation and Optimization (CGO), pp. 126–136 (2021)

19. Perelman, E., Hamerly, G., Biesbrouck, M.V., Sherwood, T., Calder, B.: Using SimPoint for accurate and efficient simulation. In: Measurement and Modeling of Computer Systems (2003)

20. Perelman, E., Hamerly, G., Calder, B.: Picking statistically valid and early simulation points. In: 2003 12th International Conference on Parallel Architectures and Compilation Techniques, pp. 244–255 (2003)
21. Ratanaworabhan, P., Burtscher, M.: Program phase detection based on critical basic block transitions. In: IEEE International Symposium on Performance Analysis of Systems and Software, ISPASS 2008, pp. 11–21 (2008)
22. Ringenberg, J., Pelosi, C., Oehmke, D.W., Mudge, T.N.: Intrinsic checkpointing: a methodology for decreasing simulation time through binary modification. In: IEEE International Symposium on Performance Analysis of Systems and Software, ISPASS 2005, pp. 78–88 (2005)
23. Sanghai, K., Su, T., Dy, J.G., Kaeli, D.R.: A multinomial clustering model for fast simulation of computer architecture designs. In: Knowledge Discovery and Data Mining (2005)
24. Sherwood, T., Perelman, E., Hamerly, G., Calder, B.: Automatically characterizing large scale program behavior. In: ASPLOS X (2002)
25. Singh, S., Awasthi, M.: Efficacy of statistical sampling on contemporary workloads: the case of SPEC CPU2017. In: 2019 IEEE International Symposium on Workload Characterization (IISWC), pp. 70–80 (2019)
26. Soares, R., Antonioli, L.F., Francesquini, E., Azevedo, R.: Phase detection and analysis among multiple program inputs. In: 2018 Symposium on High Performance Computing Systems (WSCAD), pp. 155–161 (2018)
27. Song, S., Wu, Q., Flolid, S., Dean, J., Panda, R., Deng, J.: Experiments with SPEC CPU 2017: similarity, balance, phase behavior and SimPoints (2018)
28. Vengalam, U.K.R., Sharma, A., Huang, M.C.: LoopIn: a loop-based simulation sampling mechanism. In: 2022 IEEE International Symposium on Performance Analysis of Systems and Software (ISPASS), pp. 224–226 (2022)
29. Wunderlich, R.E., Wenisch, T.F., Falsafi, B., Hoe, J.C.: Smarts: accelerating microarchitecture simulation via rigorous statistical sampling. In: Proceedings of the 30th Annual International Symposium on Computer Architecture, pp. 84–95 (2003)
30. Yi, J.J., Kodakara, S.V., Sendag, R., Lilja, D.J., Hawkins, D.M.: Characterizing and comparing prevailing simulation techniques. In: 11th International Symposium on High-Performance Computer Architecture, pp. 266–277 (2005)
31. Zhang, W., Li, J., Li, Y., Chen, H.: Multilevel phase analysis. ACM Trans. Embed. Comput. Syst. 14, 31:1–31:29 (2015)

On-Demand Triggered Memory Management Unit in Dynamic Binary Translator

Benyi Xie[1,2], Xinyu Li[1,2], Yue Yan[1,2], Chenghao Yan[1,2], Tianyi Liu[3],
Tingting Zhang[1,4], Chao Yang[5], and Fuxin Zhang[1,2(✉)]

[1] SKLP, Institute of Computing Technology, CAS, Beijing, China
{xiebenyi21b,lixinyu20s,yanyue21s,yanchenghao21s}@ict.ac.cn
[2] University of Chinese Academy of Sciences, Beijing, China
fxzhang@ict.ac.cn
[3] The University of Texas at San Antonio, San Antonio, USA
tianyi.liu@utsa.edu
[4] Loongson Technology Co. Ltd., Beijing, China
zhangtingting@loongson.cn
[5] State Grid Liaoning Electric Power Supply Co. Ltd., Shenyang, China
yangchaoneu@sina.com

Abstract. User-level Dynamic Binary Translators (DBTs) linearly map
the guest virtual memory to host virtual memory to achieve optimal performance. When the host page size exceeds the guest page size, multiple
small guest pages are mapped to a single large host page, resulting in
inappropriate permissions mapping. DBTs face security and correctness
risks accessing the inappropriately mapped host page. Our survey reveals
that most of the state-of-the-art user-level DBTs suffer from these risks.
While system-level DBT can avoid these risks through a software Memory Management Unit (MMU). However, the software MMU fully emulates guest memory management, leading to slower performance than the
linear mapping approach of user-level DBTs.

To address the balance of performance and risks, we propose a
DBT memory management method named On-Demand Triggered MMU
(ODT-MMU), that combines the strengths of both user-level and system-
level DBTs. ODT-MMU utilizes linear mapping for non-risky page
accesses and triggers a software MMU when accessing risky pages. We
implement ODT-MMU in two ways to accommodate various application scenarios: a platform-independent implementation named ODT-
InterpMMU, and a hardware-accelerated implementation named ODT-
ManipTLB. ODT-ManipTLB is designed for host Instruction Set Architectures (ISAs) that support programmable TLB. Experimental results
demonstrate that both implementations can effectively mitigate risks
associated with page size. Furthermore, ODT-ManipTLB achieves over
2000x performance improvement compared with the ODT-InterpMMU,
while maintaining comparable performance to the DBT without ODT-
MMU. Additionally, our work is applied to two industrial DBTs, XQM
and LATX.

© The Author(s), under exclusive license to Springer Nature Singapore Pte Ltd. 2024
C. Li et al. (Eds.): APPT 2023, LNCS 14103, pp. 297–309, 2024.
https://doi.org/10.1007/978-981-99-7872-4_17

Keywords: Binary translator · Memory management · Page size · TLB

1   Introduction

DBT enables the emulation of guest binaries on a host machine. Based on the emulation level of the guest, DBTs can be categorized into two types: user-level DBTs, which facilitate the migration of user applications, and system-level DBTs, which facilitate the migration of an OS. It is crucial for both types of DBTs to effectively and efficiently emulate memory management as guest binaries expect. System-level DBTs typically employ a software MMU to emulate the guest physical memory. Due to no need for emulating physical memory, user-level DBTs linearly map guest virtual memory to host virtual memory.

The linear mapping method, which reuses the host virtual memory, provides high performance for user-level DBTs. However, it introduces potential risks when discrepancies exist between the guest and host memory management. The difference in page size is the primary discrepancy between modern OSes, especially when the host page size exceeds the guest page size. Figure 1a illustrates a scenario that highlights security risks. It depicts four 4-KB private guest pages with different protection flags being linearly mapped to a 16-KB host page. The linear mapping renders four guest pages readable, writable, and executable, thereby introducing security risks such as overflow attacks. Figure 1b illustrates a scenario that highlights correctness risks arising when shared pages are used among multiple processes. DBT allocates a single 16-KB physical page to accommodate the shared 4-KB page. Consequently, the neighboring private pages are forced to be linearly mapped to the same 16-KB host physical page. This mapping causes the private pages can be overwritten by shared processes, resulting in correctness risks. Our survey reveals that most state-of-the-art user-level DBTs, including ExaGear [10,11], JIT Rosetta2[1], and user-level QEMU [5,18], suffers from the aforementioned risks, as shown in Table 1.

In contrast, system-level DBTs, such as system-level QEMU, do not encounter these risks due to the utilization of a software MMU. The software MMU fully emulates guest memory management, encompassing virtual-to-physical address translation and access permission checks. Despite its ability to mitigate the aforementioned security and correctness risks, the software MMU exhibits lower performance compared with the linear mapping approach.

On one hand, user-level DBTs utilize linear mapping, which provides high performance but entails potential risks. On the other hand, system-level DBTs employ a software MMU, which eliminates risks but exhibits lower performance. The distinctive characteristics of these two types of DBTs' memory management motivate us to propose an approach that combines their respective advantages.

---

[1] Rosetta has two versions: an Ahead-Of-Time (AOT) DBT for running X86_64 macOS applications on M-series silicon (AArch64) macOS [2], and a Just-In-Time (JIT) DBT for running X86_64 Linux applications on AArch64 Linux virtual machine [3]. Here we use the JIT version.

Table 1. Page size risks status of state-of-the-art DBTs. All of these DBTs target x86 or x86_64 Linux applications as guests. (QEMU refers to the user-level one.)

DBT	Proprietary	Host	Page size	Risks
ExaGear	Huawei	AArch64 Linux	64 KB	Existing
JIT Rosetta2	Apple	AArch64 Linux	16 KB	Existing
QEMU	–	Many ISAs Linux	8 KB/16 kB/64 KB/...	Existing
LATX (ODT-MMU)	Loongson	LoongArch Linux	16 KB	Mitigated
XQM (ODT-MMU)	Loongson	MIPS Linux	16 KB	Mitigated
QEMU (ODT-MMU)	–	Many ISAs Linux	8 KB/16 kB/64 KB/...	Mitigated

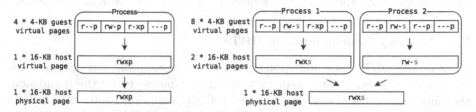

(a) Security risk caused by linearly mapping private pages. Guest permissions are inappropriately mapped to the host.

(b) Correctness risk caused by linearly mapping shared pages among processes. After the linear mapping, 12-KB data (3 * 4-KB pages) are lost from the initial 28-KB data (7 * 4-KB pages).

Fig. 1. DBT risks caused by linearly mapping small-size pages to large-size pages, for example, mapping 4-KB pages to 16-KB pages. Abbreviations: r readable, w writable, x executable, p private, s shared.

The new memory management we proposed, called on-demand triggered MMU (ODT-MMU), combines the linear mapping method with the triggering of the software MMU when risks arise. The detailed contributions of ODT-MMU are summarized as follows:

– ODT-MMU enables the utilization of linear mapping for non-risky page accesses and triggers software MMU when accessing risky pages. This approach effectively mitigates the risks related to page size and maintains the high performance of non-risky page accesses.
– To cater to various application scenarios, we implement ODT-MMU in two ways: ODT-InterpMMU, a platform-independent implementation that interprets the risky page accesses, and ODT-ManipTLB, which leverages the programmable TLB to enhance the risky page access performance.
– To the best of our knowledge, this work presents the first public analysis of the risky page accesses and the first applied solution in industrial DBTs: LATX [24] and XQM. This demonstrates the practicality of the proposed approach and showcases the effectiveness and efficiency of the ODT-MMU.

The rest of this paper is organized as follows: Sect. 2 provides a brief background and related work of DBTs' Memory Management and OS page size. Section 3 introduces the design of ODT-MMU, including the related data structures, on-demand mechanism, and two implementations: software-based ODT-InterpMMU, and hardware-based ODT-ManipTLB. Section 4 evaluates our experimental results. The last section concludes this paper.

2   Background and Related Work

This section offers an overview of memory management in DBTs, including software MMU and linear mapping, and the diverse page sizes supported by hardware and OSes. Furthermore, this section presents related work in these areas.

2.1   Memory Management in DBTs

System-level DBTs that aim to achieve full OS translation must emulate the translation of guest virtual memory to guest host memory and the permission-checking mechanism. Typically, system-level DBTs employ a software MMU to emulate the guest memory management. The software MMU consists of a software TLB and a collection of page table look-up algorithms. A guest virtual memory access is translated into tens of host instructions if the software TLB hits, otherwise, hundreds of host instructions are needed to perform page table walk, software TLB refill, and eventually memory access. Consequently, memory emulation becomes a critical bottleneck in system-level DBTs, leading to extensive research efforts focused on improving memory emulation in system-level DBTs. Work [22] analyzes the memory emulation overhead in system-level QEMU and improves the software MMU performance inspired by optimizations applied to hardware TLB. ESPT [6] and HSPT [23] embed the guest page table into the host page table to leverage host hardware MMU. Captive [20] runs DBT in virtualization mode to facilitate the host hardware memory virtualization. Dual-TLB [28] and BTMMU [9] employ the host programmable TLB to accelerate memory access. All these software MMU improvements can be utilized to optimize our ODT-MMU. For demonstration, we implement the ODT-ManipTLB by utilizing the similar mechanism used by Dual-TLB and BTMMU.

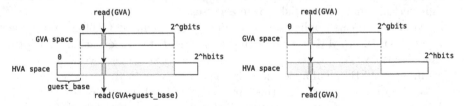

(a) Linear mapping with guest base. One guest read is translated into one host add and one host read.

(b) Linear mapping without guest base. One guest read is translated into one host read.

Fig. 2. The linear mapping from Guest Virtual Address (GVA) to Host Virtual Address (HVA) in user-level DBT.

Unlike system-level DBTs, user-level DBTs focus on running user applications on a host machine. Hence, user-level DBTs are not responsible for emulating guest physical memory. Therefore user-level DBTs typically do not use software MMU to emulate guest memory management, instead, user-level DBTs reuse the host memory management through linearly mapping Guest Virtual Address (GVA) to Host Virtual Address (HVA), as illustrated in Fig. 2. Through linear mapping, one guest memory access is translated into two host instructions: one instruction adds an offset, called *guest base*, to GVA, and another instruction performs the memory access. High-performance user-level DBTs, such as ExaGear [10], Rosetta2 [3], and LATX [24] default to set guest base to zero, thus achieving one-to-one translation for memory access. User-level QEMU [5,18] defaults to a non-zero guest base but provides an option to set the guest base to zero. Furthermore, Bintrans [17] discusses the DBT security risks introduced by the page size and provides a basic solution by temporarily changing the memory permissions. Compared with our ODT-MMU, which utilizes software MMU and needs only one OS signal, Bintrans needs three OS signals.

2.2 Page Sizes

Contemporary ISAs universally support diverse page sizes within a page table. X86_64 [1] and AArch64 [4] utilize page table walking hardware to offer several fixed page size combinations, such as x86_64's 4 KB-2 MB-1 GB combination, and AArch64's 16 KB-2 MB-32 MB-1 GB combination. MIPS [14] and LoongArch [12] achieve arbitrary page size (which must be a power of two) combinations through the software-programmable TLB. For our ODT-MMU implementations, we use a 4 KB-16 KB combination. In addition to existing page size support in industrial products, extensive research is dedicated to multiple page size support in hardware. Subblock TLB [15,21] is proposed to achieve medium-sized pages (64 KB) with high performance, surpassing the traditional superpage TLB. Skewed TLB [16,19] is introduced to support concurrently multiple page sizes within a single process using a set-associative TLB.

Table 2. The default page size for various OSes (distros) on different ISAs.

OS (Distro)	ISA	Page Size (KB)
Linux	x86/x86_64	4
Linux	UltraSPARC	8
Linux (Loongnix)	MIPS/LoongArch	16
macOS/Linux (Asahi)	AArch64	16
Linux (CentOS)	AArch64	64

Due to the hardware's support for multiple page sizes, various OSes often employ distinct default page sizes. Table 2 presents the default page sizes employed by various OSes (distros). Particularly, in the area of personal computers, macOS, Asahi Linux, and Loongnix employ 16-KB page size by default, which diverges from the traditional ISAs, like x86/x86_64 using 4-KB page size by default. In the area of servers, AArch64 CentOS employs a default page size of 64 KB, which also differs from the default page size of x86/x86_64. Moreover, there exist endeavors implementing multiple page sizes in OSes. In work [7], a multiple-page-size mechanism is implemented in IRIX OS utilizing TLB in R10000. In work [26], a similar multiple-page-size mechanism is implemented in x86 Linux OS. In work [27], a variable-page-size mechanism is implemented in MIPS Linux through variable-page-size TLB (VTLB). However, these studies primarily focus on improving performance by introducing multiple page sizes in OSes but disregard the security and correctness risks of executing small-page applications on a large-page OS, resulting in compatibility problems [13]. Furthermore, these studies typically involve modification of OS, which is not friendly to the compatibility problems, as it may introduce new compatibility problems.

3   On-Demand Triggered MMU

This section presents the design of ODT-MMU. We first introduce the related data structures and the on-demand mechanism. Then using the data structures and the on-demand mechanism as a foundation, we introduce ODT-InterpMMU, a software-based implementation that addresses the page size risks by interpreting the risky page accesses. Lastly, we introduce ODT-ManipTLB, a hardware-accelerated implementation that achieves high performance by utilizing the host's programmable TLB. Since our analysis focuses on user-level DBTs, without specifically referring to system-level DBTs, all the DBTs mentioned in the rest of this paper pertain to user-level DBTs.

3.1   Data Structures and On-Demand Mechanism

We leverage the software MMU inspired by system-level DBT to address the limitations of linear mapping. Therefore, a page table is added to user-level DBTs, called shadow page table, as shown in Fig. 3. The shadow page table only records the mappings from risky guest virtual pages to corresponding host virtual pages. The host virtual pages that are mapped in this manner are referred to as shadow pages. Additionally, a dedicated memory region, outside the linear mapped region, is allocated for these pages.

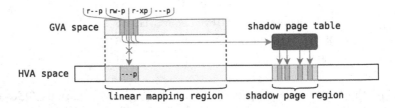

Fig. 3. Shadow page table maps risky pages to shadow page region. The linear mapping of risky pages is disabled.

Figure 4 illustrates the process of the on-demand mechanism. (1) During emulation of guest system calls related to virtual page management and permissions management, including `mmap`, `munmap`, `mprotect`, and `mremap`, (2) taking `mmap` as a specific example, if the guest tries to allocate a risky page (as shown in Fig. 1), a shadow page is allocated. (3) The linearly mapped host page is disabled by revoking its read, write, and execute permissions. (4) Consequently, if the guest attempts to access risky pages, it will trigger an OS signal due to the violation of page permissions. (5) The ODT-MMU can be invoked within the signal-handling function. Since the on-demand mechanism only modifies the permissions of risky pages, the performance of non-risky pages remains unaffected.

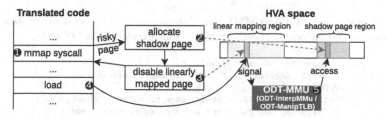

Fig. 4. The process of the on-demand mechanism.

3.2   ODT-InterpMMU: Interpreting the Risky Page Accesses

ODT-InterpMMU handles the risky memory access by interpreting it. During interpretation, the corresponding shadow page is retrieved from the shadow page table. The risky memory access is redirected to the corresponding shadow page. The outline of the ODT-InterpMMU code is depicted in Fig. 5. Within the signal handling function, the OS typically provides the Program Counter (PC), the accessed memory address (linearly mapped address), and the General Purpose Registers (GPRs). The interpretation is conducted based on the opcode of the instruction pointed at by the PC. For example, a load-byte instruction is interpreted as moving one byte from the shadow address to the destination GPR, and a store-byte instruction is interpreted as moving one byte from the destination GPR to the shadow address.

3.3   ODT-ManipTLB: Manipulating the Hardware TLB

ODT-ManipTLB leverages the host TLB for improved performance. Host ISAs like MIPS [14] and LoongArch [12] offer a VTLB that enables variable page size settings and programmability through software. The VTLB can be utilized to cache recently accessed shadow page table entries. As long as the VTLB hits, there is no overhead in accessing risky pages. Overhead only occurs when VTLB misses, and the ODT-ManipTLB is invoked as shown in Fig. 4. ODT-ManipTLB is responsible for obtaining the physical address of the shadow page and refilling the VTLB, as depicted in Fig. 6.

```
1   // Algorithm: InterpMMU(mc, lma, gprs)
2   // Input:
3   //    - mc: uint32_t (machine code)
4   //    - lma: uint64_t (linearly mapped address)
5   //    - gprs: GPRs array (General Purpose Registers)
6   // Output: None
7   uint64_t shadow_addr = shadow_page_table(lma - guest_base);
8   switch ( opcode(mc) )
9   case OPCODE_LOAD_BYTE:
10      *gprs[dest(mc)] = *(uint8_t *)shadow_addr; break;
11  case OPCODE_STORE_BYTE:
12      *(uint8_t *)shadow_addr = *gprs[dest(mc)]; break;
13  case ...
14  }
```

Fig. 5. The code of ODT-InterpMMU. The interpretation involves a switch-case statement based on the opcode of the instruction, which triggers the OS signal.

```
1   // Algorithm: ManipTLB(lma)
2   // Input: lma: uint64_t (linearly mapped address)
3   // Output: None
4   uint64_t shadow_addr = shadow_page_table(lma - guest_base);
5   // Following two funcs are implemented by kernel module
6   uint64_t physical_addr = get_physical_addr(shadow_addr);
7   refill_vtlb(lma, physical_addr);
```

Fig. 6. The code of ODT-ManipTLB. A dedicated kernel module is designed to get the physical address and refill the VTLB.

4   Evaluation

This section presents an evaluation of the experimental results of ODT-MMU. The experiments are conducted on Loongson's 3A4000 [8], which operates on Linux with a page size of 16 KB. The ODT-MMU is implemented in QEMU, targeting x86 Linux applications with a page size of 4 KB. The experiments include the following tests:

- Effectiveness tests include a collection of constructed unit tests and a real-world application - Wine [25], to evaluate the effectiveness of resolving the risks depicted in Fig. 1.
- Regression tests incorporate the industrial standard benchmark - SPEC CPU 2000, to ensure that non-risky memory accesses are not affected.
- Performance tests include a set of constructed read/write unit tests, to evaluate the performance of ODT-InterpMMU and ODT-ManipTLB.

4.1   Effectiveness Tests

Effectiveness tests aim to evaluate the effective mitigation of security and correctness risks. Unit tests are designed based on Fig. 1. To evaluate the security risks, multiple 4-KB pages with various permissions are allocated and read/written to determine whether the DBT on the 16-KB host raise segmentation fault when the reads or writes are not permitted. To evaluate the correctness risks, multiple processes are created. Among these processes, multiple shared and private 4-KB pages are allocated with various permissions. These pages are then read and written to verify whether the DBT on the 16-KB host correctly writes private data and blocks the non-permitted reads or writes by a segmentation fault. Experimental results show the private data are correctly written to private pages and no overwrite occurs in ODT-MMU QEMU. Additionally, all non-permitted reads and writes are blocked, and the permission-related results are presented in Table 3. The original QEMU is incapable of addressing the security and correctness risks, whereas ODT-MMU QEMU mitigates these risks as expected.

Table 3. Effectiveness tests for original QEMU and ODT-MMU QEMU. All test cases are derived from Fig. 1. Abbreviations: Y permitted, N not permitted.

Issue Type	Permissions	Expected Results		Original QEMU		ODT-MMU QEMU	
		Read	Write	Read	Write	Read	Write
Security	r–p	Y	N	Y	Y	Y	N
Security	rw-p	Y	Y	Y	Y	Y	Y
Security	r-xp	Y	N	Y	Y	Y	N
Security	—p	N	N	Y	Y	N	N
Correctness	r–p	Y	N	Crash	Crash	Y	N
Correctness	rw-s	Y	Y	Crash	Crash	Y	Y
Correctness	r-xp	Y	N	Crash	Crash	Y	N
Correctness	—p	N	N	Crash	Crash	N	N

Furthermore, we conduct tests on a well-known multi-process application - Wine. A typical Wine program is associated with two processes: a `wineserver` responsible for emulating the Windows kernel, and an emulated Windows application. Shared pages are utilized to share data between these processes. Our experiments demonstrate that QEMU crashes when running Windows applications such as Notepad and Tencent WeChat, whereas ODT-MMU QEMU executes these applications smoothly.

4.2   Regression Tests

To evaluate whether ODT-MMU affects the performance of non-risky memory accesses, we begin by analyzing the memory accessing behavior of the SPEC CPU 2000 Integer test suite. Since all tests within CPU 2000 Integer are single-process, the presence of risky pages is solely attributed to security risks. Figure 7 presents the statistics regarding the risky memory pages, including the number of risky pages, as well as the ratio of memory accesses that read/write the risky pages to the total number of memory accesses. Several tests, such as `164.gzip` and `300.twolf`, exhibit more than 30% memory accesses being risky. The total count of risky pages does not exceed 20 for any of the tests. The findings of Fig. 7 indicate a high concentration of risky accesses on a few pages, making

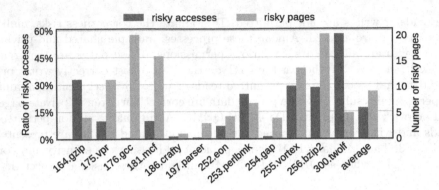

Fig. 7. The statistics of risky memory pages in SPEC CPU 2000 Integer. Left axis shows the ratio of the number of risky memory accesses to the number of all memory accesses. Right axis shows the number of risky pages.

them suitable for acceleration by VTLB, as VTLB typically incorporates 64 entries.

Subsequently, we evaluate the performance of the SPEC CPU 2000 Integer tests. The execution time of ODT-MMU QEMU (ODT-ManipTLB enabled) is normalized to that of the original QEMU, and the experimental results are illustrated in Fig. 8. The overall normalized performance hovers around 100%, suggesting that ODT-MMU has no impact on non-risky memory accesses. Conversely, when ODT-ManipTLB is enabled, several tests demonstrate a slight improvement in performance. This can be attributed to Linux's inefficient utilization of VTLB, and the enabling of VTLB in QEMU is tantamount to increasing the overall number of TLB entries, thereby slightly reducing the TLB miss rate and improving the TLB lookup performance.

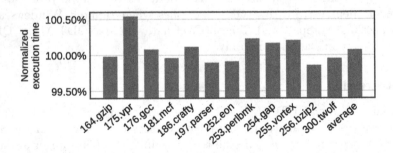

Fig. 8. The normalized execution time of ODT-MMU QEMU in SPEC CPU 2000 Integer. Normalization is achieved by dividing the execution time of ODT-MMU QEMU (ODT-ManipTLB enabled) by the execution time of the original QEMU.

4.3   Performance Tests

To evaluate the performance of risky memory accesses in ODT-MMU and original QEMU, we construct a series of read/write unit tests. Figure 9 demonstrates that ODT-InterpMMU is significantly slower than the original QEMU, which spends over 2000 ns to emulate one risky guest read/write operation. The low performance is mainly caused by the interpretation of software MMU and the trigger of OS signals for each risky read/write operation. Consistent with the findings of regression tests depicted in Fig. 8, ODT-ManipTLB exhibits a modest performance improvement compared with the original QEMU. This is because the utilization of VTLB equates to an increase in overall TLB entries, which results in fewer TLB misses and overall performance improvement.

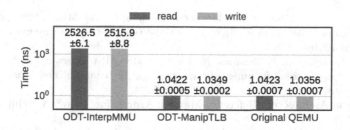

Fig. 9.   The execution time (5 digits are reserved) per guest read/write for ODT-InterpMMU, ODT-ManipTLB, and original QEMU. ODT-ManipTLB QEMU shows slightly higher performance compared with the original QEMU.

5   Conclusion

This paper focuses on analyzing memory management in user-level DBT. Our analysis has identified security and correctness risks in linearly mapping memory management utilized by user-level DBT. These risks arise when executing small-page guest applications on a large-page host OS, as the guest page permissions cannot be appropriately mapped to the host page, resulting in risky access to these pages. The importance and urgency of these risks are increasing with the current transition trend from traditional small-page OSes, such as 4-KB x86 Linux, to large-page OSes, such as 16-KB LoongArch and 16-KB AArch64 Linux. To tackle these risks, we introduce ODT-MMU, a novel DBT mechanism capable of triggering software MMU on demand. ODT-MMU includes a platform-independent implementation called ODT-InterpMMU and a hardware-accelerated implementation called ODT-ManipTLB. Both implementations effectively mitigate security and correctness risks without affecting non-risky memory accesses. Compared with ODT-InterpMMU, ODT-ManipTLB achieves a significant performance improvement of over 2000x by utilizing Loongson's programmable VTLB. Compared with the original DBT, ODT-ManipTLB does not incur noticeable performance loss. In addition to our implementations on Loongson's platform, ODT-MMU can be utilized to mitigate the security and correctness risks in other ISAs as well.

Acknowledgment. This project is funded by the 2022 National Key Research and Development Program "Security Protection Technology for Distribution Network Key Information Infrastructure" Project 3 Distribution Network Computing Equipment Security Enhancement Technology Research and Localization Development (Project No. 2022YFB3105103).

References

1. AMD: AMD64 Architecture Programmer's Manual Volume 2: System Programming (2020)
2. Apple: About the Rosetta translation environment (2021). https://developer.apple.com/documentation/apple-silicon/about-the-rosetta-translation-environment. Accessed 10 June 2023
3. Apple: Running intel binaries in Linux VMS with Rosetta (2022). https://developer.apple.com/documentation/virtualization/running_intel_binaries_in_linux_vms_with_rosetta. Accessed 10 June 2023
4. Arm: Arm Architecture Reference Manual: Armv8, for Armv8-A architecture profile (2021)
5. Bellard, F.: QEMU, a fast and portable dynamic translator. In: USENIX Annual Technical Conference, FREENIX Track (2005)
6. Chang, C.R., Wu, J.J., Hsu, W.C., Liu, P., Yew, P.: Efficient memory virtualization for Cross-ISA system mode emulation. In: International Conference on Virtual Execution Environments (2014)
7. Ganapathy, N., Schimmel, C.: General purpose operating system support for multiple page sizes. In: USENIX Annual Technical Conference (1998)
8. Hu, W., Wang, J., Gao, X., Chen, Y., Liu, Q., Li, G.: Godson-3: a scalable multicore RISC processor with x86 emulation. IEEE Micro **29**, 17–29 (2009)
9. Huang, K., Zhang, F., Li, C., Niu, G., Wu, J., Liu, T.: BTMMU: an efficient and versatile cross-ISA memory virtualization. In: Proceedings of the 17th ACM SIGPLAN/SIGOPS International Conference on Virtual Execution Environments (2021)
10. Huawei: Huawei kunpeng exagear (2022). https://mirrors.huaweicloud.com/kunpeng/archive/ExaGear/. Accessed 10 June 2023
11. Huawei: Technical constraints-introduction-user guide-binary translator (ExaGear)-Kunpeng DevKit-Kunpeng documentation: technical constraints (2023). https://www.hikunpeng.com/document/detail/en/kunpengdevps/ug-exagear/usermanual/kunpengexagear_06_0005.html. Accessed 10 June 2023
12. Loongson Technology Corporation Limited: LoongArch Reference Manual - Volume 1: Basic Architecture (2023)
13. Marcan: Asahi Linux progress report: September 2021 (2021). Accessed 10 June 2023
14. MIPS Technologies Inc.: MIPS Architecture for Programmers Volume III: The MIPS64 and microMIPS64 Privileged Resource Architecture (2014)
15. Navarro, J.E., Iyer, S., Druschel, P., Cox, A.L.: Practical, transparent operating system support for superpages. In: USENIX Symposium on Operating Systems Design and Implementation (2002)

16. Papadopoulou, M.M., Tong, X., Seznec, A., Moshovos, A.: Prediction-based superpage-friendly TLB designs. In: 2015 IEEE 21st International Symposium on High Performance Computer Architecture (HPCA), pp. 210–222 (2015)
17. Probst, M.: Dynamic binary translation (2003)
18. QEMU: QEMU, a generic and open source machine & userspace emulator and virtualizer (2003). https://github.com/qemu/qemu. Accessed 10 June 2023
19. Seznec, A.: Concurrent support of multiple page sizes on a skewed associative TLB. IEEE Trans. Comput. **53**, 924–927 (2004)
20. Spink, T., Wagstaff, H., Franke, B.: Hardware-accelerated cross-architecture full-system virtualization. ACM Trans. Archit. Code Optim. (TACO) **13**, 1–25 (2016)
21. Talluri, M., Hill, M.D.: Surpassing the TLB performance of superpages with less operating system support. In: ASPLOS VI (1994)
22. Tong, X., Koju, T., Kawahito, M., Moshovos, A.: Optimizing memory translation emulation in full system emulators. ACM Trans. Archit. Code Optim. (TACO) **11**, 1–24 (2015)
23. Wang, Z., et al.: HSPT: practical implementation and efficient management of embedded shadow page tables for cross-ISA system virtual machines. In: Proceedings of the 11th ACM SIGPLAN/SIGOPS International Conference on Virtual Execution Environments (2015)
24. Weiwu, H., et al.: Loongson instruction set architecture technology. J. Comput. Res. Dev. **60**, 2–16 (2023)
25. WineHQ: Wine, a windows compatibility layer for POSIX-compliant operating systems (1993). https://www.winehq.org/. Accessed 10 June 2023
26. Winwood, S., Shuf, Y., Franke, H.: Multiple page size support in the Linux kernel (2002)
27. Zhang, X., Jiang, Y., Cong, M.: Performance improvement for multicore processors using variable page technologies. In: 2011 IEEE Sixth International Conference on Networking, Architecture, and Storage, pp. 230–235 (2011)
28. Zhenhua, W.: A dual-TLB method to accelerate the memory access of binary translation. Master's thesis, University of Chinese Academy of Sciences, Beijing, China (2015)

MFHBT: Hybrid Binary Translation System with Multi-stage Feedback Powered by LLVM

Zhaoxin Yang[1,2], Xuehai Chen[1,2], Liangpu Wang[1,2], Weiming Guo[3], Dongru Zhao[3], Chao Yang[4], and Fuxin Zhang[1,2(✉)]

[1] SKLP, Institute of Computing Technology, CAS, Beijing, China
{yangzhaoxin21s,fxzhang}@ict.ac.cn
[2] University of Chinese Academy of Sciences, Beijing, China
{chenxuehai20,wangjingpu17}@mails.ucas.ac.cn
[3] University of Science and Technology of China, Hefei, China
{ustcgwm,zhaodongru}@mail.ustc.edu.cn
[4] State Grid Liaoning Electric Power Supply Co. Ltd., Shenyang, China
yangchaoneu@sina.com

Abstract. The shortage of applications has become a major concern for new Instruction Set Architecture (ISA). Binary translation is a common solution to overcome this challenge. However, the performance of binary translation is heavily dependent on the quality of the translated code. To achieve high-quality translation, recent studies focus on integrating binary translators with compilation optimization methods. Nevertheless, such integration faces two main challenges. Firstly, it is hard to employ complex compilation optimization techniques in a dynamic binary translator (DBT) without introducing significant runtime overhead. Secondly, the task of implementing register mapping in the compiler is challenging, which can reduce expensive memory access instructions generated to maintain the guest CPU state. To resolve these challenges, we propose a hybrid binary translation system with multi-stage feedback, combining dynamic and static binary translator, named MFHBT. This system eliminates the runtime overhead caused by compilation optimization. Additionally, we introduce a mechanism to implement the register mapping through inline constraints and stack variables in the compiler. We implement a prototype of this new system powered by LLVM. Experimental results demonstrate an 81% decrease in the number of memory access instructions and a performance improvement of 3.28 times compared to QEMU.

Keywords: Hybrid binary translation · LLVM · Optimization · Register mapping

1 Introduction

Binary translation is a technique that enables cross Instruction Set Architecture (ISA) compatibility [28]. It allows applications compiled for one ISA to run on

© The Author(s), under exclusive license to Springer Nature Singapore Pte Ltd. 2024
C. Li et al. (Eds.): APPT 2023, LNCS 14103, pp. 310–325, 2024.
https://doi.org/10.1007/978-981-99-7872-4_18

another ISA without recompilation, especially when the source code is difficult to obtain or when recompiling is costly. It also enables basic software development before the hardware can be obtained. Several factors may influence the efficiency of a binary translator, including the overhead of initialization before translation, the overhead of code translation and optimization, and the overall quality of the generated code [5, 21, 25]. Code quality holds particular significance.

Recent studies have focused on integrating binary translators with compilers like LLVM [11,18,22] to achieve high-quality translation, which allows for the utilization of diverse general-purpose optimization techniques provided by compilers. However, two main challenges arise when integrating binary translators with compilers.

The first challenge lies in minimizing additional runtime overhead caused by the time-consuming optimization algorithms provided by compilers in dynamic binary translators (DBT). HQEMU [12,15] tackles this challenge by profiling hot traces, taking advantage of the multicore resources and multithreading itself to mitigate the optimization overhead imposed by LLVM. However, the overhead of code optimization continues to grow due to the expanding number and complexity of LLVM's optimization passes. Consequently, the effectiveness of optimization may be undermined since a greater amount of time is spent on un-optimized code. Although CrossDBT [19] and HBT [23] offload part of the optimization work to the static binary translator (SBT) they integrated, they still rely on LLVM as code optimizer during execution, resulting in additional runtime overhead. Moreover, in both CrossDBT and HBT, the static translator lacks the capability to leverage feedback information [26] from the dynamic translator for additional optimization.

Another challenge arises regarding the effective maintenance of the virtual guest CPU state across the execution of translation units. Both HQEMU and CrossDBT use memory operations for maintenance purposes, resulting in the significant overhead of memory access. Although HQEMU optimizes maintenance by performing it only before guest memory access and jump instructions, the cost of memory access remains high. Utilizing register mapping can reduce maintenance memory access overhead by caching the guest CPU state in host registers. However, specific challenges arise when applying it to LLVM IR. Firstly, LLVM IR is designed to be architecture-independent, but register mapping requires direct interaction with architecture-dependent physical registers, leading to a contradiction. Secondly, it is crucial to ensure that LLVM remains a sufficient number of registers for its own utilization after register mapping.

To solve the above issues, we present MFHBT, a hybrid binary translation system combining both DBT and SBT with multi-stage feedback powered by LLVM. The system eliminates runtime code optimization overhead by offloading all code optimization work to SBT. Furthermore, the system proposes a register mapping mechanism realized through LLVM inline constraints and stack variables to reduce memory access overhead of guest CPU state maintenance.

The contributions of this paper include:

- We design a binary translation system based on LLVM. This system eliminates translation and optimization overhead caused by LLVM during execution. Moreover, it supports continuous optimization of the translated code by enabling feedback from DBT to SBT.

- We introduce a mechanism to reduce the cost of guest CPU state maintenance when using LLVM for code optimization. This mechanism combines the use of LLVM inline constraints and stack variables to provide a register mapping scheme.
- We implement a translation system, named MFHBT-LA, from x86-64 to LoongArch [27] and test its efficiency. Experiment results demonstrate an 81% decrease in the number of memory access instructions and a performance improvement of 3.28 times compared to QEMU [3]. The source code is available at https://github.com/ylzsx/MFHBT.

2   Background

2.1   Hybrid Binary Translation

Static binary translation (SBT) is an offline translation method that does not rely on program information during runtime [6]. It transforms the original binary code from guest architecture into new binary code for the host architecture prior to program execution. This approach allows for longer translation time, enabling the application of aggressive and time-consuming optimizations to generate highly efficient translated code. However, static binary translation suffers from certain limitations and incompleteness issues, such as self-modified code, which can hinder its practicality [9].

Dynamic binary translation (DBT) involves translating individual translation unit by following the execution flow and generating code using Just-In-Time (JIT) technology [2,4,17]. The generated code is subsequently executed. Due to its comprehensive understanding of program execution, dynamic binary translation effectively addresses various issues, such as self-modified code, indirect jumps, and indirect calls. However, it is important to note that DBT is sensitive to the overall cost of code generation and optimization. As a result, more complex optimization methods in the translation module are restricted, leading to inferior code quality compared to static binary translation.

To enhance the quality of the translated code while ensuring completeness, we combine SBT and DBT [1,20], thereby enhancing the overall performance of the entire binary translation system.

2.2   Maintain Guest CPU State

In binary translation, maintaining the guest CPU state is essential. This process involves acquiring the current guest CPU state prior to executing each translation unit and updating the new guest CPU state posterior to emulating the functionality of guest instructions. The commonly used methods include the memory storage method and the register mapping method. The memory storage method requires additional instructions for memory access, resulting in reduced performance compared to the register mapping method. In the register mapping method, guest registers (GRs) are mapped to host registers (HRs). After completing each translation unit, the most recent state of GRs in the guest CPU is stored in HRs. Subsequent translation units can retrieve the updated state without the need for memory access.

3   Design

3.1   Overview

We design a hybrid binary translation system that combines both the dynamic and static side to reduce the overhead of translating and optimizing at runtime, called MFHBT. This system is powered by LLVM compilation optimization and incorporates a multi-stage feedback mechanism. An overview of the system's execution process is presented in Fig. 1.

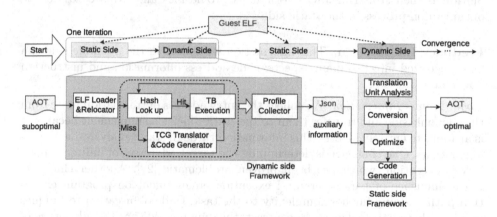

Fig. 1. Overview

During the initial iteration, the static side creates an Ahead-of-Time (AOT) file by relying solely on the translation units extracted through code mining from the guest Executable and Linkable Format (ELF) file, and no feedback information is obtained from the dynamic side. Subsequently, the dynamic side receives the AOT file and collects profiling information, which is eventually stored as a JSON file. In the second iteration, the static side examines the JSON file that was generated during the previous dynamic execution. Following that it creates superior code, which will be combined with the previous AOT file to produce a new one. The dynamic side uses this updated AOT file for execution while simultaneously collecting feedback. This iterative process continues, leading to a gradual enhancement in program performance that ultimately converges to a stable state.

The dynamic side comprises four components, functioning as ELF loading and relocation, program execution, code translation, and profile collecting. It is a lightweight binary translator that runs the high-quality generated code from the static side. Additionally, it conducts lightweight translation for basic blocks that the static side could not recognize, supplementing for the static side.

The static side is a heavyweight optimizer, built around LLVM and composed of four distinct components, functioning as translation unit analysis, instruction conversion, code optimization, and code generation. It holds two primary responsibilities: obtaining translation units and performing offline optimizations using LLVM, where the optimized code is then saved as an AOT file.

3.2 Multi-stage Feedback Mechanism

MFHBT employs a multi-stage feedback mechanism to improve the quality of generated code [7]. During each execution, MFHBT gathers information about the executed program using the profile collector on the dynamic side. This information is then stored in JSON format as profile files and utilized to aid the optimization process in the static side.

Feedback Information. This information we collect in the dynamic side can be categorized into two main aspects: code address information and instruction flow characteristics.

Code Address Information. We collect the entry address of translation units from the dynamic side and transfer them to the static side as a supplement because it is arduous to entirely identify this information through static analysis due to various factors. One challenge is determining the target addresses of indirect jumps before execution, which has been proven problematic [28]. Another challenge is the influence of parameters and execution environment on program execution paths, adding further complexity to the task. Code obfuscation techniques present additional challenges. In contrast, the dynamic side has the advantage of being able to easily identify the currently translated and executed code, which will help identify a wider range of guest code.

Instruction Flow Characteristics. We gather the instruction flow characteristics, such as hot trace paths and indirect jump target addresses [24], in our system. This information can guide further optimization in the static side, such as supplementing unrecognized translation units, expanding the range of optimization, and reordering the generated code.

Multi-stage Feedback. Our feedback mechanism operates at multiple stages, allowing each execution on the dynamic side to contribute valuable information to the static side. Factors such as program parameters, execution environment, and the program's random behavior all influence the execution path of the program. As a result, multi-stage feedback mechanism can provide more comprehensive code coverage and detailed execution flow information compared to single feedback mechanism.

Considering a program in which the execution path is influenced by the random number generated within the code. When the program is translated, it may result in different execution paths across multiple runs. During these runs, the dynamic side can capture the variations in the execution path, leading to a more thorough understanding of the program's behavior.

3.3   Register Mapping in LLVM

This paper introduces a register mapping scheme in LLVM, aiming to effectively maintain the guest CPU state. The method employs the LLVM inline constraints and stack variables, to reduce the proportion of memory access instructions in the generated code.

The implementation, depicted in Fig. 2, involves establishing a mapping between the guest and host registers. In the entry block, the mapping is established by three steps: 1) associating guest registers with LLVM stack variables, 2) binding host physical registers to virtual registers using the output constraint mechanism provided by LLVM IR inline assembly, 3) storing the virtual registers bound to host physical registers to LLVM IR stack variables. In the exit block, the mapping is built by two steps: 1) loading the guest registers from the stack variables into the virtual registers, 2) writing the virtual registers into the relative physical registers using the input constraint mechanism provided by LLVM IR inline assembly. In the translation unit, reading from and writing to the guest registers are translated to access the corresponding the stack variables.

Using stack variables does not result in unnecessary memory access because of LLVM's stack promotion optimization pass (mem2reg). This optimization pass elevates the operations involving stack variables to virtual registers, for which the LLVM backend will allocate physical registers. While extra register move operations may be required, the cost is significantly lower than memory access. Meanwhile, this approach restricts the utilization of physical registers solely at the entry and exit points of the translation unit, thereby preserving LLVM's exploration of physical registers during optimization.

The utilization of stack variables offers additional benefits. If stack variables are not used to cache guest registers, tracking the temporary virtual registers holding the latest value of the guest registers becomes complex, particularly when dealing with multiple levels of branching. However, stack variables facilitate efficient management of this tracking process by the compiler, thereby enhancing overall efficiency.

4   Implement

This section describes a prototype of an architecture-independent binary translation system named MFHBT-LA, which translates binary code from x86-64 to LoongArch. In the static side, it utilizes LLVM for offline optimization and in the dynamic side, it employs QEMU for handling code not covered by the static side. This system leverages LLVM and QEMU's support for multiple architectures.

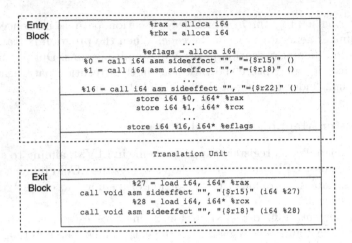

Fig. 2. An Example of Stack Translation Mode.

4.1 Dynamic Side

The dynamic side is responsible for running the pre-translated code from the static side and implementing lightweight code translation and optimization. It encompasses several tasks, including ELF loading and relocation, program execution, code translation, and profile collecting, as illustrated in the Fig. 3.

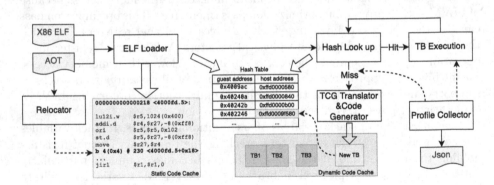

Fig. 3. The Design of Dynamic Side

ELF Loading and Relocation. This module comprises two components: the ELF loader and relocator. The ELF loader is responsible for loading the guest ELF file and the AOT file. Meanwhile, according to the information from the AOT file, it will establish a hash table and record link slots. The relocator fills the link slots by considering jump relationships in the guest program. This process helps to reduce the overhead of the context switch during execution.

Program Execution. Before each execution, the system will check whether a translation unit has been recorded in hash table based on the guest PC. If the unit is found, the corresponding code is executed until a context switch occurs, where control is transferred back to translator. If the unit is not found, translation begins.

Code Translation. The dynamic side performs translation using QEMU, stores the generated code into the dynamic code cache, and updates the hash table established in the ELF loading phase. It is important to distinguish between the translated code and the pre-translated AOT code in memory because direct linking is not possible when the translation protocols differ between the dynamic and static sides, such as in the case of emulating EFLAGS[1]. In such situations, the translator may need to synchronize certain states.

Profile Collecting. The profile collector keeps track of unrecognized code and the execution flow information, which allows the static side to utilize this information to generate higher-quality code in subsequent runs.

4.2 Static Side

The static side is responsible for implementing heavyweight optimizations in the system. It comprises four components, functioning as translation unit analysis, instruction conversion, code optimization, and code generation, as illustrated in the Fig. 4.

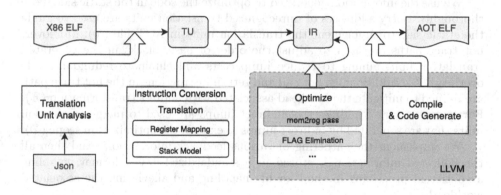

Fig. 4. The Design of Static Side

Translation Units Analysis. Translation units are obtained through two approaches: static code mining and feedback files analysis. Nonetheless, there may be cases where multiple units share the same entry address in the guest program. In such scenarios, we prioritize the unit derived from feedback files.

---

[1] The EFLAGS register is the status register that contains the current state of a x86 CPU.

Instruction Conversion. Each translation unit is translated to an LLVM IR function in two steps. Firstly, the translation unit is disassembled to guest instructions. Secondly, each guest instruction is lifted into LLVM IRs using a custom translation procedure. The focus is solely on ensuring the correctness of guest semantics, with an expectation of improved LLVM IR quality during code optimization.

Code Optimization. The obtained LLVM IR functions undergo optimization to enhance code quality. These optimizations involve various passes provided by LLVM, including mem2reg, function inlining, loop vectorize pass, and so on. Additionally, custom optimization passes and specific intrinsics for LoongArch architectures are implemented, such as the EFLAGS elimination pass.

Code Generation. The optimized LLVM IR functions are then transformed into host instructions using LLVM's code generation library and saved as a relocatable file following the ELF format, commonly referred to as an AOT file.

4.3   Multi-stage Feedback Mechanism

We implement a profile collector using various methods to collect feedback information in this paper, as shown in Fig. 5. Firstly, when the translation unit is missing in the hash table, we collect the entry addresses of unrecognized translation unit (①). Secondly, the NET algorithm [10] is used for hot trace paths collection (②). Finally, when dealing with the target addresses of indirect jumps, we keep a record of the guest PC and the target addresses (③).

We use the information generated to optimize the code in the static side more thoroughly. Entry addresses of unrecognized translation units are used to guide the static side to supplement the translation units in AOT file (④). Moreover, hot trace paths are used to adjust the order of basic blocks in the generated translation unit, aiming to reduce jump costs and eliminate redundant code overhead (⑤). Additionally, hot call and return instructions in the hot trace path are inlined to mitigate the overhead associated with address transformation (⑥). Furthermore, target addresses of indirect jumps are used to merge translation units that are separated by indirect jumps to expand the optimization scope (⑦).

We implement the gathering of various feedback information. And then all the collected information is stored in a standardized JSON format, enabling a consistent processing method for file handling and alleviating the associated workload.

In each iteration, a new AOT file is generated based on the feedback information received from the dynamic side. The ELF standard format ensures that all files are relocatable, allowing them to be linked with existing files through the use of GNU ld. This process decreases the overhead of re-generating AOT files in the static side.

4.4   Register Mapping in LLVM

We introduce a cache for each virtual register in the LLVM IR associated with a guest register to reduce the frequency of read and write operations on stack

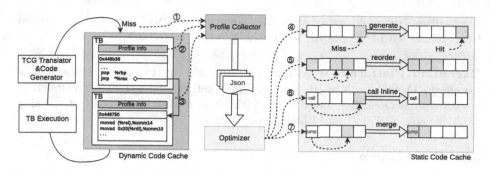

Fig. 5. The design of Multi-stage Feedback.

variables, leading to a reduced overhead of the LLVM mem2reg pass. The cache stores the most recent value of the virtual register. The value is written back to corresponding LLVM IR stack variable, only when encountering branch instructions. This approach reduces the cost of the LLVM mem2reg pass within each translation unit.

To ensure the correctness of register mapping at the entry and exit blocks of each translation unit, it is necessary to prevent the compiler from scheduling the LLVM IR instructions responsible for these mappings. To achieve this, we added priority flags to these instructions, guiding the compiler's scheduling algorithm accordingly. In MFHBT-LA, the read operations of physical registers at the entry block of a translation unit are assigned the highest priority, while the write operations of physical registers at the exit block are assigned the lowest priority. This approach effectively resolves the issue and guarantees the correctness of register mappings.

It is important to note that the register mapping mechanism does not affect the compiler's usage of physical registers or the quality of generated code, even when the number of guest registers is similar to that of host registers. Firstly, the selection of mapped registers is customizable, allowing for mapping only frequently used guest registers. Secondly, the constraints of the register mapping mechanism only apply at the entry and exit of translation units and do not interfere with the compiler's register allocation within the translation units. Therefore, compared to a purely static register mapping approach, our solution can generate high-quality code.

5 Evaluation

Benchmarks. We select the CoreMark benchmark and ten subitems from the SPEC CPU2000 INT benchmark, excluding 175.vpr and 252.eon, to evaluate the performance of our translation system. The exclusion of 175.vpr and 252.eon is due to their intensive use of floating-point operations. However we do not optimize the floating-point and vector instructions and still rely on QEMU's helper mechanism. To avoid generating AVX instructions, we compile the selected benchmarks with the options "-mno-avx -fno-tree-vectorize".

Execution Platform. We conduct testing of our translation system on a Loongson 3A5000 machine [16] running Linux kernel version 4.19.0. The machine operates at a clock frequency of 2.5 GHz. The evaluation is conducted using QEMU version v7.0.93 and LLVM version v8.0.1.

5.1   Performance

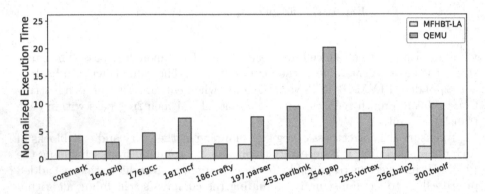

Fig. 6. Normalized execution time of MFHBT-LA and QEMU based on the native execution in CoreMark and SPEC CPU2000 INT.

We conduct a performance evaluation on three platforms: the native LA machine, QEMU, and MFHBT-LA in a stable state and calculate the normalized execution time of MFHBT-LA and QEMU based on the native program. The results, presented in Fig. 6, indicate a notable improvement in performance. MFHBT-LA exhibits a performance increase of 2.63X in the CoreMark benchmark and 3.28X in the SPEC CPU2000 INT benchmarks compared to QEMU. These findings demonstrate the superior code quality achieved through LLVM optimization compared to the translated code generated by QEMU. Furthermore, MFHBT-LA exhibite only 1.68X slower than the native execution in the SPEC CPU2000 INT.

5.2   Execution Time

Figure 7 depicts the ratio of execution time spent on the code generated in the translators. Notably, MFHBT-LA exhibits a significantly larger proportion compared to HQEMU and QEMU. The statistical data is collected using perf, which may have a slight margin of error. However, it effectively demonstrates that offloading LLVM optimization to the static side significantly reduces translation time and increases execution time spent on the code generated, consequently enhancing system performance.

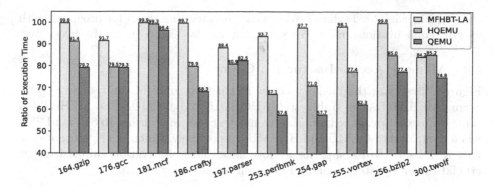

Fig. 7. Ratio of execution time to total time for the generated code of MFHBT-LA, HQEMU and QEMU.

5.3 The Performance of Convergence

We demonstrate the performance of MFHBT-LA convergence no matter when the execution path is fixed or various among different executions.

Figure 8a illustrates the relative performance of running the SPEC CPU2000 INT ref suites compared to the native program during five execution and feedback iterations. The performance reaches a stable state after two iterations, demonstrating fast convergence under a fixed execution path.

Figure 8b shows the relative performance compared to the native program of running the SPEC CPU2000 INT test, train, and ref suites in sequence. Although the three suites are various in execution path because of varying configurations and workloads, consistently improved performance is observed. This indicates that the feedback information and optimized code can be reused among different execution. This can be attributed to two main factors: (1) feedback information has a certain level of generality, resulting from factors like the limited nature of basic blocks, and (2) common execution paths exist among different runs.

Furthermore, we observe a strong resemblance between the relative performance of running ref suites in Fig. 8b and the relative performance in a stable

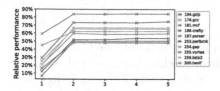

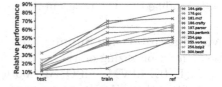

(a) The relative performance of running the SPEC CPU2000 INT ref suites compared to the native program during five execution and feedback iterations.

(b) The relative performance of running the SPEC CPU2000 INT test, train, and ref suites in sequence compared to the native program.

Fig. 8. The relative performance compared to the native program.

state in Fig. 8a. This finding further demonstrates that, even for programs with varying configurations, multiple executions can also lead to gradual convergence.

5.4   Memory Access Instruction Count

Figure 9 illustrates the memory access instruction count of the x86 native program, MFHBT-LA in stable state, HQEMU and QEMU. The MFHBT-LA achieves a substantial reduction in memory access, amounting to 81% and 65% when compared to QEMU and HQEMU, respectively, which is a significant contributing factor to its superior performance. This observation emphasizes the crucial role of register mapping in minimizing memory access.

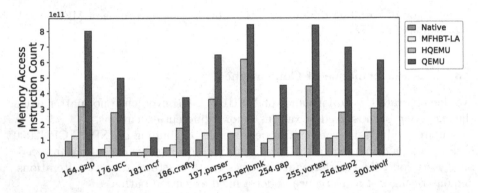

Fig. 9. The memory access instruction count for the x86 native program, MFHBT-LA, HQEMU and QEMU.

6   Discussion

Self-modifying Code. The accurate execution of self-modifying code in MFHBT is attributed to the adoption of QEMU's processing mechanism. We make slight modifications to the mechanism, resulting in the invalidation of both the dynamically generated code by QEMU and the code loaded from the AOT file when self-modification is detected. Consequently, QEMU will retranslate the code modified by the program during the subsequent execution.

Multi-architecture Support. The system is designed to be architecture independent, capitalizing on the support for multiple architectures offered by LLVM and QEMU. LLVM and QEMU both utilize Intermediate Representation (IR), TCG IR and LLVM IR, to represent program semantics, facilitating the generation of target code for various host architectures. In this work, adding a new architecture requires to implement translation procedures that convert guest instructions to LLVM IRs. Due to the optimization mechanisms provided by LLVM, the translation procedures only need to ensure correctness, rather than code quality, which accelerates the development speed of supporting a new ISA.

Real-World Applications. In addition to the benchmarks mentioned in the paper, we conduct experiments on various real-world applications, such as grep, awk, sed, and so on. Our prototype demonstrates satisfactory performance in these applications.

7 Related Work

Several conventional binary translation systems utilize a combination of binary translator and compiler. To reduce the runtime overhead of code optimization caused by compilers, HQEMU and HBT adopt different approaches. HQEMU [15], proposed by Hong et al., profiles hot traces in the execution thread, converts the TCG IR of these hot traces to LLVM IR, and implements additional optimizations in backend threads to generate superior code. This approach leverages the availability of multicore platforms to reduce the runtime overhead of code optimization. HBT [23], proposed by Shen et al., is a hybrid binary translation system based on LLVM that combines the benefits of SBT and DBT. The system offloads part of the compilation optimization cost to the SBT. Li et al. perform work to improve LLVM IR generation speed. They proposed CrossDBT [19], directly lift guest binary code to LLVM IR to avoid the additional transform overhead and local information loss compared to translate guest code to TCG IR first.

Some research works on combining static and dynamic translator to enhance the performance of the binary translation system [13,14]. Chernoff designed and implemented a binary translation system, FX!32 [8], to reduce the overhead of translation in the dynamic side. When the program execution, an AOT file generated by the static side will be loaded and executed, thus improving the performance of the system. Guan et al. proposed an approach to software cache optimization. In this approach, they rearrange the software cache layout by collecting profile information and translated code, so that the most frequently executed parts are at the top of the cache [13].

8 Conclusion

In binary translation, optimizing code quality while minimizing translation cost is crucial for improving performance. In this paper, we introduce a hybrid binary translation system with multi-stage feedback that optimizes translated code using the compiler and provides feedback to SBT based on program information from DBT. Additionally, we propose a register mapping mechanism in the compiler that reduces memory access instructions by 81% compared to QEMU in the SPEC CPU2000 INT benchmark. Our prototype, MFHBT-LA, improves performance by 3.28 times compared to QEMU in the same benchmark. As part of future work, we will optimize floating-point and vector instructions using the method proposed in this paper. Furthermore, we plan to investigate additional optimization techniques customized for specific architectures.

Acknowledgment. We would like to thank all the anonymous reviewers for their helpful comments and suggestions. This project is funded by the 2022 National Key Research and Development Program "Security Protection Technology for Distribution Network Key Information Infrastructure" Project 3 Distribution Network Computing Equipment Security Enhancement Technology Research and Localization Development (Project No. 2022YFB3105103).

References

1. Altman, E.R., Kaeli, D., Sheffer, Y.: Welcome to the opportunities of binary translation. Computer **33**(3), 40–45 (2000)
2. Bala, V., Duesterwald, E., Banerjia, S.: Dynamo: a transparent dynamic optimization system. In: Proceedings of the ACM SIGPLAN 2000 Conference on Programming Language Design and Implementation, pp. 1–12 (2000)
3. Bellard, F.: QEMU, a fast and portable dynamic translator. In: USENIX Annual Technical Conference, FREENIX Track, California, USA, vol. 41, p. 46 (2005)
4. Bezzubikov, A., Belov, N., Batuzov, K.: Automatic dynamic binary translator generation from instruction set description. In: 2017 Ivannikov ISPRAS Open Conference (ISPRAS), pp. 27–33. IEEE (2017)
5. Borin, E., Wu, Y.: Characterization of DBT overhead. In: 2009 IEEE International Symposium on Workload Characterization (IISWC), pp. 178–187. IEEE (2009)
6. Chen, J.Y., Yang, W., Hsu, W.C., Shen, B.Y., Ou, Q.H.: On static binary translation of ARM/Thumb mixed ISA binaries. ACM Trans. Embed. Comput. Syst. (TECS) **16**(3), 1–25 (2017)
7. Chen, W., Shen, L., Lu, H., Wang, Z., Xiao, N.: A light-weight code cache design for dynamic binary translation. In: 2009 15th International Conference on Parallel and Distributed Systems, pp. 120–125. IEEE (2009)
8. Chernoff, A., et al.: FX! 32: a profile-directed binary translator. IEEE Micro **18**(02), 56–64 (1998)
9. Cifuentes, Malhotra: Binary translation: static, dynamic, retargetable? In: 1996 Proceedings of International Conference on Software Maintenance, pp. 340–349. IEEE (1996)
10. Duesterwald, E., Bala, V.: Software profiling for hot path prediction: less is more. ACM SIGARCH Comput. Archit. News **28**(5), 202–211 (2000)
11. Engelke, A., Okwieka, D., Schulz, M.: Efficient LLVM-based dynamic binary translation. In: VEE 2021, pp. 165–171. Association for Computing Machinery, New York (2021)
12. Fu, S.Y., Hong, D.Y., Wu, J.J., Liu, P., Hsu, W.C.: SIMD code translation in an enhanced HQEMU. In: 2015 IEEE 21st International Conference on Parallel and Distributed Systems (ICPADS), pp. 507–514. IEEE (2015)
13. Guan, H., et al.: A dynamic-static combined code layout reorganization approach for dynamic binary translation. J. Softw. **6**(12), 2341–2349 (2011)
14. Guan, H., Zhu, E., Wang, H., Ma, R., Yang, Y., Wang, B.: SINOF: a dynamic-static combined framework for dynamic binary translation. J. Syst. Archit. **58**(8), 305–317 (2012)
15. Hong, D.Y., et al.: HQEMU: a multi-threaded and retargetable dynamic binary translator on multicores. In: Proceedings of the Tenth International Symposium on Code Generation and Optimization, pp. 104–113 (2012)
16. Hu, W., Wang, J., Gao, X., Chen, Y., Liu, Q., Li, G.: Godson-3: a scalable multicore RISC processor with x86 emulation. IEEE Micro **29**, 17–29 (2009)

17. Inoue, H., Hayashizaki, H., Wu, P., Nakatani, T.: A trace-based Java JIT compiler retrofitted from a method-based compiler. In: International Symposium on Code Generation and Optimization (CGO 2011), pp. 246–256. IEEE (2011)
18. Lattner, C., Adve, V.: LLVM: a compilation framework for lifelong program analysis & transformation. In: International Symposium on Code Generation and Optimization, CGO 2004, pp. 75–86. IEEE (2004)
19. Li, W., Luo, X., Zhang, Y., Meng, Q., Ren, F.: CrossDBT: an LLVM-based user-level dynamic binary translation emulator. In: Cano, J., Trinder, P. (eds.) Euro-Par 2022. LNCS, vol. 13440, pp. 3–18. Springer, Cham (2022). https://doi.org/10.1007/978-3-031-12597-3_1
20. Liu, I.C., Wu, I.W., Shann, J.J.J.: Instruction emulation and OS supports of a hybrid binary translator for x86 instruction set architecture. In: 2015 IEEE 12th International Conference on Ubiquitous Intelligence and Computing and 2015 IEEE 12th International Conference on Autonomic and Trusted Computing and 2015 IEEE 15th International Conference on Scalable Computing and Communications and Its Associated Workshops (UIC-ATC-ScalCom), pp. 1070–1077. IEEE (2015)
21. Payer, M., Gross, T.R.: Generating low-overhead dynamic binary translators. In: Proceedings of the 3rd Annual Haifa Experimental Systems Conference, pp. 1–14 (2010)
22. Shen, B.Y., Chen, J.Y., Hsu, W.C., Yang, W.: LLBT: an LLVM-based static binary translator. In: Proceedings of the 2012 International Conference on Compilers, Architectures and Synthesis for Embedded Systems, pp. 51–60 (2012)
23. Shen, B.Y., You, J.Y., Yang, W., Hsu, W.C.: An LLVM-based hybrid binary translation system. In: 7th IEEE International Symposium on Industrial Embedded Systems (SIES 2012), pp. 229–236. IEEE (2012)
24. Shi, H., Wang, Y., Guan, H., Liang, A.: An intermediate language level optimization framework for dynamic binary translation. ACM SIGPLAN Not. **42**(5), 3–9 (2007)
25. Spink, T., Wagstaff, H., Franke, B., Topham, N.: Efficient code generation in a region-based dynamic binary translator. In: Proceedings of the 2014 SIGPLAN/SIGBED Conference on Languages, Compilers and Tools for Embedded Systems, pp. 3–12 (2014)
26. Ung, D., Cifuentes, C.: Dynamic re-engineering of binary code with run-time feedbacks. In: Proceedings Seventh Working Conference on Reverse Engineering, pp. 2–10. IEEE (2000)
27. Weiwu, H., et al.: Loongson instruction set architecture technology. J. Comput. Res. Dev. **60**, 2–16 (2023). (in Chinese)
28. Wenzl, M., Merzdovnik, G., Ullrich, J., Weippl, E.: From hack to elaborate technique-a survey on binary rewriting. ACM Comput. Surv. (CSUR) **52**(3), 1–37 (2019)

Step and Save: A Wearable Technology Based Incentive Mechanism for Health Insurance

Qianyi Huang[1]([✉])[iD], Wei Wang[2][iD], and Qian Zhang[3][iD]

[1] Sun Yat-sen University, Guangzhou, Guangdong, China
huangqy89@mail.sysu.edu.cn
[2] Huazhong University of Science and Technology, Wuhan, Hubei, China
weiwangw@hust.edu.cn
[3] Hong Kong University of Science and Technology, Hong Kong, China
qianzh@cse.ust.hk

Abstract. The market of wearables are growing explosively for the past few years. The majority of the devices are related to health care and fitness. It is embarrassing that users easily lose interest in these devices, and thus fail to improve health condition. Recently, the "be healthy and be rewarded" programs are gaining popularity in health insurance market. The insurance companies give financial rewards to its policyholders who take the initiative to keep healthy. It provides the policyholders with incentives to lead a healthier lifestyle and the insurer can also benefit from less medical claims. Unfortunately, there are hardly any studies discussing how to design the incentive mechanism in this new emerging health promotion program. Improper design would not change policyholders' unhealthy behavior and the insurer cannot benefit from it. In this paper, we propose a mechanism for this health promotion program. We model it as a monopoly market using contract theory, in which there is one insurer and many policyholders. We theoretically analyze how all parties would behave in this program. We propose a design that can guarantee that policyholders would faithfully participate in the program and the insurer can maximize its profit. Simulation results show that the insurer can improve its profit by 40% using the optimal contract.

Keywords: Wearable technology · healthcare · incentive mechanism

1 Introduction

The market of wearable devices are booming across the global. IDTechEx analysts estimate that the market will be worth $40 billion in 2018, then accelerates to $100 billion by 2023, and finally reaches $150 billion by 2026 [16]. Various types of wearable devices are penetrating into our daily life, revolutionizing our clothes, watches, shoes, etc. The main functions of these smart devices are related

© The Author(s), under exclusive license to Springer Nature Singapore Pte Ltd. 2024
C. Li et al. (Eds.): APPT 2023, LNCS 14103, pp. 326–347, 2024.
https://doi.org/10.1007/978-981-99-7872-4_19

Fig. 1. Step and save program. The insurer would reward its policyholders who take the initiative to exercise. The intention of the insurer is to let policyholders keep fit and reduce medical expenditure.

to health condition monitoring, *e.g.*, sleep quality monitoring [24], physical activity tracking [2], and smoking detection [19]. Improving the population health is an important target of wearable technology.

According to the data published by the World Bank, health expenditure accounts for 17.1% of United States GDP [3] and the number is still increasing. The rapid growth of health expenditure casts shadow on the global economics, which has caused great concern to both households and governments. A substantial portion of the diseases and deaths are caused by unhealthy dietary habits, sedentary lifestyle, tobacco and alcohol use [10]. Wearable devices can be used to monitor users' behavior and promote a healthy lifestyle. However, a survey [18] shows that more than half of consumers no longer wear their activity trackers and a third of them stop wearing the device within six months of receiving it. Consumers lack the incentives to use the device and fail to establish healthy habits.

Recently, the "be healthy and be rewarded" programs are gaining popularity in health insurance market. With the help of wearable devices, the insurer can reward its policyholders (PHs) for their healthy behaviors. The intention of the insurer is to use financial rewards to stimulate PHs to get rid of unhealthy habits and pursue a healthy lifestyle. Thus, the insurer can reimburse less amounts of medical claims and make profits. Realizing the great potentials, many insurance companies have launched similar programs. For example, AIA Vitality members can get a $7.50 Boost Juice voucher each week for engaging in physical activity. They can also get a gift card when earning enough AIA Vitality points.

Unfortunately, there are few previous works discussing how to design the incentive mechanism in these health promotion programs. Improper goals or rewards will not stimulate PHs and the insurer may not gain profit from this program. On one hand, setting a high goal or a small reward would discourage

PHs' participation; on the other hand, giving the PHs large rewards may overran the insurer's budget. For PHs, they should have enough incentive to participate in the program, and for the insurer, it wants to maximize its profits.

In this paper, we consider the scenario of "Step and Save", as shown in Fig. 1. The insurer sets step goals for the PHs, and the PHs can get discount off their insurance premiums if their average daily step counts reach the target. To maximize its profit, the insurer needs to address two challenges. First, the insurer do not have complete information about the PHs. PHs have different personal conditions (*e.g.*, workload, economic situation), termed as *type*, which is PHs' personal information and would affect their willingness to participate in physical activity. In addition to that, PHs' original daily step counts can also affect their willingness to achieve the target. However, both PHs' types and original daily step counts are not revealed to the insurer. Second, the insurer needs to guarantee that PHs would faithfully participate in the program. Only with the reasonable expectation of PHs' behavior, the insurer can maximize its profit accordingly.

To jointly tackle these two challenges, we use contract theory [5], which is effective for mechanism design under incomplete information. The intuition is to offer each PH a proper contract item, thus it will faithfully reveal its private information. The insurer would provide several contract items (*i.e.*, step goals and corresponding discounts) for the PHs to choose. The PH would select the item that maximizes its utility. After knowing PHs' behavior, the insurer can maximize its profit accordingly.

The main contributions of this paper are as follows:

- We, for the first time, theoretically analyze the insurer and PHs' behaviors in the new emerging programs in health insurance market.
- We design the optimal feasible contract that jointly considers PHs' types and original daily step counts. It can guarantee that the PHs would truthfully participate in the program and maximize the profit of the insurer.
- We conduct extensive simulations to study the performance under various scenarios. Simulation results show that the insurer can improve its profit by 40% using the optimal contract.

2 System Model

In this section, we first present our system model and define the notations that would be used in the following sections. Then we review some concepts in contract theory.

2.1 Step and Save Program

An insurance company is promoting a health program, which encourages its PHs to exercise more by giving discounts on their premiums. It provides several options (*e.g.*, $\pi = \{[d_1, t_1], [d_2, t_2], \cdots, [d_m, t_m]\}$) for the PHs to choose. For the

PHs who choose the j-th contract item, they will get $d_j\%$ off their premiums I if their average daily steps reach the target l_j; otherwise, there is no discount for them. As there are mature techniques to authenticate/identify users [7,15,20], we assume that all the steps are taken by the legitimate PHs.

For the PHs, their daily step counts consist of two parts: S^c, the steps taken for performing daily activities (*e.g.*, get out of bed, go to dinning places) and S^e, the steps taken when participating in exercise. As pointed out in [22], S^c, the steps for daily activity (without exercise), are similar among populations. To reach the target t, they have to exercise (walk or jog) for at least $(t - S^c)$ steps.

Reaching the targets would incur cost in many ways. For example, spending more time on walking or jogging would mean less time for leisure or work [13]. It is easy to understand that only S^e would incur cost, and S^c would not. Thus, for the following discussion, we do not consider this offset value and only consider the exercising part.

The cost for each person would depend on his/her socioeconomic status, age, health situation, etc. Different PHs have different perception of how much time/comfort they sacrifice to achieve the step goal. We use θ to denote PHs' valuations over their sacrifice made for taking more steps. For PHs with large valuation, they are less willing to exercise. We assume that all PHs' valuations belong to $\boldsymbol{\theta} = \{\theta_1, \theta_2, \cdots, \theta_n\}$, where $\theta_1 > \theta_2 > \cdots > \theta_n$. According to [5], it is optimal for the insurance company to provide a contract item for each type PH. Thus, $m = n$.

Previous studies [10,23] have pointed out that physical activity can improve health status and reduce the medical expenses. We use G to denote the medical savings. For a PH who reaches t steps/day on average, the savings on its medical expense is $G(t)$. Wen *et al.* in [23] have showed that health condition is improving with increasing physical activity duration but the marginal gain is non-increasing, thus we have

$$\frac{\partial G(t)}{\partial t} > 0, \frac{\partial^2 G(t)}{\partial t^2} \leq 0. \tag{1}$$

As a common practice, only a portion of the medical expenses can be covered by the insurance. We use r to denote the reimbursement rate. We define $\bar{r} = 1 - r$.

We use C to denote the cost function. For a type-θ PH, the cost of walking t steps is $C(\theta, t)$. It is straightforward that C increases with θ and t, *i.e.*,

$$\frac{\partial C(\theta, t)}{\partial \theta} > 0, \frac{\partial C(\theta, t)}{\partial t} > 0. \tag{2}$$

It is well known that the muscle would fatigue during exercise. During walking/running periods, the speed is decreasing while the perceived difficulty is increasing. For example, the time of walking 20 thousand steps would be at least twice the time of walking 10 thousand steps and is perceived more difficult. Thus, the marginal cost is increasing with t, *i.e.*,

$$\frac{\partial^2 C(\theta, t)}{\partial t^2} > 0. \tag{3}$$

Furthermore, PHs with large valuations are more sensitive to time and comfort loss, thus we have

$$\frac{\partial^2 C(\theta,t)}{\partial\theta\partial t} \geq 0, \frac{\partial^3 C(\theta,t)}{\partial\theta\partial t^2} \geq 0 \tag{4}$$

The following paper is not limited to a concrete model of $G(t)$ or $C(\theta,t)$, but a more general discussion on the mechanism design. The insurer can substitute in the models fitting its market. For example, Duncan [10] proposed a model that G is growing linearly with physical activity engagement.

As each PH is selfish, it would choose the contract item that maximizes its utility. We use $u(\theta_i, \pi_j)$ to denote the utility of a type-θ_i PH choosing the j-th contract item.

2.2   Solution Concepts

We review the solution concepts used in this paper. The first concept is incentive compatible.

Definition 1 (Incentive Compatible). *A contract is incentive compatible if for each type-θ_j PH, it prefers to choose the contract item π_j designed for its own type, i.e.,*

$$u(\theta_j, \pi_j) \geq u(\theta_j, \pi_i), \forall i,j.$$

An accompanying concept is individual rational. We use $\pi_{Na} = [d_{Na} = 0, t_{Na} = 0]$ to denote an implicit contract, which means that a PH can choose not to participate in this program.

Definition 2 (Individual Rational). *A contract is individual rational if the utility of type-θ_j PH accepting the contract item π_j is no less than non-participating, i.e.,*

$$u(\theta_j, \pi_j) \geq u(\theta_j, \pi_{Na}).$$

The last concept is feasible contract.

Definition 3 (Feasible Contract). *A contract is feasible if it satisfies both incentive compatibility and individual rationality.*

Under feasible contract, the market is in an equilibrium. Each PH would accept the contract item designed for its type, and has no incentive to derive to another one. Similar to the PHs, the insurance company is also selfish. It will decide π to maximize its utility.

3   Feasible Contract Design

Before proceeding to discuss the feasibility of contract, we first study PHs' original daily step counts. Then, we give the necessary and sufficient conditions for feasible contract design, which would ensure that PHs would faithfully participate in the program.

3.1 Investigating PHs' Original Exercise Intensities

For different type PHs, they will engage in different levels of physical activity. They exercise for various reasons, *e.g.*, good body shape, high productivity in work, etc. For simplicity, we use the self-covered medical expenses to capture the self-motivation of PHs. As defined in Sect. 2.1, we use S_j^e to denote the original exercising steps for a type-θ_j PH. Its utility turns out to be

$$u(\theta_j, \pi_{Na}) = d_{Na} \cdot I + \bar{r} \cdot G(S_j^e) - C(\theta_j, S_j^e).$$

For the ease of expression, in the upcoming discussion, we will adopt the following notation:

$$u_0(\theta_j, t) = \bar{r} \cdot G(t) - C(\theta_j, t).$$

As PHs are rational, they would choose a value $t = S_j^e$ to maximize the above equation. We have the following lemma.

Lemma 1. *Before the health program, PHs with lower valuation exercise more than PHs with higher valuation, i.e.,*

$$S_1^e < S_2^e < \cdots < S_n^e.$$

Proof. Combing Eq. (1) and (3), we know that $\partial^2 u_0 / \partial t^2 < 0$, *i.e.*, u_0 has the maximum value when $\partial u_0 / \partial t = 0$. We prove by contradiction, assuming that $S_j^e > S_{j+1}^e$. We use C' and C'' to denote $\partial C / \partial t$ and $\partial^2 C / \partial t^2$ respectively.
We have

$$\bar{r} \cdot G'(S_j^e) = C'(\theta_j, S_j^e),$$

$$\bar{r} \cdot G'(S_{j+1}^e) = C'(\theta_{j+1}, S_{j+1}^e).$$

For $G'' \leq 0$ and $C'' > 0$, G' is non-increasing and C' is increasing. Given $S_j^e > S_{j+1}^e$ and $\theta_j > \theta_{j+1}$, we have $G'(S_j^e) \leq G'(S_{j+1}^e)$ and $C'(\theta_j, S_j^e) > C'(\theta_{j+1}, S_{j+1}^e)$. They contradict with the above two equations.
Thus, $S_j^e < S_{j+1}^e$. $\qquad\blacksquare$

Lemma 1 explains that PHs with low valuations are more likely to engage in physical activity. This is easy to understand, as PHs with large θ have high valuations of their time or comfort that they sacrifice to participate in exercise. Thus, PHs with high valuations are more reluctant to exercise.
In addition to Lemma 1, we have the following lemma.

Lemma 2. *For a type-θ_i PH accepting a contract item $\pi' = [d', t']$, its daily step count would s.t.*

$$S_i' = \begin{cases} S_i^e & \text{if } t' < S_i^e, \\ t' & \text{otherwise.} \end{cases}$$

Proof. Its utility is

$$u(\theta_i, \pi') = d' \cdot I + \bar{r} \cdot G(S_i') - C(\theta_i, S_i') = d' \cdot I + u_0(\theta_i, S_i').$$

The PH would choose an appropriate S_i' that maximizes its utility.

As $\frac{\partial u_0(\theta_i, t)}{\partial t} = 0$ when $t = S_i^e$ and $\frac{\partial^2 u_0(\theta_i, t)}{\partial t^2} < 0$, $u_0(\theta_i, t)$ is increasing when $t < S_i^e$ and decreasing when $t > S_i^e$.

For a type-θ_i PH, if the step goal set by the insurer is less than its original exercise intensity, *i.e.*, $t' < S_i^e$, it will not decrease its exercise intensity, for $u_0(\theta_i, S_i^e) > u_0(\theta_i, t')$.

If the goal is larger than its original exercise intensity, *i.e.*, $t' > S_i^e$, it will set $S_i' = t'$ and not exceed t'. This because for $\forall t > t'$, $u_0(\theta_i, t') > u_0(\theta_i, t)$.

Lemma 2 indicates that when the goals are lower than their original daily step counts, they would maintain their exercise intensity; when the goals are higher, they would increase exercise intensity to reach the goal, but not exceed it. Thus, for a type-θ_j PH, his/her utility for choosing the j-th contract is

$$u(\theta_j, \pi_j) = d_j \cdot I + u_0 \left[\theta_j, \max(t_j, S_j^e) \right].$$

The objective of the insurer is to encourage the PHs to exercise more and be more healthy. If the insurer set the goals below PHs' original daily step counts, the monetary reward will not increase their exercise intensities. Thus, the insurer will set

$$t_j \geq S_j^e.$$

3.2   Conditions for Feasible Contract

We first introduce the following lemma, which could assist in discussing the necessary and sufficient conditions for feasible contract.

Lemma 3. *For $\theta' \geq \theta$ and $t' \geq t$, we have*

$$u_0(\theta, t') - u_0(\theta, t) \geq u_0(\theta', t') - u_0(\theta', t)$$

Proof.

$$u_0(\theta, t') - u_0(\theta, t) - u_0(\theta', t') + u_0(\theta', t)$$
$$= C(\theta', t') - C(\theta', t) - C(\theta, t') + C(\theta, t)$$
$$= \int_t^{t'} \int_\theta^{\theta'} \frac{\partial^2 C(\theta, t)}{\partial \theta \partial t} \, d\theta \, dt \geq 0.$$

The last line follows because the integrand is non-negative (from Eq. (4)), and $\theta' \geq \theta, t' \geq t$.

Then, we give the necessary conditions for feasible contract.

Lemma 4. *If π is a feasible contract, we have*

$$t_1 \leq t_2 \leq \cdots \leq t_n,$$
$$d_1 \leq d_2 \leq \cdots \leq d_n.$$

Proof. For the following discussion, without loss of generality, we assume that $i < j$.

Before proceeding to the proof, we first figure out the order between t_j and S_i^e, t_i and S_j^e. For $t_j \geq S_j^e$ and $S_j^e > S_i^e$, we have $t_j > S_i^e$. We distinguish cases when $t_i > S_j^e$ and $t_i \leq S_j^e$.

Case 1: $t_i > S_j^e$, i.e., $\pi(\theta_j, \pi_i) = d_i \cdot I + u_0(\theta_j, t_i)$.

For π to be feasible, $\forall i, j$, it s.t. that

$$d_i \cdot I + u_0(\theta_i, t_i) \geq d_j \cdot I + u_0(\theta_i, t_j), \tag{5}$$
$$d_j \cdot I + u_0(\theta_j, t_j) \geq d_i \cdot I + u_0(\theta_j, t_i). \tag{6}$$

We prove by contradiction, assuming that $t_i > t_j$.
Summing up these two inequalities, we have

$$u_0(\theta_i, t_i) - u_0(\theta_i, t_j) \geq u_0(\theta_j, t_i) - u_0(\theta_j, t_j).$$

It contradicts with Lemma 3. Thus, for $i < j$, $t_i \leq t_j$.
From Inequality (6) above, we have

$$(d_j - d_i) \cdot I \geq u_0(\theta_j, t_i) - u_0(\theta_j, t_j) \geq 0.$$

The last inequality follows because $u_0(\theta_j, t)$ is decreasing when $t > S_j^e$. Thus, $d_j \geq d_i$.

Case 2: $t_i \leq S_j^e$, i.e., $\pi(\theta_j, \pi_i) = d_i \cdot I + u_0(\theta_j, S_j^e)$.

It is straightforward that $t_j \geq S_j^e \geq t_i$.
Similar to (6), we have

$$d_j \cdot I + u_0(\theta_j, t_j) \geq d_i \cdot I + u_0(\theta_j, S_j^e).$$

Then we have

$$(d_j - d_i) \cdot I \geq u_0(\theta_j, S_j^e) - u_0(\theta_j, t_j) \geq 0.$$

Thus, $d_j \geq d_i$.

Lemma 4 indicates that in a feasible contract, the rewards should increase monotonically with increasing step goals. Furthermore, the insurer would set higher step goals for PHs with small valuation and give them higher rewards. The underlying intuition is that given the same amount of rewards, PHs with small valuations are willing to exercise more. Thus, the insurer tends to give out more rewards for PHs with small valuation. Next, we give the sufficient conditions for a feasible contract.

Lemma 5. π *is a feasible contract if it* s.t.

1. *for* $\forall i$, $t_i \geq S_i^e$,
2. $t_1 \leq t_2 \leq \cdots \leq t_n$,
3. $d_1 \geq \frac{1}{I}[u_0(\theta_1, S_1^e) - u_0(\theta_1, t_1)]$,
4. *for* $j = 2, 3, \cdots, n$,

$$d_{j-1} + A \leq d_j \leq d_{j-1} + B, \tag{7}$$

where

$$A = \frac{1}{I}\left\{u_0\left[\theta_j, \max(t_{j-1}, S_j^e)\right] - u_0(\theta_j, t_j)\right\},$$

$$B = \frac{1}{I}[u_0(\theta_{j-1}, t_{j-1}) - u_0(\theta_{j-1}, t_j)].$$

Proof. We prove by induction. We use π_n to denote the contract involving type-$\theta_1, \theta_2, \cdots, \theta_n$ PHs.

When $n = 1$, there is only one contract item. According to the third condition, we have

$$u(\theta_1, \pi_1) = d_1 \cdot I + u_0(\theta_1, t_1) \geq u_0(\theta_1, S_1^e) = u(\theta_1, \pi_{Na}).$$

It satisfies both incentive compatibility and individual rationality. Thus, π_1 is feasible.

We assume that π_{k-1} is feasible. We will show that adding a new type θ_k PH and a new contract item $\pi_k = \{d_k, t_k\}$, the contract is also feasible.

We first show that it guarantees incentive compatibility. We first consider type-θ_k PHs. From the left inequality in Eq. (7), we have

$$d_k \cdot I + u_0(\theta_k, t_k) \geq d_{k-1} \cdot I + u_0\left[\theta_k, \max(t_{k-1}, S_k^e)\right].$$

The fact that π_{k-1} is feasible implies that for $i \leq k - 1$,

$$d_{k-1} \cdot I + u_0(\theta_{k-1}, t_{k-1}) \geq d_i \cdot I + u_0\left[\theta_{k-1}, \max\left(t_i, S_{k-1}^e\right)\right].$$

Combing these two inequalities, we get

$$\begin{aligned}
d_k \cdot I &+ u_0(\theta_k, t_k)\\
&\geq d_i \cdot I + u_0\left[\theta_k, \max(t_{k-1}, S_k^e)\right]\\
&\quad + u_0\left[\theta_{k-1}, \max\left(t_i, S_{k-1}^e\right)\right] - u_0(\theta_{k-1}, t_{k-1})\\
&\geq d_i \cdot I + u_0\left[\theta_k, \max\left(t_i, S_k^e\right)\right]
\end{aligned}$$

The detailed proof can be found in Appendix A.1. It indicates that type-θ_k PHs always prefer π_k over π_i for $i < k$. Next, we show that type-i PHs prefer π_i over π_k. From the right inequality in Eq. (7), we have

$$d_{k-1} \cdot I + u_0(\theta_{k-1}, t_{k-1}) \geq d_k \cdot I + u_0\left(\theta_{k-1}, t_k\right).$$

The fact that $\boldsymbol{\pi}_{k-1}$ is feasible implies that for $i \leq k-1$,

$$d_i \cdot I + u_0(\theta_i, t_i) \geq d_{k-1} \cdot I + u_0(\theta_i, t_{k-1}).$$

Combing these two inequalities, we get

$$\begin{aligned}
& d_i \cdot I + u_0(\theta_i, t_i) \\
& \geq d_k \cdot I + u_0(\theta_{k-1}, t_k) + u_0(\theta_i, t_{k-1}) - u_0(\theta_{k-1}, t_{k-1}) \\
& \geq d_k \cdot I + u_0(\theta_i, t_k)
\end{aligned}$$

In Appendix A.1, we also show that $A \leq B$. Up to now, we prove that $\boldsymbol{\pi}_k$ guarantees incentive compatibility.

Then, we show that $\boldsymbol{\pi}_k$ guarantees individual rationality. For $\boldsymbol{\pi}_k$ guarantees incentive compatible and $\boldsymbol{\pi}_{k-1}$ is feasible, we have

$$d_{k-1} \cdot I + u_0(\theta_{k-1}, t_{k-1}) \geq u_0(\theta_{k-1}, S_{k-1}^e).$$

Then,

$$\begin{aligned}
d_k \cdot I + u_0(\theta_k, t_k) & \geq d_{k-1} \cdot I + u_0\left[\theta_k, \max\left(t_{k-1}, S_k^e\right)\right] \\
& \geq u_0(\theta_{k-1}, S_{k-1}^e) - u_0(\theta_{k-1}, t_{k-1}) \\
& \quad + u_0\left[\theta_k, \max\left(t_{k-1}, S_k^e\right)\right].
\end{aligned}$$

If $t_{k-1} > S_k^e$,

$$\begin{aligned}
& d_k \cdot I + u_0(\theta_k, t_k) \\
& \geq u_0(\theta_{k-1}, S_{k-1}^e) - u_0(\theta_{k-1}, t_{k-1}) + u_0(\theta_k, t_{k-1}) \\
& \geq u_0(\theta_{k-1}, S_k^e) - u_0(\theta_{k-1}, t_{k-1}) + u_0(\theta_k, t_{k-1}) \\
& \geq u_0(\theta_k, S_k^e).
\end{aligned}$$

The second inequality holds because $t = S_{k-1}^e$ maximizes $u_0(\theta_{k-1}, t)$. The last line follows from Lemma 3.

If $t_{k-1} \leq S_k^e$,

$$\begin{aligned}
& d_k \cdot I + u_0(\theta_k, t_k) \\
& \geq u_0(\theta_{k-1}, S_{k-1}^e) - u_0(\theta_{k-1}, t_{k-1}) + u_0(\theta_k, S_k^e) \\
& \geq u_0(\theta_k, S_k^e).
\end{aligned}$$

It indicates type-θ_k PHs prefer accepting the contract over rejecting it. Thus, $\boldsymbol{\pi}_k$ guarantees individual rationality.

Therefore, we prove that $\boldsymbol{\pi}$ is feasible.

We learn that any contract satisfying the conditions in Lemma 5 is feasible, which indicates that PHs are willing to participate (individual rationality) and they would truthfully reveal their private information to the insurer (incentive compatibility). Given a feasible contract, the insurer can anticipate how the PHs would behave in the program and thus can maximize its profits accordingly.

4   Optimal Contract Design

The insurer is aimed at designing an optimal contract which could maximize its profit. In this section, we first give the optimal solution which could maximize the profit. However, the optimal solution may not preserve the feasibility of the contract. Then we give the optimal feasible solution which maximizes the profit and meanwhile preserves the feasibility of the contract.

4.1   Optimal Solution

The insurer's profit is given by

$$u(\boldsymbol{\pi}) = \sum_{i=1}^{n} N_i \cdot [r \cdot G(t_i) - r \cdot G(S_i^e) - d_i \cdot I]. \tag{8}$$

Thus, given any t_i, the insurer would set d_i to the lower bound in Lemma 5, *i.e.*,

$$d_1 = \frac{1}{I} [u_0(\theta_1, S_1^e) - u_0(\theta_1, t_1)],$$

$$d_i = d_{i-1} + \frac{1}{I} \{u_0[\theta_i, \max(t_{i-1}, S_i^e)] - u_0(\theta_i, t_i)\}$$

$$= \sum_{j=1}^{i} \frac{1}{I} \{u_0[\theta_j, \max(t_{j-1}, S_j^e)] - u_0(\theta_j, t_j)\} \tag{9}$$

where we define $t_0 = 0$. Thus,

$$u(\boldsymbol{\pi}) = \sum_{i=1}^{n} \left\{ N_i [r \cdot G(t_i) - r \cdot G(S_i^e)] - \sum_{j=i+1}^{n} N_j \cdot \right.$$

$$\left. u_0 [\theta_{i+1}, \max(t_i, S_{i+1}^e)] + \sum_{j=i}^{n} N_j \cdot u_0(\theta_i, t_i) \right\}.$$

We use $f_i(t_i)$ to denote each term in the summation, as each term is only related to t_i. Thus, we can choose t_i to maximize $f_i(t_i)$ independently. We distinguish two cases, *i.e.*, $t_i < S_{i+1}^e$ and $t_i \geq S_{i+1}^e$. We use $f_i^1(t_i)$ and $f_i^2(t_i)$ to represent $f_i(t_i)$ in these two cases, respectively.

Case 1: $t_i < S_{i+1}^e$.
    We have

$$f_i^{1''}(t) = N_i \cdot r \cdot G''(t) + \sum_{j=i}^{n} N_j \cdot u_0''(\theta_i, t) < 0.$$

$f_i^1(t)$ is maximum when $t = t_i^1$ *s.t.* $f_i^{1'}(t_i^1) = 0$.

Furthermore, $t_i^1 \geq S_i^e$ for $f_i^{1'}(S_i^e) \geq 0$.

Case 2: $t_i \geq S_{i+1}^e$.

Similarly, we have

$$f_i^{2''}(t) = N_i \left[r \cdot G''(t) + u_0''(\theta_i, t) \right]$$
$$+ \sum_{j=i+1}^{n} N_j \left[C''(\theta_{i+1}, t) - C''(\theta_i, t) \right]$$
$$< 0.$$

The last line follows because $G'' \leq 0$, $u_0'' < 0$, and $\frac{\partial^3 C(\theta, t)}{\partial \theta \partial t^2} > 0$. $f_i^2(t)$ is maximum when $t = t_i^2$ s.t. $f_i^{2'}(t_i^2) = 0$.

If $t_i^1 > S_{i+1}^e$, we know that

$$f_i^{2'}(t_i^1) = f_i^{1'}(t_i^1) - \sum_{j=i+1}^{n} N_j \cdot u_0'(\theta_{i+1}, t_i^1) > 0.$$

Then we have $t_i^2 > t_i^1 > S_{i+1}^e$. In this case,

$$f_i^1(t)_{max} = f_i^1(S_{i+1}^e) = f_i^2(S_{i+1}^e) < f_i^2(t_i^2) = f_i^2(t)_{max}.$$

The inequality follows because $f_i^2(t)$ is increasing when $t < t_i^2$.

If $t_i^1 < S_{i+1}^e$, we have that

$$f_i^{2'}(S_{i+1}^e) = f_i^{1'}(S_{i+1}^e) - \sum_{j=i+1}^{n} N_j \cdot u_0'(\theta_{i+1}, S_{i+1}^e) < 0.$$

Then we have $t_i^2 < S_{i+1}^e$. In this case,

$$f_i^2(t)_{max} = f_i^2(S_{i+1}^e) = f_i^1(S_{i+1}^e) < f_i^1(t_i^1) = f_i^1(t)_{max}.$$

The inequality follows because $f_i^1(t)$ is decreasing when $t > t_i^1$.

Thus, $f_i(t_i)$ is maximum when t_i s.t.

$$t_i = \begin{cases} t_i^1 \text{ if } t_i^1 < S_{i+1}^e, \\ t_i^2 \text{ otherwise.} \end{cases}$$

Thus, the optimal value of t_i are determined by θ_i, r and the PH distribution.

In the case where $t_i^1 < S_{i+1}^e$, $t_i = t_i^1 < S_{i+1}^e < t_{i+1}$. In the case where $t_i^1 > S_{i+1}^e$, $t_i = t_i^2 > t_i^1 > S_{i+1}^e$. In both cases, $t_i > S_i^e$. However, in the second case, there is possibility that $t_i > t_{i+1}$, which violates the second condition for feasible contract.

4.2 Optimal Feasible Solution

In this subsection, we will show how to adjust the optimal solution in Sect. 4.1 to satisfy the sufficient conditions for feasible contract.

We first claim that $f_i(t_i)$ is concave, the proof of which can be found in Appendix A.2. Then we borrow the following proposition from [14].

Lemma 6. *Let $f_i(t)(1 \le i \le k)$ be concave functions on t and $f_i(t)$ is maximum when $t = t_i$. If $t_1 \ge t_2 \ge \cdots \ge t_k$, then $\hat{t}_1 = \hat{t}_2 = \cdots = \hat{t}_k$ where*

$$\{\hat{t}_1, \hat{t}_2, \cdots, \hat{t}_k\} = \arg\max_{\hat{t}_1, \hat{t}_2, \cdots, \hat{t}_k} \sum_{i=1}^{k} f_i(t), \text{s.t.} \, \hat{t}_1 \le \hat{t}_2 \le \cdots \le \hat{t}_k.$$

Give Lemma 6, we can adjust an infeasible sequence of $\{t_i\}_{1 \le i \le n}$ to make it satisfy the conditions in Lemma 5.

If $\{t_i\}_{1 \le i \le n}$ is infeasible, then there must be a subsequence $\{t_j, t_{j+1}, \cdots t_k\}$ that is decreasing. It can be replaced by a nondecreasing sequence $\{\hat{t}_j, \hat{t}_{j+1}, \cdots \hat{t}_k\}$ according to Lemma 6. This step can be done iteratively until there is no decreasing subsequence, which indicates that second condition for feasible contract is preserved. Then, we will show that the first condition is also preserved.

Lemma 7. *The non-decreasing sequence $\{\hat{t}_i\}_{1 \le i \le n}$ s.t.* $\hat{t}_i \ge S_i^e.$

Proof. If $\{t_i\}_{1 \le i \le n}$ is nondecreasing, then $\hat{t}_i = t_i \ge S_e^i$. If a subsequence $\{t_j, t_{j+1}, \cdots t_k\}$ is decreasing, then

$$t_j > t_{j+1} > \cdots > t_k \ge S_k^e > \cdots > S_{j+1}^e > S_j^e.$$

We have $f_j'(S_k^e) > 0, f_{j+1}'(S_k^e) > 0, \cdots, f_k'(S_k^e) \ge 0$. We write $F(t) = \sum_{i=j}^{k} f_i(t)$. Then $F'(S_k^e) = \sum_{i=j}^{k} f_i'(S_k^e) > 0$, indicating that $F(t)$ is increasing when $t = S_k^e$. Thus, $\hat{t}_j = \hat{t}_{j+1} = \cdots = \hat{t}_k > S_k^e > \cdots > S_{j+1}^e > S_j^e.$

Combining Lemma 5 and 6, we conclude that $\{\hat{t}_i\}_{1 \le i \le n}$ is the optimal feasible solution. Given $\{\hat{t}_i\}_{1 \le i \le n}$, the insurer can set the rewards as in Eq. (9). In this way, PHs will truthfully participate in the program and the insurer can maximize its profits.

5 Numeric Results

In this section, we show the simulation results.

In [10], Duncan gave the model for savings estimation. With regard to physical activity, Duncan reported that each year a PH can save \$306 for per hour high intensity activities per week. We choose two models for $G(t)$: $G_1(t) = c_1 \log(t+1)$ and $G_2(t) = c_2\sqrt{t}$. They both satisfy the properties of G. We estimate that high intensity activity is equivalent to 100 steps/min. Based on this information, we can estimate c_1 and c_2.

Similarly, we choose two models for $C(\theta, t)$: $C_1 = \theta t^2$ and $C_2 = \theta t^3$. They also satisfy the properties of C. In [13], Finkelstein *et al.* reported that if paid \$9.7, participants are willing to exercise for one more hour than the control group. We set this average valuation to be the mean value of θ. The remaining θ values are evenly distributed in the range $\left[0.5\bar{\theta}, 1.5\bar{\theta}\right]$.

By default, we use G_1 and C_1 and set $r = 0.6$, $n = 15$.

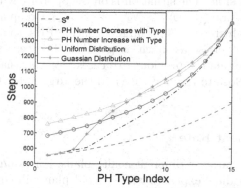

(a) Step goals under different PH distributions.

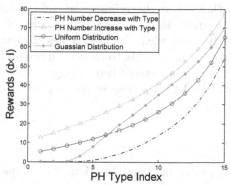

(b) Rewards under different PH distribution.

Fig. 2. Contract under four different PH distributions.

5.1 PH Distributions

As shown in Sect. 4, the optimal solution varies with PH distribution. We show how the insurer would optimize the design under different PH distributions. Although the optimal design is generic for all kinds of PH distributions, here we discuss four cases: 1) PHs' number decreasing with type, $i.e.$, $N_1 < N_2 < \cdots < N_n$; 2) PHs' number increasing with type, $i.e.$, $N_1 > N_2 > \cdots > N_n$; 3) Uniform distribution; 4) Gaussian Distribution.

In Fig. 2, we show the optimal contract under four different type distributions. S^e does not depend on PH distribution. When PHs' number is decreasing with type ($i.e.$, $N_1 < N_2 < \cdots < N_n$), most PHs have small valuations. For the purpose of profit maximization, the insurer would set low rewards for large valuation PHs, so as to reduce small valuation PHs' interest in these contract items. Accordingly, it can set high step goals for small valuation PHs and maintain the rewards as low as possible. The situation is on the opposite when PHs' number is increasing with valuation ($i.e.$, $N_1 > N_2 > \cdots > N_n$). Compared to the previous case, it would set high step goals for large valuation PHs, so as to encourage the majority of PHs to exercise as much as possible. The case with uniform type distribution falls between the previous two cases. For Gaussian distribution, the small index part is close to the first case and the large index part is close to the second case.

5.2   Reimbursement Rate

Reimbursement rate varies in different health plans. For example, the silver plan will cover 70% of medical expenses while a gold plan will cover 80%. We show how the optimal contract would vary with the reimbursement rate. We assume that PHs' types follow Gaussian distribution.

Figure 3(a) shows that when the reimbursement rate is large, the insurer prefers PHs to exercise more than the case when the reimbursement rate is small. This is intuitive because when the insurer has to cover a large portion of medical expenses, it would like its PHs to exercise more and be healthy.

Conversely, when the reimbursement rate is large, PHs are reluctant to exercise. Thus, as shown in Fig. 3(b), the insurer has to give them higher rewards to stimulate them.

5.3   Insurer's Profits

We study the insurer's profits in this subsection. We compare the optimal contract with the baseline, in which the insurer does not separate different types of PHs, neither consider their original daily step counts, and provides only one contract item $[d^*, t^*]$ for all PHs. We use exhaustive search to find the optimal d^* and t^*.

In Fig. 4, we show the insurer's profit in the baseline and the optimal contract under four combinations of $G(t)$ and $C(\theta, t)$.

1. $G_1(t) = c_1 \log(t + 1), C_1(\theta, t) = \theta t^2$;
2. $G_1(t) = c_1 \log(t + 1), C_2(\theta, t) = \theta t^3$;
3. $G_2(t) = c_2 \sqrt{t}, C_1(\theta, t) = \theta t^2$;
4. $G_2(t) = c_2 \sqrt{t}, C_2(\theta, t) = \theta t^3$.

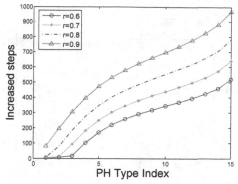

(a) Increased exercise level under different re-imbursement rates.

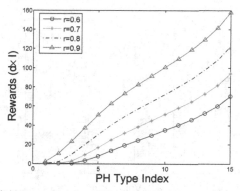

(b) Rewards for PHs under different reim-bursement rates.

Fig. 3. Contract under four different reimbursement rates.

Figure 4 shows that compared with the baseline, in all four cases, the insurer can achieve higher profits using the optimal contract design. The results are averaged over the four distributions in Sect. 5.1.

According to [5], it is optimal to design a contract item for each type PHs. In this problem, paid the same amount of rewards, PHs with small valuation will exercise more than the PHs with large valuation. Thus, the insurer will prefer to allocate the financial incentives to PHs with small valuations. In the baseline mechanism, the insurer can not optimize the allocation. Furthermore, if $t^* < S_k^e$ for type-θ_k PHs, they can get the rewards without increasing their physical activity intensity. The rewards to these PHs will not change their behavior, and thus no savings for the insurer. On average, the profits in optimal contract design is 1.39 times of the profits in the baseline.

We also compare the optimal design with the baseline when n varies from 5 to 20. The results are shown in Fig. 5. On average, the insurer can improve its profit by 40%.

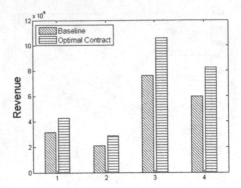

Fig. 4. The insurer's profits in the baseline and optimal contract.

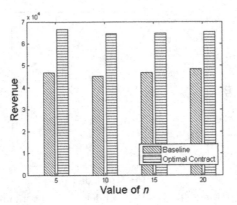

Fig. 5. The insurer's profits when n varies from 5 to 20.

6 Discussion

6.1 Investment in Wearable Devices

In this paper, we assume that every PH owns an activity tracker, such as Nike+, Fitbit, etc. In practice, wearable devices are not so widespread yet. Some insurers may distribute fitness trackers to its PHs for free [4], others may cooperate with device vendors and provide discount off these devices [1].

The cost for wearable device can be regarded as a constant. The insurer's profit should be Eq. (8) minus a constant term. However, the constant term would not change the optimal solution to the maximization problem. Thus, the optimal solution is valid when the insurer takes the cost of devices into account.

6.2 Privacy Concerns of PHs

In this paper, we do not consider the privacy concerns of PHs and assume that PHs are willing to share their fitness data with the insurer. We believe that this assumption is reasonable for three reasons. First, studies show that users are willing to trade personal information for better experience and savings. A study from IBM [17] reveals that consumers are willing to share their location, mobile number and social handle with retailers for personalized shopping experience. Similarly, Cisco [6] reports that 74% of consumers would allow driving habits to be monitored to save on insurance/service maintenance. Second, unlike blood pressure or glucose levels, the daily step counts are not sensitive information. Last, the users only need to share the aggregate statistics, such as monthly or annual average, not all the details. The insurer cannot infer further private information about the PHs.

7   Related Works

Extensive works study the effectiveness of financial incentives for health behavior change, including weight loss, smoking cessation and attendance for vaccination or screening [13,21]. There is evidence showing that finical incentives can encourage healthy behavior change. However, the effectiveness depends on various factors, such as ages, socioeconomic status, etc [13]. In this study, we focus on physical exercise intensity and use *type* to separate different cost-effectiveness groups of populations.

There are also a number of research related to health-care intervention programs [10,11]. In [10], Duncan present a literature review of population health management programs, reporting that investment in health management programs can bring financial returns, including both savings for medical expenditure and improved productivity at workplace. In this paper, we discuss how to encourage PHs to participate in physical activity. From the insurer's point of view, we give the optimal contract design, maximizing the insurer's profits.

Contract theory is widely used in job market, supply chain planning and insurance market. Besides, it also has applications in spectrum trading [8,12,14] and smartphone collaborative computing [9]. In our case, the PHs' incentives comprise of two parts: the finical rewards from the insurer and the self-motivation to keep fit, which complicates the discussion. We jointly consider these two sources of incentives and present the optimal contract design.

8   Conclusion

In this paper, we study the emerging health promotion programs in insurance markets and model the market using contract theory. We theoretically analyze how the insurer and PHs would behave in this program. We give the optimal feasible contract design, which can guarantee that PHs would truthfully participate in the program and maximize the profit of the insurer. We conduct extensive simulations to study the performance under various scenarios. Simulation results show that the insurer can improve its profit by 40% using the optimal contract. It provides a promising solution to tackle the increasing health expenditure all over the world.

Acknowledgements. This research is supported in part by the Key-Area Research and Development Program of Guangdong Province (No. 2020B0101390001) and in part by the National Natural Science Foundation of China (No. 62002150).

A   Appendices

A.1   Supplementary Proof for Lemma 5

Here we provide supplementary proof for Lemma 5. As $i \leq k - 1$, $t_{k-1} \geq t_i$.

To prove that

$$u_0 \left[\theta_k, \max(t_{k-1}, S_k^e) \right] + u_0 \left[\theta_{k-1}, \max \left(t_i, S_{k-1}^e \right) \right]$$
$$-u_0(\theta_{k-1}, t_{k-1})$$
$$\geq u_0 \left[\theta_k, \max \left(t_i, S_k^e \right) \right],$$

we distinguish five cases:

Case 1: $t_i \geq S_k^e > S_{k-1}^e$.

$$u_0 \left(\theta_k, t_{k-1} \right) + u_0 \left(\theta_{k-1}, t_i \right) - u_0(\theta_{k-1}, t_{k-1}) \qquad \geq u_0 \left(\theta_k, t_i \right).$$

The inequality follows from Lemma 3.

Case 2: $S_{k-1}^e \leq t_i < S_k^e$ and $t_{k-1} \geq S_k^e$.

$$u_0 \left(\theta_k, t_{k-1} \right) + u_0 \left(\theta_{k-1}, t_i \right) - u_0(\theta_{k-1}, t_{k-1})$$
$$\geq u_0 \left(\theta_k, t_{k-1} \right) + u_0 \left(\theta_{k-1}, S_k^e \right) - u_0(\theta_{k-1}, t_{k-1})$$
$$\geq u_0 \left(\theta_k, S_k^e \right).$$

The first inequality holds because $u_0(\theta_{k-1}, t)$ is decreasing when $t > S_{k-1}^e$.

Case 3: $S_{k-1}^e \leq t_i < S_k^e$ and $t_{k-1} < S_k^e$.

$$u_0 \left(\theta_k, S_k^e \right) + u_0 \left(\theta_{k-1}, t_i \right) - u_0(\theta_{k-1}, t_{k-1}) \geq u_0 \left(\theta_k, S_k^e \right).$$

The inequality holds because $u_0(\theta_{k-1}, t)$ is decreasing when $t > S_{k-1}^e$, and then $u_0 \left(\theta_{k-1}, t_i \right) > u_0(\theta_{k-1}, t_{k-1})$.

Case 4: $t_i < S_{k-1}^e$ and $t_{k-1} \geq S_k^e$.

$$u_0 \left(\theta_k, t_{k-1} \right) + u_0 \left(\theta_{k-1}, S_{k-1}^e \right) - u_0(\theta_{k-1}, t_{k-1})$$
$$\geq u_0 \left(\theta_k, t_{k-1} \right) + u_0 \left(\theta_{k-1}, S_k^e \right) - u_0(\theta_{k-1}, t_{k-1})$$
$$\geq u_0 \left(\theta_k, S_k^e \right).$$

The first inequality holds because $u_0(\theta_{k-1}, t)$ is decreasing when $t > S_{k-1}^e$.

Case 5: $t_i < S_{k-1}^e$ and $t_{k-1} < S_k^e$.

$$u_0 \left(\theta_k, S_k^e \right) + u_0 \left(\theta_{k-1}, S_{k-1}^e \right) - u_0(\theta_{k-1}, t_{k-1}) \geq u_0 \left(\theta_k, S_k^e \right).$$

The inequality holds because $u_0(\theta_{k-1}, t)$ is increasing when $t < S_{k-1}^e$.

In summary, type-θ_k PHs always prefer π_k over π_i.

Next, we show that $A \leq B$.

If $t_{j-1} > S_j^e$,

$$A = \frac{1}{I}\left[u_0(\theta_j, t_{j-1}) - u_0(\theta_j, t_j)\right]$$

$$\leq \frac{1}{I}\left[u_0(\theta_{j-1}, t_{j-1}) - u_0(\theta_{j-1}, t_j)\right] = B.$$

The inequality follows from Lemma 3.

If $t_{j-1} \leq S_j^e$,

$$B = \frac{1}{I}\left[u_0(\theta_{j-1}, t_{j-1}) - u_0(\theta_{j-1}, t_j)\right]$$

$$\geq \frac{1}{I}\left[u_0(\theta_{j-1}, S_j^e) - u_0(\theta_{j-1}, t_j)\right] \geq A.$$

A.2 Prove the Concavity of $f_i(t_i)$

Prove that

$$f_i(t_i) = \begin{cases} f_i^1(t_i) \text{ if } t_i < S_{i+1}^e, \\ f_i^2(t_i) \text{ otherwise,} \end{cases}$$

is a concave function.

Proof. For $f_i^{1''} < 0$ and $f_i^{2''} < 0$, $f_i^{1'}(t_i)$ and $f_i^{2'}(t_i)$ is decreasing. Furthermore, $f_i^1(S_{i+1}^e) = f_i^2(S_{i+1}^e)$ and $f_i^{1'}(S_{i+1}^e) = f_i^{2'}(S_{i+1}^e)$. But $f_i^{1''}(S_{i+1}^e) \neq f_i^{2''}(S_{i+1}^e)$. Thus, $f_i'(t_i)$ is defined but $f_i''(t_i)$ is undefined when $t_i = S_{i+1}^e$.

To show that $f_i(t)$ is concave, we need to show that $\forall x_1, x_2$ and $\forall \lambda \in [0, 1]$,

$$\lambda f_i(x_1) + (1 - \lambda)f_i(x_2) \leq f_i(\lambda x_1 + (1 - \lambda)x_2).$$

Without loss of generality, we assume that $x_1 \leq x_2$. We distinguish four cases:

Case 1: $x_1 < S_{i+1}^e$ and $x_2 < S_{i+1}^e$.

It is intuitive because f_i^1 is concave.

Case 2: $x_1 \geq S_{i+1}^e$ and $x_2 \geq S_{i+1}^e$.

It is also intuitive because f_i^2 is concave.

Case 3: $x_1 < S_{i+1}^e$, $x_2 \geq S_{i+1}^e$ and $\lambda x_1 + (1 - \lambda)x_2 < S_{i+1}^e$.

We write $x_0 = \lambda x_1 + (1 - \lambda)x_2$. Then,

$$x_1 - x_0 = (\lambda - 1)(x_2 - x_1), x_2 - x_0 = \lambda(x_2 - x_1).$$

$$\lambda f_i(x_1) + (1-\lambda)f_i(x_2) - f_i(x_0)$$
$$= \lambda \left[f_i^1(x_1) - f_i^1(x_0) \right] + (\lambda - 1) \left[f_i^1(x_0) - f_i^1(S_{i+1}^e) \right]$$
$$+ (\lambda - 1) \left[f_i^2(S_{i+1}^e) - f_i^2(x_2) \right]$$
$$= \lambda f_i^{1\prime}(a)(x_1 - x_0) + (\lambda - 1)f_i^{1\prime}(b)(x_0 - S_{i+1}^e)$$
$$+ (\lambda - 1)f_i^{2\prime}(c)(S_{i+1}^e - x_2)$$
$$= (\lambda - 1)\left[f_i^{1\prime}(a) - f_i^{2\prime}(c) \right](x_2 - S_{i+1}^e)$$
$$+ (\lambda - 1)\left[f_i^{1\prime}(a) - f_i^{1\prime}(b) \right](S_{i+1}^e - x_0).$$

According to Mean Value Theorem, $a \in [x_1, x_0]$, $b \in [x_0, S_{i+1}^e]$, and $c \in [S_{i+1}^e, x_2]$. Because $f_i^{1\prime}(t)$ and $f_i^{2\prime}(t)$ is decreasing, $f_i^{1\prime}(a) \geq f_i^{1\prime}(b) \geq f_i^{1\prime}(S_{i+1}^e) = f_i^{2\prime}(S_{i+1}^e) \geq f_i^{2\prime}(c)$. Furthermore, we have $x_2 \geq S_{i+1}^e > x_0$ and $\lambda \leq 1$. Thus,

$$\lambda f_i(x_1) + (1-\lambda)f_i(x_2) - f_i(x_0) \leq 0,$$

meaning that $f_i(t)$ s.t. the condition for concavity in this case.

Case 4: $x_1 < S_{i+1}^e$, $x_2 \geq S_{i+1}^e$ and $\lambda x_1 + (1-\lambda)x_2 \geq S_{i+1}^e$.
We note that $f_i^2(t) \geq f_i^1(t)$ always holds. Thus,

$$\lambda f_i(x_1) + (1-\lambda)f_i(x_2) - f_i(x_0)$$
$$= \lambda f_i^1(x_1) + (1-\lambda)f_i^2(x_2) - f_i^2(x_0)$$
$$\leq \lambda f_i^2(x_1) + (1-\lambda)f_i^2(x_2) - f_i^2(x_0)$$
$$\leq 0.$$

The last line follows because f_i^2 is concave.

Therefore, we prove that $f_i(t_i)$ is a concave function.

References

1. AIA vitality. https://www.aiavitality.com.sg/memberportal/partners/fitbit
2. Fitbit. https://www.fitbit.com/
3. Health expenditure, total (% of GDP). https://data.worldbank.org
4. Manulife. https://www.manulifemove.hk/en/gift/
5. Bolton, P., Dewatripont, M.: Contract Theory. MIT Press, Cambridge (2005)
6. Cisco, Cisco Customer Experience Research - Automotive Industry Global Data (2013)
7. Cornelius, C., Peterson, R., Skinner, J., Halter, R., Kotz, D.: A wearable system that knows who wears it. In: MobiSys 2014, pp. 55–67. ACM (2014)
8. Duan, L., Gao, L., Huang, J.: Cooperative spectrum sharing: a contract-based approach. IEEE Trans. Mob. Comput. **13**(1), 174–187 (2014)
9. Duan, L., Kubo, T., Sugiyama, K., Huang, J., Hasegawa, T., Walrand, J.: Incentive mechanisms for smartphone collaboration in data acquisition and distributed computing. In: INFOCOM 2012 (2012)

10. Duncan, I.: Managing and Evaluating Healthcare Intervention Programs. Actex Publications (2014)
11. Duncan, I.G.: Healthcare Risk Adjustment and Predictive Modeling. Actex Publications (2011)
12. Feng, X., Zhang, Q., Zhang, J.: Hybrid pricing for TV white space database. In: INFOCOM 2013 (2013)
13. Finkelstein, E.A., Brown, D.S., Brown, D.R., Buchner, D.M.: A randomized study of financial incentives to increase physical activity among sedentary older adults. Prev. Med. 47(2), 182–187 (2008)
14. Gao, L., Wang, X., Xu, Y., Zhang, Q.: Spectrum trading in cognitive radio networks: a contract-theoretic modeling approach. IEEE J. Sel. Areas Commun. 29(4), 843–855 (2011)
15. Gong, L., et al.: Experiences of landing machine learning onto market-scale mobile malware detection. In: Proceedings of the Fifteenth European Conference on Computer Systems, pp. 1–14 (2020)
16. Hayward, J., Chansin, G., Zervos, H.: Wearable Technology 2016–2026-Markets, players and 10-year forecasts (2016)
17. IBM, Greater expectations: consumers are asking for tomorrow, today (2014)
18. Ledger, D., McCaffrey, D.: Inside wearables: how the science of human behavior change offers the secret to long-term engagement. In: Endeavour Partners, Cambridge, MA, USA (2014)
19. Parate, A., Chiu, M.-C., Chadowitz, C., Ganesan, D., Kalogerakis, E.: RisQ: recognizing smoking gestures with inertial sensors on a wristband. In: MobiSys 2014 (2014)
20. Ren, Y., Chen, Y., Chen, Y., Chuah, M.C.: User verification leveraging gait recognition for smartphone enabled mobile healthcare systems. IEEE Trans. Mob. Comput. 14, 1961–1974 (2015)
21. Sutherland, K., Christianson, J.B., Leatherman, S.: Impact of targeted financial incentives on personal health behavior a review of the literature. Med. Care Res. Rev. 65(6 suppl), 36S-78S (2008)
22. Tudor-Locke, C., Bassett, D.R., Jr.: How many steps/day are enough? Sports Med. 34(1), 1–8 (2004). https://doi.org/10.2165/00007256-200434010-00001
23. Wen, C.P., et al.: Minimum amount of physical activity for reduced mortality and extended life expectancy: a prospective cohort study. The Lancet 378(9798), 1244–1253 (2011)
24. Zhang, J., Zhang, Q., Wang, Y., Qiu, C.: A real-time auto-adjustable smart pillow system for sleep apnea detection and treatment. In: IPSN 2013 (2013)

Machine Learning and Data Analysis

Spear-Phishing Detection Method Based on Few-Shot Learning

Qi Li[✉] and Mingyu Cheng

Beijing University of Posts and Telecommunications, Beijing 100876, China
{liqi2001,chengmingyu}@bupt.edu.cn

Abstract. With the further development of Internet technology, various online activities are becoming more frequent, especially online office and online transactions. This trend leads that the network security issues are increasingly prominent, the network security situation is more complex, and the methods and means of attacks are emerging in endlessly. Due to the characteristics of spear-phishing such as target accuracy, attack durability, camouflage concealment and damage severity, it has become the most commonly used initial means for attackers and APT organizations to invade targets. Thus, automated spear-phishing detection based machine learning and deep learning have become the focus of researchers in recent years. However, because of a smaller range and less attack frequency, the number of spear-phishing emails is very limited. How to detect spear-phishing based on machine learning and deep learning with small samples has become a key issue. Meanwhile, in machine learning and deep learning, few-shot learning aims to study a better classification model trained with only a few samples. Therefore, we propose a spear-phishing detection method based on few-shot learning that combines the basic features and the message body of emails. We propose a simple word-embedding model to analyzes the message body, which can process the message body of different lengths into text feature vectors with the same dimension, thus retaining the semantic information to the greatest extent. Then the text feature vectors are combined with the basic features of emails and input into commonly used machine learning classifiers for detection. Our proposed simple word-embedding method does not require the complex training of the model to learn a large number of parameters, thereby reducing the dependence of the model on a large number of training data. The experimental results show that the method proposed in this paper achieves better performance than the existing spear-phishing detection method. Especially, Especially, the advantages of our detection method are more obvious with small samples.

Keywords: few-shot learning · spear-phishing email · machine learning

1 Introduction

With the development of Internet technology, email has become not only an indispensable communication means in people's daily work, but also an important channel for obtaining work information or documents. Therefore, more and more attackers tend to use email as

© The Author(s), under exclusive license to Springer Nature Singapore Pte Ltd. 2024
C. Li et al. (Eds.): APPT 2023, LNCS 14103, pp. 351–371, 2024.
https://doi.org/10.1007/978-981-99-7872-4_20

the carrier of malicious links or files, they always utilize social engineering to induce the recipients to click malicious links or download malicious attachments. Compared with the attack through malware directly, phishing emails have their special characteristics. For example, phishing emails have less technical requirements for attackers and it does not require the attackers to master the zero-day vulnerability or develop specific attack tools. Instead, it is usually centered on social engineering, that is, the attacker only needs to construct a seemingly innocuous email of interest to the recipients. In conclusion, phishing emails have become a popular way of network attack because of its lower cost and higher validity.

Spear-phishing is a special form of the phishing email. Compared with the general phishing email, it has the characteristics of target accuracy, attack durability, camouflage concealment and damage severity. At the beginning of the attack, the attacker needs to continuously investigate the target receiver or organization. After collecting enough personal information of the receiver, the attacker will carefully construct an exclusive email and send it at an appropriate time. Since the content of the email is closely related to the receiver, the success rate of the spear-phishing is usually high. According to the framework of "adversarial tactics, techniques, and common knowledge (ATT&CK)" proposed by MITRE, spear-phishing is often used as a starting point for advanced persistent threat (APT) attacks [1]. Many active APT organizations, such as OceanLotus and SideWinder, usually tend to use emails to deliver malware to their targets [2, 3]. There is evidence that the members of important organizations such as governments, companies, enterprises and authorities are the groups that are most vulnerable to phishing attackers [4]. Once the attack is successful, it will result in a leak of confidential data and bring serious damage for businesses, nonprofit organizations, governments and even national security.

Due to the huge damage caused by spear-phishing in recent years, relevant institutions and enterprises have begun to study automated detection methods to filter harmful emails. In the early days, researchers tried to analyze emails from multiple dimensions, including the sender's IP, domain, and subject keywords. They set up a blacklist or whitelist to filter out malicious emails [5–10]. However, the attackers can easily bypass the detection by forging identities or addresses. With the development of dynamic debugging technology, the sandboxes are widely used in phishing mail detection and have achieved good results [11, 12]. However, in recent years, attackers have begun to use anti-sandbox or cloud attachments technology to evade detection from anti-virus engines [13], even many attackers don't carry malicious attachments directly in the emails. At the same time, the statistics of Lawrence Berkeley National Lab shows that none of the successful spear-phishing attacks involved a malicious attachment [14]. In order to make up for the shortage of current methods, researchers introduced artificial intelligence to the detection of malicious emails. They first extracted a variety of email characteristics (mainly including sender's IP, sender's domain, sending time, embedded links, etc.), and then combined sandbox results to detect the potential malicious emails. Only few researchers take the semantic information into account into the detection process [15, 16]. It is well known that the content of the email shows the attacker's inducing skill and diction habits, which are very helpful for describing the characteristics of attacking organizations. In our previous work, we analyzed the message body of the email and use long-short term memory (LSTM) to judge whether an email is valid or not through the content of the email. However, this method cannot be used in spear-phishing detection directly. In spear-phishing, the attacker is more cautious, with a smaller range and less attack frequency, so the number of training samples cannot meet the demands of deep learning. Therefore, it is necessary to introduce the few-shot learning method to detect the most harmful attack.

In this paper, we proposed a few-shot learning method to detect spear-phishing emails, which extracted features from the mail header and message body respectively. When analyzing the message body of an email, we proposed a simple word-embedding method that used concatenated pooling to optimize features of the content. This method can reduce the dependence on model complexity, therefore perform better results without a large amount of training data. Moreover, in order to solve the problem caused by different lengths of training data, we used concatenated pooling to obtain vectors with consistent dimensions, which avoid information loss caused by padding and truncation during data processing. After processing the message body, we combined the processed result with other features as an input vector of machine learning methods.

The rest of the paper is organized as follows: In Sect. 2, we introduce the related works. In Sect. 3, we describe the framework of spear-phishing detection proposed in detail. The methods are presented in Sect. 4, including feature extraction of mails and processing of the body of mails. Section 5 details the experiment and evaluates the results. In Sect. 6, we conclude our work.

2 Related Work

2.1 Spear-Phishing Detection Technology

The traditional detection methods of phishing emails are mainly divided into three categories: detection methods based on the black-and-white list, methods based on sandbox and methods based on using machine learning and deep learning model.

The detection method based on blacklist and whitelist compare the URL connection and IP with lists in database. Currently, the commonly used blacklist of phishing websites includes Phishitank and Openphish. Jain et al. designed a method to automatically update the whitelist through historical data, so as to realize the reliability analysis of email domain name [8]. This method can complete the detection of phishing emails through simple and convenient query operations. However, since it relies on the comprehensive blacklist and whitelist, the attacker can bypass the detection by changing the IP address and URL link of email, which makes this method invalid for the unknown attack detection of the phishing email.

The detection method based on sandbox uses sandbox technology to analyze the static characteristics and dynamic behavior of phishing email attachments. Han et al. proposed a new sandbox tool to detect attachments of email [12], but this method cannot be applied to encrypted attachments. Besides, with the emergence of anti-sandbox technology, it is difficult to catch malicious behaviors of attachments simply using sandbox technology. At the same time, sandbox-based detection method cannot be applied to detecting phishing emails with cloud attachment.

Recently, the detection method based on machine learning and deep learning is the focus of attention in research [17–26]. This method trains machine learning or deep learning model by extracting the features to detect phishing emails. Du et al. proposed an anti-phishing technology to detect phishing emails by extracting mail features and calculating information entropy [27]. Peng et al. use natural language processing technology to detect phishing emails by extracting keyword information of message body [28]. In the detection of spear-phishing emails, it is very important to analyze the header characteristics and the message body of emails. Han et al. extracted the origin feature, text feature, attachment feature and recipient feature of email, and used KNN graph to realize the campaign attribution and early detection of spear-phishing emails [15]. Wang et al. raise a detection method for spear-phishing emails based on authentication considering the attacker's stylometric feature, gender feature and personality feature [16]. In addition, Grant et al. propose a new method which uses features derived from an analysis of fundamental characteristics of spear-phishing attacks and combines with a new nonparametric anomaly scoring technique for ranking alerts [14]. However, this method can only detect the spear-phishing emails, but cannot determine the organization, which is an important problem in the analysis of spear-phishing attack.

2.2 Few-Shot Learning Methods

With the development of artificial intelligence technology, few-shot learning has become the focus of current researchers. As we all know, machine learning and deep learning model need to complete the target task through a large number of data training, while few-shot learning aims to solve the model's dependence on large-scale data, and only using a small number of samples can get better results by prior knowledge. The methods of few-shot learning are mainly divided into three categories, including methods based on data, model and algorithm [29].

The data-based method is often called data augmentation through the operation of samples to get a richer and more sufficient sample set, which can support the training of the model. In the field of computer vision, data augmentation methods for images usually include image flipping, rotation, scaling, clipping, translation and adding noise [30, 31]. In the field of natural language processing, the easy data augmentation for text classification tasks mainly include synonym replace, random insert, random swap and random delete [32]. At the same time, the back translation method is also an important method, through the use of machine translation and back translation to complete data augmentation. In the field of speech recognition, methods such as adding noise, time shift, volume adjustment, speed adjustment, stretching signal and random same type extraction and splicing are often used [33]. In addition, the generation model can also be used to generate data similar to real data to complete data augmentation. Although there are many ways of data augmentation, however this method can only alleviate the problem of insufficient samples to some extent, and its ability is very limited.

The model-based methods include multi-task learning, metric learning and external memory-based methods. Multi-task learning method uses common information shared across tasks and specific information of each task to spontaneously learn multiple learning tasks. Embedding learning embeds all the samples in the training set into a low-dimensional separable space through a function F, then embeds the samples in the testing set into this low-dimensional space and calculates the similarity between the test samples and all the training samples to selects the tags of the samples with the highest similarity as the label of the test samples. Koch et al. explore a method for one-shot image recognition based on Siamese networks which employ a unique structure to naturally rank similarity between inputs [34]. Snell et al. propose typical networks for the problem of few-shot classification, which introduce the idea of mixed density estimation [35]. Sung et al. put forward that the difference between the relation network whose difference with other models is that the relation network autonomously learns an optimal measure function instead of a certain measure function given by humans, and realizes zero-shot learning to a certain extent [36]. Geng et al. propose a new induction network to learn generalized class wise representations, innovatively combining the dynamic routing algorithm with the typical meta-learning framework [37].

The algorithm-based method is to find the optimal parameters from the perspective of algorithm theory, corresponding to the optimal hypothesis space. Meta-learning is one of the most important ways, learning good initialization parameters, and then in the new task, as long as the initialization parameter is updated iteratively, it can adapt to the new task. The most classic model of this method is Model-Agnostic Meta-Learning, which can quickly adapt to new tasks with only a small amount of data by adjusting one or more gradients based on the initial parameters [38].

3 Simple Word-Embedding Model

The appropriate analysis of the message body will significantly improve the detection effect, but the current spear phishing detection methods did not make full use of the message body. In the process of semantic information utilization, there are some key problems that need to be solved.

First, due to the accurate target and low frequency of the spear-phishing attack, the number of email samples is quite small, which is not enough to support the deep learning model. However, when using machine learning to detect, we need to transform the message body information into a feature vector. How to choose an appropriate text vectorization method is the second key problem to be solved. Thirdly, since the different content of the message body, the length of the constructed message vector will be inconsistent. But the machine learning algorithm needs feature vectors with the same dimension. The existing approach usually addresses this problem by truncating or padding, which will result in missing or redundant information.

To solve the problems mentioned above, we proposed a simple word-embedding model. As shown in Fig. 1, the proposed model includes three important parts, that are vectorization of the message body, hierarchical-max pooling and hierarchical-min pooling.

- In vectorization of the message body, we segment the message body and use word2vec method to transform the message body into vector sequences. In word2vec, we use 128-dimensional word vectors, which fixes the final feature vectors of the message body to a length of 2 * 128 dimensions, and it is concatenated with the basic features of emails.
- In hierarchical-max pooling, we first use local max pooling to select the significant elements of the word vector, which can extract the feature with high representation ability. Then, the global average pooling is used to retain spatial information and

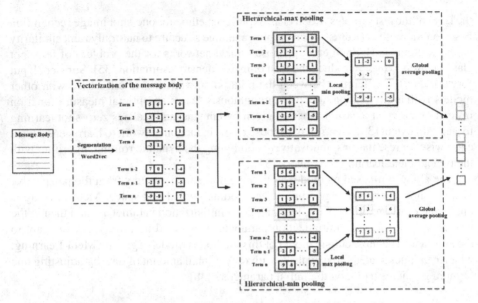

Fig. 1. The structure of our simple word-embedding model

word order. Meanwhile, the global average pooling can solve the problem of different lengths of the message body by calculating the average of all vector sequences.

- In hierarchical-min pooling, we use local min pooling to select the most easily ignored information in the vectors, which can reflect the attacker's characteristics in a subtle way. Similarly, the global average pooling is used to aggregate the intermediate features extracted from all local windows.

3.1 Hierarchical-Max Pooling

When dealing with the text classification or prediction task, the max pooling layer is usually used to extract the significant part of the word vector, that is, the keywords of the email. However, max pooling doesn't consider the spatial information and word order, which are very important in NLP. Therefore, we introduced the average pooling, and design a hierarchical pooling structure based on max pooling and average pooling.

Max Pooling: Since some keywords in a sentence or an article are important for prediction task or classification task, max pooling is used to extract these features from each dimension of word vectors, which is very similar to the max pooling in convolutional neural network. The formula of max pooling is shown as follows:

$$Z_j^{max} = \max_{i=1...L} v_{ij} \tag{1}$$

where v_{ij} is the j-th dimension of the first vector in the text, L is the length of the text, Z_j^{max} is the max value of all vectors in the j-th dimension, Z^{max} is the result of max pooling. According to the max pooling, we can ignore the words which are less relevant to the target task.

Average Pooling: Average pooling is the simplest strategy to transform a word vector sequence into a feature vector. This method calculates the average value of elements on a given word vector sequence by the following formula:

$$z_j^{average} = \frac{1}{L} \sum_{i=1}^{L} v_i \qquad (2)$$

where v_i denotes the i-th vector in the message body, and L is the length of the text. The average pooling operation takes the average value of all word vectors in each dimension, and then obtains the feature vector which has the same dimension with the original word vector. Obviously, the average pooling strategy takes the elements of each sequence into account through a simple average operation, and gives each word vector the same weight. Unlike max pooling, the contribution of each word to the final feature vector is the same in average pooling.

Hierarchical-Max Pooling: Both average pooling and max pooling do not consider word order and spatial information, which are of great significance in dealing with text problems. Therefore, in this paper, we use the hierarchical pooling model to analyze the message body. For a given text vector $\mathbf{v} = \{v_1, v_2, \cdots, v_L\}$, the local window denoted as $v_{i:i+n-1}$, and there are n consecutive words in the local window, $v_i, v_{i+1}, \cdots, v_{i+n-1}$. In the process of hierarchical-max pooling, we first complete the local max pooling by the $v_{1:n}, v_{1+s:n+s}, v_{1+2s:n+2s}, \cdots, v_{L-n+1:L}$ stride-sliding local window, where n denotes the size of the sliding window, and s denotes the stride. The process of sliding is similar to that of the convolution neural network. After the local max pooling, we aggregate the intermediate features extracted from all windows through the global average pooling operation, and finally form the text feature vector. On the one hand, the hierarchical-max pooling strategy retains the construction information from a single word window (i.e. n-gram) to the text sequence, that is, this method can obtain the local spatial information of the text sequence, instead of learning fixed-length representations for the n-grams that appears in the corpus, which is similar to the bag of n-gram method.

3.2 Hierarchical-Min Pooling

In the traditional method of extracting text features, max pooling is used to select the part with high representation ability of the vector, but this method cannot retain the most easily ignored information in the vector, which can reflect the attacker's characteristics in a subtle way. Therefore, we combined features extracted by hierarchical-min pooling with features extracted by hierarchical-max pooling, so as to retain the information of email as much as possible.

Min Pooling: In the field of computer vision, since the pixel of images is distributed in the range of 0 to 255, only max pooling is usually used which can extract the key features. Instead, if we use min pooling, we will often get all zero feature maps and can't extract the key texture features of the image. However, in the word embedding method, each dimension of word vector after word2vec is not limited in the range from 0 to 255. At this time, the min pooling will extract features different from the max pooling, which is easy to be ignored, but they can reflect the attacker's characteristics in a subtle way. The formula for the min pooling is as follows:

$$Z_j^{min} = \min_{i=1...L} v_{ij} \tag{3}$$

Hierarchical-Min Pooling: After local min pooling, we use global average pooling to process feature vector, which is similar to the process of local hierarchical-max pooling.

Concatenated Pooling: Due to the difference between the max pooling and the min pooling in the processing of text information, it is unreasonable to use a pooling method alone to extract information. Therefore, in order to retain the original semantics of the statement to the greatest extent, we use the concatenated pooling method. For a word vector, the results of hierarchical-max pooling and hierarchical-min pooling are combined together to form the concatenated pooling feature vector.

4   Spear-Phishing Detection Method Based on Few-Shot Learning

In our spear-phishing detection method, we first preprocess the email and extract key discrete features. For the message body, we first use word2vec to vectorize the message body, and then input the feature vector to simple word-embedding model to implement dimension reduction and further refine the semantic information, which can obtain a lightweight word vector that reflects the information of semantics and word order at the same time. Finally, we combine the discrete features with the feature vector of the message and input them to the machine learning model for detection (Fig. 2).

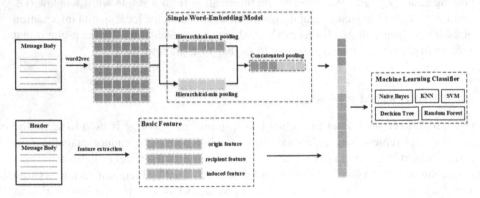

Fig. 2. The framework of spear-phishing detection method based on discrete feature and message body of the mails

4.1   Basic Feature Extraction

In this paper, we select some wildly used features commonly used in spear-phishing detection and the details of features are shown in Table1.

Table 1. The basic feature of email

Type of the feature	Abbreviation	Feature
Origin feature	ADO	attacker's domain
	SIP	source IP
	OCT	origin country
	SDT	sent date
Recipient feature	RDO	recipient's domain
	OIN	organization information
Induced feature	CLK	containing link or not
	CSL	containing short-links or not
	CPT	containing picture or not
	CKW	containing key words or not(such as "click", "download")

These features are divided into three categories: origin feature, recipient feature, and induced feature. The origin feature reflects the sender's attributes of the email, such as domain, IP and origin country which can uniquely identify the attackers and reflect the organizational characteristics. Besides, we also extract the day of week as an additional categorical feature. In the recipient feature, we extract the recipient's IP, domain name, and recipient's organization and industry information to reflect the recipient characteristics of the email, that is, the target attribute in spear-phishing. However, these header features of emails, especially the origin feature, can be easily forged by attackers to improve the concealment of identity. To this end, in our method, we also extract induced features. Because the contents of emails can reflect the attacker's potential attack habits, which are often carefully constructed by the attacker for the target, such as using phishing links or short links, embedding pictures and obvious induced word.

4.2 Visualization and Explanation of Message Body Feature Vector

In Sect. 3, we have described the simple word-embedding model in detail. In order to demonstrate the effectiveness of the model more intuitively, we visualize the organizational characteristics of the feature vector. We use the t-distributed stochastic neighbor embedding (t-SNE) algorithm to map the high-dimensional features of all samples to a two-dimensional space according to Ref. [41]. In Fig. 3, we demonstrate the feature distribution of 7 APT organizations (Krast, Layork, Elderwood, Nitro, Bisrala, Darkmoon, Samskams). We can find that samples of the same organization are clustered, and there are also obvious divisions between different organizations. Especially, due to the limitation of the number of samples and the two-dimensional space, the distribution of Bisrala's email sample is more scattered. However, the overall effect of visualization shows that the simple word-embedding model proposed in this paper can retain the characteristics of mail samples from different organizations.

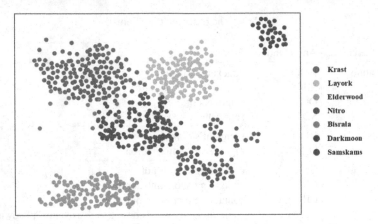

Fig. 3. The feature visualization of our simple word-embedding method representation

4.3 Feature Fusion

In feature fusion, we use the simple word-embedding model to process the message body to obtain a text feature vector, $V_{message}$. Subsequently, $V_{message}$ is concatenated with the discrete feature vector of the mail, $V_{existing}$, to obtain the final email representation vector, $V_{email} = (V_{message}, V_{existing})$, which will be input into the machine learning model.

4.4 Classifier

To choose the appropriate classifier, we try five different machine learning algorithms including KNN, Naive Bayes, Decision Tree, Random Forest, and Support Vector Machine. KNN algorithm classifies the samples by selecting the labels of data adjacent to the samples in the feature space. Naive Bayes algorithm is based on the assumption that the characteristics of the samples are independent of each other, and uses Bayes principle to calculate the probability of samples belonging to each category. Decision Tree selects the key feature of samples through entropy or Gini index, and summarizes a set of classification rules. Random Forest classifies samples by integrating the results of multiple Decision Tree classifiers. Support Vector Machine calculates the distance from the sample points to the hyperplane to finds the maximum margin hyperplane to realize the classification task.

5 Experiments and Result Discussion

5.1 Datasets

The dataset of phishing emails in this experiment contains 1342 mails from 7 organizations [15]. The origin organization of each email is determined manually. In order to ensure the balance of data samples, we will select a small number of balanced samples from each class as training data, which will improve the effectiveness of the model.

In few-shot learning, the number of training samples are very limited, and researchers usually use n-way k-shot to describe the setting of training data. Usually, n-way k-shot refers to randomly selecting n classes with k samples in each class. Such a process is called a task. In each task, the training set is called support set, and the test set is called query set. For example, 5-way 10-shot 5-query means to select 5 class in complete dataset, 10 samples from each class as the support set and 5 samples as the query set. Such a process is called an episode and one task includes many episodes. Following the standard experimental setup in few-shot learning, we carried out 7-way classification tasks for 1-shot, 5-shot and 10-shot respectively, and set the query set size to 15.

5.2 Experimental Setup and Evaluation Criteria

All experiments carried out in the Ubuntu 14.04. LTS environment, using python 3.5.4 and Keras 2.1.2 neural network library to build networks. We use Tensorflow 1.4.1 as a backend computing framework. CPU server is Inter(R) Xeon(R) CPU E5–2637 v4 @ 3.50 GHz, GPU is TITAN(X) (Pascall).

In the experiment, we choose accuracy, precision, recall Macro F1 and Micro F1 as the evaluation criteria. In each task, the evaluation criteria will be calculated separately, and the final evaluation criteria of the model is calculated by averaging results of all randomly generated episodes on the testing dataset. The formulas of the metrics are as follows:

$$\text{Acc} = \frac{1}{n}\sum_{i=1}^{n}\text{Acc}_i = \frac{1}{n}\sum_{i=1}^{n}\left(1 - \frac{errors_{num}}{sum}\right) \times 100\% \tag{4}$$

$$P = \frac{1}{n}\sum_{i=1}^{n}P_i = \frac{1}{n}\sum_{i=1}^{n}\frac{TP}{TP+FP} \times 100\% \tag{5}$$

$$R = \frac{1}{n}\sum_{i=1}^{n}R_i = \frac{1}{n}\sum_{i=1}^{n}\frac{TP}{TP+FN} \times 100\% \tag{6}$$

$$\text{Macro}\,F1 = \frac{1}{n}\sum_{i=1}^{n}F1_i = \frac{1}{n}\sum_{i=1}^{n}\frac{2\times P_i \times R_i}{P_i + R_i} \tag{7}$$

$$\text{Micro}\,F1 = \frac{2\times P \times R}{P+R} \tag{8}$$

where TP, FP, FN represent True Positive, False Positive, False Negative respectively. A represents the accuracy, which refers to the proportion of correct results predicted by the model. P, R and F1 are calculated by dividing the multi-classification evaluation into the multi binary-classification evaluation, and calculating the average value. P represents the precision, which refers to the proportion of the samples identified as a certain class correctly. R represents the recall, which refers to the proportion of all samples of a certain class that are correctly identified as that class. Macro F1 is calculated by averaging the F1 score of each classification. Micro F1 is calculated by the sum of TP, FP and FN in each binary-classification respectively.

5.3 Experimental Results

1) The influence of different method of word2vec
In the processing of the message body, we transform the message body into vector sequences. Different schema of word2vec will affect the performance of our simple word embedding model. Therefore, we design some experiments to choose the optimal one.

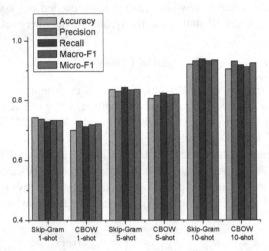

Fig. 4. The result of using different feature vectors

- CBOW: This method uses surrounding words to predict the center word. The input of the model is the word vector corresponding to the context of the target word, and the output is the word vector of the target word.
- Skip-gram: This method uses the center word to predict surrounding words. The input of the model is the word vector of the center word, and the output is the word vector corresponding to the context of the target word.

As shown in Fig. 4, the accuracy of Skip-gram method is higher than that of CBOW method in the message body analysis to be solved in this paper, so we use the feature vector based on Skip-gram.

2) Comparison with other simple word-embedding method
Term Frequency (TF) and Term Frequency-Inverse Document Frequency (TF-IDF) are two commonly used and simplest word-embedding methods, which use the characteristics of the bag-of-word model. We take these two methods as the baseline in this paper. At the same time, we also compare the performance of the proposed method with other commonly used simple word-embedding methods, including average pooling, max pooling and hierarchical pooling (max pooling and average pooling). The experimental results are shown in Fig. 5.

From the results in Fig. 5, the proposed simple word-embedding model is significantly better than TF, TF-IDF and commonly used simple word-embedding methods.

The hierarchical pooling is the closest to the results of the proposed method, because the structure of hierarchical pooling is the most similar to our proposed method, retaining the spatial information. However, the existing simple word-embedding methods fail to combine local features with global features, or lose the details that are easy to be ignored. Our proposed method not only integrates the max pooling and the min pooling, but also combines the local features and the global features through the global average pooling to retain the original semantics, so as to extract the characteristics of the attacker in the message body to the greatest extent.

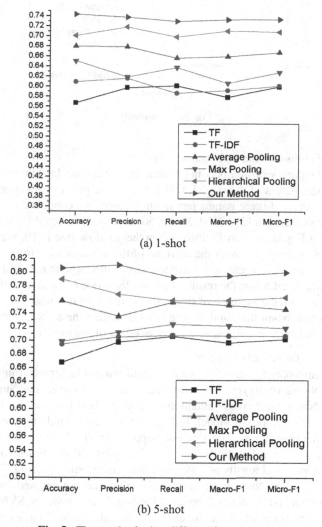

(a) 1-shot

(b) 5-shot

Fig. 5. The result of using different feature vectors

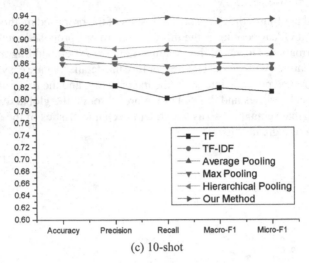

(c) 10-shot

Fig. 5. (*continued*)

3) The effect of sliding window parameters

In the proposed simple word-embedding model, the size and stride of the sliding window are the super parameters of the model, which need to be given in advance. In order to explore the influence of these parameters in our method, we conduct experiments with window size selected from {5, 10, 20, 30, 40, 50} and stride selected from {1, 3, 5, 10}.

As shown in Fig. 6, we can find that when the window size is 10, the accuracy of the model reaches the peak. With the increase of the window size, the accuracy has a obvious decline, which is because the window size is too large to extract local features with fine-grained. In addition, the results show that the stride has a small influence on the experiments, but with the increase of stride, the accuracy of the model has a significant decline. Moreover, when the window size is smaller than the stride, the word vectors cannot be fully utilized, which leads to the poor effect of the model.

4) The influence of different classifier

To choose the appropriate classifier, we try five different machine learning algorithms including KNN, Naive Bayes, Decision Tree, Random Forest, and Support Vector Machine. In KNN, we use cross-validation to select the best K value. For Naive Bayes, we use Gaussian Naive Bayes model. In Decision Tree and Random Forest model, we use Gini coefficient index as criterion. For Support Vector Machine, the linear kernel function is selected according to the number of samples and the dimensions of feature vector. The experimental results of different classifiers are shown in Fig. 7.

The results of KNN, Naive Bayes and Decision Tree are similar, and Random Forest is slightly better than KNN, Naive Bayes and Decision Tree. However, SVM has the best detection effect, because when the dimension of feature vector is large enough but the number of samples is small, the linear kernel can still achieve a good classification effect, which makes SVM model show its natural advantages even when facing the problem of small samples.

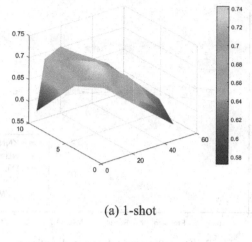

(a) 1-shot

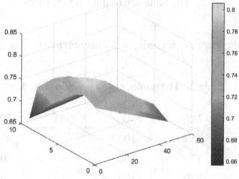

(b) 5-shot

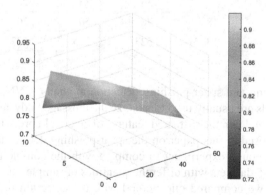

(c) 10-shot

Fig. 6. The effect of window size and stride

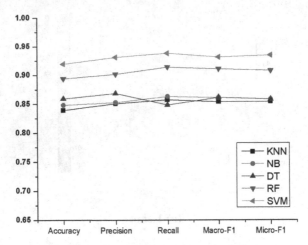

Fig. 7. The influence of different classifiers

5) Comparison with other spear-phishing detection method

Table 2. The number of samples in dataset

Organization\Datasets	DS_1	DS_2	DS_3	DS_4	DS_5
Krast	157	100	50	20	10
Layork	139	100	50	20	10
Elderwood	770	100	50	20	10
Nitro	153	100	50	20	10
Bisrala	12	12	12	12	10
Darkmoon	33	33	33	20	10
Samskams	78	78	50	20	10
Total	1342	523	295	132	70

In traditional phishing and spear-phishing detection methods, CNN, LSTM and other deep learning models are usually used to analyze the message body, and machine learning models are used to learn the extracted features of emails. In order to verify the effect of the method proposed in this paper on the spear-phishing detection with small samples, we designed enough experiment to compare with the commonly used detection methods. We set up 5 datasets with different quantities of samples, as shown in Table 2. In the experiment, we compared our method with the detection methods using only deep learning models (CNN and LSTM). In addition, we compare our method with the methods proposed by Han et al. and Wang et al. Han et al. extracted the origin feature, text feature, attachment feature and recipient feature of the email and used KNN graph. Wang et al. proposed an authentication-based spear-phishing detection method, paying more attention to the attacker characteristics reflected in the email, including stylometric feature, gender feature and personality feature.

It can be seen from the results in Fig. 8 that when the number of samples is sufficient, the detection effect of the CNN and LSTM models is slightly better than our proposed method, but as the number of samples decreases, the detection effect of the deep learning

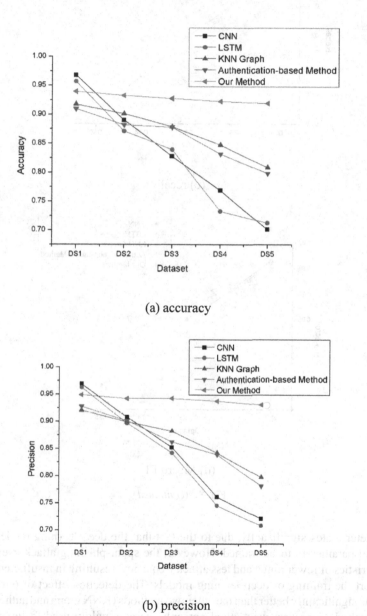

(a) accuracy

(b) precision

Fig. 8. The result of comparing with other spear-phishing detection method

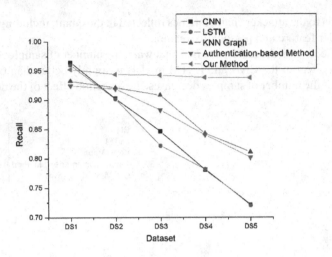

(c) recall

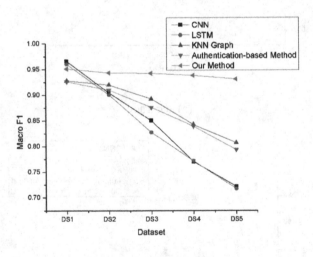

(d) Macro F1

Fig. 8. (*continued*)

model deteriorates significantly, due to the fact that the deep learning model contains too many parameters to be trained. However, the spear-phishing attack event has the characteristics of fewer range and less attack frequency, resulting in insufficient samples to support the training of deep learning models. The detection effect of our proposed method is significantly better than the other two methods (KNN graph and authentication-based method). Because our method not only extracts wildly used features, but also uses the entire message body of emails to the detection, instead of only the statistical

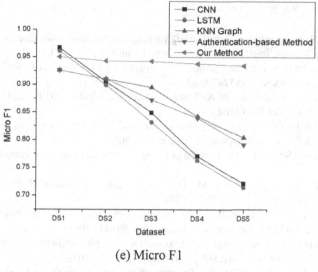

(e) Micro F1

Fig. 8. (*continued*)

characteristics of the message body. In that way, the original semantic information of the message body can be retained to the greatest extent.

6 Conclusion

In this paper, we analyzed the existing spear-phishing attack detection methods. We found that, the detection method based on the artificial definition of features may cause incomplete feature extraction due to the lack of prior knowledge while the detection method based on deep learning has high requirements on training samples. In order to slove this problem, we proposed a spear-phishing detection method based on few-shot learning, which can work well with limited labeling samples. On the one hand, we extracted the wildly used features such as attacker IP, target domain, induction keywords and so on. On the other hand, the simple word embedding-model is used to output the word vector of message body information with small samples. Then, we combine these two kinds of characteristics together and input them into the machine learning model for classification, including KNN, NB, DT, RF, SVM. Moreover, we also determined the optimal values of window size and stride of the sliding window in simple word-embedding model through sufficient experiments. The experimental results show that the spear-phishing detection method based on few-shot learning proposed in this paper has a better effect than the existing spear-phishing detection methods. Especially, our method can achieve better performance with small samples.

References

1. The MITRE Corporation: Adversarial Tactics, Techniques, and Common Knowledge (ATT&CK), Tactics, initial access. https://attack.mitre.org/tactics/TA0001/
2. FreeBuf: Analysis on the attack samples of vulnerability exploitation of (2017). https://www.freebuf.com/articles/web/155747.html
3. FreeBuf: Attack event report of APT organization SideWinder (2019). https://www.freebuf.com/articles/paper/213799.html
4. Fireye: Best defense against spear-phishing attacks (2018). https://www.fireeye.com/current-threats/best-defense-againstspearphishing-attacks.html
5. Jansson, K., von Solms, R.: Phishing for phishing awareness. Behav. Inf. Technol. **32**, 584–593 (2013)
6. Nikolaos, T., Nikos, V., Alexios, M.: Browser blacklists: the utopia of phishing protection. E-Bus. Telecommun. **554**, 278–293 (2014)
7. Wang, Y., Agrawal, R., Choi, B.: Light weight anti-phishing with user whitelisting in a web browser. In: 2008 IEEE Region 5 Conference, pp. 39–42 (2008)
8. Jain, A., Gupta, B.: A novel approach to protect against phishing attacks at client side using auto-updated white-list. EURASIP J. Inf. Secur. **1**, 2016 (2016)
9. Marchal, S., François, J., State, R.: Proactive discovery of phishing related domain names. In: Balzarotti, D., Stolfo, S.J., Cova, M. (eds.) RAID 2012. LNCS, vol. 7462, pp. 190–209. Springer, London (2012). https://doi.org/10.1007/978-3-642-33338-5_10
10. Cao, Y., Han, W., Le, Y.: Anti-phishing based on automated individual white-list. In: Proceedings of the 4th ACM Workshop on Digital Identity Management, pp. 278–293 (2008)
11. Nissim, N., Cohen, A., Glezer, C., Elovici, Y.: Detection of malicious PDF files and directions for enhancements: a state-of-the art survey. Comput. Secur. **48**, 246–266 (2015)
12. Han, X., Kheir, N., Balzarotti, D.: PhishEye: live monitoring of sandboxed phishing kits. In: ACM SIGSAC Conference on Computer & Communications Security, pp. 1402–1413 (2017)
13. FreeBuf: APT-C-12, Nuclear Crisis Action Revealing (2018). https://www.freebuf.com/column/176675.html
14. Ho, G., Sharma, A., Javed, M., Paxson, V., Wagner, D.: Detecting credential spearphishing in enterprise settings. In: 26th USENIX Security Symposium (2017)
15. Han, Y., Shen, Y.: Accurate spear phishing campaign attribution and early detection. In: Proceedings of the 31st Annual ACM Symposium on Applied Computing, pp. 2079–2086 (2016)
16. Wang, X., Zhang, C., Zheng, K., Tang, H., Tao, Y.: Detecting spear-phishing emails based on authentication. In: IEEE International Conference on Computer and Communication Systems, pp. 450–456 (2019)
17. Tewari, P., Singh, R.: Machine learning based phishing website detection system. Int. J. Eng. Res. Technol. **4**, 172–174 (2015)
18. Jain, A., Gupta, B.: A machine learning based approach for phishing detection using hyperlinks information. J. Ambient Intell. Humaniz. Comput. 2015–2028 (2018)
19. Jain, A., Gupta, B.: Comparative analysis of features based machine learning approaches for phishing detection. In: International Conference on Computing for Sustainable Global Development, pp. 2125–2130 (2016)
20. Abdelhamid, N., Thabtah, F., Abdel-jaber, H.: Phishing detection: a recent intelligent machine learning comparison based on models content and features. In: IEEE International Conference on Intelligence & Security Informatics, pp. 72–77 (2017)
21. Chiew, K., Tan, C., Wong, K., Yong, K., Tiong, W.: A new hybrid ensemble feature selection framework for machine learning-based phishing detection system. Inf. Sci. **484**, 153–166 (2019)

22. Sahingoz, O., Buber, E., Demir, O., Diri, B.: Machine learning based phishing detection from URLs. Expert Syst. Appl. **117**, 345–357 (2019)
23. Yadollahi, M., Shoeleh, F., Serkani, E., Madani, A., Gharaee, H.: An adaptive machine learning based approach for phishing detection using hybrid features. In: International Conference on Web Research, pp. 281–286 (2019)
24. Zhu, E., Chen, Y., Ye, C., Li, X., Liu, F.: OFS-NN: an effective phishing websites detection model based on optimal feature selection and neural network. IEEE Access **7**, 73271–73284 (2019)
25. Phoka, T., Suthaphan, P.: Image based phishing detection using transfer learning. In: Annual International Conference on Knowledge and Smart Technology, pp. 232–237 (2019)
26. Smadi, S., Aslam, N., Zhang, L.: Detection of online phishing email using dynamic evolving neural network based on reinforcement learning. Decis. Support Syst. **107**, 88–102 (2018)
27. Du, Y., Xue, F.: Research of the anti-phishing technology based on e-mail extraction and analysis. In: International Conference on Information Science & Cloud Computing Companion, pp. 60–65 (2014)
28. Peng, T., Harris, I., Sawa, Y.: Detecting phishing attacks using natural language processing and machine learning. In: IEEE International Conference on Semantic Computing, pp. 300–301 (2018)
29. Wang, Y., Yao, Q., Kwok, J., Ni, L.: Generalizing from a few examples: a survey on few-shot learning. ACM Comput. Surv. **1**(1) (2020)
30. Huynh-The, T., Hua, C., Kim, D.: Encoding pose features to images with data augmentation for 3-D action recognition. IEEE Trans. Industr. Inf. **16**(5), 3100–3111 (2020)
31. Liu, Z., et al.: Automatic diagnosis of fungal keratitis using data augmentation and image fusion with deep convolutional neural network. Comput. Methods Program. Biomed. **187** (2020)
32. Wei, J., Zou, K.: EDA: easy data augmentation techniques for boosting performance on text classification tasks. In: Conference on Empirical Methods in Natural Language Processing & International Joint Conference on Natural Language Processing (2019)
33. Park, D., et al.: SpecAugment: a simple data augmentation method for automatic speech recognition. In: Conference of the International Speech Communication Association (2019)
34. Koch, G., Zemel, R., Salakhutdinov, R.: Siamese neural networks for one-shot image recognition. In: International Conference on Machine Learning (2015)
35. Snell, J., Swersky, K., Zemel, R.: Prototypical networks for few-shot learning. In: Annual Conference on Neural Information Processing Systems, vol. 30 (2017)
36. Sung, F., Yang, Y., Zhang, L., Xiao, T., Torr, P., Hospedales, T.: Learning to compare: relation network for few-shot learning. In: IEEE/CVF Conference on Computer Vision and Pattern Recognition, pp. 1199–1208 (2018)
37. Geng, R., Li, B., Li, Y., Ye, Y., Jian, P., Sun, J.: Few-shot text classification with induction network. In: Conference on Empirical Methods in Natural Language Processing (2019)
38. Finn, C., Abbeel, P., Levine, S.: Model-agnostic meta-learning for fast adaptation of deep networks. In: International Conference on Machine Learning (2017)
39. Shen, D., et al.: Baseline needs more love: on simple word-embedding-based models and associated pooling mechanisms. In: Annual Meeting of the Association-for-Computational-Linguistics, pp. 440–450 (2018)
40. Pan, C., Huang, J., Gong, J., Yuan, X.: Few-shot transfer learning for text classification with lightweight word embedding based models. IEEE Access **7**, 53296–53304 (2019)
41. Maaten, V., Hinton, G.: Visualizing data using t-SNE. J. Mach. Learn. Res. **9**, 2579–2625 (2008)

Time Series Classification Based on Data-Augmented Contrastive Learning

Junyao Wang[1], Jiangyi Hu[2], Taishan Xu[3], Xiancheng Ren[3],
and Wenzhong Li[1(✉)]

[1] State Key Laboratory for Novel Software Technology, Nanjing University,
Nanjing 210023, China
`junyaowang@smail.nju.edu.cn`, `lwz@nju.edu.cn`
[2] State Grid Chongqing Electric Power Company, Chongqing 400014, China
[3] Nari Technology Co., Ltd., Nanjing 211106, China

Abstract. Time series classification has become a popular research topic in data mining and has a wide range of applications in many fields in daily life. When analyzing and classifying time series, it is challenging to address their dynamic distribution characteristics and preserve key temporal information. In this paper, we propose a novel time series classification algorithm based on data-augmented contrastive learning. The proposed model consists of four parts, the Data Augmentation module, the Encoder, the Feature Space Contrastive Learning module and the Classifier. The four parts work together to jointly accomplish the task of time series classification. During the process of training the time series representation encoder, we adopt a loss function combining contrastive loss and classification loss to optimize the encoder, which can learn label-related representations from time series data and extract internal features. We conduct extensive experiments based on 30 open datasets, which show that the proposed method outperforms the state-of-the-art baseline algorithms.

Keywords: Contrastive Learning · Data Augmentation · Time Series Classification · Representation Learning

1 Introduction

Time series data is a set of observation data sequentially arranged in the order of time. Time series exist in all aspects of daily life, almost any data that needs to consider the order can be converted into time series to process. Many areas involve time series analysis, such as weather forecasting, medical ECG (electrocardiogram) analysis, futures price trend prediction, behavior recognition, etc.

This work was partially supported by the Natural Science Foundation of Jiangsu Province (Project "Research on Frontier Basic Theory and Method of Security Defense for Power Systems with High-dimensional Uncertain Factors", Grant No. BK20222003).

© The Author(s), under exclusive license to Springer Nature Singapore Pte Ltd. 2024
C. Li et al. (Eds.): APPT 2023, LNCS 14103, pp. 372–389, 2024.
https://doi.org/10.1007/978-981-99-7872-4_21

Time series can accurately visualize the pattern and trend over time of a set of data, which can reflect the internal or external development of the target.

Time series analysis has become one of the hottest topics in the field of data mining. Time series classification is an important part of time series analysis, which refers to classifying time series into different categories or labeling them correspondingly. Time series classification algorithms have been widely used in many fields, which have great impact on daily life, such as speech recognition [10] and gait recognition [31]. In the medical field, time series classification can be used for the classification of ECG signals to detect diseases such as myocardial infarction [28]. In the financial field, time series classification can be used to determine financial fraud [30], predict futures price trend [19], etc.

Unlike regular data, time series data contains temporal information internally, and it is necessary to consider the characteristics of time series and retain the key temporal information when analyzing and classifying them, which requires special modeling and processing of time series.

Deep neural network has achieved great success in the field of computer vision (CV) [25,33,36], natural language processing (NLP) [9,27,38], speech recognition [6,15,24], etc., reaching or even surpassing the performance of humans in some tasks. Data of both natural language processing and speech recognition tasks are temporal in nature, which is one of the main characteristics of time series. This similarity has inspired the enthusiasm of applying deep learning to time series research. Most time series representation and classification methods are inspired by experiences from CV and NLP. These fields have strong inductive biases, such as transformation-invariance and cropping-invariance, but these assumptions are not always applicable in modeling time series [39]. The distribution and semantics of a time series may change over time, and the cropped sub-series may have a different distribution compared to the original time series. Therefore, when applying deep learning to time series classification, more effective and applicable modeling and classification approaches for time series data are needed.

Contrastive learning is a self-supervised learning technique that does not require manual labeling of data and is a discriminative representation-based learning framework [2,12,26]. The samples are compared with similar and dissimilar samples, and the model is optimized through the calculation of contrastive loss, which makes the feature representations of similar samples closer and those of dissimilar samples more distant. Compared with traditional models, the comparative learning model is simple to construct and has low manual burden. It enhances the generalization ability and robustness of the model by automatically constructing positive and negative pairs, which is not limited by the scale of labeled data.

The application of contrastive learning in the study of time series classification algorithms can greatly improve the effectiveness of time series classification algorithms and will also reduce the burden of labeling data manually to some extent. However, as self-supervised learning, contrastive learning fails to take labels into consideration and this will lead to poor performance in some classification tasks. In this paper, we propose a novel method to combine the labels of time series and contrastive learning using a data-augmented approach. The proposed model consists of four parts, the Data Augmentation module, the Encoder, the Feature Space Contrastive Learning module and the Classifier. The four parts work together to jointly accomplish the task of time series classification. During the process of training the time series representation encoder, we use a loss function combining contrastive loss and classification loss to optimize the encoder, which can learn label-related representations from time series data and extract internal features and greatly accomplish the time series classification task. We conduct extensive experiments based on 30 open datasets, which show that the proposed method outperforms the state-of-the-art baselines in time series classification tasks.

The major contributions of this paper are summarized as follows:

- We propose a novel time series classification algorithm based on Data-Augmented Contrastive Learning. The proposed model consists of four parts, the Data Augmentation module, the Encoder, the Feature Space Contrastive Learning module and the Classifier. The four parts work together to jointly accomplish the task of time series classification.
- During the process of training the time series representation encoder, we propose a loss function combining contrastive loss and classification loss to optimize the encoder. Therefore the proposed encoder can learn label-related representations from time series data and extract internal features and greatly accomplish the time series classification task. By choosing positive and negative pairs according to the labels, we propose a novel data-augmented contrastive learning method to form time series presentation.
- We conducted extensive experiments of classification performance on 30 time series datasets from the UCR Archive. The experimental results show that our time series classification algorithm outperforms the baseline algorithms.

The rest of the paper is organized as follows. In Sect. 2, we summarized the related works of this paper, and analyzed the advantages and disadvantages of existing algorithms. In Sect. 3, we gave a brief definition of the time series classification problem. In Sect. 4, we proposed our method, Data-Augmented Contrastive Learning, to solve the time series classification problem. In Sect. 5, we conducted extensive experiments to compare the performance of our method and the baselines on time series classification tasks. In Sect. 6, we concluded the model proposed in the paper and the results of this experiment.

2   Related Work

We summarize the related work in terms of time series classification, time series representation learning, and contrastive learning.

2.1   Time Series Classification

Time series classification is a popular topic in data mining and many scholars have proposed efficient algorithms to address time series classification problem.

Before the extensive use of deep learning in studying time series classification algorithms, Dynamic Time Wrap (DTW) was often used as a measure of similarity between time series, while the k-NN algorithm was used for clustering, and the two were combined for time series classification work [29]. Some scholars also use Bag-of-Patterns (BOP) [17], Time Series Forest (TSF) [5], and Shapelet-based methods [13] to conduct time series classification.

Compared with traditional machine learning methods, deep learning methods using neural networks reduces the difficulty of designing feature extraction methods. By overlaying layers with different functions, more abstract and high-dimensional features are easy to be obtained, which can make the model perform better on time series classification tasks. Deep learning models in time series classification can be divided into two categories: generative models and discriminative models [14].

Generative Model for Time Series Classification. Generative models are trained in an unsupervised manner prior to the learning phase of the classifier, with the goal of finding a good representation of the time series prior to the training process of the classifier [14].

Bengio et al. introduced a generalized denoising autoencoders that can be used to process both continuous and dispersed data [1]. Unlike the usual convolutional neural networks that require max pooling between layers, Mittelman et al. proposed an undecimated fully convolutional neural network for time series modeling [23]. Wang et al. proposed a cycle deep belief network model for multivariate time series classification [34], where deep belief network was used to find the intrinsic structure of the data and learn the representation applicable to the original data. Malhotra et al. proposed a deep recurrent neural network called TimeNet [22], which is trained in an unsupervised manner to extract features of time series. Ma et al. proposed a functional echo state network [20], which changed the output weights of the numerical variables of the echo state network to a time-varying output weight function, and introduced a temporal aggregation operator in the output layer, making this echo state network usable as a classifier with better performance than the single-algorithm approach.

Discriminative Model for Time Series Classification. A discriminative deep learning model is a classifier (or regressor) that directly learns the mapping between the raw input of a time series (or its hand engineered features) and outputs a probability distribution over the class variables in a dataset [14].

Wang et al. proposed three models of multilayer perceptron, convolutional neural network and residual neural network applied to end-to-end time series classification [35]. Lin et al. proposed group-constrained convolutional recurrent neural network [18], which combines a convolutional neural network part that can be used to extract high-level features and a recurrent neural network part that enhances the temporal features of the time series data.

2.2   Time Series Representation

Time series representation learning usually does not require manual feature engineering and allows an end-to-end learning process on the raw time series data to automatically extract the features of the time series to facilitate downstream work tasks.

Zerveas et al. proposed a transformer-based framework for multivariate time series representation learning [40]. Eldele et al. proposed a time series representation learning method which employs temporal and contextual contrasting [7]. Franceschi et al. proposed an unsupervised scalable representation learning method for multivariate time series [8], which can cope with the problem of embedding time series data of different sequence lengths as well as unlabeled time series data. Yang et al. proposed a time-series multimodal representation learning model that uses a correlated recurrent neural network (CorrRNN) to fuse multiple naturally temporal input modalities that can simultaneously learn joint representations and temporal dependencies between modalities [37]. Yue et al. proposed a universal framework for learning representations of time series in an arbitrary semantic level, namely TS2Vec, which applies hierarchical contrasting to learn scale-invariant representations within augmented context views [39].

2.3   Contrastive Learning

In classical contrastive learning, Oord et al. proposed a representation learning method using Contrastive Predictive Coding (CPC) that can effectively extract suitable representations from high-dimensional data [26]. He et al. proposed a method for unsupervised visual representation learning called momentum contrast (MoCo) [12], and the model has performed well in several different tasks such as ImageNet classification. Chen et al. proposed a framework for simple contrast learning for visual representations (SimCLR) [2] to learn the best representation of the image in an unsupervised manner.

As the self-supervised and unsupervised contrastive learning has gained rapid development, there are also scholars who studied supervised contrastive learning. Khosla et al. proposed a supervised contrastive learning approach that introduces the labels of the data into the contrastive loss function to optimize the representation [16].

3   Problem Definition

Univariate time series $X = [x_1, x_2, ..., x_T]$ is a set of ordered real values, where the real number T is the length of X. The M-dimensional multivariate time series $X = [X^1, X^2, ..., X^M]$ consists of M distinct univariate time series, where $X^i \in \mathbb{R}^T$. The dataset $D = \{(X_1, Y_1), (X_2, Y_2), ..., (X_N, Y_N)\}$ is the set of (X_i, Y_i), where X_i can be univariate time series or multivariate time series, and Y_i is the label corresponding to the time series. The goal of time series classification is to learn a function f that maps each time series X_i to the corresponding class label Y_i.

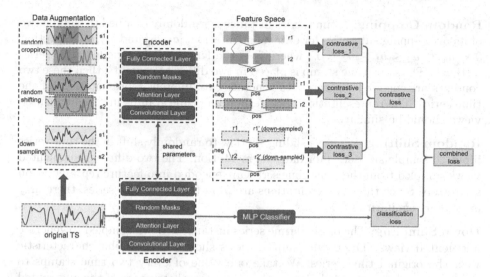

Fig. 1. Time series classification model based on data-augmented contrastive learning (DACL).

4 Method

4.1 Model Architecture

We proposed a time series classification model based on data-augmented contrastive learning (DACL), which is shown in Fig. 1. It is mainly composed of four parts, the Data Augmentation module, the Encoder, the Feature Space Contrative Learning module and the Classifier.

The original time series data are fed into the Data Augmentation module to generate augmented views. Then the augmented views are encoded by the encoder for contrastive learning in feature space to get contrastive loss. Meanwhile, the raw data are fed into the encoder which shares parameters with the encoder mentioned before. A multilayer perceptron (MLP) classifier is used to classify the representations and get the classification loss. The combined loss is consist of the contrastive loss and the classification loss to adjust the parameters of the encoder and the classifier.

The four parts of the model work together to accomplish the time series classification task. The details are explained as follows.

4.2 Data Augmentation

The Data Augmentation module is the main part of the DACL model. The original time series data are fed into this module to generate augmented views for contrastive learning. Here we introduce three methods for data augmentation: random cropping, random shifting and down sampling.

Random Cropping: A time series instance is randomly cropped to sample two of its overlapping sub-series for data augmentation, $[a_1, b_1]$ and $[a_2, b_2]$, such that $0 < a_1 \leq a_2 \leq b_1 \leq b_2 \leq T$, where T is the length of the original time series instance. The same time stamp is placed in two different contexts, then these two contexts are encoded separately to generate two different representations of the time series. The representation of corresponding time stamps in two augmented views should be similar.

Random Shifting: We use a sliding window to randomly shift in the time series input to sample sub-series for data augmentation. The two different augmented views sampled from the same time series are encoded into feature representation separately. Since these representations are from the same time series, there may exist more similarities.

Down Sampling: The original time series instance is down sampled to generate augmented views. The down sampled views should have similar characteristic with the original time series. We take one value of every two time stamps to generate the down sampled view so that the general structure of the augmented view will not differ too much from the original time series.

The methods we use to generate augmented data are very useful to help the encoder learn deeper features from the time series by contrastive learning.

4.3   Encoder

Here we need a powerful encoder for feature extraction of the time series, and we refer to the encoder in TS2Vec [39] to encode the time series. The encoder f_θ consists of four parts: a fully connected layer, a layer for random masks, an attention layer and a convolutional layer.

The fully connected layer, for each input time series X_i, maps the value $X_{i,t}$ on each timestamp to a high-dimensional latent vector $z_{i,t}$. Then the latent vector is randomly masked to generate an augmented view so that the encoder will have better generalization ability. Different from the encoder of TS2Vec [39], an attention layer is introduced to help the encoder focus more on important parts of the time series. After that we use the convolution layer to extract the contextual representation for each time series.

After passing into such an encoder, the time series X_i will be encoded into a feature vector $r_i = \{r_{i,1}, r_{i,2}, ..., r_{i,T}\}$, where $r_{i,t} \in \mathbb{R}^K$, and K is the dimension of the representation vector.

4.4   Feature Space Contrastive Learning

In order to better learn the internal feature of time series, we conduct contrastive learning in the feature space. After the Data Augmentation module and the Encoder, the original time series are encoded into representations of different augmented views. By contrastive learning, we can adjust the parameters of the encoder so that it can form more discriminative feature representations.

Since three methods are used in Data Augmentation, we also introduce three different methods to choose the positive pairs and the negative pairs for contrastive learning accordingly.

- For the augmented views generated from random cropping, the representations on the same timestamp in the two augmented contexts of the same original time series input act as positive pairs, while the representation on the different timestamp or from different time series input act as negative pairs.
- For the augmented views generated from random shifting, the whole representation of two augmented views from the same original time series act as positive pairs, while the augmented views from different time series input are negative pairs.
- For the augmented views generated from down sampling, the whole representation of the down-sampled view and the original time series input act as positive pairs, while the augmented views from different time series input are negative pairs.

The contrastive loss is calculated as below:

$$\mathcal{L} = -log\frac{exp(sim(z_1, z_2)/\tau)}{\sum_{k=1}^{2N} \mathbb{1}_{[k \neq 1]} exp(sim(z_1, z_k)/\tau)}, \tag{1}$$

where τ is temperature parameter, $sim(\cdot)$ represents the similarity between two representation vectors, and z_k represents the training samples in a batch.

The whole contrastive loss is as below:

$$\mathcal{L}_{contrastive} = \frac{1}{S} \sum_{i=1}^{S} \mathcal{L}, \tag{2}$$

where the S is the number of all the contrastive loss.

4.5 Classifier

We use a multilayer perceptron (MLP) as the classifier to classify the representation of different time series. Thanks to the encoder, the representation of time series should have the ability to better extract the feature of time series. So we can use a simple MLP to accomplish the time series classification task.

Meanwhile, the classifier is also used to help the encoder better learn the feature of time series. All the data augmentation and feature space conrtastive learning methods are used to learn the internal features of time series rather than the categorical features. So the result of the classifier can be used to adjust the encoder as well. The classification loss is combined with the contrastive loss to adjust the encoder so that the encoder can learn both the internal features and the categorical features, which is useful for time series classification task.

When calculating the classification loss, the raw time series input is passed into the encoder to generate a feature representation of the original time series.

The feature representation of the time series is passed into the classifier to obtain the predicted class values. The predicted category values and the true time series label are used to calculate the classification loss of the time series. Let the original time series data be X_i and the label be Y_i, and after the encoder f_θ, the feature representation r_i of the time series is obtained, and then the feature representation r_i is passed into the classifier to get the predicted category value of the original time series $\hat{Y}_i$. The classification loss function is as below:

$$l^{(i)}_{classification} = CrossEntropy(\hat{Y}_i, Y_i). \tag{3}$$

The total classification loss is as below:

$$\mathcal{L}_{classification} = \frac{1}{N} \sum_{i=1}^{N} l^{(i)}_{classification}. \tag{4}$$

4.6   Overall Process

In the DACL model, the original time series data are fed into the Data Augmentation module to generate augmented views. Then the augmented views are encoded by the encoder for contrastive learning in feature space to get contrastive loss $\mathcal{L}_{contrastive}$. Meanwhile, the raw data are fed into the encoder and the representations are classified by the classifier to get the classification loss $\mathcal{L}_{classification}$. In order to learn the internal features of the time series and the differences between time series categories, we combine the contrastive loss and the classification loss and get the combined loss of the time series representation module as below:

$$\mathcal{L}_{combined} = \lambda_1 \times \mathcal{L}_{contrastive} + \lambda_2 \times \mathcal{L}_{classification}, \tag{5}$$

where λ_1 and λ_2 are the weighing parameters, which are used to adjust the weights of the two loss functions. The combined loss are used to adjust the encoder and the classifier. After the training process, the model can be used to classify the time series.

The four parts of the model work together to accomplish the time series classification task.

5   Experiments

In this section, we evaluate the performance of the proposed method on time series classification.

5.1   Datasets

In order to be able to better test the performance of the model, this experiment was conducted on real-world time series datasets, the well-known UCR Archive [4]. The UCR Archive is a widely used set of standard datasets for time

Table 1. Description of Datasets.

Name	Train	Test	Class	Length	Type
ArrowHead	36	175	3	251	Image
Beef	30	30	5	470	Spectro
BirdChicken	20	20	2	512	Image
Car	60	60	4	577	Sensor
FaceAll	560	1690	14	131	Image
FaceFour	24	88	4	350	Image
FiftyWords	450	455	50	270	Image
Fish	175	175	7	463	Image
GunPoint	50	150	2	150	Motion
LargeKitchenAppliances	375	375	3	720	Device
Meat	60	60	3	448	Spectro
OSULeaf	200	242	6	427	Image
PhalangesOutlinesCorrect	1800	858	2	80	Image
ScreenType	375	375	3	720	Device
SonyAIBORobotSurface2	27	953	2	65	Sensor
Symbols	25	995	6	398	Image
ToeSegmentation2	36	130	2	343	Motion
Yoga	300	3000	2	426	Image
ACSF1	100	100	10	1460	Device
FreezerSmallTrain	28	2850	2	301	Sensor
Fungi	18	186	18	201	HRM
GestureMidAirD3	208	130	26	Vary	Trajectory
HouseTwenty	40	119	2	2000	Device
MelbourncPedestrian	1194	2439	10	24	Traffic
PickupGestureWiimoteZ	50	50	10	Vary	Sensor
PigAirwayPressure	104	208	52	2000	Hemodynamics
PigCVP	104	208	52	2000	Hemodynamics
PLAID	537	537	11	Vary	Device
SmoothSubspace	150	150	3	15	Simulated
UMD	36	144	3	150	Simulated

series classification tasks, with 85 datasets at the time of its release in 2015 and 43 new time series datasets added in 2018 [3], covering a wide range of fields including finance, medicine, and machinery. Each dataset contains a series of time-series data that have been labeled. Most of the datasets have time series data of fixed length, while a few datasets contain time series data of variable length. Currently, UCR Archive is widely used for the benchmark test of time series classification algorithms.

In the experiments, we randomly selected 30 datasets from the UCR Archive based on different time series lengths, the size of the training and test sets, the number of dataset categories, and the domain of the data source. The datasets cover a wide range of domains such as spectrum, sensor, image, and traffic, where the sequence length, data size, and number of categories of time series are distinguishable enough to test the behavior and performance of the model under various situations. The details of the selected datasets are described in Table 1.

5.2   Baselines and Performance Metrics

The choice of baselines and performance metrics is crucial to the measurement of the performance of a new algorithm.

Baselines. The baselines used in this experiment are: TS2Vec, T-Loss, TNC, TS-TCC, TST and DTW. These baselines are all state-of-the-art or classical algorithms in the time series classification field, and this experiment use them to compare with the model based on data-augmented contrastive learning called **DACL** proposed in this paper.

– *TS2Vec* [39] is a general framework for learning time series representations at any semantic level. The TS2Vec model conducts contrastive learning hierarchically in an augmented contextual view, where the representation of any sub-series in the time series can be derived by a simple aggregation of the representations of the corresponding timestamps. Then, a SVM with a RBF kernel is trained upon the time series representations to complete the classification task.
– *T-Loss* [8] is an unsupervised scalable representation learning method for multivariate time series. This framework can cope with the problem of embedding time series data of different sequence lengths as well as unlabeled time series data. After the embedding of the original time series data is completed, a classifier is used to classify the embedded time series.
– *TNC* [32] is an unsupervised representation learning framework for time series with temporal neighborhood coding. They consider that time series are locally smooth and time series signals in the neighborhood are distinguishable from those not in the neighborhood, and the model learns time series representations by finding neighborhoods in the time series. The classifier can be trained upon the time series representations learned from the training to accomplish the time series classification task.
– *TS-TCC* [7] is a time series representation learning method which employs temporal and contextual contrasting. This model can learn the representation of unlabelled time series using unsupervised learning. The model augments the data with various transformations of the time series based on transformation consistency, uses the transformed series as a positive pairs for contrastive learning. This method learns the representations of the time series and then uses a classifier to complete the classification work.

- *TST* [40] is a transformer-based framework for multivariate time series representation learning. The model uses unsupervised pre-training to improve the performance of the model by training a transformer encoder to extract dense vector representations of unlabeled multivariate time series. The representation got from the training can be used to get the predicted classification results using the softmax function, and the cross-entropy loss function is used to fine-tune the pre-trained encoder to optimize the classification results.
- *DTW* [29] is dynamic time wrapping algorithm which is recognized as an extremely effective algorithm for measuring the similarity of time series. The k-NN algorithm is one of the commonly used classification algorithms, which will use the class of the k closest sample points to classify the sample points [11]. Use the combination of DTW and k-NN to classify the time series.

Performance Metrics. The performance metric we use to evaluate the performance of these methods on time series classification task is *accuracy*. In a multi-classification task, accuracy is defined as the ratio of the number of correctly classified samples to the total number of samples. Suppose a multi-classification task with a total number of N samples and a total number of K categories, and for each category j of the classification task, the number of samples correctly classified to that category is TP_j, then accuracy is calculated as follows:

$$Accuracy = \frac{\sum_{j \in [1,K]} TP_j}{N}. \tag{6}$$

5.3 Results

This experiment compares the performance of the six time series classification baselines mentioned above on the 30 time series datasets and evaluates the performance of the models using accuracy as a performance metric. The detailed experimental results are shown in Table 2.

5.4 Analysis

As shown in the table, the overall performance of the model proposed in this paper exceeds that of the baselines on 19 out of 30 time series datasets, which indicates that our model is able to accomplish the time series classification task well. The model proposed in this paper provides stable performance on time series classification tasks when facing time series datasets with variable length of sequences.

The trained time series encoder of our model can well extract the internal features of time series and the differences between time series classes, which can be used in other downstream tasks. By embedding the time series, the time series representations can reflect the deeper patterns of the time series and facilitate other data mining work subsequently.

The t-distributed stochastic neighborhood embedding (t-SNE) can reduce the dimension of high-dimensional vector data and can be used for visualization of high-dimensional data [21]. In this experiment, the t-SNE method is used to reduce the dimensions of time series representations and visualize them in order to be able to observe the encoding ability of the encoder. The t-SNE visualization results on four of the datasets, SonyAIBORobotSurface2, SmoothSubspace, Fish and Car are shown in Fig. 2, Fig. 3, Fig. 4 and Fig. 5. It can be seen from the data visualization results that the encoder is able to extract the features from the time series and can map the time series data of the same category to close locations in space, which can facilitate the downstream work. It can be seen that during the period of training from the original data to 1000 iterations, as the number of

Table 2. Comparison of performance of different time series classification algorithms.

Dataset	DACL (Ours)	TS2Vec	T-Loss	TNC	TS-TCC	TST	DTW
ArrowHead	0.811	**0.857**	0.766	0.703	0.737	0.771	0.703
Beef	**0.833**	0.767	0.667	0.733	0.600	0.500	0.633
BirdChicken	**0.900**	0.800	0.850	0.750	0.650	0.650	0.750
Car	**0.883**	0.833	0.833	0.683	0.583	0.550	0.733
FaceAll	**0.862**	0.771	0.786	0.766	0.813	0.504	0.808
FaceFour	**0.955**	0.932	0.920	0.659	0.773	0.511	0.830
FiftyWords	0.756	**0.771**	0.732	0.653	0.653	0.525	0.690
Fish	**0.943**	0.926	0.891	0.817	0.817	0.720	0.823
GunPoint	**0.993**	0.980	0.980	0.967	**0.993**	0.827	0.907
LargeKitchenAppliances	**0.869**	0.845	0.789	0.776	0.848	0.595	0.795
Meat	**0.950**	**0.950**	**0.950**	0.917	0.883	0.900	0.933
OSULeaf	0.831	**0.851**	0.760	0.723	0.723	0.545	0.591
PhalangesOutlinesCorrect	**0.819**	0.809	0.784	0.787	0.804	0.773	0.728
ScreenType	0.451	0.411	0.416	**0.509**	0.419	0.419	0.397
SonyAIBORobotSurface2	**0.930**	0.871	0.889	0.834	0.907	0.745	0.831
Symbols	0.944	**0.976**	0.963	0.885	0.916	0.786	0.950
ToeSegmentation2	**0.923**	0.892	0.900	0.831	0.877	0.615	0.839
Yoga	0.840	**0.887**	0.837	0.812	0.791	0.830	0.836
ACSF1	**0.910**	0.900	0.900	0.730	0.730	0.760	0.640
FreezerSmallTrain	0.848	0.870	0.933	**0.982**	0.979	0.920	0.759
Fungi	0.935	0.957	**1.000**	0.527	0.753	0.366	0.839
GestureMidAirD3	**0.354**	0.292	0.285	0.292	0.177	0.154	0.323
HouseTwenty	0.849	0.916	**0.933**	0.782	0.790	0.815	0.924
MelbournePedestrian	**0.961**	0.959	0.944	0.942	0.949	0.741	0.791
PickupGestureWiimoteZ	**0.960**	0.820	0.740	0.620	0.600	0.240	0.660
PigAirwayPressure	**0.755**	0.630	0.510	0.413	0.380	0.120	0.106
PigCVP	**0.865**	0.812	0.788	0.649	0.615	0.596	0.154
PLAID	0.540	0.561	0.555	0.495	0.445	0.419	**0.836**
SmoothSubspace	**1.000**	0.980	0.960	0.913	0.953	0.827	0.827
UMD	0.986	**1.000**	0.993	0.993	0.986	0.910	0.993

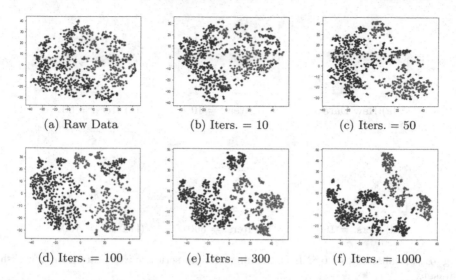

Fig. 2. Visualization of t-SNE embedding of time series representation on the SonyAI-BORobotSurface2 dataset.

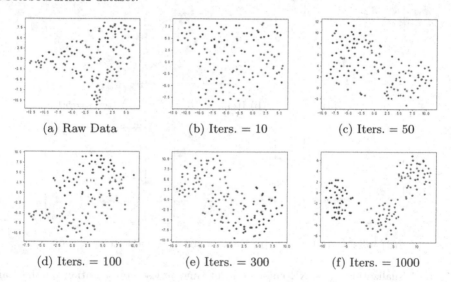

Fig. 3. Visualization of t-SNE embedding of time series representation on the Smooth-Subspace dataset.

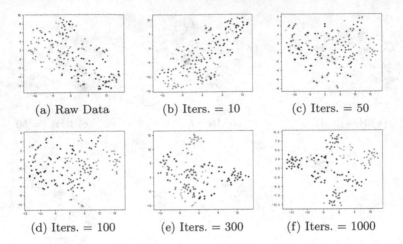

Fig. 4. Visualization of t-SNE embedding of time series representation on the Fish dataset.

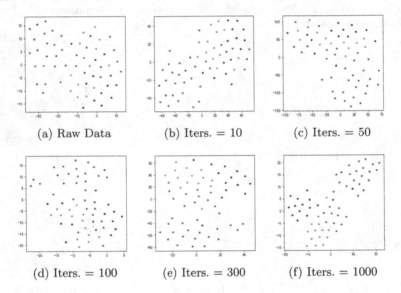

Fig. 5. Visualization of t-SNE embedding of time series representation on the Car dataset.

iterations increases, the greater the differentiation of the representations between different categories of time series in the dataset, the better the embedding effect, which proves that the encoder is able to learn the effective representations well.

6 Conclusion

This study analyzes the classic and advanced algorithms of time series classification, summarizes the advantages and disadvantages of current time series classification algorithms, and proposes a time series classification algorithm based on data-augmented contrastive learning, which combines the method of contrastive learning with the task of time series classification. The proposed model consists of four parts, the Data Augmentation module, the Encoder, the Feature Space Contrastive Learning module and the Classifier. The four parts work together to jointly accomplish the task of time series classification. We conduct extensive experiments based on 30 open datasets, and the overall classification performance of our model outperformed the baseline algorithms.

References

1. Bengio, Y., Yao, L., Alain, G., Vincent, P.: Generalized denoising auto-encoders as generative models. In: Advances in Neural Information Processing Systems, vol. 26 (2013)
2. Chen, T., Kornblith, S., Norouzi, M., Hinton, G.: A simple framework for contrastive learning of visual representations. In: International Conference on Machine Learning, pp. 1597–1607. PMLR (2020)
3. Dau, H.A., et al.: The UCR time series archive. IEEE/CAA J. Autom. Sin. 6(6), 1293–1305 (2019)
4. Dau, H.A., et al.: The UCR time series classification archive (2018). https://www.cs.ucr.edu/~eamonn/time_series_data_2018/
5. Deng, H., Runger, G., Tuv, E., Vladimir, M.: A time series forest for classification and feature extraction. Inf. Sci. 239, 142–153 (2013)
6. Deng, L., et al.: Recent advances in deep learning for speech research at Microsoft. In: 2013 IEEE International Conference on Acoustics, Speech and Signal Processing, pp. 8604–8608. IEEE (2013)
7. Eldele, E., et al.: Time-series representation learning via temporal and contextual contrasting. In: Proceedings of the Thirtieth International Joint Conference on Artificial Intelligence, IJCAI 2021, pp. 2352–2359 (2021)
8. Franceschi, J.Y., Dieuleveut, A., Jaggi, M.: Unsupervised scalable representation learning for multivariate time series. In: Advances in Neural Information Processing Systems, vol. 32 (2019)
9. Gardner, M., et al.: Allennlp: a deep semantic natural language processing platform. arXiv preprint arXiv:1803.07640 (2018)
10. Geurts, P.: Pattern extraction for time series classification. In: De Raedt, L., Siebes, A. (eds.) PKDD 2001. LNCS (LNAI), vol. 2168, pp. 115–127. Springer, Heidelberg (2001). https://doi.org/10.1007/3-540-44794-6_10
11. Guo, G., Wang, H., Bell, D., Bi, Y., Greer, K.: KNN model-based approach in classification. In: Meersman, R., Tari, Z., Schmidt, D.C. (eds.) OTM 2003. LNCS, vol. 2888, pp. 986–996. Springer, Heidelberg (2003). https://doi.org/10.1007/978-3-540-39964-3_62
12. He, K., Fan, H., Wu, Y., Xie, S., Girshick, R.: Momentum contrast for unsupervised visual representation learning. In: Proceedings of the IEEE/CVF Conference on Computer Vision and Pattern Recognition, pp. 9729–9738 (2020)

13. Hills, J., Lines, J., Baranauskas, E., Mapp, J., Bagnall, A.: Classification of time series by shapelet transformation. Data Min. Knowl. Disc. **28**, 851–881 (2014)
14. Ismail Fawaz, H., Forestier, G., Weber, J., Idoumghar, L., Muller, P.A.: Deep learning for time series classification: a review. Data Min. Knowl. Disc. **33**(4), 917–963 (2019)
15. Khalil, R.A., Jones, E., Babar, M.I., Jan, T., Zafar, M.H., Alhussain, T.: Speech emotion recognition using deep learning techniques: a review. IEEE Access **7**, 117327–117345 (2019)
16. Khosla, P., et al.: Supervised contrastive learning. Adv. Neural. Inf. Process. Syst. **33**, 18661–18673 (2020)
17. Lin, J., Li, Y.: Finding structural similarity in time series data using bag-of-patterns representation. In: Winslett, M. (ed.) SSDBM 2009. LNCS, vol. 5566, pp. 461–477. Springer, Heidelberg (2009). https://doi.org/10.1007/978-3-642-02279-1_33
18. Lin, S., Runger, G.C.: GCRNN: group-constrained convolutional recurrent neural network. IEEE Trans. Neural Netw. Learn. Syst. **29**(10), 4709–4718 (2017)
19. Livieris, I.E., Pintelas, E., Pintelas, P.: A CNN-LSTM model for gold price time-series forecasting. Neural Comput. Appl. **32**, 17351–17360 (2020)
20. Ma, Q., Shen, L., Chen, W., Wang, J., Wei, J., Yu, Z.: Functional echo state network for time series classification. Inf. Sci. **373**, 1–20 (2016)
21. Van der Maaten, L., Hinton, G.: Visualizing data using t-SNE. J. Mach. Learn. Res. **9**(11) (2008)
22. Malhotra, P., TV, V., Vig, L., Agarwal, P., Shroff, G.: Timenet: pre-trained deep recurrent neural network for time series classification. arXiv preprint arXiv:1706.08838 (2017)
23. Mittelman, R.: Time-series modeling with undecimated fully convolutional neural networks. arXiv preprint arXiv:1508.00317 (2015)
24. Nassif, A.B., Shahin, I., Attili, I., Azzeh, M., Shaalan, K.: Speech recognition using deep neural networks: a systematic review. IEEE Access **7**, 19143–19165 (2019)
25. O'Mahony, N., et al.: Deep learning vs. traditional computer vision. In: Arai, K., Kapoor, S. (eds.) CVC 2019. AISC, vol. 943, pp. 128–144. Springer, Cham (2020). https://doi.org/10.1007/978-3-030-17795-9_10
26. Oord, A.V.D., Li, Y., Vinyals, O.: Representation learning with contrastive predictive coding. arXiv preprint arXiv:1807.03748 (2018)
27. Otter, D.W., Medina, J.R., Kalita, J.K.: A survey of the usages of deep learning for natural language processing. IEEE Trans. Neural Netw. Learn. Syst. **32**(2), 604–624 (2020)
28. Pyakillya, B., Kazachenko, N., Mikhailovsky, N.: Deep learning for ECG classification. In: Journal of Physics: Conference Series, vol. 913, p. 012004. IOP Publishing (2017)
29. Senin, P.: Dynamic time warping algorithm review. Information and Computer Science Department University of Hawaii at Manoa Honolulu, USA, vol. 855, no. 1–23, p. 40 (2008)
30. Seyedhossein, L., Hashemi, M.R.: Mining information from credit card time series for timelier fraud detection. In: 2010 5th International Symposium on Telecommunications, pp. 619–624. IEEE (2010)
31. Shajina, T., Sivakumar, P.B.: Human gait recognition and classification using time series shapelets. In: 2012 International Conference on Advances in Computing and Communications, pp. 31–34. IEEE (2012)

32. Tonekaboni, S., Eytan, D., Goldenberg, A.: Unsupervised Representation Learning for Time Series with Temporal Neighborhood Coding. arXiv e-prints arXiv:2106.00750 (2021). https://doi.org/10.48550/arXiv.2106.00750
33. Voulodimos, A., Doulamis, N., Doulamis, A., Protopapadakis, E., et al.: Deep learning for computer vision: a brief review. Comput. Intell. Neurosci. **2018** (2018)
34. Wang, S., Hua, G., Hao, G., Xie, C.: A cycle deep belief network model for multivariate time series classification. Math. Probl. Eng. **2017** (2017)
35. Wang, Z., Yan, W., Oates, T.: Time series classification from scratch with deep neural networks: A strong baseline. In: 2017 International Joint Conference on Neural Networks (IJCNN), pp. 1578–1585. IEEE (2017)
36. Wu, Q., Liu, Y., Li, Q., Jin, S., Li, F.: The application of deep learning in computer vision. In: 2017 Chinese Automation Congress (CAC), pp. 6522–6527. IEEE (2017)
37. Yang, X., Ramesh, P., Chitta, R., Madhvanath, S., Bernal, E.A., Luo, J.: Deep multimodal representation learning from temporal data. In: Proceedings of the IEEE Conference on Computer Vision and Pattern Recognition, pp. 5447–5455 (2017)
38. Young, T., Hazarika, D., Poria, S., Cambria, E.: Recent trends in deep learning based natural language processing. IEEE Comput. Intell. Mag. **13**(3), 55–75 (2018)
39. Yue, Z., et al.: Ts2vec: towards universal representation of time series. In: Proceedings of the AAAI Conference on Artificial Intelligence, vol. 36, pp. 8980–8987 (2022)
40. Zerveas, G., Jayaraman, S., Patel, D., Bhamidipaty, A., Eickhoff, C.: A transformer-based framework for multivariate time series representation learning. In: Proceedings of the 27th ACM SIGKDD Conference on Knowledge Discovery & Data Mining, pp. 2114–2124 (2021)

From Ledger to P2P Network: De-anonymization on Bitcoin Using Cross-Layer Analysis

Che Zheng[1], Shen Meng[2(✉)], Duan Junxian[3], and Zhu Liehuang[2]

[1] School of Computer Science and Technology, Beijing Institute of Technology,
Zhong Guan Cun South Street, Beijing 100081, China
chezheng@bit.edu.cn

[2] School of Cyberspace Science and Technology, Beijing Institute of Technology,
Zhong Guan Cun South Street, Beijing 100081, China
{shenmeng,liehuangz}@bit.edu.cn

[3] National Laboratory of Pattern Recognition, Chinese Academy of Sciences
Institute of Automation, Zhong Guan Cun East Road, Beijing 100190, China
junxian.duan@ia.ac.cn

Abstract. Cryptocurrency has the characteristics of decentralization and anonymization, which have emerged and attracted widespread attention from various parties. However, cryptocurrency anonymization breeds illegal activities such as money laundering, gambling, and phishing. Thus, it is essential to deanonymity on Cryptocurrency transactions. This paper proposes a cross-layer analysis method for Bitcoin transactions deanonymization. Through acquiring large-scale original transaction information and combining the characteristics of the network layer and the transaction layer, we propose a propagation pattern extraction model and associated address clustering model. We achieve the matching of the suspected transaction with the originator's IP address for high precision and low overhead. Through experimental analysis in a real Bitcoin system, the cross-layer method can effectively match the original transaction with the target node, which reaches an accuracy of 81.3% and is 30% higher than the state-of-the-art method. By controlling several factors, such as different times and nodes, the characteristics of the extracted transaction propagation pattern can be proved reasonable and reliable. The practicality and effectiveness of the cross-layer analysis are higher than that of a single-level scheme.

Keywords: Bitcoin transactions · Deanonymization · Propagation path · Address clustering · Cross-layer analysis

1 Introduction

Since the birth of Bitcoin [1], attention to cryptocurrencies has continued to rise. According to CoinMarketCap [2], a leading blockchain digital currency statistics

© The Author(s), under exclusive license to Springer Nature Singapore Pte Ltd. 2024
C. Li et al. (Eds.): APPT 2023, LNCS 14103, pp. 390–416, 2024.
https://doi.org/10.1007/978-981-99-7872-4_22

site, there are already more than 25,000 cryptocurrencies and a total market cap of more than $1 trillion as of June 2023. Cryptocurrencies have gained the trust and popularity of many users due to their significant features, such as decentralization and anonymity of transactions.

However, the anonymous feature of trading is a double-edged sword. On the one hand, users do not need to disclose their identity information to third-party agents, which protects users' privacy. On the other hand, due to the anonymity of the user, cryptocurrencies are often used for money laundering, drug trafficking, and terrorist crimes [3], and this phenomenon intensifies as the anonymity of cryptocurrencies continues to grow. In response to the illegal transactions of unscrupulous individuals, researchers have launched a confrontational analysis of the anonymity mechanism of cryptocurrencies to discover real identity information.

The existing solutions mainly focus on a single-level, which can only be traced to specific stages in the Bitcoin transaction process, and it is difficult to achieve a more precise goal. According to the process of generating, forwarding, and verifying transactions in the Bitcoin network, the existing methods include the research of the network layer and the transaction layer. The research of the network layer aims to link users' pseudonyms to their real-world IP addresses by analyzing the transaction propagation data [4,5].

The research of the transaction layer is mainly dedicated to discovering the relationship between anonymous peers from public transactions, e.g., transaction graph analysis [6,7] or cluster analysis [8,9].

This paper mainly focuses on designing an effective and efficient deanonymization method by combining the analysis of the network layer and the transaction layer. The core of the study is to locate originating transactions and pseudonyms based on a specific IP address of originators (i.e., peers who generate transactions). As each peer can either generate new transactions or forward transactions generated by other peers, the transaction deanonymization problem can be abstracted as a transaction refinement process, where originated transactions are extracted from massive available transactions.

To extract suspected originating transactions through cross-layer data analysis, there still exist two main challenges: 1) *Network layer*: transaction deanonymization requires the frequent collection of Bitcoin network information, such as network topology and propagation path, which may introduce an interference with the network functionalities and cause high communication overhead. Due to factors such as node dynamics and network delays, making it difficult to distinguish between the originating transaction and the forwarding transaction through the transaction propagation information. 2) *Transaction layer*: the data we can obtain in the transaction layer is limited and the historical block data cannot be attached for clustering. It is also important to consider the calculation error caused by different class sizes in the process of cluster analysis. Therefore, it remains a challenging task to conduct the information collection process in a more efficient way.

To tackle these challenges, we propose the underlying network forwarding pattern and Bitcoin address associated attribute to analyze the originating transaction characteristic. During the extraction, every node in the network is considered and the multi-probe will be used to avoid misjudgment. Furthermore, regularization is used to solve the class scale problem. To reduce the network interference and the communication overhead, we choose two probe nodes to receive transaction information rather than generating transactions and collect the propagation path passively. By combining multi-probe, we generate fewer transactions to adapt to the transmission pattern.

Compared with our previous work [10], the novelty of this paper includes the new data analysis scheme by combining the network layer and transaction layer to find the originating transactions. The additional contributions beyond the original paper [10] are as follows:

- We develop the multi-probe combination to optimize the calculation process in the propagation pattern extraction. When the number of transactions for training the pattern is reduced exponentially, the multi-probe can ensure that there are enough nodes connected to assign weights without causing more interference to the network.
- We design the clustering regularization model in the transaction layer, which can effectively optimize the output results without relying on the threshold and can effectively match the specific IP address with its transaction addresses in the wallet.
- We demonstrate the effectiveness, precision and overhead of the proposed method in the real-world Bitcoin system, which is suitable for networks at different times and different nodes. The results show that it achieves 81.3% precision on average, which is 30% higher in comparison with the state-of-the-art method.

To the best of our knowledge, this is the first attempt to combine the underlying network layer with the transaction layer for Bitcoin deanonymization. The rest of this paper is organized as follows. Section 2 introduces the relevant background and previous works. The system architecture of our method is presented in Sect. 3, which is followed by the design details of the propagation pattern matching model in Sect. 4 and the associated address clustering model in Sect. 5. Next, we evaluate the performance of our method in Sect. 6. After a brief discussion in Sect. 7, the conclusion of this study is presented in Sect. 8.

2   Background and Related Work

This section provides a basic overview of the Bitcoin system, including the generation of a transaction with pseudonyms and a special focus on the transaction forwarding mechanism, and then presents an overview of existing deanonymization methods.

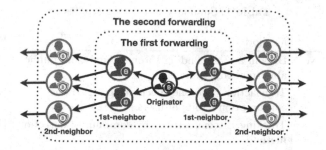

Fig. 1. Transaction forwarding mechanism in Bitcoin network.

2.1   Background of Bitcoin System

Transaction Address. The process of the Bitcoin transaction is pseudony-mous, meaning that funds are not tied to real-world entities but rather Bitcoin addresses. To heighten financial privacy, a new Bitcoin address can be generated for each transaction [11]. For example, hierarchical deterministic wallets gener-ate pseudorandom "rolling addresses" for every transaction from a single seed, while only requiring a single passphrase to be remembered to recover all corre-sponding private keys. There are random and multiple addresses for one Bitcoin transaction, which are different from the entity address of the user's local loca-tion. In order to distinguish them, we call the Bitcoin address and IP address respectively hereafter.

Transactions Inputs and Outputs. A transaction includes one or more inputs and one or more outputs. When a user sends a Bitcoin, the user specifies each address and the number of Bitcoins sent to that address in the output [12]. The use of multiple inputs corresponds to the use of multiple coins in a cash transaction. When the output of one transaction becomes the input of another transaction, the Bitcoin has already been spent. As with cash transactions, the number of addresses for payment may over the expected amount. In this case, use the extra output to return the change to the payer. In another case, if the remaining amount of one address is insufficient to pay for the amount of one transaction, use the other addresses as input together.

Transaction Forwarding. A transaction in Bitcoin system consists of one or more input addresses and one or more output addresses. These addresses are known as pseudonyms of Bitcoin users. When a transaction is generated by an originator, it will be broadcasted to all the other nodes in the Bitcoin network. To forward transactions, each node connects to a limited number of nodes, which are referred to as neighbors [13]. According to the parameter settings in the Bitcoin system, the number of neighbors each node has is at most 125, including 8 outgoing neighbors and 117 incoming neighbors [14].

An example illustrating the transaction forwarding process is exhibited in Fig. 1. The originator first sends the transaction to its neighbors (i.e., 1st-neighbor nodes), who, in turn, forwards the transaction to their neighbors (i.e.,

Table 1. Summary of existing studies

Category	Methods	References
Transaction layer approaches	Bitcoin address finding through analyzing public abnormal transactions	[15, 16]
	Transaction timezone speculating based on consumption habits of users	[7]
	Tracking Bitcoin activity by community detection method	[17]
	Extending existing heuristics with methods for identifying peel chain	[9]
Network layer approaches	Transaction classification by the forwarding patterns in underlying network	[18]
	Transaction originator inference by the first forwarding node in propagation path	[4]
	Bitcoin client node deanonymization by its neighbor nodes	[5, 19]
	AS is used as a man-in-the-middle to monitor the transactions of a specific Bitcoin client	[20]
	Transaction address obtainment by sending fake information proactively	[21]

2nd-neighbor nodes). The forwarding process continues until the transaction reaches every node in the network.

Actually, the forwarding of a transaction does not happen immediately when a peer receives the transaction. Every 100 milliseconds one neighbor node is randomly selected from the list of all peers' neighbors, and the queue for outgoing forwarding messages is flushed for this node [5]. In the meanwhile, the mechanism may prevent the other neighbor nodes from receiving the forwarded transaction.

2.2 Summary of Existing Studies

Based on the characteristics of the Bitcoin system, a transaction needs to be forwarded by other nodes from the originator, and the transaction is broadcasted in the whole network. We briefly summarize the existing studies on Bitcoin deanonymization, which can be classified into two categories, as shown in Table 1.

The first category attempts to discover the relationship among users from publicly available transaction information, for instance, it can discover that grouping pseudonyms are likely to belong to the same user. The second category aims at associating user pseudonyms with real-world IP addresses through analyzing transaction propagation information in Bitcoin network.

Correlation Analysis of Transaction-Layer Information. To find the relationship between Bitcoin pseudonyms, the transaction graph and input-output information are employed for correlation analysis. Narayanan and Shmatikov [6] employed the information from IMDb (Internet Movie Database) with the same user to deanonymize Netflix prize data scts. Reid et al. [15] and Liao [16] speculated the source Bitcoin address and the funds' flow of transaction from public transaction address. DuPont [7] determined the frequent period of the transaction according to the consumption habits of the public. Kappos et al. [9] propose a clustering method for peel chain, and further verifies the effectiveness of the co-spending clustering method through this method. Cazabet [17] used complex network analysis and community detection to match multiple addresses with its Bitcoin users. Moreover, the precision of these approaches will be significantly affected when users adopt a one-off address strategy or transaction obfuscation strategy.

Linkability Analysis of Network-Layer Propagation Information. Existing deanonymization approaches usually leverage the transaction propagation information in Bitcoin underlying network to exploit the linkability between pseudonyms and IP addresses. Koshy et al. [18] classified distinct transaction relay patterns and designed heuristics to hypothesize transaction ownership. Dan Kaminsky et al. [4] proposed the Sybil attack to assume that the first forwarding node IP address of a new transaction is owned by the original sender. Biryukov et al. [5] put forward a transaction traceability mechanism based on neighbor nodes. In the following work, Biryukov [19] developed a TOR middle-man attack and "Address cookies" to identify specific clients. Ethan Heilman [21] used a set of IP address controlled to form an unsolicited incoming connection with the victim and sent fake network information continuously to obtain the transaction address. Muoi et al. [20] exploit the vulnerability of the BGP protocol to perform man-in-the-middle attacks against specific Bitcoin nodes to monitor transactions issued by Bitcoin clients from the AS level. In the above discussion, the solution might cause serious interference to the underlying network, even requiring more computing resources.

2.3   System Architecture

The Novelty of this Paper. The method proposed in this paper matches the Bitcoin node IP address with its originating transactions. The method possesses several advantages over previous methods: 1) It does not need to connect to all peers to collect forwarding information and causes less interference. 2) It is independent of the network environment and overcomes the random delay. 3) It allows the training of different probability models to fit the distribution function in different network environments. The process of continuous iterations can make the model more universal. 4) The scheme of cross-layer breaks through the limitation of single-level traceability.

3   System Overview

Based on the research on existing work, we have optimized the deanonymization scheme by combining the network layer and the transaction layer. In this

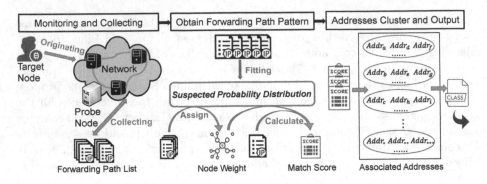

Fig. 2. An overview of system architecture.

section, we propose an innovative deanonymization architecture and introduce the workflow of each step in it.

Due to the characteristics of the anonymity and dynamics of nodes in the Bitcoin system, we are trying to reduce the interference to the network, which focuses on a specific target node with a known IP address in advance.

Suppose that the uncontrollable target node needs to be matched with its originating transaction. Based on the existing traceability methods, we intend to propose a cross-layer method to build a matching mechanism for the originating transaction, which combines the characteristics of the transaction propagation mode in the underlying network layer and the characteristics of the Bitcoin address usage mode of the initiator in the transaction layer. After establishing a monitoring network to obtain transaction information, the basic transaction forwarding path pattern and associated bitcoin address cluster are used to output suspicious originating transactions.

An overview of the system architecture is shown in Fig. 2, which consists of three main components. The first component collects forwarding information of all transactions in the Bitcoin network and then feeds this information to the rest two components for further analysis. The second component calculates the matching score of suspected originating transactions via an underlying network propagation pattern. The pattern extracted through the transaction forwarding path when broadcasting to the whole network. The matching score means the similarity between the transaction and the originating transaction according to the weight of each forwarding node. The third component refers to the optimization model by using the associated address clustering via the transaction layer. The core of the clustering is to use the associated input addresses of the per transaction to filter abnormal transactions and improve predicted accuracy.

In order to collect forwarding information of all transactions in the Bitcoin network, we design a monitoring network and the network topology is shown in Fig. 3. There are three types of important nodes and other forwarding nodes to constitute this monitoring network. The target node is who we are going to concentrate on. The controllable node and the probe are the new members of the network.

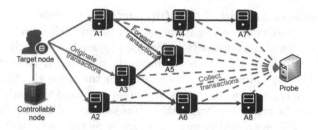

Fig. 3. Network topology for collecting transaction forwarding information in Bitcoin network.

We assume that the target node is similar to other nodes because of the regular pattern in the transaction forwarding mechanism. It is possible that we have difficulty in connecting the target node owing to the unstable network environment. To find out the originating transactions of the uncontrollable target node, we use a controllable node to connect the target node with single point connection, indicating that the target node is the only one to forward transactions firstly. It equals to that the transaction is originated by the target node when the controllable node generates a transaction.

We develop the probe program based on the Bitcoin open source code to monitor the target node and obtain the forwarding path list for each transaction. The Bitcoin node realizes the connection by saving the IP address, the port of neighbor nodes, the forwarding transaction information, and the Block information. Through simulating the connection between Bitcoin nodes, the probes are accessible to collect transaction information forwarded by other nodes or originated by the target node. A probe node which can receive transaction information rather than generating transaction to collect the propagation path passively.

3.1   Description of Workflow

This section describes the details involved in the architecture in Sect. 2.3, including the process from acquiring transactions in the network to finding the originating transactions, which can reduce errors caused by propagation delays and applies to uncontrollable nodes.

Suppose it is required to match an uncontrollable target node with its originating transactions. Based on the previous method, we combine the characteristics of the transaction propagation pattern in the underlying network layer and the Bitcoin address usage pattern of the originator in the transaction layer to construct an originating transaction matching mechanism. After establishing the monitoring network to collect transaction information, we use probability distribution function and node weight assignment to extract the characteristics of the transaction forwarding pattern. Then we leverage the associated address clustering analysis to output the suspected originating transactions.

Step 1. Collecting the individual transaction by probe

To extract the underlying propagation pattern mainly relies on the forwarding path characteristics of the transaction. We use probes, the controllable node and the target node to form a monitoring network, introduced in Sect. 2.3, which is used to collect the transactions transmitted in the network. The probes will record the transactions associated with the target node and the sequence in which one of the nodes forwards the originating transactions of the target node. The information of each forwarded transaction arrives at the probe will be recorded, including the hash value of the transaction, the forward node IP address, and the arrival time. Then, we can sort the different nodes according to the time when the forwarded transaction reaches the probe.

Step 2. Extracting the propagation pattern from underlying network

The transaction created by the target node will be firstly sent to their neighbors. When we know about the neighbor nodes' information of the target node, we can count the probability that the neighbor node appears in the forwarding path of one originating transaction. The parameter to fit is illustrated in Sect. 4. Then, we extract the pattern that the transaction is an originating transaction when a certain node appears in a particular position. As the dynamic of neighbor nodes that are not easy to be continuously connected. We assign the node weight depending on the probability where the node appears in the originating transaction forwarding path. Then, we calculate the matching score for each collected transaction with the pattern extracted. The higher the score, the more likely the transaction is originated by the target node.

Step 3. Outputting the suspected originating transactions optimized by associated address clustering

In order to avoid threshold selection and ignore abnormal transactions to increase the accuracy of matching suspected originating transactions, as there are multiple inputs in one transaction from the usage pattern of Bitcoin addresses, we perform an associative address clustering for optimization. The definition of the clustering will be presented in Sect. 5.1. After clustering, when the score of a certain class is the highest, we output it and the transactions in it are inferred to the originating transactions.

4   Matching Score Calculation via Propagation Pattern Speculation

Since the nodes are using the forwarding dynamics in the underlying network, a regular pattern of forwarding paths still exists. To handle the effect of the dynamics of network and forwarding, we calculate the square error as the loss function to speculate the propagation pattern of the originating transactions. In addition, we also propose a node weight model based on a multi-probe to improve the matching precision for the suspected originating transactions without knowledge of specific nodes.

The symbols used in this section are defined as shown in the following Table 2.

4.1   Propagation Pattern Extraction Using Forwarding Path

We assume that an originating transaction of the target node has a similar propagation pattern when it forwarded in the underlying network layer. Therefore, we speculate on the suspected originating transaction of the target node by extracting forwarding features and matching.

Since the number of online server nodes in the Bitcoin network exceeds 10,000 per day, the network delays between different nodes and probes are different, resulting in a difference in the order of forwarding transactions and the order in which the transactions reach the probe nodes. Therefore, the accuracy of the forwarding path obtained using a single probe node is low. In this regard, by deploying multiple probe nodes to establish monitoring networks, multiple propagation paths can be obtained for the same transaction.

Table 2. Notations in calculation

Notation	Definition
M	The transaction set of originating
A	The controllable node who is used to simulate the target node
$\mathcal{N}$	The IP address set of neighbor nodes
r_i	Arbitrary IP address collected in the network
$\sigma_{\mathcal{N}}$	The indicative function for the neighbor node IP address
$\mathbb{T}$	All forwarded transactions captured by probe
$\mathcal{T}$	All originating transactions captured by probe
$\sigma_{\mathcal{T}}$	The indicative function for the originating transactions
$\bar{L}_i$	The forwarding path list of transaction T_i without target node
$\mathcal{R}$	The IP addresses set of forwarding nodes
$\mathcal{P}$	The set of p probes
c_p	The number of node connection of probe p

For computational cost considerations, we deploy two probes to collect transaction information forwarded in the underlying network layer. By listening instead of generating or forwarding transactions, the probe can sort the collected forwarding information in order of time arrival to obtain a forwarding path list for a transaction. By leverage two probes, we can connect to more nodes in the underlying network, get more accurate forwarding information, and even reduce overhead.

By analyzing the forwarding path of each transaction through the forwarding information in the underlying network layer, we find that several nodes who forward information advanced are important nodes in most cases. We can empirically judge the probabilities $p_N^*(k)$ represents the probability of neighbor node appearing in position k in originating transaction $\mathcal{T}$. In the collected forwarding path list of non-original transactions, we can find out that the position of important nodes is generally more backward. The $\bar{p}_N^*(k)$ stands for the probability of a neighbor node appearing in position k in a non-originating transaction.

By combining the $p_N^*(k)$ and $\bar{p}_N^*(k)$ of two forwarding paths from different transactions, we can calculate the probability $SusPro$ to extract the characteristics of the transaction propagation pattern. With that in mind, if the forwarding path of a transaction is similar to the propagation pattern we extract, then the transaction is more likely to be the originating transaction we are looking for.

Based on the above idea, we use Algorithm 1 to fit the $SusPro$ distribution function $p_N(k, b)$, where k represents the position of neighbor node in forwarding path. The b is the parameter vectors to be fitted for the probability distribution function.

Algorithm 1. Fitting the $SusPro$ distribution function

Require:
$M, A, \mathcal{N}$
Ensure:
$p_N(k, b)$
1: Deploy the probes and obtain forwarding path list.
2: Use a controllable node A as the target node to originate M transactions;
3: Capture the transaction set $\mathbb{T}$ and $\mathcal{T}$;
4: Obtain forwarding path list $\bar{L}_i = \left\{ r_k^{(i)} | (k = 1, 2, ..., l) \right\}$;
5: **if** $r_i \in \mathcal{N}$ **then**
6:     $\sigma_\mathcal{N}(r_i) = 1$;
7: **else**
8:     $\sigma_\mathcal{N}(r_i) = 0$;
9: **end if**
10: **for each** $T_i \in \mathcal{T}$ **do**
11:     Calculate $p_N^*(k)$ by Equation (1);
12: **end for**
13: **for each** $T_i \notin \mathcal{T}$ **do**
14:     Calculate $\bar{p}_N^*(k)$ by Equation (2);
15: **end for**
16: Use Equations (3) to speculate the $SusPro$;
17: According to Equations (4), the loss functions by the square error are selected to fit $p_N(k, b)$;

We leverage the controllable nodes A to simulate originating transactions and extract the pattern of propagation between forwarding nodes in the underlying network. We conduct an analysis of $SusPro$ according to the forwarding path information of the known originating transactions collected by the probe, where the $T_j \in \mathbb{T}$. First of all, we use Eq. (1) to calculate the probability of the position k corresponding to the neighbor node in the originating transaction.

$$p_N^*(k) = \frac{\sum_{j=1}^m \sigma_\mathcal{N}\left(r_k^{(j)}\right) \times \sigma_\mathcal{T}(T_j)}{|\mathcal{T}|} \tag{1}$$

In addition, the T_j stands for transaction j captured by probe. And the $\sigma_N\left(r_k^{(j)}\right)$ is the characteristic function represents the node $r_k^{(j)}$ whether is a neighbor node of the target node, which the k means the node position in forwarding path. In the same way, we define the calculation process of $\bar{p}_N^*(k)$ for non-original transactions as shown in Eq. (2).

$$\bar{p}_N^*(k) = \frac{\sum_{j=1}^{m} \sigma_N\left(r_k^{(j)}\right) \times (1 - \sigma_T(T_j))}{(|\mathbb{T}| - |\mathcal{T}|)} \tag{2}$$

Then, we combine the $p_N^*(k)$ and $\bar{p}_N^*(k)$ to speculate the propagation pattern as the discrete empirical probabilities function $\widetilde{p}_N(k)$. When the neighbor nodes from $\mathcal{T}$ appear in position k of forwarding path list, the function is expressed in Eq. (3).

$$\widetilde{p}_N(k) = \frac{p_N^*(k)}{p_N^*(k) + \bar{p}_N^*(k)} \tag{3}$$

Next, we need to fit appropriate $p_N(k, b)$ according to the distribution of empirical probability $\widetilde{p}_N(k)$. During fitting the $SusPro$, we calculate the square error as the loss function of $p_N(k, b)$, which is shown in Eq. (4).

$$min \sum_{k=1}^{l} (p_N(k, b) - \widetilde{p}_N(k))^2 \tag{4}$$

The Levenberg-Marquardt method is employed to fit the parameter b. Subsequently, we can obtain $p_N(k, b)$ by real-world Bitcoin network. We describe the reliability of $SusPro$ in Sect. 6.2.

4.2   Node Weight Assignment Using Multi-probe

In the actual Bitcoin transaction system, since most nodes will refuse our request to obtain their neighbor nodes, it is difficult to directly obtain the neighbors' information of the target node. Additionally, the neighbor node may be randomly selected to forward the originating transaction, which may cause the low precision of outputting the real originating transactions. If we consider each forwarding node, we can design a model to assign weights to each forwarding node, which is more practical rather than depending on whether the neighbors are forwarding.

We assume that transactions forwarded by important nodes (neighbor nodes) can be presumed to be originating transactions, while transactions forwarded by more important nodes are more like originating transactions. After knowing the $SusPro$ for each position k, if the node at this position is not a neighbor node, we assign the weight w_{r_i} for every node r_i to confirm the degree of importance in the forwarding path list.

Since the monitoring range of a single probe is limited, it is not possibly connected to all nodes in the underlying network. When performing weight assignment, it is impossible to do it for all nodes, which may affect the precision of matching the originating transaction propagation pattern. Therefore, we use a multi-probe (define the p probes) to connect to the whole network, to extract accurate propagation patterns with less training data, and to traverse as many nodes as possible when assigning node weights. We propose a method the focuses on the target node, which is described in Algorithm 2.

At the beginning of Algorithm 2, we let the controllable node connect to the target node with a single point. The information will only be forwarded to the target node when we originate a transaction T_i, which seems that the transaction is originated by the target node. Through analyzing the forwarding path of the transactions captured by the probe p, we can obtain the distance weight $w_{r_v^p}$ from the target node to the other nodes r_v^p.

Before assigning the weights, we need to fit the probability $\hat{p}_N(k, c)$ of the important nodes appearing in different positions in the forwarding path. The effectiveness of the probability is verified in Sect. 6.2. The loss function by calculating the square error is shown in Eq. (5).

$$min \sum_{k=1}^{l} (\hat{p}_N(k, c) - p_N^*(k))^2 \tag{5}$$

After fitting the parameter vector c of $\hat{p}_N(k, c)$, we can define the distance weight of a node r_v^p, as shown in Eq. (6).

$$w_{r_v^p} = \sum_{i=1}^{M} \sum_{k=1}^{l} \left(\sigma_{\{r_v^p\}} \left(\bar{r}_k^{(i)} \right) \times \hat{p}_N(k, c) \right) \tag{6}$$

Obviously, the $w_{r_v^p}$ depends on the $SusPro$ that the node appears in the originating transactions and the frequency of occurrence. And the $SusPro$ needs to be universally applicable to all forwarding transactions. The node appear in more forwarding paths, the cumulative weight is greater. However, if some nodes in the network are not connected, we will not get total transaction forwarding paths in the propagation process. Therefore, multi-probe coordination is needed to obtain more paths for analysis, so that the nodes can be assigned weights more accurately.

However, when there are too many probe nodes, although they can connect to more nodes in the network, they will also cause interference to the network. In our consideration, we only leverage two probes, that is, $p = 2$. By combining the two probes, the amount of test data in the propagation pattern extraction process is reduced, and we will have twice as much analyzable data.

Algorithm 2. Node weight assignment using multi-probe

Require:

M, A, p probes

Ensure:

Node weight set $\mathcal{W} = \left\{ w_{r_i^p} | i = 1, 2, ..., s \right\}$

1: Deploy the probe p, use another controllable node connect to the target node A with a single point to originate M transactions;

2: Capture transaction set $\mathcal{T}$;

3: Obtain forwarding path list set $\{\bar{L}_i^p\}$ by probe p, $\bar{L}_i = \left\{ r_k^{(i)} | (k = 1, 2, ..., l) \right\}$;

4: Take Equation (5) to fit the probability $\hat{p}_N(k, c)$;

5: **for each** p in $\mathcal{P} = \{1, 2, ..., p_{max}\}$ **do**

6:     **for each** $\bar{L}_i^p$ in $\{\bar{L}_i^p\}$ **do**

7:         $\mathcal{R} \leftarrow \mathcal{R} \cup \bar{L}_i^p$

8:     **end for**

9:     Get the IP address set $\mathcal{R} = \{r_v^p | v = 1, 2, ..., s\}$;

10:    Calculate the node weight $w_{r_v^p}$ according to Equation (6);

11: **end for**

12: Get the node weight set $\mathcal{W}$ of captured nodes;

4.3 Matching Score Calculation

The precision of weight assignment to the nodes is higher when there are more nodes connected to the probes. Therefore, in the scenario of multi-probe monitoring Bitcoin transactions, we can improve the precision of the final score by combining multi-probe to evaluate the same transaction.

In order to accurately evaluate whether a transaction is an originating transaction, we use the *SusPro* and the weight $w_{r_i^p}$ of the node corresponding to a certain position k to calculate the matching score. When the matching score of a transaction is high, the transaction is closer to the propagation pattern we extracted, and it is more likely to be the originating transaction.

Matching scores of the transaction is not only based on binarization whether it is forwarded by neighbor nodes, but is also determined by the node weight between the target and other nodes. For a transaction T_i that remains unknown whether it is originated by the target node, we calculate its matching score based on the $p_N(k, b)$ by extracting the propagation pattern and weight of the nodes who forwarded the transactions captured. The method of calculating the matching score S_{T_i} of a transaction T_i for probe p is shown in Eq. (7).

$$S_{T_i}^{(p)} = \left(\prod_{k=1}^{l} \left(1 - p_N(k, b) \times w_{r_k^{(i)}} / \|\mathcal{W}\|_\infty \right) \right)^{-1} \tag{7}$$

Where $\|.\|_\infty$ represents the infinite norm of a vector consisting of all the elements in a set. The $S_{T_i}^{(p)}$ reaches which score can be outputted as the originating transaction will be depended on threshold selection.

After node weight assignment, we propose the calculation method of the matching score by combining the node weights. Since the accuracy of the node weight depends on the number and quality of nodes connected in the network (i.e., the degree of importance or proximity to the target node), the node weight assignment using multi-probe can be applied to the matching score calculation.

However, considering the more nodes connected to the probe, the more likely the weight assignment is to match the real situation, we will homogenize each probe to the same transaction and multiply it by a scale factor, and then combine it as the final matching score of a single transaction. The calculation of combining the multi-probe is presented in Eq. (8). Where the p represents the node weight are depended on the probe p.

$$S_{T_i} = \frac{1}{\sum_{p=1}^{p_{max}} c_p} \left(\sum_{p=1}^{p_{max}} c_p S_{T_i}^{(p)} \right) \tag{8}$$

There are four main factors affecting the result: the network delay t_λ, the routing distance from the target node to other nodes t_{d_1}, the routing distance from these nodes to the probe node t_{d_2}, and the random delay of transaction forwarding t_ε. The time interval t from the time when transaction originating to the time that the probe node receives the transaction can be expressed as shown in Eq. (9):

$$t = t_\lambda + t_{d_1} + t_{d_2} + t_\varepsilon \tag{9}$$

It can be seen that the network delay is stable and the node network relationship is unchanged, the time interval of the same node can be regarded as applying a random disturbance on a fixed interval. This model is suitable for situations where nodes do not change neighbor nodes frequently in a short time.

5   Associated Address Clustering Optimization Model

In the process of speculating the originating transaction, the controllable node may be used to send multiple transactions using a single point connection with the target node. We can record the hash of originating transactions, then select a suitable threshold with a better accuracy rate and a transaction recall rate based on the score. However, due to the fact that there are many uncontrollable factors in the real network environment, we recommend that the threshold should be used according to the actual situation. Even so, the target node may not be connected by the probe, so it is still having difficulty in threshold selection or selection failure when judging the originating transaction. In the following, we will give a way to bypass the threshold to output the originating transaction.

5.1   Clustering Using Associate Addresses

Original bitcoin whitepaper [1] has been indicated that the addresses used as an input to a transaction can be cluster together. The goal of the method coincides

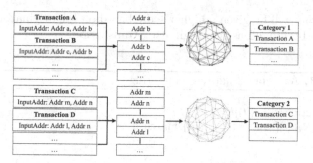

Fig. 4. The example of optimizing the output with associated address clustering. Suppose the transaction A have two inputs with Addr a and Addr b, and the transaction B with inputs Addr b and Addr c. When the probe captured these two transactions, they will be clustered to Category 1 according to that they have the same inputs Addr b, and the same as Category 2. By parity of reasoning, we aggregate the associated transactions into a single category until there is no longer any association between the categories.

with the goal we want to match the transaction address to the target node, so the focus of optimization from the suspicion of a single transaction to a relationship between all the suspected transactions.

The core of the associated address clustering optimization is to use the address clustering to filter abnormal transactions and improve accuracy. When we backtracked blocks in a month, the clustering relationship can be defined as follows: **1)** when multiple addresses are sent to one or more addresses, the addresses of multiple inputs are determined to be one class, **2)** in zero-input transactions, the output addresses are in one class (i.e., miners mining transaction), **3)** in the case of overlapping addresses between one class and another class, the two classes are combined into one class.

The example of clustering using associate addresses as shown in Fig. 4.

There is no need to empirically choose the threshold for the transaction score. It is possible to find real-origin transactions but lower scores due to the unstable factors, which can increase the recall rate. And it is possible to filter out non-origin transactions with higher scores due to unstable factors, which can increase the accuracy. To meet the high accuracy requirements, we use a single input address clustering algorithm, which is the most accurate clustering algorithm from others. The algorithm description as shown in Algorithm 3.

Under Algorithm 3, we have the class label for each transaction. Suppose a Bitcoin user often uses the same IP address and the same associate Bitcoin addresses to send a transaction. In this way, we can take association address clustering to divide the multiple transactions captured by a probe into multiple classes and mark these classes. In addition, if different transactions in a class are captured multiple times, then the class has a higher probability of being the class corresponding to the real originator. Furthermore, if the two suspected transactions for the same input address have a clustering relationship, then the two transactions will be given a higher score based on the original score, and are more likely to be judged as the originating transaction.

Algorithm 3. Associated address clustering

Require:

One set transaction $\mathbb{T} = \{T_i | i = 1, 2, ..., n\}$

Input address $\mathcal{R}_i = \{\gamma_s | s = 1, 2, ..., m\}$ matched

transaction T_i

Ensure:

Class label $\mathcal{U} = \{\mho_{T_1}, \mho_{T_2}, ..., \mho_{T_n}\}$ matched for

transaction T_i

 1: **for each** $T_i \in \mathbb{T}$ **do**

 2:      $\mho_{T_i} \leftarrow i$

 3: **end for**

 4: **for each** $i \in [1, n]$ **do**

 5:      **for each** $j \in [i + 1, n]$ **do**

 6:          **if** $\mathcal{R}_i \cap \mathcal{R}_j \neq \oslash$ **then**

 7:             $Target \leftarrow \mho_{Tj}$

 8:             **for each** $T_k \in \mathbb{T}$ **do**

 9:                 **if** $\mho_{T_k} = Target$ **then**

10:                    $\mho_{T_k} \leftarrow \mho_{T_i}$

11:                 **end if**

12:             **end for**

13:          **end if**

14:      **end for**

15: **end for**

5.2 Outputting the Classes Through Normalization

Transaction clustering based on the associated address can effectively reduce the scale of false positives without using the threshold output method. According to the input address of the transaction, there will be overlapping rules for clustering, and the class score will be calculated according to the matching score of each transaction.

If the cluster score only depends on the score of a single transaction in the class, when the total number of transactions is large enough, there may be a large number of abnormal (with a high score) transactions in the small-scale class, resulting in the final class score abnormally high. Therefore, under this clustering rule, some small-scale classes are not effective enough to make their scores normal. When the class size increases, it is foreseeable that the abnormally scored transactions will be stable at a smaller scale. So we introduce a regularization in the cluster score, and the class size will have an impact on the final score.

After we obtain the *SusPro* corresponding to the target node represented by $p_N(k, b)$ and the weight $\mathcal{W}$ of each node, we will conduct the clustering. The hybrid method to output the suspected transaction class as shown in Algorithm 4.

In order to make the class scale also be used as an element in the calculation of the class score, we take the average score of a transaction in a class to multiply the natural logarithm of the number of elements in this class as the final class score. After obtaining the score for each transaction, the score S_i of each transaction class u is calculated according to Eq. 10, where $T_j \in C_{luster_i}$, $|C_{luster_i}| = N$.

$$S_i = \frac{1}{N} \sum_{j=1}^{N} S_{T_i} \cdot \ln N = \frac{\ln N}{N} \sum_{j=1}^{N} S_{T_i} \tag{10}$$

However, where a class with a large average class size may be filtered out, and when the number of transactions generated by the user is not enough, the accuracy is lowered. Therefore, it is necessary to do a step of screening before regularization, that is, regularization is only performed for classes with higher average scores, but not for classes with large scales but low average scores. Then, a class with a high final matching score will be output.

The method can effectively avoid the occurrence of high-scoring non-original transactions in the small scale class, which would make the class scores highly, and finally determines the failure of the originating transaction class. And the average score can effectively avoid the significant deviation of the class score caused by the abnormality of individual transaction scores in the large scale class. In order to make the difference of the transaction to be more obvious, we normalize the average score that converts the number to a decimal between $(0, 1)$ and gets transaction with a significantly higher score. We consider that the transaction with the highest score is the originating transaction of the target node, and the inputs of these transactions are the associate Bitcoin addresses of the target node.

Algorithm 4. Transaction originating decision

Require:
$p_N(k, b)$, $p_N^*(k)$ obtained in Algorithm 1
Time of duration t_s during one *session*
Ensure:
Score set $\mathbb{S} = \{S_i | i \in \mathcal{U}\}$ of one transaction class
1: **while** begin one *session* **do**
2:     Get $\mathcal{W}$ from algorithm 2;
3:     Use probe to catch transaction continued for t_s;
4: **end while**
5: Obtain a set of transactions $\mathbb{T}$ captured by the probe, and the transaction T_i corresponding to the input address $\mathcal{R}_i$, forwarding path list;
6: Clustering the transaction $\mathbb{T}$ captured according to Algorithm 3, then obtain the class label $\mho_{T_i}$ corresponding to each transaction T_i;
7: Get the class label set $\mathcal{U} = \{u_e | e = 1, 2, ...z, \}$;
8: Calculate score S_{T_i} of transactions according to Equation (8);
9: Obtain S_i of transaction classes according to Equation (10);

---

6   Performance Evaluation

In this section, we evaluate the performance of the proposed method, including the preliminary in Sect. 6.1, the evaluation of propagation pattern effectiveness in Sect. 6.2, the comparison of identifying precision in Sect. 6.3, the overhead of the deanonymization in Sect. 6.4, and the evaluation of cross-layer analysis and single-layer method in Sect. 6.5.

6.1   Preliminary

Method to Compare. In order to present a comprehensive understanding of the contribution of our approach, we employed the method proposed by A. Biryukov et al. [5] for comparison, which is referred to as **Neigh** hereafter. The method needs to be under the connection with all the nodes in the whole network, which also needs to mark six neighbor nodes of each target node. According to the position of nodes in forwarding path list, if three neighbor nodes appear in the top ten positions, the transaction is considered to be an originating transaction.

The method we proposed uses data analytics to realize the Bitcoin transactions deanonymization. We proposed a model combined with the probability distribution function fitting and the node weight assignment, which is referred to as **Prow** hereafter. To avoid interference with the Bitcoin system, we only conduct experiments on one target node.

To ensure data authenticity and universality, the partial transactions are originated during the dispersed time period of one day, and different neighbors are selected between different sessions.

Experimental Settings. In our experiments, we use two controllable nodes to verify the effectiveness of the method. The controllable node A is used as the target node under a real network environment. Another controllable node B was used to originate transactions to calculate the probability distribution of neighbor nodes. A probe node was adopted in the experiment to monitor the Bitcoin network and collect the forwarding information to obtain forwarding list. Among them, the probe node deploys the crawling program, which can effectively collect the transaction information forwarded in the underlying network. The controllable nodes deploy the Bitcoin client, which can independently create the transaction and check the information of the neighboring nodes.

6.2   Evaluation of Propagation Pattern Effectiveness

In our preliminary considerations, In order to accurately identify whether a transaction is originated by the target, we need to verify whether the $p_N(k, b)$ is universal in the real network. We calculate the $p_N^*(k)$ of neighbor nodes and fit its parameters through experiments as followed.

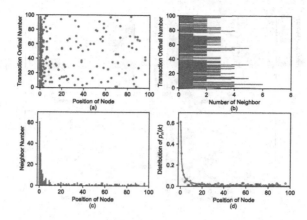

Fig. 5. The distribution of neighbors appearing in each location. The (a) shows the position where the neighbor appears in the list of 100 transactions, (b) shows the number of neighbors in the forwarding path list of 100 transactions, (c) shows the number of neighbors appearing in each position in the list, and (d) shows the probability of neighbors appearing in each position in the list.

If we know a controllable node A and a probe node, we first use A to originate 100 transactions as different groups in different time periods intermittently. And we know the neighbor nodes of the controllable nodes in these groups of transactions. When the probe monitors the network, we obtain the forwarding path lists and have received more than 120,000 pens transactions forwarded by all nodes. Based on the position of known neighbors in the known forwarding list, we calculate the probability of neighbors appearing in each location as shown in Fig. 5.

According to the probability of neighbors appearing in each position, we find the higher the position in the forwarding list, the more probably it is the neighbor node. Therefor, we assume the inverse function $\hat{p}_N(k,c)$ in the Eq. (11). Then, we can obtain the $c_1 = 0.3963$, $c_2 = -0.3601$, $c_3 = -0.0005$.

$$\hat{p}_N(k,c) = \frac{c_1}{k - c_2} - c_3 \tag{11}$$

In view of the feasibility of the neighbor probability in the forwarding list, we select 3,000 transactions that are not in our originating transactions. We count the $\bar{p}_N^*(k)$ distribution of our neighbor nodes in the forwarding path list, and the result can be found in Fig. 6.

Similarly, we describe the probability of neighbors appearing in each position in non-originating transaction as $\hat{p}_N(k,d)$. We assume the exponential function to fit the parameter d as presented in Eq. (12). We obtain the $d_1 = 0.0081$, $d_2 = 56.5202$, $d_3 = -0.0321$.

$$\hat{p}_N(k,d) = d_1 \times ln(k + d_2) + d_3 \tag{12}$$

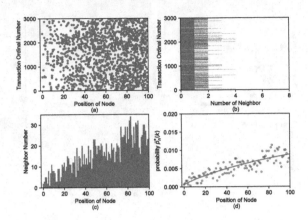

Fig. 6. The distribution of known neighbors appearing in each location in non-originating transaction.

Under the Eq. (11) and Eq. (12), we can calculate the probability of whether the transaction is originated when neighbor nodes appear in a certain position in the forwarding list. Then, we describe the function $p_N(k, b)$ as shown in Eq. (13).

$$p_N(k, b) = \frac{\hat{p}_N(k, c)}{\hat{p}_N(k, c) + \hat{p}_N(k, d)} \tag{13}$$

According to the transaction collection and probability analytics in the real Bitcoin network, the probability distribution of the originating and non-originating transactions is matched with the *SusPro* in the suspected probability calculation model.

In order to prove that the probability of the neighbor nodes appearing in different positions is not randomly selected, which are used in the node weight assignment model and refer to the $p_N^*(k)$. We select sixty transactions in six time periods of a day, as shown in (a) of Fig. 7.

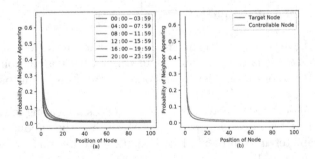

Fig. 7. Feasibility analysis of the $p_N^*(k)$ distribution in different time of the day and different nodes in current network.

The result demonstrates that the $p_N^*(k)$ distribution of different times is similar to each other. Almost the same result through conducting experiments of each time period of the day proves that the $p_N^*(k)$ distribution is applicable to any time of the day.

At the same time, in order to prove that the probability is applicable to other nodes connected in the current network, we choose the other controllable node which is used to simulate the target node. In the same network, we analyze the known transactions from the two nodes and check the neighbors of them. Then, we select forty transactions separately to compare the $p_N^*(k)$ distribution as shown in (b) of the Fig. 7. The result shows that the probability distribution is similar to each other. As a result, we can reasonably apply the $p_N^*(k)$ distribution of the controllable node to the target node.

6.3   Comparison of Precision

This experiment aims to compare the **Neigh** method with our **Prow** method in terms of precision and recall rate by outputting the originating transactions. In the existing studies, all the nodes in the Bitcoin network need to be continuously connected when the probe collects information, which may cause network congestion on the Bitcoin network. However, there is no need to consider the different resource requirements. As a result, we only use probes to connect a part of nodes.

We assume that the two methods have the same transaction propagation paths, through which, we can obtain the neighbor node information accurately. In order to implement the previous method, we mark the six neighbors of the target node. If the top ten of the forwarding path list has three neighbors, we output the suspected originating transactions. Additionally, we obtain the matching score of each transaction through our method. Besides, we output the originating transactions that over the threshold θ. For different requirements, we can select different θ referring to the ROC curve. In this experiment, we selected 0.075 to be the threshold, which ensures the precision rather than the recall rate.

In order to clearly compare the two methods, we select six rounds of experimental transaction data for conducting comprehensive analytics. The number of transactions per round is recorded. On average, the probe received 5,925 transactions on each round of experiments. We estimate the precision and recall rate of two methods on average of six rounds.

As shown in Table 3, the precision reached up to 81.3% and the recall rate was 26.3%. In the case of the same network environment and experimental settings, the precision was 51.3% and the recall rate was 24.8% through the application of the previous method. Although rarely correct transactions are found in the previous method, it represents that the strategy can ignore most abnormal transactions. Comparing the precision and the recall rate of the previous method, we can find that our method has higher precision.

Our method has the advantage that we do not depend on the network environment and neighbors. It is difficult to guarantee continuous connection to the

Table 3. Comparison of our method and existing studies

Rounds	Transactions	Precision (%)		Recall (%)	
		Prow	Neigh	Prow	Neigh
1	5159	100	67	18	30
2	4978	100	60	20	15
3	5821	86	89	30	35
4	8703	27	22	40	20
5	6276	75	50	30	19
6	4614	100	20	20	30

whole network, and there are some non-originating transactions and some uncontrollable forwarded transactions in the real environment. Therefore, we may get an inaccurate forwarding path list when the neighbor node forwards with random delay. Especially, our method is dependent on the weight of the node. We calculate the whole forwarding node rather than the neighbors who may not be connected.

6.4   Evaluation of Overhead

In this section, we evaluate the network interference caused by the process of calculating *SusPro*, and find the balance between lower cost and higher precision.

In order to find the transaction with the highest matching score, we need to fit the appropriate $p_N(k, b)$. As the target node may not be connected, we mainly evaluate the $\widetilde{p}_N(k)$ according to Eq. (3). In the definition of Eq. (1) and (2), it is required $p_N^*(k)$ and $\bar{p}_N^*(k)$, which is calculated from the originating transactions and all captured transactions. In the procedure to obtain $p_N^*(k)$, we need to originate some transactions, which may cause the network interference. Consequently, we design experiments to find a balance between lower interference and higher precision.

To simplify the procedure of fitting the parameter b, we need to fit it according to the parameter c in Eq. (5). Assuming the $c = (c_1, c_2, c_3)$, the $p_N(k, b)$ may be the most suitable function for high precision to calculate the matching score when c_1, c_2, c_3 are determined. We use 80 originating transactions in total to fit the 3 parameters and the result is shown in Fig. 8.

As shown in the Fig. 8, when the number of transactions reaches 50, the parameters c_1 and c_2 tend to be stable. That is, the probability distribution is no longer affected by other factors. Thus, it is in the balance between lower cost and higher precision, which is more practical than we justified in Sect. 4.2. Additionally, it is also more practical than the existed method which needs to connect all the node in the network to collect transactions.

Among them, we found that the Bitcoin system will no longer allow the transaction to be forwarded when the number of transactions reaches 24 in each round. Therefore, we take 8 rounds to test with 10 transactions per round. During

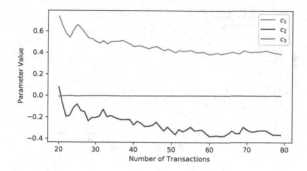

Fig. 8. Evaluation of the balance between lower interference and higher precision.

the analysis, we find that when we reduce the number of transactions per round, the parameters will be greatly affected by the network delay and cause unstable fluctuations. As a result, it is recommended that we can use more transactions per round but less than 24 to fit the suitable parameters. The result means that the cost of learning the pattern matching model is 40 transactions, and it only takes one day in terms of time cost. Different topological networks need to be established for different source nodes, and different propagation mode models can be trained.

6.5 Effectiveness of Clustering in Cross-Layer Analysis

In this section, we will show that the clustering plays a crucial role in improving the accuracy and recall rate in cross-layer analysis. We define the method without clustering named *Naive Threshold*, and we take the total number of originated transactions as the prior threshold θ. Then we output the top θ transactions of the matching score as the suspected originating transaction to calculate the accuracy and recall rate. At this time, the accuracy is equal to its recall rate.

Refer to clustering, the class with the highest score is used as the suspected transaction class, and the transactions in it are the suspected originating transactions. Compare to the *Native Threshold*, the accuracy is 100% when the recall rate is not 0%, so the accuracy of clustering is constantly grater, which will increase the accuracy to 100% in most cases.

Therefore, we simulate the target to originate transactions by 5 rounds, and 10 transactions per round, which means the $\theta = 10$. And we only compare the recall rate between the two methods to output the suspected transactions. As shown in Fig. 9, it can be seen that the recall rate is significantly improved after using the clustering, so the clustering plays an important role in our method.

Obviously, in the evaluation we can cluster transactions together, there is random use of duplicate addresses or single-input addresses. If each transaction with a single input, then a large number of transactions will be required to realize clustering.

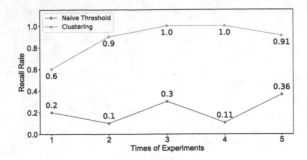

Fig. 9. Comparison the recall rate of the *native threshold* and clustering.

However, we will take block #557916 in the Bitcoin network as an example to illustrate that transaction clustering is widespread in the Bitcoin system. There are a totally 2,824 transactions in this block, and after we use the clustering method, there are 1,006 transactions with a clustering relationship, and finally obtain 195 classes with more than 2 transactions. The average number of transactions in each of these classes was 5, and there are up to 17 transactions in one class.

Therefore, we are reasonably simulating the real Bitcoin trading scenario and further confirm that the clustering can optimize the matching results, which is suitable for most target nodes to find its originating transactions.

7   Discussion

We proposed a cross-layer method to realize Bitcoin transactions deanonymization. Our method may reveal the privacy of Bitcoin users. The following suggestions are put forward for protecting the privacy and resisting traceability: 1) Bitcoin peers can make deals in a private network such as Tor, the originating IP address, and the originating transactions have been hidden layer by layer. 2) Bitcoin users can select a single address to send a transaction. Besides, they can also back up Bitcoin address with multiple IPs, which may reduce the fitting precision of the $p_N^*(k)$ distribution. 3) The users can send each transaction by changing several neighbors during a single session, which may effectively reduce the precision of node weight assignment.

On the other hand, we have gotten the originating transaction class of one IP address belongs to the target trader. We judge that the input address is the originating address through each transaction, so we can match the transaction address and IP address of the Bitcoin trader, which achieve the identification of originator. When conditions permit, many address classes can be obtained in the whole Bitcoin network. By monitoring the transactions of these address classes, when we obtain the $p_N^*(k)$ distribution, and the node with the highest score is found according to the node weight model, then we can consider the node as the suspected originating node.

8   Conclusion

In this paper, we proposed an effective method to realize the deanonymization of large-scale Bitcoin transactions based on cross-layer data analytics. By employing the matching score calculation via propagation pattern speculation and associated addresses clustering, we could output the originating Bitcoin transactions from large-scale captured transactions. The experimental results showed that the proposed method is more practical compare with the existing methods in terms of precision and resource utilization. In addition, we reduced the deviation caused by network dynamics, and cross-layer data analysis is more practical than single-level traceability. In future work, we will find the IP address by tracking the related transactions with the node weight assignment model or other more efficient methods.

Acknowledgment. This work is partially supported by National Key R&D Program of China with No. 2020YFB1006100, China National Funds for Excellent Young Scientists with No. 62222201, Beijing Nova Program with Nos. Z201100006820006 and 20220484174, NSFC Project with No. 61972039, Beijing Natural Science Foundation with Nos. M23020, L222098 and 7232041.

References

1. Nakamoto, S.: Bitcoin: a peer-to-peer electronic cash system. Decentralized Bus. Rev. 21260 (2008)
2. Cap, C.M.: Cryptocurrency market capitalizations—coinmarketcap (2019). Accessed 15 Jan 2019
3. Foley, S., Karlsen, J.R., Putniņš, T.J.: Sex, drugs, and bitcoin: how much illegal activity is financed through cryptocurrencies? Rev. Financ. Stud. **32**(5), 1798–1853 (2019)
4. Kaminsky, D.: Black OPS of TCP/IP. Black Hat USA 44 (2011)
5. Biryukov, A., Khovratovich, D., Pustogarov, I.: Deanonymisation of clients in bitcoin P2P network. In: Proceedings of the 2014 ACM SIGSAC Conference on Computer and Communications Security, pp. 15–29 (2014)
6. Narayanan, A., Shmatikov, V.: Robust de-anonymization of large sparse datasets. In: 2008 IEEE Symposium on Security and Privacy (S&P 2008), 18–21 May 2008, Oakland, California, USA, pp. 111–125. IEEE Computer Society (2008)
7. DuPont, J., Squicciarini, A.C.: Toward de-anonymizing bitcoin by mapping users location. In: Proceedings of the 5th ACM Conference on Data and Application Security and Privacy, pp. 139–141 (2015)
8. Meiklejohn, S., et al.: A fistful of bitcoins: characterizing payments among men with no names. In: Proceedings of the 2013 Conference on Internet Measurement Conference, pp. 127–140 (2013)
9. Kappos, G., Yousaf, H., Stütz, R., Rollet, S., Haslhofer, B., Meiklejohn, S.: How to peel a million: validating and expanding bitcoin clusters. In: 31st USENIX Security Symposium (USENIX Security 2022), pp. 2207–2223 (2022)
10. Shen, M., Duan, J., Shang, N., Zhu, L.: Transaction deanonymization in large-scale bitcoin systems via propagation pattern analysis. In: Yu, S., Mueller, P., Qian, J. (eds.) SPDE 2020. CCIS, vol. 1268, pp. 661–675. Springer, Singapore (2020). https://doi.org/10.1007/978-981-15-9129-7_45

11. McMillan, R.: How bitcoin lets you spy on careless companies. wired.co.uk (2014)
12. Kroll, J.A., Davey, I.C., Felten, E.W.: The economics of bitcoin mining, or bitcoin in the presence of adversaries. In: Proceedings of WEIS, vol. 2013. Citeseer (2013)
13. Ron, D., Shamir, A.: Quantitative analysis of the full bitcoin transaction graph. In: Sadeghi, A.-R. (ed.) FC 2013. LNCS, vol. 7859, pp. 6–24. Springer, Heidelberg (2013). https://doi.org/10.1007/978-3-642-39884-1_2
14. Yang, B., Garcia-Molina, H.: PPay: micropayments for peer-to-peer systems. In: Proceedings of the 10th ACM Conference on Computer and Communications Security, pp. 300–310 (2003)
15. Reid, F., Harrigan, M.: An analysis of anonymity in the bitcoin system. In: PASSAT/SocialCom 2011, Privacy, Security, Risk and Trust (PASSAT), 2011 IEEE Third International Conference on and 2011 IEEE Third International Conference on Social Computing (SocialCom), Boston, pp. 1318–1326 (2011)
16. Liao, K., Zhao, Z., Doupé, A., Ahn, G.-J.: Behind closed doors: measurement and analysis of cryptolocker ransoms in bitcoin. In: 2016 APWG Symposium on Electronic Crime Research (eCrime), pp. 1–13 (2016). IEEE
17. Remy, C., Rym, B., Matthieu, L.: Tracking bitcoin users activity using community detection on a network of weak signals. In: Cherifi, C., Cherifi, H., Karsai, M., Musolesi, M. (eds.) COMPLEX NETWORKS 2017 2017. SCI, vol. 689, pp. 166–177. Springer, Cham (2018). https://doi.org/10.1007/978-3-319-72150-7_14
18. Koshy, P., Koshy, D., McDaniel, P.: An analysis of anonymity in bitcoin using P2P network traffic. In: Christin, N., Safavi-Naini, R. (eds.) FC 2014. LNCS, vol. 8437, pp. 469–485. Springer, Heidelberg (2014). https://doi.org/10.1007/978-3-662-45472-5_30
19. Biryukov, A., Pustogarov, I.: Bitcoin over tor isn't a good idea. In: 2015 IEEE Symposium on Security and Privacy, SP 2015, 17–21 May 2015, San Jose, pp. 122–134 (2015)
20. Tran, M., Choi, I., Moon, G.J., Vu, A.V., Kang, M.S.: A stealthier partitioning attack against bitcoin peer-to-peer network. In: 2020 IEEE Symposium on Security and Privacy, San Francisco, pp. 894–909. IEEE (2020)
21. Heilman, E., Kendler, A., Zohar, A., Goldberg, S.: Eclipse attacks on bitcoin's peer-to-peer network. In: 24th {USENIX} Security Symposium ({USENIX} Security 2015), pp. 129–144 (2015)

Robust Online Crowdsourcing with Strategic Workers

Bolei Zhang$^{(\boxtimes)}$, Jingtao Zhang, Lifa Wu, and Fu Xiao

School of Computer, Nanjing University of Posts and Telecommunications,
Nanjing 210046, China
{bolei.zhang,b20032220,wulifa,xiaof}@njupt.edu.cn

Abstract. Crowdsourcing has facilitated a wide range of applications by leveraging public workers to contribute large number of tasks. However, most prior works only considered static environments and overlooked the system dynamics. In practice, the task set to be allocated is time-varying and the workers may be strategic when deciding whether to accept the tasks. In this paper, we formulate the online crowdsourcing problem as a sequential optimization problem, where a requestor needs to allocate tasks repeatedly to the workers to maximize the long-term cumulative utility. To deal with the dynamics, we first build an environmental model to predict the system dynamics. The model can also embed the tasks into a fixed lower-dimensional space. Next, we propose a multi-agent reinforcement learning algorithm to optimize the allocation mechanism for the requestor. The underlying intuition is that the mechanism can be robust even with adversarial workers. In the experiment, we conducted extensive experiments to evaluate the performance. The results validate that our method can achieve the best performance in almost all cases. The results are robust when deployed in an adversarial environment.

Keywords: Crowdsourcing · Reinforcement Learning · Adversarial Policy Optimization · Strategic Workers

1 Introduction

Crowdsourcing, which leverages the power of dispersed participants for contributing services, has been adopted in a variety of applications, such as image labeling, spatial-temporal environment sensing, and data gathering. The crowdsourcing mechanism generally involves allocating *a large number of tasks* to *public groups of workers*, which is a double-edged sword: On one hand, it has the advantage of low costs, high flexibility and diversity; On the other hand, the dynamics from the tasks and workers also bring unpredictability and uncertainties.

In a typical crowdsourcing scenario (depicted in Fig. 2), the platform has a large time-varying set of tasks to be allocated. Public workers may arrive asynchronously at the platform. When a worker arrives, the requestor should allocate one of the tasks to the worker, along with some monetary payment as

© The Author(s), under exclusive license to Springer Nature Singapore Pte Ltd. 2024
C. Li et al. (Eds.): APPT 2023, LNCS 14103, pp. 417–433, 2024.
https://doi.org/10.1007/978-981-99-7872-4_23

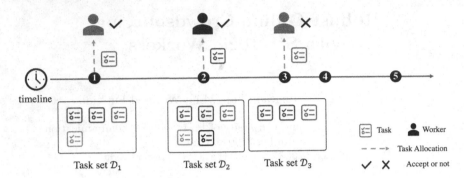

Fig. 1. An illustration of the crowdsourcing process.

incentives. The worker can then decide whether to finish the task, based on the task difficulty and amount of incentives. The requestor's objective is to allocate the tasks for high quality and low payment. Prior works have adopted methods such as combinatorics [3,15], reverse auctions [8,13], and game-theory [17,23]. As the tasks can be allocated repeatedly, recent works are also considering online learning algorithms such as reinforcement learning (RL) [5], so that the long-term cumulative utility can be maximized.

Despite the progresses that were made, most prior works have either assumed static worker cost or invariable task set. In practice, both the task set and the worker costs can be dynamic. As presented in Fig. 1, tasks can be added to or removed from the task set, and the workers may be strategic or even adversarial against the requestor to make decisions. Such scenarios pose significant challenges for optimal crowdsourcing, as historical allocation experience can not be utilized directly. In online crowdsourcing, understanding the environment dynamics is crucial for an optimal allocation: On one hand, the requestor should determine how to allocate new tasks based on task semantics. On the other hand, it is critical to infer the workers' strategies for a robust allocation.

In this work, we propose a model-based RL algorithm for robust online task allocation in crowdsourcing. The main idea is to build a variational environmental model, and query with this model to optimize the allocation mechanism. The model can predict the environment dynamics with supervised learning. It also encodes the tasks to a fixed-size embedding space, so that the RL can allocate variable task set. The objective is then formulated as a two-player max-min game between the requestor and the workers. By optimizing the objective, the requestor's allocation mechanism can be robust even with adversarial workers. Under the supervised environmental model, it is natural to adopt "centralized training, decentralized execution" (CTDE) framework to optimize the requestor's allocation policy.

Extensive experiments are conducted to validate the effectiveness of our approach. We first show that our algorithm can converge steadily in the training phase. In the execution phase, our algorithm can still outperform other baselines significantly. We also validate the performance of our algorithm w.r.t different values of the hyper-parameters. The results show that: 1) With stronger adversarialness from the workers, our algorithm can still be robust and have high performance; 2) The transition model has high accuracy when predicting the system dynamics.

The main contributions can be summarized as:

- We formulate the crowdsourcing problem with strategic workers as a two-player max-min problem, where the workers are assumed to be adversarial against the requestor.
- We propose a variational environment model to predict system dynamics. The model can also embed the tasks to a lower fixed-dimension space.
- Under the environmental model, we adopt the multi-agent SAC to find the optimal robust crowdsourcing mechanism.
- Extensive evaluations demonstrated that our algorithm can have high performance across different system settings.

The rest of this paper is organized as follows. We first introduce the related works in Sect. 2. Next, we present the preliminaries and formulate as a max-min optimization problem in Sect. 3 and Sect. 4. Our method is presented in Sect. 5. The experiments are conducted in Sect. 6. Finally, we conclude our paper in Sect. 7.

2   Related Work

Crowdsourcing has attracted enormous attentions in recent years, due to its flexibility and cost-efficiency. One of the key challenges in crowdsourcing is to optimally allocate the tasks to recruit high quality workers with low payment. A lot of effort has been devoted to designing efficient incentive mechanisms [19,20], such as auction mechanism [11,13], dynamic pricing [14,22], deep reinforcement learning [5,10]. The related works have studied how to allocate tasks, ensure task qualities and select appropriate workers. Now we briefly review the related literature in this field.

When allocating tasks, Alabbadi et al. [1] proposed a task scheduling model based on multi-objective optimization. Their method can efficiently allocate tasks in spatial crowdsourcing. Zhao et al. [23] used a game-theoretical method for fair task allocation. They adopted improved evolution game theory to minimize the difference between the returns. For ensuring the task qualities, Niu et al. [12] proposed a machine learning approach for ensuring the task qualities. Their method can eliminate the noisy input from the environment and the sensor devices. Lu et al. [12] proposed a multi-objective worker selection algorithm. Moreover, they designed an enhanced evolution algorithm for efficient mobile crowdsensing. For incentive mechanisms, Chi et al. [4] adopted a multi-strategy repeated game for incentivizing the workers, so that the workers can provide long-term high quality tasks. These works focused on matching the workers with the tasks, and often ignored the workers' willingness for accepting the tasks.

As the worker costs are often private, auction mechanism has been widely considered, where the workers first bid a cost for completing the task, and the platform assigns the tasks based on the bids. Yang et al. [21] designed an auction-based incentive mechanism, which is computationally efficient, individually rational, profitable, and truthful. Wang et al. [18] integrated multi-attribute auction and two-stage auction to maximize the platform utility. One key advantage of auction mechanism is that it can help to ensure that tasks can be assigned at their true market value, which reduces the risk of underpricing or overpricing. However, auctions are usually complex and time-consuming, and may not be suitable for crowdsourcing with large number of tasks and workers.

In the pricing mechanism, the requestor directly sets prices (payments) for each task, and the workers can choose whether to accept the payment. As the requestor and the workers make sequential decisions, the problem is often modeled as a Stackelberg game. Under this model, Yang et al. [21] addressed this scenario and modeled the platform as the leader for pricing, and the workers as the follower. Tong et al. [16] proposed a matching-based approach to deal with the uncertainty of the true supply in spatial crowdsourcing. Miao et al. [14] proposed a dynamic pricing mechanism that leveraged a deep time sequence model to learn the effect of bonuses on workers' quality for crowd tasks. Most dynamic pricing mechanisms only considered the sequential behaviors of the requestor, and overlooked the sequential behaviors of the workers.

Due to the dynamics of the environment and worker valuations, recent works are considering online learning algorithms such as multi-armed bandit (MAB) and RL. An et al. [2] adopted MAB method to select workers to improve service quality. However, their algorithm neglected the effect of the decisions on the system state. While in RL, the next state must also be considered when making decisions. Liu et al. [9] used RL for mobile crowdsensing, where the objective is to maximize the energy efficiency, data collection ratio, and geographic fairness, while minimizing energy consumption simultaneously. Zhu et al. [24] optimize the mechanism by first predicting the mobility of vehicles. However, the dynamics of the candidate task set and the strategic behaviors of the workers were seldom considered. In practice, the set of tasks is often regarded as the agent action, and it can be difficult to deal with dynamic action space in RL. Moreover, the strategic behaviors of the workers may lead to non-stationary of the requestor's decision process.

3 Preliminaries

3.1 Markov Decision Process

In RL, the environment is often modeled as a Markov Decision Process (MDP), which can be represented as a set of tuples $\mathcal{M} = \langle \mathcal{S}, \mathcal{O}, \mathcal{A}, \mathcal{R}, \mu_0, \gamma \rangle$, where $\mathcal{S}$ is the state space; The observation $\mathcal{O}$ is a subset of the state: $\mathcal{O} \subseteq \mathcal{S}$; $\mathcal{A}$ is the action space; $\mathcal{T} : \mathcal{S} \times \mathcal{A} \rightarrow \mathcal{S}$ is the transition model for generating the next state; $\mathcal{R} : \mathcal{S} \times \mathcal{A} \rightarrow \mathbb{R}$ is the reward function; μ_0 is the initial state distribution; $\gamma \in [0, 1)$ is a discount factor. At each step t, when an agent observes the state $s_t \in \mathcal{S}$ and executes an action $a_t \in \mathcal{A}$, it will then be transitioned into a new state s_{t+1} and receives an immediate reward $r_t(s_t, a_t)$, according to the transition function $T(s_{t+1}, r_t | s_t, a_t) \in \mathcal{T}$. The agent aims to learn an optimal policy $\pi^*(\cdot)$ to maximize the discounted cumulative reward: $\mathcal{J}(\pi) = \mathbb{E}_{s_0 \sim \mu_0, a_t \sim \pi(\cdot | s_t), s_{t+1} \sim T(\cdot | s_t, a_t)} [\sum_{t=0}^{T} \gamma^t r_t(s_t, a_t)]$.

Suppose $\rho^\pi(s, a) = (1 - \gamma) \cdot \pi(a_t | s_t) \sum_{t=0}^{\infty} \gamma^t P_\mathcal{T}^\pi(s)$ is the normalized occupancy measure for a policy $\pi(\cdot)$, where $P_\mathcal{T}^\pi(s)$ denotes the density of state s visited by π under $\mathcal{T}$ at time step t. The discounted cumulative reward can also be expressed as: $\mathcal{J}(\pi) = \mathbb{E}_{(s,a) \sim \rho_\mathcal{T}^\pi} [r(s, a)]$.

3.2 Soft Actor-Critic

Soft Actor-Critic (SAC) is an algorithm that optimizes a stochastic policy in an off-policy way. SAC trains the policy to maximize a trade-off between expected return and entropy to encourage exploration. The objective with the expected entropy of the policy can be written as:

$$\mathcal{J}(\pi) = \sum_{t=0}^{T} \mathbb{E}_{(s,a) \sim \rho^\pi} [r(s, a) + \omega \mathcal{H}(\pi(\cdot | s))]$$

where ω is a hyperparameter for the relative importance of the entropy term, and $\mathcal{H}$ is the entropy function. The policy can be reparameterized with a neural network transformation: $a = f_\phi(\epsilon; o)$, where ϵ is a noise sampled from some fixed distribution. The soft value function V_π is defined to include the entropy bonuses from every timestep:

$$V_\pi(s) = \mathbb{E}_\pi \left[\sum_{t=0}^{T} \gamma^t \left(r(s_t, a_t) + \omega \mathcal{H}(\pi(\cdot | s_t)) \right) \middle| s_0 = s \right],$$

Similarly, the action-value function $Q_\pi(s, a)$ is defined as:

$$Q_\pi(s, a) = \mathbb{E}_\pi \left[\sum_{t=0}^{T} \gamma^t R(s_t, a_t, s_{t+1}) \right.$$
$$\left. + \omega \sum_{t=1}^{T} \gamma^t \mathcal{H}(\pi(\cdot | s_t)) \middle| s_0 = s, a_0 = a \right],$$

3.3 Robust Adversarial Reinforcement Learning

To find a robust policy, Robust Adversarial Reinforcement Learning (RARL) assumed that the environment is dynamic against the agent. Therefore, the problem can be formulated as a two-player zero-sum game:

$$\pi = \arg \max_{\pi \in \Pi} \min_{\hat{\pi} \in \hat{\Pi}} V_{\pi, \hat{\pi}}, \tag{1}$$

where $\hat{\pi}$ is the adversary policy of the environment. The intuition behind the definition is that the algorithm can have high performance even with adversarial environment. The algorithm for RARL can alternate between optimizing the agent policy and the adversary's policy. In our work, we assume the workers are adversarial against the requestor with an additional lower bound constraint.

4   System Model

In this section, we first introduce the system setting of online crowdsourcing with strategic workers. Next, we formulate the problem as a max-min optimization problem.

4.1   The Crowdsourcing Setting

In the crowdsourcing problem, the workers may arrive asynchronously and randomly. We therefore discretize the environment into T steps: $\{0, 1, 2, ..., T-1\}$, where a worker arrives at each step t. A snapshot of the crowdsourcing at the tth step is presented in Fig. 2. As illustrated, at this step, the requestor q has a dynamic set of tasks $\mathcal{D}_t$ to be allocated, e.g. annotating a set of images, sensing different locations, or completing questionares. When a worker w arrives, the requestor will choose a task $d_t \in \mathcal{D}_t$ and payment p_t to the worker. Afterwards, the worker can decide whether to accept the task. The decision is represented as a binary value δ_t.

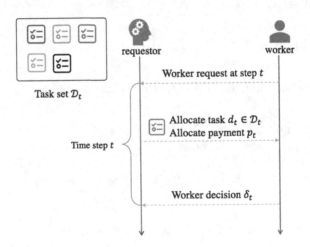

Fig. 2. A snapshot of allocation at step t.

According to the above setting, the requestor makes sequential decisions to allocate the tasks and payment. We can therefore model the requestor's decision process as an MDP. The main elements can be defined as follows:

Observation (o_t^q): When making decisions, the requestor can only observe partially the state $o_t^q \subseteq s_t^q$. Typically, the requestor can observe the task content, the context information, and partial information of the worker. The partial information of the worker includes the historical trajectories and task qualities, but does not include the utility of the worker.

Action (a_t^q): The action of the requestor includes two parts: the task d_t and the payment p_t, i.e., $a_t^q = (d_t, p_t)$. The task $d_t \in \mathcal{D}_t$ is represented as the semantic vector, such as the pixels of an image, or text description of a questionare. The payment p_t is a scalar value. Note that in the crowdsourcing scenario, new tasks may arrive dynamically. Therefore, the action space d_t often has high dimension and is not fixed.

Reward (r_t^q): As each task can be allocated multiple times, the marginal gain for finishing the tasks will decrease. Let N_t^d be the number of times that the task d is finished at step t. The immediate reward function for the requestor can be formulated as:

$$r_t^q(s_t^q, d_t, p_t) = \delta_t g_t(w, d_t) \frac{\log(N_t^d + 1) - \log N_t^d}{p_t + \kappa}, \qquad (2)$$

where $g_t(w, d_t)$ represents quality of task d_t finished by worker w. κ is a constant value for smoothing the denominator. According to this formulation, the requestor prefers higher quality $g_t(w, d_t)$, higher coverage $\log(N_t^d + 1) - \log N_t^d$, higher success ratio δ_t, and low payment $\frac{1}{p_t + \kappa}$.

The major notations are listed in Table 1. For ease of brevity, in the following, the time quotation t may be temporarily omitted. We use the symbol $'$ to denote the elements in the next step.

4.2 Problem Formulation

In practice, the workers are also strategic to make decisions: they may deceive the requestor temporarily to pursue higher long-term utility. The strategic behaviors can lead to the non-stationary of the environment: when allocating tasks and payments under the same system state, the requestor may have different expected reward. Moreover, it is intricate to infer the workers' utility as the workers may be strategic. Instead, in this work, we consider robust crowdsourcing with adversarial training. The underlying intuition is that the allocation strategy can be robust even in the worst case when the workers behave adversarially. Formally, we regard the workers as homogeneous and formulate the problem as a two-player max-min game. Let π_q and π_w be the policy functions for the requestor and the worker, V_{π_q, π_w} be the expected value function of the requestor under the policies. The problem is defined as follows:

Problem 1. Given a constant C, find an optimal policy π_q and π_w from the set Π_q, Π_w, defined by:

Table 1. Key parameter table of system model

Notation	Definition
$\mathcal{D}_t$	the task set to be allocated at step t
W	the set of workers
N_t^d	the number of times that task d is finished at step t
$a_t^q = (d_t, p_t)$	the action of the requestor: allocated task d_t and payment p_t at step t
$z_t^q = (z_t^d, p_t)$	the task embedding d_t and payment p_t
$\tilde{a}_t^q = (\tilde{d}_t, p_t)$	the regenerated value for the task d_t and payment p_t
δ_t	the binary decision value of the worker at step t
g_t	the task quality at step t
o_t^q	the requestor's observation at step t
r_t^q	the requestor's reward at step t
r_t^w	the reward of the worker at step t
α	the weight for the variational encoder
β	the weight for the transition model
γ	the discount factor

$$\max_{\pi_q \in \Pi_q} \min_{\pi_w \in \Pi_w} V_{\pi_q, \pi_w},$$
$$\text{s.t.} \sum_{t=0}^{T} p_t \geq C. \tag{3}$$

The constraint indicates that the workers need to ensure the cumulative payment received is above a threshold C. The objective indicates that the requestor's allocation policy should be robust with adversarial workers. The problem can be written as a Lagrangian under the KKT conditions:

$$\max_{\pi_q \in \Pi_q} \max_{\lambda \geq 0} \min_{\pi_w \in \Pi_w} (V_{\pi_q, \pi_w} + \lambda(C - \mathbb{E}_{\pi_w}[\sum_{t=0}^{T} p_t])), \tag{4}$$

where λ is a non-negative Lagrange multiplier. In the implementation, we regard the parameter λ as a fixed hyperparameter, which is easier for model training. As C is a constant, the objective can be reformulated as:

$$\max_{\pi_q \in \Pi_q} \min_{\pi_w \in \Pi_w} (V_{\pi_q, \pi_w} - \lambda \mathbb{E}_{\pi_w}[\sum_{t=0}^{T} p_t]), \tag{5}$$

5   Methods

In this section, we first show how to build a supervised environment model to allocate dynamic tasks. Next, we consider the strategic behaviors of the workers under this model to optimize the allocation policy.

5.1   The Environment Model

According to the system setting, the candidate task set $\mathcal{D}_t$ is time-varying, and the workers are strategic to make decisions. To consider the dynamics from the tasks and workers, we first build a supervised environment model. The environment model takes current system state and the requestor's action as input, and predicts the next state and the requestor reward. It can be represented as: $\hat{T}(o'_q, r_q | o_q, d, p)$.

As the task set is variable and has high-dimension, it is difficult to adopt RL directly under this model. To adapt to dynamic action set, in this work, we propose to embed the original task into a lower fixed-dimension latent space. In particular, we introduce an action encoder function $E(\cdot)$, which maps the origin action (task) d to a fixed-size embedding: $z_d = E(d)$, $z_d \in \mathbb{R}^K$. We also introduce a decoder network $D(\cdot)$ to regenerate action representation: $\tilde{d}$. With the encoder-decoder structure, the tasks can be embedded into a lower dimensional space for RL. Let θ_e, θ_d, θ_t be the parameters of the networks respectively. The parameters can be optimized by maximizing the following objective:

$$\mathcal{L}(\theta_s, \theta_e, \theta_d) = \mathbb{E}_{o_q, a_q, o'_q \sim \rho^\pi} [\underbrace{\mathbb{E}_{z_d \sim E(d)} [\log(D(\tilde{d} | z_d; \theta_d))]}_{\text{decoder}}$$

$$+ \beta \underbrace{\mathbb{E}_{z_d \sim E(d)} [\log(\hat{T}(o'_q, r | o_q, z_d, p; \theta_t))]}_{\text{transition model}}$$

$$- \alpha \underbrace{D_{KL}(E(z_d | d; \theta_e) || \mathcal{N}(0, \mathbf{I}))]}_{\text{variational encoder}},$$

where α and β are non-negative hyperparameter weights. The function $\hat{T}(\cdot | o_q, z_d, p; \theta_t)$ simulates the environment transition, and $D(\cdot | z_d; \theta_d)$ maps the action embedding to the original action. In this formulation, the first item maps the embedding vector z_d to the original action space d. The second term uses maximization likelihood estimation to predict the next state o'_q and the reward r, based on the current state o_q, task embedding z_d and payment p. In the third term, we use KL-divergence to encourage disentangling property in the inferred action embedding. The above objective function optimizes the transition model $\hat{T}(o'_q, r | o_q, z_d, p; \theta_t)$, the action encoder $E(z_d | d; \theta_a)$ and the decoder $D(\tilde{d} | z_d; \theta_d)$ jointly. Figure 3 shows the network structure of the action embedding process.

The objective is similar to that of variational autoencoder [7] with an additional environment transition model $\hat{T}(o'_q, r | o_q, z_d, p; \theta_t)$. In fact, the two parts can benefit from each other. With the environment transition model, the action embedding can potentially have a more disentangling representative embedding.

With the action embedding, the transition model can utilize the action more efficiently. In the implementation, we use isotropic Normal distribution for the KL-divergence term to reduce the likelihood terms to mean squared error.

5.2 Adversarial Policy Optimization

In practice, the workers can also be strategic when deciding whether to accept the task and payment. As formulated in Eq. 5, the workers can be regarded as adversarial agent that maximizes the long-term cumulative reward. Therefore, we define the worker reward as:

$$r_w(o_q, a_q, \delta) = \delta(\tau p - (1 - \tau)r_q(o_q, a_q)), \tag{6}$$

where $\tau \in [0, 1]$ is the coefficient for the adversarialness of the workers. When $\tau = 0$, the workers are fully adversarial to minimize the requestor's reward. When $\tau = 1$, the workers aim to maximize the received payments. By setting different values of τ, The workers can achieve a trade-off between received payments and adversarialness.

Now, we can now formulate the problem as a two-agent RL problem. Note that we are optimizing the policies only from the perspective of the requestor: the worker observation can be denoted as $o_w = (o_q, a_q)$. Thus, it is natural to adopt the "centralized training, decentralized execution" (CTDE) mechanism: During training, the algorithm can take the global information to evaluate the state-action value functions: $Q_q(o_q, a_q, a_w)$ and $Q_w(o_q, a_w, a_q)$; In the execution, only local observation is used to infer the policy function: $\pi_q(z_d, p|o_q)$ and $\pi_w(a_w|o_q, a_q)$, where a_w is the probability that the worker accepts the task, i.e., $a_w = P(\delta = 1)$. In the experiment, the state-action value functions and the policy functions are all implemented with neural networks. The network structures are illustrated in Fig. 4.

According to the network structures, we can adopt multi-agent SAC for policy optimization. Compared to the single-agent case, we use centralized critic functions $Q_l(o_q, a_q, a_w)$, $l \in \{q, w\}$ to evaluate the expected return by taking the actions of both the requestor and the worker as input. More concretely, let ϕ_q and ϕ_w be the parameters of the policy networks of the requestor and the worker. The approximate gradient of the expected return can be written as:

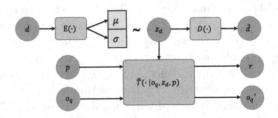

Fig. 3. The network structure of the transition model and action encoder-decoder.

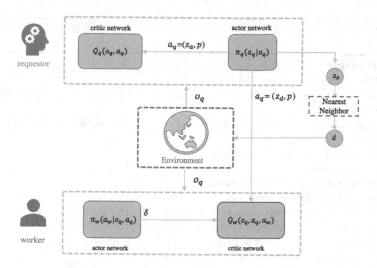

Fig. 4. The network structure of our method.

$$\hat{\nabla}_{\phi_l} J_l(\phi_l) = \nabla_{\phi_l} \log \pi_l(a_l|o_l) + (\nabla_{a_l} \log \pi_l(a_l|o_l)$$
$$- \nabla_{a_l} Q_l(o_l, a_l)) \nabla_{\phi_l} f_{\phi_l}(\epsilon; o_l), \tag{7}$$

where $l \in \{q, w\}$, $f_{\phi_l}(\epsilon; o_l)$ represents a neural network transformation for the action embedding in SAC, and ϵ is a noise sampled from some fixed distribution. The parameters of the centralized action-value functions can be updated with the stochastic gradients to minimize the soft Bellman residual:

$$\nabla_{\psi_l} J_l(\psi_l) = \nabla_{\psi_l} Q_l(o_q, a_q, a_w)(Q_l(o_q, a_q, a_w)$$
$$- r_l(o_q, a_q, a_w) - \gamma V_{\psi_l}(o'_l)), \tag{8}$$

With the encoder-decoder network, the requestor's policy network can directly output the task action in the embedding space. To execute in the origin space, we retrieve the closest task (nearest neighbor) in the embedding space, i.e. $d = \arg\min_{d' \in \mathcal{D}_t} ||z_d - p_e(d')||_2$.

The details of our approach is presented in Algorithm 1. We first initialize the networks with random parameters (Line 3–4). We also construct a replay buffer $\mathcal{R}$ with an empty set (Line 5). In each step, the requestor action embedding z_d is first sampled from the policy network $\pi_q(\cdot)$, and is mapped to the original action space d (Line 8–11). After executing the requestor action, the worker action δ can also be sampled from $\pi_w(o_w)$ and executed in the environment (Line 13–14). The tuples $(o_q, a_q, \delta, r_q, r_w, o'_q)$ in each step are stored in the replay buffer $\mathcal{R}$ (Line 16). In the training phase, we can sample a mini-batch tuples from the replay buffer, and update the network parameters according to the stochastic gradients (Line 19–24).

Algorithm 1: Robust Online Crowdsourcing with Strategic Workers (ROC)

---

1 **Input**: Hyperparameter $\alpha, \beta, \kappa, \lambda$;

2 **Output**: Requestor policy $\pi_q(\cdot)$;

3 Initialize the transition model $\hat{T}(\cdot)$, action encoder $E(\cdot)$, action decoder $D(\cdot)$ randomly;

4 Initialize policy networks $\pi_q(\cdot)$, $\pi_w(\cdot)$ and action-value networks $Q_q(\cdot)$, $Q_w(\cdot)$ randomly;

5 Initialize the replay buffer $\mathcal{R} = \emptyset$;

6 **for** *each step* **do**

    /* Execution in the environment   */

7   **for** *each worker w arrives* **do**

8   Get the requestor observation o_q from the environment;

9   Compute action embedding $a_q = (z_d, p) = \pi_q(o_q)$;

10   Retrieve the closest action $d = \arg\min_{d' \in \mathcal{D}_t} \|E(d') - z_d\|_2$;

11   Execute action $\tilde{a}_d = (d, p)$ in the environment;

12   Get worker observation $o_w = (o_q, \tilde{a}_d)$;

13   Compute worker action $\delta = \pi_w(o_w)$;

14   Compute worker reward $r_w(o_q, a_q) = \delta(\lambda p_t - r_q(o_q, a_q))$;

15   Execute action δ in the environment;

16   Get requestor's reward r_q and next observation o'_q;

17   Store $(o_q, \tilde{a}_q, \delta, r_q, r_w, o'_q)$ into $\mathcal{R}$;

18   **end**

    /* Train the networks   */

19   **for** *each gradient step* **do**

20   Sample a mini-batch of $(o_q, z_q, p, \delta, r_q, r_w, o'_q)$ from $\mathcal{R}$;

21   Update the parameters of $E, D, \hat{T}$;

22         $\theta \leftarrow \theta - \eta_e \nabla_\theta \mathcal{L}(\theta_s, \theta_e, \theta_d)$;

23   Update the policy parameters with $\phi_l \leftarrow \phi_l - \eta_l^\pi \nabla_{\phi_l} \mathcal{J}_l(\phi_l)$, where $l \in \{q, w\}$;

24   Update the critic parameters with $\psi_l \leftarrow \psi_l - \eta_l^Q \nabla_{\psi_l} \mathcal{J}_l(\psi_l)$, where $l \in \{q, w\}$;

25   **end**

26 **end**

---

6   Evaluation

6.1   Experiment Settings

The Environment. In the experiments, we collect real historical data to build a simulation environment. The crowdsourcing is an image labeling task with 20 121 images. The images are from 236 categories. The encoder network first uses ResNet-50 to extract embeddings with size 1 024. Images within the same category generally have similar embeddings. In the experiments, the initial set has $15,000$ images. We then add or remove 5 images from the set randomly at each step. We also limit the payment of the requestor at each round to be within $[0, 1]$.

In this environment, there are 1 024 workers. We assume the workers have random adversarialness, i.e., the coefficient τ for each worker is sampled from a uniform distribution $[0, 1]$. We use a random normal vector with size $1,024$ to represent each worker initially. When the workers accept tasks, the worker representation is updated as the average of accepted tasks embeddings, to reveal the experience of this worker. The quality $g(w, d_t)$ can then be computed as the normalized cosine distance between the worker and the task.

Model Parameters. In the RL algorithm, both the actor network and the critic networks have three 64-unit fully connected (FC) layers. The first two FC layers are followed by a ReLU layer for activation, and a batch norm layer. The output of the actor network consists of the mean and variance values of N workers from the policy distribution [6]. In the transition networks, the encoder uses 2 64-unit fully connected layers out output z_d with size 64. The decoder uses 3 64-unit fully connected layers to regenerate the embeddings with size 1 024. The transition model also has 3 64-unit fully connected layers to predict the next state and reward.

By default, κ is set as $\log 2$, so that the reward of the requestor is between $[0, 1]$. The environment model hyper-parameters α and β are set as 1. In the third experiment, it can be validated that other values of α and β can still achieve high accuracy. The adversarial coefficient τ is set as 0.5, so that ROC can deal with the adversarialness and self-interest simultaneously. We will also validate the performance of ROC with other values of τ.

Baselines. We compare our algorithm with the following baselines:

- *Random*: In the Random method, the images are allocated to the workers randomly, and the payment is sampled from a uniform distribution within $[0, 1]$;
- *Greedy*: In this method, the worker is allocated the image that has the highest quality. The payment is proportional to the quality.
- *SL (Supervised Learning)*: We use a supervised time-series algorithm (XGboost) to predict each worker's decision based on the historical features. The worker is then allocated the task with the highest quality, and the payment is allocated with the highest reward.

6.2 Results

In this part, we conduct experiments to answer the following questions: 1. What is the performance of the ROC when compared to other baselines? 2. Can the environment models accurately predict the system dynamics? 3. Can our method be robust in an adversarial environment?

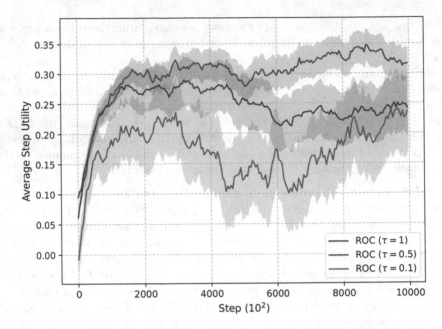

Fig. 5. The convergence of ROC with different values of τ.

Convergence During Training. In the first experiment, we train ROC algorithm with different values of τ as 0.1, 0.5, 1. When $\tau = 0$, the workers will always deny the task requests. The algorithm is evaluated in the online environment without exploration for every 100 steps. We train each algorithm 3 times. The shaded area denotes one-standard derivation. The results are presented in Fig. 5. As presented, all the algorithms can converge steadily in the training phase. When $\tau = 0.1$, the workers are more adversarial. Therefore, the algorithm is conservative when allocating the payment. At beginning, the variance is large since the requestor and the workers form a zero-sum game. When τ becomes large, the workers are less adversarial, and the algorithm has smaller variance. When τ is 1, the workers concentrate on maximizing the received payments and the requestor can also have higher expected returns. In ROC, we use default value as $\tau = 0.5$. In this case, the algorithm achieves the highest performance and convergence rate.

Table 2. The average step utility of the requestor.

τ	0.1	0.5	1
Random	0.032 ± 0.034	0.047 ± 0.031	0.049 ± 0.025
Greedy	0.059 ± 0.024	0.124 ± 0.024	0.152 ± 0.022
SL	0.093 ± 0.024	0.158 ± 0.026	0.193 ± 0.024
ROC ($\tau = 0.1$)	$\mathbf{0.223 \pm 0.047}$	0.237 ± 0.054	0.225 ± 0.057
ROC ($\tau = 0.5$)	0.205 ± 0.041	$\mathbf{0.309 \pm 0.038}$	0.271 ± 0.041
ROC ($\tau = 1$)	0.151 ± 0.025	0.244 ± 0.047	$\mathbf{0.279 \pm 0.062}$

6.3   Performance in the Execution

Next, we compare different algorithms in the execution phase w.r.t. different worker adversarialness in the online environment. The average worker adversarialness are 0.1, 0.5, and 1. In the execution phase, the ROC algorithms will not explore for random actions. The results are presented in Table 2. As presented, Random algorithm has poor performance in different settings, as it ignores the heterogeneity of the tasks and workers. The variance is also large in the Random algorithm. Greedy has better performance since the tasks are allocated to the worker with high quality. However, Greedy did not fully consider the worker decisions. In SL, both the tasks and workers are considered. But the algorithm is not sequential, and the workers strategies are not considered. In ROC algorithms with different values of τ, all the algorithms achieved high performance in different settings. Among them, ROC ($\tau = 0.5$) has the steadies performance, as it simultaneously considered the received payments and the adversarialness of the workers.

In this experiment, we can also validate the robustness of ROC. When $\tau = 0.1$, ROC ($\tau = 0.5$) can still have high performance close to ROC ($\tau = 1$). This shows that ROC can be robust in an almost fully adversarial environment.

6.4   The Accuracy of Environmental Models

In this part, we validate the accuracy of the environmental models w.r.t different values of α and β. When α is large, the algorithm has higher disentangling ability. When β is large, the environment gives higher weight to the transition part. As the environment models are regression to predict the state, reward and action, we use 3 metrics for validation: r2-score, mean squared error (MSE), and mean average precision error (MAPE).

Table 3 shows the metrics when regenerating the action embeddings. Table 4 shows the metrics when predicting the system state and reward. As presented, the environment model can achieve high accuracy in different settings. When α and β are both equal to 1, the transition model can reach a proper trade-off between the regenerating the actions and predicting the system state.

Table 3. The model accuracy for regenerating the actions.

α	β	MSE	R2	MAPE
0.5	1	3.15×10^{-4}	0.812	0.029
1	1	2.79×10^{-4}	0.833	0.026
2	1	3.42×10^{-4}	0.803	0.031
1	0	2.75×10^{-4}	0.841	0.0285
1	100	3.92×10^{-4}	0.785	0.035

Table 4. The model accuracy for predicting the environment state and reward.

α	β	MSE	R2	MAPE
1	1	0.013	0.755	0.026
1	100	0.011	0.772	0.023

7   Conclusion

This paper studied the problem of online crowdsourcing with strategic behaviors. In particular, the crowdsourcing aims to allocate a large time-varying set of tasks to public strategic workers. The advantages of the proposed method can be summarized as follows: First, we propose to build an environment model to predict the environment states and requestor reward. The model can also embed the tasks into a fixed lower dimensional space. Second, a multi-agent RL algorithm is used to optimize the allocation for the requestor, so that the adversarial behaviors from the workers can also be considered. Third, empirical analyses validate the effectiveness and robustness of our algorithm.

In the future work, we will try to deploy our algorithm in the real environment. One of the major challenges is the gap between online environment for deployment and the simulation for training. Our method has already show promising in the robustness. We will also improve the transferability in the future.

References

1. Alabbadi, A.A., Abulkhair, M.F.: Multi-objective task scheduling optimization in spatial crowdsourcing. Algorithms **14**(3), 77 (2021)
2. An, N., Wang, R., Luan, Z., Qian, D., Cai, J., Zhang, H.: Adaptive assignment for quality-aware mobile sensing network with strategic users. In: 2015 IEEE 17th International Conference on High Performance Computing and Communications, 2015 IEEE 7th International Symposium on Cyberspace Safety and Security, and 2015 IEEE 12th International Conference on Embedded Software and Systems, pp. 541–546. IEEE (2015)
3. Bhatti, S.S., Fan, J., Wang, K., Gao, X., Wu, F., Chen, G.: An approximation algorithm for bounded task assignment problem in spatial crowdsourcing. IEEE Trans. Mob. Comput. **20**(8), 2536–2549 (2020)
4. Chi, C., Wang, Y., Li, Y., Tong, X.: Multistrategy repeated game-based mobile crowdsourcing incentive mechanism for mobile edge computing in internet of things. Wirel. Commun. Mob. Comput. **2021**, 1–18 (2021)
5. Ding, Y., et al.: A city-wide crowdsourcing delivery system with reinforcement learning. Proc. ACM Interact. Mob. Wearable Ubiquitous Technol. **5**(3), 1–22 (2021)
6. Haarnoja, T., et al.: Soft actor-critic algorithms and applications. arXiv preprint arXiv:1812.05905 (2018)
7. Kingma, D.P., Welling, M.: Auto-encoding variational bayes. arXiv preprint arXiv:1312.6114 (2013)

8. Li, Y., Li, Y., Peng, Y., Fu, X., Xu, J., Xu, M.: Auction-based crowdsourced first and last mile logistics. IEEE Trans. Mob. Comput. (2022)
9. Liu, C.H., Dai, Z., Zhao, Y., Crowcroft, J., Wu, D., Leung, K.K.: Distributed and energy-efficient mobile crowdsensing with charging stations by deep reinforcement learning. IEEE Trans. Mob. Comput. $20(1)$, 130–146 (2019)
10. Liu, C.H., et al.: Curiosity-driven energy-efficient worker scheduling in vehicular crowdsourcing: A deep reinforcement learning approach. In: 2020 IEEE 36th International Conference on Data Engineering (ICDE), pp. 25–36. IEEE (2020)
11. Liu, S., et al.: Truthful online double auctions for mobile crowdsourcing: an on-demand service strategy. IEEE Internet Things J. $9(17)$, 16096–16112 (2022)
12. Lu, Z., Wang, Y., Tong, X., Mu, C., Chen, Y., Li, Y.: Data-driven many-objective crowd worker selection for mobile crowdsourcing in industrial iot. IEEE Trans. Industr. Inf. $19(1)$, 531–540 (2021)
13. Mak, T.S.H., Lam, A.Y.: Two-stage auction mechanism for long-term participation in crowdsourcing. IEEE Trans. Comput. Soc. Syst. (2022)
14. Miao, X., Peng, H., Gao, Y., Zhang, Z., Yin, J.: On dynamically pricing crowdsourcing tasks. ACM Trans. Knowl. Discov. Data (TKDD) $17(2)$, 1–27 (2022)
15. Tong, Y., Chen, L., Zhou, Z., Jagadish, H.V., Shou, L., Lv, W.: Slade: a smart large-scale task decomposer in crowdsourcing. IEEE Trans. Knowl. Data Eng. $30(8)$, 1588–1601 (2018)
16. Tong, Y., Wang, L., Zhou, Z., Chen, L., Du, B., Ye, J.: Dynamic pricing in spatial crowdsourcing: a matching-based approach. In: Proceedings of the 2018 International Conference on Management of Data, pp. 773–788 (2018)
17. Wang, R., Zeng, F., Yao, L., Wu, J.: Game-theoretic algorithm designs and analysis for interactions among contributors in mobile crowdsourcing with word of mouth. IEEE Internet Things J. $7(9)$, 8271–8286 (2020)
18. Wang, Y., Cai, Z., Zhan, Z.H., Gong, Y.J., Tong, X.: An optimization and auction-based incentive mechanism to maximize social welfare for mobile crowdsourcing. IEEE Trans. Comput. Soc. Syst. $6(3)$, 414–429 (2019)
19. Wang, Y., Gao, Y., Li, Y., Tong, X.: A worker-selection incentive mechanism for optimizing platform-centric mobile crowdsourcing systems. Comput. Netw. 171, 107144 (2020)
20. Wu, Z., Li, Q., Wu, W., Zhao, M.: Crowdsourcing model for energy efficiency retrofit and mixed-integer equilibrium analysis. IEEE Trans. Industr. Inf. $16(7)$, 4512–4524 (2019)
21. Yang, D., Xue, G., Fang, X., Tang, J.: Incentive mechanisms for crowdsensing: crowdsourcing with smartphones. IEEE/ACM Trans. Netw. $24(3)$, 1732–1744 (2015)
22. Zhang, W., Hong, Z., Chen, W.: Hierarchical pricing mechanism with financial stability for decentralized crowdsourcing: a smart contract approach. IEEE Internet Things J. $8(2)$, 750–765 (2020)
23. Zhao, Y., Zheng, K., Guo, J., Yang, B., Pedersen, T.B., Jensen, C.S.: Fairness-aware task assignment in spatial crowdsourcing: game-theoretic approaches. In: 2021 IEEE 37th International Conference on Data Engineering (ICDE), pp. 265–276. IEEE (2021)
24. Zhu, X., Luo, Y., Liu, A., Tang, W., Bhuiyan, M.Z.A.: A deep learning-based mobile crowdsensing scheme by predicting vehicle mobility. IEEE Trans. Intell. Transp. Syst. $22(7)$, 4648–4659 (2020)

Distinguished Work from Student Competation

New Filter2D Accelerator on the Versal Platform Powered by the AI Engine

Wenbo Zhang[✉], Tianshuo Wang, Yiqi Liu, Yiming Li, and Zhenshan Bao

Faculty of Information Technology, Beijing University of Technology, Beijing, China
zhangwenbo@bjut.edu.cn

Abstract. Filter2D, as a fundamental operator of CNN, has vital optimization and acceleration significance in computer vision (CV) applications, so it is designed as the CCFSys-CCC2023 competition CV track. Based on the CCC2023 competition designated Versal ACAP Architecture, we proposed the AI Engine (AIE) kernel and AIE graph design scheme and reconstructed the programmable logic (PL) and Processing System (PS) accordingly. Results show that, compared to the only PS scheme, our design achieve about 104.51~139.41 speedup on the specified platform Versal ACAP, which overcame all other 50+ group and won the championship of CCC2023.

Keywords: Filter2D · Hardware Accelerator · Heterogeneous Architecture · Versal · ACAP

1 Introduction

Filter2D, which is a widely used operation in image processing and video processing, will reduce the noise and details in images. So Filter2D block plays a vital role for image smoothing, image sharpening and edge detection [10, 15, 20]. Besides, it is the most frequent operator in convolution neural networks (CNN) and it is essential to optimizing Filter2D for improving the speed of CNN.

Filter2D is template operation that can divide the whole computational problem into local templates, and it is suitable for achieving directional acceleration. However, considering the spatial dependence of input data, it is necessary to adjust the algorithm to adapt hardware for better performance. In the past, many scholars optimized two-dimensional convolution and CNN based on hardware architectures such as CPU, GPU, FPGA, etc. We reinterpret the traditional issue with Versal ACAP architecture [5], an AMD/Xilinx designed next-generation heterogeneous computing platform which includes scalar engines, adaptive engines, and intelligent engines.

Compared to the related work, the major contributions of our work are summarized as follows:

Supported by AMD University Program.

© The Author(s), under exclusive license to Springer Nature Singapore Pte Ltd. 2024
C. Li et al. (Eds.): APPT 2023, LNCS 14103, pp. 437–449, 2024.
https://doi.org/10.1007/978-981-99-7872-4_24

- We proposed a set of accelerator optimization design ideas based on the characteristics of AI Engine in Versal ACAP.
- We design the Filter2D hardware accelerator based on our proposed design ideas and verified in the VCK5000 node of HACC@NUS
- We submit our design and results to CCFSys-Customized Computing Challenge (CCC) 2023 [3] committee and win the first place winner award for both CV and DSP group with highest processing resolution and FPS.

The rest of this paper is organized as follows. Section 2 shows the related work of Filter2D and CNN accelerator. Section 3 introduces our system model and accelerator design. Section 4 contains the emulation result, hardware result and our analysis. Section 5 makes the conclusion of this paper and looks forward to future work.

2   Related Work

Filter2D, as widely known as 2D convolution, is characterized by substantial number of template calculations and cross-row memory access. Based on these features, numerous scholars have spent a lot of time optimizing on CPU [13,19]. However, with the challenges such as CNN that require compute multiple large-scale convolutions, the training efficiency of the network is severely hampered by the limitations of CPU computing power. Consequently, researchers gradually explored the optimization of Filter2D on GPU [14,16], which possess superior parallel computing capabilities. Nonetheless, due to potential communication bottlenecks between computation nodes in GPU, it is difficult to fully utilize the accessing data. Application Specific Integrated Circuit (ASIC) [8,18], on the other hand, offers a good choice with the architecture that allows for in-memory computing.

Compared with ASIC, Field Programmable Gate Array (FPGA) overcome the drawbacks of long development cycles and limited scalability associated with ASIC [7], enabling them to keep up with the latest advancements in the AI field. Numerous scholars have conducted research on FPGA, including optimizing algorithms [9,12] to adapt to existing hardware architectures and introducing double-buffering-based memory for the mismatch between computation throughput and memory bandwidth. Ma et al. [17] proposed an efficient convolution acceleration strategy based on loop-unrolling Single Instruction Multiple Data (SIMD) architecture. However, their proposed architecture, which stores both feature maps and weights in on-chip memory, results in excessive consumption of FPGA storage resources.

AMD/Xilinx recognized the potential of SIMD architecture and introduced the AI Engine Array [2], which supports SIMD, into FPGA with the PS+PL. This led to the development of the Versal ACAP architecture [6]. Xijie et al. [11] focused on embedded systems and proposed a highly scalable and re-configurable CNN accelerator, called XVDPU. Jinming et al. [21] introduced a matrix multiplication and addition accelerator along with the code generation framework CHARM, suitable for various classical networks. However, their work was primarily focused on embedded development environment such as VCK190 board, which had limited on-chip resources, making it challenging to deploy third-party libraries. In the case of VCK5000, which is specifically designed for server application acceleration, it is crucial to take compatibility with third-party libraries into account.

3   System Model and Accelerator Design

Figure 1 is the top-level design of our work which makes full use of the advantage of Versal ACAP heterogeneous platform. Because the Versal ACAP architecture contains three different frameworks: AI Engine (AIE), Programmable Logic (PL) and Processing System (PS). We will introduce each part of the design in the following subsection.

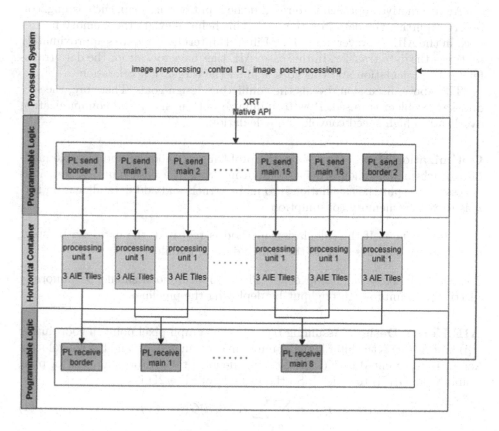

Fig. 1. Top-Level Design

3.1   AI Engine

Problem Setting and Design Objectives. To compute an output feature point, we need to compute the output with the corresponding input feature point and the surrounding data using the convolution kernel. Therefore, its most significant memory access characteristic is cross-row data access. Nevertheless, in order to high-speed interact between the accelerator and the program, we have to compress the image to one-dimensional streaming data. In this case, the first key problem is raised: How to achieve high-speed convolution calculations with the sequential input data stream?

Assuming we are dealing with a filtering kernel of $n \times n$, the simplest and easiest way is to cache n-1 rows and calculate with the n rows input. However, due to the distributed memory architecture adopted by the AIE array, each tile can only use a maximum of 32KB of memory. As the resolution gradually increases, the memory space in the AIE tile is far from sufficient to support caching of n-1 rows of data. Therefore, it's essential to partition and preprocess data.

An alternative approach is to rebuild the input feature map, such as img2col, before inputting the data into the AIE. This helps alleviate the memory bottleneck in the AIE. However, for a $n \times n$ Filter2D filtering, it requires approximately n^2 times the data transfer. In this case, AIE tiles have to wait for the data transfer for the calculation and this goes against the target of acceleration.

The above discussion reveals the conflicting design goals. Therefore, the second key problem is raised: How to minimize both memory and communication overhead in high-speed convolution calculations?

Optimization Rules. Transform the problem into modular and scalable modules. Each module should finish computing while the data input. If not, it is necessary to split the calculation into more kernels and add data allocation kernels to reduce memory consumption.

Task to Modules: If the calculation method is repeated, the data can be split, and multiple modules process the source data in parallel.

Distribute Module Computing Load: The computing load should be uniformly distribute to improve throughput by deploying the pipeline.

AIE Kernel Design. Assuming $G(i, j)$ is the graph pixel point in coordinates (i,j) and $K(i, j)$ is the filter kernel number in coordinates (i,j) and the convolution kernel is represented as K(i, j). G(i, j:k) denotes the vector composed of pixel points from G(i, j) to G(i, k). So the formula of Filter2D is

$$Filter2D(i,j) = \sum_m \sum_n K(m,n)G(i+m, j+m) \tag{1}$$

In AIE 8 int32 multiplication and addition (MAC) operations can be completed within one instruction [1] ,so we rebuild the Eq. 1 to make full use of the SIMD feature of AIE array,

$$Filter2D(i,j:j+7) = \sum_m \sum_n K(m,n)G(i+m, j+m:j+m+7) \tag{2}$$

Example. Taking 3×3 Filter2D on a 3×10 image slice as an example. In Fig. 2, the image is divided into 9 vectors that circle with different colors. These vectors correspond to the nine weights in the 3×3 kernel. Therefore, we can 8 parallel calculate the Filter2D by MAC the image and kernel in the same color.

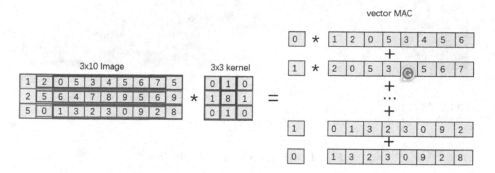

Fig. 2. 8 parallel int32 3x3 Filter2D computing

AIE Graph Design. Because the different rows' calculations are independent, we separate them to distribute the computational load to other tiles. To compute efficiently, we divide the module into 3 tiles, as Fig. 3.

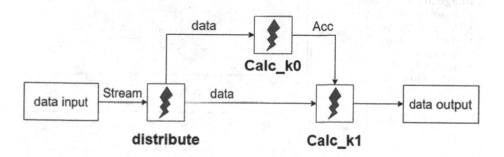

Fig. 3. AIE Filter2D Compute Unit

The compute unit contains three tiles. The Calc_K0 computing core handles two-thirds of the convolution computation, while the Calc_K1 computing core is responsible for others and accumulating Calc_K0 results. Due to the different data ranges of the two computing core, we used a distributed core to distribute the data for two computing cores.

Besides, we accelerate the computations in each processing with the pipeline, as shown in Fig. 4.

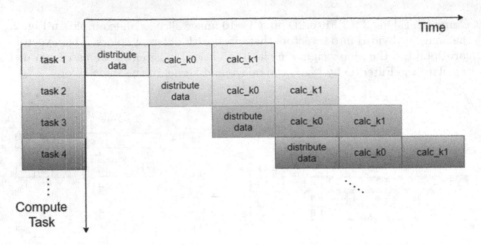

Fig. 4. AIE processing unit pipeline

Although one processing unit could finish the whole convolution operations, to improve speed, we slice the image and use multiple processing units to run simultaneously. The segmentation scheme is shown in Fig. 5.

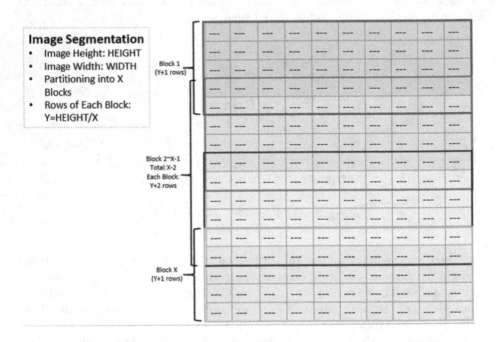

Fig. 5. The slicing method of image

In summary, we expand our design and used 18 processing units in the current scheme. Though, the more blocks the image is segmented into, the more processing units, the shorter the calculation time. However, it's vital to take hardware resource limitations into account, such as the number of AIE and PL interactive ports.

3.2   Programmable Logic Design

Data Mover. Usually, data is stored in the DDR. We need PL kernels transform the memory block to data stream. Given that the first and last slices have fewer rows than the middle blocks. We categorize the PL kernel into 4 kinds: pl_send_border for send border slice, pl_send_main for send middle slice, pl_receive_boarder for receive border slice, pl_receive_main for receive middle slice.

So there are 27 PL kernels that serve for the 18-way AIE input and output. The data flow is shown in Fig. 6.

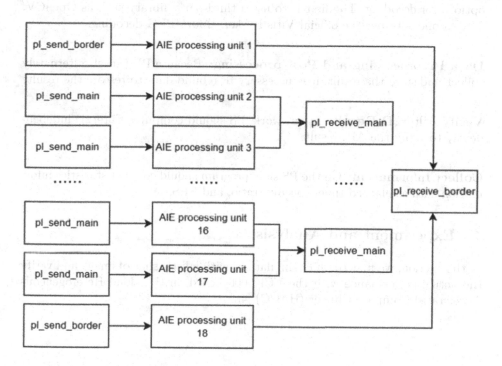

Fig. 6. The slicing method of image

JPEG Decoder. This decoder is used to complete the task of Filter2D through hardware decoding even without third-party libraries, such as OpenCV, to load images.

3.3   Processing System Design

The Processing System (PS) of VCK5000 is the x86 host which is connected by PCIE. And developers can use common x86 development tools and libraries to develop and optimize applications. On the PS side, run the application that the user wants to accelerate, and call the accelerator through Xilinx Runtime (XRT). For simplicity in this work, we only focus on deploying a 3×3 Filter2D operation on Super Definition (SD) gray-scale images.

Here is the functional design of PS:

Sequence Control. The program is employed with C++17 standard and XRT Native API for sequence control and application acceleration. Before the accelerator cores are called, the PS program should open the device and load the compiled xclbin file into the device through XRT.

Image Decoder: The input data comes from JPEG files and there are two options for decoding. The first is to use a third-party library such as OpenCV. The second is to use the official Vitis PL kernel for JPEG decoding.

Data Preprocessing and Post-processing: Because PL kernels alternately collect and store the result, it is necessary to rebuild data to restore the result.

Verify Filter2D Result: In our work, PS should computes Filter2D independently to verify the AIE result.

Collect Information: On the PS side, program should conduct statistics information such as elapsed time, speedup ratio, and FPS.

4   Experiment and Analysis

In this section, we first conduct simulations with a little slice of image and verify the actual performance with the VCK5000 board on the cloud Heterogeneous Accelerated Compute Cluster (HACC) [4].

4.1   Experiment Setup

Experiment Environment
  Our experiment environment is shown in Table 1

Table 1. Experiment Environment

Vitis version	2022.2
experimental platform	AMD/Xilinx VCK5000 Versal Develop Card
card driver	xilinx_vck5000_gen4x8_xdma_2_202210_1
third-party library	OpenCV 4.2.0

Benchmarks. In the experiments, we use the following three metrics to show effect of our design.

Makespan: the total time required to complete Filter2D.

Speedup Ratio: the ratio of the execution time of one program compared to another program.

FPS: Frame per second.

4.2   Experiment Result

Experiment Emulation. To get the performance evaluation of AIE, we simulate our work with Vitis and check result with Vitis Analyzer.
  Due to the time consuming of AIE simulation, we choose 64 × 64 as an example rather than real 8K image. For the 8K images, the actual hardware result will be presented in following sections.

Memory Usage Emulation: Figure 7 is part of the Array view of Vitis Analyzer and we only focus on a processing unit. Green lines indicates the direction of data flow while the red blocks means the memory usage. Apparently, our design make full use of tile's local memory.

Makespan Emulation: The trace view of Vitis Analyzer is shown in Fig. 8. In Fig. 8, the work load of multiple tiles are basically balanced, and it takes 1138ns to process the 64 × 64 image. We can estimate the makespan of 8K images: $7680/64 \times 4320/64 \times 1138 \approx 9.2$ ms, which is highly consistent with the hardware makespan.

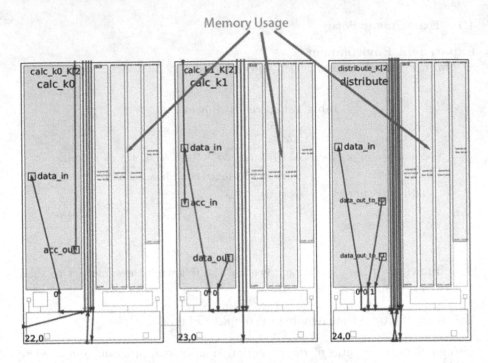

Fig. 7. Processing unit memory usage

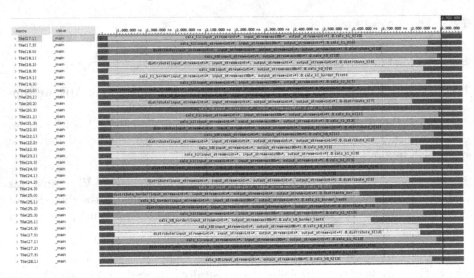

Fig. 8. AIE tiles trace

Hardware Result. We comply with the requirements of the competition and verify our hardware result based on cloud HACC@NUS.

The Heterogeneous Accelerated Compute Clusters (HACC) program is a special initiative to support novel research in adaptive compute acceleration for high performance computing (HPC). Five HACCs have been established at some of the world's most prestigious universities. Each cluster is specially configured to enable some of the world's foremost academic teams to conduct state-of-the-art HPC research.

Our baseline is the Filter2D in PS independently. We initially considered taking the Filter2D in Vitis Libraries as the baseline. However, the official solution requires preloading data into local memory and cannot support 8K resolution images. Therefore, as a compromise, we set the ratio between the makespan of Filter2D on the PS side independently and the makespan of our Filter2D solution.

As shown in Table 2, our design can effectively accelerate Filter2D of several sizes. The makespan of 8K (9.82 ms) is basically consistent with our Vitis emulation estimation results (9.2 ms). In addition, the speedup ratio gradually increases with increases in image resolution. The reason for our analysis should be that the AIE makespan includes the time for PL data handling and process synchronization. When the image size increases, this part of time remains basically unchanged and affects the acceleration ratio in smaller resolutions.

Table 2. The hardware result of different image resolution

image resolution	average AIE makespan (ms)	average PS makespan (ms)	speedup ratio	FPS
7680 × 4320	9.82	1369.22	139.41	101.87
4096 × 2160	2.93	370.38	126.41	341.30
1280 × 720	0.43	44.94	104.51	2325.58

Besides, our work was submitted and evaluated by the CCFSys-CCC 2023 committee. In the CV group, our design outperformed all other competitors by delivering the highest speedup ratio, FPS and image resolution. As a result, we won the first place for both CV and DSP groups.

5 Conclusion and Future Work

In this paper, we propose our accelerator design ideas based on the features of Versal ACAP AI Engine and verify our accelerator design in emulation and hardware nodes of HACC. Our design was demonstrated on the CCFSys-CCC 2023 and won the first place winner award.

However, there are still some aspects that need to research in future work.

- Associated operator of neural network
  Although we only attempted the Filter2D, its design ideas can be effectively extended to the CNN models. In the future, we will explore the optimization design of typical operators for various neural networks.

- Versal ACAP heterogeneous system automation design
  As a heterogeneous computing platform, Versal ACAP contains three different frameworks. It's important to research the automation design for enhancing development efficiency.

Acknowledgement. We thank the support the AMD/Xilinx for board and software donation and support from AMD/Xilinx Heterogeneous Accelerated Compute Cluster at NUS. We thank all the reviewers and CCFSys-CCC committee for their valuable feedback.

References

1. AMD/Xilinx: AI engine API and intrinsics user guide
2. AMD/Xilinx: AI engine white paper
3. AMD/Xilinx: CCFSys-CCC2023. https://ccfsys-ccc.github.io/2023/
4. AMD/Xilinx: CCFSys-CCC2023. https://www.amd-haccs.io/index.html
5. AMD/Xilinx: Versal ACAP. http://www.xilinx.com/versal
6. AMD/Xilinx: Versal ACAP AI engine architecture manual - AM009. https://docs.xilinx.com/r/en-US/am009-versal-ai-engine/
7. Bai, L., Zhao, Y.M., Huang, X.M.: A CNN accelerator on FPGA using depthwise separable convolution. IEEE Trans. Circuits Syst. II-Express Briefs **65**(10), 1415–1419 (2018). https://doi.org/10.1109/tcsii.2018.2865896. Go to ISI: //WOS:000446155600027
8. Chen, X.M., Han, Y.H., Wang, Y., IEEE: communication lower bound in convolution accelerators. In: 26th IEEE International Symposium on High Performance Computer Architecture (HPCA), pp. 529–541. International Symposium on High-Performance Computer Architecture-Proceedings (2020). https://doi.org/10.1109/hpca47549.2020.00050. Go to ISI: //WOS:000531494100040
9. Deng, H.P., et al.: 3D-VNPU: a flexible accelerator for 2D/3D CNNs on FPGA. In: 29th IEEE Annual International Symposium on Field-Programmable Custom Computing Machines (FCCM), pp. 181–185. Annual IEEE Symposium on Field-Programmable Custom Computing Machines (2021). https://doi.org/10.1109/fccm51124.2021.00029. Go to ISI: //WOS:000681289100021
10. Gilan, A.A., Emad, M., Alizadeh, B.: FPGA-based implementation of a real-time object recognition system using convolutional neural network. IEEE Trans. Circuits Syst. II-Exp. Briefs **67**(4), 755–759 (2020). https://doi.org/10.1109/tcsii.2019.2922372. Go to ISI ://WOS:000522403100031
11. Jia, X., et al.: XVDPU: a high performance CNN accelerator on the versal platform powered by the AI engine. In: 2022 32nd International Conference on Field-Programmable Logic and Applications, FPL, pp. 209–217. International Conference on Field Programmable Logic and Applications, AMD; Intel; Groq; Twosigma; Lattice Semicond; XILINX; Maxeler; Two Sigma (2022). https://doi.org/10.1109/FPL57034.2022.00041. 32nd International Conference on Field-Programmable Logic and Applications (FPL), Belfast, North Ireland, Aug 29-Sep 02, 2022
12. Thomas K, A., Poddar, S., Mondal, H.K.: A CNN hardware accelerator using triangle-based convolution. J. Emerg. Technol. Comput. Syst. **18**(4), Article 78 (2022). https://doi.org/10.1145/3544975

13. Kelefouras, V., Keramidas, G.: Design and implementation of 2D convolution on X86/X64 processors. IEEE Trans. Parallel Distrib. Syst. **33**(12), 3800–3815 (2022). https://doi.org/10.1109/tpds.2022.3171471. Go to ISI: //WOS:000831139000004

14. Kim, H., Song, W.J.: Las: locality-aware scheduling for GEMM-accelerated convolutions in GPUs. IEEE Trans. Parallel Distrib. Syst. **34**(5), 1479–1494 (2023). https://doi.org/10.1109/TPDS.2023.3247808

15. Li, G.D., Min, L.Q., Zang, H.Y.: Color edge detections based on cellular neural network. Int. J. Bifurcation Chaos **18**(4), 1231–1242 (2008). https://doi.org/10.1142/s0218127408020963. Go to ISI: //WOS:000257292300022

16. Lym, S., Lee, D., O'Connor, M., Chatterjee, N., Erez, M.: Delta: GPU performance model for deep learning applications with in-depth memory system traffic analysis. In: IEEE International Symposium on Performance Analysis of Systems and Software (ISPASS), pp. 293–303. IEEE International Symposium on Performance Analysis of Systems and Software-ISPASS (2019). https://doi.org/10.1109/ispass.2019.00041. Go to ISI: //WOS:000470201600033

17. Ma, Y.F., Cao, Y., Vrudhula, S., Seo, J.S.: Optimizing the convolution operation to accelerate deep neural networks on FPGA. IEEE Trans. Very Large Scale Integr. (VLSI) Syst. **26**(7), 1354–1367 (2018). https://doi.org/10.1109/tvlsi.2018.2815603. Go to ISI: //WOS:000437031400013

18. Mo, H., et al.: 9.2 a 28nm 12.1 TOPS/W dual-mode CNN processor using effective-weight-based convolution and error-compensation-based prediction. In: 2021 IEEE International Solid-State Circuits Conference (ISSCC), vol. 64, pp. 146–148 (2021). https://doi.org/10.1109/ISSCC42613.2021.9365943

19. Moradifar, M., Shahbahrami, A.: Performance improvement of gaussian filter using simd technology. In: 2020 International Conference on Machine Vision and Image Processing (MVIP), pp. 1–6 (2020). https://doi.org/10.1109/MVIP49855.2020.9116883

20. Ye, J.Y., Shen, Z.Y., Behrani, P., Ding, F., Shi, Y.Q.: Detecting usm image sharpening by using CNN. Signal Process.-Image Commun. **68**, 258–264 (2018). https://doi.org/10.1016/j.image.2018.04.016. Go to ISI: //WOS:000447572100023

21. Zhuang, J., et al.: CHARM: composing heterogeneous accelerators for matrix multiply on versal ACAP architecture. In: Proceedings of the 2023 ACM/SIGDA International Symposium on Field Programmable Gate Arrays, FPGA 2023, pp. 153–164. Association for Computing Machinery, New York (2023). https://doi.org/10.1145/3543622.3573210

Author Index

© The Editor(s) (if applicable) and The Author(s), under exclusive license
to Springer Nature Singapore Pte Ltd. 2024
C. Li et al. (Eds.): APPT 2023, LNCS 14103, pp. 451–452, 2024.
https://doi.org/10.1007/978-981-99-7872-4

Printed in the United States
by Baker & Taylor Publisher Services

Printed in the United States
by Baker & Taylor Publisher Services